To Bruce,
with very best wishes,

Jeremy

Revolution and the Republic

A History of Political Thought in France since the Eighteenth Century

JEREMY JENNINGS

OXFORD
UNIVERSITY PRESS

OXFORD
UNIVERSITY PRESS

Great Clarendon Street, Oxford OX2 6DP

Oxford University Press is a department of the University of Oxford.
It furthers the University's objective of excellence in research, scholarship,
and education by publishing worldwide in

Oxford New York

Auckland Cape Town Dar es Salaam Hong Kong Karachi
Kuala Lumpur Madrid Melbourne Mexico City Nairobi
New Delhi Shanghai Taipei Toronto

With offices in

Argentina Austria Brazil Chile Czech Republic France Greece
Guatemala Hungary Italy Japan Poland Portugal Singapore
South Korea Switzerland Thailand Turkey Ukraine Vietnam

Oxford is a registered trade mark of Oxford University Press
in the UK and in certain other countries

Published in the United States
by Oxford University Press Inc., New York

© Jeremy Jennings 2011

British Library Cataloguing in Publication Data

Data available

Library of Congress Cataloging in Publication Data
Library of Congress Control Number: 2011929431

Typeset by SPI Publisher Services, Pondicherry, India
Printed in Great Britain
on acid-free paper by
MPG Books Group, Bodmin and King's Lynn

ISBN 978–0–19–820313–1

1 3 5 7 9 10 8 6 4 2

In memory of Jack Greenleaf

Acknowledgements

In the course of the years spent writing this book I have incurred many debts and it is a pleasure to record my thanks to the friends, colleagues, and institutions that have provided invaluable support.

Between 1997 and 2000 I was in receipt of a research grant from the Economic and Social Research Council; in 1998, 2002, 2006, and 2007 I received research funding from the British Academy; and in 2008–9 received a grant through the Research Leave programme of the Arts and Humanities Research Council. The latter enabled me to finish this project.

In 2002–3 I had the extreme good fortune to be a visiting fellow at the Columbia University Institute for Scholars at Reid Hall in Paris and I gratefully acknowledge the help and support of the Institute's Director, Danielle Haase-Dubosc, and of Michaela Bacou and Brune Biebuyck. In 2006 I had the great honour of holding the post of Vincent Wright Professor at the Institut d'Études Politiques in Paris and wish especially to thank Patrick Le Galès and his colleagues at CEVIPOF for making this such a memorable and productive experience. In 2005–6 I was Visiting Research Fellow at the Institute for Advanced Study at Indiana University, Bloomington, and express my deepest appreciation for the support I received from its director, Ivona Hedin. Jeff Isaacs, Russell Hanson, and Elinor Ostrom of the Indiana University Department of Political Science were never less than generous and enthusiastic hosts.

I would also like to thank the libraries and librarians who provided invaluable assistance over many years of research. In addition to the staff at the Bibliothèque Nationale in Paris and of the Rare Books Room of the British Library in London, my thanks go to the library of the Musée Social in Paris and in particular to the late Colette Chambelland and to Michel Prat.

On a number of occasions I have been able to discuss ideas developed in this volume at conferences organized by Liberty Fund. These have always proved to be immensely rewarding and enriching meetings and through them I have had the opportunity to converse at length in the most supportive of surroundings with scholars from across the world. Special thanks go to Liberty Fund Fellows Christine Dunn Henderson and Mark E. Yellin.

Such has been the length of time I have spent working on this project that during the course of its writing I have taught at the Universities of Swansea, Birmingham, and London. In each case it is a pleasure to record my thanks to these institutions and to my colleagues, both past and present. In London I have benefited greatly from the friendship, conversation, and advice of Richard Bellamy, Richard Bourke, Angus Gowland, Simon Green, Colin Jones, Daniel Johnson, Chandran Kukathas, Cécile Laborde, Ian Malcolm, Niall O'Flaherty, Mark Pennington, Richard Shannon, Quentin Skinner, Georgios Varouxakis, Robert Willer, and, as always, Julian Jackson.

It goes without saying that I owe an enormous debt to colleagues and friends in France. These are too numerous to list. However, I wish in particular to express my thanks to Patrice Gueniffey, Lucien Jaume, and Farhad Khosrokhavar. Above all, I take this opportunity to express my warmest thanks to Christophe Prochasson who, for almost thirty years, has been my friend and guide. Through him I extend my thanks to the Prochasson and Cœuré families for their unfailing generosity and kindness. I similarly thank my good friends Marie-Laurence and Jean Netter.

Much of the best work on French intellectual history comes out of North America and I have been exceptionally fortunate in having had the opportunity to make the acquaintance of and learn from many colleagues working there. Among those I would especially like to thank are: Barbara Allen, Richard Boyd, Henry C. Clark, Bryan Garsten, Alan Kahan, Herman (Gene) Lebovics, Mark Lilla, Daniel J. Mahoney, Samuel Moyn, Jennifer Pitts, Helena Rosenblatt, Filippo Sabetti, David Schalk, James T. Schleifer, Steven Vincent, Charles Walton, Cheryl Welch, Richard Wolin, and, last but by no means least, my dear friend and collaborator Aurelian Craiutu.

On another continent, I express my thanks to Eduardo Nolla.

I would also like to thank Stephanie Ireland and Briony Ryles at Oxford University Press and Jane Robson for excellent copy-editing.

Sadly my first university teacher and head of department, Jack Greenleaf, died before this book was completed. It is to his memory that it is dedicated.

Jeremy Jennings

London, May 2010

Contents

Introduction
Revolution and the Republic

I

When, in January 1789, Louis XVI summoned the Estates-General to meet in Versailles he could little have imagined that, less than three years later, the monarchy itself would be overthrown and that, soon afterwards, he would be executed in the Place de la Révolution. In that short period of time, the feudal order had been destroyed, the aristocracy had been abolished, the Catholic Church had been deprived of both its property and its independence, and, no less significantly, the Republic had been proclaimed on 22 September 1792. 'Nobody', William Doyle has written, 'could have predicted that things would work out as they did.'[1]

What occurred during the French Revolution is central to the argument of this book.[2] Our starting point is that these tumultuous events marked the decisive moment in the history of modern France, even though, in an often repeated phrase, the Revolution was something of a mistake. What the revolutionaries of 1789 intended, in other words, was not what came out of the Revolution and this was so because at its heart was a process of *dérapage*.[3] The Revolution was 'blown off course' by a series of factors, most notably economic mismanagement, divisions within the revolutionary elite, the flight of the king and his recapture at Varennes in June 1791, and, most importantly, the declaration of war against France's neighbours in the following year. The Revolution thus deviated from the path envisaged by the members of the National Assembly in the summer of 1789. What many of its leaders appear to have wanted was a modernized monarchy and a reformed constitution based broadly upon the model of England and the separation of powers. This was swiftly rejected as the Revolution rushed headlong towards a fundamental reconstruction of society.

Unless otherwise stated the place of publication is Paris.

[1] William Doyle, *The Origins of the French Revolution* (Oxford, 1988), 213.
[2] Gary Kates (ed.), *The French Revolution: Recent Debates and New Controversies* (London, 1998) and Robert Alexander, *Re-writing the French Revolutionary Tradition* (Cambridge, 2003).
[3] François Furet and Denis Richet, *La Révolution française*, 2 vols. (1965–6).

Nothing quite like the French Revolution had been seen before.[4] It was seen by its participants and by those who viewed it from afar as a revolution precisely because it sought to change all aspects of life. This included the calendar and currency; weights and measures; place and street names; the description of physical space and time; as well as public and religious festivals. 'While debating about clocks and hats', Lynn Hunt has written, 'the deputies were developing their notions about politics, representation and hierarchy.'[5] The manner in which a person spoke or dressed came to be as politically significant as what they wrote or did. Far from being unimportant, this figured as part of the attempt to create a 'new man'.[6] The end pursued came to transcend that of mere constitutional reform and became that of the creation of a virtuous people. To refer again to Lynn Hunt: 'the social and economic changes brought about by the Revolution were not revolutionary. . . . In the realm of politics by contrast virtually everything changed.'[7]

We need not dwell upon the protracted debate about the origins of the Revolution.[8] Recent accounts, far from emphasizing the mounting class conflict between nobility and bourgeoisie[9] or the Revolution's social and economic causes, have located these origins in two unrelated phenomena: the bankruptcy of the French state following the financially ruinous involvement in the American War of Independence and the economic crisis of 1788 arising from the general harvest failure of that year. As François Furet explained with something of a rhetorical flourish:[10] 'From 1787, the kingdom of France had been a society without a State.' Beyond the façade of monarchical authority, there lay only 'panic and disorder'. The Revolution simply took over an 'empty space', in the process filling the enormous vacuum created by the sudden and near-total collapse of the once-mighty Bourbon monarchy. Yet, and this is at the heart of so much that was to follow, 'the revolutionary consciousness, from 1789 on, was informed by the illusion of defeating a State that had already ceased to exist'. Out of this came 'the ideology of a radical break with the past' and with this arose 'a tremendous cultural drive for equality'.[11]

---

[4] For a more nuanced perspective see Michael Sonenscher, *Before the Deluge: Public Debt, Inequality, and the Intellectual Origins of the French Revolution* (Princeton, 2007).

[5] Lynn Hunt, *Politics, Culture and Class in the French Revolution* (Berkeley and Los Angeles, 1984), 79.

[6] Mona Ozouf, *L'Homme régénéré: Essais sur la Révolution française* (1989), 116–57.

[7] Hunt, *Politics, Culture and Class*, 221.

[8] See Doyle, *Origins*, 7–40, and Peter R. Campbell (ed.), *The Origins of the French Revolution* (London, 2006).

[9] See Sarah Maza, *The Myth of the French Bourgeoisie: An Essay on the Social Imaginary, 1750–1850* (Cambridge, Mass., 2003). Maza's bold thesis is that 'the French bourgeois did not exist'.

[10] See Furet, *La Révolution française* (2007). For a commentary on Furet's work, see Ran Halévi, *L'Expérience du passé: François Furet dans l'atelier de l'histoire* (2007) and Tony Judt, 'François Furet (1927–1997)', *New York Review of Books* (6 Nov. 2002), 41–2. As Furet expressed it in *Le Monde* published on 19 May 1992: 'What continues to astonish me in retrospect is that in an event that was so dominantly and so extraordinarily political, people for so long wanted to see either social transformation or the emergence of capitalism.'

[11] Furet, *Interpreting the French Revolution* (Cambridge, 1981), 24–5.

There are various dimensions to this account. One, drawing upon the work of Guy Chaussinand-Nogaret,[12] suggests that the nobility were not the reactionary and closed caste they were so often taken to be. 'In cultural development and in the political and social thought of the Enlightenment', Chaussinand-Nogaret wrote, 'nobles played a role as important as the representatives of the Third Estate.' Moreover, from the 1760s onwards, the nobility took on the idea of merit and showed themselves as eager as, if not more than, the bourgeoisie to take advantage of the new commercial opportunities afforded by the market.[13] Through marriage the differences between nobility and middle classes were becoming increasingly blurred, even though this process was not occurring as quickly as the latter might have wished. This in turn produced a political programme that would be advanced by the aristocratic representatives of the National Assembly. 'Despotism, favouritism, intrigue, irresponsibility, waste', Chaussinand-Nogaret wrote, 'these were the governmental vices that the nobility sought to reform'. In broad terms, this meant constitutional government, an end to privilege and equality before the law.

What went wrong? At a minimum: two things. First, in the summer of 1789 the nobility jumped both ways. One group, sheltered (in Chaussinand-Nogaret's phrase) from 'the contaminations of the age', opposed innovation: the other 'welcomed the boldest reforms'. Second, and more seriously, the nobility 'became the victims of their own line of thought'. By questioning the authority of their right to hereditary power they irretrievably undermined their own legitimacy. This argument finds support in more recent work by William Doyle. Prior to the Revolution, Doyle contends, the French nobility were 'the most open elite in Europe'; but during the Revolution itself, he suggests, they proved to be their own 'most fateful' enemies.[14]

A related part of this argument focuses upon the emergence of the ideology and rhetoric of anti-nobilism. Here we can draw upon the thesis advanced by Patrice Higonnet.[15] Recognizing that 'the distance between most nobles and most bourgeois was not great in 1789', Higonnet nevertheless contends that there existed differences, if not of substance, then of style, and that these fed powerfully into perceptions of what existed, thus distorting the 'supposed realities of the situation'. To that extent, Higonnet rightly states, 'the actions of the nobles had little to do with their fate'. Rather, what mattered was the evolution of the attitude of the bourgeoisie towards the nobility. This passed through various stages. Armed with

---

[12] Guy Chaussinand-Nogaret, *La Noblesse au XVIIIe siècle: De la féodalité aux lumières* (1976).

[13] See also Daniel Roche, *France in the Enlightenment* (Cambridge, Mass., 1998), 418. Of the debate concerning the so-called 'commercial nobility' Roche writes: 'The controversy reveals a society in which the highest levels of the bourgeoisie and the highest levels of the aristocracy tended, in terms of economic practice and social relations, to break the legal framework of orders and classes in such a way as to form a single existential group that can be seen as the predecessor of the notables in nineteenth-century bourgeois society. At the same time, however, a substantial segment of the society was unwilling to give up existing privileges.'

[14] William Doyle, *Aristocracy and its Enemies in the Age of Revolution* (Oxford, 2009). See also Jay M. Smith, *Nobility Reimagined: The Patriotic Nation in Eighteenth-Century France* (Ithaca, NY, 2005).

[15] Patrice Higonnet, *Class, Ideology and the Rights of Nobles during the French Revolution* (Oxford: 1981).

the 'hopelessly unrealistic' expectation that 'the gift of citizenship would transform potentially selfish individuals and make them good', the view in 1789 was that, if the nobility was to be abolished, then the nobles themselves could be transformed (as, indeed, some of them set out to demonstrate). After 1791, in an atmosphere of what Higonnet describes as 'opportunistic anti-nobilism', the nobility were increasingly seen as being both corrupt and treacherous, and therefore to be excluded from the nation. Next came the 'ideological anti-nobilism' of the Jacobins. It was at this point that the physical eradication of the nobility through the Terror became 'the symbolic representation of social regeneration'. 'Only in 1799', Higonnet concludes, 'did the bourgeoisie finally understand that all property owners should make common cause'. Again this argument receives support from Doyle. 'The less threatening nobles became', he writes, 'the more ferociously they were threatened.'[16]

To that extent the bourgeoisie, contrary to what for many years was the prevailing Marxist account of the Revolution, actually acted against their own economic interests, allying themselves with the urban poor and the peasantry in defence of what Higonnet terms an 'abhorrent economic and social levelling'. Why was this so? As Furet pointed out, as early as August 1789 the leaders of the Revolution began to believe that it was time to 'stop' the Revolution, but 'each of these successive rallyings took place only after its leaders had taken the Revolution a step further in order to keep control of the mass movement and to discredit rival factions'. At each moment, in other words, those who wished to bring the Revolution to a close found themselves extending it in order to defeat their opponents. In consequence, the leaders of the Revolution came to embrace ever more radical positions and, with each new phase, the attachment to, first, constitutional monarchy and, then, constitutional government itself became ever weaker.

Here we arrive at the heart of the drama of the Revolution. How could a series of reforms which had set out to abolish privilege and to establish legal and civil liberty lead to a decade of bloody turmoil and produce a new form of revolutionary government?[17] To find an answer to this conundrum we need to provide responses to three questions.

To begin: what, if any, was the connection between 1789, the Revolution that produced the Déclaration des Droits de l'Homme et du Citoyen, and 1793, the Revolution that produced the Reign of Terror? As summarized by Patrice Gueniffey, there have been three answers to this question.[18] The 'counter-revolutionary' answer, articulated first during the Revolution itself, saw 1793 as the 'necessary outcome' of 1789, as the moment which revealed its awful and bloody truth. The 'revolutionary' answer, given its clearest expression in the mid-nineteenth century, saw 1793 as an accident, as the product of civil war and foreign invasion, and therefore as having 'no connection whatsoever with the principles of the Revolution'. The third answer is of more recent origin. This sees the Terror, 1793, as a 'contingent' product of 'the

---

[16] Doyle, *Aristocracy*, 309.
[17] See Keith Michael Baker, 'Transformations of Classical Republicanism in Eighteenth-Century France', *Journal of Modern History*, 73 (2001), 32–53.
[18] Patrice Gueniffey, *La Politique de la Terreur* (2000), 199.

culture of the Revolution'. It was there in embryo in 1789 but needed the circumstances of foreign invasion and civil war to bring to the fore 'passions and ideas
which were not easily compatible with the establishment of political liberty'.[19] 'There
were no revolutionary circumstances', Furet wrote, 'there was a Revolution that fed
on circumstances'.[20]

Second, what was the Terror?[21] This is not easily answered as even the revolutionaries themselves were far from agreeing about what it was. At a minimum,
however, it took three different forms. There was, first of all, the spontaneous and
collective violence associated with the punitive (and usually savage) acts of the
people directed against their opponents. Prison massacres and mob lynchings were
two of its forms. This was violence with no particular aim but vengeance. It both
preceded and post-dated the Revolution and was not specific to it. Jean-Paul Marat,
from the moment he published the first issue of *L'Ami du peuple* on 12 September
1789, was its most tireless advocate. As Gueniffey indicates, Marat's view was that
the enemies of the Revolution should be stoned to death, stabbed, shot, hanged,
burnt, impaled, or torn to pieces. Next there was Terror as the calculated, premeditated, rational, and strategic use of violence as an instrument and as a means
designed to develop what might be termed a logic of example. The execution
of Louis XVI would fall into this category. The aim was to terrorize the 'enemies'
of the Revolution into silence. There was, next, Terror as extermination, the use of
violence to eradicate the enemies of people through their systematic execution. It
was not a question of punishment but of annihilation. The ultimate symbol of this
last stage was *la Sainte Guillotine*, an instrument of execution capable of beheading
the twenty-two leaders of the Girondin faction (one of whom was already dead) in
twenty-five minutes.[22] In terms of chronology, the Revolution went from the first
form of Terror to the third, the definition of the Revolution's enemies being
gradually extended to include ever greater numbers of people. The actual figures
involved were relatively small, with approximately 16,000 people being guillotined
in a nine-month period covering 1793–4. However, these increased dramatically
with the war against the Revolution's opponents in the Vendée and the Revolution's felt need to come up with more inventive and thorough means to dispatch its
opponents.[23]

Let us look at two examples of how the Terror worked. The first is the famous
'Law of Suspects' passed on 17 September 1793, eleven days after the Convention
declared that Terror was 'the order of the day'. This piece of legislation empowered
the State to arrest anyone who 'either by their conduct, their contacts, their words
or their writings, showed themselves to be supporters of tyranny, federalism or the
enemies of the people'. This included those who could have been said to have either
'misled' or 'discouraged' the people. Virtually anybody could have fallen foul of

---

[19] Furet, quoted ibid. 200.
[20] Furet, *Interpreting the Revolution*, 62.
[21] See Gueniffey, *La Politique de la Terreur*.
[22] See Daniel Arasse, *La Guillotine et l'imaginaire de la Terreur* (1987).
[23] Amongst the many attempts to secure a speedier process of execution were plans to build a
guillotine capable of the simultaneous execution of several victims.

such a law, especially as the only evidence required to establish guilt was denuncia-tion by a loyal patriot. The sole punishment for those found guilty was death.[24] The second example illustrates how Terror operated against groups or regions which opposed the Revolution. We will pass over the systematic massacre of the people of the Vendée in western France by the so-called *colonnes infernales* in January 1794 and mention only the fate of the city of Lyons after it had rallied to the cause of counter-Revolution. When it finally surrendered, the Committee of Public Safety decreed that the entire city was to be destroyed in an act of collective punishment, its very name was to disappear and was to be replaced by that of Ville-Affranchie. There was too much work for the guillotine to do, so condemned men were blown into open graves by cannon and gunfire.

The truth is that the Terror developed a logic of its own, threatening or punishing people not for what they did but for what they were or represented. This is why the category of 'suspect' was at its heart. Moreover, it was a 'system' that perpetuated itself. Its defenders liked to portray the Terror as a temporary measure designed to meet exceptional circumstances. However, once installed, it operated not just as a system of arbitrary and absolute power but as something that could not be stopped or even slowed down. Rather the pace of its operation accelerated, in the end engulfing most of the revolutionaries themselves, including Robespierre, his own crime being the 'suspicion' or 'rumour' that he intended to marry the daughter of Louis XVI and have himself crowned as king.

The third question is: who were the Jacobins? It would be a mistake to see the Jacobins as a single homogeneous bloc or party. Initially they took the title of the Société des Amis de la Constitution, later becoming the Société des Amis de la Liberté et de l'Égalité. Members of this society were so called for the reason that they originally met in a former convent of Dominican or 'Jacobin' monks. Whilst its leadership was concentrated in Paris, with Robespierre and those who later constituted the Committee of Public Safety at its heart, there also existed a network of provincial clubs which, at their height, brought together between 100,000 and 200,000 activists who saw their task as that of supporting and implementing the policies of the new regime. Initially the Jacobins were not clearly distinguishable from the other groups that aspired to lead the Revolution, but by 1793 they had distanced themselves from the moderates, such that the Terror of 1793–4 was very much their affair. Not only did the Jacobins implement it but they also provided its political and moral justification.

It is the question of what the Jacobins stood for (and, more generally, what was their significance) that has generated the most controversy. As Patrice Gueniffey has observed: 'through their capacity to embody what was most radical in the French Revolution, and consequently to embody the Revolution itself, the Jacobins passed into the two centuries which followed as legend, history, tradition, heritage, theory

---

[24] At first substantial numbers of suspects were acquitted but over time this number was dramatically reduced as a percentage of those placed on trial. See Gérard Walter, *Actes du Tribunal Révolutionnaire* (1986).

and practice'.[25] As for Robespierre himself, [26] as Furet remarked, he had 'the strange privilege of becoming an *embodiment*'. 'Robespierre', he wrote, 'is an immortal figure not because he reigned supreme over the Revolution for a few months, but because he was the mouthpiece of its purest and most tragic discourse.'[27]

Above all, this was a discourse that assigned a new goal to the Revolution: that of attaining the reign of virtue and of bringing about a return to a natural, prelapsarian order.[28] 'Considering', Robespierre declared, 'the extent to which the human race has been degraded by the vice of our former social system, I am convinced of the need to bring about a complete regeneration . . . to create a new people.'[29] How did the Jacobins envision their model of virtue? At its core was a quest for simplicity and a rejection of what were seen as the imperfections, the shallowness, and false appearances of the corrupt present. Robespierre, who gloried in his mythical status as the 'Incorruptible', was its very incarnation. Immune from ordinary passions (there is no evidence that Robespierre engaged in any sexual activity),[30] he above all others was best placed to denounce the failings and prejudices of ordinary mortals. No one could better tear away the 'masks' behind which were hidden depravity, avarice, and ambition.

This can be illustrated by citing one example of Robespierre's rhetoric. Robespierre detested the theatre. He did so because, of all the arts, it more than any other was a world of appearance, and therefore was capable of corrupting an innocent people. 'The princesses of the theatre', Robespierre announced, 'are no better than the princesses of Austria. Both are equally depraved and both should be treated with equal severity.'[31] Actors, and especially pretty actresses, were to be denied access to the ranks of the people. Moreover, Robespierre extended this argument to politics itself. In a remarkable tirade delivered before the Jacobins on 8 January 1794 Robespierre compared the opponents of the Revolution to actors, where the politically and morally corrupt followed each other in a succession of different 'masks'.[32] 'It is always', Robespierre declared, 'the same scene, the same theatrical action'. Conversely, it was his sense of his own moral purity that provided the Jacobins with the audacity first to denounce and then to physically destroy their opponents, repeating with hypnotic regularity the denunciation of their moral turpitude and crimes. 'I sometimes fear', Robespierre announced shortly before

---

[25] Patrice Gueniffey, 'Jacobinisme', in François Furet and Mona Ozouf, *Dictionnaire critique de la Révolution française: Idées* (1992), 243. See also Patrice Gueniffey, 'Robespierre', ibid., *Acteurs*, 247–71.

[26] See Ruth Scurr, *Fatal Purity: Robespierre and the French Revolution* (London, 2007).

[27] Furet, *Interpreting the Revolution*, 56, 61. For a selection of Robespierre's speeches in English: see Slavoj Žižek (ed.), *Robespierre: Virtue and Terror* (London, 2007).

[28] See Lucien Jaume, *Le Discours Jacobin et la démocratie* (1989) and Mona Ozouf, '"Jacobin": Fortune et infortunes d'un mot', *L'École de la France: Essais sur la Révolution, l'utopie et l'enseignement* (1984), 74–90.

[29] *Œuvres de Maximilien Robespierre*, x. *Discours de 27 juillet 1793–27 juillet 1794* (1967), 12.

[30] Scurr, *Fatal Purity*, 102, indicates that upon his arrival in Paris Robespierre acquired a mistress. The evidence is not conclusive.

[31] *Œuvres de Maximilien Robespierre*, x. 101.

[32] See Paul Friedland, *Political Actors: Representative Bodies and Theatricality in the French Revolution* (Ithaca, NY, 2002).

his own fall from power, 'that in the eyes of posterity I will be sullied by the impure proximity of wicked men'.[33]

The second point of reference for the Jacobin model of virtue was the classical world of Greece and Rome. Turning their backs on the Christian tradition, it was Solon, Lycurgus, and Brutus who were their heroes, with a clear preference being expressed for Sparta over Athens. As Robespierre's most loyal supporter, Saint-Just, was to remark, the world had been empty since the Romans. Here was fertile terrain for the florid imaginations of the revolutionaries, as they dwelt upon a world where there was no industry, no commerce, no luxury, no big cities, only the rustic simplicity of peasant farmers and the sublime heroism of citizen-soldiers. It was also an exclusively male world, public space being reserved only for the activities of men and for supposedly male virtues.

Most of all, it was a world which saw public participation in the communal affairs of the State as the source of moral worth. The good individual was the good citizen and the good citizen was the good patriot. Saint-Just summed this up when he said that the 'good citizen' was ardent, pure, austere, and disinterested. There, he proclaimed, was the 'character of a patriot'.[34] The common good was always to take precedence over the individual interest; the public realm was at all times to have priority over the private sphere. The Jacobins were unambiguous about this. 'A man who lacks public virtues', Robespierre announced, 'cannot have private virtues.'[35] Again, this had an overt political message. What, Robespierre asked, have the 'enemies' of the Revolution understood by virtue? 'By this word', he responded, 'they have all understood fidelity to certain private and domestic obligations; but they have never understood it in terms of public virtues, never as selfless devotion to the cause of the people.'[36]

Accordingly, the moral regeneration of the individual—at times for Robespierre it was also a physical regeneration, achieved through the regimentation and control of a citizen's diet and clothing[37]—could best be secured in a communal setting and it was this that explained the fascination of the Jacobins for civic festivals. Of these, the most portentous and imposing were the ceremonies constructed around the cult of the Supreme Being.[38] This new civic religion was to purge the individual of everything that was to distinguish him or her from the civic body. All divisions would disappear before the universal religion of nature.[39]

How did this lead to the Terror? Everything indicates that the Jacobins believed that moral regeneration would be spontaneous and would be grounded upon the innate moral goodness of the people. Once the aristocratic prejudices and practices of the old order had been removed and once, most importantly, the people had

[33] *Œuvres de Maximilien Robespierre*, x. 567.
[34] Quoted in Jaume, *Le Discours Jacobin*, 211.
[35] *Œuvres de Maximilien Robespierre*, x. 520.
[36] Ibid. 531.
[37] Ibid. 15–20.
[38] See Mona Ozouf, *La Fête révolutionnaire, 1789–99* (1976).
[39] See 'Sur les Rapports des idées réligieuses et morales avec les principes républicains, et sur les fêtes républicains', *Œuvres de Maximilien Robespierre*, x. 443–62.

been placed in an appropriately beneficial educational environment, virtue would reign triumphant. Everyone could participate in this renewal, even the former noble and Catholic priest. Indeed, so embracing was this vision of universal fraternity and moral harmony that it could even welcome the foreigner.

However, real human beings, with their earthly passions, presented the Jacobins with something of a problem. Not everyone showed themselves prepared to be convinced by this vision of the sublime; opponents refused to go away; dissenting voices continued to be heard; well-intentioned measures for reform produced practical disasters. The only explanation could be the continued existence of selfishness and wickedness. So, with mounting intensity, the Jacobins deployed a rhetoric that contrasted 'virtue', 'truth', 'purity', and 'people' with that of 'vice', 'falsehood', 'corruption', and 'individuals'. There could be no compromise with such 'evil' and therefore death could be perceived as the rational alternative to a failure or absence of virtue.

Thus, the remorseless logic of extermination could begin. The corrupt, the traitors, the turncoats, the backsliders, the opportunists, the cowards, the moderates, the false revolutionaries, the immoral, those lacking in virtue, all could be removed. Robespierre's speeches are littered with such language, possibly his favourite derogatory expression being that of *fripon* or rascal. The world was full of such unworthy characters, all of them eager to subvert the government of the Republic. Yet each purification, each wave of executions, seemed only to leave France still divided between the pure and the wicked, necessitating renewed zeal. Category upon category of people became the objects of suspicion, up to and including the revolutionaries themselves, such that they started to slaughter one another, with Robespierre being obliged in each case to further radicalize the process, if only to keep his own head. So, little by little, there emerged an ideology of Terror, which not only justified its use but also identified its victims. Terror was to be an emanation of virtue and the guillotine was to be the means of separating the good from the wicked.[40]

Its clearest definition came in Robespierre's speech before the Convention on 5 February 1794.[41] 'Within the scheme of the French Revolution', Robespierre declared, 'that which is immoral is impolitic, that which is corrupting is counter-revolutionary.' If, he went on, 'the mainspring of popular government in peacetime is virtue, amid revolution it is at one and the same time *virtue and terror*: virtue, without terror, is ill-fated; terror, without virtue, is impotent.' Terror, therefore, was 'nothing but prompt, severe, inflexible justice'. Slowness of judgement amounted to impunity, to punish oppressors was 'clemency' and to pardon them was a 'barbarity'. No one except the guilty had anything to fear but to tremble was itself a sign of guilt.[42]

---

[40] Furet, *Interpreting the Revolution*, 69–70.
[41] For key speeches by Robespierre, Saint-Just, and Couthon in support of the Terror see *L'Impossible Terreur* (1989).
[42] *Œuvres de Maximilien Robespierre*, x. 350–66.

What was needed for the guilty to be punished? Here Robespierre and his colleagues had no doubts: revolutionary government.[43] This, Robespierre acknowledged, was a concept that was 'as new as the revolution that had produced it'. Its definition and description could not be found 'in the books of writers on politics', because they had not foreseen the Revolution. Yet, with astonishing prescience, Robespierre understood exactly what it was, and so made the all-important distinction between revolutionary and constitutional government. 'The goal of constitutional government', he clarified, 'is to conserve the Republic; that of revolutionary government is to establish it. The Revolution is the war of liberty against its enemies; the Constitution is the regime of victorious and peaceful liberty.' Under a constitutional government, it was sufficient to protect the individual from the abuses of public power; under a revolutionary government the public power was obliged to defend itself against all the factions that attacked it, 'deploying without cease new and rapid means in response to new and pressing dangers'. Revolutionary government owed its citizens the full weight of its protection; towards its enemies it owed 'only death'. Revolutionary government, in short, was government without limits, government in a vacuum, government as absolute power. It was, to cite Robespierre's most famous phrase, 'the despotism of liberty against tyranny'. Its goal was nothing less than 'the salvation of the people'.[44]

How could such a revolutionary government come to an end? This was possible only when all the enemies of the Revolution had been defeated. But this, as defined by the revolutionary project, was not a possibility. The alternative was the death of the revolutionaries themselves. 'Is not', Robespierre asked, 'the death of the founders of the liberty itself a triumph?' Only the 'tomb' would bring them 'rest'. 'I', he announced, 'do not believe in the necessity of life.' On 30 July 1794 Robespierre, having first tried to kill himself, was granted his wish, leaving behind, as he said in his final speech, 'only a terrible truth and death'.[45]

The men who secured Robespierre's dramatic removal from power and his execution had as their goal not only that of preserving their own lives but also that of terminating the Revolution. The Constitution of Year III, promulgated during the summer of 1795, sought to establish the Republic upon a secure and stable basis, limiting popular sovereignty, protecting individual liberties, and locating power in the hands of an educated elite.[46] First, however, France had to extract herself from the Terror, a task which entailed much more than the execution of Robespierre and his closest associates.[47] The administrative and organizational structure of the Terror had to be dismantled and those deemed responsible needed to be judged. This was an entirely new experience, and was not one to be accomplished either quickly or easily. Nor was the restoration of justice without its own acts of arbitrary

---

[43] 'Rapport sur les Principes du gouvernement révolutionnaire fait au nom du Comité du Salut Public', ibid. 273–7.

[44] Ibid. 357.

[45] Ibid. 567.

[46] See Michel Troper, *Terminer la Révolution: La Constitution de 1795* (2006).

[47] Bronislaw Baczko, *Comment sortir de la Terreur: Thermidor et la Révolution* (1989). See also Sophie Wahnich, *Les Émotions, la Révolution française et le présent* (2009).

revenge. As Benjamin Constant was to observe shortly afterwards: 'nothing is rarer than the passage from arbitrary power to the rule of law'.[48]

But the Terror left an even more enduring problem. What sense could be made of it? How could it be explained? What had been the cause of its genesis? Did its original source lie in the people or in their leaders? How could its reappearance be prevented? There is an argument, recently advanced by Patrice Gueniffey, which sees the resort to Terror as the 'fate' not just of the French Revolution but of all revolutions. Seen as such, the use of Terror is integral to the logic of revolution itself, its employment intrinsic to a situation where power is used absolutely and without limits.[49] Gueniffey is probably correct and, it could be argued, it was precisely this truth that was perceived by Edmund Burke as early as 1790. But this was not an argument available to those who sought simultaneously to understand their own immediate past and to move France forward towards the establishment of a more enduring and less threatening regime.[50]

No one better represented this endeavour than Benjamin Constant. In the uncertain years that followed the establishment of the Directory in 1795 he published a series of brilliant pamphlets designed to alert France to the need to break with what he termed her 'revolutionary habits'. These habits included an enthusiasm for counter-revolution.[51] Most persuasive of all was his text *Des effets de la Terreur*, published in May 1797. Here Constant set out to demolish all of the arguments which suggested that the Terror had been somehow either 'inevitable' or 'beneficial'. It had not saved the Republic. It had not overcome the obstacles faced by the Revolution. It had not created a 'new people'. It had not prepared France for a 'free constitution'. Rather, Constant argued, it had destroyed the 'public spirit' of the people, prepared them for 'servitude', and produced the vicious circle of crime following crime. Worse still, the savage events that had accompanied the birth of the First Republic had led people 'to conflate the Republic with the Terror, the republicans with their executioners'.[52]

What then did the future hold? With his usual lucidity, Constant realized that there could be no return to the past. If people wanted rest, that rest 'had to be found in the Republic' because, if not, the alternative was 'to recommence, in the opposite direction, the terrible path that France has taken and to return to tyranny by revisiting the river of blood which had flowed in the name of liberty'.[53] Like it or not, in other words, France's future was inextricably linked with the republican form of government, in whatever shape that might be. Somehow or other, that

---

[48] Benjamin Constant, *Des Réactions politiques* (1797), 92.

[49] Gueniffey, *La Politique de la Terreur*, 226.

[50] See Andrew Jainchill, *Reimagining Politics after the Terror: The Republican Origins of French Liberalism* (Ithaca, NY, 2008).

[51] In addition to *Des Réactions politiques*, see *De la Force du Gouvernement actuel de la France et de la necessité de s'y rallier* (1796) and *Des Suites de la contre-révolution de 1660 en Angleterre* (1799).

[52] Constant, *Des effets de la Terreur* (Lausanne, 1948), 45. The text was originally published in May 1797.

[53] Constant, *De la Force du Gouvernement actuel*, 109.

regime had to be built and consolidated. The choice, Constant averred, was a stark one: between 'order and liberty on one side, anarchy and despotism on the other'.[54]

Which path would France take? Constant himself feared the worst, correctly perceiving that, for many, the exercise of arbitrary power had not lost its attractions. Accordingly, the stark choice he set out for France was one that was to remain well beyond the final decade of the eighteenth century. Here perhaps we should again refer to Robespierre. The Revolution, in a very real sense, came to an end with his fall. The dream of recreating human beings and of rebuilding society from top to bottom was over. Yet, as Robespierre knew, even in death he was leaving behind a powerful legacy. In his final, passionate, and furious speech, denouncing enemy after enemy, he again called upon his fellow revolutionaries to draw upon all their resources of courage. For, if they did not, the consequences were clear. France, he told them, would suffer 'a century of civil wars and of calamity' and they, in turn, would perish. What followed was accurately to bear out this sombre prediction. It is that century of civil war and calamity that provides the political backdrop for the ideas examined in this volume.

II

If the dramatic course taken by the Revolution of 1789 could not have been foreseen, the same might perhaps not be said of the collapse of the social and political order that was soon to be known as the *ancien régime*. Successive attempts at financial and institutional reform—both half-hearted and genuine—had all come to nothing, a situation greatly acerbated by the inertia of the kindly but irresolute Louis XVI. In the end the French monarchy ran out of both money and ideas. If few now take seriously the claim, beloved of Marxist historians such as Georges Lefebvre, that the decisive and determining cause of the French Revolution was the rise of the capitalist bourgeoisie,[55] it would equally be a mistake to believe that the Revolution was entirely without social origins. The actions of the peasantry and of the people of Paris in the summer of 1789 were proof alone of this. More interesting from our perspective, however, was the realm of public opinion. Never before had it been so powerful or (as the unfortunate Queen Marie-Antoinette was to discover) so fickle.

Here recent investigations into how people lived, worked, dressed, consumed, and spoke—*l'histoire des choses banales*[56]—have successfully opened up the way for ground-breaking studies of the press, book-selling and readership, education, religious rituals, public festivals, and sexual habits. Thus, by moving away from the 'great texts' of the High Enlightenment towards the actual diffusion and vulgarization of books and pamphlets (including pornographic ones) of

---

[54] Constant, *De la Force du Gouvernement actuel*, 3.
[55] But see Henry Heller, *The Bourgeois Revolution in France, 1789–1815* (New York, 2006).
[56] Daniel Roche, *Histoire des choses banales* (1997).

eighteenth-century low life,[57] it became possible to provide an entirely novel account of the cultural origins of the French Revolution. They were to be found, as Roger Chartier has shown, in the de-Christianization of French society and the de-sacralization of the monarchy. By separating the person of the monarch from the divine, these long-term trends meant that the institution itself could be subject to ridicule and profanity.[58] Likewise, by looking at 'perceptions and conceptions, customs and practices' of the people, Daniel Roche in his *La France des Lumières* has revealed how the 'popular representation' of the monarchy came under severe strain—there was, he writes, 'a demand for irreverence, transgression, and subversion'—leading ultimately to 'a major symbolic crisis' affecting 'the organic structure of the Ancien Régime state'. The people, he continues, discovered the existence of a 'void' at the heart of the 'principal royal functions'. Ultimately, Roche contends, the 'divine right monarchy acknowledged its helplessness', paving the way for a series of crises crystallized around two main areas of conflict: the need to solve the kingdom's financial problems and the question of whether representation in the recalled Estates-General should take a traditional or new form. In the end, the decision was made to double the number of representatives from the Third Estate but to preserve voting by order. The polarizing consequences of this decision and of the elections that were to follow had a dramatic impact upon the course of events in the summer of 1789.

If attention has fallen upon the manner in which the Bourbon monarchy was stripped of its sacred aura, so too it has focused upon the producers of ideas themselves and, more broadly, the structural dimensions of intellectual life in France. Moreover, what these inquiries serve to reveal and to emphasize are the significant levels of continuity between the intellectual practices of pre- and post-revolutionary France. This also constitutes an important backdrop to the political ideas to be discussed in this volume.

As is well known, Jürgen Habermas has argued that intellectuals were the representatives of an emergent public sphere.[59] As the eighteenth century evolved, French *philosophes* in the *salons*, German philosophers in reading societies, and English writers in coffee houses came together in a social space in order to participate, as independent thinkers, in the open discussion of matters of cultural and political interest. The French case is especially intriguing. In the seventeenth century everything was done to bring a rising republic of letters under royal patronage, principally through such institutions as the Académie Française and the Académie des Sciences. Similar, if less powerful and prestigious, institutions were created in the provinces.

---

[57] See Robert Darnton, 'The High Enlightenment and Low-Life Literature in Pre-Revolutionary France', *Past and Present*, 51 (1971), 81–115. See also Simon Burrows, *A King's Ransom: The Life of Charles Théveneau de Morande, Blackmailer, Scandalmonger and Master-Spy* (London, 2010).

[58] See Roger Chartier, *Les Origines culturelles de la Révolution française* (Paris, 1991). Chartier's argument is that the 18th cent. saw the emergence of a new way of reading texts, less based on authority and religion, and more 'free, casual and critical' in character.

[59] Jürgen Habermas, *The Structural Transformation of the Public Sphere: An Inquiry into a Category of Bourgeois Society* (Cambridge, Mass., 1989). See also Didier Masseau, *L'Invention de l'intellectuel dans l'Europe du XVIIIe siècle* (1994).

Freed from the vagaries of aristocratic benefaction, men of letters nevertheless found themselves compromised, implicated in the broader project of absolutist state-building and the greater glory of the monarchy.[60] In 1662 a report presented to Louis XIV on the use of the arts 'for preserving the splendour of the king's enterprises' listed ninety men of letters and their aptitudes to serve the monarch. This advice was duly followed and from 1663 onwards sizeable pensions were awarded to writers and scholars. Particular attention was given to historians, with the appointment of historiographers royal. Over a century later, in 1774, the Baron de Breuteuil, future first minister of Louis XVI, wrote a memorandum exploring the question of 'how to make use of men of letters', a text that, according to Munro Price, 'argued that the monarchy should stop treating writers as enemies, as Louis XV had done in his last years, and instead make friends of them through patronage'.[61]

As both Daniel Roche and Dena Goodman have observed,[62] the *salons* of eighteenth-century Paris played a key role in reducing this degree of dependency upon the State. Here conversation and discussion reigned supreme, and did so in an atmosphere that became ever less frivolous and ever more preoccupied with the advance of knowledge. Under the governance of their often-competing female hosts, the *salons* brought together people of diverse social backgrounds and nationalities, but at their heart were the *philosophes*.

'Without being fully conscious of it', writes Pierre Lepape, the *philosophes* 'formed a new social group characterized by their unfettered use of knowledge and by their demand for complete liberty of expression, a dispersed community united at the level of ideas by the same creed of the search for truth by means of reason and experimentation.'[63] It was Voltaire—in the three entries in his *Dictionnaire philosophique* (1764) devoted to 'Philosophes', 'Gens de Lettres' and 'Lettres, Gens de lettres, ou lettrés'— who first provided their collective self-portrait and who, in his famous defence of Calas, gave form to a new type of political engagement. Having no power but in his words and pen, he attacked arbitrary power and the miscarriage of justice in the name of humanity and praised what he termed 'independence of mind'.[64] The transformation that occurred over the century was accurately summarized (and criticized) in 1805 by Louis de Bonald, one of the most articulate voices of Catholic reaction. Asked to comment on the influence of *gens de lettres*, he replied: 'If, in the century of Louis XIV, the Académie Française had proposed a similar subject for discussion, it would have spoken of the *duties* of *gens de lettres*. Today it is a question of their *independence*.'[65]

---

[60] See Daniel Roche, *Les Républicains des lettres: Gens de culture et Lumières au XVIII siècle* (1988), 151–71 and Peter Burke, *The Fabrication of Louis XIV* (New Haven, Conn., 1992), 49–59.

[61] *The Fall of the French Monarchy* (London, 2003), 50.

[62] Roche, *France in the Enlightenment*, 443; Dena Goodman, *The Republic of Letters: A Cultural History of the French Enlightenment* (Ithaca, NY, 1994), 12–52. See also Antoine Lilti, *Le Monde des salons: Sociabilité et mondanité à Paris au XVIII siècle* (2005). Lilti's account emphasizes the aristocratic practices of sociability typical of the *salons* and downplays the role of radical ideas.

[63] Pierre Lepape, *Voltaire Le Conquérant: Naissance des intellectuels au siècle des Lumières* (1994), 269.

[64] Opponents were far less charitable: see Joseph de Maistre, *Œuvres* (2007), 557.

[65] Louis de Bonald, 'Réflexions sur les questions de l'indépendance des gens de lettres, et de l'influence du théâtre sur les mœurs et le gout, proposées pour le sujet de prix par l'institut national, à sa séance de 29 juin 1805', in *Œuvres complètes*, x (1838; repr. Geneva, 1982), 58.

Here was a model that was to be replicated endlessly in future years, the man of letters raised to the status of what Paul Bénichou referred to as 'a secular spiritual power'.[66] Ironically, the enemies of the *philosophes* were obliged to adopt similar strategies and techniques.[67]

Central to the appearance of this new social category was the influence of a market economy that undermined traditional commercial and social relations. It was in this context that the great nineteenth-century critic Sainte-Beuve could speak of 'la littérature industrielle'.[68] Extending this argument, Christophe Charle has shown how the growth of the book trade—built upon an expansion of the reading public—and an expanding free press in the nineteenth century further served to enhance the autonomy of the writer. These factors, when combined with the gradual expansion of higher education, led to a significant increase in the numbers employed within the university and literary sectors of the economy, a development which itself gave rise to the concept of a literary bohemia existing in penury at the margins of conventional society. Moreover, as the power and authority of the Catholic Church continued to wane, men of letters came more and more to replace the priest as both society's guide and its repository of values. To refer to Christophe Charle again, he has shown how, as the nineteenth century progressed, the figures of the poet, the artist, the prophet, and, finally, the scientist were in turn accorded the status of being the voice of humanity. In summary, writers and intellectuals more generally were able over time to reduce their dependence upon both Church and State.

However, it would be a mistake to over-emphasize the innovatory aspects of the public sphere in the post-revolutionary period. The *salons* continued to play a key role as institutions of intellectual and political sociability until well into the nineteenth century.[69] If they were eclipsed during the Revolution, they were to an extent reconstituted by aristocratic émigrés forced into exile and were then revived in France under the Directory and, even more so, with the advent of the First Empire in 1804. According to Stephen Kale, between 1815 and 1848 the *salons* 'became the principal centres of elite political networking and discussion' and remained relatively free from repressive interference by the State. For example, the dominant political figure of the July Monarchy, François Guizot, arranged his social life around the *salon* of his mistress, the Princess Lieven. Likewise, Alexis de Tocqueville attended the *salons* of the Duchesse de Rauzannot, Madame de Castellane, and the Duchesse de Dino, the latter presided over by the illustrious Charles-Maurice de Talleyrand, Prince of Benevento. Under the July Monarchy

---

[66] Paul Bénichou, *Le Sacre de l'écrivain 1750–1830: Essai sur l'avènement d'un pouvoir spirituel laïque dans la France moderne* (1996). See also Priscilla Parkhurst Clark, *Literary France: The Making of a Culture* (Berkeley and Los Angeles, 1987), 126–58.

[67] Didier Masseau, *Les Ennemis des philosophes: L'Antiphilosophie au temps des Lumières* (2000), 273–320. See also Darrin M. McMahon, *Enemies of the Enlightenment: The French Counter-Enlightenment and the Making of Modernity* (Oxford, 2001).

[68] 'Quelques Vérités sur la situation en littérature', in C. A. Sainte-Beuve, *Portraits Contemporains* (1846), 327–46.

[69] Steven Kale, *French Salons: High Society and Political Sociability from the Old Regime to the Revolution of 1848* (Baltimore, 2004).

Tocqueville was a regular attendee at the *salon* of the Princess Belgiojoso and at several other foreign *salons* in Paris.[70]

The decline of the *salons* was a gradual, rather than a precipitate, one and they continued to flourish until their near-extinction in the late nineteenth century, receiving their last and possibly greatest literary invocation in the novels of Marcel Proust. Kale himself suggests several factors to explain their decline, not the least of which were the rise of parliamentary politics and a collapse of the aristocratic conception of the role of women, but the point is that the *salons* were replaced by new forms of intellectual sociability. Amongst these new sites were to be the newspaper editor's office, the publishing house, and the offices of the many literary and political reviews that flourished in the Paris of the *Belle Époque* and beyond. The weekly discussions that took place in the tiny Latin Quarter office of Charles Péguy's *Cahiers de la quinzaine* were fairly typical of the latter, as were later to be those at *La Nouvelle Revue Française* (under André Gide) and *Les Temps modernes* (under Jean-Paul Sartre). The Parisian café—of which there were an estimated 40,000 in the 1880s—also came to occupy a central place in intellectual life, with those of Saint-Germain-des-Prés becoming synonymous with French intellectual life.[71] These varied institutions, with their discrete practices, have served to give a distinctive character to the manner in which political ideas have been expressed and articulated in France.

Nor should we ignore the restraints upon intellectual production in the periods both before and after 1789. Despite the growing importance of the Republic of Letters during the eighteenth century, writers for the most part continued to be drawn from the traditional elites of the *ancien régime* and few were those who were able to live by their pen alone. The reality for most was the garret, the café, and 'the columns of third-rate reviews'.[72] The Revolution, in overthrowing monarchical and feudal power, largely put an end to royal and aristocratic patronage, leaving men of letters at the mercy of a commercial market that offered only limited economic support. Not surprisingly, therefore, the numbers involved still remained small, as was the readership of books, journals, and the popular press. The most prestigious review of the age, the *Revue des Deux Mondes*, had only 350 subscribers in 1831 and still as few as 2,500 in 1846 (compared with the 13,500 subscribers to the *Edinburgh Review* in 1818). Despite a significant increase in the number of titles, the average circulation of provincial newspapers in this period was in the region of 700–1,500 copies. It is estimated that the number of new book titles rose from 800 in 1789 to 7,600 in 1850 and to 12,000 in the decade of the 1890s, but those like Victor Hugo and Émile Zola who earned a living from writing alone remained the exception.[73]

[70] André Jardin, *Tocqueville: A Biography* (Baltimore, 1998), 398–9.
[71] See Antony Beever and Artemis Cooper, *Paris After the Liberation 1944–1949* (London, 1995).
[72] Robert Darnton, 'The Facts of Literary Life in Eighteenth-Century France', in Keith M. Baker (ed.), *The Political Culture of the Old Regime* (Oxford, 1987), 261–92.
[73] See Clark, *Literary France*, 37–60.

Censorship during the eighteenth century was generally agreed to be largely inefficient and ineffective—many books and newspapers banned in France were simply imported from the Netherlands and Britain—but it did exist and continued to make life difficult for those not prepared to toe the official line. There was, according to Charles Walton, 'a widespread consensus that the State should maintain and reinforce moral values, customs, and manners'.[74] As Benjamin Constant was later to remind his readers, in 1767 edicts were passed which condemned to death authors of writings calculated to stir up people's minds.[75] In 1789 the 'free communication of ideas and opinions' was recognized through Article 11 of the Déclaration des Droits de l'Homme et du Citoyen, but, to refer again to Walton, the 'surveillance, repression and manipulation' of expressions of political opinions by the State continued to exist. Building upon a law on sedition passed in July 1791, the legislation of the Terror made the publication and expression of anti-patriotic and defamatory opinion a crime punishable by death. Napoleon I quickly re-established the censorship of books and the press, frequently subjecting journalists and writers to prosecution. For example, Destutt de Tracy's important *Commentaire sur l'Esprit des lois de Montesquieu* was first published anonymously in Philadelphia in 1811,[76] whilst the liberal periodical *Le Censeur*, edited by Charles Comte and Charles Dunoyer, was closed down altogether. Press freedom (within limits) was reaffirmed in the constitutional charter of 1814 and further strengthened through a series of laws in 1819 (thereby enabling the press to play an important role in the downfall of Charles X in 1830) but the Villèle government ended jury trial for press offences so as to increase the likelihood of guilty verdicts. Restrictions continued under the July Monarchy after 1830. The September laws of 1835 increased the amount of caution money required by the government before a newspaper could be started and such was the general penury of the press that journalists were frequently compared to prostitutes. 'The Restoration', wrote Tocqueville in 1843, 'was one long and imprudent battle by the government against the press. The years which have followed the July Revolution have presented the same spectacle with the difference, however, that under the Restoration it was the press that finished by defeating the government whilst in our day it is the government that has triumphed over the press.'[77] Controls over publishing media were augmented under the Second Republic (when newspapers were banned from saying anything insulting about the President) and again in the early years of the Second Empire (the amount required as caution money was raised

---

[74] *Policing Public Opinion in the French Revolution: The Culture of Calumny and the Problem of Free Speech* (Oxford, 2009), 10.

[75] Benjamin Constant, *Principles of Politics Applicable to All Governments* (Indianapolis, 2003), 152. Constant was mistaken about the date: the edicts were passed in 1757.

[76] See Gilbert Chinard, *Jefferson et les Idéologues d'après sa correspondance inédite* (Baltimore, 1925), 31–96.

[77] Alexis de Tocqueville, 'Lettres sur la situation intérieure de la France', *Œuvres complètes* (1985), iii/2. 112. The French press, Tocqueville contended, had more power than its American opposite number. This was because it was concentrated in one place—Paris—and in fewer hands.

in 1852).[78] They were not relaxed with the advent of the Third Republic. Writing in 1873, the historian Edgar Quinet could comment that '[t]he condition of the writer is worse in France than in any other place in Europe: the law treats him as a suspect and surrounds him with mistrust and traps'.[79] It was only in 1881 that controls over the publication of books and newspapers were completely removed.

This new-found freedom, when combined with reduced production costs, improved distribution methods, and higher levels of literacy, encouraged a flourishing daily and periodical press, but this in turn brought a press that was both corrupt and controlled by financial interests.[80] Press restrictions were reimposed in the 1890s (in response to violence by anarchist groups) whilst the 1881 Act was suspended in 1940 with the fall of France and the beginning of the Vichy regime. In 1944 a set of ordinances banned any papers that had appeared under the German occupation and sought to protect the press from what were seen as dangerous commercial interests. This attempt to preserve the press from monopoly control was achieved at the expense of heavy reliance upon state subsidy. Newspaper sales per head of the population in France were lower than in any other industrialized western European country, except Italy. Moreover, at the height of the Algerian conflict in the late 1950s the State sought systematically to intimidate editors and journalists through the confiscation of their publications.

State control and censorship of the opera and the theatre—activities suspected of engendering unruly behaviour and of encouraging the expression of public opinion—were finally abolished only in 1907. If, in the eighteenth century, the *cause célèbre* was the production of Beaumarchais's *La Folle Journée, ou le Mariage de Figaro*, for her part, Sheryl Kroen has shown how the staging of Molière's anticlerical *Tartuffe* became a source of popular demonstration against the religious policies of both Church and State during the Restoration and how, as a consequence, its performance was frequently banned by the authorities (as indeed it had been during the reign of Louis XIV).[81] To that extent, calls for aesthetic purity, often justified in terms of art for art's sake, were frequently a reflection and product of political repression. After the Second World War radio and television broadcasting were a state monopoly. A powerful, and at times heavily interventionist, Ministry of Information oversaw the content of radio and television programmes, thereby ensuring that broadcasters could not forget that, in President Pompidou's words, they were 'the voice of France'. Only in the 1980s did the State begin to loosen its grip.

Likewise the State—especially in the period between the Restoration and the 1848 Revolution—kept a watchful eye over what was taught in universities and did not hesitate to remove troublesome academics when necessary. Both François

---

[78] Jules Simon commented of the laws operating under the Second Empire that 'it would be easy to show that [they] give to the administration the means to kill whatever paper they wish with extreme ease': *La Liberté politique* (1871), 208.

[79] Edgar Quinet, *La République, conditions de la régénération de la France* (1873), 120.

[80] See Christophe Charle, *Le Siècle de la presse* (2004).

[81] Sheryl Kroen, *Politics and Theatre: The Crisis of Legitimacy in Restoration France, 1815–1830* (Berkeley, Calif., 2000).

Guizot and Jules Michelet were to fall victim to this practice. More oppressive still, the State resorted to imprisonment of those writers taken to be its opponents. In 1832 this fate was to befall two leaders of the Saint-Simonian movement, Prosper Enfantin and Michel Chevalier, and later afflicted Félicité de Lamennais, Alexis de Tocqueville, Pierre-Joseph Proudhon, and many others in the nineteenth century. Charles Maurras, the principal ideologue of the monarchist movement in the twentieth century, was imprisoned for his support for the Vichy regime. Many other writers were subject to the arbitrary exactions of the post-Second World War *épuration*. The State also upon occasion exacted the death penalty: Condorcet in the eighteenth century and Robert Brasillach in the twentieth century being two of the unfortunate victims.[82]

But both the pre- and post-1789 French State has had more in its armoury than these formal instruments of control. It could ennoble. It could accord prestige. It could grant favours. After the Revolution, in other words, patronage was modified rather than abolished. For example, the young (and then monarchist) Victor Hugo received a modest annual stipend from Louis XVIII,[83] whilst after 1830 Chateaubriand lived off a sizeable pension provided by the exiled Bourbon monarch. Sainte-Beuve, Alexandre Dumas, Alfred de Musset, and many others received sinecures from the July Monarchy. Others, more numerous but more humble in aspiration, were prepared to accept employments from the State that were largely honorary and entailed few formal time-consuming duties. As Philip Mansel has commented, 'inside many French writers there was a courtier struggling to get out'.[84]

Moreover, the great academic and literary institutions of the State, first created under the *ancien régime* and later reformed and enhanced under the First Empire and subsequent Republics, lost none of their power to seduce. Alexis de Tocqueville was by no means alone in devoting considerable time and energy to securing election to the Académie des Sciences morales et politiques and the Académie Française, nor in seeking to block the election of his rivals. Even in death—as has been the case with Voltaire, Rousseau, Condorcet, Victor Hugo, Émile Zola, André Malraux, and, most recently, Alexandre Dumas—the State, with all the symbolic authority at its disposal, can honour its writers by moving their remains to the hallowed site of the Panthéon. Lesser mortals can be offered one of the many honorific titles of distinction and recognition that the Republic, as much as any other of France's regimes, has used, in the words of Olivier Ihl, as a 'systematic instrument of governance'.[85] From Rousseau to Georges Sorel, from Paul Nizan to the writers of today's *Le Monde diplomatique*, there has been no shortage of commentators who have accused their fellows of undue subservience to the State.

---

[82] Condorcet committed suicide before the day of his execution.

[83] The son of a Bonapartist general, Hugo effectively became official poet to the royal court: see Graham Robb, *Victor Hugo* (London, 1997).

[84] Philip Mansel, *Paris between Empires 1814–1852* (London, 2001), 311.

[85] Olivier Ihl, 'Emulation through Decoration: A Science of Government?', in Sudhir Hazareesingh (ed.), *The Jacobin Legacy in Modern France* (Oxford, 2002), 158–82. For a more extensive discussion see Olivier Ihl, *Le Mérite et la République: Essai sur la société des émules* (2007).

If Voltaire provided the first clear definition of the *philosophe*, he also illustrated another structural dimension of French intellectual life: banished from Paris, his career can be read as a sustained attempt to return to the capital. With the decline of the court in Versailles, the scene became, and still is, Paris, producing a geographical concentration of intellectual life which retains the capacity to bedazzle the foreign visitor.[86] In 1734 Marivaux felt able to comment that 'Paris is the world; the rest of the earth is nothing but its suburbs.'[87] Accordingly, as Dena Goodman has observed: 'over the course of the eighteenth century, aspiring young men of letters would pour into Paris from the provinces'.[88] This is a view confirmed by Madame de Staël. '[A]s those who are endowed with intellect feel the need to exert it', she wrote, 'so all who had any talent made their way immediately to the capital in the hope of obtaining employment.'[89] Accordingly, 'le désert français',[90] the barren and sleepy world beyond Paris's ancient city walls, has had as its corollary the unrealistic hopes and frustrations suffered by generations of aspiring intellectuals from the provinces who, like Balzac's 'great man in embryo', the poet Lucien Chardon of *Les Illusions perdues*, have scrambled for success and recognition in the metropolis.

Paris was also the capital of print.[91] Publishing and consuming most of the nation's book output, its libraries drew in scholars and the curious whilst its theatres and its concert halls attracted huge crowds. Paris's population was substantially more literate than elsewhere in the country. It was also more cosmopolitan, drawing in exiles and visitors from all over Europe and America and (later) from Africa and Asia.[92] Rebuilt and embellished by the mid-nineteenth-century urban transformation masterminded by the Baron Haussmann, Paris was to be not merely the capital of France but the city of modernity and the metropolis of the civilized world.[93] Moreover, the city of Baudelaire's *flâneur* itself became the subject of literary and artistic exploration and myth.

For all the loss of universal pretensions, little has changed over the last two hundred years or more. In Paris are still to be found all the great institutions of French intellectual life, its foremost educational establishments, its great museums, the major publishing houses, the daily and periodical press, and, not unimportantly, the centres of political and administrative power.[94] 'Centralisation', Jean-Paul Sartre

---

[86] See Patrice Higonnet, *Paris, Capital of the World* (Cambridge, Mass., 2002); Colin Jones, *Paris, Biography of a City* (London: 2004); Andrew Hussey, *Paris: The Hidden City* (London, 2006) and Graham Robb, *Parisians* (London, 2010).

[87] Quoted in Jones, *Paris, Biography*, 204.

[88] Goodman, *Republic of Letters*, 24.

[89] Germaine de Staël, *Considérations sur la Révolution française* (1983), 415.

[90] This phrase is associated with Jean-François Gravier's *Paris et le désert français* (1947).

[91] Mansel, *Paris between Empires*, 307–28, refers to Paris as the 'City of Ink'.

[92] See Lloyd S. Kramer, *Threshold of a New World: Intellectuals and the Exile Experience in Paris, 1830–1848* (Ithaca, NY, 1988).

[93] As part of the plan to showcase Paris as a world capital, four international exhibitions were held in 1855, 1867, 1878, and 1889. The last received over 32 million visitors.

[94] Further evidence of the dominance of Paris and the surrounding region is provided by the size of its population. As Graham Robb recounts, in 1801 more people lived in Paris than in the next six biggest cities combined. By 1886 the figure has risen to the next sixteen cities combined: see *The Discovery of France* (London, 2007), 3–18.

wrote, describing the situation of the writer in 1947, 'has grouped us all in Paris.'[95] A 'busy American' or 'trained cyclist', he added, could meet all the people he needed to know in twenty-four hours. Nowhere has this been truer than in the field of education. Here, as the work of Jean-François Sirinelli has revealed, the picture has been, and still is, one of a small and self-contained intellectual elite.[96]

If Dena Goodman makes the point that, in the eighteenth century, young men of letters flocked to the capital, she also comments that they 'were in no hurry to leave Paris'. In later years this proved less to be the case, as we must not forget the numerous voyages undertaken voluntarily by French writers to such countries as Italy, Germany, England, Russia/the Soviet Union,[97] America,[98] the Orient, and, more recently, Maoist China and Castro's Cuba. But Goodman's observation contains more than a grain of truth. When Simone de Beauvoir visited New York for the first time in January 1947, for example, she was shocked to discover that she could love another city as much as she loved Paris.[99]

The fact is, however, that quite frequently France's turbulent political history gave her writers no choice but to leave the capital. An astonishing number of the authors cited in this book spent either a small or a significant part of their careers in exile. If, as the example of Voltaire illustrates,[100] this was the case under the *ancien régime*, it was equally true during the period of the Revolution and the First Empire. Joseph de Maistre, sharing the enforced exile of many royalist sympathisers, wrote most of his diatribes against the Revolution in St Petersburg, whilst Madame de Staël, after years of involuntary travel across Europe, published her influential *De l'Allemagne* in London. It was also true of the Second Empire, when important exiles included Edgar Quinet, Jules Michelet, Jules Barni, Louis Blanc, and, most famously, Victor Hugo, who, like Chateaubriand before him, sought refuge in the Channel Islands. The experience was repeated under the Vichy regime, when Raymond Aron and Simone Weil followed General de Gaulle to London and others, such as Claude Lévi-Strauss and Georges Bernanos, found a safer haven in the United States[101] or further afield in Latin America. The July Monarchy forced Étienne Cabet into exile and even the Third Republic drove Émile Zola abroad as he sought to avoid imprisonment after the publication of his open letter denouncing the miscarriage of justice involving Captain Alfred Dreyfus.[102] As Madame de Staël commented, 'the fear of such an exile was

[95] Jean-Paul Sartre, *What is Literature?* (London, 1967), 125.

[96] *Génération intellectuelle: Khâgneux et Normaliens dans l'entre-deux guerres* (1988).

[97] See in particular Astolphe de Custine's *La Russie en 1839* (1843).

[98] See Durand Echeverria, *Mirage in the West: A History of the French Image of America* (Princeton, NJ, 1957).

[99] Simone de Beauvoir, *L'Amérique au jour le jour* (1997), 104.

[100] See Ian Davidson, *Voltaire in Exile: The Last Years, 1753–78* (London, 2005).

[101] See Jeffrey Mehlman, *Emigré New York: French Intellectuals in Wartime Manhattan, 1940–44* (Baltimore, 2000) and Emmanuelle Loyer, *Paris à New York: Intellectuels et artistes français en exil 1940–1947* (2005).

[102] See Lloyd S. Kramer, 'S'exiler', in Duclert and Prochasson, *Dictionnaire critique de la République* (2002), 1042–50.

sufficient to reduce all the inhabitants of the principal city of the empire to slavery'.[103]

Parisian dominance has taken another important form. Prior to, and immediately after, the Revolution, the linguistic map of France was immensely complex, constituting a rich mosaic of languages and dialects, many such as Breton and Alsatian quite distinct from French.[104] As Daniel Roche comments: 'in the eighteenth century, learned people began to think of these dialects and patois in terms of Parisian linguistic superiority: these impure tongues spoken by peasants and others threatened the purity of Paris'.[105] What occurred, following the policies introduced during the Revolution and after intended to silence these diverse tongues,[106] was the progressive triumph of the capital, with the result that France became increasingly characterized by linguistic homogeneity. By the end of the nineteenth century, the schoolteachers of the Third Republic, the so-called 'black hussars', had ensured that few, if any, linguistic barriers stood in the way of the circulation of (Parisian) ideas. As a consequence, the defence of France's indigenous languages, as with the cause of regionalism more generally, was until recently largely consigned to the advocates of Catholic and monarchical reaction.[107]

Moreover, this provides a clue to the important cleavages that were to inform so much of French intellectual debate in the two centuries that followed the Revolution. Linguistic diversity was a reflection of regional and territorial fragmentation and this in turn had overlaid upon it a conflict between landed interests and the emerging industrial wealth of France's towns and cities. This powerful tension was only further exacerbated by the efforts of political elites to forge a national culture, especially when this entailed a challenge to the historically established corporate privileges of the Church. At issue was the control of values and of community norms, and this explains why one of the fundamental political questions of the age was all too frequently that of the control of education and of the educational system. The broader point is that the nationalization of intellectual life that occurred in France during the nineteenth century was a reflection of the nationalization of politics itself.[108]

There is one further important structural dimension of French intellectual life meriting our attention. Recent research has shown that the emergence of the intellectual during the Dreyfus Affair at the end of the nineteenth century was intimately bound up with the ideal of the hero and with the themes of honour,

---

[103] De Staël, *Considérations*, 283. See Angelica Goodden, *Madame de Staël: The Dangerous Exile* (Oxford, 2009).

[104] Robb, *Discovery of France*, 50–70.

[105] *France in the Enlightenment* (Cambridge, Mass., 1998), 240.

[106] See Michel de Certeau, Dominique Julia, and Jacques Revel, *Une politique de la langue: La Révolution française et le patois* (1975) and Rita Hermon-Belot, *L'Abbé Grégoire: La Politique et la vérité* (2000), 322–57.

[107] The personal and political dimensions of the issues surrounding linguistic diversity have been explored in Mona Ozouf's *Composition française: Retour sur une enfance bretonne* (2009).

[108] See Jack Hayward, *Fragmented France: Two Centuries of Disputed Identity* (Oxford, 2007). See Daniele Caramani, *The Nationalization of Politics: The Formation of National Electorates and Party Systems in Western Europe* (Cambridge, 2004).

masculinity, and manhood.[109] For the anti-Dreyfusards, intellectuals were persistently (and easily) depicted as being weak, ineffectual, and therefore feminine, whilst those of the pro-Dreyfus cause were only too ready to portray themselves as men of action (and also to cast doubt about the sexual preferences of their opponents). On both sides, association with the feminine was part of a strategy of delegitimation.

Nevertheless, the Dreyfus Affair marked something of a minor breakthrough for women as intellectuals.[110] Denied the right to vote, they were entitled to sign petitions (as twenty-three did with the 1898 *manifeste des intellectuels*) whilst the Dreyfusard Ligue des Droits de l'Homme opened up its membership to them. The feminist journal *La Fronde* actively campaigned for the Dreyfusard camp, notwithstanding that several popular women writers were prominent supporters of the nationalist Ligue de la Patrie Française.[111] More generally, the *Belle Époque* saw women entering the literary establishment for the first time and taking advantage of the new educational opportunities allowed them by the Third Republic.[112]

Yet, for all their presence in the imagery of the Republic, women were largely denied a public voice and scarcely existed as intellectuals. This was a far cry from the world of the eighteenth-century *salon*, where women played a leading role in the shaping of political debate, or from the heady excitement created by what Carla Hesse describes as 'the unprecedented opportunities for women' of the revolutionary decade itself.[113] Post-revolutionary France, as Madame de Staël recognized, provided a far less favourable terrain for female involvement in political and intellectual life. '[S]ince the Revolution', she remarked, 'men have thought it politically and morally useful to reduce women to the most absurd mediocrity.' It was the fate of women 'who cultivated literature', she concluded, to suffer ridicule under monarchies and hate under republics.[114]

In post-revolutionary France access to education was restricted for women, as was career choice. Women were discouraged from reading (on the grounds that it was a dangerous and unfeminine activity) whilst those who did publish were largely restricted to the writing of domestic manuals and needed the authorization of their husbands to negotiate with a publisher. Women existed not as individuals but as

[109] See Venita Datta, *Birth of a National Icon: The Literary Avant-Garde and the Origins of the Intellectual* (New York, 1999); John Cerullo, 'Living the Dreyfusard Life: Violence, Manhood and the Intellectuals', paper presented to the French Historical Studies Association, Boston, Mass., 1996; and Christopher E. Forth, *The Dreyfus Affair and the Crisis of French Manhood* (Baltimore, 2004).

[110] See Françoise Blum, 'Itinéraires feministes à la lumière de l'Affaire', in Michel Leymarie (ed.), *La Postérité de l'affaire Dreyfus* (Lille, 1998), 93–101.

[111] See Mary Louise Roberts, *Disruptive Acts: The New Woman in Fin-de-Siècle France* (Chicago, 2002), 107–64.

[112] See Geraldi Leroy and Julie Bertrand-Sabiani, *La Vie littéraire à la Belle Époque* (1998). One should also not lose sight of the fact that many non-French female writers came to Paris: see Shari Benstock, *Women of the Left Bank, Paris 1900–1940* (London, 1994).

[113] Carla Hesse, *The Other Enlightenment: How French Women Became Modern* (Princeton, NJ, 2001), 42. See also Lucy Moore, *Liberty: The Lives and Times of Six Women in Revolutionary France* (London, 2006).

[114] Germaine de Staël, *Politics, Literature and National Character* (New Brunswick, NJ, 2000), 234–5.

members of families and therefore economic independence was refused them (including that enjoyed by men from an expanding cultural market in which women had no right to intellectual property).[115] As Hesse observes: 'In legal terms, the Old Regime thus ended for women of letters, not in 1789 or 1793, nor even with the achievement of the suffrage in 1946, but in 1965 when they finally achieved legal and financial independence within marriage.'[116]

There were exceptions to this picture of exclusion, but even someone with the force of character of George Sand (née Aurore Dupin, baronne Dudevent) felt oddly diffident and ill at ease in the world of politics.[117] That world was a male world, requiring the masculine qualities of reason and intelligence, the idea of the 'public man' being an object of honour and virtue, whilst that of a 'public woman' was an object of shame. The unstable crowd was feminine; women, when they entered politics, were a source of disorder.[118] Such a vision was easily deployed by the many currents of anti-feminism that have littered France's recent past,[119] but it was also central to France's dominant republican culture. As Michelle Perrot has written: 'the creation of a universalist and individualist citizenship has placed women in an inescapable position . . . Within this framework, women are more than ever reduced to their bodies, fettered to a constraining femininity.'[120] Only as individuals, and not as women, could they make demands upon a system that continues to be characterized by what Françoise Gaspard has described as 'l'homo-socialité politique masculine'.[121]

The argument that the subordination of women is integral to France's revolutionary and republican culture has most forcefully been advanced by American historians, notably Joan Landes and Joan Scott.[122] Here the view is that, if the Revolution initially opened up possibilities for the involvement of women in politics, these were quickly closed down, with women again being confined to a purely domestic role. This, for Joan Scott, is exemplified in the treatment received by Olympe de Gouges, authoress of the *Déclaration des Droits de la Femme et de la Citoyenne*. In 1793, she writes, 'de Gouge was read as an embodiment of the danger of chaos and unlawfulness', as a threat to 'rational social order and for the

---

[115] See Annie Prassoloff, 'Le Statut juridique de la femme auteur', *Romantisme*, 77 (1992), 9–14.
[116] Hesse, *The Other Enlightenment*, 78.
[117] See Michelle Perrot, *Les Femmes ou les silences de l'histoire* (1998).
[118] See Michelle Perrot, *Femmes politiques* (1998). The exclusion of women from the public world of politics was also mirrored in their progressive exclusion as economic actors in the market place: see Victoria E. Thompson, *The Virtuous Marketplace: Women and Men, Money and Politics in Paris, 1830–1870* (Baltimore, 2000).
[119] See Christine Bard (ed.), *Un siècle d'antiféminisme* (1998).
[120] Perrot, *Les Femmes*, 276.
[121] Françoise Gaspard, 'L'Antiféminisme en politique', in Bard, *Un siècle*, 340.
[122] See Joan Landes, *Women and the Public Sphere in the Age of the French Revolution* (Ithaca, NY, 1988) and *Visualising the Nation: Gender, Representation and the Revolution in Eighteenth-Century France* (Ithaca, NY, 2001); Joan Wallach Scott, *Only Paradoxes to Offer: French Feminists and the Rights of Man* (Cambridge, Mass., 1996). See also Olwen Hufton, *Women and the Limits of Citizenship in the French Revolution* (Toronto, 1992); Lynn Hunt, *The Family Romance of the French Revolution* (Berkeley, Calif., 1992), 151–91; and Dorinda Outram, *The Body and the French Revolution: Sex, Class, and Political Culture* (New Haven, Conn., 1989).

meanings of masculinity and femininity on which it had come to depend'. Arrested in July of that year, she was subsequently executed. This was not simply the result of her criticism of Robespierre and her support for the Girondin policy of federalism. As Scott goes on to explain: 'For the Jacobins, women's entire social function could be read literally from her body's reproductive organs, and especially from her breasts. . . . women as breast-nurturers but not creator. Man as citizen—the conqueror of nature. The differences between women and men were taken to be irreducible and fundamental.'[123] Virtue was a male category: a woman who sought to challenge that assumption could legitimately be subject to repression.

Scott's analysis of the fate of Olympe de Gouges highlights another important dimension to this question. Her overall point is that 'in France, until 1944, the common ground for individuality, as for citizenship, was masculinity',[124] but in this particular case she wants to argue that the views put forward by de Gouges constituted a direct challenge to 'the Revolution's continuing definition of women as passive citizens'. At the heart of the Revolution was a debate about representation, a debate that focused upon the definition of 'those capable of self-representation and those who could only be represented, those with and without autonomy'.[125] Women did not possess the capacity for autonomy.

III

How do these points relating to the structural dimensions of French intellectual life bear upon the issues raised by our discussion of the French Revolution? First, the emphasis upon the political history of the Revolution is not incompatible with an awareness of the importance of cultural and social practices. This was an argument made forcefully by Pierre Rosanvallon in his 2002 *Leçon inaugurale* to the Collège de France.[126] Political ideas and events, Rosanvallon stated, cannot be studied in isolation from the complex phenomena which make up a political culture. If this was true in general, it was especially the case in France where, according to Rosanvallon, politics 'does not only have as its function the guaranteeing of liberties and the regulation of collective life, as is the case in England and the United States'. From the Revolution onwards, on this view, politics has been intimately entwined with the social and the cultural, with the latter deriving much of their meaning and shape from the former. The political (*le politique*) denotes far more than the activity of politics narrowly defined (*la politique*).

Second, the Revolution, and the Republic it produced, gave birth to a prolonged and immensely sophisticated debate about what it meant to be a member of a political community and how that political community was to be organized. It was a debate about the very fundamentals of politics. In this lies what might be regarded as its endless fascination and richness. Here again arguments developed by

---

[123] Scott, *Only Paradoxes*, 49–50.   [124] Ibid. 10.   [125] Ibid. 35.
[126] Pierre Rosanvallon, *Leçon inaugurale* (2002). See 'Inaugural Lecture, Collège de France' in Samuel Moyn (ed.), *Pierre Rosanvallon: Democracy Past and Future* (New York, 2006), 31–58.

Rosanvallon provide enlightenment. At the heart of the issues raised by political modernity, he contends, is the 'indeterminate' character of democracy. Who or what is the subject of that democracy? Which has the superior claim, the political equality embodied in universal suffrage or the demands of rational governance? How can the sovereignty of the people be given a satisfactory institutional structure? Should emancipation within a democracy take the form of greater individual autonomy or social participation? Such questions, he argues, demonstrate that, as both a concept and a practice, democracy is marked by 'tensions' and 'equivocation'. Yet, as Rosanvallon has further argued, what occurred specifically in France during and after the Revolution was a failure properly to conceptualize the nature of representative democracy.[127] The far from uncontroversial charge is that the aspiration towards social unity combined with the principle of equality born with the Revolution produced what he terms a 'democracy of integration' which has been unresponsive to the demands of pluralism.[128]

Moreover, Rosanvallon continues, the 'central question' which came to preoccupy the 'French political imagination' remained that of who held power rather than what form that power should take, 'the dynamic of sovereignty' pushing France between the opposites of absolute monarchy and a radical republic, with no thought to sovereignty's limitation. It has been, Rosanvallon writes, 'the kings of war and the kings of glory who [the French] admire'. Their ideal has been only to 'democratise absolutism', a secret aspiration given flesh in the 'republican monarchism' of General de Gaulle's Fifth Republic.[129] 'If the French in 1789', Rosanvallon writes, 'invented equality, they subsequently established a catalogue of the diseases and problems of modern democracy rather than their solutions. It is a specific form of universalism that is put forward by French democracy: far from constituting a model it is better seen as an inventory of the profound difficulties associated with political modernity.'[130] From this perspective, the Revolution of 1789 and the Republic that followed set out principles of political sovereignty and representation that were fundamentally flawed, and whose consequences were to be played out in French politics over the next two hundred years.

This is by no means a view shared by all. It would not be endorsed by those contemporary advocates of republicanism who still remain deeply hostile towards the claims of a pluralist democracy. Nor would this view secure the support of all the historians working in the field. For example, 1998 saw the publication of Patrice Higonnet's *Goodness beyond Virtue: Jacobins during the French Revolution.*[131]

---

[127] This is the subject matter of three volumes: *Le Sacre du citoyen: Histoire du suffrage universel en France* (1992); *Le Peuple introuvable: Histoire de la représentation démocratique en France* (1998); *La Démocratie inachevée: Histoire de la souveraineté du peuple en France* (2000).

[128] See Pierre Rosanvallon, *Le Modèle politique français: La Société civile contre le jacobinisme de 1789 à nos jours* (2004). Rosanvallon's subject here is what he terms 'la culture politique de la généralité'.

[129] See Pierre Rosanvallon, *La Monarchie impossible: Les Chartes de 1814 et 1830* (1994), 149–81.

[130] Pierre Rosanvallon, *Le Sacre du citoyen: Histoire du suffrage universel en France* (1992), 455.

[131] (Princeton, NJ, 1998). See also Anne Sa'adah, *The Shaping of Liberal Politics in Revolutionary France: A Comparative Perspective* (Princeton, NJ, 1990). Whilst recognizing that it would be 'tendentious' to present revolutionary Jacobinism as a form of liberalism, Sa'adah nevertheless argues that Jacobinism presented 'a second model of liberal politics, even more wary of political power than its

Breaking with the recent revisionist account of the Revolution associated with François Furet, Higonnet's book amounts to a defence of the Jacobins and attempts to attribute the descent into Terror to what he repeatedly describes as 'instincts' or habits of mind rather than to the ideology of the Jacobins themselves. The Terror, he writes, was 'a brutalized, backward-looking gesture of despair', drawing upon 'long habits of absolutist politics and intolerant religion'. The 'nobility' of the Jacobins' message—described as the 'desire to harmonize the private and the public through purposeful and libertarian civic-mindedness'—needs to be separated from their 'flaws, errors and liabilities'. This has important conclusions. 'Jacobinism', he writes, 'can still be a model for modern democrats'. It puts to shame 'our own inactive allegiance to socially inert and pluralistic democracy'.

For all that this account of the nature of Jacobinism is both implausible and unconvincing, it nevertheless underscores the continued importance and interest of the events which surrounded this experience. As all those who witnessed the Revolution realized, nothing like it had been seen before. So too they understood that the world would never be the same again. It was not just the language of politics that changed but its location and its actors. A whole new vocabulary of politics came into existence. Court politics was replaced by street politics. Aristocrats departed the stage, to be replaced by the people and those who presumed to speak in their name. New institutional forms of politics appeared. With this, the style of politics, as well as the values embodied in politics as an activity, was dramatically revised. So also were the very goals of politics. Gone were its limited ambitions and its preoccupations with dynastic rivalries: in came a vision of politics that placed it, for good or ill, at the centre of human existence and that saw political activity as a means of social transformation and regeneration. All of this was to be a source of dramatic instability and contestation, flowing beyond the borders of France and beyond the confines of the revolutionary decade.

How might these complex patterns of thinking be studied? What form will our analysis and discussion take? Pierre Rosanvallon has spoken of what he terms 'a conceptual history of politics'. The argument in this volume will take something of this form. The structure of the book will not therefore be crudely chronological. Nor will it work its way systematically through a list of authors and their texts. Rather, it will focus upon a set of core concepts and ideas around which political theory and practice have been structured in France since the eighteenth century, acknowledging both that concepts gain their meaning from their respective historical contexts and from how they are used by historical actors. If conceptual change during this period was extensive, the surprise (perhaps) is that a society characterized by such social and political instability provides evidence of considerable conceptual continuity over time. The potential range of material that could be covered is vast and it would be folly to aspire to anything like comprehensive or encyclopedic coverage. Accordingly, the material under consideration is structured around a loose, but overarching, organizational principle: namely, that political

Anglo-American counterpart' (p. 197). In her view, Jacobinism established 'the primacy of the liberal agenda in France'.

thought in France can be read as a continuous and open-ended debate about the meaning of the Revolution of 1789 and the form of republican government that it gave rise to. The individual chapters are not ordered according to any strict unilinear sequence—indeed, it might well be judged to be the case that they can be read individually and out of sequence—but the book as a whole does possess a certain narrative logic which moves the argument forward to the present day. Having (hopefully) reached this point, the reader should not expect a series of resounding and forthright conclusions. The aim is to provide what might be seen as a broad conspectus of the French political tradition as it has evolved over the past two hundred years and more. It is in the nature of such an account that it can never be complete or definitive. The questions we ask of a political tradition change as our own preoccupations themselves change. To paraphrase Alexis de Tocqueville, however, it is to be hoped that the subject matter of what follows will be the object of both admiration and alarm, and certainly not of indifference.

1

Rights, Liberty, and Equality

I

As was noted by both Pierre-Louis Roederer and Madame de Staël,[1] the driving passion of the Revolution of 1789 was that of equality. More specifically, and as Roederer made abundantly clear, the ambition was to attain not an equality of wealth but an 'equality of rights'.[2] The principal motivating force of the Revolution, Roederer explained, was not to free lands and persons from all servitude nor to free industry from all restraint, but rather to put an end to privilege. Indeed, such was the fervent hostility to privilege, and to the inequalities it was taken to embody, that the assault upon it demanded not just the abolition of those privileges associated with the First and Second Estates (the clergy and the aristocracy) but also the destruction of all privileges held by cities, provinces, bodies of magistrates, and corporations. Accordingly, on the night of 4 August 1789 the privileges of these institutions were abolished, thus simultaneously bringing to an end what was henceforth to be known as the *ancien régime* and producing for the first time an association of equal and individual citizens living under a set of laws common to all. The Abbé Sieyès eloquently expressed the mood of the time when he proclaimed that: 'By their very nature, all privileges are unjust, odious and in opposition to the supreme goal of political society.'[3]

This same sentiment was acknowledged by the Déclaration des Droits de l'Homme et du Citoyen where it was affirmed that: 'Men are born and remain free and equal in their rights'. Article VI of the Déclaration further indicated that the law was to be the same for all and, most importantly, that: 'All citizens . . . are equally eligible to all dignities and to all public positions and occupations, according to their abilities, and without distinction except that of their virtues and their talents.' Article XIII, recognizing the injustice of the tax privileges of the nobility and the clergy, stipulated that taxation 'should be equitably distributed among all the citizens in proportion to their means'. Equality, therefore, was to be achieved by and through the law, which itself was to embody equality through its generality and

---

[1] Pierre-Louis Roederer, *L'Esprit de la Révolution de 1789* (1831) and Germaine de Staël, *Considérations sur la Révolution française* (1983), 221.

[2] Roederer, *L'Esprit de la Révolution*, 9. See pp. 52–6.

[3] Emmanuel Sieyès, *Essai sur les privilèges* (1789), in *Qu'est-ce que le Tiers État?* (1982), 3. See Roberto Zapperi (ed.), *Emmanuel-Joseph Sieyes: Écrits politiques* (1985) and Michael Sonenscher (ed.), *Emmanuel Sieyès: Political Writings* (Indianapolis, 2003).

universality. The most tangible expression of equality was that access to public offices was to be based not upon birth but upon merit. All of these principles, although they pre-date the inauguration of the First Republic, became part of the heritage of republicanism and, in varied forms, have appeared in subsequent Republican constitutions.

Several points should be noted. The first is that equality was not listed amongst the 'natural and inalienable rights of man'. These were restricted to 'liberty, property, security and the resistance to oppression'. The tension between the potentially rival claims of liberty and equality was established at the outset. Roederer's view was that everything the Revolution accomplished with regard to liberty followed either directly or indirectly from the desire to establish an equality of rights.[4] Next, civil equality did not entail political equality. The promise of equal participation in the formation of the general will was quickly withdrawn as constitutional theorists—with Sieyès foremost among them—sought to reduce the political influence of the people with a variety of ingenious proposals, most notably the distinction between active and passive citizens. Finally, the attainment of civil equality did not require the imposition of economic equality. If, following the night of 4 August and in line with the attack upon privilege, what constituted property was radically transformed (one could no longer own government offices as property, for example), the right to property, and therefore the right to the unequal ownership of wealth, remained 'inviolable and sacred'. This right could only be taken away when demanded by 'public necessity'.

Little attention was given to the need to assess the competing demands of natural rights and social utility. This was understandable in the circumstances. The Déclaration des Droits de l'Homme et du Citoyen was first and foremost a political and not a philosophical document. However, as we now know, the doctrine of universal natural rights could be profoundly subversive of the existing order and, indeed, it was not to be long before this became evident to many, if not to all. Indeed, much the same could be said of the doctrine of natural rights as Jean-Paul Rabaut Saint-Étienne said of the Revolution as a whole: 'it had only one principle: that of reforming abuses; but as everything in this dominion was an abuse it resulted from it that everything was changed'.[5] If this quickly led critics of the Revolution to categorize the language of rights as part of an unholy conspiracy organized and led by the *philosophes*, it provided the supporters of the Revolution with a set of problems which stubbornly refused to go away in succeeding years. How, in short, could a recognition of individual rights, now proclaimed as the bedrock of a newly fashioned political community, be given institutional expression and be made compatible with what were to become mounting demands for the realization of civil, political, and economic equality? To this question there were to be innumerable, conflicting answers.

---

[4] Roederer, *L'Esprit de la Révolution*, 10.
[5] Jean-Paul Rabaut Saint-Étienne, *Précis historique de la Révolution* (1792), 200.

II

The Déclaration des Droits de l'Homme et du Citoyen embodied 'the authentic voice of those who made the Revolution—men of property not primarily concerned about social questions, but anxious to ensure that despotic, irresponsible government should never again bring the country to the brink of chaos'.[6] Thus, in the numerous outline *déclarations* submitted to the newly constituted National Assembly during August 1789 hopes for the regeneration of France were invariably framed in terms of the avoidance of the abuse of power through the protection of the rights of man.[7] Likewise, the rights enunciated were deemed to be natural rights, owing nothing to God and religion, and to be of universal validity and application. A declaration of rights, the Marquis de Lafayette told the National Assembly, should express 'eternal truths' and should 'recall the sentiments that nature has engraved in the heart of every individual'.[8]

So too the Déclaration was the product of a specific moment in French history.[9] Although it decisively rejected the claims of historical precedent, a universalistic discourse could not hide the fact that the document finally approved on 26 August 1789 very much reflected the necessities of the situation.[10] If this was true of individual articles—Article XVII, for example, not only sought to defend property from arbitrary abuses by the State but also covered the need to ensure that the peasantry should indemnify their *seigneurs* for the loss of their seigneurial rights which took place on the night of 4 August[11]—it applied with similar force to the document as a whole where the desire to indulge in metaphysical speculation was counter-balanced by the need to give legitimacy to the new National Assembly and its activities in a situation where a political void was fast threatening to engulf France in a wave of urban and rural violence. The text itself is incomplete, as on 27 August it was decided as a matter of urgency to move on to the more pressing task of formulating a new constitution.

The Déclaration des Droits de l'Homme et du Citoyen, then, emerged under the pressure of a profound political crisis. Nevertheless, as events unfolded during the summer of 1789 there appears to have been a genuine and widespread feeling that a declaration of rights, preferably operating as a preface to a written (and

---

[6] William Doyle, *Origins of the French Revolution* (Oxford, 1988), 205.

[7] See Christine Fauré (ed.), *Les Déclarations des droits de l'homme de 1789* (1988).

[8] *Archives Parlementaires*, 8 (1875), 221.

[9] See Dale Van Kley, 'From the Lessons of French History to Truths for All Times and All People: The Historical Origins of an Anti-Historical Declaration', in Van Kley (ed.), *The French Idea of Freedom: The Old Regime and the Declaration of 1789* (Stanford, Calif., 1994), 72–113.

[10] See Marcel Gauchet, 'Droits de l'homme', in François Furet and Mona Ozouf (eds.), *Dictionnaire critique de la Révolution française: Idées* (1992), 121–38; Elisabeth Guibert-Sledziewski, 'Raison politique et dynamique des lois dans la Déclaration', *Droits*, 8 (1988), 33–9; Jacques Godechot, 'Les Droits de l'homme et la Révolution française', *Società Italiana di storia del diritto: Atti del IV congresso internazionale* (Florence, 1982), 979–82.

[11] See Jean Morange, 'La Déclaration et le droit de propriété', and Jean-Jacques Bienvenu, 'Impôt et propriété dans l'esprit de la Déclaration', *Droits*, 8 (1988), 101–10 and 135–42.

monarchical) constitution, was not only required but desirable.[12] Approximately thirty such *déclarations*—with that of Arnaud Gouges-Cartou running to as many as seventy-one articles[13]—were placed before the National Assembly, with even the Comte d'Antraigues, a supporter of the royal veto, feeling able to remark that it was 'absolutely necessary' to produce a declaration of rights because 'if one day the sky again were to unleash the plague of despotism ... the people would be able, by preserving the memory of the *Déclaration des droits du citoyen*, to recapture it and to create a new constitution'.[14] More typical was the view, expressed by the Comte de Castellane, that the more men knew their rights the more they would cherish the laws that protected them.[15] Equally evident was the feeling that any declaration of rights should be characterized by simplicity and clarity of expression. I want, the Protestant Jean-Paul Rabaut Saint-Étienne announced on 18 August, 'such lucidity, veracity and directness in its principles ... that everyone should be able to grasp and understand them, that they might become a children's alphabet, that they should be taught in schools'.[16]

Nor, despite the confusion as to what they might be, did there appear to be much doubt that these rights were 'self-evident'. More significant was the claim, advanced by Jean-Louis Second, that these rights were not to be discovered in history nor in 'the charters and archives of nations' but 'from within man, from within his nature, from within the eternal archives of justice and reason'.[17] Durand de Maillane amplified this argument when, in seeking a return to the 'true principles of our monarchy', he spoke of the need to reclaim the rights 'due to man and his nature ... rights against which neither time nor force could do anything'.[18] The claims of prescriptive tradition and status, in short, were simply jettisoned without recall.

The most persuasive and eloquent exponent of a constitution and a declaration designed to protect the natural and civil rights of the citizen was undoubtedly Emmanuel Sieyès.[19] Having announced the advent of the Revolution with an attack on privilege and a defence of the claims of the Third Estate, in his famous phrase, 'to be something', Sieyès next provided the National Assembly with a carefully crafted and detailed document entitled *Préliminaire de la Constitution: Réconnaissance et exposition raisonnée des droits de l'homme et du*

---

[12] See Keith Michael Baker, 'The Idea of a Declaration of Rights', in Van Kley, *French Idea of Freedom*, 154–96.
[13] Arnaud Gouges-Cartou, 'Projet des Déclaration des droits', in Fauré, *Les Déclarations*, 203–17.
[14] Cte d'Antraigues, 'Au Sujet de la Déclaration des droits de l'homme et du citoyen', in Fauré, *Les Déclarations*, 172.
[15] Cte de Castellane, 'Sur la Déclaration des droits', in Fauré, *Les Déclarations*, 134.
[16] *Archives Parlementaires*, 8 (1875), 453.
[17] Jean-Louis Seconds, 'Essai sur les droits des hommes, des citoyens et des nations; ou addresse au roi sur les états généraux et les principes d'une bonne constitution', in Fauré, *Les Déclarations*, 60.
[18] Pierre-Toussaint Durand de Maillane, 'Opinion sur les divers plans de Constitution, et la Déclaration des droits de l'homme et du citoyen', in Fauré, *Les Déclarations*, 140–1.
[19] See Jean-Denis Bredin, *Sieyès: La Clé de la Révolution française* (1988); Murray Forsyth, *Reason and Revolution: The Political Thought of the Abbé Sieyès* (Leicester, 1987); William H. Sewell Jr, *A Rhetoric of Bourgeois Revolution: The Abbé Sieyes and What is the Third Estate?* (Durham, NC, and London, 1994); and Pasquale Pasquino, *Sieyès et l'invention de la constitution en France* (1998).

citoyen,[20] a text premised upon the belief that the primary purpose of any constitution was to protect and extend the rights of man and the citizen. Thus Sieyès's introductory remarks led him to the initial conclusion that 'the social state does not establish an unjust inequality of rights by the side of a natural inequality of means: on the contrary, it protects the equality of rights against the natural and harmful inequality of means'.[21]

Sieyès then felt able to assert that the first of man's rights was the 'ownership of his person' and to argue from this that it followed that man also had the right to ownership of his own actions and labour. When combined with the Lockean maxim that the mixing of one's labour with an object provided an entitlement to ownership this produced a definition of liberty in terms of the enjoyment of one's 'personal' and 'territorial' property and the overall conclusion that 'every citizen had the right to remain, to go, to think, to speak, to write, to print, to publish, to work, to produce, to protect, to transport, to exchange and to consume'.[22] The only limitation to the exercise of these rights was infringement upon the rights of others and as such, in Sieyès's view, was a matter to be settled by law. The principal threats to their enjoyment were deemed to come in the form of 'malevolent citizens', abuses by the 'public power', and external attack.

Where Sieyès moved beyond the Lockean position was in his argument that, in addition to the legitimate expectation that a citizen's rights and liberties would be protected, the citizen had a 'right' to the benefits of association, amongst which he included public works, poor relief, and a system of education. Eschewing the details of their provision, Sieyès nevertheless commented that 'it is sufficient here to say that the citizenry as a whole have a right to everything that the State can do in their favour'.[23]

All of the above rights were categorized by Sieyès as natural and civil rights, with the latter appearing, not without ambiguity, to be distinguishable from the former by their more obvious social origin. Both categories, however, were to be differentiated from political rights. If all citizens enjoyed natural and civil rights—everyone, Sieyès affirmed, had a right to the protection of their person, property, and liberty—only a restricted number, the so-called 'active' citizens, had a right to participate in the affairs of the public power. 'The difference between these two types of rights', Sieyès explained, 'is that natural and civil rights are those for the maintenance and development of which society is formed whilst political rights are those by which society is formed'.[24] Explicitly excluded from the possession of political rights were women ('in their present condition'), children, foreigners and those not contributing financially to the support of the 'public establishment'. For those described by Sieyès as 'the real shareholders of the great social enterprise', on the other hand, equality of political rights was to be a fundamental principle.

---

[20] Three versions of this document exist. The version cited here is the one read before the National Assembly on 20–21 July 1789: see Fauré, *Les Déclarations*, 91–107.
[21] Ibid. 95.   [22] Ibid. 96.   [23] Ibid. 99.   [24] Ibid. 101.

The outline *déclaration* which followed—with thirty-two articles, later amended to thirty-seven[25]—was intended to summarize these 'eternal rights' in a codified and easily accessible form. It is interesting to note, therefore, that if Sieyès concentrated upon emphasizing the rights to liberty, property, and security, the specifics of the *déclaration* included the right to free speech, freedom of the press, the right to travel, and the inviolability of letters. All citizens were to be equally subject to the law and no one could be arrested or imprisoned without just cause. Moreover, it was, according to Marcel Gauchet,[26] this *déclaration* and not that presented by Lafayette, nor indeed that of the *sixième Bureau* (which on 19 August had received by far the highest number of votes), that played the decisive role in shaping the final document approved on 26 August.[27] Starting from the premise that 'ignorance, forgetfulness or contempt of the rights of man are the sole causes of public misfortune and the corruption of government', the Déclaration des Droits de l'Homme et du Citoyen went on *inter alia* to assert that natural rights existed prior to the formation of society, that the only legitimate limitation upon their enjoyment was the rights of others, and that these limits could only be established by legislation. In this way, with both astonishing speed and audacity, the members of the National Assembly established rights as the basic language of the new politics.

Why then when, as Jeremy Waldron has observed,[28] the belief in universally applicable principles of justice and right had lost all 'philosophical respectability' did the language of the rights of man occupy such a central place in the deliberations of the National Assembly during the months of July and August 1789? In part (although this must not be exaggerated)[29] the explanation lies in the immense prestige accorded to the American precedent, a prestige given greater force by the strong personal relationships that existed between such figures as Jefferson and Franklin and those who initially led the Revolution. For example, the philosopher and mathematician Condorcet, who in 1789 was one of the most tireless advocates of the need for a declaration of rights, did not hesitate to cite with approval the simplicity and wisdom of the American declaration of 1776 and of Virginia's Bill of Rights or to draw attention to the numerous commercial and moral benefits which had resulted from their application.[30] 'The spectacle of a great nation where the rights of man are respected', he wrote in 1787, 'is of use to all the others, despite differences in climate, morals and constitutions.'[31] A further influence was the

---

[25] 'Déclaration des droits du citoyen français', ibid. 219–24.

[26] Gauchet, 'Droits de l'homme'.

[27] 'Motion de M. le Mquis de La Fayette relativement à la Déclaration des droits de l'homme', in Fauré, *Les Déclarations*, 87; 'Projet de Déclaration des Droits de l'homme et du citoyen, discuté dans le sixième Bureau de l'Assemblée nationale', ibid. 231–4.

[28] Jeremy Waldron, *Nonsense upon Stilts* (London, 1987), 18.

[29] See François Furet, 'From Savage Man to Historical Man: The American Experience in Eighteenth-Century French Culture', in Furet, *In the Workshop of History* (Chicago, 1984), 153–66, and Marcel Thomann, 'Origines et sources doctrinales de la déclaration des droits', *Droits*, 8 (1988), 55–70.

[30] Jean-Antoine-Nicolas Caritat, marquise de Condorcet, 'De l'Influence de la Révolution d'Amérique sur l'Europe', *Œuvres de Condorcet* (1847), viii. 3–113.

[31] Ibid. 13.

remonstrances of the French law courts, the *parlements*.[32] As J. H. Shennan has shown, starting out from conservative premises the vocabulary of the magistrates of Paris shifted ground dramatically during the eighteenth century, with new implications and meanings being attached to such words as 'man', 'humanity', and 'society'. 'The concept of specific rights for legally constituted groups', he writes, faded 'before that of the universal rights of man'.[33]

More generally, if the Déclaration des Droits de l'Homme et du Citoyen was not a direct product or expression of the Enlightenment, the members of the National Assembly were nevertheless able to turn to the *philosophes* for inspiration as part of what Alexis de Tocqueville was later to describe as their 'revolutionary education'.[34] Locke, Rousseau, the physiocrats, and others, misinterpreted and radicalized, provided, in Cheryl Welch's words, 'a ready-made vocabulary of revolution' and one that was imbued with the language of natural rights.[35] Despite the criticisms directed against arguments from 'nature' during the eighteenth century by writers such as David Hume and d'Alembert such formulations, as Dan Edelstein has shown,[36] continued to be commonplace and to retain their credibility. To paraphrase Diderot, many were those who believed that the best legislation was that which conformed most closely to nature. To take but one example: Condorcet, using a sensationalist epistemology that in the hands of Helvétius had produced a crude utilitarianism, insisted that the facts of human nature logically gave rise to principles of universal rights and justice.[37] 'We call these rights *natural*', Condorcet wrote in 1787, 'because they derive from the nature of man, because from the moment that a sensate being capable of reasoning and of having moral ideas exists, it follows as an obvious and necessary consequence that he must enjoy these rights, that he cannot be deprived of them without injustice.'[38] Such was the unproblematic character of these rights, according to Condorcet, that only the right to equality needed explanation.[39]

---

[32] See William Doyle, 'The Parlements', in Keith Baker (ed.), *The French Revolution and the Creation of Modern Political Culture*, i. *The Political Culture of the Old Regime* (Oxford, 1987), 157–68.

[33] J. H. Shennan, 'The Political Vocabulary of the Parlement of Paris in the Eighteenth Century', *Società italiana di storia del diritto: Atti del IV congresso internazionale*, 951–64. Of less importance were the *cahiers de doléances* prepared for the meeting of the Estates-General; see George V. Taylor, 'Revolutionary and Nonrevolutionary Content in the *Cahiers* of 1789: An Interim Report', *French Historical Studies*, 7 (1971–2), 479–502. See Lucien Jaume (ed.), *Les Déclarations des droits de l'homme* (1989), 75–91.

[34] See Wolfgang Schmale, 'Les Droits de l'homme dans la pensée politique des Lumières', in Antoine de Baecque, *L'An 1 des droits de l'homme* (1988), 332–53.

[35] Cheryl Welch, *Liberty and Utility: The French Ideologues and the Transformation of Liberalism* (New York, 1984), 7. See also André Jardin, *Histoire du Libéralisme politique: De la crise de l'absolutisme à la constitution de 1875* (1985), 94–112.

[36] *The Terror of Natural Right: Republicanism, the Cult of Nature and the French Revolution* (Chicago, 2009).

[37] See Keith M. Baker, *Condorcet: From Natural Philosophy to Social Mathematics* (Chicago, 1975), 195–263.

[38] Condorcet, 'Lettres d'un bourgeois de New-Haven à un citoyen de Virginie', *Œuvres de Condorcet*, ix. 14.

[39] Condorcet, 'Idées sur le despotisme: à l'usage de ceux qui prononcent ce mot sans entendre', ibid. 166.

Thus the language of rights, for all its philosophical frailty, retained a definite plausibility and amongst France's political representatives in the summer of 1789 attained almost the status of a common linguistic currency. Ironically, however, the limitations to its popularity were immediately visible, even in the debates within the National Assembly that surrounded the actual formulation of the Déclaration des Droits de l'Homme et du Citoyen. For men such as Sieyès the recent American experience provided not so much an example to be followed as something that France, imbued with a universalistic spirit, could improve upon. Such a belief implicitly assumed that the situations faced by the two nations were not necessarily comparable. This was made explicit by Rabaut Saint-Étienne on 18 August when he stated categorically that 'the circumstances are not the same: [America] was breaking with a distant parent State; it was the case of a new people destroying everything in order to renew everything'.[40] It was this theme that was repeatedly developed by Lally-Tollendal when he argued that the differences between a colonized people freeing itself from a far-away government and an 'ancient' people which had experienced the same form of government for fourteen centuries and been ruled by the same dynasty for eight centuries were immense, and so much so that any statement of natural rights in France had of necessity to be accompanied by the immediate disclosure of 'positive' rights in a written constitution. 'I ask', Lally-Tollendal stated, 'that this declaration of rights should be as short, as clear and as concise as possible; that, having established the principle, its correct application is speedily carried out in order that others might not be able to apply it incorrectly; that, having transported man to the forests, he is brought back at once to the midst of France.'[41]

In short, whilst Lally-Tollendal remained committed to a declaration of rights, he recognized that unless these rights could be quickly located in a precisely defined, concrete context they ran the risk of unleashing excess and disorder. Others amongst the *monarchiens* or moderates were not slow to take up and to amplify this theme.[42] 'We will never abandon our rights', Jean-Joseph Mounier declared, 'but we should not exaggerate them. We must not forget that the French are not a new people, recently emerged from the depths of the forest in order to form an association, but a society of 24 million men which wishes to strengthen the ties between its various parts, which wishes to regenerate the kingdom so that the principles of a true monarchy might be forever sacred.'[43] The French people, having freed itself from servitude, now needed to establish the empire of law.

It was initially the Comte de Mirabeau who most forcefully expressed what were perceived to be the dangers and absurdity of undue abstraction. As early as 15 June 1789 when opposing the proposal of the *citoyen-philosophe* Sieyès to

---

[40] *Archives Parlementaires*, 8 (1875), 452.
[41] Ibid. 222–3, 458.
[42] See Robert Griffiths, *Le Centre perdu: Malouet et les « monarchiens » dans la Révolution française* (Grenoble, 1988).
[43] *Archives parlementaires*, 8 (1875), 214.

rename the Estates-General as the 'Assemblée des représentants connus et verifiés de la nation française', he commented that

> it is not always expedient, it is not always appropriate to consult only what is right without regard to the circumstances ... The metaphysician, travelling on a map of the world, crosses everything without difficulty, has no trouble either with mountains or deserts or rivers or chasms; but when he wishes to make a journey, when he wishes to arrive somewhere, he must always remember that one walks on the ground and that he no longer inhabits an ideal world.[44]

Before the National Assembly in August this same logic was deployed to demonstrate the impossibility of formulating a declaration of the rights of man capable of application to all political associations and all forms of government when those responsible were necessarily constrained by 'local circumstances' and which, 'given a people grown old amongst anti-social institutions', would attain nothing more than 'relative perfection'. Speaking on behalf of the *comité des cinq* Mirabeau indicated, for example, that in their endeavour to formulate a declaration of rights they had experienced great difficulty 'in distinguishing between what belonged to the nature of man and the modifications it had received in this or that particular society'.[45]

Mirabeau's own solution to what he perceived as the dangers implicit in any declaration of rights was to argue that in these circumstances wisdom consisted in the recognition of the virtues of a *juste milieu*. Others showed themselves to be less sanguine when faced with the possibility (and the reality) of social chaos and anarchy. During August 1789 the most resolute opponent within the National Assembly of a declaration of rights proved to be Pierre-Victor Malouet. His argument, in summary, was that, if in America the morals, tastes, and circumstances of the new nation were conducive to the existence of democracy and liberty, this was far from the case in France, where there existed 'a vast multitude of men without property' who, with good reason, at times became enflamed by 'the spectacle of luxury and opulence'. While such inequality might be regrettable it nevertheless remained the case that those in a 'dependent condition' had to recognize the 'legitimate limits' to their 'natural liberty'. As such, there was no purpose in telling 'men deprived of understanding and means' that they were 'equal in rights to the most powerful, to the most fortunate'. 'Why', Malouet proclaimed, 'begin by transporting [man] to a high mountain in order to show him his limitless dominion when upon descending he will find constraints at every step?' The end result would only be disaster.[46]

One dimension of this argument was that, if man had rights, as a member of society he also had duties and obligations. The fear, voiced explicitly by the Comte de Sinety, was that by talking only about rights men would be encouraged to

---

[44] *Œuvres de Mirabeau: Discours et Opinions* (1835), i. 103.
[45] *Archives parlementaires*, 8 (1875), 438–9, 453–5.
[46] 'Opinion de M. Malouet sur la Déclaration des droits de l'homme', in Fauré, *Les Déclarations*, 161–4. For Malouet's account of this turbulent period see *Mémoires de Malouet* (1868), i. 309–43.

display their 'natural leaning' towards egoism, to the detriment of their fellows and of society as a whole. This 'destructive vice', in Sinety's view, could be overcome if any declaration of the rights of man was in turn accompanied by a statement of the duties of the citizen.[47] It was this contention that was supported by the Abbé Grégoire and others in a stormy debate that took place on 4 August, with Grégoire arguing that, when France was experiencing 'a moment of insurrection' by a people for long 'tormented by tyranny', it was necessary that man should know 'not only the circle that he can traverse but also the barrier that he cannot cross'.[48] On this occasion, the motion to place duties by the side of rights was defeated by 570 votes to 433.

Writing some three years later Rabaut Saint-Étienne was to comment that the National Assembly had made known their rights to French citizens in much the same way as 'a sick father, with not long to live, hands over to his heir the title of his possessions and of his money'. It was by no means certain, in other words, that the assembly would survive for long enough to pass the laws which followed from the principles outlined in the Déclaration des Droits de l'Homme et du Citoyen.[49] This proved to be the case. Condorcet, for example, in a pamphlet entitled *Réflexions sur ce qui a été fait et ce qui reste à faire*,[50] commented upon the 'anarchy' and 'hatred' that had resulted from a vaguely worded and defective declaration of rights. It was, he argued 'the false impression that the people had seized of their rights, in imagining that the tumultuous will of a town, a borough, a village, and even a district, is a form of law and that the will of the people, in whatever manner it was manifested, had the same authority as a will expressed in a prescribed form by a recognized law' that was at the heart of the problem. The people, Condorcet remarked plaintively as the unfolding of the Revolution pushed him nearer to his own personal tragedy, must recognize that they could not ask for more than they had been given.

The dramatic events that followed can only be sketched in brief outline. The declaration of rights approved by the National Assembly at the end of August 1789 was eventually to figure as a preamble to the revised monarchical constitution, approved on 14 September 1791. Three months earlier, however, Louis XVI had attempted to flee France, only to be intercepted with other members of his family at Varennes and forced to return to Paris in abject humiliation.[51] Although given a second chance to prove his loyalty to the new regime, the monarch's days were now effectively numbered. In the spring of 1792 France (recklessly) declared war against Austria and soon found herself being invaded, with the capital itself in danger.

[47] André-Louis-Esprit, comte de Sinety, 'Exposition des motifs qui parassissent devoir déterminer à reunir à la Déclaration des droits de l'homme et du citoyen, celle des devoirs du citoyen', in Fauré, *Les Déclarations*, 175–81.

[48] Henri-Baptiste, abbé Grégoire, 'Opinion sur la necessité de parler des devoirs dans la Déclaration des droits de l'homme et du citoyen', in Fauré, *Les Déclarations*, 189–90. See also de Baecque, *L'An 1 des droits de l'homme*, 121–5.

[49] Rabaut Saint-Etienne, *Précis historique*, 191–2.

[50] *Œuvres de Condorcet*, ix. 441–68.

[51] See Mona Ozouf, *Varennes: La Mort de la royauté* (2005).

Amid mounting chaos, on 10 August the Tuileries Palace was stormed, in one insurrectionary gesture overturning both the constitution and the king. A month later, France was declared a republic, with Louis XVI being subsequently put on trial and executed in January 1793.

The new legislative assembly, now known as the Convention, had therefore both to save France from defeat and to promulgate a new constitution. To its credit, it did both, although at a high price. In the first instance, this momentous task fell to the group of deputies known as the Girondins, led by Brissot and armed with the intellectual support of Condorcet. Given the dramatic circumstances, discussion of the rights of man received only intermittent attention. Nevertheless, by the time that the Girondins fell from power in early June 1793 they had secured the approval of a new declaration of rights (running to thirty articles).[52] Largely inspired by Condorcet's proposals of February of that year,[53] this new declaration included as rights both the right to equality and the right to what was termed 'la garantie sociale'. There was however much agonizing about the force to be given to both the right to property and the right to insurrection, the Girondins showing themselves eager to protect the former and to restrict the latter to legal means. Mounting popular discontent combined with the ferocious assault of the Jacobins made this position increasingly difficult to sustain. Robespierre, leading the Montagnard attack, damned the proposals of the Girondins, denouncing a declaration of rights made 'not for man, but for the rich, for the monopolists, for the speculators, for tyrants'.[54]

A few weeks later the Girondins were removed forcibly from power, the Jacobins losing no time in presenting their own declaration of the rights of man and the citizen on 24 June 1793. The right to equality was now firmly established as one of the four natural rights of man, with the right to property losing its 'inviolable and sacred' status. If the right to resist oppression was characterized as a consequence of these rights, its importance was underlined with the description of insurrection as 'the most sacred of rights and the most necessary of duties'. Despite this change of tone and emphasis, the definition of the right to liberty as the right to do whatever did not infringe the rights of others remained essentially unchanged, as did the definition of property. Indeed, property was now specified as the right which 'belonged to every citizen to enjoy and to dispose of his goods, his income, the fruits of his labour and his industry as he pleases'.[55] Similarly, if the end of society was described as 'the common good', the egalitarian impetus was restricted to the recognition of the 'sacred debt' owed by society towards its members and the vague commitment to find work or the means of subsistence for those without employment. Robespierre's proposal for the progressive taxation of income was ignored.

---

[52] See Jaume, *Les Déclarations*, 262–4.
[53] Ibid. 240–3.
[54] Speech by Robespierre on 24 April 1793: see *Œuvres de Maximilien Robespierre*, ix. *Discours Septembre 1792–27 Juillet 1793* (1958), 461.
[55] See Jaume, *Les Déclarations*, 299–303.

Beyond this, the declaration of rights that was to act as a preamble to the republican constitution of Year 1 set out a series of individual and collective rights intended to protect the citizen from an oppressive government. All, like the new constitution itself, were to be suspended with the proclamation of the decree that revolutionary government was to operate 'until the return of peace'.

Amongst the victims of the Terror were not only both Georges Danton and Condorcet, but also Olympe de Gouges, executed on 3 November 1793. Her crimes, in the eyes of the Jacobins, were many, but here she merits attention because of her remarkable text, *Les droits de la femme*, dedicated to Marie-Antoinette, Queen of France, and penned in 1791. By any standards, this must be one of the most subversive documents ever written. It bristles with irony and scorn, lampooning the universalistic pretensions of the Revolution, parodying the seventeen articles of the declaration of 1789. 'Law and justice', de Gouge proclaimed, 'consist in restoring all that belongs to others; thus the only limits to the exercise of the natural rights of women are perpetual male tyranny.' Woman, she continued, 'has the right to mount the scaffold; she must equally have the right to mount the rostrum'. De Gouges claimed for women the same rights as those enjoyed by men. Property should belong to both sexes. Careers and positions should be open to women as for men. Women should be granted an equal share not only of wealth but of public administration. Men and women should be equal in the eyes of the law.

Nothing came of these demands, the Jacobins effectively banning women from public life. A decade later the Napoleonic Civil Code of 1804 reversed even the limited improvement to the legal status of women introduced during the Revolution. Much the same occurred with formulations of rights in general. As Jacques Godechot has written, the Constitution of 1795, which followed the removal of the Jacobins from power, 'was drawn up with the aim of preventing a return to the regime of Year II, that is, the dictatorship of a group of men who believed themselves to be directly mandated by the "people"'.[56] What this meant has been lucidly summarized by Marcel Gauchet. 'With Thermidor', he writes, 'the hour of duties sounded'.[57] Accordingly, the declaration of rights approved by the Convention on 22 August 1795 came replete with a set of nine specific duties, each clearly intended to encourage the individual citizen to obey the law, respect property, and serve the *patrie*.[58] Just as significantly, the rights proclaimed were no longer taken to be natural but to be those enjoyed by men in 'society'. Reference to men being born free and equal in rights was dropped, with equality now being defined simply as equality before the law. The right to resist oppression was removed, as was any mention of the rights to free speech and freedom of the press. In this way it was hoped that the revolutionary and insurrectionary potential of the rights of man would be curbed. Four years later, the Constitution of Year VIII, drafted with Napoleon Bonaparte in mind, simply dispensed with a declaration of rights altogether.

---

[56] Jacques Godechot, *Les Constitutions de la France depuis 1789* (1970), 94.
[57] Marcel Gauchet, *La Révolution des droits de l'homme* (1989), 257.
[58] See Jaume, *Les Déclarations*, 307–9.

III

It was among the increasingly vociferous ranks of Catholic and monarchical reaction that criticisms of the merits of the language of the rights of man came most frequently to be heard. Initially supporters of the monarchical cause in the National Assembly, such as Durand de Maillane, showed little restraint in deploying the language of natural rights to defend their position, believing that the proclamation of rights would play an indispensable part in returning the monarchy to its 'pure and noble origin'.[59] Quickly, however, the supporters of a constitutional settlement on the moderate right began to have grave doubts about the potential dangers of this strategy. The Comte de Montlosier, future member of the Club Monarchique, concluded his *Essai sur l'art de constituer les peuples ou Examen des opérations constitutionnelles de l'assemblée nationale de France* with a forty-page outline entitled 'Aperçu d'un projet de constitution', replete with its own 'Déclaration des droits de l'homme'.[60] In this he had few kind words for the declaration of 26 August 1789. If, Montlosier argued, there were two types of revolution—one which followed the dictates of reason and of nature, another which was prepared in 'silence' and in the 'shadows'—so too there were two ways of formulating a declaration of rights. The best method was 'to take man as he is today', within society as it existed, in order to examine 'the best place for him in this situation'. The incorrect method was to look at the nature of man in isolation, abstracted from all 'social conventions'. The latter, 'analytical' process, while it might be appropriate for a solitary thinker in the calm of his study and distanced from events, when applied to the highly charged context of an assembly comprised of 'twelve hundred people', had produced a set of 'true, ambiguous or false maxims' which, taken together, lacked either 'structure or coherence'. What sense, Montlosier remarked, did it make to suggest that ignorance, forgetfulness, and contempt for the rights of man were the sole causes of public misfortune? What about superstition, fear, the desire to dominate, pride, necessity, hunger, laziness, and epidemics? In what possible way could man be said to be born free and equal in rights? Of what sort of liberty were they talking? Physical liberty? Moral liberty? And if man 'were to remain free only in this manner', Montlosier mocked, 'I think that of all creatures he would truly be the greatest slave'. Moreover, it was not at all clear what was meant by such terms as property, security, and resistance to oppression. The end result was that a set of 'philosophical adages' had become a weapon used by man against society itself.

Montlosier's own statement of rights took on a very different complexion, beginning with a proclamation that personal slavery was against the nature and rights of man and that the right of property was grounded in the right of all men to own what they had produced through their labour. It ended with the assertion that,

---

[59] Pierre-Toussaint Durand de Maillane, 'Opinion sur les divers plans de Constitution', 137–50.
[60] François-Dominique de Reynaud, comte de Montlosier, *Essai sur l'art de constituer les peuples ou Examen des opérations constitutionnellles de l'Assemblée nationale de France* (1790).

as all social conventions had to be freely endorsed, 'every man had accordingly the right to leave the association and to betake his person, his wife, his children, and his property where he pleases and as he pleases'. His declaration, he believed, was in accord with the real desires, wishes, and affections of men.

A year later Montlosier placed himself firmly on the side of counter-revolution, bewailing what he termed the 'altar raised by delirium, vanity and cupidity' that had become contemporary France and calling for the instigation of civil war.[61] Nevertheless, he counselled the émigrés not to re-enter France in the spirit of vengeance lest they be left 'only with genealogical charts to set against the charter of the rights of man'. A return to the monarchy and to religion, he warned, must not be an excuse for a return to the abuses of the *ancien régime*. Such pleas for conciliation were not to be found in the writings of Antoine de Rivarol. Nor was a toleration of the language of rights.

Riverol's earliest works—for example, the *Dissertation sur l'universalité de la langue française*[62]—pre-date the Revolution and were to provide the philosophical support for what was to become the most immediate, brilliant, scurrilous, and vehement attack upon the principles of 1789. Specifically, Rivarol denied the veracity of Condillac's sensationalist epistemology, arguing that sentiment preceded sensation, doubted that man either should or could be dissected into his constituent parts, and believed that truth and wisdom were embodied in language. As in nature everything was in harmony and proportion, so it followed that 'the man who analyses, whether as a chemist or as a reasoner, can only . . . decompose and kill'.[63] In Rivarol's opinion, it was precisely this 'analytical' spirit that inspired the *philosophes* and which accounted for their numerous dangerous errors.[64] They had mistaken resemblance between men for the equality of man. They had failed to realize that it was not 'truth' but 'fixity' that mattered and that 'genius in politics consists not in creating but in preserving and . . . [that] it is not the best law but the most stable which is the good one'.[65] There was no such thing, Rivarol argued, as 'universal justice': all judgements were 'relative' and reflected 'fear and need'. Did not animals have the same right to pleasure and life as men? Yet we hunted and killed them. In similar fashion, 'if nature were suddenly to produce a race superior to ours we would be at once as culpable as the sharks and the wolves'.[66] Nor was it possible to talk of man's original goodness. Men were born with 'good' physical organs and 'useful' needs but as moral beings they did not exist. It was, in sum, not 'without effort and without aiding nature that [man] becomes finally the supreme social and rational being'. Men therefore needed government, religion, and

---

[61] François-Dominique de Reynaud, comte de Montlosier, *Des Moyens d'opérer la contre-révolution* (1791).
[62] Antoine de Rivarol, *Dissertation sur l'universalité de la langue française* (1784). See Jean Lessay, *Rivarol* (1989).
[63] Antoine de Rivarol, *De la philosophie moderne* (1797), 5.
[64] See *De l'homme intellectuel et moral*, in *Œuvres complètes* (1808), i. 1–390.
[65] Rivarol, *De la philosophie moderne*, 21.
[66] Ibid. 57.

morality to protect and elevate them. Moreover, men by nature were social, not solitary, beings. It was the 'solitary condition' that was the 'artificial condition'.

All of these arguments were brought to bear by Rivarol in an analysis of the Revolution which from the summer of 1789 onwards—in, for example, the articles he contributed to the *Journal politique national*[67]—retained a remarkable level of consistency and coherence. As events unfolded, these articles repeatedly turned their attention to the Déclaration des Droits de l'Homme et du Citoyen. Here, in the form of this 'dangerous' and 'criminal preface', was a text which ignored practice and experience, confused the savage with the 'social' man, and mistook 'natural independence' for 'civil liberty'. Why, Rivarol asked, talk to the citizen of rights that he will never exercise? Why tell men that they are equal when it would be better to tell them frankly that they are very unequal, that 'one is born strong and another weak'? Why precede a constitution with a statement of 'metaphysics' that earlier legislators had had the good sense to hide from public inspection?

Furthermore, the people, 'la vile canaille', would not understand such a declaration of rights. 'Philosophy', Rivarol wrote, 'being the product of lengthy meditation and an entire life, ought not and cannot be presented to the people who are always at the beginning of life.'[68] They worked for six days and on the seventh day had time only for rest and religion. They imitated truth with as much conviction as they were likely to be seduced by error. In the hands of the people, therefore, what had been formulated as a 'defensive arm' would quickly become a means of offence. Having been granted civil equality, the people would demand the absolute equality of ownership. A hatred of rank would become a hatred of all authority. 'With this declaration in their hands', Rivarol announced, 'the negroes in our colonies and the servants in our houses could chase us from our inheritance.'[69] As for the soldier told to defend private property, he would reply that the earth belonged to all men and that he wanted his fair share. 'What would you say', Rivarol asked, 'to this sophist armed with your *declaration of rights* and a gun? He would take your goods as a *man of nature*, enjoy them as a *citizen* and defend them as a *soldier*.' In brief, if you encouraged the ignorant to believe that rights should be equal, the result would be 'blood, ruin, and death'.

Behind Riverol's charge that talk of natural rights in a society grounded in social and economic inequality was foolish and incautious nonsense lay the belief (or realization) that civilization, constantly threatened by the barbarism lurking beneath it, was only ever a fragile construction. Equally, if Rivarol accepted that the Church and the royal court were in part responsible for France's current ills, he nevertheless remained convinced that only a monarchy and an hereditary aristocracy, combined with the institutions of private property, the family, and an established religion, could restore order. Inspired by a hatred of the rich, a misplaced enthusiasm for the sovereignty of the people had effectively dissolved the body politic, producing a 'reign of terror', the guillotine, and an altogether new

[67] Rivarol, *Œuvres complètes*, iv. 1–390; repr. as *Journal politique national* (1989).
[68] Rivarol, *De la philosophie moderne*, 15.
[69] Rivarol, *Journal politique national*, 113.

species of revolutionary government which, like a 'hungry tyrant', devoured the people of France. The blame lay with the *philosophes* for having undermined the foundations of the *ancien régime*.

In these ideas, and indeed in others voiced by Rivarol, one can see prefigurations of the central themes raised by theorists of the counter-revolution from the 1790s onwards.[70] The Revolution was the product of a conspiracy organized and led by the *philosophes*. It was an expression of atheism, of Protestantism, and of individualism. It was an act of Providence and a display of divine displeasure with a sinful France. All republics, all political systems resting upon a spurious and unrealizable doctrine of popular sovereignty and natural rights, were doomed to collapse. The Revolution had brought into existence an entirely new form of government whose destructive powers and potential knew almost no limits. Only a restored and purified monarchy could terminate this anarchy. It was Joseph de Maistre and Louis de Bonald who turned these disparate positions into a coherent doctrine of reaction and who, in *Considérations sur la France*[71] and *Théorie du pouvoir politique et religieux dans la société civile, démontrée par le raisonnement et par l'histoire*,[72] gave them their classic expression.

Of the two, the writings of Maistre are the more vivid and elegant. Rarely however do they focus directly upon either the doctrine of natural rights in general or the Déclaration des Droits de l'Homme et du Citoyen in particular. Rather, like Rivarol, Maistre used the metaphor of the 'revolutionary chariot' to characterize an event which he took not only to be 'satanic' and 'radically bad' but that he also believed to be beyond the control of men. In the works of man, Maistre contended, 'everything is as wretched as their author': all comes to naught when the chains which bind us to the Supreme Being are broken. Accordingly, man's efforts at constitutional reform were foolhardy. The removal from power of the Jacobins amounted to no more than a few scoundrels killing a few other scoundrels. This profound scepticism took a multitude of forms. It meant, importantly, that Maistre did not share the enthusiasm of many for the example of the American constitution. Not only would the American republic not last but, he wagered, Washington would be neither built nor become the capital city! His views on the doctrine of natural rights followed from these conjectures. If all new constitutions were vain monuments to folly, all talk of rights was abstract nonsense. As Maistre lucidly announced: 'The Constitution of 1795, like its predecessors, was made for man. But there is no such thing as *man* in the world. In my lifetime I have seen Frenchmen, Italians, Russians, etc.; thanks to Montesquieu, I even know that *one*

---

[70] See Jacques Godechot, *The Counter Revolution* (London: 1972), 32–4.

[71] Joseph de Maistre, *Considérations sur la France* (1797) in *Œuvres* (2007), 175–289. See Richard Allen Lebrun, *Throne and Altar: The Political and Religious Thought of Joseph de Maistre* (Ottawa, 1965); Richard A. Lebrun, *Joseph de Maistre: An Intellectual Militant* (Kingston and Montreal, 1988); Owen Bradley, *A Modern Maistre: The Social and Political Thought of Joseph de Maistre* (Lincoln, Neb., and London, 1999).

[72] Louis de Bonald, *Théorie du pouvoir politique et religieux dans la société civile, démontrée par le raisonnement et par l'histoire* (1796) in *Œuvres complètes* (1864), i. 121–954. See David Klinck, *The French Counterrevolutionary Theorist Louis de Bonald (1754–1840)* (New York, 1996).

can be Persian. But as for *man*, I declare that I have never in my life met him; if he exists he is unknown to me.'[73]

It was in the writings of Louis de Bonald that the Déclaration des Droits de l'Homme et du Citoyen was subjected to the most searching criticism. Bonald's thought was built around a series of improbable tripartite divisions and proceeds by way of deduction and analogy from a set of first principles—for example, that one cannot speak about man without speaking about God—to what are taken to be a set of 'fundamental axioms of politics or of the science of society'. Thus a properly ordered society is one with 'a will which commands, a love which directs and a force which executes', whilst at the same time it is taken to be axiomatic that 'in a situation where all men wish to dominate . . . it is necessary that a single man dominates or else all men destroy each other'. What Bonald wished to establish through the use of this conceptual paraphernalia was that there were certain relationships between men that were 'necessary' and that, if respected, they formed the basis of what he termed a 'constituted society', a society that secured the primary goal of the mutual preservation of its members through the protection of men and of their property.

The prime example or 'model' of a 'constituted society' provided by Bonald was that of ancient Egypt. Here was a form of government incorporating a public religion, a monarchy respecting fundamental laws, and hereditary distinctions. It was to be contrasted with Asiatic despotism and with the unstable systems characteristic of classical Greece and Rome. If it had a modern equivalent, it was to be found among the German tribes that had destroyed the Roman Empire. The dominant trait of a 'constituted society', however, was that the will, love, and force within it were always 'general' and not 'particular'. 'I agree', wrote Bonald, 'with a theology which posits an uncontrolled will, a disproportionate self-love, a depraved or criminal action as the source of all our disorders and the origin of all our ills.'[74] For a society to survive, it was necessary that a general love of others should prevail over a private love of self.

Explicitly stated was Bonald's conviction not only that there existed only one true form of constitution for a political society but also that to negate its fundamental laws was to ensure social disintegration and decline. So, in a republic—where by definition the entire natural order was upturned and where God was dethroned—there no longer existed a general body but a collection of individuals. Individual pleasure and happiness, not general well-being, became the goal. All laws were arbitrary and not even an effective army or police force could survive. In republics, Bonald affirmed, 'the present is everything: they have no thought for the future'.[75]

It was precisely in this context, in a 'non-constituted society', that legislators, perceiving the 'radical vice' of their own legislation, committed the further error of seeking to complement fundamentally erroneous laws with 'preliminary declarations of imagined rights and alleged duties'.[76] The clearest example of such

---

[73] Maistre, *Considérations*, 235.
[74] Bonald, *Théorie du pouvoir*, 142.
[75] Ibid. 204.   [76] Ibid. 161.

stupidity masquerading as truth, in Bonald's opinion, was, not surprisingly, the Déclaration des Droits de l'Homme et du Citoyen of 1789.[77] It was a series of indeterminate maxims and propositions in which only 'the logic of the passions' was clearly visible. No sooner had its 'double-meanings' been promulgated than France awoke from sleep into convulsion and it was through this 'distorting light' that everyone examined their position in society. Men in high office were ashamed of having usurped authority, those of inferior rank of having prostituted their allegiance. Wealth, even to the property owner, seemed a wrong and poverty an injustice. No one was contented with their lot and society as a whole became divided 'like two armies face-to-face' about to begin a senseless and ungodly battle in which 'success could only be a calamity'. Those who appealed to the last article of the Déclaration affirming that property was a sacred and inviolable right were countered by those who appealed to the first article affirming that men are born and remain free and equal. Finally, 'after many lengthy and bloody errors', people began to realize that one should talk less of man's rights and more of his duties. But this was not sufficient to stop the carnage: France had already returned to a 'barbarous' and 'savage' condition.

Thus, Bonald's charge was that, in a situation where the idea of law had been consistently secularized and in which a total transformation of society had been carried out in its name, a declaration of the rights of man was singularly incapable of putting a break upon human passions. Not without irony, Bonald denied that the 1789 declaration was an example of metaphysics and this for the good reason that it was so manifestly defective and in error. He doubted that the language of rights could ever be used in a precise and expedient manner. Right, he argued, meant rule, from *dirigere*, but used indiscriminately it had come to express all relationships, even the most contradictory. If therefore this 'many-headed expression' was convenient for everyday conversation, 'in politics it expresses nothing of worth and had been deadly'. Equally, Bonald concluded that the words 'nature' and 'natural' had been misunderstood, with the result that the *philosophes* had incorrectly associated natural right and natural law with the nascent and original state of man and society. 'The true nature of society', Bonald argued by contrast, 'was the highest state of society, in the same way that the true nature of man and his necessary state is society in general'. It was, in other words, the constitutive and statutory laws of a society that were its natural laws, that embodied what was just, reasonable, and necessary, and it was because this had not been recognized that people had been preached such absurd nonsense about the disorders inflicted upon man by society. Like Maistre, Bonald had only contempt for the supposed merits of the 'entirely man-made' American republic: its enthusiasts proclaimed it to be eternal when it had only existed for a mere fifteen years. It would inevitably disintegrate.[78]

Similarly, Bonald rejected the view that natural laws were somehow 'engraved' upon the heart and therefore did not require any 'visible authority' or instruction to

---

[77] Bonald, *Législation Primitive, considérée dans les derniers temps par les seules lumières de la raison* (1800), in *Œuvres complètes*, (1864), i. 1050–1402.
[78] Bonald, *Théorie du pouvoir*, 347–50.

make them known. A wiser philosophy, he argued, would recognize that these truths needed to be inculcated and that this could be achieved by, amongst other things, the influence of a good education and of good laws. Above all, Bonald found a place for religion in this process and so much so that it was imperative that laws be imprinted with the sacred character of divinity. Human justice, he believed, could not be separated from divine justice. Civil legislation needed to draw inspiration not from the pagan world (as had been the case with the *philosophes*) but from the eternal principles of Christianity, from the Ten Commandments. Men, in short, should be taught what they owed to God and to each other before being told what they can do to others. One day, Bonald believed, governments—enlightened by their own errors and mistakes—would realize that these long-established truths formed the foundation of all social and moral order. 'Therefore', Bonald concluded, 'the sovereign legislator must be placed at the head of all legislation and we must get this philosophical truth, the most philosophical of truths, into our minds: that the revolution began with a declaration of the rights of man and that it will only finish with a declaration of the rights of God.'[79]

Among supporters of the monarchical cause, therefore, the language of rights was progressively abandoned as support for a moderate constitutional settlement hardened into outright opposition towards the Republic and all its ills. At first suspected only of undue abstraction, the language of rights was progressively superseded by a harsher discourse which associated talk of rights with a rampant egalitarianism and which came increasingly to hold the entire natural law philosophy of the eighteenth century responsible not just for the disorder of the Revolution itself but also for the Terror. Faced with the political, moral, and social disintegration of France, for the theorists of counter-revolution there was no room for compromise with such an atheistic doctrine.

IV

It was not only from the perspective of the post-revolutionary resurgence of Catholic thought that the Déclaration des Droits de l'Homme et du Citoyen was subject to censure and disparagement. The logic and epistemological bases of natural law were treated with growing scepticism among philosophers as the eighteenth century progressed and, if its rhetoric continued to enjoy considerable popular esteem, it was utilitarianism—in the shape, for example, of Helvétius's *De l'Esprit*—that came to occupy a central place in Enlightenment philosophical and political thinking. Certain writers, most notably Condorcet, had little difficulty in recognizing the threat posed to rights by utilitarian principles but others—attempting to rescue what perhaps could not be saved—showed little hesitation in attempting to break out of the straitjacket imposed by David Hume's distinction between fact and value and, as a consequence, in deriving rights from the basic needs and

[79] Bonald, *Législation Primitive*, 1133.

capacities of human nature. However, the tension between the potentially competing claims of utility and rights remained and would be cruelly exposed in the decade
after 1789. The primary locations of this debate were the *salon* of Helvétius's widow
at Auteuil and the Institut National des Sciences et des Arts, founded in 1795.
Its principal participants were the group of writers who were to be known as the
Idéologues.[80]

In the case of Condorcet, a refusal to endorse a utilitarian logic which
countenanced the transgression of the rights of the minority in the interests of
the 'greater number', and therefore condemned society to 'perpetual war', brought
with it the deployment of a sophisticated probabilistic analysis of voting behaviour
designed to demonstrate that a pure democracy of the type envisaged by Rousseau
was appropriate neither to contemporary France nor indeed to any situation where
the existence of the unenlightened many posed a threat to the emergence of a
rational politics.[81] It was this that explained his opposition to the Jacobin constitution of 1793. Nevertheless, it was recognized by many that the principle of the
equality of rights, when grounded in a conception of the natural equality of man,
appeared to offer the possibility, however unwelcome, of demands for greater
political and (even) economic equality. For example, Condorcet had no logical
alternative but to argue that political rights should be extended to include women.
In an important text entitled *Sur l'admission des femmes au droit de cité. 3 juillet
1790*[82] he drew the following conclusions: 'the rights of men result solely from the
fact that they are sensate beings, capable of acquiring moral ideas and of reasoning
about these ideas. Thus women, having the same capacities, necessarily have the
same rights.'[83] The only serious grounds for denying political rights to women
were those of social and public 'utility' but this, Condorcet contended, was the
language of tyrants and justified slavery. 'It was', he argued, 'in the name of public
utility that the Bastille was filled, that books were censored.' Such motives could
never outweigh the claims of 'un véritable droit'.

It was this conundrum that was faced by those prepared to conflate a discussion of
rights and utility. An early illustration of this is provided by the two best-known texts
of the Comte de Volney: *La Loi naturelle ou principes physiques de la morale*, published
in 1789,[84] and *Les Ruines ou Méditations sur les Révolutions des Empires*, published in
1793.[85] Nature, Volney argued, had given to all men 'the same organs, the same
sensations, and the same needs'.[86] From this it followed that all men had the same
rights to the use of their possessions and that all men had an equal right to life and to
the means which sustained it. The good therefore was defined in terms of 'everything

---

[80] Welch, *Liberty and Utility*, and Martin S. Staum, *Minerva's Message: Stabilizing the French Revolution* (Montreal and Kingston, 1996). See also B. W. Head, *Ideology and Social Science: Destutt de Tracy and French Liberalism* (Dordrecht, 1985); Emmet Kennedy, *A Philosophe in the Age of Revolution: Destutt de Tracy and the Origins of Ideology* (Philadelphia, 1978); and François Azouvi (ed.), *L'Institution de la raison: La Révolution culturelle des idéologues* (1992).

[81] See Baker, *Condorcet*, 225–48.

[82] *Œuvres de Condorcet*, x. 119–30.

[83] Ibid. 122.   [84] Volney, *Œuvres complètes* (1821), i. 251–310.

[85] Ibid. 1–245.   [86] Ibid. 102.

which tends to preserve and to perfect man' and the bad as 'everything which tends to destroy or diminish man'. Yet, when confronting himself with the possibility that these 'eternal and immutable laws' might engender a descent into anarchy—France, he readily acknowledged, was a country 'divided into two unequal and contrasting bodies', the people and the privileged—he showed no hesitation in resorting to a series of soothing maxims designed to alleviate any such fears. 'We are men', Volney has the people remark, 'and experience has taught us well that each one of us tends to rule and to enjoy life at the expense of others.'[87] In Volney's opinion, therefore, the people would accept with equanimity that the task of establishing 'the true principles of morality and reason' was best left to 'hommes choisis', to experts. In similar fashion, Volney believed that the rules of behaviour which would operate in the new society could be reduced to one overriding principle: 'the simplicity of manners'. This he defined as 'the narrowing of needs and desires to what is truly useful to the existence of the citizen and his family: that is, the man of simple tastes has few needs and lives happily with little'.[88] Discord within society, Volney contended, thereby disclosing the inspiration behind the entire educational programme of the *Idéologues*, derived not from the order of things themselves but from the manner in which they were 'perceived' and 'judged'. We had to be taught to see things as they really were.

Nevertheless, among those who came to gravitate around the *salon* at Auteuil the emphasis in the first place fell resolutely upon the defence of the rights of man and if this was to an extent the result of philosophical confusion it did not prevent Destutt de Tracy, arguably the most important of the *Idéologues*, from formulating the very first hostile response to Edmund Burke's diatribes against the Revolution or from deflecting criticism of the Déclaration des Droits de l'Homme et du Citoyen in the process. Burke, Destutt de Tracy argued, was not only wrong to suggest that France would have been better advised to follow the English constitutional model but, he continued, 'if our declaration of rights is a load of nonsense, our conduct is an excellent commentary on it. It was at the moment when America busied herself with nonsense that she became invincible to the whole force of England.'[89] The real problems for the *Idéologues*, however, began as the demands of the Parisian populace, the *sans-culottes*, became ever more strident and as France lurched towards Jacobin dictatorship.

P. C. F. Daunou, for example, began his *Essai sur la constitution*[90] with a biting and detailed attack upon the Déclaration des Droits de l'Homme et du Citoyen. 'We have drawn up', he wrote, 'seventeen articles whose incoherence, ambiguity and lack of precision have served as a prelude to injustice, to the feebleness of our laws, to the constitutional humiliation of our people, and to our long-drawn-out disasters'.[91] The source of these errors, he argued, lay in what he described as the 'synthetic method' used to formulate the original declaration, a method which had

---

[87] Ibid. 100. [88] Ibid., p. 305.
[89] Antoine-Louis-Claude Destutt de Tracy, *M. de Tracy à M. Burke* (1790).
[90] Pierre-Claude-François Daunou, *Essai sur la constitution* (1793).
[91] Ibid. 2.

led subsequently to the continued merging of natural, civil, and political rights into one amorphous and confused block. To formulate a new, more complete, and better structured declaration, Daunou argued, 'we ought to go back to the origin of our moral ideas: that is, to the first sensation which showed us a man unnecessarily preventing another from satisfying his needs'.[92] On this account, it was out of the relationships between men—principally those of injury and oppression—that natural rights were born. Moreover these rights—detailed by Daunou as the natural rights to liberty, equality, and the resistance to oppression—themselves quickly gave rise to a set of civil rights—essentially the rights to security and to property—that had their origin in a 'social contract' associating 'the force of all for the maintenance of the rights of everyone'. Finally, political rights emerged as each of the contractees realized that they should 'combine in order to establish the means to guarantee natural and civil rights'.[93] The outline declaration that followed—in which it was made explicitly clear that strict equality in the ownership of property was an impossibility—was intended to refute criticism that such principles were a matter of 'pure speculation, inapplicable to the current condition of both morals and society'.

The significance of this argument was at least two-fold. By taking as his starting point the analysis of the relationship between men and thereby dismissing 'the figure of a primordial man enclosed in the solitude of his needs', Daunou effectively shifted the emphasis away from the natural to the social.[94] The threat to the established order posed by the concept of a state of nature where all were equal, in other words, was diminished. Second, in purely political terms, it provided Daunou with the grounds for arguing that the exercise of executive power should be neither abused nor weak. 'The civil right to property', Daunou commented, in *Rémarques sur le plan proposé par le comité du salut publique*,[95] 'is the only possible tie between twenty-five million individuals joined together in an indivisible republic: all other systems will create anarchy.' If he acknowledged the dangers that flowed from an excessively unequal distribution of wealth, Daunou ceased to refer to the right to resist oppression, preferring to talk instead of preserving 'the right to petition and the right to assemble, peacefully and without arms'.

Another, altogether more sophisticated, attempt to deprive the language of rights of its radical dimensions was made by Daunou's fellow *Idéologue*, the journalist and politician Pierre-Louis Roederer.[96] Writing in *De la philosophie moderne et de la part qu'elle a eue à la Révolution française*,[97] Roederer devoted nearly fifty pages to

---

[92] Pierre-Claude-François Daunou, *Essai sur la constitution* (1793) 7.   [93] Ibid.

[94] Gauchet, *La Révolution des droits de l'homme*, 282.

[95] Pierre-Claude-François Daunou, *Rémarques sur le plan proposé par le comité du salut public* (1793), 5.

[96] See Kenneth Margerison, *P-L. Roederer: Political Thought and Practice during the French Revolution* (Philadelphia, 1983). See also Ruth Scurr, 'Social Equality in Pierre-Louis Roederer's Interpretation of the Modern Republic, 1793', *History of European Ideas*, 26 (2000), 105–26, and 'Pierre-Louis Roederer and the Debate on the Forms of Government in Revolutionary France', *Political Studies*, 52 (2004), 251–68.

[97] Pierre-Louis Roederer, *De la philosophie moderne et de la part qu'elle a eue à la Révolution française* (1799).

challenging the argument advanced by Rivarol that the new 'analytical' philosophy was predominantly destructive. 'If', he wrote, 'the Revolution was not a necessary product of philosophy, the Terror was less a necessary product of the Revolution and even less the fruit of philosophy itself.'[98] In so doing he denied Rivarol's charge that the declaration of 1789 was a 'criminal' and 'impossible' text, contending that to affirm rights was also (implicitly) to impose duties and that the text had recognized the limits to liberty in a 'social state'. He further argued that neither the constitution of 1791 nor that of 1793 had asserted that 'man was naturally equal without restriction'. Nor, he claimed, had any *philosophe* endorsed a doctrine of 'natural equality'.

Despite these assurances, in the *Cours d'organisation sociale*,[99] written some six years earlier, Roederer had been obliged to go to great lengths to show that property must be included amongst the natural rights of man and therefore must not be restricted. Starting from what he described as our 'anatomical and physiological' knowledge of men, Roederer had little difficulty in arguing that morality in general had its origin in man's desire to satisfy his needs and therefore that the primary guarantors of subsistence—namely, liberty, security, and property—must be categorized as 'an abridgement of the rights of man'.[100] The point was that these rights pre-dated what Roederer described as 'le pacte social', indeed that the very purpose of such a pact was to ensure the protection of rights deemed to be inherent to the nature of man. Recognizing that of these rights it was the right to property that was the most contested, Roederer went on to provide an extensive defence of property and its hereditary possession that combined the language of Locke with that of social utility.

The Lockean dimension of Roederer's argument was clearly visible in his assertion that 'it is a natural right that an object becomes the possession of the first man who, in order to satisfy his needs, mixes his labour with it'.[101] To challenge this was to challenge a man's right to live. In response to those who argued that a man required possession only of the product of the earth and not of the earth itself, Roederer replied that a man needed not only food today but also to be free of worries for the future. Property, in other words, provided security as well as liberty. The argument from utility, in contrast, asserted that common ownership was effective neither as a means of satisfying human needs nor of enhancing overall production. The needs of individuals varied and only private property could ensure the expenditure of the amount of labour appropriate to their satisfaction. Moreover, it was not merely a question of enjoying the benefits of property but of developing the means of production through *industrie* and the division of labour. The inequality of wealth, Roederer added, was not a necessary consequence of private property and it could in any case be diminished through the introduction of what he described as 'des institutions douces'. He categorically denied Robespierre's charge that private property was a source of waste and luxury.

---

[98] Ibid. 29. See 'De la Terreur', in Roederer, *L'Esprit de la Révolution de 1789*, 197–233.
[99] Pierre-Louis Roederer, *Cours d'organisation sociale*, in *Œuvres complètes* (1859), viii. 129–305.
[100] Ibid. 137.   [101] Ibid. 235.

The argument, then, is that as the language of rights became embedded in Robespierrean discourse and subverted into an instrument of Jacobin dictatorship, men of a liberal disposition such as Daunou and Roederer found themselves increasingly ill at ease with a form of speech that threatened to turn an equality of rights into an aspiration towards both political and economic equality. One dimension of this—displayed with brilliance by the Abbé Sieyès—was a penchant for increasingly complex constitutional and electoral arrangements designed to place limitations upon the powers of popular sovereignty. Another was to argue that formal declarations of rights were superfluous and largely ineffective as a means of preventing the abuse of power.[102] Still another was the attempt to develop a political economy which sought to unite patterns of industriousness—especially frugality—with the republican manners associated with moderate wealth and the absence of social hierarchy.[103] More generally, in the years immediately following the fall of the Jacobins, the *Idéologues* sought to stabilize the Republic and to place it upon solid institutional foundations. If Roederer spoke of the need to provide a government which combined 'rectitude' with 'strength',[104] the physician Pierre Cabanis argued for a government 'capable of efficiently protecting its citizens without ever being able to subvert public liberty'.[105] A large republic of 30 million inhabitants, the latter argued, needed 'a vigorous executive power'.[106] For his part, Destutt de Tracy developed a detailed programme, covering educational, economic, and domestic reform, that in political terms focused upon the need to restructure the State and to ensure the rigorous application of 'repressive laws'.[107]

Of greater significance was the attempted development of *idéologie* itself. As conceived by Destutt de Tracy, *idéologie*, or the science of thought and action, was the fundamental building block upon which the possibility of all human advance rested. This, in turn, entailed an almost limitless enthusiasm for the possibilities of conceptual reform, a characterization of religious belief and speculative metaphysics as obsolete sources of ignorance, and the search for means of perfecting our intellectual capacities. Less clear is the extent to which Destutt de Tracy was able to resolve the tension arising from his need to reconcile an advocacy of limited government with a philosophical position pointing towards government by an educated elite and a conception of objective interests. Even less certain is the extent to which the *Idéologues*, when faced with the demise of civil and political liberties, rekindled their original enthusiasm for the language of rights. Cheryl Welch takes the view that the search for stable government led the *Idéologues* to emphasize 'the utilitarian side of the revolutionary legacy'.[108] Martin Staum, by contrast, asserts

---

[102] Jean-Baptiste Say, 'Quelques idées sur le projet de Constitution de la Commission des Onze', *Décade philosophique littéraire et politique*, 6 (1795), 79–90.

[103] Richard Whatmore, *Republicanism and the French Revolution: An Intellectual History of Jean-Baptiste Say's Political Economy* (Oxford, 2001).

[104] Pierre-Louis Roederer, *Du Gouvernement* (1795), 14.

[105] Pierre Cabanis, *Quelques considérations sur l'organisation sociale en général et particulièrement sur la nouvelle constitution* (1799), 1.

[106] Ibid. 39–40.

[107] Destutt de Tracy, *Quels sont les moyens de fonder la morale chez un peuple?* (1798).

[108] Welch, *Liberty and Utility*, 6.

that 'the *Idéologue* confrontation with arbitrary power led to a resurgence of the language of rights'.[109]

To resolve this issue we should look at the two most important treatises on politics provided by the *Idéologues* in the periods of the First Empire and of the Restoration: Destutt de Tracy's *Commentaire sur 'l'Esprit des lois' de Montesquieu*, written in 1806–7 and first published in French in 1817,[110] and Daunou's *Essai sur les garanties individuelles qui réclame l'Etat actuel de la société*, published in 1819.[111]

Daunou provided a compelling account of the iniquities of arbitrary and despotic government. It was a self-perpetuating system that corrupted men and rested upon ambition and hatred. Nevertheless, as a counter-model he spoke of the need for guarantees of, rather than rights to, personal liberty, domestic security, and the development of *industrie* through production and trade. Liberty itself was defined as the 'full enjoyment of these individual guarantees',[112] with their safeguard resting not in 'general propositions' but in the 'positive rules' associated with long-established practice. Amongst the desirable practices listed were freedom of opinion and trial by jury. 'Nowhere', Daunou wrote, in stark contrast to the position he had adopted in his *Essai sur la constitution* of 1793, 'will I have resort to abstract principles, to the hypothesis of the social pact, to a discussion of its clauses, or to the anterior or natural rights that it presupposes.'[113]

Destutt de Tracy's *Commentaire sur 'l'Esprit des lois' de Montesquieu* was written for Thomas Jefferson. In a footnote to the text he kindly commented that the declaration of rights presented by Jefferson's friend, Lafayette, to the National Assembly on 11 July 1789 remained 'the best that had been produced'.[114] In the main body of the text, however, he argued that such declarations were a sign of political immaturity. It was far better to preface a constitution with a set of general principles which had their origin in 'the observation of man' and which, Destutt de Tracy believed, could be reduced to three 'eternal verities': governments are made for the governed; there should never exist in society a power that could be changed only by recourse to violence or that, when changed, altered the entire workings of society; governments should always seek to preserve the independence of the nation and the liberty of its members.[115] In general terms, therefore, Destutt de Tracy recommended a system of what he termed 'national government', resting upon free but indirect elections, civil liberty (including freedom of the press and from arbitrary arrest), legal but not economic equality, and a society in which every citizen would benefit from the liberalization of commerce and industry. However, the limitations of his attachment to rights were amply demonstrated by his argument that women should be excluded from public life. 'Women', he wrote, 'as sensate and reasoning beings, certainly have the same rights and, roughly

---

[109] Martin Staum, 'Individual Rights and Social Control: Political Science in the French Institute', *Journal of the History of Ideas*, 48 (1987), 422.

[110] Destutt de Tracy, *Commentaire sur 'l'Esprit des lois' de Montesquieu*, in *Œuvres* (1819).

[111] Pierre-Claude-François Daunou, *Essai sur les garanties individuelles que réclame l'Etat actuel de la société* (1819).

[112] Ibid. 210.   [113] Ibid. 6.

[114] Destutt de Tracy, *Commentaire*, 255.   [115] Ibid. 252–3.

speaking, the same capacities as men; but they are not called upon to assert these rights and to employ this capacity in the same way.' Women, in short, were destined for 'domestic functions' and men for 'public functions'.[116] More telling still was Destutt de Tracy's definition of liberty as the 'power to exercise one's will'. To be free was to be able to do what one wished.[117]

This argument received its fullest expression in the fourth part of Destutt de Tracy's *Elémens d'Idéologie*, the *Traité de la volonté et de ses effets*.[118] The contention was that our needs and means, rights and duties, derived from the faculty of the will and this in turn was defined entirely in terms of the desire to maximize pleasure and to minimize pain. Liberty was understood as the power to execute our will, to act according to our desires, and therefore was 'the solution to all our ills, the fulfilment of our desires, the satisfaction of our needs'.[119] As such, liberty was to be equated with happiness. Our rights were equal to our needs and, consequently, the 'rights of one person are nothing to do with the rights of another'.[120] Our duty was to satisfy these needs 'without any extraneous consideration'. Restrictions upon our rights only emerged with the appearance of the social conventions associated with the concepts of justice and injustice but this changed merely the means of implementation and not the substance of our duty. The goal of the 'good society', accordingly, was always to augment the power of each person by making that of others converge with it and by preventing them from reciprocally nullifying each other.[121] Viewed thus, society could be described as 'purely and uniquely a continuous series of exchanges'[122] and therefore the remainder of Destutt de Tracy's argument focused upon an analysis of the mechanisms of production and distribution.

There was much of merit in Destutt de Tracy's argument, not least his fulminations against the desire for luxury displayed by *les oisifs* and his determination to defend the merits of the various categories—be they manufacturers or merchants—who comprised *la classe laborieuse*. This entailed, first, a rejection of the physiocratic notion that agriculture was the primary source of wealth and, second, a repudiation of the attachment of the physiocrats to a centralized state as a vehicle of economic progress. At issue was a fundamental disagreement about the nature of productive activity, Destutt de Tracy wishing to argue that to produce was to give to things a utility that they did not previously possess and, therefore, that all labour from which utility arose was productive. But his text does indicate how far the utilitarian equation of liberty with the satisfaction of individual desires left him with the troubling conclusion that what made one form of social organization preferable to another was only the extent to which it enhanced the happiness of its members. The argument was not framed in terms of the protection of rights—be they natural, civil, or political—and the actual form a government took—beyond the distinction between 'national' and 'special' governments—was not considered to be over-important. The government that governed best, that maximized our liberty, was the

---

[116] Destutt de Tracy, *Commentaire*, 193.   [117] Ibid. 154.
[118] Destutt de Tracy, *Elémens d'Idéologie*, iv. *Traité de la volonté et de ses effets* (1815).
[119] Ibid. 110.   [120] Ibid. 130.
[121] Ibid. 137.   [122] Ibid. 144.

government that made us the happiest.[123] This was a far cry from the sentiments informing the debates of the National Assembly in 1789.

V

It would take a mind of far greater subtlety than that possessed by any of the *Idéologues* to appreciate the dangers of this unwillingness properly to discriminate between the claims of utility and those of rights. 'Right', Benjamin Constant recognized, 'is a principle, utility is only a result' and to subject the former to the latter was like subjecting 'the eternal rules of arithmetic to our daily interests'. Nothing could excuse a man who assisted a law he believed to be iniquitous, a judge who sat in a court he knew to be illegal, or a henchman who arrested a man he knew to be innocent in order to deliver him up to the executioner. To justify that statement, Constant not only outlined what he took to be the ambiguities inherent in the concept of utility (especially as it had been set out by Jeremy Bentham) but also fell back upon a position that, in his view, had been the guiding thread behind the aspirations of 1789: 'all citizens possess individual rights independently of every social and political authority and any authority that violates these rights becomes illegitimate'. For Constant, these rights were summarized as the rights to individual and religious liberty, freedom of speech, the possession of property, and protection from arbitrary interference. Most importantly, they were to be enjoyed by all and could not therefore be abrogated in the name of some utilitarian calculation.[124]

That the restored Bourbon monarchy proved itself unable to honour even the modest concessions made to such a doctrine in the Charte of 1814 was itself testimony to the limited appeal of the language of rights. Much the same occurred with the advent of the July Monarchy of Louis-Philippe. The Charte of 1830, like its predecessor, reaffirmed many of the basic principles of the declaration of 1789— equality before the law, the equal eligibility of all for civil and military posts, the inviolability of property—but did so without speaking of the rights of the individual citizen.[125] This was probably sufficient to guarantee France further years of political turmoil.

Other pressing matters were on the horizon. During the revolutionary decade, what was understood by property was essentially land. Suggestions for the redistribution of private wealth, for example, usually took the form of demands for periodic redivision of landed property—the Jacobins opposed primogeniture for this reason— rather than the socialization of the means of production. This began to change in the early decades of the nineteenth century as it became increasingly obvious to some that the bourgeoisie appeared to be the principal beneficiaries of the emerging industrial

---

[123] Destutt de Tracy, *Commentaire*, 161.
[124] See Stephen Holmes, *Benjamin Constant and the Making of Modern Liberalism* (New Haven, Conn., 1984), 125–7 and Biancamaria Fontana, *Benjamin Constant and the Post-Revolutionary Mind* (New Haven, Conn., 1991), 114–17.
[125] See Pierre Rosanvallon, *La Monarchie impossible: Les Chartes de 1814 et de 1830* (1994).

system. This was a view that received dramatic confirmation with the uprising by starving workers in Lyons in 1834. The eradication of pauperism, as it became known, called for radical measures. To these demands were then added, especially from 1840 onwards, a secularized religious impulse that saw the attainment of equality as being the key component in the advance towards the rediscovered goal of fraternity.[126] A good example of this style of thinking is Pierre Leroux's *De l'Égalité*, where equality was described as 'a divine law' anterior to all others and where Christianity was repeatedly characterized as conveying the same message as the revolutionary triptych of 'Liberty, Equality, and Fraternity'.[127]

No one gave clearer expression of this republican attachment to equality than socialist Louis Blanc. Liberty, 'without equality and fraternity, its two immortal sisters', Blanc wrote, would only produce 'the liberty of the savage condition'.[128] This was what existed under the capitalist system of unbridled competition. Blanc's response, set out famously in *L'Organisation du travail*,[129] was to recommend the establishment of *ateliers sociaux*, workshops for which funds would be put forward by government. This was not to be a system of enforced collectivization or of state-imposed equality but one where equality would emerge through the principle and practice of association. The end to be pursued was unambiguous. It was one where 'all men have an equal right to the full development of their unequal faculties, the instruments of production belonging to everyone like the air and the sun'.[130]

From this perspective, liberty was seen not just as a 'right' but as the 'ability' to exercise our faculties to the full. If, therefore, Blanc recognized the importance of those liberties that he himself listed as liberty of the press, of conscience, and of association, he believed that our conception of liberty had to be extended so as to embrace a range of liberties that would abolish the servitude arising from poverty and hunger. These he described as the liberty to life, to pursue one's aptitudes, to choose a job, and the liberty that would arise from physical abundance. Only when the latter had been satisfied would it be possible to speak of 'l'homme libre'.[131] By liberty, then, was meant not just the narrow conception of the absence of restraint but something tied to a different vision of society: the *social* Republic.

With the Revolution of February 1848 and the fall of the July Monarchy, republicans for the first time saw the opportunity of establishing a Republic that would embody not just the political equality of the ballot box but also the social and economic demands they had campaigned for over the last decade.[132] The former goal was attained (almost without debate) through the proclamation of direct and universal male suffrage but on the latter questions there proved to be no

---

[126] See Marcel David, *Le Printemps de la fraternité: Genèse et vicissitudes 1830–1851* (1992). See also Michel Borgetto, *La Devise 'Liberté, Égalité, Fraternité'* (1997) and Mona Ozouf, 'La Révolution française et l'idée de fraternité', in *L'Homme régénéré: Essais sur la Révolution française* (1989), 158–82.

[127] Pierre Leroux, *De l'Égalité* (Boussac, 1848). This text was first published in 1838.

[128] Louis Blanc, 'La Liberté', *Le Nouveau monde: Journal historique et politique*, 8 (1850), 1–12.

[129] Blanc, *L'Organisation du travail* (1840).

[130] Blanc, 'La Liberté', 3.

[131] Ibid. 5–6.

[132] See Maurice Agulhon, *1848 ou l'apprentissage de la République 1848–1852* (1973).

agreement. Work for some 100,000 people was created through the establishment of national workshops but these, despite popular protest in support of them, were quickly closed. At the heart of the question were the newly formulated claims to 'the right to work' and 'the right to assistance'. As on previous occasions, the passions aroused and arguments deployed over these issues were clearly visible in the debates of the National Assembly as its members sought to define the principles of the new constitution.[133]

Let us note that the deputies began by discussing whether the constitution should be preceded by a preamble outlining general principles and rights. Despite the familiar arguments that such a preamble would be 'vague', 'obscure', 'theatrical', and 'metaphysical', serving no useful purpose, it was the proponents of a preamble, bolstered by the rhetorical power of poet Alphonse de Lamartine, who carried the day.[134] Next, the deputies turned their attention to the content of the preamble and specifically to the question of whether it should include the right to work. Discussion was nothing if not animated, as all those involved recognized that the outcome would define the character of the February Revolution itself. 'The rights which you have declared to date', argued the socialist Victor Considérant, 'are old rights, those that can be called bourgeois rights; the right to work is a new right, it is the right of the workers.'[135] If it were not granted the workers would conclude that the revolution was over. Other speakers, such as parliamentary deputies Ledru-Rollin and Crémieux, continued this theme, locating demands for a recognition of the right to work within the tradition of 'the great revolution'. More typical was the measured response of the deputy for the Indre, Rollinat. Responding to Alexis de Tocqueville's charge that the February Revolution ran the risk of making the State 'the master of every man', he countered that 1848 was 'a social revolution in the sense that it sought to secure the continuous and progressive improvement of the physical and mental state of the people through means consistent with the sacred right of property'.[136] The workers therefore had to accept that work was both a right and a duty and, if they did so, the State would help them within 'the limits of the possible'. The State, in short, would recognize 'the right not to die of hunger'.

As the political tide turned against the radicals—in June 1848 an uprising by Parisian workers was ruthlessly crushed by the army led by General Cavaignac—it was the arguments of Adolphe Thiers against the right to work that secured the greater audience.[137] A reluctant supporter of the Republic,[138] Thiers's contention was that all societies rested upon three fundamental principles: property, liberty,

---

[133] See François Luchaire, *Naissance d'une constitution: 1848* (1998); Piero Craveri, *Genesi di une constituzione: Libertà et socialismo nel dibattito constituzionale del 1848 in Francia* (Naples, 1985).

[134] *Le Moniteur Universel: Journal Officiel de la République Française*, 251 (6 Sept. 1848), 2333.

[135] Craveri, *Genesi di une constituzione*, 123–4.

[136] *Le Moniteur Universel*, 258 (14 Sept. 1848), 2458.

[137] Adolphe Thiers, *Discours de M. Thiers, prononcés à l'Assemblée nationale dans la discussion de la constitution, septembre et octobre 1848* (1848): repr. in *Discours parlementaires de M. Thiers* (1880), viii. 57–106.

[138] Adolphe Thiers (1797–1877) was one of the major intellectual and political figures of 19th-cent. France. A liberal conservative, he later became the Third Republic's first head of government.

and competition. It was through work that one acquired property. It was though work that one expressed one's liberty. It was through work that one attempted to do better than one's neighbour. Everyone, Thiers argued, benefited from these principles, including the worker, whose standard of living had risen steadily over the past forty to fifty years. To codify the right to work, however, would encourage laziness and idleness; it would bankrupt industry and bankrupt the State. Even more seriously, it was an invitation to insurrection. Have you, Thiers asked his fellow deputies in the phrase reminiscent of Rivarol's argument in the 1790s, thought of 'the danger in which you will find yourselves when [the unemployed] present themselves before you, armed not just with the imposing demands that arise from their misery but also with an article of your constitution?'[139] For the State to offer help, as it should do, was not the same thing as to grant a right.[140]

Louis Blanc's reply was spirited to say the least.[141] Accepting that the right to property derived from work, he insisted that the ownership of property when not a consequence of work was 'illegitimate' and that work which did not result in the ownership of property was 'oppressive'. More to the point, he argued that if 'man has the right to life, by the same token he should have the right to the means to preserve it'.[142] At the level of the individual this entailed a recognition of the right to work; at the level of society it demanded the replacement of a system of competition by a system of association: socialism

Nevertheless, it was the argument against the right to work that carried the day, leaving the preamble to the Constitution with no more than a recognition of the obligation of the Republic, 'through fraternal assistance, to secure the existence of those citizens in need, either by providing them with work within the limits of its resources or, for want of a family, by giving help to those who are not in a position to work'.[143]

Where did this now place discussion of rights, liberty, and equality within republican discourse? For guidance we can turn to Charles Renouvier's *Manuel Républicain de l'Homme et du Citoyen*, written in 1848 and commissioned by the Ministry of Public Instruction as a civic catechism for the new Republic.[144] If the text itself betrays both the heated debates of the period as well as Renouvier's conviction that the Republic should embody 'justice' and 'fraternity', it also relied upon a formal, legalistic definition of liberty as 'the power to do everything that does not harm others, everything that does not infringe upon the rights of others'.[145] The 'principal

---

[139] *Discours de M. Thiers*, 50. A similar statement was made by Duvergier de Hauranne: 'Let us imagine that, in a situation of crisis, a million workers, or 500,000 if you wish, arrive with the article of your constitution in their hands and ask you for work and for a wage when the coffers of the State are empty, when taxes are not being paid, when there is no credit left: what would you do?' *Le Moniteur Universel*, 257 (13 Sept. 1848), 2419.

[140] See also Thiers, *De la propriété* (1848).

[141] Louis Blanc, *Le Socialisme: Droit au Travail: Réponse à M. Thiers* (1848).

[142] Ibid. 78.

[143] See Luchaire, *Naissance d'une constitution*, 219–20.

[144] Charles Renouvier, *Manuel Républicain de l'Homme et du Citoyen* (1848). Quotations are from the 1904 edn. See Marie-Claude Blais, *Au principe de la République: Le Cas Renouvier* (2000).

[145] Renouvier, *Manuel Républicain*, 145.

liberties' that were 'natural' and that it was the responsibility of the Republic to guarantee for its citizens were taken to be 'the liberty of conscience, the liberty of speech, the liberty to write and to publish'. To these were then added three more liberties: 'individual liberty', defined as the right not to be accused, arrested, or detained without proper authority; 'political liberty', described as the right of the citizen to obey only those laws authorized by his representatives and to pay only those taxes to which he had consented; 'the liberty to assemble and to associate', where special mention was made of the activities of religion and politics.

The complications began to arise when Renouvier considered liberties associated with the right to property. 'The most important outcome of a well-ordered Republic', he wrote, 'is to guarantee for each citizen the protection of his person, of his rights and of everything that belongs to him.'[146] This included a citizen's property, described as 'the fruits of a man's work'. Accordingly, Renouvier concluded that a law taking away the right to property 'would very much diminish the liberty of man, would place the citizen in a position of too great a dependence upon the Republic'.[147] Property was a stimulant to work and a cause of material progress.

What did this mean for an understanding of equality? Renouvier's starting point was that all men were 'born equal in rights' and that this was affirmed through 'the empire of law'. The emphasis therefore fell upon the civil equalities declared in 1789: 'The law of the Republic does not accept any distinction between citizens based upon birth or any hereditary possession of power. Civil and political functions can never be held as property.'[148] The law, in terms of both protection and punishment, was the same for all. Equality of conditions, however, was to be rejected because 'it could be established only by depriving citizens of their liberty'.

How, then, could equality be made compatible with liberty? Renouvier's answer, in true *quarante-huitard* fashion, was to call upon the sentiment of fraternity. 'It is', he wrote, 'fraternity that leads citizens, brought together through their representatives in parliament, to reconcile all their rights, in such a way that they remain free men whilst, as far as possible, becoming equals.'[149]

What substance could be given to this aspiration? Renouvier was clear that the rights of property were not without limits and that industry and commerce could, to an extent, be subject to public regulation. Unfettered competition had led to abuses and exploitation. He therefore specifically recommended that the State should provide cheap credit, that associations of workers should be allowed to run factories and workshops, and that land should be redistributed more equally. The interesting part of Renouvier's argument, however, lay elsewhere. If Renouvier went further by embracing what he termed 'the right to work and to subsistence through work', he gave a similarly prominent place to what was to become one of the great republican *leit-motifs* of the future: 'the right to receive an education'.[150] This education was to be the same for all. It was to be not merely a technical education but also a moral and civic education. Its aim was 'to elevate the soul'. Henceforth, it was to be education, rather than the pursuit and implementation

---

[146] Ibid. 161.   [147] Ibid. 169.   [148] Ibid. 203–4.
[149] Ibid. 206.   [150] Ibid. 207.

of demands for economic equality, that would be the motor of republican equality.[151]

Renouvier's text, therefore, tried its best to produce a synthesis of republican thinking that would preserve the radical aspiration towards greater equality whilst seeking to avoid the rhetorical excesses of those who challenged the very right to property. It is intriguing to note that, when faced with the hypothetical situation of there being too many people for the number of jobs available, Renouvier's response was not to contemplate further assaults upon the right of property but rather to suggest that the Republic should establish a colonial empire. 'The earth', he wrote, 'is vast and still largely unpopulated. Could we not, if the need arose, create new Frances overseas?'[152] Similarly, Renouvier's text was imbued with the desire to reconcile Christianity with the cause of the Republic: fraternity was nothing but 'the application to society of the doctrine of Christ'. In this his position was not much different from that of such liberals as Alexis de Tocqueville who, while opposing the right to work, regarded the act of helping the poor as 'Christianity applied to politics'.[153] Moreover, the descent of the Second Republic into a revived and modernized form of Bonapartism left Renouvier bitterly disillusioned and recognizing that the philosophy of the Republic had to be grounded on more than vague humanitarian sentiment. On this project, beginning with the *Essais de critique générale* and ending with *Science et la morale*, he was to spend the best part of the next twenty years.[154]

Nor was Renouvier to be alone in this, as there can be no doubt that a significant transformation in the thinking of republicans took place during the years of Napoleon III's Second Empire. Moreover, that transformation was diverse in both content and intellectual inspiration, republicanism drawing upon a wide variety of ideological and political influences.[155] By way of illumination, we can turn our attention to the writings of Jules Barni as a guide to what arguably became the dominant republican position on the related issues of rights, liberty, and equality.[156]

Like Renouvier, Barni spent a significant proportion of these years engrossed in the study of Immanuel Kant, producing a series of commentaries and translations of his major works. He did much of this during the 1850s in what amounted to self-imposed internal exile—having resigned from his teaching position following

---

[151] Recognition of the right to a free education (as well as the surveillance of all educational institutions by the State) was accepted through Article 9 of the 1848 Constitution. It was a source of immediate controversy. The liberal Catholic Comte de Montalembert described it as a form of 'intellectual communism': *Le Moniteur Universel*, 263 (19 Sept. 1848), 2497.

[152] Renouvier, *Manuel Républicain*, 214.

[153] *Le Moniteur Universel*, 257 (13 Sept. 1848), 2418.

[154] See Blais, *Au principe de la République*. See Charles Renouvier and François Pillon, 'La doctrine républicaine, ou ce que nous sommes, ce que nous voulons', *La Critique philosophique, politique, scientifique, littéraire*, 1 (1872); repr. in Stéphane Douailler *et al.*, *Philosophie, France, XIXe siècle* (1994), 727–53.

[155] See Philip Nord, *The Republican Moment: Struggles for Democracy in Nineteenth-Century France* (Cambridge, Mass., 1995).

[156] On Barni, see Sudhir Hazareesingh, *Intellectual Founders of the Republic: Five Studies in Nineteenth-Century French Political Thought* (Oxford, 2001), 227–80.

Louis Napoleon's *coup d'état* in 1851—and then during the following decade in Switzerland, where he held an academic post. With the fall of the Second Empire he returned to France, later to secure election as a parliamentary representative for the Somme in 1872, and again in 1876. He died in 1878 and, despite his major contribution to republican thinking, was quickly forgotten, even by his fellow republicans.

The similarity with Renouvier was not limited to their mutual admiration for Kantian philosophy, however. Like the latter, in 1872 Barni published his own *Manuel Républicain*.[157] This text built upon Barni's earlier *La Morale dans la démocratie*,[158] published in 1868. Barni did not disguise his desire to escape from the misplaced equation of politics with the pursuit of virtue. This, he announced, 'had been the error of the republics and the philosophers of antiquity'.[159] Moreover, it had been perpetuated by such eminent eighteenth-century philosophers as Rousseau, Mably, and 'even Montesquieu'. Each, in Barni's view, had not embraced 'the modern spirit' which, he argued, 'gives greater autonomy and liberty to the individual conscience, frees it from the intemperate yoke of politics and encloses the latter within the limits of the law'.[160] It followed that the first duty of the State was to respect and protect the 'natural rights' of all citizens and therefore that liberty should be defined in terms of the absence of arbitrary restraint and interference upon the actions of individuals.[161] 'Liberty in its essence', Barni wrote, 'consists of the faculty that allows man to direct and to organize himself, in a word to be *his own master*, and not to be the property of someone else.'[162] He gave this definition of liberty further description by specifying that it included the ability of each person 'to think and to speak freely, to work freely and to make free use of the fruits of his labour'.[163] Displaying the distance separating him from the Jacobin tradition, he commented that to curtail liberty in order to protect it was just an excuse for arbitrary power. 'It is time', Barni wrote, 'to finish with these theories which, in the name of securing liberty in the future, only serve the interests of tyranny today or of despotism tomorrow.'[164] The proper role of government was not to govern men but to teach them to govern themselves.

There are at least three features of Barni's account of republican liberty that merit further comment. Each tells us something about how republicanism was to develop in the years following the establishment of the Third Republic in 1870. The first is Barni's oft-repeated conviction that liberty must not be confused with either 'licence' or 'fanaticism'. 'There is no republic worthy of its name and that will last without the proper habits of liberty', he wrote.[165] Liberty, in other words, had to be informed by a comprehensive set of republican values, values that obliged every citizen to seek personal moral improvement and to respect the dignity of others. The conservative, not to say bourgeois, character of this moralized vision of

---

[157] Jules Barni, *Manuel Républicain* (1872).
[158] Jules Barni, *La Morale dans la démocratie* (1868). See also Jules Barni, *Ce que doit être la République* (Amiens, 1872).
[159] Barni, *La Morale*, 13.
[160] Ibid. 14–15.   [161] Ibid. 143.   [162] Barni, *Manuel Républicain*, 2.
[163] Ibid.   [164] Barni, *La Morale*, 166.   [165] Barni, *Manuel Républicain*, 103.

liberty was shown in the central place allotted to hard work, sobriety, chastity, the sanctity of the family, and respect for the law. Next, rejecting the arguments of Pierre-Joseph Proudhon, Barni unequivocally included the right to property as one of the fundamental rights of the individual. 'Not only has a man the right to make use of his own physical person', he wrote, 'but he also has that of working as he wishes, as long as he respects the same right in others.'[166] The right of the individual to own property, Barni contended, was the condition and source of the prosperity of society and it must be respected by government. Charity and self-help, rather than 'the organization of work by the State', would provide the best solutions to the misery of the poor. Recognition of the right to work would only lead society to 'despotism and ruin'. Thirdly, Barni extended his definition of liberty of thought to include 'liberty of conscience' and from this concluded that a state religion was an affront to such a liberty. Two things followed from this. Most obviously, Barni endorsed the call for a complete separation of Church and State. Next, he placed renewed emphasis on the importance of the provision of primary (and, where appropriate, secondary) education by the Republic. Taking up the theme announced by Renouvier, the first obligation of the Republic was to provide instruction for the people. Without this—as the disastrous experience of the Second Empire of Napoleon III all-too-vividly demonstrated—the liberty granted the people through universal suffrage would become an instrument of domination and despotism.[167]

How did these arguments have an impact upon Barni's views on equality? If liberty was 'the first principle of republican government', then equality was its 'necessary corollary'.[168] What this entailed, he argued, was equality before the law, civil equality, and political equality. It meant 'no more privileges, no more distinctions, no more castes, and no more classes' but it did not necessitate 'the strict levelling of all wealth', as this would denote the end of liberty.[169] The first duty of the citizen was to respect the law and this was to be accompanied by a willingness to subordinate personal self-interest before the common good. The good citizen was to display 'the virtue of abnegation'. As Barni commented, 'the love of equality does not denote a hatred of all superiority'. It was not driven by envy.[170] Not once in this analysis, as Barni acknowledged, was the word socialism mentioned, although 'the social question' was not forgotten. The aim was to ensure that 'the workers and the bosses, the poor and the rich, no longer form two antagonistic classes in society, as too often occurs today'.[171] The solution lay in 'good will', 'individual effort and a sense of solidarity'. The amelioration of the condition of the workers, in other words, rested less upon the actions of the State than upon the sentiment of fraternity, of belonging to the same family and loving each other as brothers. 'Citizens', Barni proclaimed, 'be *human* towards each other; the observance of this simple maxim will smooth out many difficulties and, better than the army, will secure social peace.'[172]

---

[166] Barni, *La Morale*, 150.
[167] See Barni, *Ce que doit être la République*.
[168] Barni, *Manuel Républicain*, 3.
[169] Ibid. 5.   [170] Ibid. 103.   [171] Ibid. 112.   [172] Ibid. 105.

Yet the most telling example of Barni's willingness to accommodate his understanding of equality to the forces of social conservatism was shown in his statement
that equal political rights should be denied to women. As he explained: women
were the equal of men 'as moral beings' and everything should be done 'to
emancipate women from all degrading tutelage'. This meant removing the 'injustices' of the Napoleonic Civil Code. However, Barni went on, 'in general the life
appropriate to women is not political life but private life'. 'Their proper place', he
explained, 'is not in the public forum but in the domestic home', supporting their
husbands and caring for their children. In any case, direct involvement in politics was
unnecessary as women possessed their 'natural representatives and deputies in the
form of their fathers, their brothers, their husbands and their sons'.[173]

Here then was a definition of rights, liberty, and equality that would come to
predominate amongst republicans from the 1870s onwards. How can this long
process of evolution be summarized? Republicans like Barni sought to detach the
language of rights and of liberty from the threat of tyranny and dictatorship (in
the shape of Jacobinism and Bonapartism) and thus to ally it to a stable, property-
owning democracy. It provided republicans with a political programme that could
appeal to an emerging new middle class and to a conservative peasantry. Just as
importantly, it sought to delegitimize radical and socialist understandings of liberty
within republicanism. Within this discourse, equality came to mean an equality
of rights and (in theory at least) an equality of opportunity but not an equality of
outcome. It was understood as civil equality (principally equality before the law)
rather than as an equality of wealth. In the key area of schooling, it meant that all
pupils, irrespective of their beliefs, were to be treated in an equal manner and,
increasingly, that education was to be perceived as the primary route to personal
emancipation and autonomy. Having removed all property qualifications from the
franchise, political equality existed in the form of universal male suffrage. Women
were not to enjoy rights equal to those of men. Despite this grave anomaly, the
State was under an obligation to treat all citizens equally. Inequalities of treatment
could only be justified in terms of the general interest.

What followed in the final decades of the nineteenth century were a set of
measures intended to turn this vision into a reality. The republicans, once they had
secured political control of the Republic after 1879, introduced a series of reforms
designed to enhance the liberty of the individual citizen and to extend social justice.
These covered such areas as freedom of speech and of the press, the right to hold
public meetings, as well as the key reforms granting the right to join a trade union
and the right to strike.[174] These measures were accompanied by legislation reforming the labour code, regulating hours of work, introducing industrial injuries
insurance, and encouraging arbitration in industrial disputes. Legislation enacted

[173] Barni, *La Morale*, 33–49, 126–38. Philip Nord shows how republicans reacted against the
infamous immorality and corruption associated with the imperial court: 'To the wiles of the
imperial coquette, republicans counterposed the virtues of the *femme de foyer*', Nord, *Republican
Moment*, 229.
[174] See Jean-Marie Mayeur, *Les Débuts de la IIIe République 1871–1898* (1973), 108–110.

in the early 1880s introduced free and compulsory secular education in state schools. For these reasons this period has sometimes been regarded as the 'golden age' of republican liberties.

A less glowing picture is revealed in Jean-Pierre Machelon's *La République contre les libertés?*[175] In his account, the pursuit of stability and order meant that striking workers, protesting anarchists, religious congregations, and civil servants felt the full force of state repression as the fundamental liberties of certain categories of individuals were disregarded in the name of social peace. The result was growing disillusionment and discontent amongst the working-class movement as well as renewed hostility towards the Republic from the Catholic Church.

The preoccupation with social peace also produced its quintessential ideological expression in the shape of the doctrine of *solidarité*.[176] As one of the doctrine's supporters, the philosopher Célestin Bouglé, was to comment: *solidarisme* was, in effect, to become 'the official philosophy of the Third Republic'.[177] Seeking to steer a mid-way course between free-market liberalism and collectivist socialism, its emphasis fell upon encouraging the practices of association, cooperation, and mutuality. Fiercely secular in orientation, it saw an education freed from the influence of the Catholic Church as the best means of developing both the moral and civic conscience of the individual citizen.[178]

The most famous exponent of the doctrine of *solidarité* was Léon Bourgeois.[179] Bourgeois was no minor figure. Amongst his many public offices, he was minister for public instruction between 1890 and 1892 and again in 1898. In 1896, the year in which he published *Solidarité*, he formed his own short-lived government. He later went on to be president of both the Chamber of Deputies and the Senate. Drawing upon the work of philosopher Alfred Fouillée and in particular his *La Science sociale contemporaine*,[180] Bourgeois's resolutely scientific argument was that the concept of *solidarité* should replace that of *fraternité* in republican thinking, for the simple reason that, while the latter was abstract and meta-physical, the former could be empirically grounded. The 'law of solidarity', he believed, demonstrated the 'reciprocal dependence' that existed between human beings, and as such was 'universal'. Accordingly, from an observation of situations of reciprocity it would be possible to establish a 'theory of rights and duties' that was 'neither abstract nor subjective but concrete, objective, in line with the

---

[175] Jean-Pierre Machelon, *La République contre les libertés?* (1976). This is not a view fully shared by Philip Nord. '[T]he Third Republic', he argues, was 'a democratic regime that sprang from and then nurtured a resurrected civil society': see Nord, *Republican Moment*, 246–53. See also Pierre Rosanvallon, *La Démocratie inachevée: Histoire de la souveraineté du peuple on France* (2000), 313–35.

[176] See Jean-Fabian Spitz, *Le Moment républicain en France* (2005) and Marie-Claude Blais, *La Solidarité: Histoire d'une idée* (2007).

[177] *Le Solidarisme* (1907), 1. See also Alfred Croiset (ed.), *Essai d'une philosophie de la solidarité: Conférences et discussions* (1902).

[178] See Ferdinand Buisson, *La Foi laïque: Extraits de discours et d'écrits (1878–1911)* (1912).

[179] Léon Bourgeois, *Solidarité* (1896).

[180] (1880). See also Fouillée, *La Propriété sociale et la démocratie* (1884) and *Les Éléments sociologiques de la moralité* (1905).

necessities of nature, and thus definitive'.[181] All individuals would come to recognize the mutual debt they owed towards each other and through this it would be possible to secure an 'equitable distribution' of benefits and costs, advantages and obligations. Thus, Bourgeois concluded, 'the doctrine of solidarity appears as the development of the philosophy of the eighteenth century and as the culmination of the social and political theory of the French Revolution'.[182]

What this meant, as he subsequently made clear on numerous occasions, would have greatly pleased all those who in the 1790s had voiced their doubts about the political wisdom of using the language of rights. The Revolution, Bourgeois argued, had given men their liberty and had made them equal in rights but it had taken a further century for people to realize that 'this liberty would not be assured to all if everyone, not recognizing a limit to their own liberty and profiting from the personal strength and advantages given to them by chance, made use of liberty in a selfish fashion'. It was therefore necessary, Bourgeois declared, 'to complete the declaration of the rights of man by adding a declaration of duties'.[183]

---

[181] Bourgeois, *Solidarité*, 86.   [182] Ibid. 156.
[183] This remark was made in a speech by Bourgeois in 1900, repr. in *Solidarité* (1904), 234. See also p. 210.

2

Absolutism, Representation, and the Constitution

I

'The cause of the evil, Sire', wrote Jacques Turgot, principal minister to the newly crowned Louis XVI, 'derives from the fact that your nation has no constitution.'[1] The consequences, as detailed in the *Mémoire sur les municipalités*, were grave. France, Turgot went on, 'is a society composed of different orders that are badly united and of a people in which there are few social ties between its members'. Everyone was concerned with their own selfish interests. There was no sense of the public good 'because the common interest was neither visible nor known'. Taxes were not paid. Commerce was stifled. Every town and village existed like 'a separate little republic'. Wherever possible the authority of the crown was circumvented, with the result that the king was 'forced to decree on everything' and was thus seen as being 'at war with his people'.

The solutions proposed—but never implemented, as Turgot was removed from office a year later in 1776—amounted to the introduction of a system of national instruction designed to produce 'an educated and virtuous people' and, more importantly in our context, a root and branch reorganization of municipal representation from the level of the village upwards. The intention of the latter was to allow a more accurate assessment of individual tax liabilities and a more efficient provision of public works. The most striking feature of this dimension of the proposed reforms, however, was that participation in the hierarchy of representative assemblies was to be based not upon the traditional orders of French society but upon a property qualification. All of those with a financial stake in society were, in one way or another, to have their say. Similarly, it is clear that the role of these assemblies was not to give voice to the will of the nation but rather to inform the monarch in order that he might better make decisions. The sovereign could, if he so chose, directly address the highest of the nation's assemblies but were he to do so it would only be to indicate the revenue required by the State.

The aim, then, was to give France an ordered and efficient representative structure so as to place the kingdom upon a sound financial footing. The result

---

[1] 'Mémoire au Roi, sur les Municipalités, sur la hiérarchie qu'on pourrait établir entre elles, et sur les services que le gouvernement en pourrait tirer', *Œuvres de Turgot* (Osnabrück, 1844), ii. 504.

of this new constitution would be such, Turgot assured the king, that 'in a few years, Your Majesty will have a new people, the first amongst peoples. In place of the corruption, cowardice, intrigue and greed that is to be found everywhere, there will everywhere be virtue, disinterestedness, honour and zeal.'[2] We know that Turgot's *Mémoire* was never presented to Louis XVI and that in the years that followed neither administrative nor financial reform were pursued with any success, an impasse that led not to the emergence of Turgot's 'new people' but to the eventual disintegration and bankruptcy of the State. With the failure of the Assembly of Notables, convened in January 1787 at Versailles, to agree to a programme of fiscal reform, the king was left with little alternative but to convoke the Estates-General for its first meeting since the beginning of the seventeenth century. Financial necessity was now to drive France towards a fundamental reappraisal of what had been understood by sovereignty, representation, and the constitution.

'By 1789', William Doyle has written, 'the universal demand was for a constitution, a clear and inviolable body of law which set explicit limits to governmental power and defined the rights of all citizens.'[3] This assumed that France did not have a constitution already. Was this so? Until well into the eighteenth century what was understood by the notion of a constitution was far from clear. Turgot, for example, took a constitution to be less a form of government than the way in which a society was organized and structured. This was undoubtedly one of the common usages.[4] Another, which had its origin in Roman and canon law, was an understanding of the constitution as the body of laws, edicts, rulings, and declarations which emanated from authority, be it emperor, monarch, or the Church. It was the latter understanding which had the greater currency. Moreover, it was undoubtedly the case that French monarchs felt themselves constrained by a set of fundamental laws that should not be transgressed.[5] Here we might note the complaint made by the exiled future Louis XVIII and Charles X in September 1791 that their elder brother, Louis XVI, had no right to concede to the destruction of the old constitution. Indeed, it was not until 1800 that Louis XVIII abandoned his plans to restore the 'Ancienne Constitution'. In this sense the kingdom possessed a constitution grounded in custom and past practice, existing prior to and independently of the will of any one individual or group of individuals.

The first of these fundamental laws concerned the dynastic right to the French throne. Succession was secured not by election but through the direct male line, excluding women and illegitimate offspring. When Louis XIV sought to overturn this command in the so-called 'affair of the bastards' it was seen as a gross violation

---

[2] Ibid. 549.
[3] William Doyle, 'The Parlements', in Keith Michael Baker (ed.), *The Political Culture of the Old Regime* (Oxford, 1987), i. 157.
[4] Marina Valensise, 'La Constitution française', in Baker, *Political Culture*, 441–67.
[5] Doyle, 'The Parlements', 157.

of the fundamental laws of the realm—the king was not free to dispose of the crown as he wished—and was quickly reversed by Louis XV in 1717.[6] The second fundamental law stipulated that the royal domain was inalienable. As the kingdom was not the personal property of the monarch he had no right to give any part of it away. Over time this sentiment hardened into the more formal distinction between the person of the king and the institution of the State, with the former seen increasingly as the administrator rather than the proprietor of the latter.[7] This carried with it the connotation that the monarch should seek to live off his own means and resources. He could not tax at will. However, the costly wars embarked upon by Louis XIV, followed by the financially ruinous involvement in the Seven Years War and French intervention in the American War of Independence, transformed taxation from a gift granted to the king by his grateful subjects into an unwelcome and increasingly onerous imposition from above. It seemed increasingly as if the monarch was serving his own interests rather than the general welfare of his people.

Similarly, the fundamental laws of the kingdom dictated not only that the monarch should act justly and in accordance with the dictates of the Catholic Church but that he should also respect the customs of the realm. In particular, the sovereign was bound to acknowledge the privileges and 'liberties' enjoyed by the innumerable bodies, corporations, and organizations that patterned French society. The extension of royal authority, therefore, could only be obtained by challenging and destroying these legal and fiscal privileges, a process intensified by the search for ever-increasing sums of revenue. This long-drawn-out conflict arguably came to a head with the so-called Maupeou Revolution of 1771 when the king's chancellor sought to break the opposition of the French *parlements*, and especially that of Paris, to his proposed reforms. By exiling the magistrates of the Paris *parlement*, Maupeou demonstrated that the powers of even the most exalted intermediary bodies could be ignored and that monarchs could act without restraint. 'It was now clear to everybody', Doyle writes, 'that subjects of the French king had no rights, and no institutions, that the monarch was not able, or prepared, to violate.'[8]

There were at least two possible responses to this situation. The first was to attempt to reverse the decomposition of the ancient constitution by making a return to what were seen as its primitive origins. The second, and more compelling, response was to acknowledge the need, as Keith Baker comments, 'for a restatement of the principles of the political order, a reconstitution of the body politic'.[9] It was

---

[6] The principles governing occupancy of the French throne were known as those of representative succession. This meant that, in legal terms, the new monarch was taken to be the same person as the previous king. Louis XIV went to such lengths to subvert this principle because he knew that if the boy king Louis XV died without an heir, the throne would pass to Philip V of Spain, thus reopening the prime cause of the war of the Spanish Succession.

[7] See Herbert H. Rowan, *The King's State* (New Brunswick, NJ, 1980). Rowan's argument is that French monarchs never entirely abandoned the practices of 'proprietory dynasticism', continuing to the end to conflate their own and their family's interests with those of the State.

[8] Doyle, 'The Parlements', 164.

[9] Keith M. Baker, 'French Political Thought at the Accession of Louis XVI', *Journal of Modern History*, 50 (1978), 283.

in this context that the meaning attributed to the idea of a constitution changed irrevocably, and with radical implications. Henceforth it was to be understood as the arrangements determining the manner in which the institutions of the State and of public authority operated. More than this, given the descent of the monarchy into what was widely perceived to be despotism, the demand was increasingly made and heard that these arrangements should correspond to the deliberate choice of the nation. For some this was perceived in terms of a foundational contract between monarch and citizen but at a minimum it denoted an acceptance that individuals 'had the right to modify or to recreate the legal forms of their common existence'.[10]

What form was this to take? How could the deliberate choice of the nation be expressed and represented? The traditional argument was that it was the monarch in his own person who represented the people.[11] That same logic denied all other claims. However, with each crisis, the crown seemed less and less to serve the general welfare and this understanding of representation became increasingly untenable. The strongest rival claim came from the *parlements*. These were not parliaments in the conventional sense but rather courts of law which, in addition, had the important function of registering, if not initiating, all new laws. Although they could not reject legislation, they had the right to 'remonstrate', to point out deficiencies and defects in what was being proposed. As they defiantly pursued this role, they came more and more to see themselves as acting as a restraint upon the abuse of royal authority. In the process a significant transformation occurred. In original conception, the function of the *parlements* was to represent the king to the nation and, in return, to inform the monarch if his subjects were in distress. As a consequence of their almost interminable conflicts with the crown during the eighteenth century, the *parlements* now presumed to speak to the monarch on behalf of and as the representatives of the nation. 'The parlementary opposition', Daniel Roche writes, 'developed four themes . . . : the right of the sovereign courts to represent the nation; the nation's right to accept or reject taxes; individual rights; and the separation of powers.'[12] None of these themes, and least of all the first, was accepted by the crown, which repeatedly restated its representative prerogatives.

The crown was not alone in rejecting the presumptions of the *parlements*. For some, the *parlements* were to be distrusted because they represented not the interests of the nation but the corporate order. For others, the ease with which the crown had dissolved and humbled the *parlements* demonstrated that they were not capable of representing the nation effectively or of defending the people's interests. Moreover, there was a body which, for all its imperfections, had superior claims to fulfil this function: the Estates-General.

On 8 August 1788 the king, bowing to increasing pressure, convoked the Estates-General for 1 May of the following year. As this indicates, the Estates-General was summoned to assemble only at the will of the monarch. Keith Baker makes clear that in its traditional role it represented the nation not 'as a separate

---

[10] François Furet and Ran Halévi, *La Monarchie républicaine: La Constitution de 1791* (1996), 56.
[11] See Keith M. Baker, 'Representation', in Baker, *Political Culture*, 469–92.
[12] Daniel Roche, *France in the Enlightenment* (Cambridge, Mass., 1998), 470.

entity apart from the king, but as a multiplicity of orders and Estates made one only by (and in) the royal presence'.[13] It had no legislative function because it exercised no public will. This explains why the members of the Estates-General were called upon to present *cahiers de doléances* before the king. They could not act on behalf of the communities or corporate bodies which had chosen them but could simply make known their grievances. Furthermore, respect for the traditional form of their convocation meant that the Estates-General would meet not as one body but as three separate orders.

How then might this complex, and changing, pattern of representation be summarized? Again we can refer to Keith Baker. The traditional logic of representation, he writes, derived from 'the essential relationship' between the monarch and a particularistic social order. Neither the *parlements* nor the Estates-General could stand for or speak on behalf of the whole: the latter in particular could be no more than mandatories of their community. 'Representation from above, deputation from below', Baker states, 'such is the traditional juridical formula of the Old Regime'.[14] The problem was that each successive crisis of government heightened the sense of a crisis of authority, leading this whole theory of representation to unravel bit by bit, such that if the king might plausibly claim to represent the (bankrupt) State he could no longer claim to represent the nation as a whole. The question thus became: who, if not the monarch, could speak on behalf of the nation and by what mechanism could the nation, if at all, be represented?

This question went to the heart of the theoretical structure of the monarchy, for the simple reason that it challenged the claim that the king alone embodied the sovereign public will. This is how, with extreme clarity and vigour, Louis XV defined his understanding of his own sovereignty in the *discours de la flagellation* of 3 March 1766:

> It is in my person that sovereign power resides. . . . It is from me alone that my courts derive their authority; and the plenitude of this authority, which they express only in my name, remains always in me . . . It is to me alone that legislative power belongs, without any dependence and without any division. . . . The whole public order emanates from me, and the rights of the nation . . . are necessarily joined with mine and rest only in my hands.[15]

Remarkably, Louis XVI repeated this formula almost word for word as late as 1787.[16] How could this theory of sovereignty be justified?

Writing in *Philosophy and the State in France*[17] Nannerl Keohane has argued that, in the context of the absolutist theory of the *ancien régime*, 'Frenchmen who welcomed consolidation of power in the monarchy were . . . not unconcerned with the securities and liberties of subjects. They believed that concentrated power

---

[13] Baker, 'Representation', 471.

[14] Ibid.

[15] Quoted in William Doyle, *The Oxford History of the French Revolution* (Oxford, 1989), 38.

[16] See Michel Antoine, 'La Monarchie absolue', in Baker, *Political Culture*, 8, and Ruth Scurr, *Fatal Purity: Robespierre and the French Revolution* (London, 2007), 57.

[17] Nannerl O. Keohane, *Philosophy and the State in France* (Princeton, NJ, 1980), 7.

provided more effective protection for all the members of a community than divided power.' The point is a straightforward one. The Anglo-American tradition has taken it to be axiomatic both that power must be checked and divided if it is not to be abused and that the protection of the rights of the individual by the State is of fundamental importance. It is only thus that freedom can be said to exist. Yet, as Nannerl points out, in France from the sixteenth century until well into the eighteenth century, the first of these key conditions for a liberal polity was 'rejected outright' whilst the second was 'commonly ignored'. This made sense in the context of a society which was both divided and parcellized and in which not only was a strong State necessary to secure civil peace but also where that State—in the form of an absolute monarchy—came to embody claims to represent the generality, as opposed to the partiality and particularity, of society's interests. As Ellen Meiksins Wood has commented: 'The king embodied the *public* aspect of the State as against the private character of his subjects.'[18] In this situation the central political question was that of rendering royal power 'more truly public', of cleansing it of particularistic influences, of ensuring that *la monarchie absolue* did not descend into *la monarchie arbitraire*.[19] The moral prescription—as Bossuet made plain in his *Politique tirée des propres paroles de l'Ecriture Sainte*, first published in 1709—was that the divinely ordained monarch should work for the greater good of the kingdom. If kings were not subject to the penalties of the laws, they must themselves be just and owed to the people the example of justice-keeping.[20]

This is not the place to explore the vexed question of whether the absolute monarchy in pre-revolutionary France was a myth or a reality.[21] Research over the last thirty years or more has served to indicate that it was at best a tendency or direction towards which policy moved rather than an established form of government.[22] Only royalist propaganda taken at face value has led us to believe that the crown triumphed over all its opponents.[23] It was, however, the propaganda generated by the crown that did so much to establish the widely and long-held belief that there could exist a single superior and sovereign will capable of expressing the permanent and common interests of the entire nation, despite the fact that the monarchy had little possibility of actually imposing that will. Here we might take one glorious (and enduring) example: the gardens of the Palace of Versailles. Summarizing the scale of this magnificent achievement, Ian Thompson writes that it 'was packed with messages about the military might of France, about technological progress, the superiority of French art over Italian, the commanding reach of the

---

[18] Ellen Meiksins Wood, 'The State and Popular Sovereignty in French Political Thought: A Genealogy of Rousseau's "General Will"', *History of Political Thought*, 4 (1983), 287.

[19] Pierre Rosanvallon has made a similar point. See 'Political Rationalism and Democracy', in Samuel Moyn (ed.), *Pierre Rosanvallon: Democracy Past and Future* (New York, 2006), 127–8.

[20] See Jacques-Benigne Bossuet, *Politics Drawn from the Very Words of Holy Scripture*, tr. Patrick Riley (Cambridge, 1999), 85. According to Bossuet there was 'nothing more distinct' than the distinction between absolute and arbitrary government.

[21] See Fanny Cosandey and Robert Descimon, *L'Absolutisme en France* (2002).

[22] See Regnheld Hatton (ed.), *Louis XIV and Absolutism* (London, 1976) and David Parker, *The Making of French Absolutism* (London, 1983).

[23] Roger Mettam, *Power and Faction in Louis XIV's France* (Oxford, 1980).

Most Christian King and the futility of insurrection. Even the little fleet that bobbed around the Grand Canal was an effective piece of propaganda about France's status as a maritime power.'[24] At the time of the death of Louis XIV in 1715 France might have been 'impoverished, vanquished [and] riddled with internal dissent',[25] but there still remained a powerful conviction that *la monarchie absolue* received justification as an appropriate response to the conditions of urban and religious unrest of the recent past. Furthermore, the fear of a return to the wars of religion occupied a central place in the minds and memories of the French people.[26] Thus, the absolute monarchy figured as a mechanism designed to enhance, rather than to diminish, the security and liberty of the individual.

Such a view received its most coherent theoretical justification in the writings of Jean Bodin, and especially in *Les six livres de la République*, first published in 1576.[27] In Bodin's celebrated phrase, sovereignty was an 'absolute and perpetual power'. It was not only supreme but also indivisible. The source and the exercise of sovereignty were deemed to have the same location: the monarch alone. As such, Bodin's theory was designed to counter all claims—and principally those voiced by Protestants—to the effect that sovereignty had its origins amongst the people and therefore that a right to rebellion existed.

A version of this argument is visible in the response of Bossuet to the views advanced by Pierre Jurieu in his *Lettres Pastorales* of 1689.[28] Exiled in Holland, the Calvinist Jurieu contended that it had been the people who, out of prudence, had created the sovereign and who therefore were the source of sovereignty. Accepting that the people themselves could not exercise sovereignty, it was nevertheless the sovereignty of the people that was the source of all authority: it was the people who made kings. The authority of the sovereign over the people, thus, derived from 'a mutual pact' and one that specified that while the sovereign had the right to punish the guilty he had no right to punish the innocent. 'Never', Jurieu wrote, 'did the people have the intention of giving to the sovereign the power to abuse its laws, its liberty, its religion and its life.' As the scriptures taught us, there was no legitimate 'power without limits', nor therefore was there such a thing as 'passive obedience without limits'. Accordingly the removal of James II from the throne of England and his replacement by William of Orange had been legitimate because James II had broken his pact with the people.

Bossuet's reply first doubted the biblical accuracy of Jurieu's account: the Jews had not lived for three centuries without a sovereign. Rather, obedience to the sovereign was in accordance with the precepts of Jesus Christ and had subsequently been confirmed by the scriptures, by tradition, and by the example

---

[24] Ian Thompson, *The Sun King's Garden: Louis XIV, André Le Nôtre and the Creation of the Gardens of Versailles* (London, 2006), 285.
[25] Mettam, *Power and Faction*, 319.
[26] David A. Bell, *The Cult of the Nation: Inventing Nationalism, 1680–1800* (Cambridge, Mass., 2001), 30–2.
[27] See Jean Bodin, *On Sovereignty* (Cambridge, 1992).
[28] Pierre Jurieu, *Lettres Pastorales XVI—XVII—XVIII (1689), suivies de la réponse de Bossuet Cinquième Avertissement aux protestants (1690)* (Caen, 1991).

of the early Church. Far from being the 'sovereign power', therefore, the people had no legitimate mechanism—'neither arms, nor assemblies, nor any authority whatsoever'—through which it could oppose the monarch. Only the Protestants, Bossuet argued, had thought otherwise, and all had failed to recognize that 'anarchy' and 'bloody civil wars' would be the consequences of their sinful doctrines. If 'Cromwell and his fanatics' were the 'true authors of the crime' against the person of Charles I, their justification lay in those maxims asserting 'the absolute sovereignty of the people over kings [and] the primordial contract between peoples and kings'. Jurieu had specifically denied this charge, arguing that it was not 'legitimate to oppose kings to the point of cutting off their head', but Bossuet observed that he had no grounds for doing so and no grounds for placing limitations upon the power of the people, no matter how unreasonable their actions. Moreover, Bossuet pointed out, Jurieu had singularly failed to offer anything like a convincing definition of either the people or its powers. Those who 'flattered the people', he concluded, were invariably 'the henchmen of tyranny'.[29] Much of what was to occur during the summer of 1789 and its immediate aftermath was prefigured in this exchange of views. Even at that late date, many were those who believed that the interests of the people and those of the crown could not be separated and that the sole sovereign authority resided in the person of the monarch.

The same disposition also brought with it a pervasive distrust of those intermediary powers and voluntary associations that later French liberals were to consider as one of the all-important guarantees of English liberty. Estates, *parlements*, the Church, and other similar bodies were seen as feudal remnants voicing private (and therefore selfish) corporate concerns and even when defended by Montesquieu came to be conflated with aristocratic power and what was known as the *thèse nobiliaire*. This was not all. To quote Ellen Meiksins Wood again: 'Even in more radical attacks on royal absolutism, the public will of the State was not generally opposed, as in England, by asserting private interests or individual rights against it. Nor was the common good redefined as a public interest essentially constituted by private interests.'[30] Rather what tended to happen was that the precise location of the source and principle of generality was transferred away from the monarch towards some other institution deemed capable of expressing its superior claims. The Huguenot constitutionalists, for example, simply shifted its setting from the king to the public councils of the people, thereby confronting 'absolutism on its own terms by stressing the particularity of the monarch'. The charge, in other words, was not so much that the sovereign might have said 'L'État, c'est moi' but that he acted as if he believed that 'L'État, c'est à moi'.[31]

[29] See Lucien Jaume, *La Liberté et la loi: Les Origines philosophiques du libéralisme* (2000), 37–93.

[30] Meiksins Wood, 'The State and Popular Sovereignty', 309.

[31] Herbert H. Rowan, 'L'État, c'est à moi: Louis XIV and the State', *French Historical Studies*, 2 (1961–2), 83–98.

The conclusion drawn by Keohane is unambiguous. 'Many of Rousseau's authoritarian passages', she writes, 'were restatements of hoary arguments in French absolutist thought.'[32] Nowhere was this more evident than with the concept of 'la volonté générale'. It came replete with the injunction not only that sovereignty should be neither divided nor restricted but also with the call for the total alienation of each individual and of his rights to the community. Rousseau's innovation lay not with the concept of sovereignty but in his denial that the sovereign will could be indefinitely identified with one individual. By doing this he opened up the way for the all-important redescription of sovereignty as the will of all those citizens who made up the membership of the political body. In this fashion was the theory of absolute monarchy transformed into the radical alternative of absolute popular sovereignty. The misunderstanding has been to believe that in either case a concern for the liberty of the individual was absent. Moreover, this discloses one of the most important elements of continuity between pre- and post-revolutionary France. 'It is no exaggeration to say', Lucien Jaume writes, 'that the totality of revolutionary debate up to Bonaparte is marked by the doctrine of the *indivisibility of sovereignty*, a concept which the Revolution did not forge but which it had taken up from the monarchy.'[33]

II

During the summer and into the autumn of 1789 virtually no one challenged the principle of monarchy. As Madame de Staël was later to comment, the desire was to secure a 'monarchie tempérée'.[34] Nevertheless, a dramatic transfer of power took place. The Estates-General, convened at Versailles in early May, initially sat, in line with tradition, as three separate orders. The Third Estate, nominally representing 95 per cent of the population, soon proposed that the three Estates should conduct their deliberations as one body. Initially rebuffed, they pressed on alone, on 17 June giving themselves the title of National Assembly. Three days later, finding themselves locked out of the building where they met, the deputies of the Third Estate reassembled at a nearby tennis court and swore not to dissolve themselves before France had been given a new constitution. In the following days, they were joined by the majority of the members of the clergy and then, on 25 June, by forty-seven representatives of the nobility. The new body was to vote not by order but by head. On 7 July it gave itself a new name: the National *Constituent* Assembly, thereby indicating its clear intention to provide France with a new constitution and effectively transferring the location of sovereignty to itself. A week later, the people of Paris, fearing military repression, stormed the Bastille. Having lost control of

---

[32] Keohane, *Philosophy and the State*, 442.

[33] Lucien Jaume, *Échec au Libéralisme: Les Jacobins et l'État* (1990), 15. See also Lucien Jaume, 'Citoyenneté et souveraineté: Le Poids de l'absolutisme', in Baker, *Political Culture*, 515–34.

[34] Anne-Louise Germaine de Staël, *Des circonstances actuelles qui peuvent terminer la révolution et des principes qui doivent fonder la république en France* (1979), 160.

events, Louis XVI had no alternative but to concede. His fate was now in the hands of those who claimed to lead the Revolution.[35]

As was so often the case, it was the Abbé Sieyès who most clearly articulated the logic that informed the new situation. His pamphlet, *Qu'est-ce que le Tiers Etat?*, published in January 1789, clearly set out the grounds for this transfer of sovereignty. For Sieyès, the only legitimate source of power derived from the nation: all other forms were contrary to the 'common interest'. 'The nation', he proclaimed, 'existed before everything else; it is the origin of everything. Its will is always legal; it is the law itself.'[36] And for Sieyès the nation was constituted by the Third Estate alone, for the simple reason that it, rather than the aristocracy and the clergy, laboured to produce the wealth upon which the nation rested. To that extent, the Third Estate was 'Everything': it was 'a complete nation'. It followed from this, Sieyès argued, that the 'representatives' of the Third Estate were the 'rightful depositaries of the national will' and that they could, therefore, 'without error, speak in the name of the entire nation'.[37]

These arguments were advanced before the Third Estate had established its political ascendancy. Once it had done so, the challenge became that of translating these claims into constitutional principles and practices.[38] Most obviously, this was in part quickly achieved through the Déclaration des Droits de l'Homme et du Citoyen, Article 3 of which declared that sovereignty resided in the nation whilst Article 6 specified that the law was an expression of the general will. No mention was made of the king. If this much could be agreed upon relatively easily, there was markedly less unanimity when the deputies addressed the issue of the composition of the National Assembly and the related question of the legitimacy or otherwise of the royal veto.[39]

In the first instance, the intellectual leadership of the Revolution fell to the group known as the *monarchiens* and loosely clustered around the figure of Jean-Joseph Mounier. Their dominance was short-lived (Mounier himself resigned his seat in October 1789 and returned home to Grenoble) but during the summer of that year the documents they produced as members of the constitutional committee provided the focus of debate.[40] Starting from a definition of liberty as the absence of interference and its need for protection through law, the *monarchiens* not only dismissed the idea that the classical world could figure as a political model for contemporary France (damning what were described as the 'sophisms of the uncritical admirers of the Greeks and the Romans') but also

---

[35] See Marcel Gauchet, *La Révolution des pouvoirs: La souveraineté, le peuple et la représentation 1789–1799* (1995).

[36] Emmanuel Sieyès, *Qu'est-ce que le Tiers État?* (1982), 66.

[37] See Pasquale Pasquino, *Sieyès et l'invention de la constitution de France* (1998), 53–72.

[38] See Keith Baker, *Inventing the French Revolution* (Cambridge, 1994), 252–305.

[39] See J. K. Wright, 'National Sovereignty and the General Will: The Political Program of the Declaration of Rights', in Dale Van Kley (ed.), *The French Idea of Freedom: The Old Regime and the Declaration of Rights of 1789* (Stanford, Calif., 1994), 199–233.

[40] See esp. Jean-Joseph Mounier, 'Considérations sur les Gouvernements et principalement sur celui qui convient à la France', *Archives Parlementaires*, 8 (1875), 407–22; speech by the Comte de Lally-Tollendal, ibid. 514–22; Jean-Joseph Mounier, 'Principes du gouvernement Français', ibid. 523–7.

showed themselves as possessing a perceptive appraisal of the dangers of arbitrary government, be it in the form of the despotism either of a single individual or of the 'multitude'. In so doing, they advocated the claims of representative, as opposed to direct, democracy, believing the latter to be entirely inappropriate to a modern state. If, in the circumstances, they were prepared to accept that sovereignty resided in the nation—politically, there was no alternative—they strongly contended that its exercise could only be secured by non-mandated representatives sitting in two chambers so constructed as to represent the diverse interests of the whole country and to secure sound and responsible legislation. 'To be the source of sovereignty and to exercise sovereignty', Mounier commented, 'are very different things.'[41] Similarly, the *monarchiens* also recommended the separation of executive and legislative power. As Mounier further explained: 'In order to avoid tyranny, it is absolutely indispensable to ensure that the power to make laws is not in the hands of those who implement them.'[42] In short, the preservation of individual liberty demanded the division of sovereignty and this could best be achieved in a system of representative and constitutional government. Seeking to build upon experience, rather than philosophical principle, the constant point of reference was the English constitution. The institutions of government had to take into account 'the weakness and the passions of men'.[43]

By early September 1789 the *monarchiens* had been swept aside, defeated decisively in the vote for a second chamber by 490 votes to 89. Why did they lose? Two reasons can be highlighted. The first is that to call for two parliamentary chambers and to endorse the English model was taken to be either implicit or explicit support for aristocratic power and privilege and very few people in the summer of 1789, never mind later, were prepared to stand up for the aristocracy. The opponents of Mounier and his friends persistently lampooned the supposed merits of England's constitution, frequently citing Rousseau's quip that the English were only free once in every five years when they voted in elections and that the use of their freedom showed that they did not merit it.[44] The brochure published by Charles-Philippe-Toussaint Guiraudet in 1789, *Qu'est-ce que la nation et qu'est-ce que la France?*, accurately captures these sentiments. To introduce such a system into France would be to institute the 'most terrible of governments: hereditary aristocracy' and to rekindle the 'ashes of feudalism'. The role of the people was to destroy 'these gothic and absurd divisions'.[45]

The second reason is more complex and relates to the Rousseauian rhetoric permeating so many of the speeches made before the National Assembly. The

---

[41] See esp. Jean-Joseph Mounier, 'Considérations sur les Gouvernements et principalement sur celui qui convient à la France', *Archives Parlementaires*, 560.

[42] Ibid. 409.

[43] Ibid. 412. 'In matters of government', Mounier wrote, 'many philosophers have followed the example of Plato by creating republics which could only ever exist in their books.'

[44] See Mounier, in *Archives Parlementaires*, 8 (1875), 563. For an example of the use of the Rousseauian critique of England see the remarks of Pétion, ibid. 533.

[45] Charles-Philippe-Tousssaint Guiraudet, *Qu'est-ce que la nation et qu'est-ce que la France?* (1991), 35–45.

constitutional debates of the summer of 1789 abound with references to the general will and all too frequently it was asserted that the general will could not err. There was no broad agreement about who embodied or who could express that general will, but among the opponents of the two-chamber model there was the firm conviction that, through the Revolution, the nation had been reborn. A revolution had taken place in the 'hearts' of the people, Jean-Baptiste Salle declared, to the extent that 'the French today are everything that they could be'.[46] Shorn of privilege and of the prejudices of the past, as Rabaud de Saint-Étienne remarked, France had no need of a system which would be able to accommodate diverse and conflicting interests. Jacques-Guillaume Thouret made a similar point when he remarked that 'a second chamber is being proposed as a way of achieving equilibrium, but since all the orders are merged together there are no more diverse interests to protect'.[47] Again Sieyès had pointed the way. Purged of 'two hundred thousand heads' (a somewhat unfortunate reference to the aristocracy and the clergy in view of what was to come) what, he asked, had the nation to fear from itself? It 'alone could express its own will'.[48] Thus reconfigured as the nation, the people were deemed to possess a unitary will. Rabaut Saint-Étienne set out the institutional logic which applied to such a situation. Given that the power to govern belonged to the nation in its entirety, '[t]he sovereign is a single, simple thing, since it is made up of the collective whole without exception; therefore legislative power is single and simple; and if the sovereign cannot be divided, nor can legislative power, for there are no more two, three or four legislative powers as there are two, three, or four sovereigns'.[49]

Not everyone agreed. The *monarchiens* in particular did not accept this rosy picture of a nation reborn, frequently reminding their fellow deputies of what an uneducated populace had done to Socrates. Nor was there agreement about the precise location of the general will that could not err. As one deputy had the temerity to put it: 'Everyone says that the law is the expression of the general will but everyone adapts the meaning of this to fit his own system. Some understand this will to be made manifest through the deputies . . . others believe that to this we should add the will of the monarch. . . . still others want a Senate.' Casting Rousseau to the wind, he himself concluded that 'the general will is that of the majority of French citizens'.[50]

Of one thing we should be clear: among the deputies assembled in Versailles during the summer of 1789 there was wide agreement that a republican form of government was only appropriate to small states and that as France quite definitely

---

[46] Salle, in *Archives Parlementaires*, 8 (1875), 530.

[47] Thouret, ibid. 580. Thouret was later to be executed by the Jacobins.

[48] Sieyès, *Qu'est-ce que le Tiers État?*, 81, 61. Rhetorically at least, Sieyès went so far as to embrace the argument that the aristocracy were not a natural part of the French nation, inviting them to return to the forests of Germany from whence they apparently came.

[49] Jean-Paul Rabaut Saint-Etienne, in *Archives Parlementaires*, 8 (1875), 569. For a contemporary analysis of why the argument for a single chamber was destined to fail see Antoine Barnave, *De la Révolution et de la constitution* (Grenoble, 1988), 116–22.

[50] Jean-Baptiste Crénier, *Archives Parlementaires*, 8 (1875), 550.

did not fall into this category some form of reformed monarchy was most to be desired. As Mounier explained: 'In drawing up the constitution of France, we need very much to take into account the large population of the kingdom. An association which is so numerous is so far distant from nature that we must not imagine that it can be governed by simple means, such as those which might be adequate for a town or a small province.' A monarchy, he further specified, was appropriate for all peoples whose population exceeded 'two to three hundred thousand men'.[51] Various arguments were adduced to support this view—not least the need for a strong executive power in a large state—but prominent among these was the recognition that it was only in small states that all the citizens could be assembled together. In such societies the general will could easily be known—as even the Duc de la Rochefoucauld acknowledged[52]—but in a large state no such simple mechanism was available.

It was this argument that provided the context in which the deputies discussed the second of the key constitutional issues they faced: the necessity or otherwise of the royal veto. Again, the *monarchiens* were the first to present their case. This was the way that Pierre-Victor Malouet defended the right of the king to possess an absolute veto on all legislation. 'It is true', he began, 'that sovereignty resides in the nation.' However, he continued, 'it is both useful and necessary for the repose and happiness of a large nation that there exists in its midst a pre-eminent authority, whose functions, whose powers, are so constituted that the person who possesses it has none of the cares and ambitions which drive other men and where the increase in his own fortune coincides with that of the general happiness.' Such was the origin of royal authority, as the nation had passed over to the monarch 'an element of its sovereignty which it could not exercise itself'. This position of lofty detachment and personal disinterestedness contrasted markedly with that of the nation's freely elected representatives: their will and ambition could contradict 'the general will and interest'. From this, it followed that 'the royal veto is a right and a national prerogative conferred upon the head of the nation in order that he may confirm and guarantee whether a decision taken by the representatives is or is not the expression of the general will'.[53] Three points can be highlighted here. The first is that the fear of popular disturbance and the 'will of the majority' was such that the *monarchiens* had no desire to see measures vetoed by the monarch returned to the people for discussion, hence the veto was to be absolute rather than suspensive. Next, we can note that the *monarchiens* persisted in the pre-1789 belief that the monarch, as sovereign, transcended the partiality and particularity of individual or corporate interests. Thirdly, they expressed a widely held apprehension about and distrust of the logic of representation in the form of a popular assembly.

Their opponents rejected the first two, although not the third, of these points. The people, they countered, were no longer ignorant and were becoming increasingly enlightened. Second, the monarch, as the Calvinist Rabaut Saint-Étienne made clear, should not be mistaken for the 'permanent representative of the nation'

---

[51] Mounier, ibid. 412.   [52] Ibid. 548.   [53] Ibid. 535–7.

if only because the two words 'permanent' and 'representative' should never be conjoined and because no function was less open to hereditary possession than representation. The king, he announced, 'could not be at one and the same time representative, head, legislator and executive'.[54] Moreover, to the extent that the monarch acted according to his own particular will he, if not the general will, could err. Nor, crucially, was the monarch alone in this, for, as the critics of the absolute veto themselves recognized, if the general will could not err, then the will of the representatives of the nation could most certainly be in error. This was clearly stated before the Assembly by both the Abbé Grégoire and Rabaut Saint-Étienne.[55] It was for this reason that, displaying their Rousseauian distrust of representation to the full, they both called not for an absolute but for a suspensive veto. In this way, disputed legislation could be passed back to the people in order that they, the possessors of sovereign power, could reaffirm the general will in the face of a corrupted or misguided representative assembly. As Jean-Baptiste Salle remarked: 'A man can be mad, but not a great nation: a great nation which reflects upon its interests, which decides for itself, could not will its own ill.'[56] It was these arguments which carried the day, with the result that the king was granted the right to suspend the introduction of legislation for up to six years.

How might we make sense of this seemingly paradoxical conclusion? Patrice Gueniffey, at the beginning of his detailed study of elections and electoral systems during the revolutionary period,[57] not only makes the point that the problem of representation was central to the Revolution but that the dream of the Revolution was to create a perfect symmetry between 'the will and the interests of the citizens'. This was to be done by introducing a system which would eschew all mediation between the individual elector and the sovereign, thereby assuming that those electors were able to give 'collective expression' to their will. The Revolution, he comments, 'was made against a power that was radically distinct from society, against the division of interests which opposed orders, communities and individuals'.[58] This categorical rejection of mediation and of the representation of private interest denoted 'a pre-democratic conception of democracy' and one that was to become 'the unpassable horizon of revolutionary political culture'.[59] For the time being, at least, the suspensive veto of the monarch seemed compatible with the expression of the general will of the nation.

These arguments also indicated that representatives were subject to a strong element of suspicion and so much so that, from the very outset of the Revolution, demands were made that they should be subject to surveillance and sanction.[60] To take but one example, Jean-Baptiste Salle, in recognizing that 'the first duty of a free people is to entrust its liberty to no one', called for the frequent renewal of representatives, constant public scrutiny and publicity of their actions, and the

---

[54] Ibid. 569.   [55] Ibid 567, 571.   [56] Ibid. 530.

[57] Patrice Gueniffey, *Le Nombre et la Raison: La Révolution française et les élections* (1993).

[58] Ibid. 24.

[59] Ibid. See Pierre Rosanvallon, *Le Peuple introuvable: Histoire de la représentation démocratique en France* (1998).

[60] See Patrice Gueniffey, *La Politique de la Terreur* (2000), 81–6.

right of the people to make 'the most vigorous and imperative protests'.[61] It was at this point that the next stage of the argument came into play, in the shape of the Abbé Sieyès's powerful discourse on the royal veto, delivered before the Assembly on 7 September.[62]

Sieyès argued against the royal veto on a number of grounds, not least because no one's vote could count twice. More profoundly, he believed that the veto, whether absolute or suspensive, was a form of arbitrary power. 'I can only see it', he announced, 'as a *lettre de cachet*[63] launched against the national will, against the entire nation'. It was, however, what followed that was the most interesting and innovative part of his speech. 'I know', Sieyès remarked, 'that we have come to consider the voice of the nation as if it were something other than the voice of the representatives of the nation, as if the nation could speak otherwise than through its representatives.' This was both false and dangerous because it ran the risk of splitting and dividing France up into 'an infinite number of small democracies, held together only by the ties of a general confederation'. France, Sieyès replied, was not a collection of states but 'a unitary whole, composed of integral parts'. In short, the proposals of men such as Rabaut Saint-Étienne and Salle would return France to the 'chaos of customs, regulations, and prohibitions' that had typified the *ancien régime*.

What, in Sieyès's view, was the alternative? 'In a country that is not a democracy (and France is not a democracy)', Sieyès pronounced emphatically, 'the people can only speak and can only act through its representatives'. There were four dimensions to this argument. The first was the recognition that all of the people, even 'the multitude without education', should have a say in the framing of legislation as of right. Next, Sieyès applied the principles of the division of labour to the political process.[64] Modern European societies, he argued, were based upon commerce, agriculture, and production. They were 'vast workshops', where most people existed at the level of 'work machines'. Consequently, 'the very great majority of our fellow citizens have neither the education nor the leisure to occupy themselves directly with the laws that ought to govern France'. At best they could choose representatives 'more capable' than themselves. To this Sieyès then added the standard argument applying to large states: 'Since it is obvious that the five to six million active citizens, spread out across twenty-five million leagues, can never meet together, the best that they can aspire to is to form a legislature through representation.' Finally, such an arrangement would produce good decisions. Representatives would 'deliberate', learn the views of others, benefit from 'mutual enlightenment', before taking a decision in line with the views of 'the majority'.

Stated thus, a key dimension of Sieyès's argument is missing. Meaningful deliberation amongst representatives was clearly not possible if they were mandated

---

[61] Salle, in *Archives Parlementaires*, 8 (1875), 533.

[62] Ibid. 592–7. This text can also be found in Furet and Halévi, *La Monarchie républicaine*, 406–17, and Roberto Zapperi (ed.), *Emmanuel-Joseph Sieyès: Écrits politiques* (1985), 229–44. See also Bronislaw Baczko, 'Le Contrat social des Français: Sieyès et Rousseau', in Baker, *Political Culture*, 493–513.

[63] *Lettres de cachet* were used by the monarch to imprison individuals without trial and were taken to be one of the most powerful symbols of arbitrary power under the *ancien régime*.

[64] See Zapperi, *Emmanuel-Joseph Sieyès*, 25–90, 245–71.

by their electors. Therefore, they should not be. The collective will of the entire nation could not be expressed if representatives were obliged to articulate the uninformed and partial views of their constituents. For these reasons, Sieyès insisted that, although the deputy was elected directly by his *baillage*, 'he is the deputy of the entire nation; all the citizens are his constituents'. The representative's job was to 'propose, to listen, to dialogue, to modify his opinion, in order finally to form in common a common will'. The voice of 'the people or the nation' had no other location than 'the national legislature'. What mattered was not unity of discussion but 'unity of decision'.

Sieyès acknowledged that it was not 'absolutely impossible' that the nation's representatives should act in error but he remained convinced that they, rather than some 'external mechanism', were best placed to rectify their error. The re-election of one-third of the deputies each year would be sufficient to ensure that the assembly could benefit from the experience of its members whilst guaranteeing that it 'would never become aristocratic'. On the substantive issue of the royal veto Sieyès failed to convince his fellow deputies. Nevertheless, this speech served to highlight dilemmas facing those framing the new constitution that refused to go away. Again we can refer to Gueniffey's analysis of the election systems introduced during the Revolution for clarification. As he points out, the initial objective was to construct a system of representation capable of 'interpreting and voicing the general will of the nation'.[65] This was to be attained through the expression of the individual wills of the people combined with rational deliberation. The revolutionaries, therefore, found themselves faced by 'the contradictory demands of number and reason'. It was arguably the Abbé Sieyès who understood this better than anyone else.

The reality of this contradiction came fully into view when, on 20 October 1789, the deputies began debating the questions of who should be entitled to be an elector and who should be eligible for election.[66] Five criteria were applied to settle the first question. To be an elector one had to be a (male) French citizen, be over 25 years of age, have lived at the same address for the previous year, pay the equivalent of three days' unskilled labour in taxes, and not be a servant. This produced approximately 4.4 million 'active' citizens. Women, minors, servants, and vagabonds were excluded on the grounds that their position of dependence prevented them from freely and independently exercising their will. The servant, for example, would vote as instructed by his master. The decisive distinction, however, was not between 'active' and 'passive' citizens but between electors and those eligible for elected office. The electoral system was to be based on indirect election in two stages. Active citizens had the right to choose a representative from electors who paid taxes to the equivalent of ten days' labour. These in turn were to meet in departmental assemblies, where the deputies themselves were chosen, each of which had to be paying at least a silver mark (*le marc d'argent*) in taxes. The latter was

---

[65] Gueniffey, *Le Nombre et la Raison*, 36.
[66] In addition to Gueniffey, *Le Nombre et la Raison*, see Malcolm Crook, *Elections in the French Revolution: An Apprenticeship in Democracy, 1789–1799* (Cambridge, 1996), 30–53.

equivalent to fifty-four days labour and reduced those eligible to around 50,000. By making this distinction between voting and function, in short, the Assembly clearly intended to neutralize the possible negative effects of the sovereignty of number. Those chosen to represent the nation would be men of enlightenment and of independent means. They would also have a stake in the maintenance of society. Having dismissed a second parliamentary chamber as a bastion of aristocracy, the National Assembly duly introduced its own rampart against the radicalism and ignorance of the multitude.

Sieyès was obsessed by national unity.[67] If this was clear from his views on representation, so too it was revealed in his concern to redraw the administrative map of France in order to eradicate the vestiges of the *ancien régime*. Without territorial reorganization, he announced in his *Observations sur le Rapport du Comité de Constitution concernant la nouvelle organisation de la France*,[68] 'the provinces will retain forever their sense of separateness, their privileges, their pretensions, their jealousies'. What followed was a plan to redivide France upon purely geometric lines. The intention, however, was to help the Breton and the Provençal 'to acquire the quality of citizen', one day 'to carry the name of being French'. Proposals upon similar lines were shortly afterwards placed before the National Assembly by Sieyès's colleague, Jacques-Guillaume Thouret.[69] Despite opposition, Thouret's scheme was broadly approved, with the result that France found itself divided into eighty-four departments of roughly equal size. Reform of municipal administration soon followed. Summarized by Furet and Halévi, 'the dominant preoccupation' was not 'to safeguard the liberties of the provinces with regard to central power, but on the contrary to subordinate in a harmonious way the different parts of the realm to the supreme law, as expressed by the National Assembly'.[70]

The same logic informed the conviction that legislation should not be subject to judicial review. The framers of the new political order deliberately set out to weaken the capacity of the judiciary to curtail the legislative and executive branches of government on the grounds that the courts of the *ancien régime*—the *parlements*—had restrained the monarchy in a reactionary manner. As sovereignty, one and indivisible, was to be located in the will of the citizens as expressed in law, it came to be seen that the National Assembly alone could give voice to the general will, leaving the courts with the modest role of resolving private disputes. The judiciary, as such, performed a function rather than existed as a constitutional power. As Laurent Cohen-Tanugi explained: 'Legislation was the supreme source of law; judges could only apply it, not review it.'[71] This hostility to judge-made law remained in place throughout subsequent regimes and only began to change, albeit unintentionally, with the creation of the Conseil constitutional under the Fifth

---

[67] Jean-Denis Bredin, *Sieyès: La Clé de la Révolution française* (1988), 167.

[68] See Zapperi, *Emmanuel-Joseph Sieyès*, 245–71.

[69] For the three speeches made by Thouret in defence of these proposals see Furet and Halévi, *La Monarchie républicaine*, 435–61.

[70] Ibid. 201.

[71] Laurent Cohen-Tanugi, 'From One Revolution to the Next: The Late Rise of Constitutionalism in France', *Tocqueville Review*, 12 (1990–1), 55–60.

Republic after 1958. Even then there were many republicans who remained deeply suspicious of moves towards the institutionalization of an *État de droit*.[72]

Similarly, the memory of the arbitrary abuse of executive power during the *ancien régime* was such that the National Assembly sought consistently to reduce the prerogatives of the executive. If the monarch was not to possess the right to dissolve the assembly, so he was not to have the right to convoke it or to interfere in the manner in which it carried out its business. Although nominally head of the executive, all orders emanating directly from the monarch had to be counter-signed by one of his ministers. To emphasize this reduction in status, the monarch was now said to rule 'by the grace of God and by the constitutional law of the State'. Moreover, the fear of renewed 'ministerial despotism' led the Assembly not only to claim the right to censure ministers but also to enforce their dismissal. In addition, the Assembly consistently circumvented the executive by setting up its own committee structure.[73]

How might these important developments be summarized? First, breaking with the traditions and practices of the *ancien régime*, it was quickly established that a constitution worth its name should have a clearly written and coherent form. Its authors were to be the nation acting as sovereign through its representatives. Next, although in form a constitutional monarchy, the constitution that came to be promulgated on 3 September 1791 effectively transferred power to an assembly in the name of the people. Moreover, it was explicitly assumed that if a people were sovereign, then this was a sufficient condition to ensure that it was free, and therefore that the rights of the individual would be protected. Accordingly, those framing the constitution paid scant attention to the need for a separation or balance of powers. There was to be one parliamentary chamber, indirectly elected upon the basis of a broadly based male suffrage. Unease about the legitimacy of representation meant that representatives were placed under constant surveillance and were subject to frequent reselection. A similar distrust of executive power meant that the latter found itself weakened and in a subordinate position to the legislative assembly.[74]

The Constitution of 1791 was still-born.[75] The flight of Louis XVI from Paris and his capture at Varennes saw to that. Nevertheless a set of constitutional principles had been established that were broadly adhered to by the constitutions of both 1793 and 1795, the former pushing these principles in a radical direction, the latter seeking to re-establish stability following the Terror. The constitution of 1793 or Year I, for example, reaffirmed the sovereignty of the people; further extended the suffrage (making it direct and universal for males); maintained the practice of a single legislative assembly; reduced the power of the executive (by conferring it upon twenty-four ministers elected by the legislative assembly and

---

[72] See my 'From "Imperial State" to "l'État de droit": Benjamin Constant, Blandine Kriegel and the Reform of the French Constitution', *Political Studies*, 44 (1996), 488–504.

[73] See Guy Antonetti, *La Monarchie constitutionnelle* (Paris, 1998), 11–36.

[74] See Stéphane Rials, 'Une doctrine constitutionnelle française?', *Pouvoirs*, 50 (1989), 81–95.

[75] See Jacques Godechot, *Les Constitutions de la France depuis 1789* (1995), 33–67.

drawn from names selected by primary assemblies at departmental level); disregarded any reference to the process of judicial review; and reduced the mandate of assembly representatives to one year only.

However, there were two significant innovations. Such was the passion of the Jacobins for a form of democracy that was both transparent and egalitarian that the supremacy of the legislative assembly was to be counter-balanced by the direct expression of the will of the people. Under the constitution this could take two forms: the people were explicitly granted the right to insurrection as well as the right of legislative veto.[76] This itself reflected the deep, and unresolved, unease felt by the Jacobins towards the process of representation. If within their own organization the Jacobins made repeated resort to the practice of denunciation, this was even more evident with regard to those who claimed to represent the people. Robespierre's speeches and articles in the period 1792–3 are a ceaseless tirade against those deputies who placed private interest before the general interest.[77] The people, he argued, had not overturned 'the despotism of the throne' in order to witness the installation of a 'privileged class' of corrupt and venal representatives. 'The source of all our ills', he proclaimed, 'lies in the absolute independence that the representatives have claimed for themselves without consulting the nation itself.' This 'representative despotism' had enslaved the nation.[78] There was, therefore, need for a new assembly that would be 'pure, incorruptible', peopled by 'virtuous men', by 'patriots'. The infidelities arising out of the process of representation could only be overcome if the representative shared the simplicity and honesty of morals that characterized the people.

At times both Robespierre and Saint-Just suggested that the root of the problem lay in the ability of corrupt, aristocratic factions to insert themselves between the French people and their representatives—'I dare to say', Saint-Just commented, 'that the Republic would soon flourish, if the people and its representatives were to have the dominant influence, and if the sovereignty of the people was purged of aristocrats and their agents'[79]—but the weight of their argument was directed against what Robespierre himself designated as 'the most cruel and most indestructible of all tyrannies': 'absolute representative government'.[80] Against the representative claims of private, local, or sectional interest, in other words, were to be deployed the counter-claims of neither number nor reason but of the sovereignty of the moral good. Only the Jacobins themselves could speak in its name.[81]

The republican constitution of 1793 was approved by popular referendum during the summer of that year. If 1.1 million electors gave their approval, 4.3 million abstained. No sooner had this occurred than its application was suspended, as the government of the Republic was declared to be revolutionary until the 'return of peace'. A year later, Robespierre, Saint-Just, and about eighty of their close supporters

[76] See Jacques Godechot, *Les Constitutions de la France depuis 1789* (1995), 79–92.
[77] See *Œuvres complètes de Robespierre*, iv (1939).
[78] Ibid. 328.
[79] Louis-Antoine de Saint-Just, 'Sur les personnes incarcérées', in *L'Impossible Terreur* (1989), 52.
[80] *Œuvres complètes de Robespierre*, iv. 146.
[81] See Lucien Jaume, *Le Discours Jacobin et la démocratie* (1989), 255–385.

(including Robespierre's brother) were executed as the Jacobins were removed from power. In the difficult days and months that followed their overthrow on 9 Thermidor, constitutional issues were left in abeyance but by the following year the question of devising a new constitution again came to the fore.

There is no need to pay detailed attention to these discussions.[82] The constitution of 1793 was judged to be both unworkable and dangerous, sacrificing the rights and liberties of individuals to the sovereign will of the assembly. What was to replace it? There is a view that the constitution of 1795 amounted to only a rhetorical rejection of its Jacobin predecessor.[83] While this analysis has a considerable element of truth—there were points of continuity with the constitutions of both 1791 and 1793—the new constitution approved by the Convention sought to learn from the lessons of the recent past and to establish a structure that would place the Republic upon a secure foundation and prevent a return to revolutionary dictatorship.[84] It attempted to do this in a variety of ways. The suffrage was reformed through the reintroduction of both a property qualification and a system of indirect election; sovereignty was defined not in terms of the nation but 'in essence' as the possession of 'the universality of French citizens'; the right of citizens to veto legislation was removed.

More complex were the provisions for the organization of both legislative and executive power. For the first time, France was to possess two legislative chambers, the Conseil des Cinq-Cents and the Conseil des Anciens, membership of which was to be decided upon by the same electorate, even if their composition and powers were to differ. If the first chamber had the right of legislative initiative, the second could approve or reject, although not amend, legislation. The executive was to be composed of a Directory of five members, each elected for five years. The Conseil de Cinq-Cents was to nominate ten names for each position, whilst the Conseil des Anciens selected the successful candidates by secret ballot. The Directory itself possessed significant powers, including the right to nominate both generals and judges. It could not, however, dissolve the legislative body nor veto legislation. Ministers—of which there were seven—were responsible to the Directory and were not allowed to meet as a group. The assumption that age and a family were a barrier to radicalism was also evident in the stipulation that members of the Directory had to be over 40 years of age. Similar age restrictions applied to the two chambers.

The committee responsible for formulating the new constitution was largely composed of former supporters of the moderate Girondins. If the main public advocate of the committee's work was Boissy d'Anglas,[85] by general agreement the principal author of the Constitution of Year III was the future *Idéologue*, Daunou. Sieyès refused to get involved and made known his opposition to the proposals before the Convention. He feared, rightly, that the strict division between the

---

[82] See Gauchet, *La Révolution des pouvoirs*, 125–86.

[83] Michel Troper, *La Séparation des pouvoirs et l'histoire constitutionnelle française* (1980), 188–200.

[84] See Godechot, *Les Constitutions*, 101–41. One notable feature of this constitution is how detailed it was, running to 377 articles. The constitution of 1793 had only 124 articles.

[85] See Gérard Conac and Jean-Pierre Machelon (eds.), *La Constitution de l'an III: Boissy d'Anglas et la naissance du libéralisme constitutionnel* (1999).

legislative and executive branches of government would quickly lead to deadlock. He also proposed, in what was for him a significant innovation, the establishment of a *jury constitutionnaire* which would annul any legislation that did not conform to the fundamental laws of the constitution.[86] However, the new constitution's supporters were of the opinion that it would make impossible a return to despotism through the institutionalization of what Boissy d'Anglas did not hesitate to term 'the balance of powers'. Herein lies the controversy. The prevailing opinion has been that the new constitution gave only modest expression to these constitutional principles.[87] Against Sieyès's advice, for example, no mechanism was introduced to ascertain the constitutionality of laws. On this view, the executive remained subordinate to the legislative, which itself was only artificially split into two chambers for 'technical' reasons. However, to a certain extent the power of the executive *vis-à-vis* the legislative branch was strengthened and the very introduction of two legislative chambers marked an important shift from what had been quickly established as an article of revolutionary faith. It thus denoted a tentative break with the logic that located an indivisible sovereignty within a single representative assembly. An element of equilibrium, if not strict balance, was obtained, with the firm intention of protecting the people from the abuses of their own power.

The Directory has had few friends or admirers, even if historians are now inclining to see it in a more positive light.[88] Determined to hold on to power, the Thermidorians, as the dominant group of deputies were now known, not only (illegally) removed royalist deputies from the legislative chambers in September 1797 but repeated the manœuvre a year later when newly elected Jacobin deputies were purged before they had the opportunity to take up their seats. Even the regime's initial supporters began quickly to doubt that it could survive. The early enthusiasm to be found in Madame de Staël's *Rélexions sur la paix intérieure*,[89] penned in 1795 in the confident expectation that the Thermidorian Republic would overcome divisions between royalists and republicans and bring 'repose' to France, gave way to the more sober appraisal evident in her *Des circonstances actuelles qui peuvent terminer la Révolution et des principes qui doivent fonder la République en France* published three years later, where she recognized that this 'bad constitution' was inadequate to the tasks demanded of it. The Directory, she commented, might 'save the vessel from shipwreck but it could not navigate it to port'. Like many others, she concluded that a regime that could only remain in existence by flouting the constitution had to be reformed. Above all, the executive needed to be given the means to govern.[90]

[86] See Pasquino, *Sieyès et l'invention de la constitution*, 181–96.

[87] See Michel Troper, *Terminer la Révolution: La Constitution de 1795* (2006).

[88] See James Livesey, *Making Democracy in the French Revolution* (Cambridge, Mass., 2001); Howard G. Brown, *Ending the French Revolution* (Charlottesville, Va., 2006) and Andrew Jainchill, *Reimagining Politics after the Terror: The Republican Origins of French Liberalism* (Ithaca, NY, 2008). For an overview of historiographical debates associated with the Directory see Malcolm Crook, *Napoleon Comes to Power: Democracy and Dictatorship in the Revolutionary Era* (Cardiff, 1998).

[89] See *Œuvres complètes de Mme La Baronne de Staël* (1820), ii. 95–172.

[90] De Staël, *Des circonstances actuelles*, 155–221. See also Benjamin Constant, *Des Suites de la contre-révolution de 1660 en Angleterre* (1799).

This was also the opinion of the Abbé Sieyès. Elected to the Directory in June 1799, he began immediately to plot its downfall, turning first to the young general Barthélemy Joubert and then, after the former's death in Italy, to Napoleon Bonaparte.[91] The latter's triumphant, if mysterious, return from his military campaign in Egypt set the scene for what was later to be known as the *coup d'état* of 18 Brumaire. At the time, the dissolution of the Directory under the threat of force was seen as something both necessary and inevitable and broadly to be welcomed.

Sieyès (on this occasion, incorrectly) imagined that he would now have the chance to provide France with the constitution he believed that she had long required. Power was immediately handed over to an 'executive consulate' composed of Sieyès, the regicide Roger Ducos, and Bonaparte himself. Their task was to provide France with yet another new constitution, something they did in approximately one month. Universal male suffrage was restored but in such a manner as to make its operation almost meaningless. Sieyès got his way over the introduction of a 'Sénat conservateur', membership of which was for life and whose function was to scrutinize the legality of all laws and all actions by government. The legislative was to be divided into two chambers, one of which would discuss legislation whilst the other would vote upon it. Neither possessed the right of legislative initiative. Where Sieyès was rebuffed was in the matter of executive power. Granted extensive authority, there were to be three Consuls, each serving for ten years, but of these one—Bonaparte—was to be designated as First Consul. It was to be in this office that real power was to be located.[92]

'Citizens', it was immediately declared, 'the revolution is established on the principles with which it began. It is finished.' Technically, the Republic still existed, although in 1802 Bonaparte had himself proclaimed Consul for life, further extending his already considerable powers and reducing the powers of the legislative branch (which was now to assemble only at the behest of the government). At this point, as Jacques Godechot remarked, 'Napoleon was already more powerful than Louis XIV'.[93] Two years later, at a ceremony held in the cathedral of Notre-Dame and attended by Pope Pius VII, Napoleon crowned himself emperor, a scene immortalized by the painter David. The emperor's crown was to be passed on by hereditary succession, through the male line. Should there be (as seemed likely) no male successor, Bonaparte granted himself what no monarch of France had ever possessed: the right of adoption.

In this way the experiment of the First Republic came to its sorry conclusion. Chateaubriand, writing at his most royalist in his text *De Buonaparte, Des Bourbons*, reached the following conclusion.[94] The French, in seeking to create 'a society without a past and a future', had tried 'various forms of republican government', only in the 'light of experience' to conclude that monarchy was the most appropriate form of government for the country. Yet, he continued, 'we believed our faults

---

[91] Isser Woloch, *Napoleon and his Collaborators: The Making of a Dictatorship* (New York, 2001).

[92] See Godechot, *Les Constitutions*, 151–62.

[93] Ibid. 166.

[94] François-René de Chateaubriand, *De Buonaparte, des Bourbons, et de la nécessité de se rallier à nos princes légitimes pour le bonheur de la France et celui de l'Europe*, in *Grands Écrits politiques* (1993), i. 49–129.

to be too great to be pardoned'. Some feared for their lives. Others feared for their newly acquired wealth. Above all, human pride prevented people from accepting that they had made a mistake. And so they chose Napoleon Bonaparte to rule them. The republicans believed him to be one of their own, 'the popular leader of a free State'. The royalists saw him as the French George Monk who would restore the monarchy. Everyone believed in him. Everyone was to have their hopes dashed. 'Never', Chateaubriand wrote, 'did a usurper have such an easy or more brilliant role to play.' He was, Chateaubriand concluded, 'a false great man', leaving France impoverished and weakened by political incompetence and reckless wars.

To this criticism of Napoleon we will return but, at this point, we might pause to reflect upon the dramatic and momentous changes and developments that had taken place in the decade after 1789. The fragile and beleaguered constitutional structure of the *ancien régime* had been comprehensively dismantled, at times almost by accident and chance, the monarchy quickly being replaced by a republican system that few had considered to be a workable or practical alternative. In revolutionary circumstances, driven as much by disturbance in the streets and in the countryside as by debates within the National Assembly and subsequent assemblies, those representing what was now indisputably conceived of as the French nation had grappled (in some cases, at the cost of their own lives) with a set of fundamental issues stubbornly resisting resolution. Once the modest proposals for constitutional reform of the *monarchiens* had been ditched by the late summer of 1789, the Revolution found itself in the grip of a set of doctrines relating to sovereignty and representation that eluded their implementation into a stable republican institutional form. Only the Abbé Sieyès seems to have grasped what was required in this novel situation—his thinking steadily evolving over the decade towards a fuller appreciation of the need for representative deliberation, a strong executive, and judicial review—but even he, for all his reputation as the constitutional 'oracle', could not prevent the slide into Bonapartist dictatorship.

For the time being, therefore, the Republic remained curiously without content. When the monarchy was abolished in September 1792, nothing was said about the character of the regime that would follow. By default, therefore, it came to be associated with violence and terror.[95] Attempts to stabilize the Republic proved fruitless. Yet a conceptual revolution of immense significance had taken place. This, at least, could not be reversed.

III

When Napoleon Bonaparte's Empire came to an ignominious end in 1814, very few people, if any, contemplated a return to the Republic.[96] The monarchy was

---

[95] This was the view of Georges Weill in his classic study, *Histoire du parti républicain en France de 1814 à 1870* (1900).

[96] See Pamela Pilbeam, *Republicanism in Nineteenth-Century France, 1814–1871* (London, 1995), 60–154.

restored, only for it to be briefly overturned after Napoleon's escape from Elba, and then restored again with his defeat at Waterloo by Wellington's army. Louis XVIII, it was said, had returned to France in 'the baggage train of the enemy'. A legal and illegal White Terror followed. If the former was extensive (between 50,000–80,000 public officials were expelled from their posts and 5,000 people put on trial for political crimes), the latter was particularly murderous and brutal (especially in the south where religious differences between Catholics and Protestants added fuel to the fire). The persecution of opponents of the Restoration did much to forge a bond between republicans and Bonapartists.

Nevertheless, in the years that immediately followed, republicanism was largely reduced to an inchoate existence among shadowy conspiratorial groups and societies, many of whom translated their marginality into a belief in an insurrectionary route to power. A more coherent republican movement began to emerge after the Revolution of 1830 and the inauguration of the July Monarchy. The republicans were idealists, patriots, believers in justice, and saw themselves as the true heirs of the Revolution of 1789. Ominously, to cite Pamela Pilbeam, 'they could not agree on a precise model', some appealing to the National Assembly, others to the Convention, whilst some retained a thinly disguised admiration for Robespierre.[97] The protests that erupted in February 1848, leading to the hasty abdication of Louis-Philippe and the birth of the Second Republic, found the republicans not only weak but divided, both ideologically and organizationally. It was to these individuals, however, that (quite expectedly) was to fall the task of steering France towards yet another constitution.

One of the first decisions of the Provisional government of the Second Republic was to declare elections (by universal male suffrage) for a Constituent Assembly, thereby reviving the constitutional practices of 1789 and 1792. Nearly 8 million votes (out of an electorate of 9.4 million) were cast, with the result that the radical wing of the republican movement found itself a minority in the new assembly. If members of the legal profession comprised by far the largest single group, among the deputies were to be found an astonishing, if not unrivalled, selection of literary and intellectual talent. By the side of poet and historian Alphonse de Lamartine were to be found Félicité de Lamennais, the socialists Louis Blanc, Pierre Leroux, and Philippe Buchez, the historian Edgar Quinet, Alexis de Tocqueville, the writer Victor Hugo, and the anarchist Pierre-Joseph Proudhon. Lesser luminaries included Victor Considérant, Alexandre Ledru-Rollin, the liberal Catholics Henri-Dominique Lacordaire and Charles de Montalembert, and economic pamphleteer Frédéric Bastiat.[98] In the first few months, it was Lamartine who effectively dominated the chamber.[99]

If the Constituent Assembly of the Second Republic found it no easy task to agree upon the rights to be accorded to its citizens, questions relating to the organization of executive and legislative power proved equally problematic. However,

[97] Ibid. 107.
[98] See Michel Winock, *Les Voix de la liberté: Les Écrivains engagés au XIXe siècle* (2001), 315–46.
[99] For Lamartine's political views see Renée David (ed.), *Alphonse de Lamartine, la politique et l'histoire* (1993).

they were subject to the most extensive and detailed discussion. The assembly set up a constitutional committee, which began work in late May 1848. Its report was passed on to the fifteen *bureaux* of the assembly, who in turn reported back to the committee on 24 July. The committee then revised its proposals, placed them before the Assembly, with discussion of each article taking place between 4 September and 27 October. Amended, the proposals were reviewed again by the committee, and received final approval by the Assembly on 4 November 1848.[100] 'Never perhaps', wrote Maurice Deslandres in 1933, 'has any constitution been so meticulously and so lengthily drawn up; if it was not perfect it was certainly not for want of thought and labour.'[101]

There were certain areas of relative agreement. In line with the traditions established in the 1790s, the first article of the constitution affirmed that 'sovereignty resides in the universality of French citizens'. Despite the doubts of some, and references in debates (as in the past) to the cases of servants and the illiterate, the suffrage was granted to all males over 21 years of age. Voting was to be both secret and direct, with voters choosing from lists of candidates for each *département*. Without the latter, as one deputy explained, France would only see the election of candidates representing 'the interest of the village, the *canton*, the *arrondissement*, and not general interests'. The priest and the landowner, it was feared, would dominate in each locality.[102] Article 34 stipulated that deputies, elected for three years, represented not their *département* but 'France in her entirety', whilst Article 35 specified that they could not be put under a specific mandate by their electors. The emphasis therefore again fell upon ensuring the independence of representatives from particular or sectional interests. This was not to be the last echo from the past. Under Article 32, the Assembly, as the expression of the national will, was deemed to sit 'permanently'. When it chose to adjourn, a commission composed of its members would have the right to recall the Assembly 'in a case of emergency'.

More contentious was the debate surrounding the familiar question of whether the Republic should operate with one or two parliamentary chambers. Two things stand out here. The first is that it was at this point that the divisions between 'les républicains de la veille ou du lendemain' became most evident. The former, those who had been republicans before 1848, tended to support a one-chamber arrangement, whilst the latter, those who had converted (often with deep misgivings) to the Republic after the Revolution of 1848, usually inclined towards a two-chamber model. Secondly, the debates of 1848 were in many respects a rerun of those of the revolutionary decade after 1789.

This, for example, was how Alexis de Tocqueville defended the call for two chambers.[103] To believe, he argued, that a two-chamber system amounted to the institutionalization of aristocratic power was a mistake and rested upon a

[100] See François Luchaire, *Naissance d'une constitution: 1848* (1998), 193–270.
[101] Maurice Deslandres, *Histoire constitutionnelle de la France de 1789 à 1870* (1933), ii. 345.
[102] Piero Craveri, *Genesi di una costituzione: Libertà et socialismo nel dibattio constituzionale del 1848 in Francia* (Naples, 1985), 138.
[103] Ibid. 129–31.

misunderstanding of the proper functioning of parliamentary institutions. There were at least three justifications that could be provided to support such a model. Executive power needed to be strong but in order to prevent it from abusing its power there was room for another body which could control certain of its actions (the signing of treaties, etc.). Executive power was placed in 'a perilous position' when it found itself confronted by a single chamber. Conflict would be inevitable; with the result that one or the other would quickly destroy its opponent. Next, a single chamber would be consumed by what Tocqueville described as 'legislative intemperance', the desire to legislate 'without cease'. 'The body that represents all ideas, all interests,' he argued, 'drives everything forward, destroys everything: it is irresistible.' Finally, he made the point that if the existence of two chambers could not prevent a revolution, it could at least militate against poor government causing revolutions. There would exist 'a diversity of views' from which both would profit.[104]

In short, Tocqueville and his allies did everything possible to refute the charge that the argument for two chambers was an argument in defence of aristocratic power. It is this that explains why their frequent point of reference was no longer the English monarchical constitution but rather the American republican model.[105] Tocqueville himself added a new preface to the 12th edition of *De la Démocratie en Amérique*, in which he argued that the principles of the American constitution were 'indispensable for all Republics'.[106] He similarly told the electors of Cherbourg that 'in America, the Republic is not a dictatorship exercised in the name of liberty; it is liberty itself, the real and true liberty of all the citizens'.[107]

From this perspective, the emphasis fell upon seeking to ensure that legislation was subject to scrutiny by different groups of people who, although representing the same 'democratic' interest, would 'moderate' the possibly impetuous and ill-considered actions of a single chamber possessed of the inclination to believe that it alone spoke in the name and with the authority of the 'national will'. 'Do not doubt', Duvergier de Hauranne told his parliamentary colleagues, 'that in voting for two chambers we will satisfy the need for order, the need for moderation, the need for stability, which is what the entire country now demands: by voting for two chambers we will prove that we wish to bring the revolutionary crisis to an end and to return to an era of legal government.'[108]

Discussion of the relevance of the American constitutional model was by no means confined to the parliamentary chamber and its constitutional commission. The text of the American constitution was reprinted in several new editions and it

---

[104] See Lucien Jaume, 'Tocqueville et le problème du pouvoir exécutif en 1848', *Revue Française de Science Politique*, 41 (1991), 739–55.

[105] See René Rémond, *Les-États-Unis devant l'opinion française 1815–1852* (1962), 831–58; Odile Rudelle, 'La France et l'expérience constitutionnelle américaine: Un modèle présent, perdu, retrouvé', in Marie-France Toinet (ed.), *Et la Constitution créa l'Amérique* (Nancy, 1988), 35–52; and Marc Lahmer, *La Constitution Américaine dans le débat français, 1795–1848* (2001), 291–381.

[106] Alexis de Tocqueville, *Œuvres complètes* (1961), i/1, pp. xliii–xliv.

[107] Ibid. (1990), iii/3. 44–5.

[108] *Le Moniteur Universel* (26 Sept. 1848), 2596.

was the subject of frequent commentary in the press.[109] It was also debated in numerous brochures and pamphlets.[110] The most vigorous and articulate member of the 'American school' was Édouard Laboulaye.[111] In 1849 Laboulaye was appointed to the chair of comparative law at the Collège de France. His inaugural lecture was entitled *De la Constitution Américaine et de l'Utilité de son étude* (1850). In 1849 he had published his *Considérations sur la Constitution*. The latter text began with a full-blooded criticism of socialist wishful thinking and of abstract declarations of rights. Laboulaye then presented a systematic critique of those constitutional proposals—specifically, a unicameral chamber and a weak executive—that ignored the lessons to be learnt from America. It was not a question of slavishly copying the American constitution but of recognizing the merits of a system that had brought internal peace, prosperity, and liberty. In 1851 Laboulaye returned to this theme in his *La Révision de la constitution: Lettres à un ami*.[112]

The proponents of the two-chamber American model readily acknowledged that public opinion was against them. Despite the fact that, in their view, the correctness of their position was proven by both reason and experience—principally, the descent of one-chamber government into revolutionary dictatorship contrasted with the long-established stability and success of the American constitution—their fear was that the rhetoric of the past, littered as it was with references to the indivisibility of sovereignty and the unity of the national will, would carry the day. This proved to be the case. The report drawn up by the constitutional committee and presented to the Assembly by Armand Marrast spoke in the following terms: 'Sovereignty is one; the nation is one; the national will is one. Why therefore should we want the delegation of sovereignty to be divisible, national representation to be split into two, the law, which emanates from the general will, to give a double expression to a single thought?'[113] The same text justified this position by reference to what it took to be an incontestable fact: 'the homogeneity of the French people'.

Time and time again the opponents of the two-chamber model returned to this theme. For example, Marcel Barthe, deputy for the Basses-Pyrénées, argued: 'If we consider the elements making up our country, we find a people that is completely

---

[109] See e.g. Clarigny, 'Des institutions républicains en France et aux Etats-Unis', *Le Constitutionnel* (10 and 24 June, and 5 July 1848) and J. A. Dréollé, 'Lettres sur la Constitution américaine', *L'Opinion publique* (28 Nov., 10 and 19 Dec. 1848). The latter cited Tocqueville's 'excellent work' but went on to contrast the political immaturity of the French with the maturity of the Americans. Above all, see Michel Chevalier, 'Étude sur la Constitution des États-Unis', *Le Journal des Débats, Politiques et Littéraires* (25 May, 6, 15, and 22 June, 4, 11, and 21 July 1848).

[110] See e.g. Hyacinthe Colombel, *Quelques réflexions concernant la Constitution qu'on élabore pour la France* (Nantes, 1848); J. Magne, *Esquisse d'une Constitution: Ce que la France républicaine pourrait, avec avantage, emprunter aux institutions des Etats-Unis* (1848); and Abel Rendu, *Les deux Républiques* (1850).

[111] See Walter D. Gray, *Interpreting American Democracy in France: The Career of Edouard Laboulaye* (Newark, NJ, 1994).

[112] Both *Considérations sur la Constitution* and *La Révision de la Constitution* were repr. in *Questions constitutionnelles* (1872).

[113] 'Rapport fait au nom de la commission de Constitution, après avoir entendu les représentants délégués des bureaux, par le citoyen Armand Marrast, représentant du peuple. Séance du 30 août 1848', in Luchaire, *Naissance d'une constitution*, 203.

homogeneous ... there exists only one great nation, speaking the same language, living under the same laws, the same administration, the same rules; from one extremity to the other there exists a nation indivisible in all of its parts.' Moreover, this homogeneity was written into the course of French history. 'If we consider', Barthe continued, 'our history we see that since the first centuries of the monarchy, it has constantly moved towards unity, something that has been attained through the greatest of efforts and the most generous of sacrifices ... Our forefathers, with their victories and their blood, made this unity.' Here was to be found 'the greatness and the strength of France'. For good measure, Barthe then added that the French 'love equality more than they love liberty'.[114]

Similar arguments were advanced by other deputies, the focus invariably falling upon the idea that unity was the special 'genius' of France. Again these views found an echo in wider public discussion. For example, Émile Dehais, in a text specifically designed to refute the arguments presented by François Guizot in his *De la Démocratie en France*, countered that 'of all states, the United States is the one upon which we should least model ourselves. This is why. France is the most unitary country that exists and the republic of the United States is federal. To claim to give to the one certain fundamental institutions of the other and to rely upon the example of this other in order to demonstrate the necessity of these institutions is to prove almost nothing.'[115]

It was Alphonse de Lamartine, the supreme orator of the 1848 Revolution, who brought the parliamentary debate to a close. The pages of *Le Moniteur Universel* record that when he stood up to speak he was received with 'a deep silence'. What, he began, was a constitution if not 'the exterior form of a people'? It should not be something arbitrary but should express the 'reality of the nature of the nation'. Following this logic, why did both England and the United States have two chambers? With regard to the former, Lamartine indicated that he blushed to reply because everyone knew the answer: England was 'almost exclusively an aristocracy'. In France, by contrast, the only aristocracy that existed was the 'aristocracy of enlightenment, the aristocracy of intelligence'. There was no theocracy, no military caste, and no privilege: all were judged on their personal merit. What of America's Senate? What reality did it represent? The need for federalism rather than the spirit of democracy was the answer. It revealed the 'imperfection' and 'the shortcomings of national unity' in America and was the continuation of a form of 'anarchy'. The French nation, by contrast, displayed 'a completely democratic unity', a unity of rank, of origin, and of interest, given expression through 'the sovereignty of all'. To contemplate the creation of a second parliamentary chamber, therefore, was to run the risk of artificially introducing an element of aristocracy and of division into France. Moreover it was to propose a weakening of the sovereignty of the French nation.[116]

[114] *Le Moniteur Universel* (27 Sept. 1848), 2606.
[115] Émile Dehais, *Du Gouvernement de la France, précédé d'une lettre à M. Guizot sur la Démocratie* (1851), 214.
[116] *Le Moniteur Universel* (28 Sept. 1848), 2620–2.

The opportunity of reply fell to liberal monarchist Odilon Barrot, who again called upon the deputies to remember the need for a mechanism that would 'moderate' the 'all-powerful' nature of 'French democracy'. Not surprisingly, the amendment to introduce two chambers was decisively defeated by 530 votes to 289. Moreover, the deputies believed that on the outcome of this debate depended the future of the Republic. They were to be mistaken, and this was because almost their next decision was to approve the direct election of the president. This was their great constitutional innovation and this also was their great political error. The argument against the direct election of the president was clear enough. Sovereignty resided in the people and was expressed through the election of their parliamentary representatives to a single chamber. Therefore the head of the executive should be chosen by and be responsible to that assembly. To do otherwise, as the future president of the Third Republic, Jules Grévy, announced, would be to recreate 'a veritable monarchical power', endowed with the moral authority that would inevitably flow from direct election by universal suffrage. The assembly would quickly become the instrument of executive power.

The most considered response came from Alexis de Tocqueville. At the committee stage Tocqueville let it be known that 'the excessive influence of the President would be an immense danger', but he nevertheless supported the view that ministers should be responsible to the president and that the latter should possess the initiative for legislation. Without this there would exist 'anarchy' and the absence of power at the heart of the executive. He made the further suggestion that France might adopt the two-level American electoral college model for choosing the president (a recommendation that was rejected), but Tocqueville carried the day with the argument that to secure election a candidate must receive a majority of the votes cast. Where this was not the case, the right to choose the president would fall to the parliamentary assembly.[117]

Tocqueville next entered the fray when he defended the report of the constitutional committee before the Assembly. Here his argument was grounded in the need for a separation of powers. To institute a system where the head of the executive was nominated by the Assembly would be to make a return, 'purely and simply', to the Convention of 1793. It would be as if the president did not exist. The executive would be reduced to following the orders of the Assembly. 'We will not have the Terror', Tocqueville argued, 'but we will have bad government, a loud, tyrannical government, a changing, violent, unreflecting, thoughtless government, without a sense of tradition or wisdom, the sort of government you get when a single chamber possesses not only the plenitude of legislative power but also the plenitude of executive power.' It would also be, Tocqueville added, 'a deeply corrupting and corrupted government'.[118]

Again, it was to be the eloquence of Lamartine that inspired the deputies to vote 627 against 180 in favour of the direct election of the president. If the opponents of

---

[117] Craveri, *Genesi di una costituzione*, 146–53, 198–201. For Tocqueville's own account, see Tocqueville, *Souvenirs* (1999), 223–45.

[118] *Le Moniteur Universel* (6 Oct. 1848), 2724–5.

this proposal feared that it would split the sovereignty of the nation into two irreconcilable parts, it is also clear that they felt deep misgivings about how the electorate would choose to cast their votes. It was by no means guaranteed that the candidates of the Republic would carry the majority. Tocqueville himself alluded to this in his own speech, arguing nevertheless that the people would feel betrayed if they were denied the right to elect the president themselves. In 'the deep fibres of her being, in her heart', he argued, France was 'profoundly republican' and if the people showed hesitation it was only because they sensed that the inauguration of the Republic might mean more than a change of France's 'political constitution'. Once they had been reassured, he concluded, fears about the outcome of the vote would be allayed.

Lamartine took up this theme with his usual persuasiveness and lack of political judgement. There was, he proclaimed, no need to fear a repeat performance of the 18 Brumaire because the latter had been the product of 'long years of terror' combined with the promise of future military victories. Rather, 'the true danger' for the Republic lay in the 'disaffection' of the people. How better to overcome this, how better to secure the loyalty and affection of each citizen, how better to encourage the expression of their republican sympathies, than to involve them directly in choosing the person who would be the head of the executive? By doing so, Lamartine contended, not only would a government be produced that was 'more universal, more popular' but it would also make it 'more difficult, more odious, more inexcusable' to attack the Republic.[119]

Lamartine was quickly proven to be mistaken. Already, in June 1848, Louis Napoleon Bonaparte, nephew of the emperor, had been triumphantly elected to the Assembly in four constituencies. Two days after Lamartine made his case, the Assembly decided that all male French citizens over the age of 30 should be eligible to stand for the office of president. Amendments to the effect that members of the Bourbon, Orleanist, and Bonapartist dynasties should be excluded were rejected. Two weeks later, on 26 October, Louis Napoleon declared himself to be a candidate, being swept to victory on 10 December with over 5.4 million votes. His nearest rival, Cavaignac, secured only 1.4 million. Lamartine received a derisory 7,910.

It would be wrong to attribute this outcome solely to the form of the Constitution itself. The otherwise undistinguished figure of Louis Napoleon owed his popularity to the myth created around the memory of the emperor during the previous two decades[120] and to the fact that, rightly or wrongly, he appeared as a guarantor of order. Many also believed that he would be an easily manipulated figurehead. Nevertheless, his election was precisely the outcome that the *républicains de la veille* most wanted to avoid. The fear of the abuse of executive power—shared even by those who had wished to see an enhanced executive—was such that the provision for the direct election of the president was accompanied by the stipulation of a four-year, non-renewable term of office. The same article of the

[119] *Le Moniteur Universel* (7 Oct. 1848), 2737–9.
[120] See Natalie Petiteau, *Napoléon: De la mythologie à l'histoire* (1999), 57–105.

constitution also specified that a president could not be replaced by members of his immediate family. From the outset it seemed doubtful that the new president would accept these limitations. Moreover, Louis Napoleon's election immediately exposed the ambiguities of a constitution that accorded the legitimacy deriving from universal suffrage to two potentially rival bodies. To which one the government of the day was to be responsible was far from clear. Louis Napoleon quickly exploited these ambiguities to the full.

Elections in May 1849 confirmed that the republicans were in a minority. In line with this result Louis Napoleon first appointed a government headed by Odilon Barrot and in which Tocqueville held the post of minister of foreign affairs. At the end of October this government was dismissed by the president and replaced by one more to his own liking, thereby foreclosing any lingering parliamentary reading of the constitution. From this point onwards, opponents of the regime were subject to systematic repression, forcing many of the leaders of republicanism into exile. Press censorship was tightened. Political clubs were disbanded. Government officials and schoolteachers deemed to be untrustworthy were dismissed. In May 1850 the principle of universal male suffrage was abandoned through the introduction of a three-year residence requirement for all voters, thus removing approximately 3 million citizens from the electoral list. The following year it was formally proposed before the Assembly that the constitution be revised in order to permit the re-election of Louis Napoleon. When this proposal failed to secure the three-quarters of the votes cast required to ratify revision, the resort to a *coup d'état* became inevitable. This duly followed, with military precision, on 2 December 1851, the anniversary of Napoleon's crowning as emperor in 1804 and of his victory at the battle of Austerlitz in 1805. A plebiscite was immediately arranged for 21–22 December, when the 'French people' were asked if they wished Louis Napoleon Bonaparte to remain in power and to grant him the authority to propose a new constitution. There were 7,436,216 votes for and only 646,737 against.

Less than a month later, on 14 January 1852, a new constitution was proclaimed.[121] A prefatory proclamation by the president disclosed its logic. In his opinion, Louis Napoleon let it be known, for the past fifty years the 'administrative, military, judicial, religious [and] financial' organization of France had rested upon the principles and practices of the Consulate and the Empire. It was his intention, therefore, to bring France's political institutions into line with those of 'this epoch' and thus to return to the model established by the Constitution of Year VIII (1799). Accordingly, Louis Napoleon was to remain president for the next ten years. The office of president was granted extensive powers. A popularly elected assembly, significantly reduced in size, was to have the right to discuss and vote but not initiate legislation. Ministers were not to be drawn from it and the president could summon and dissolve it at will. A Senate, composed of not more than 150 members, for the most part appointed for life by the president,[122] had the

---

[121] See Godechot, *Les Constitutions*, 287–319. On the logic underpinning this 'illiberal democracy' see Rosanvallon, *La Démocratie inachevée: Histoire de la souveraineté en France* (2000), 181–221.

[122] All cardinals, marshals, and admirals were members as of right.

job of verifying the constitutionality of all laws. It met in secret. Finally, there was to be a Conseil d'État, with members again chosen by the president, responsible for the framing of all legislation.[123]

It came as no surprise when, less than a year later on 7 November 1852, the Senate proposed to revise the constitution in order to reinstitute the title of emperor. Approved by popular referendum two weeks later, on 2 December the inauguration of the Second Empire was officially proclaimed, with Louis Napoleon taking the title of Napoleon III.[124]

IV

Napoléon le Petit, as Victor Hugo contemptuously referred to him,[125] proved to be a far more durable and successful opponent than many had thought possible. If few were the writers who rallied to the cause of the Second Empire (Prosper Merimée and Sainte-Beuve were two notable exceptions), many found themselves either forced into exile or reduced to silence. Opportunities to express or to display dissent were extremely limited and when, in 1859, Napoleon III declared an amnesty there were many who refused to return to such ignominy. Hugo, for example, remained in exile on the Channel island of Guernsey until September 1870, returning only after the emperor's military defeat and capture at Sedan.

Nevertheless, the regime itself underwent considerable evolution over the next eighteen years, progressively moving towards a recognizably less authoritarian and more parliamentary form. The Senate became a legislative assembly, no longer sitting in secret, whilst the lower chamber found its powers of initiative and scrutiny greatly extended. In 1869 it was decreed that ministers could be drawn from either body. The final stage in this process came with what effectively amounted to the proclamation of a new, liberal constitution in May 1870. Approved with a massive majority by popular referendum, the future of the empire seemed secure.

What happened next is too well-known to require detailed recounting. Napoleon III recklessly engaged in yet another foreign adventure and found himself obliged to abdicate as the French army suffered a series of humiliating reverses at the hands of its Prussian adversaries. If a criminal act brought the Second Empire into existence, an act of folly brought it to a close. The Second Empire, even less than the Directory, has

---

[123] The Conseil d'État had its origins in the Conseil du Roi, the term first appearing in 1578. In its modern form, it was established through Article 52 of the Constitution of Year VIII, Napoleon Bonaparte intending it to be a synthesis of the traditions of the *ancien régime* and the innovations introduced by the Revolution. It again came up for serious discussion with the advent of the Second Republic, when its defenders tended to see the Conseil d'État as a way of giving substance to the concept of the separation of powers. Significantly, its members were to be chosen by the Assembly. Under the Constitution of the Second Empire it was the President who decided upon its membership.

[124] When Napoleon Bonaparte abdicated in June 1815 he did so in favour of his son, the so-called King of Rome and the child from his marriage in 1810 with the archduchess Marie-Louise, daughter of the Emperor Francis I of Austria. Within the Bonapartist dynasty he was subsequently regarded as Napoleon II.

[125] Victor Hugo, *Napoléon le Petit* (London, 1852).

therefore had few admirers, republicans in particular refusing to see any merit in either the usurper or his regime. Loose morals and corruption, both vividly described in the journals of the Goncourt brothers, have been taken to be its hallmarks.[126] Only relatively recently, beginning with two studies by Theodore Zeldin,[127] did this picture begin to change.

Specifically, Sudhir Hazareesingh has argued that the years before 1870 saw 'the emergence of a vibrant democratic political culture in France'.[128] Mass voting associated with the regular plebiscites called by the emperor was at the heart of this process of transformation. On this view the years of the Second Empire were ones marked by institutional experimentation and political development, with signifi-cant levels of continuity existing into the early years of the Third Republic. Hazareesingh has contended further that this period was also one when 'the mainstream republican movement made the momentous transition from the classical problematic of Revolution to the concerns of democratic modernity'.[129] If the broad picture is one characterized by a growing awareness of the short-comings of excessive centralization and, therefore, of the need for the devolution of power, the more limited contention is that, amongst republicans themselves, 'the centralist ideology of Jacobinism was challenged, subverted, and eventually crea-tively redefined by republican conceptions of the good life which stressed the significance of territorial politics and local forms of civic engagement'.[130] Ground-ed in an unremitting hostility to the arbitrary and authoritarian abuse of power by Napoleon III, republicans focused their attention upon the merits of municipal democracy.

These developments provide the backdrop to the final section of this chapter. By taking two examples—the writings of Louis Blanc and Jules Barni—it will be shown how discussion of issues relating to sovereignty, the constitution, and representation evolved in this period. To conclude, we will look briefly at the constitutional debates surrounding the origins of the Third Republic.

As has already been shown, Louis Blanc was one of the principal theorists of republican socialism. In 1848 it was he who did more than anyone else to campaign for a recognition of the right to work. Like many others, he soon found himself in exile. There he engaged in almost perpetual quarrels with his fellow republicans. In particular, he quickly responded to the demands for direct democracy articulated by men such as Victor Considérant and Ledru-Rollin. Time and time again he entered this debate, recalling the figures of Montesquieu, Rousseau, and Robespierre, reliving the events of the 1789 Revolution. At the heart of his argument was the frequently repeated charge that calls for 'government by the people themselves'

---

[126] See Alain Plessis, *De la fête impériale au mur des fédérés (1852–1871)* (1973).

[127] Theodore Zeldin, *The Political System of Napoleon III* (London, 1958) and *Emile Ollivier and the Liberal Empire of Napoleon III* (Oxford, 1963).

[128] Sudhir Hazareesingh, *From Subject to Citizen: The Second Empire and the Emergence of Modern French Democracy* (Princeton, NJ, 1998).

[129] Ibid. 317.

[130] Sudhir Hazareesingh, *Intellectual Founders of the Republic: Five Studies in Nineteenth-Century French Political Thought* (Oxford, 2001), 4.

amounted to calls for no government at all. They would lead to federalism and inevitably would produce a descent into chaos.

Blanc's response rested upon two central claims. The first was that direct government by the people only made sense where the people were one, where there was unity of the will, and where there were no conflicting interests. For good measure, he added that the people would also have to be subject to the reign of virtue.[131] Given what Blanc termed the 'condition of a lack of solidarity in which we live' this was palpably not the case. It was nonsense to speak of the people as if they were one person and spoke with one voice. Rather, in these circumstances, the result would be a 'babélisme universel', with 37,000 'microscopic assemblies' each speaking in the name of their own sovereign and consumed by their own disagreements, each subject to intrigue and uncertainty. In place of the 'Republic, one and indivisible' would be substituted a 'Republic split into pieces'. Next, Blanc argued that, given the 'state of ignorance' in which France's 37,000 communes were to be found, to contemplate direct democracy was to consider handing authority over to 'prejudice', 'the spirit of routine', 'darkness', and 'confusion'. It was to push a faith in universal suffrage to the point of absurdity.

Blanc insisted that, despite recent 'errors',[132] his own faith in the merits of universal suffrage remained as strong as ever. He did not doubt that the people were sovereign or that the law should be the expression of their will. As such, the sovereignty of the people was both 'sacred' and 'inalienable'. He was also ready to accept the principle, advanced by his opponents, that 'sovereignty could have no other representative than itself'. However, he did believe that sovereignty could and should be delegated. The great error of those who recommended 'direct legislation', Blanc argued (echoing the Abbé Sieyès in the process) was to fail to realize that the 'making of laws corresponded to a function, which should be judged . . . according to the division of labour'. Not every citizen could spend all their time in discussion and some were better placed than others to perform this function. The challenge was to put in place a system of universal suffrage that would operate according to 'the true principles of democracy'.

According to Blanc, representation was an important function but 'the relationship of dependence which existed between the elected member and his electors' had to be acknowledged. The representative was a *mandataire* and if he did not perform his job properly he should be subject to immediate recall.[133] In order to maintain a concordance of views between an elected member and his constituents, a representative should be in place for one or two years at most. Blanc also indicated that he was in favour of a system of proportional representation designed to facilitate the articulation of minority opinion.[134] In other words, it was possible to invent

---

[131] See Louis Blanc, 'De la vertu considerée comme principe du governement', in *Questions d'aujourd'hui et de demain.Première série: Politique* (1873), 23–43.

[132] See Blanc, 'De la Présidence dans une République', ibid. 319–45. In this text Blanc explained why the French peasantry voted for Louis Napoleon.

[133] Blanc, 'Du Mandat impéritif', ibid. 347–66.

[134] Blanc, 'De la représentation proportionelle des minorités', ibid. 239–56.

mechanisms capable of ensuring that the sovereignty of the people was faithfully represented.

When reflecting upon the form of election to be put in place, Blanc made it clear that he opposed a two-tier system—on the grounds that it would recreate 'a truly aristocratic class'—and also election based upon single-member constituencies. His preference was for a list system. To accept the single-member constituency model, he contended, was in effect to side with the forces of monarchism and of counter-revolution, for the reason that it would be 'to accept the dominance of small corrupt towns, to prostitute universal suffrage to purely local interests, to sacrifice in advance the virtues of talent to the mediocrity of intransigence, of merit to wealth'.[135] He spoke elsewhere of the all-pervasive influence of the *clocher*, of the church bell-tower, of narrow-minded religious parochialism. With single-member constituencies, in other words, sovereignty would be 'localized' and it would be handed over to the enemies of the Republic. It was at this point that Blanc conjured up the experience of the great Revolution. Would it have been possible to defend France and the Republic in 1793 from its internal and external enemies if they had existed as 37,000 'scattered parts', if (here citing Robespierre) they had been reduced to an arena for 'quibblers', their 'energy' and 'genius' dissipated by the 'obscure debates' in 'local assemblies'? The forces of 'militant democracy' embody-ing 'the unity of the *patrie*', he argued, would have been consumed by their enemies.[136]

To that extent, Blanc wrote, 'I preserve my faith in the traditions of revolution-ary unity'.[137] It was in the name of unity and through unity that France had been saved. Blanc, therefore, wholeheartedly embraced what he saw as the necessity for 'political unity' and, consequently, the benefits of 'political centralisation'.[138] There was need for a 'single point' to give 'active and strong direction to the general interests' of society as a whole and that point could only be located in Paris. His opponents, he claimed, wished to reduce Paris to something less than a 'thirty-thousandth part' of France and to destroy its 'intellectual dominance'. It had been Paris, however, that had stormed the Bastille and Paris that had brought the royal family back from Versailles as prisoners. For fifty years Paris had been 'the insomnia of kings'. 'If', Blanc went on, 'you break or relax the network of communes which has Paris as its nub, political unity would disappear and with that the nation.'[139] Blanc's considered view, therefore, was that if Paris should not smother or suffocate France, then it should at least 'shine', it should inspire and lead. This did not mean, he argued, that he supported dictatorship, because if political centralization was a necessity then, by the same token, administrative centralization was 'detestable'.

---

[135] Blanc, 'Du Suffrage universel', ibid. 235.
[136] See esp. Louis Blanc, *Plus de Girondins* (1853). Blanc attributed the Terror to exceptional external circumstances and saw it as a 'temporary and desperate means of national defence': see 'Lettre sur la terreur', *L'Impossible Terreur* (1989), 67–82.
[137] Blanc, *La République Une et Indivisible* (1851), 90.
[138] Blanc, *L'Etat et la commune* (1866).
[139] Blanc, *La République Une et Indivisible*, 88–9.

The problem was that, if France did not have the former, it certainly had the latter, and it was this that was the 'cause of oppression and ruin'.

Thus Blanc found himself defending France's communes as a valuable form of associational life and as the building blocks upon which the 'edifice' of the nation and the State was built. Nevertheless, the force of his argument, sustained over many years into the 1860s, was that the State was the principal source of national unity and that it was a force for progress and enlightenment. It was to be through that centralized state that the liberty of the individual would be given political expression and would be attained. The fragmentation and decentralization of that political power—especially when taken as far as an endorsement of the federalism of the Girondins—would lead to the disintegration of the nation and the triumph of reaction. Most intriguing of all was the remarkable metamorphosis that Blanc seemed to believe would occur as the people expressed its indivisible sovereign will. Through the mechanism of representation and a single parliamentary chamber, the ignorance and narrow-mindedness of the individual (provincial) citizen was to be transformed into the unitary, revolutionary will of the *patrie*. It was a transfiguration no less miraculous than that which occurred when the monarch, in his person, was taken to embody the sovereign public will of a deeply fractured polity.

Views similar to those held by Louis Blanc continued to be widely articulated by writers and publicists within the Jacobin tradition and who persisted in believing that the Second Empire could be analysed and understood by analogy with the events of the 1790s. The transition to the concerns of political modernity came rather from those who were prepared to look Napoleon III's regime squarely in the face and, perhaps also, to acknowledge that there were important lessons to be learnt.

As we saw in the previous chapter, Jules Barni played a key role in the reformulation of republican understandings of liberty and equality. His views on constitutional matters and the territorial organisation of the State were no less innovatory. Again, we can make a comparison between the views of Charles Renouvier and those of Barni. In his text of 1848 Renouvier had been content to make a few general references to the nature of the Republic and the location of sovereignty. Barni's *Manuel Républicain*, by contrast, gave a detailed presentation of the institutional arrangements appropriate to a republic, systematically drawing upon his experience of exile in Switzerland. In so doing he fully reflected the impact of the experience of the Second Empire upon republican thinking.[140]

According to Barni, universal suffrage was 'the fundamental feature of any republic worthy of the name'. Given that, in practice, it was impossible for the people to 'deliberate' on all matters of public interest, representatives had to be chosen. However, in line with earlier republican thinking, Barni contended that these representatives were to be 'mandated' and that these mandates were to be 'limited, temporary and revocable'. In this way the people would preserve 'the sovereignty which belonged to it and of which it can only divest itself by committing suicide'. Again, in practice, Barni recognized that this sovereignty translated into 'the law of

[140] Jules Barni, *Manuel Républicain* (1872), 11–96.

the majority', but his memory of the *coup d'état* of 1851 was such that this was combined with an insistence that this must not be confused with 'the despotism of number'. 'All absolute power', he wrote, 'is a usurpation of the rights of citizens'.

The real innovations in Barni's argument became evident when he addressed issues concerned with the institutional structures and geographical location of power. Breaking with the centralist tradition of republicanism, Barni embraced municipal liberty. Each commune, he contended, should, as far as possible, govern itself, like 'a small republic within a large one'. The same went for intermediary bodies such as *cantons*. 'In general', he wrote, 'we should allocate to central government or to the State only what the communes and the intermediary bodies either cannot do or cannot do well.' In this way public life would be more vibrant, citizens would be more active, and the State would cease to be overburdened. The traditional republican fear of political disintegration was, however, not entirely absent from Barni's mind. Municipal independence was not to be a pretext for 'the despotism and pretensions of local powers' and therefore the State had an obligation to ensure that 'this decentralization' did not compromise the rights of individuals and the public interest.

Next, Barni openly embraced the separation of legislative, executive, and judicial power, thereby dismissing republican claims that no limits could be placed upon the sovereignty of the people as expressed through law. When all three powers were combined in either one person (Bonapartism) or one assembly (republicanism) the result was despotism and 'caesarism'. Of central importance was the independence of the judiciary, as under the Second Empire the judicial system had become 'an instrument of domination and corruption in the hands of the government'.

With regard to legislative power, Barni sought to ensure not only that elections were held regularly (every two years was his recommendation) but that it was recognized that the fundamental purpose of legislative activity was to ensure 'the liberty of citizens'. The purpose of government, in brief, was not to secure the reign of virtue. Just as intriguing was Barni's comment that the State should allow 'each member and each group within society to act and to develop with the greatest amount of independence possible'. In this way would general prosperity be secured.

What of the thorny question of whether parliament should have one or two chambers? Again, Barni broke with republican tradition by recognizing the merits of a second chamber—it allowed for greater reflection in the discussion and passing of laws—even if he ultimately opted for the one-chamber option. This, however, was on the pragmatic grounds that, in the present circumstances, a two-chamber arrangement might foster a return of 'aristocratic pretensions'.

Finally, it was Barni's reflections upon executive power that most clearly displayed the impact of the experience of Second Empire upon his thinking. Executive power was to be subordinate to, but not absorbed by, the legislative power. Most importantly, everything had to be done to prevent executive power from becoming a form of 'personal government'. The Second Republic's system of electing a president via direct universal suffrage was therefore not to be reinstituted. Nor, indeed, did Barni recommend that the office of president should be continued. His preference was for a form of ministerial committee or *conseil d'état*, not elected by direct universal suffrage, but chosen by the legislative chamber. To avoid an undue and debilitating dependence upon the latter the executive power was to be nominated for the same period of time as the parliamentary chamber. Just as evident was Barni's desire to diminish the extravagance and excess associated with the executive offices of the State, to reduce the so-called dignified or symbolic functions of the State to more modest proportions. If this meant that the Republic would eschew the systematic dispensation of public honours—he attributed the creation of the Légion d'honneur to the 'Machiavellian genius of Bonaparte'—it also meant that it would have no need of the lavish expenditure associated with the courts of both the *ancien régime* and the Bonapartist Empires.

On 4 September 1870 the existence of the Third Republic was proclaimed from the balcony of the *hôtel de ville* in Paris. The task of the provisional government was first to resolve the outcome of the war with Prussia and then to provide France with yet another new constitution. If the first was attained by the signing of the treaty of Frankfurt in May 1871 (entailing the secession to Prussia of the eastern provinces of Alsace and Lorraine), the second turned out to be an unusually long-drawn-out process. On the eve of the unexpected collapse of the Second Empire republicans represented at best a small and divided group, and this minority position was confirmed by the elections that took place on 8 February 1871. Of the 645 deputies, 400 were self-proclaimed supporters of monarchical restoration. During the next few months, and certainly following the brutal suppression of the Paris Commune by an unrepentant Adolphe Thiers, opinion began to swing towards the Republic, but it was by no means clear that the restoration of the monarchy could be averted.

Fortunately for the republicans, divisions within the competing houses of the royal family and the obstinacy of the principal pretender to the throne, the Comte de Chambord,[141] provided them with more time, and little by little the constitutional edifice of the Third Republic was put into place. This was neither without its setbacks nor without its compromises. In May 1873 Thiers was forced to resign as head of government, to be replaced by the conservative and pro-monarchist MacMahon, but that same year, on 20 November, a law was passed confirming that the president of the Republic would be elected for seven years. Two years later, beginning on 6 January 1875, the Assembly began the discussion of what came to be a set of constitutional laws that confirmed and gave form to the existence of the Third Republic. The first significant step was the passing of the so-called Wallon amendment which, in specifying the manner in which the president would be elected, also required that the new regime be republican, bicameral. and parliamentary. Subsequent articles followed in rapid succession, leading to the passing of a law on the organization of the Senate on 24 February and, the following day, a law on the organization of legislative and executive power. A further constitutional law, passed in July 1875, filled out the details of these arrangements.[142]

[141] See Steven Kale, *Legitimism and the Reconstruction of French Society, 1852–1883* (Baton Rouge, La., 1992).
[142] See Godechot, *Les Constitutions*, 331–8.

The constitution of the Third Republic therefore rested upon a President, possessing substantial executive power, who was to be elected by both parliamentary chambers; a Senate, composed of 225 members elected by indirect suffrage for nine years and of 75 members who sat for life, possessing legislative power; and, finally, a Chamber of Deputies, elected by direct (male) universal suffrage, with primary legislative responsibility. In effect, what was produced was a balanced constitution with, to quote the classic text of David Thomson, 'elements of democracy, oligarchy, and even monarchy'.[143] It is also interesting to note that, if the doctrine of the separation of powers was not accepted in its pure form, it was taken sufficiently seriously, as Maurice Vile pointed out, to ensure that 'ministers refrained from exercising their vote in the Chamber, even when defeat might result from their abstention'.[144] Indeed, it is easy to imagine that Mounier and his fellow *monarchiens* would have been happy with such constitutional arrangements! Certainly, this time the 'American school' seemed to have won the day.[145]

For many republicans, such a level of compromise proved a bitter pill to swallow. Jules Barni, in one of the many speeches he gave around this time before the Union républicaine de la Somme, spoke of his fear that what would be created was 'a Republic surrounded by monarchical institutions'.[146] Louis Blanc, as his *Histoire de la Constitution du 25 février 1875* amply revealed,[147] simply could not be reconciled to a situation where the republicans had made all the compromises in order to 'receive nothing, absolutely nothing'. An important part of Blanc's denigration of the new constitution was that these compromises had been made by republicans who had never gone into exile and by a new generation determined to secure power at almost any price.

After 1875 the republicans continued to make electoral progress, confirming their majority status in the elections which followed President MacMahon's foolhardy dissolution of the Chamber of Deputies. Not long afterwards they also took control of the Senate. In 1879 MacMahon was replaced by one of the republican heroes of 1848: Jules Grévy. *La Marseillaise* became the national anthem; 14 July, the anniversary of the storming of the Bastille, became a national holiday, and parliament, following the revision of Article 9 of the constitution, returned from Versailles to Paris.

Did this mean that further constitutional revisions were needed in order to remove the offensive vestiges of monarchical and aristocratic power? On this the republicans proved to be divided, but the moderates carried the day, with the result that the only significant revision was ratified in 1884, when it was affirmed that the republican form of government itself could not be subject to revision, that members of the Bourbon, Orleanist, and Bonapartist families were ineligible for the office of president, and that there were no longer to be members of the Senate who sat for life.

---

[143] David Thomson, *Democracy in France since 1870* (Oxford, 1980), 102.
[144] M. J. C. Vile, *Constitutionalism and the Separation of Powers* (Oxford, 1967), 243.
[145] See Rudelle, 'La France et l'expérience constitutionnelle américaine', 44–51.
[146] *Discours de MM Jules Barni et Eugène Delattre* (Amiens, 1872), 10.
[147] (1882).

The arguments against further revision were most forcefully articulated by one of the great political presences of the period, Jules Ferry.[148] This is how Ferry characterized his republican opponents on the left. They are, he proclaimed, 'the passionate and resolute opponents of the system of two chambers and the Presidency of the Republic; they are unitarians, believers in simplicity. They dream of a single chamber, without counterbalances, without rules, doing whatever it wants to do in the world.'[149] For them, the Republic stood for 'perpetual agitation, incessant change'. It was 'the Revolution on the march . . . the headlong rush towards the unknown, towards the absolute'.[150] For Ferry, by contrast, the miracle was that a new constitution, 'made by monarchists against the republicans', had 'saved the Republic'. The task ahead, the task of 'a less idealist, less dreamy generation', therefore, was 'to administer, to govern, to strengthen the Republic' and this was best done, in his view, through 'good sense, work and a love of progress'. This meant that the republicans should focus not upon vague, unrealizable schemes but upon the important practical questions that concerned 'the intellectual, moral and material elevation of the most numerous and poorest classes' of French society.[151] What mattered was 'the stability of the Republic'. Moreover, this could, and should, be attained without the distractions which would arise from the needless revision of the constitution. It was a nonsense, Ferry countered, to claim that the constitution was monarchical because the president had the right to dissolve parliament and because there existed two parliamentary chambers. History showed that those republics possessing two chambers had been the only ones that had endured. As for the right of dissolution, it was no more monarchical than the president himself was a monarch: it was 'the means of resolving insoluble conflicts, which in the United States could persist indefinitely without causing a problem, but which here could not exist without paralysing national life'. To take away the right of dissolution from the president, he concluded, would be 'to relegate him to the rank of a nominal and decorative institution'.[152]

Of course, it was precisely this that occurred in practice. The tradition quickly developed of only electing a president who would not be inclined to use his powers and who was content to be a figurehead. Moreover, the Senate, despite that the fact that in later years it was able to block important legislation relating to the introduction of income tax and the female suffrage, came to play a largely subordinate and quiescent role. By default, therefore, the balanced constitution gave way to government by assembly and, in this way, the republican ideal prevailed.

---

[148] See Jules Ferry, *La République des citoyens*, 2 vols (1996); François Furet (ed.), *Jules Ferry, fondateur de la République* (1985); and Jean-Michel Gaillard, *Jules Ferry* (1989). Elected as a republican deputy in 1869 Ferry was an unequivocal opponent of what in his electoral address he termed 'the fantasies of personal government'. He subsequently played a key role in the establishment of the Third Republic, serving as Minister of Education (1879–83) and twice as Prime Minister (1880–1, 1883–5).

[149] Ferry, *La République des citoyens*, ii. 145.

[150] Ibid. 376.

[151] Ibid. 183.

[152] 'Extrait du discours préparé pour le 14 fevrier 1889', in Furet, *Jules Ferry*, 144.

What this meant was made vividly clear in the decades that were to follow. The passion, not to say nostalgia, for unity and unanimity remained an abiding obsession amongst republicans—so much so that political parties were viewed as sources of division. Like the *parlements* of the *ancien régime* and the factions of the Revolution, they were seen as intermediary powers bent upon subverting the general will. Thus, throughout the Third Republic and into the Fourth Republic the majority of parliamentary deputies remained without party affiliation. Parliamentary majorities, therefore, were not constructed through the ballot box but in the parliamentary chamber itself. Moreover, in the absence of party programmes, the emphasis within the chamber fell upon discussion and participation. Good laws were to be the result of long deliberation, with the individual deputy esteemed above all for his eloquence and powers of argumentation. As Nicolas Rousselier observes, 'for a long time the parliamentary republic rested upon the ideal of "Athenian" democracy, submitting as many laws as possible to the deliberation of the "magistrates" of the people, each free to vote as his conscience dictated'.[153]

What happened as a consequence was that France became a prey to a weak executive and the regular fall of governments. The Chamber of Deputies, dominated by the individual deputy and lacking any sense of party discipline, was famously likened to a mirror in which France would not recognize herself. Unsurprisingly, it was not to be long before calls for stronger and more effective government were heard. In the late 1880s, these were to focus upon the mercurial figure of General Boulanger, in later years—and especially in the inter-war period—they were to be phrased in terms of the need to respond to pressing social and economic problems.[154] Arguably these issues were only resolved with the establishment by General de Gaulle of the Fifth Republic in 1958.

However, we might have been misled by this conventional picture. As we have seen, the monarchs of the *ancien régime* saw themselves as the physical embodiment of sovereign power. This claim was sustained not only by the ideology of divine right and the invocation of the fundamental laws of the realm but also by a public ritual of astonishing sophistication. At the palace of Versailles a ceremonial form was played out which embraced all aspects of the monarch's life. Protocol and etiquette determined all. Portraits, medallions, and other artistic artefacts deliberately fostered and enhanced the monarch's public image. Miraculous powers of healing were attributed to the royal touch.[155] As Jennifer Jones has written, 'French absolutism was a theatre-state in which Versailles was the stage and Louis the playwright and principal player.'[156]

---

[153] 'Deux formes de représentation politique: le citoyen et l'individu', in Marc Sadoun (ed.), *La Démocratie en France* (2000), i. 263–4.

[154] See also Rousseillier, *Le Parlement de l'Éloquence: La Souveraineté de la délibération au lendemain de la Grande Guerre* (2000) and 'Le Système politique: Représentation et délibération', in Serge Berstein and Michel Winock (eds.), *L'Invention de la démocratie* (2003), 355–79.

[155] See Gérard Sabatier, *Versailles, ou le figure du roi* (1999).

[156] Jennifer M. Jones, *Sexing La Mode: Gender, Fashion and Commercial Culture in Old Regime France* (Oxford and New York, 2004), 9.

In the Third Republic there was no shortage of reflection upon the powers of the president.[157] But there was broad agreement that the president was not the *locus* of power, only its representative. The people, after all, were sovereign. This was why, to many, the assassination of President Sadi Carnot in 1894 seemed such a pointless act. It was to destroy only the person and not the republican regime itself. And yet the presidents themselves, cast in their modest role, were not immune from replicating the ceremonial practices that had graced the courts of the *ancien régime*. As Christophe Prochasson has shown,[158] the presidency of Félix Faure (1895–9) was marked by a self-conscious element of ritual. The president's good health, robust physique, and clothing were a matter of public display. His passion and prowess as a hunter (in the royal forests) was proof of his physical courage. His presidential visits were choreographed in meticulous detail to secure maximum effect, his arrival greeted with cheers of both 'Vive la République' and 'Vive Félix Faure'. No voyage was complete without a gesture to the poor or the sick (with doctors testifying to the beneficial effects upon their patients). The members of Faure's family were an integral part of the presidential entourage and themselves became objects of veneration.

There were many republicans who felt deeply uneasy about this theatricalization and personalization of presidential power, preferring the holders of the presidential office to be content with providing a modest example of hard work and sobriety. The fact remains, however, that the Republic, like the Bourbon monarchy before it, was not immune from the temptation of giving physical representation and symbolic expression to an indivisible sovereignty as a means of overcoming the tensions of a divided polity.

[157] See e.g. Joseph Barthélemy, *Le Rôle du pouvoir exécutif dans les Républiques modernes* (1906) and Henri Leyrat, *Le Président de la République, son rôle, ses droits, ses devoirs* (1913).

[158] Christophe Prochasson, 'Le Corps de Félix: Corps et records du président Félix Faure', in Jacques Julliard (ed.), *La Mort du roi: Essai d'éthnologie politique comparée* (1999), 197–230. See also Avner Ben-Amos, *Funerals, Politics, and Memory in Modern France, 1789–1996* (Oxford, 2000).

3

Sovereignty, the Social Contract, and Luxury

I

If political thought in nineteenth-century France was preoccupied with questions about rights and the constitution, so too it was haunted by the excesses and disorder of the Revolution. In this Jean-Jacques Rousseau occupied centre stage.[1] Whether loved or loathed, Rousseau came to be seen not just as the theorist of the social contract but also as the prophet of popular sovereignty, and therefore as the patron of a modern state that had swept away all before it. As Alexis de Tocqueville commented, Rousseau 'became and he was to remain the sole teacher of the Revolution in its youth'.[2]

To show how this was the case and what it meant for the development of political thought in France the central part of this chapter will seek to examine three strands of political opinion, each of which in its day exercised considerable influence and (in two cases) power: that associated with Catholic Reaction and the post-Napoleonic Restoration (Joseph de Maistre, Louis de Bonald, and the young Félicité de Lamennais); the liberalism of Benjamin Constant and the writer-politician François Guizot; and, thirdly, the anarchism of Pierre-Joseph Proudhon. For all their ideological differences each shared a horror of what they saw as the Rousseau-inspired radical political and social change of Robespierre's Jacobin dictatorship. First, however, the chapter will address the context and content of Rousseau's theory of social contract, assessing the significance of his ideas and the innovations they entailed. It will then briefly allude to the long-standing debate about the influence of Rousseau upon the Revolution of 1789.

It would be wrong to overstate Rousseau's originality. Long before him those not prepared to accept that sovereignty had its origin in either paternal power or divine right had been ready to concede that its source was to be found in the people. What marked Rousseau out from his predecessors was that they, unlike him, saw sovereignty as being only the people's temporary possession, as something that was to be handed over to the appropriate authority as soon as possible, only rarely (and in some cases never) to be reclaimed. Pufendorf, for example, even went so far as to define the handing over of the right to govern by a

---

[1] See Jean Roussel, *Jean-Jacques Rousseau en France après la Révolution, 1795–1830* (1972).
[2] Alexis de Tocqueville, *The Old Regime and the Revolution* (Chicago, 2001), ii. 57.

defeated people as a meaningful form of consent. Not only was Rousseau unwilling to grant that sovereignty could be given away either under duress or by tacit agreement but he even opposed its voluntary and unforced transfer. Sovereignty was not like a piece of property that could be freely disposed of: it was an inalienable possession, part of an individual's very humanity. Rousseau's contribution was therefore to attribute not just the origin but also the exercise of sovereignty to the people.[3]

The implications of these ideas upon Rousseau's conception of contract were necessarily profound, and this because the 'fundamental' problem he thus set himself was nothing less than that of squaring the circle: namely, how 'to find a form of association that will defend and protect the person and goods of each associate with the full common force, and by means of which each, uniting with all, nevertheless obeys only himself and remains as free as before'.[4] The contrast with the position endorsed by Thomas Hobbes could not have been starker. As Hobbes perceived it, the human condition was so bleak that men could only escape from the war of all against all by agreeing to transfer their right to govern and to adjudicate in disputes to the single sovereign power of Leviathan. The trade-off was a straightforward one: life and an element of liberty in exchange for obedience to the sword. For Rousseau there was to be no trade-off, there were to be no losses, only gains. Men could have both liberty and law if they were able to construct a society where they ruled themselves.[5]

For Rousseau therefore there was to be only one contract of association and no pact of submission. 'Each individual', he wrote, 'recovers the equivalent of everything he loses.' But something 'remarkable' took place when the contract was signed. The individual, in Rousseau's phrase, was 'doubly committed', first to his fellow contractees and secondly as a member of the community in relation to the sovereign. Individuals thus found themselves to have entered into a reciprocal agreement not just with the body of which they were to become members but also with a sovereign deemed henceforth to possess a moral personality. The latter point was fundamental. Rousseau, as much as Hobbes, was aware that a contract where everyone was free to decide upon its terms and when it was to be observed was a recipe for disaster. To prevent the inevitable descent into a 'state of nature' where the association would be either 'tyrannical or void' Rousseau therefore had resort not to the usual strategy of two contracts (the first of which ensures that society is not dissolved even if government is dissolved) but to a fiction: the general will. Its existence as something which was 'always rightful and always tends to the public good' was sufficient to allow Rousseau to stipulate that it was the sovereign

[3] Robert Derathé, *Jean-Jacques Rousseau et la science politique de son temps* (1970). See Patrick Riley, *The General Will Before Rousseau: The Transformation of the Divine into the Civic* (Princeton, NJ, 1986).

[4] Rousseau, 'The Social Contract', in *The Social Contract and Other Later Political Writings* (Cambridge, 2007), 49–50.

[5] The contrast between the positions adopted by Hobbes and Rousseau was noted by Diderot in his entry on 'Hobbisme' in the *Encyclopédie*.

and the sovereign alone who was the sole judge of the contract's implementation. The State was only viable upon this condition.

Rousseau's contract was thus in one sense anything but contractual. Postulated was a pact between a collectivity considered as a single moral person and each of its members taken individually. From this it followed that of the two contracting parties it was only one—the individuals concerned—who could be in breach of the agreement entered into. By an altogether different route we arrived therefore at a conclusion similar to that of Hobbes: the social contract gave absolute power to the sovereign over his subjects.

If this was so, it was partly because Rousseau, unlike John Locke, did not view the foundational contract either as a means of regulating the required balance between rights-bearing individuals and government or of securing the liberal functioning of institutions. For him, as for Hobbes, the contract was constitutive of society itself. Where, however, Rousseau diverged from Hobbes was in the end envisaged. As Robert Derathé correctly observed, for Hobbes that end was civil peace, whilst for Rousseau it was ensuring that men could unite without giving up any of their liberty.

The argument here is sufficiently well-known as not to need detailed clarification. As Rousseau explained: 'what man loses by the social contract is his natural freedom and an unlimited right to everything that tempts him and he can reach: what he gains is civil freedom and property in everything he possesses'.[6] Expressed differently, there was no other solution to our problems than the substitution of the arbitrary relations existing between men by the obedience of the citizen to the law. To that end, it was necessary that the members of the association should transform themselves from a group of isolated individuals with many different wills into a community with a common will or interest. As we passed from the state of nature into civil society, justice was to replace instinct as a rule of conduct and in this way we obeyed only rules that we had prescribed for ourselves and thus enjoyed untrammelled 'moral freedom'.

Given the controversy caused by this proposition and its related claim that individuals could be forced to be free, it is interesting that it was precisely at this point of the argument of *Du Contrat social* that Rousseau chose to declare that 'the philosophical meaning of the word *freedom* is not my subject here'. In a way his concerns were more mundane and straightforward. What he, unlike so many of his predecessors ('Grotius and the rest' as Rousseau described them), was eager to reject was the idea that the individual could contract into anything and under any circumstances and that in this way the rights of slavery, conquest, and despotism could be justified. Rousseau always opposed such a conception of contract and he did so for the good reason that 'to renounce one's freedom is to renounce one's quality as a man'.

What the reader was to make of this has been open to a wide-range of interpretation. Rousseau himself, given his belief that sovereignty could not be subject to

---

[6] Rousseau, 'Social Contract', 53–4.

the procedure of representation, was convinced that his ideas could be applied, if at all, only to states whose geographical area did not exceed that of a small city. Political simplicity, exemplified by 'troops of peasants... attending to affairs of State under an oak tree', was to be the preferred model and it was only later (in his reflections upon the projected governments of Corsica and Poland) that these strictures were to be relaxed. In *Du Contrat social* itself Rousseau refused to stipulate 'definitively' what was the 'best' form of government, suggesting that it could be judged in terms of population growth, thereby handing the entire matter over to the *calculateurs*, whom he exhorted, in almost Benthamite fashion, to 'count, measure, compare'.

More profoundly, Rousseau's musings upon the social contract and the society to which it was to give rise tied in with the broader Rousseauian theme of how both individuals and peoples could be structured for virtue. At a psychological level— and with Rousseau these are numerous—the argument is that Rousseau's formulations were not derived from the lived experience of the Genevan republic (as he claimed) but were rather an enlarged projection of his own being, with virtue measured by the citizen's willingness to be subsumed by the mythic self he had elaborated in his writings.[7] 'There is no subjection so perfect', Rousseau wrote in *Emile*, 'as the one which retains the appearance of liberty.'

To Rousseau's contemporaries it was precisely this preoccupation with virtue that struck the deepest chord. 'Jean-Jacques', Robert Darnton writes in *The Great Cat Massacre*,[8] 'opened up his soul to those who could read him right, and his readers felt their own souls elevated above the imperfections of ordinary existence.' Here the key texts were the *Confessions* (nothing quite like its intimate and often sordid self-examination had been seen before)[9] and the *Nouvelle Héloïse* (which had run to some seventy editions by 1800) and not *Du Contrat social*. Julie's pure love for Saint-Preux and her (inevitable) exemplary death were such as to shape the *sensibilité* of virtually an entire generation of admirers and so much so, as Emmet Kennedy has argued, that 'almost single-handedly Rousseau precipitated an affective revolution'.[10] The cult of Rousseau worship that sprang up shortly after his death—celebrated by, among others, Marie-Antoinette, Queen of France—had this rather than any specific political doctrine as its object. It was moreover this sensibility, this longing for moral elevation, purity, and transparency, which was to be magnified out of all proportion in the Revolution that began in 1789.

---

[7] Carol Blum, *Rousseau and the Republic of Virtue: The Language of Politics in the French Revolution* (Ithaca, NY, and London, 1986), 72.

[8] Robert Darnton, *The Great Cat Massacre* (New York, 1984), 249.

[9] Prosper de Barante, writing in *De la Littérature française pendant le dix-huitième siècle* (1809), 189, was later to comment: 'It is indeed a singular occurrence that a man who sought to secure the esteem and even the admiration of posterity should do so by recounting the smallest details of a life which had nothing of greatness, which displayed no actions of distinction, and which, on the contrary, was full of revolting behaviour and unpardonable offences.'

[10] Emmet Kennedy, *A Cultural History of the French Revolution 1762–1791* (New Haven, Conn., and London, 1989), 112.

II

The question of Rousseau's (and more broadly the Enlightenment's) connection with the French Revolution has long been the cause of controversy and debate. Over eighty years ago Daniel Mornet meticulously reconstructed the reading patterns of pre-revolutionary France and to his surprise discovered that *Du Contrat social* scarcely figured at all. The imagined connecting link appeared to have vanished. For all Mornet's errors this view continued for many years to have its adherents and was most forthrightly restated by Joan McDonald.[11] Her view was that Rousseau had been little read, and even less understood, by those who made the Revolution but that nevertheless both the revolutionaries and their opponents made ceaseless appeal to his authority. It was, she argued, the 'memory' and 'the myth of Rousseau rather than his political theory which was important in the mind of the revolutionary generation'.[12] This thesis was subsequently challenged by Roger Barny in an important article which stated categorically that Rousseau's 'specifically political works, far from being unknown, influenced a number of the future revolutionary leaders and, in a more general way, contributed to the formulation of some of the most important themes of bourgeois political thought'.[13] McDonald's thesis was further contested by R. A. Leigh's bibliographical researches which revealed that *Du Contrat social* had indeed been frequently republished in the period immediate prior to the Revolution. The picture was further complicated with the appearance of Norman Hampson's *Will and Circumstance: Montesquieu, Rousseau and the French Revolution*. Hampson's contention, backed up by the analysis of five key revolutionary figures (Mercier, Brissot, Robespierre, Saint-Just, and Marat), was that both Montesquieu and Rousseau had acted as the principal influences in the intellectual apprenticeship of the revolutionaries, even though their ideas were basically antithetical. This, he writes, 'did not stop virtually all the political writers of the 1780s from borrowing from both at once'.[14]

The force of Hampson's argument was that whilst the revolutionaries took Montesquieu, and not Rousseau, as their guide there was the hope that calmer waters would be reached. The former's conception of a pre-existing *esprit général* informing and fashioning society and its political institutions made possible the recognition and equilibrium of competing interests but under Rousseau's tutelage these interests had to be dissolved into the general will, by force if necessary. By the same token Rousseau taught the revolutionaries that as long as a sovereign acted for the public good it could not infringe the liberty of its subjects. They learnt too that politics—'everything is rooted in politics', Rousseau wrote in his *Confessions*—was

[11] Joan McDonald, *Rousseau and the French Revolution 1762–1791* (London, 1965).
[12] Ibid. 172.
[13] Roger Barny, 'Jean-Jacques Rousseau dans la Révolution', *Dix-Huitième Siècle*, 6 (1974), 62.
[14] Norman Hampson, *Will and Circumstance: Montesquieu, Rousseau and the French Revolution* (London, 1983), 58.

the instrument of social regeneration and emancipation. If need be there could also be resort to the genius of the lawgiver. It is hard then not to agree with François Furet when he writes that Rousseau's 'political thought set up well in advance the conceptual framework of what was to become Jacobinism and the language of the Revolution'.[15]

This view has now become something of a commonplace. It was restated most recently by James Swenson is his *On Jean-Jacques Rousseau: Considered as One of the First Authors of the Revolution*, a title chosen specifically to recall that of the book published by Louis-Sébastien Mercier in 1791. Of the political situation in 1789, Swenson writes, 'Rousseau provided the conceptual terms in which the struggle developed.'[16] Similarly, according to Marcel Gauchet, 'whether Rousseau had been read a lot or a little before the Revolution is of minor importance: he was the author of the moment. He was the thinker exactly appropriate to what the circumstances required.'[17]

It is not difficult to find evidence to support this view. To take one slightly comic example, we can cite the debate which took place in the Constituent Assembly in August 1791 concerning the raising of a statue in Rousseau's honour. The debate quickly turned to the idea of moving Rousseau's remains to the Panthéon and ended with a disagreement about who exactly owned his body and who, therefore, had the right to make this decision. Nevertheless, there could be no doubting the admiration for Rousseau amongst those present at this discussion. Repeatedly cited as the author of both *Du Contrat social* and *Émile*, this much-persecuted 'extraordinary man' and 'universal genius' was accredited with being the first to have established both the equality of rights among men and the sovereignty of the people and with having been 'the first founder of the French Constitution'.[18]

Moreover, this interpretation of Rousseau's influence upon the Revolution accords with the views of many of the participants. If we pass over Augustin Barruel's famous contention that the Revolution was from start to finish a 'conspiracy' led by philosophers against both Church and State—a conspiracy in which Rousseau inevitably figured amongst the *gens de lettres* and thus as a member of 'the most wicked and dangerous group of citizens'[19]—it is sufficient to glance briefly at Jean-Joseph Mounier's *Recherches sur les Causes qui ont empêche les Français de devenir libres et sur les moyens qui leur restent pour acquérir la liberté*, published while Mounier was in exile in 1792. Mounier, as may be recalled, had been a supporter of moderate constitutional reform and it was he who later enunciated the formula that, if the *philosophes* had not caused the Revolution, the latter had produced their influence. How, Mounier asked, could a revolution that had set out to eradicate arbitrary power lead to chaos? The answer was simple. Out of ignorance and

---

[15] François Furet, *Interpreting the French Revolution* (Cambridge, 1981), 31.

[16] James Swenson, *On Jean-Jacques Rousseau: Considered as One of the First Authors of the Revolution* (Stanford, Calif., 2000), 192.

[17] Marcel Gauchet, *La Révolution des pouvoirs: La Souveraineté, le peuple et la représentation 1789–1799* (1995), 57.

[18] *Archives Parlementaires*, 29 (1875), 755–61.

[19] Augustin Barruel, *Mémoires pour servir à l'histoire du jacobinisme* (Chiré en Montreuil, 1973), 217.

laziness those who purported to set France free had turned to Rousseau and *Du Contrat social*, 'the worst book', Mounier commented, 'which has ever been written about government'. It was from his 'principles of anarchy' that these 'modern legislators' had taken their ideas. In their speeches and proclamations they had 'without cease drawn upon the expressions of J.-J. Rousseau'.[20]

How might the matter of Rousseau's influence in the French Revolution be summarized? First, Rousseau was read by all sections of society, from the aristocracy downwards.[21] Next, he was read in diverse and contradictory ways and those who cited Rousseau often did so for no better reason than to give added authority to their own views. Robespierre is a good example of this. Thirdly, if Rousseauian discourse undoubtedly permeated the revolutionary decade and if those who aspired to lead the revolution sought occasionally to put Rousseau's ideas directly into practice, then equally the actions of the revolutionaries frequently contradicted anything Rousseau might have said. Bernard Manin, for example, points out that Jacobin policies on the economy and taxation owed nothing to Rousseau. He also reminds us that Robespierre specifically indicated that the theory of revolutionary government underpinning the Terror could not 'be found in the books of writers on politics'.[22]

Stated in this way, however, we have no sense of the emotional (and frequently tearful) frenzy that Rousseau induced amongst his disciples. The community born out of the social contract was to be frugal, hard-working, virtuous, distrustful of wealth, free of corruption, trusting to the simple qualities of the people cast as the repositories of all that was naturally good. Armed thus, men such as Robespierre and Saint-Just had little difficulty affirming their own rhetorical and moral ascendancy over opponents who bore the mark of evil. What happened when the people, corrupted by despotism, were found to be unworthy of the love that had been invested in them was the recourse to an ever-extensive dictatorship, with the general will supposedly articulated by a twelve-man Committee of Public Safety.

The revolutionaries, then, were not just millenarians: they were 'Rousseauist millenarians'.[23] Moreover, the hypnotic effect of their actions was such as to bequeath to France a living tradition and style of politics—what Pierre Rosanvallon has termed a 'political culture of generality'—that was deeply imbued with Rousseauian notions. The bare bones of what virtually amounted to a revolutionary catechism can be easily sketched out.[24] Sovereignty belonged to the people. There were no limits to sovereignty because the field of politics was itself without limits. It was the task of the community to ensure that the general will was respected and it alone had the right to decide upon the sacrifices that were to be demanded of each

---

[20] Mounier, *Recherches sur les causes* (179, 1973), 147–58.

[21] Roger Chartier, *Les Origines culturelles de la Révolution française* (1990), 105–7.

[22] Bernard Manin, 'Rousseau', in François Furet and Mona Ozouf (eds.), *Dictionnaire critique de la Révolution française: Idées* (1992), 457–81.

[23] Norman Hampson, 'The Heavenly City of the French Revolutionaries', in Colin Lucas (ed.), *Rewriting the French Revolution* (Oxford, 1991), 53.

[24] See Jacques Julliard, *La Faute à Rousseau* (1985) and Rosanvallon, *Le Modèle politique français: La Société civile contre le jacobinisme de 1789 à nos jours* (2004).

individual. The role of government was limited to the execution of the general will as expressed by the people as sovereign. Money and the activities it engendered were the source of corruption and moral decline. The goal of politics was that of transformation and regeneration. Its political expression was to be the one and indivisible Republic. By general agreement, therefore, Rousseau's greatness lay in his advocacy of liberty and in his recognition that this would demand the destruction of all past forms of tyranny. For many in France he was the philosopher of fraternity.

III

In the immediate aftermath of the fall of Robespierre there was no shortage of commentary upon Rousseau's work. Almost without exception a connection was made between Rousseau and the events of the Revolution and invariably Rousseau's influence was seen in strongly negative terms. Time and time again his influence was attributed to his seductive style and to the naivety, if not the malice, of his readers. Clearly too there was a sense that his influence persisted and that his ideas still needed to be refuted. A work such as that by Pierre Landes, *Principes du droit politique, mis en opposition avec ceux de J.J. Rousseau sur le Contrat social*, for example, consisted of a point by point refutation of Rousseau's ideas, beginning with the contention that, far from being born free, man was born weak and therefore in need of authority rather than liberty.[25] Written slightly later, Gabriel-Jacques Dageville's *De la Propriété politique et civile* argued, against Rousseau, that the 'true' social contract could only be that made between property owners to defend their property and thus that Rousseau's contract, as had been demonstrated by the events of the Revolution, could only lead to disorder and the disintegration of society.[26] Given the persistence of these fears, Rousseau's works virtually vanished from booksellers' shelves and under Napoleon no edition of *Du Contrat social* was published.

Nowhere was the hostility and distrust directed towards Rousseau's ideas more evident than among those writers who, like Rousseau, believed that sovereignty was one and absolute but who saw the origin of that sovereignty as found not among the people but in God. Of these no one put the case more succinctly than Joseph de Maistre. Written in exile between 1794 and 1796, his *Étude sur la souveraineté* amounted to a systematic attempt to demolish the very foundations of Rousseau's thought.[27]

---

[25] Pierre Landes, *Principes du droit politique, mis en opposition avec ceux de J. J. Rousseau sur le Contrat social* (1801).

[26] Gabriel-Jacques Dageville, *De la propriété politique et civile* (1813).

[27] Joseph de Maistre, 'Étude sur la souveraineté', in *Œuvres complètes* (Lyons, 1884), i. 309–554. A revised version of this text has been publ. under the title of *De la Souveraineté du peuple: Un anti-contrat social* (1992). See also Joseph de Maistre, 'Examen d'un écrit de J.-J. Rousseau: Sur l'inégalité des conditions parmi les hommes', in *Œuvres complètes*, vii. 507–66. In English see Maistre, *Against Rousseau: 'On the State of Nature' and 'On the Sovereignty of the People'* (Montreal and Kingston, 1996).

There was no doubt in Maistre's mind that Rousseau had been one of those responsible for both the outbreak and the horrors of the Revolution. Robespierre and Marat could not have committed their crimes had Rousseau and the other *philosophes* not undermined the bases of France's pre-1789 Christian order. Rousseau's particular achievement (and again special mention was made of his seductive 'eloquence') was everywhere to have spread 'contempt for authority and the spirit of insurrection'. Nor did Maistre have any doubts about Rousseau's motives. Rousseau, Maistre wrote, could never forgive God for not making him either a duke or a peer of the realm. His work was infused with 'a certain plebeian anger directed against all forms of superiority'.[28]

However, the core of the theocratic argument directed by Maistre against Rousseau lay in the assertion that man was by nature 'sociable' and therefore that it made no sense to speak of man existing prior to the existence of society. The latter, Maistre argued, was 'the direct result of the will of the Creator who wanted that man should be what he always and everywhere had been'. It followed therefore that it was 'a major error' to conceive of society as a 'choice' based upon human consent, deliberation, or what Maistre described as 'a primitive contract'. The confusion, he believed, derived in part from a misunderstanding about what was meant by the word 'nature' and in this context he was sure that such anomalous examples as the 'American savage' had little to teach us. It was absurd to seek the character of a being in its most undeveloped and untypical form. By the same token a people could not be said to pre-date the existence of sovereignty. A sovereign, in Maistre's view, was necessary to make a people and therefore society and sovereignty both appeared at precisely the same time. 'There was', Maistre wrote, 'a people, some kind of civilization and a sovereign as soon as men came into contact with each other.'

The same logic also told Maistre that the very power which had decreed the existence of the social order and of sovereignty had also willed 'modifications to sovereignty according to the different character of nations'. Nations, Maistre believed, quite definitely had different characters and from this were derived different forms of government that in each case were suited to the conditions. Thus, to ask in the abstract, as Maistre interpreted Rousseau to have done, what was the best possible form of government was to pose an insoluble question. 'From these incontestable principles', Maistre continued, 'derives a conclusion which is no less so: that the social contract is a chimera. Because if there are as many governments as there are different peoples, if the various forms of these governments are perforce prescribed by the power which has given to each nation its moral, physical, geographical and commercial qualities, then it is no longer possible to speak of a pact.'[29] In short, each people had the type of government that suited it and none of them had been either chosen or self-consciously created.

As such Rousseau, in addition to his many personal faults and the immense damage he had caused, was cast as 'the mortal enemy of experience'.[30] If history

---

[28] Maistre, 'Étude sur la souveraineté', 457.
[29] Ibid. 329.   [30] Ibid. 456.

taught us (as Maistre believed it did) that monarchy was the most natural and universal form of government and that no pure form of democracy had ever existed, this had in no way prevented Rousseau from proclaiming that the 'sole legitimate government' was one he himself acknowledged was made for gods, was suitable only for small states, and for a people with a simplicity of morals.[31] So also Rousseau judged democracy not by how it actually worked—'Of all the monarchs', Maistre wrote, 'the hardest, the most despotic, the most intolerable, is the monarch people'[32]—but in terms of its theoretical perfection: hence the general will was by definition always right. The whole thing, from the idea of the social contract upwards, was nothing more than 'un rêve de collège'.[33]

Just as importantly there lay beneath this critique of Rousseau an alternative (and, Maistre believed, more compelling) account of the origin of society and of the nature of government. Joseph de Maistre's 'general thesis' was that human beings were relatively powerless and therefore were incapable of any significant level of creative activity. They were also tainted by original sin and hence were not, as Rousseau believed, potentially perfect. From this Maistre found himself in agreement with Hobbes. Society, he wrote, 'is in reality a state of war and here is to be found the necessity of government: given that man is evil he must be governed; wherever several people want the same thing there must be a superior power over everyone who can adjudicate and who can prevent them from fighting each other . . . a being who is both social and evil must be put under the yoke'.[34] Government was therefore not a vehicle for human liberation but was rather a necessary remedy for the consequences of original sin. To limit the power of the sovereign was to destroy it. If there was a difficulty, it was not that the sovereign should not exercise his will 'invincibly' but that he should be prevented from exercising it 'unjustly'.[35] This was to be avoided by ensuring that power derived from the papacy rather than from Rousseau's 'blind multitude'. How then was the legitimacy of a government to be assessed? For Maistre, all governments, given their divine source, were good governments but the best were those that provided the greatest sum of happiness to the greatest number of people over the longest period of time. Ultimately this could be measured not by the maxims of 'human reason' but by the simple criterion of their longevity or duration.

The overall import of Joseph de Maistre's argument, as all his writings testify, was that the Revolution of 1789, directly inspired by Rousseau's 'disastrous principles', had been a frontal assault upon what he chose to describe as 'the eternal laws of nature'. By divorcing politics from religion and by mistakenly seeking to rebuild society upon the foundation of a man-made contract, chaos and disorder had inevitably followed.

This was to be a refrain taken up by the ideologists of Catholic counter-revolution on a regular basis, none more so than Louis de Bonald. The writings of Bonald have neither the brilliance nor the trenchancy of those of Maistre, but

---

[31] Ibid. 482.   [32] Ibid. 502.   [33] Ibid. 489.
[34] Maistre, 'Examen d'un écrit de J.-J. Rousseau', 563.
[35] Maistre, 'Étude sur la souveraineté', 422.

they again demonstrate that central to the counter-revolutionary defence of both throne and altar was the perceived need to refute Rousseau's ideas, in this case by demonstrating how Rousseau's own arguments could be used to subvert the very ideas for which he was taken to stand.

Louis de Bonald began his magisterial *Théorie du pouvoir politique et religieux dans la société civile, démontrée par le raisonnement et par l'histoire*,[36] first published in 1796 and written in exile in Heidelberg, with a statement effectively denying the possibility of ever reconstructing society from first principles. 'Man', he proclaimed, 'has always wanted to set himself up as the legislator of religious society and of civil society and to provide a constitution for each of them: I believe it possible to show that man can no more give a constitution to religious and political society than he can give weight to a body or dimensions to matter.'[37] In short, the constitution of society was as natural and as immune to human action as the physical constitution of man himself. As such all forms of political voluntarism—of which Rousseau's ideas were a prime example—were nothing less than deviations from what Bonald regarded as 'the fundamental axioms of politics or of the science of society'. Indeed, he went so far as to suggest that *Du Contrat social* would have been better published under the lugubrious title of *Méthode à l'usage des sociétés pour les éloigner de leur inclination naturelle, ou de la nature*.

What Bonald took these axioms to be is, to say the least, somewhat complicated. His argument, never quick in pace, moved forward by way of deduction and analogy, and was built around a series of tripartite divisions. As we saw in our earlier discussion of Bonald's critique of the rights of man, the central claim was that a properly constituted society was one in which the elements of will, love, and force were in harmony and that certain relationships between men were 'necessary' and must therefore be respected if the lives and property of a society's members were to be preserved. At this point our focus must be on the first of Bonald's categories: *la volonté*.

Given that God had created man in his own image, how could society's descent into turmoil be explained? Bonald's reply was in accord with what he took to be the teachings of theology. These, he argued, saw 'an unrestrained will, an uncontrolled love of self, immoral or criminal action as the source of all our disorders and as the origin of all our tribulations'.[38] From this there had followed war between men and their decline into 'a savage state', a war made more destructive by the fact that men were not born, as philosophy proclaimed, equal in rights but unequal in strength. 'The necessary effect', Bonald wrote, 'of the increase of the human race is to bring men closer together; the necessary effect of the unleashing of their wills and their strength is to destroy them'.

How, then, could these conflicting and opposed wills be brought into harmony so as to ensure the predominance of what Bonald termed 'the general will of society'? That general will, he insisted, could not be interpreted as either the

---

[36] Louis de Bonald, 'Théorie du pouvoir politique et religieux dans la société civile, démontrée par le raisonnement et par l'histoire', in *Œuvres complètes de M. de Bonald* (1864), i. 121–954.
[37] Ibid. 121.   [38] Ibid. 142.

particular will of one man, or indeed as 'the will of all men taken together'. Nor should the general will be mistaken for 'the will of the people'. 'The will of a people in their entirety, even if it is unanimous', Bonald continued, 'is only the sum of its particular wills', each of which was necessarily selfish and destructive. The truth of this distinction between 'the will of all' and 'the general will', Bonald twice contended, had even been recognized, if only to be ignored, by Rousseau himself. It represented 'the most complete refutation of his work'.

Rousseau was thus charged with deploying a rhetoric of constant self-contradiction. But it was precisely this rhetoric that had been deployed by the revolutionaries as they set out to create a republic. Under such a regime, Bonald argued, society became nothing more than a collection of individuals and accordingly the general will was dissolved into the sum of individual and particular wills, with individual pleasure and happiness, not general well-being, becoming its goal. In these circumstances, society progressively disintegrated, reverting back to its 'primitive state' where men sought only to secure their own dominance. To such a state had France been reduced during the Revolution, with 'hunger, misery, and death' everywhere made visible.

Indeed, in Bonald's eyes, France had become the very 'negation' of a properly constituted society. 'There arose', he proclaimed,

> a single power and a constitution came into existence. But, by God, what a power and what a constitution! It has its fundamental laws and its public religion: it is the cult of *Marat*. It has its single and general power: it is *death*. It has its social superiors: they are the *Jacobins*, the priests of this cult and the agents of this power. This power has a representative: it is the instrument of torture. This monarch has its ministers: they are its executioners. It has its subjects: they are its victims. Nothing like it has ever been seen on the earth before.[39]

Here, then, was the result of the philosophical confusion sown by Rousseau's theory of the general will. But the sting in the tale of Bonald's case against Rousseau was that if the popular will could not be said to constitute the general will, then the will of the monarch certainly could. 'It is clear', Bonald wrote, 'that, in a constituted society, the monarch is the law, since the law is the expression of the general will which he in turn dispenses and represents: in his capacity as monarch therefore he could not wish to violate the law, that is to say, to wish to destroy what the general will of society wishes to preserve'. Rousseauian logic was thus turned on its head, with the monarch, rather than the people, embodying a general will which seemingly could not err.

Thus, Bonald's overall assessment of Rousseau's achievements was disarmingly straightforward. He had, Bonald declared, 'sacrificed society for man, history for his own opinions, and the universe for Geneva'.[40] Was it, however, as simple as that? Bonald began his *Théorie du pouvoir politique et religieux dans la société civile* by stating unapologetically that his text frequently cited the works of both Montesquieu and Rousseau. How, he asked, could one write about politics without

---

[39] Ibid. 304. [40] Ibid. 129.

referring to *De l'Esprit des lois* and *Du Contrat social*, when, even if both were full of errors, they presented 'a synthesis of all past and present politics'? For all Bonald's desire to see an atheistic revolution brought to an end and a hereditary monarchy restored, in other words, he nevertheless reluctantly had to acknowledge the scale of Rousseau's achievement.

As might be clear, Bonald associated philosophy in general with the desire to destroy religion. The doctrine of the sovereignty of the people, on this view, by 'dethroning God', led inevitably to atheism. Writing after the Restoration of the monarchy, and thus after the tide of revolutionary change appeared to have turned, the young Félicité de Lamennais was to adopt a strikingly similar attitude. To those unfamiliar with the details of Lamennais's religious and political itinerary this might seem surprising because, if Lamennais is now remembered, it is almost always as the disciple of democracy and the defender of the oppressed, as the excommunicated priest whose radicalism was voiced under the banner of 'Dieu et la liberté'. Yet for the royalist Lamennais of the *Essai sur l'indifférence en matière de la religion*, published in 1817,[41] everything was clear: the Reformation had given birth to Descartes, who himself had engendered the philosophy of the eighteenth century, which in turn had produced 1789, 1793, and the Revolution's catalogue of crimes. In this woeful sequence, the atheistic doctrines of Rousseau—described by Lamennais as the 'Genevan sophist'—had played a very significant role.

The opening sentence of Lamennais's text made the message plain. The unhappiest of centuries was not one that was attracted by error but one which neglected and scorned the truth. The real enemy was indifference because this ultimately was 'incompatible with order and the very existence of society'. Locke, Kant, and Descartes were in turn taken to task for their contribution to our scepticism whilst our salvation was deemed to lie in a divinely inspired *sensus communis* embodying our collective certitudes. Philosophy, by denying the mysteries of Christianity, destroyed morality and undermined the bases of religious and political authority in society. Rousseau, Lamennais conceded, was not an atheist but the force of his argument was that all religions were equally good and equally true, thus relegating faith to a matter of climate and degrees of latitude. The way was then open for an acceptance of all vices and all crimes and what Lamennais described as 'a vast shipwreck of all truths and all virtues'. It is here that we again see the near-obligatory recognition of Rousseau's literary talents—'Never', Lamennais wrote, 'did anyone make such skilful use of words'—but the result nevertheless was 'a shapeless assemblage of incoherencies, absurdities, and contradictions'.[42]

Rousseau the deist, in other words, had led us unerringly towards uncertainty and indifference and thence to the destruction of society itself. But the same disastrous results were also obtained by another dimension of Rousseau's philosophy: contract theory. 'Never', Lamennais commented, 'was there a doctrine so absurd, so deadly and so degrading as this.'[43] What were the grounds of Lamennais's dissent?

---

[41] Félicité de Lamennais, *Essai sur l'indifférence en matière de la religion* (1817).
[42] Ibid. 95.   [43] Ibid. 328.

In the first instance, no society had been seen to originate in this way and it was a ridiculous idea to imagine that society owed its existence to a random collection of individuals meeting by chance 'in the woods'! Second, every pact implied sanctions to ensure that it was observed but where in Rousseau's writings was a convincing description of these sanctions to be found? There was nothing, Lamennais argued, to stop people from reclaiming their sovereignty. Far from creating the 'tranquillity of order' the contract would only establish a conflict between particular wills and between sovereign and subject, with force alone as the final arbiter. 'When the force of the sovereign prevails,' Lamennais wrote, 'one has despotism; when the force of the people carries the day, one has anarchy.'[44] Nor was Lamennais convinced that anything changed with the signing of the social contract. Each individual remained as he was before, sovereign of himself and independent of all wills but his own, and therefore subject to nothing else but the will of the strongest. Moreover, Rousseau could come up with no better reason for adhering to the contract than self-interest. On this fragile basis, Lamennais contended, did philosophy seek to ground society.

The criticism did not stop there. Once the doctrine of the social contract had been accepted by the people it had turned society into one vast arena where only private interests dominated. What Rousseau understood by liberty was in reality only a form of servitude, characterized by a hatred of 'all institutions, all laws, and all social distinctions'. Governments acted solely upon the basis of self-preservation and self-aggrandizement and much the same was true of the masses. 'If', Lamennais wrote, the latter 'are allowed for one minute to sense their power they will abuse it in order to destroy everything and will run headlong towards anarchy believing all the time that they are marching towards liberty'. Armed with the theory of the general will and the belief that it was always right, 'the people had no need to justify their acts; they could legitimately do whatever they wished, even destroy or annihilate themselves'.[45] In short, the same doctrine which had dethroned God and had dethroned kings, had in turn dethroned man and reduced him to the level of an animal. Turmoil followed turmoil, revolution followed revolution, and a country which had been the 'ornament' and the 'queen' of Europe had been reduced to providing the human race with 'a great and terrible lesson'.

Lamennais's conclusion was unambiguous and placed Rousseau at the heart of the century's ills. Once philosophy had told man that his reason was the source of truth and that his will was the source of power, truth became nothing more than what appealed to his inclinations and power was reduced to naked force. The members of society, with their equal rights and their contrary interests, would destroy themselves down to the last man were it not for the fact that the strongest would enslave the weakest and would make his will the sole law and the sole standard of justice. 'Such', Lamennais wrote, 'is the necessary result of the absurd social contract thought up by philosophy, and which is in reality only a blasphemy declaring war against society and against God.'[46] Upon the ruins of religion, society

---

[44] Ibid. 330.   [45] Ibid. 354.   [46] Ibid. 345.

would be consumed by divorce, adultery, selfishness, corruption, barbarism, luxury, and cupidity, descending into nothingness.

The sadness in all of this is that, as the papacy remained true to its conception of the unity of throne and altar and as it allied itself increasingly with Europe's temporal powers, Lamennais found himself ever more drawn to the sufferings of Europe's Catholic peoples and from this onwards to a defence of liberty of conscience, liberty of the press, and liberty of education. He supported the Revolution of 1830, only then (as we shall see later) to be quickly disillusioned by the July Monarchy's failure to support similar uprisings across Europe. He was then to find himself in the liberal and republican camp. This should not lead us to forget the sustained ferocity of his assault upon Rousseau.

The response of those who most forcefully articulated the counter-revolutionary rejoinder to Rousseau's writings was therefore not without ambivalence. They too felt the power and persuasiveness of his ideas, even though they had no doubts about what had been their profoundly destabilizing consequences for France. If they thought that the idea of a social contract was a ridiculous invention, they could most of all not forgive Rousseau for stealing sovereignty from God and giving it to the people. Like Rousseau, however, they believed that sovereignty should be neither limited nor divided. Was the response of the writers of French liberalism any less ambivalent?

Liberalism in France was a multifaceted affair.[47] Stated simply, with the outbreak of the Revolution there were those who were prepared to clothe their calls for reform within the doctrine of natural rights and with this came a willingness to speak of a pact or contract as the origin of civil society. One example of this was Pierre Daunou's *Essai sur la constitution*,[48] published in 1793. Another was Pierre-Louis Roederer's imposing *Cours d'organisation sociale*, published in the same year.[49] If anything the prevailing influence in both cases was Lockean rather than Rousseauian, the emphasis falling upon the contract as a means of protecting pre-existing rights (and especially the right to property). Roederer, for example, stated that: 'When the needs of men have made known their natural rights to them and led them to unite together, they enter a contract of union and this is the social pact; they subsequently draw up the conditions of their union and from this civil law is born. The social pact and civil law are therefore only guarantees . . . of the natural rights of man.'[50] Moreover, with time—and specifically with the radicalization of the language of rights which accompanied the rise of the Jacobins—the enthusiasm for such a style of argument waned considerably. Writers such as Daunou and Roederer, as we saw earlier, became associated with the group known as the *Idéologues*, and with this, along with their colleagues Cabanis and Destutt de Tracy, became increasingly preoccupied with the need to establish and preserve

---

[47] See Lucien Jaume, *L'Individu effacé: Ou le paradoxe du libéralisme français* (1997).
[48] Pierre Daunou, *Essai sur la constitution* (1793).
[49] Pierre-Louis Roederer, 'Cours d'organisation sociale', in *Œuvres complètes* (1859), viii. 129–305.
[50] Ibid. 137.

social peace and order. For men such as these it was to be the maxim of utility, rather than anything to be found in the writings of Rousseau, that was to act as their guide.

This is not to say that Rousseau now ceased to trouble the consciences of those who sought, against the odds, to keep alive the flame of French liberal opinion. Rousseau continued to do so and this was primarily because of the principal theoretical presupposition upon which the social contract was thought to rest: popular sovereignty. Here we can again turn to the arguments provided by Rousseau's fellow Swiss Protestant, Benjamin Constant. Writing in *De l'esprit de conquête et de l'usurpation*, published in 1814, Constant commented: 'It will be apparent, I believe, that the subtle metaphysics of *Du Contrat social* can only serve today to supply weapons and pretexts to all kinds of tyranny, that of one man, that of several or that of all, to oppression either organized under legal forms or exercised through popular violence.'[51] In the later *Commentaire sur l'ouvrage de Filangieri* he spoke of the 'terrible consequences and incalculable dangers' of Rousseau's theories.[52] The unpublished text, written between 1806 and 1810 and which like Constant's famous work of 1815 carried the title *Principes de politique*, was even more specific, attributing 'all the misfortunes of the French Revolution' to 'his eloquent and absurd theory'. 'It would be only too easy to show', Constant wrote, 'that the most erroneous sophisms of the most ardent apostles of the Terror were nothing else than perfectly legitimate conclusions drawn from the principles of Rousseau.'[53] Nevertheless, he was quick to add: 'I do not wish to join Rousseau's detractors. At present they are numerous enough . . . He was the first to make a sense of our rights popular; his voice has awakened generous hearts and independent minds.'[54] Elsewhere he was to refer to Rousseau as 'one of the great geniuses of the eighteenth century'.[55]

Where Constant found himself in agreement with Rousseau was in an acceptance that 'there are only two sorts of power in the world: one, illegitimate, is force; the other, legitimate, is the general will'.[56] All authority, Constant argued, whether it be a monarchy or a republic, should rest upon the latter principle. Where he diverged from Rousseau, however, was in his understanding of the precise nature and extent of the sovereignty that was to embody that will. As perceived by Rousseau, the general will was translated into the unlimited sovereignty of the

---

[51] Benjamin Constant, 'De l'esprit de conquête et de l'usurpation', in *De la liberté chez les Modernes* (1980), 186.

[52] Benjamin Constant, *Commentaire sur l'ouvrage de Filangieri* (1822), 51.

[53] Benjamin Constant, *Principes de politique, applicables à tous les gouvernements (version 1806–1810)* (1st publ. 1980), 44.

[54] This statement appears twice in Constant's writings, as a footnote in 'De l'esprit de conquête et de l'usurpation' and as part of the text to the unpubl. version of *Principes de politique*.

[55] Benjamin Constant, *De la Doctrine politique qui peut réunir les parties en France* (1816), 37.

[56] The following discussion of Rousseau's ideas is found in two locations: *Principes de politique, applicables à tous les gouvernements (1806–10)*, 33–49 and 'Principes de politique, applicables à tous les gouvernements représentatifs et particulièrement à la constitution actuelle de la France' (1815), in *De la liberté chez les modernes*, 269–78.

people and for Constant it was precisely the absence of limits upon that sovereignty that posed the gravest threat to liberty. 'When', he wrote, 'you establish that the sovereignty of the people is unlimited, you create and you toss at random into society a degree of power which is too large in itself, and which is bound to constitute an evil, in whatever hands it is placed.' Constant, like John Stuart Mill after him, was eager to establish that there was a part of human existence that 'by necessity remains individual and independent' and that therefore should properly remain beyond social control. Rousseau, he remarked, had 'overlooked this truth', thus providing 'the most fearsome support for despotism'.

This was the very heart of the problem, for what Rousseau had forgot or had misunderstood was that, as soon as the sovereign sought to make use of his power, as soon as the practical organization of authority was begun, the sovereign had to delegate power, thus destroying the very qualities the sovereign was said to embody. Whether we liked it or not, we were, in other words, submitting ourselves to those who acted in the name of all. We were not entering into a condition equal for all but one in which certain individuals derived exclusive advantage and were above the common condition. Not everyone would gain the equivalent of what they would lose because the result of the contract was 'the establishment of a power which takes away from them whatever they have'. If there was a parallel to be drawn it was with what Constant described as 'Hobbes's whole dreadful system'. The absolute character of the contract envisaged was such as to ensure the continuous violation of individual liberty irrespective of whether sovereignty was exercised in the name of the monarch or of democracy. What no tyrant would do in his own name, he could easily do in the name of the authority granted him through the unlimited power of the general will.

Rousseau, Constant wrote, was appalled by the consequences of his own argument and by the 'monstrous force' he had created. So appalled, in fact, that he set out a series of conditions that effectively destroyed the principle he had just proclaimed. By announcing that sovereignty could be neither delegated, alienated, nor represented he was, in other words, declaring that it could not be exercised at all. Constant's own answer was to argue that no authority, not even that exercised in the name of the people, should be unlimited and then to recommend a set of political institutions drawing heavily upon the English model so despised by Rousseau. Of even greater consequence (as we shall see in the next chapter) was his attempt to outline a conception of liberty thought to be appropriate to the modern age. Here Rousseau was cast irredeemably amongst the advocates of ancient liberty.

What the latter point indicates is that Constant's discussion of Rousseau figured at the core of his thinking. Indeed, it should be noted that both versions of the *Principes de politiques* commenced with an analysis of the ideas contained in *Du Contrat social*. The same is also to an extent true of another dominant representative of liberal opinion during the period of the Restoration: François Guizot. He too sought to restore political stability to post-revolutionary France but in contrast to Constant he focused less upon formulating what Lucien Jaume has termed a 'libéralisme du sujet' than upon establishing the bases of a system of representative government appropriate to the new conditions in which France now found herself. The crucial factor here was Guizot's conviction that power should reside in the hands of those who had the 'capacity' to govern properly.[57] 'Capacity', he wrote, 'is nothing else than the ability to act according to reason . . . It is the sole principle in virtue of which the limitation of electoral rights can be properly designated.'[58]

It was after the restoration of the monarchy in 1814 that Guizot set out to elucidate the principles upon which such a system would rest. He opposed equally those who wished to continue the revolution and those who, as he put it, wished 'to begin the counter-revolution'. Like Constant, therefore, he was preoccupied with the question of the definition and practice of sovereignty, rejecting the claims of both popular and divine sovereignty on the grounds that each, being absolute, would lead inevitably and necessarily to tyranny. 'The true theory of sovereignty', Guizot explained, founded upon 'the radical illegitimacy of all absolute power, whatever may be its name and place, is the principle of representative government.'[59] It is at this point that Rousseau, the adversary of representation, came to occupy a central place in Guizot's argument.[60]

Guizot began by denying that a contract of the kind envisaged by Rousseau was the bond of human association. 'Society and government', he wrote, 'are born together and coexist necessarily.' Society commenced therefore at the moment when the relations between men ceased to be determined by force, when men came, in Guizot's words, to recognize the 'law of reason'. 'The contract which binds men to the laws of justice and of truth', Guizot thus believed, 'is no more their work than are the laws themselves.' Moreover, it was not within the power of men either to break this contract or to forget it with impunity. Next, Guizot had to challenge the most fundamental of Rousseau's assumptions: namely, that the will of the individual was the source of the sovereign's legitimacy and power.

This was done in two stages. The first was to recognize that, for Rousseau, all representation was 'delusive and impossible' and therefore that all forms of representative government were illegitimate. On this view, representation of the will was simply an impossibility and all power founded upon such representation was tyrannical. The logical conclusion, which Guizot granted had been acknowledged by Rousseau, was that all 'great States' were illegitimate and therefore that 'it was necessary to divide society into small republics in order that, once at least, the will

---

[57] It is in this context that Pierre Rosanvallon has spoken of the desire of Guizot and his fellow *doctrinaires* to establish 'l'ordre capacitaire': see *La Démocratie inachevée: Histoire de la souveraineté du peuple en France* (2000), 93–126.

[58] François Guizot, *Histoire des origines du gouvernement représentatif en Europe* (1851), ii. 230. This text is based upon lectures given in Paris between 1820 and 1822. In English tr. see *The History of the Origins of Representative Government in Europe* (Indianapolis, 2002).

[59] Guizot, *Histoire des origines*, 13.

[60] In addition to the argument contained in lecture 10 of vol. ii of *Histoire des origines*, Guizot's critique of Rousseau is to be found in the pages of *Philosophie politique: de la souveraineté*. Written during the early 1820s and never completed, it was first publ. in full only recently: see Guizot, *Histoire de la civilisation en Europe* (1985), 305–89.

of each citizen might give its consent to the law'. This, as we know, had been a solution that had appealed to many republicans in the early 1790s but Guizot wanted to push the argument further, arguing that even if this could be done, 'the problem would be far from being resolved'. 'What does it matter', Guizot pointed out, 'if a law should have emanated from my will yesterday if today my will has changed? Can I only will once? Does my will exhaust its rights in one single act?' Seen in this light it was impossible for the individual to contract into any obligation that determined his future conduct. What an individual no longer wills, Guizot remarked with devastating accuracy, 'has no more right over him than the will of a stranger'. Pushed to this extreme conclusion, it was therefore not just large states, but all states, all constitutions, and all laws that were illegitimate. Men could not contract into any obligations whatsoever. The result would be the dissolution of society itself.

However, the principal error, according to Guizot, lay not in the practical implications of Rousseau's theories, which were palpably ridiculous, but in the principle itself. Rousseau had simply misunderstood the proper nature of representation. This was the second strand of Guizot's argument. 'It is not true', Guizot proclaimed, 'that man should be absolute master over himself, that his will should be his legitimate sovereign, that at no time and by no right does anyone have power over him if he does not consent.' Beyond and distinct from the will of the individual, Guizot wanted to argue, lay a 'law which is called either reason, morality, or truth' and unless it was followed the use we made of our liberty was either absurd or criminal. Thus man had no right to act arbitrarily or according to the dictates of his 'solitary will' and no one, therefore, had the right to impose a law because he willed it nor oppose a law because it was against his will. Rather, the legitimacy of power rested not in the will of the person who exercised it but 'in the conformity of its laws with eternal reason'. Reason alone, Guizot confirmed, is the 'sole source of legitimate power'.

Guizot sought to prove this argument by referring to the fact that both children and imbeciles were denied the right to exercise their will without supervision. What was true of them, he commented, is 'true of man in general: the right to power is derived from reason, never from will'. It was what Guizot took the political consequences of this to be that were pregnant with significance. The sum total of reason was dispersed unequally between those individuals who made up society and thus the principal concern needed to be that of bringing these 'fragments' together so as to constitute a government and to realize 'public reason and public morality'. 'What we call *representation*', Guizot concluded, 'is nothing else than a means to arrive at this result.'

We will later examine Guizot's theory of representative government in more detail but, to summarize, the intended force of his argument against Rousseau was that the sovereignty of reason was to be contrasted with that of the sovereignty of 'number' and with this that the claims of democracy and of universal suffrage were to be rejected in favour of a limited franchise which would assure the predominance of 'capacity'. It was the attempt to secure that end which was to dominate the thinking of liberals in France in the period before 1848.

Yet, paradoxically, Guizot's position was closer to that of Rousseau's than he realized, for had not the latter explicitly refused to equate the general will with the will of the majority and had he not also argued that it existed independently from the selfish and private wills of all? To that extent, Rousseau's general will was not far removed from Guizot's concept of 'public reason', as both were meant to embody the common good. Nevertheless, in the process of developing his argument, Guizot had hit upon a criticism of Rousseau that was to be taken up by people with far more radical intentions: any form of contract which bound our will in the future was a restriction of our individual liberty. In England this objection had first been voiced by William Godwin in his *Enquiry Concerning Political Justice*;[61] in France it was taken up by the first self-proclaimed anarchist, Pierre-Joseph Proudhon.[62]

Proudhon was not a man known for being moderate towards those he disagreed with and his attitude towards Rousseau was no exception to this rule. First of all, Proudhon was in no doubt that Rousseau was directly responsible for what he described as 'the great deviation of "93"' and for the society of 'frightful chaos and demoralization' that it had produced. Rousseau, in brief, was unambiguously identi-fied with a tradition that, in Proudhon's eyes, had been 'bewitched by politics': Jacobinism. Further, it was within this tradition that Rousseau's concept of social contract was to be located. Rousseau, Proudhon argued, understood 'nothing of the social contract' and because this was so he had articulated 'an offensive and defensive alliance of those who possess against those who do not possess'. It was 'a contract of hatred', a 'monument of incurable misanthropy', a 'coalition of the barons of property, commerce, and industry against the disinherited proletariat', an 'oath of war'. Less excitedly he remarked: 'tyranny, claiming divine right, having become odious, [Rousseau] reorganizes it and makes it respectable, or so he says, by making it proceed from the people'. The fundamental error, as Proudhon saw it, was to see only the political relations that existed between men and therefore to see the contract as an agreement between citizen and government. In such an agreement there was 'necessarily alienation of a part of the liberty and of the wealth of the citizen . . . it is an act of appointment of arbiters, chosen by the citizens without any preliminary agreement . . . the said arbiters being clothed with sufficient force to put their decisions into practice and to collect their salaries'.

The import of Proudhon's argument, therefore, was that Rousseau had provided a spurious, if brilliantly oratorical, defence of the domination of the state, in this case the one and indivisible Jacobin Republic. Yet Proudhon, unlike other critics of Rousseau, did not want to abandon the idea of contract altogether. Far from it, in fact: it was precisely the idea of what Proudhon termed 'free contract' that would lead to the dissolution and ultimate disappearance of the State. The key argument here was what Proudhon saw as the transition from distributive justice, defined as the reign of law and as feudal, governmental, and military rule, to commutative justice, the dominance of the economic and industrial system. It was by moving

---

[61] William Godwin, *Enquiry Concerning Political Justice* (Harmondsworth, 1976), 212–16. Godwin's text was first publ. in 1798.

[62] See Pierre-Joseph Proudhon, *Idée générale de la Révolution au XIXe siècle* (1851).

away from politics to economics that his preferred model of decentralized and pluralistic self-government—mutualism—would come into existence.

A proper contract, Proudhon argued, was not one between those governed and those governing (as Rousseau believed) but excluded government and was one between individuals as individuals. What characterized this contract was that it was an agreement for equal exchange, in which several individuals organized themselves for a definite purpose and time. Each contractee was therefore mutually obliged to provide a certain amount of goods, services, and work in exchange for other goods, services, and work of equal value. Beyond this, each of the contractees was perfectly independent. The contract therefore was 'essentially reciprocal': it implied no obligation upon the parties concerned except that which resulted from their personal promise of reciprocal delivery. Just as importantly, it was not subject to any external authority. 'When I agree with one or more of my fellow citizens', Proudhon wrote, 'it is clear that my own will is my law; it is myself who, in fulfilling an obligation, am my own government.' Likewise, by agreeing upon a contract, individuals indicated their willingness to 'abdicate all pretensions to govern each other'. More than this, Proudhon envisaged that this system of contract could be extended indefinitely throughout society, producing a community that would be composed of an intricate web of contracts freely agreed upon by the individuals concerned. 'It implies', Proudhon wrote, 'that a man bargains with the aim of securing his liberty and his well-being without any personal loss.'

Seen in this light it was what Proudhon described as 'the constitution of value' that was 'the contract of contracts'. Each contract was to be based upon a 'just price' for the goods and services exchanged and this, in Proudhonian terms, made possible the realization of what he regarded as a pattern of justice that was 'totally human and nothing but human'. All conflicting interests were reconciled and all divergences were unified. 'Everything else', Proudhon wrote, 'is war, the rule of authority.'

Proudhon's case against Rousseau, therefore, was that he had fundamentally misinterpreted the idea of the social contract as it had emerged out of the sixteenth century. This 'revolutionary tradition', born out of the quarrel between the Catholic Bossuet and the Protestant Jurieu, had given us 'the idea of the social contract as the very antithesis of government': under the guise of eloquence and paradox, Rousseau had turned it into the very opposite.

IV

When the July Monarchy collapsed in 1848 the constitutional and political questions that had engulfed France in the 1790s resurfaced with a vigour that seemed hardly to have diminished over the preceding five decades. Yet this time the names of Montesquieu and Rousseau were rarely cited.[63] When they were, as was the case with Pierre Leroux before the Constituent Assembly, it was to

---

[63] François Luchaire, *Naissance d'une constitution: 1848* (1998), 45.

encourage its members to seek new guides as they sought to frame the constitution of the Second Republic. France, he believed, needed a new 'political science' which would avoid the Montesquieu and Rousseau-inspired errors of the past.[64] If not explicitly cited, however, the influence of Rousseau's ideas was not difficult to discern. This was especially so in the pronouncements of those such as Victor Considérant and Ledru-Rollin as they advocated a system of direct democracy. Again one claim was that representation would put an end to the sovereignty of the people.

As might be anticipated, the orthodox republican response came from Louis Blanc in the form of the familiar argument that, strictly speaking, Rousseau's ideas could only be applied to societies characterized by 'a very small state, a people that was easy to bring together, citizens who knew each other, a pronounced simplicity of morals, high levels of equality in both rank and fortune, little or no luxury'. Where this did not exist, Blanc asked, had Rousseau not countenanced the separation of executive and legislative power? Had he not also acknowledged the need for a legislator? Anything else would lead to a return to federalism and therefore to the chaos produced by the Girondins.[65]

As it was, the constitution of the Second Republic did not need an element of Rousseauian democracy to push it towards a speedy disintegration. The provision that the president was to be directly elected for a fixed and non-renewable period was sufficient to do the job. In these circumstances, as Sudhir Hazareesingh has argued,[66] Rousseau was subject to 'systematic exclusion' from republican memory. When not forgotten, however, an important transformation occurred, as was illustrated by views of Jules Barni.

Written in exile, the second volume of Barni's *Histoire des Idées morales et politique en France au dix-huitième siècle* amounted to a detailed analysis of Rousseau's ideas seen through the perspective of Barni's enthusiastic neo-Kantianism.[67] The most striking innovation in Barni's argument was not only that Rousseau was freed of responsibility for the Terror and the acts of the Convention but that he was now seen in an unambiguously favourable light as the philosopher not of 1793 but of 1789. The Déclaration des Droits de l'Homme et du Citoyen, Barni wrote, was 'the putting into practice of the ideas of *Du Contrat social*'.[68] It was Rousseau's idea that had inspired the abolition of the feudal order and that had led to the demand of the Third Estate that voting was to be by head. In no way, Barni continued, was Rousseau responsible 'for the politics of the slaughterhouse that sullied the French Revolution and that made possible the resuscitation of Caesarism in the France of the nineteenth century'.[69] In moral terms, Rousseau stood for the recognition of

[64] *Le Moniteur Universel: Journal Officiel de la République française*, 250 (6 Sept. 1848), 2317–18.
[65] See esp. Louis Blanc, *Plus de Girondins!* (1851) and *La République Une et Indivisible* (1851).
[66] Sudhir Hazareesingh, *Intellectual Founders of the Republic: Five Studies in Nineteenth-Century French Political Thought* (Oxford, 2001), 293.
[67] Jules Barni, *Histoire des Idées morales et politiques en France au dix-huitième siècle* (1867), ii.
[68] Ibid. 296.   [69] Ibid. 300.

the inner voice of conscience, whilst in politics he was the advocate of republican equality and the sovereignty of the people.[70] He understood and showed that the liberty of man was inalienable. At bottom, Barni wrote, 'the principle of Rousseau is nothing else than that of the free adhesion of citizens to the political institutions and to the laws under which they live and which they are required to obey; and this principle is nothing else than that of liberty, without which man is nothing more than a slave or a machine'.[71] In this way Rousseau could be read as an unremitting critic of the Second Empire of Napoleon III.

But Barni was also alive to the fact that in Rousseau's theory of the State 'the liberty of the individual and the rights of the human person are not sufficiently recognized or safeguarded'. This was where Kant came to Barni's rescue. The source of Rousseau's errors, Barni argued, lay in his preoccupation with unity, an enthusiasm grounded in an admiration for the 'ancient city'. Rousseau, he commented, 'too easily forgets when he speaks of the people that if it can be seen as a person . . . this person is not strictly and absolutely *one*, and that it is composed of as many persons as there are individuals in the State and that the general will which arises from it can never have in reality the ideal and abstract unity which he attributes to it'.[72] That weakness, Barni contended, could be overcome by supplementing Rousseau with a reading of the author of *The Critique of Pure Reason*, thus allowing us to move from the potential for 'civil despotism' to the realization of 'philosophical liberty'.

In short, if, as Barni wished, Rousseau was to have an appeal for the moderate republicans who were to set out to construct the edifice of the Third Republic from the 1870s onwards, it had to be a Rousseau who could be said to lend support to the reforming, but not radical, programme upon which the regime was to be constructed. He had to be seen as an advocate of modern and not ancient democracy and as an opponent of governmental despotism, as someone whose views would no longer inspire fear and who would not scare away the bourgeoisie.

If this strategy failed, however, there was always the device of falling back upon the figure of Rousseau as a writer.[73] As we have seen, even the most ardent opponent of Rousseau found it difficult not to acknowledge his literary abilities. His was a style that overcame the most hard-hearted hostility. What better then than to focus upon this rather than upon anything that Rousseau might have said about politics? And this indeed was to be one of the primary ways in which the Third Republic came to celebrate his genius. Standing before the statue of Rousseau on the Montagne Sainte-Geneviève on the day of its inauguration in February 1889, Jules Simon of the Académie Française put the case beautifully. Rousseau, he proclaimed, was 'above all a great writer'. The literary style was the man. 'I do not

[70] This was the theme of the chapter devoted to Rousseau in Barni's *Les Martyrs de la libre-pensée* (1880), 230–56. The book is composed of lectures given in Geneva in the early 1860s.

[71] Barni, *Histoire des Idées*, 223.

[72] Ibid. 259.

[73] See Jean-Marie Goulemot and Eric Walter, 'Les Centenaires de Voltaire et Rousseau: Les Deux Lampions des Lumières', in Pierre Nora (ed.), *Les Lieux de mémoire* (1997), i. 351–82. Between 1878 and 1912 (the bicentenary of his birth), Goulemot and Walter argue, Rousseau acquired 'the status of a great national writer' who had devoted his life to 'the triumph of French culture'.

know', he went on, 'to which Jean-Jacques Rousseau [this statue] has been raised: whether it be the author of *Emile* or the author of *La Nouvelle Héloise* or the author of *Du Contrat social,* but it is to the incomparable writer, to one of the masters of our language, that the Académie Française dedicates it.'[74]

Rousseau was thus domesticated, removed from the political passions his writings had done so much to foster during the nineteenth century. In the same way that the language of rights and of liberty was detached from the threat of tyranny and of dictatorship and that compromises were made by republicans over the constitution, so too the radical dimensions of Rousseauian thinking were now underplayed, bequeathing a Rousseau made more palatable to a Republic which appeared to prize stability and order above all. Yet, in truth, the enigma remained. As we have seen, the experience of the French Revolution had been such as to convince many of Rousseau's readers that his doctrine of the social contract and the general will had merely transposed the absolutism of government onto another plane, producing a catastrophe without precedent. Exactly how and why this might have happened was what continued to intrigue and horrify his many readers. There was no clear answer to this conundrum. Moreover, what made both this fascination with Rousseau and the extent of his impact all the more remarkable, as Bertrand de Jouvenel commented as long ago as 1947, was that virtually everything Rousseau believed in had since been either 'rejected or condemned' by the evolution of society. As Jouvenel pointed out, Rousseau preferred 'the countryside to the town, agriculture to commerce, simplicity to luxury, the equality of citizens in an unsophisticated economy to their inequality in a complex economy, direct solidarity between men whose interests were the same to indirect solidarity between men whose different interests were complementary'.[75] The world described and desired by Rousseau, in other words, had become increasingly removed from the realities of French society.

V

The general outline of Rousseau's anti-modernist argument was clearly visible in *Du Contrat social,* but the groundwork for this position had been laid in his earlier discourses and in his response to the criticisms these had engendered. According to Rousseau, the first source of evil was inequality. From this had arisen riches. From riches were born luxury and idleness. Out of luxury came the fine arts. Out of idleness came the sciences.[76] Rousseau's opinion was that, as everything beyond what was absolutely necessary was a 'source of evil', it would be 'exceedingly imprudent' to multiply our needs.[77]

---

[74] Jules Simon, *Inauguration de la Statue de Jean-Jacques Rousseau: Le dimanche, 3 Fevrier 1889* (1889).

[75] Bertrand de Jouvenal, 'Essai sur la politique de Rousseau', preface to Jean-Jacques Rousseau, *Du contrat social* (1992), 124.

[76] 'Observations by Jean-Jacques of Geneva', in Rousseau, *The Discourses and Other Early Political Writings* (Cambridge, 1997), 45.

[77] 'Last Reply', in Rousseau, ibid. 84. See Renato Gallieni, *Rousseau, le luxe et l'idéologie nobiliare: Étude socio-historique* (Oxford, 1989).

This, as Rousseau readily recognized, had turned out not to be the case. From a situation where, in the state of nature, the inequality existing among men had been 'scarcely perceptible' had arisen a 'nascent inequality' which had not only come to characterize civil society in general but which had also given rise 'to the most horrible state of war'.[78] Men were consumed by ambition and jealousy. Competition, rivalry, and conflict of interest defined their relations with each other. 'Savage man and civilised man', Rousseau told his readers,

> differ so much in their inmost heart and inclinations that what constitutes the supreme happiness of the one would reduce the other to despair. The first breathes nothing else but repose and freedom. . . . By contrast, the Citizen, forever active, sweats, scurries, constantly agonises in search of ever more strenuous occupations . . . He courts the great whom he hates, and the rich whom he despises; he spares nothing to attain the honour of serving them.[79]

Such was the sorry outcome of our enslavement to luxury and inequality.

The manner in which these ills could be rectified was set out in the third of Rousseau's famous discourses, the *Discours sur l'économie politique*, published in Diderot and d'Alembert's *Encyclopédie* in 1755.[80] The guiding principle was that 'the first and most important rule of legitimate or popular government . . . is . . . to follow in everything the general will'. From this Rousseau set out what he described as a series of general rules of political economy, the second of which included the prescription that citizens must be taught to be good. This, however, was not possible if society remained subject to division and 'the tyranny of the rich'. Therefore, Rousseau stated, 'it is one of the most important functions of government to prevent extreme inequalities of fortune'. This was to be done 'not by taking away wealth from its possessors, but by depriving all men of the means to accumulate it; not by building hospitals for the poor but by securing citizens from being poor'.

Rousseau sketched out how this was to be done in some detail. If 'the right to property is the most sacred of all the rights of citizenship', by the same token, 'the distribution of provisions, money and merchandise in just proportions . . . is the true secret of finance'. Taxes thus became primarily not a means of raising revenue for the State but of constructing a just society. Where then should taxes fall?: 'on the productions of the frivolous and all too lucrative arts, on the importation of all pure luxuries, and in general on all objects of luxury'. To this was added an extensive list of items which were to be taxed out of existence. These would include: servants in livery, carriages, rich furniture, fine clothes, spacious courts and gardens, public entertainments of all kinds, as well as useless professions such as dancers, singers, and actors.

---

[78] 'Discourse on the Origin and Foundations of Inequality among Men', in Rousseau, *Discourses*, 113–88.
[79] Ibid. 186–7.
[80] 'Discourse on Political Economy', in Rousseau, *Social Contract*, 3–38.

How such a society might operate in the contemporary world was described in Rousseau's reflections on the projected reformation of the government of Poland.[81] If the Poles were to escape from their present situation of anarchy and to enjoy free and just government they needed to choose an economic system based upon agriculture and the arts necessary for life. If they did so, Rousseau speculated, 'Luxury and indigence will sensibly disappear together, and the Citizens cured of the frivolous tastes opulence fosters and of the vices associated with poverty, will place their cares and their glory in serving the fatherland well, and find their happiness in their duties.'[82] Eliminating all luxury, Rousseau conceded, was an extremely difficult undertaking and it could not be rooted out solely through sumptuary laws. It had to be extinguished from men's hearts and this could only be done through the acquisition of healthier and nobler tastes. Thus every young Pole was to be subject to a civic education, his eyes firmly fixed upon the fatherland and his body acquainted with regular physical exercise. The intention would be to accustom each child 'to rule, to equality, to fraternity, to competitions, to living under the eyes of their fellow citizens and to seeking public approbation'.[83]

In summary, Rousseau provided a comprehensive indictment of a society based upon inequality and one where the pursuit and enjoyment of luxury had replaced a simple life lived according to the dictates of virtue. We had lost our innocence and our morals. We were slaves to vice. The poor grovelled in their misery whilst the idle rich were honoured for their possession of superfluous opulence. In our fellow human beings we saw only competitors and 'everyone pretends to be working for the profit or reputation of the rest, while only seeking to raise his own above theirs and at their expense'.[84]

To his own satisfaction at least, Rousseau had proved that this had not been so in our original state. Selfishness had not always been the engine of human behaviour. Love of oneself (*amour de soi*) had been replaced by self-love (*amour propre*) and it had been out of this transformation that had merged the activity of commerce. It was only in modern, commercial societies that calculations of self-interest drove and determined the actions of individuals.[85]

We catch a glimpse of the importance attached by Rousseau to the argument against commerce and luxury if we consider his response to the writings of the now little-known Jean-François Melon. In 1734 Melon published his *Essai politique sur le commerce*.[86] At the time it achieved a level of notoriety for the simple reason that,

---

[81] 'Considerations on the Government of Poland and on its Projected Reform', ibid. 177–269. Rousseau also sketches out a response to this corruption of society in his constitution for Corsica. Corsica was to remain a predominantly agrarian society where barter would replace money as a form of exchange and where commercial activity and international trade would be kept to a minimum. There would be no division of labour.

[82] Ibid. 229.

[83] Ibid. 191.

[84] 'Preface to "Narcissus"', in Rousseau, *Discourses*, 100.

[85] See Pierre Force, *Self-Interest Before Adam Smith: A Genealogy of Economic Science* (Cambridge. 2003), 34–47.

[86] Publ. originally in 1734, references are to the edn. in Osnabrück, 1966. Born in Tulle in 1675 Melon occupied a variety of governmental functions, acting as secretary to the financier John Law. He died in 1738.

in addition to an advocacy of a set of mercantilist measures, it contained a chapter unambiguously praising the benefits of the pursuit and enjoyment of luxury.[87] According to Melon, if commerce could be defined as 'the exchange of the superfluous for what is necessary',[88] then luxury was 'an extraordinary sumptuousness which flows from wealth and the security provided by government'. Yet, luxury could be given no precise meaning, because desires were 'relative to time and persons'. Furthermore, Melon disputed the claim that luxury encouraged immorality, contending that it had certain moral benefits: most notably, it was the 'destroyer of sloth and idleness'. Melon was also eager to point out the futility of seeking to regulate luxury out of existence. With Rousseau's Geneva clearly in mind, he commented that such a society more resembled 'a community of recluses than a society of free men'. He similarly disputed the efficacy of sumptuary laws, believing them fundamentally flawed in both design and intention. Crucially, such laws disregarded the human motive of emulation.

From this followed a key claim and one that brought Melon's argument close to that of Bernard Mandeville's renowned *The Fable of the Bees* of 1714. 'What does it matter to a state', Melon asked, 'if through foolish vanity an individual is ruined by vying with the retinue of a neighbour?' Ruin was a punishment well-deserved, but the only outcomes of a legislator seeking to prevent such behaviour would be to reduce the workers to 'dangerous idleness', 'restrict liberty', and take away a motive for industry. Why, he went on, should extravagant expenditure be damned? What concern was it of ours if someone paid an excessive price for frivolous objects? Unspent, this money would remain 'dead to society'. Used in the pursuit of luxury, it paid the gardener, fed and clothed his children, and encouraged him to work with an eye to a better future. Given away as charity to beggars, that same money would only encourage their debauchery. On this view, therefore, the pursuit of luxury produced benefits for society as a whole and contributed to the well-being of the State.

Melon was neither the first nor the last to write about the subject of luxury.[89] The word 'luxe' entered the French language in 1606 as the synonym for 'superfluity'. In 1694, the *Dictionnaire de l'Académie Française* tied its meaning to that of 'excess', with an implied note of moral condemnation.[90] At this time, criticism of luxury largely focused upon the lavish expenditure of the court at Versailles, as was testified by Fénelon's abidingly popular text *Les Aventures de Télémaque*, with its praise of simplicity, labour, and the virtues of agriculture.[91] Kings, Fénelon contended, might be poisoned by excessive authority but luxury empoisoned an entire nation and, as such, it was 'almost incurable'. Yet, by the mid-century,

---

[87] Ibid. 742–9.

[88] Ibid. 709. See Michael Cardy, 'Le "Nécessaire" et le "superflu"', *Studies in Voltaire and the Eighteenth Century* (Oxford, 1982), ccv. 183–90.

[89] See Christopher J. Berry, *The Idea of Luxury: A Conceptual and Historical Investigation* (Cambridge, 1994), 126–76, and Maxine Berg and Elizabeth Eger (eds.), *Luxury in the Eighteenth Century: Debates, Desires and Delectable Goods* (Houndmills, 2003).

[90] Philippe Perrot, *Le Luxe: Une richesse entre faste et confort XVIIIe—XIXe siècle* (1995), 34 n. 2.

[91] François de Fénelon, *Telemachus* (Cambridge, 1994).

censure had extended beyond the aristocratic culture of the court to embrace a series of broader concerns relating to the activity of consumption itself and its impact upon the whole fabric of French society. The increase in commercial prosperity was associated with a growing materialism that brought with it a series of ills, not the least of which was taken to be a confusion of ranks.[92] Moreover, the scale and intensity of the debate was quite astonishing. Daniel Roche has estimated that, in France alone, between 1736 and 1786 over 100 texts were published that dealt with the issue of luxury.[93]

Montesquieu, for example, rejected the argument against luxury in letter 106 of his *Lettres persanes* and he returned to the theme at some length in *De l'Esprit des lois*, devoting much of book 7 to the examination of sumptuary laws in republics and monarchies and book 20 to the relationship of laws to commerce.[94] Diderot also took up the theme of luxury, most notably in his *Observations sur le Nakaz*.[95] Here, however, the stress fell upon the benefits that accrued from the expenditure of the rich man. 'He makes his nation worth visiting for foreigners; he provides a livelihood for a large numbers of citizens who are consumers and who give a price to the fruits of the earth', Diderot wrote. Nevertheless, Diderot, like Montesquieu, also drew a distinction between good and bad luxury. If the latter united the vices of opulence and poverty, the former produced the flourishing of the sciences and prosperity for all. He also rejected the key claim of the physiocratic school that economies such as those of England which derived their wealth from trade, manufacturing, and the production of luxury goods rested upon unstable and 'sterile' foundations. As Diderot commented, 'the principle of the physiocrats, carried to excess, would condemn a nation to being no more than peasants'.[96]

Nevertheless, and as indicated by Rousseau himself, it was Melon who brought the subject of luxury to the fore. This is explained in part by the fact that when Voltaire published his controversial poem *Le Mondain*, he attached to his reply to his critics a letter written by Melon to the Comtesse de Verrue.[97] The Comtesse de Verrue was there cited by Melon as an example of the wisdom of his doctrine that luxury was necessary for the circulation of money and the maintenance of industry. Further controversy arose because Voltaire openly indicated his preference for the modern world over a Garden of Eden characterized by physical austerity. The rich, Voltaire argued, were born to spend their money and the poor were there to receive

---

[92] Sarah Maza, *The Myth of the French Bourgeoisie: An Essay on the Social Imaginary, 1750–1850* (Cambridge, Mass., 2003), 55.

[93] Roche, *Histoire des choses banales* (1997), 88.

[94] Montesquieu, *Persian Letters* (Harmondsworth, 1973), 193–6. See Catherine Larrère, 'Montesquieu on Economics and Commerce', in David W. Carrithers, Michael A. Mosher, and Paul A. Rahe (eds.), *Montesquieu's Science of Politics* (Lanham, Md., 2001), 335–74, and Roger Boesche, 'Fearing Monarchs and Merchants: Montesquieu's Two Theories of Despotism', *Western Political Quarterly*, 44 (1990), 741–61.

[95] Diderot, *Political Writings* (Cambridge, 1992), 124–5, 130–1.

[96] Ibid. 125.

[97] See *Œuvres complètes de Voltaire* (Oxford, 2003), xvi. 273–313. See Ellen Ross, 'Mandeville, Melon and Voltaire: The Origins of the Luxury Controversy in France', *Studies in Voltaire and the Eighteenth Century* (Oxford, 1976), clv. 1897–1912.

it. Colbert and Solomon, both of whom 'through luxury [had] enriched the state', rather than the classical heroes of Greece and Rome, were the objects of Voltaire's praise. Voltaire took up this theme on many subsequent occasions—his *Diction-naire philosophique*, for example, contained an entry on luxury—and he continued to refer favourably to Melon, citing him as 'a man of sense, a good citizen and an excellent philosopher'.[98]

It was however the Marquis de Saint-Lambert's who, in a long essay for the *Encyclopédie*, best set out the arguments both for and against luxury.[99] Six were cited in favour of luxury: luxury contributed to the growth of population; it enriched states; it facilitated the circulation of money; it softened manners and spread the private virtues; it was favourable to the advance of knowledge; and it increased the wealth and happiness of citizens. Against this were the arguments that luxury encouraged the decline of the 'useful' arts; it ruined the countryside; it led to depopulation; it produced a confusion of social ranks; and it weakened our sense of honour and our love of country. Saint-Lambert's text endeavoured to show that all of these assertions could be contradicted by the facts and thus that the effects of luxury—beneficial or otherwise—were relative to the situation in which it was to be found. 'In this regard', he wrote, 'luxury is for peoples what it is for individuals; the multitude of gratifications must be in keeping with the means to enjoy them.'[100]

Saint-Lambert was therefore clear in his own mind that the consequences of what he termed 'disordered luxury' were truly deleterious. Extreme cupidity and the pursuit of frivolous wealth induced a progressive decline. Subject to especial opprobrium were those who performed no function in society and the *nouveaux riches* who quickly became addicted to their idleness. In their desire to escape boredom they sought ever more indulgent and extraordinary forms of gratification. Intriguingly, Saint-Lambert here made reference to what he termed 'mad emulation'.

However, Saint-Lambert also detailed the conditions in which luxury could be of benefit to society as a whole. There would be no sudden fortunes. Extreme poverty and extreme wealth would be rare. Luxury would not be detached from usefulness. All classes would appreciate and enjoy the fine arts. Most importantly, 'luxury and the passions leading to it must be subordinated to a spirit of community and to the goods of the community'.[101] Governments, therefore, should not be indifferent to the manner through which people acquired their wealth and the way they chose to spend it. In particular, the well-being of one group of people could not be sacrificed for the well-being of another. Accordingly, the first objective had to be to put 'luxury back in order'. With the exception of controls on imported luxury goods, Saint-Lambert stipulated, this would not entail new sumptuary laws, nor would it require new agrarian laws or new divisions of property. It would be sufficient to end privileges in manufacturing, make state finance less lucrative, and to punish idleness. From this would follow the imperceptible increase and dispersion of both

---

[98] See *Œuvres complètes de Voltaire* (Oxford, 2003), xvi. 273–313. See Ellen Ross, 'Mandeville, Melon and Voltaire: The Origins of the Luxury Controversy in France', *Studies in Voltaire and the Eighteenth Century* (Oxford, 1976), clv. 276–81.

[99] See *Œuvres complètes de Diderot* (1821), xvii. 235–77.

[100] Ibid. 247.   [101] Ibid. 250.

wealth and luxury. As Saint-Lambert concluded, 'I beg my readers to rid themselves alike of the prejudices of Sparta and of Sybaris.'[102]

It is apparent from his text that Saint-Lambert was aware that the debate about luxury now took a predictable and standard form.[103] In particular Saint-Lambert mirrored the wider concern (evident also in the writings of Helvétius and Condillac) to distinguish between the good and bad uses of luxury and to specify that luxury could not be divorced from considerations of social utility. There was, however, no such measured response from Rousseau. In his 'Last Reply' to the criticisms directed at his *Discours sur les sciences et les arts* he made the following comment:

> It is true that up to now, luxury, although often prevalent, had at least at all times been viewed as a fatal source of infinitely many evils. It was left for M. Melon to be the first to publish the poisonous doctrine whose novelty brought him more followers than did the soundness of his reasoning. I am not afraid to be alone in my century to fight these odious maxims which only tend to destroy and to debase virtue, and to make for rich people and wretches, that is to say for wicked people in either event.[104]

Moreover, as the century proceeded, there was no lessening in the argument between the pro- and anti-luxury camps. Indeed, it would run right up to the outbreak of the Revolution itself, providing the critics of luxury in particular with powerful arguments with which to attack both the court and the leisured aristocracy. Indeed, as John Shovlin has shown, these debates help explain why the financial crisis that engulfed the monarchy played such an important role in determining the origins of the Revolution itself.[105]

Here we might cite two texts by way of supporting evidence. Butel-Dumont's *Théorie du luxe, ou traité dans lequel on entreprend d'établir que le luxe est un ressort non seulement utile mais même indispensablement nécessaire à la prospérité des États*,[106] and the Abbé Pluquet's *Traité philosophique et politique sur le luxe*.[107] Taking diametrically opposed views on the whole issue, the former was content to define luxury in morally neutral terms as those things which were 'superfluous' and not 'strictly necessary',[108] whilst the latter denounced it as 'the use of objects producing agreeable sensations considered necessary by man, although by the laws of nature the use of these objects and the agreeable sensations they produce are neither necessary or useful to life or health, nor necessary for the happiness of man'.[109] If Pluquet was to devote more than 900 pages to developing this theme, repeatedly disparaging the ideas of Melon, Bernard Mandeville, David Hume, and the other 'panegyrists of luxury' in the process, Butel-Dumont was content with a more modest 400 pages designed to prove his argument that the most powerful

---

[102] Ibid. 276.

[103] Berry, *Idea of Luxury*, 137.

[104] Rousseau, 'Last Reply', 84.

[105] Shovlin, *The Political Economy of Virtue: Luxury, Patriotism and the Origins of the French Revolution* (Ithaca, NY, 2006).

[106] (1771), 2 vols.

[107] (1786), 2 vols.

[108] Butel-Dumont, *Théorie du luxe*, i. 121.

[109] Pluquet, *Traité philosophique*, i. 79.

peoples and states were those that pursued luxury and that it was far better for states to reduce their expenditure than to impose 'inept' sumptuary laws.

To these texts can be added Gabriel Sénac de Meilhan's *Considérations sur les richesses et le luxe*,[110] published on the eve of the Revolution and intended as a detailed refutation of the ideas put forward by Jacques Necker in his *De l'Adminis-tration des finances de la France*.[111] Necker's argument had been that it was a mistake to attribute luxury uniquely to changes in morals, the nature of govern-ment, or the acquisition of the New World. Luxury had its origin 'in the natural course of things', and specifically in 'the advancement of science' and, at best, government could temper the taste for it. In response, the greater part of the almost 500 pages of Sénac de Meilhan's text was devoted to the wholesale castigation of the political, social, and moral consequences of luxury. Great states preserved them-selves not because of, but despite, their luxury. 'The immortal author of *Téléma-que*', he wrote, 'better understood and made known the problems arising from luxury than most of those who have explored the subject.'[112]

Published only three years earlier, Antoine-Prosper Lottin's *Discours contre le luxe: Il corrompt les moeurs et détruit les Empires*,[113] began by announcing that combating luxury was 'the most important and patriotic of subjects', and then proceeded, in addition to pillorying 'the eternal inconstancy of fashions' and the reduction of society to a 'perpetual ball', to itemize how luxury destroyed the arts, the sciences, letters, industry, agriculture, public morals, and manners, before finally destroying empires themselves. Citing Montesquieu and the example of the decline of the Spanish Empire, Lottin contended that wealth did not guarantee the greatness of a state. Rather this lay in a people devoted to agriculture and the 'useful arts' and one imbued with a sense of virtue and courage. For these writers, in summary, the luxury debate was certainly no frivolous and ephemeral matter of taste and fashion but one of the most important and far-reaching questions of the age. At issue was nothing less than the fate of the absolute monarchy and the aristocratic order.

It was, of course, a perpetual refrain in the writings of Rousseau that he alone had correctly observed the maladies of the age and that he alone was inspired by a love of humanity that was so strong that he was obliged to speak out. Everyone else, he believed, spoke only of 'commerce and money'. As we have seen, this was not true and Rousseau was by no means alone in his condemnation of luxury. But, for once perhaps, Rousseau might be excused his rhetorical excesses, for it was indeed the case that writers in France, and elsewhere in Europe, were beginning to grapple with issues relating to trade, to finance, and to the market in a way that they had not done previously.[114] Did the advent of the French

---

[110] (1787).
[111] Jacques Necker, *De l'Administration des Finances de la France* (1784). Vol. iii 57–75 is devoted to 'Considérations sur le luxe et sur le progrès'.
[112] Sénac de Meilhan, *Considérations sur les richesses*, 174.
[113] (1783).
[114] See Henry C. Clark, *Compass of Society: Commerce and Absolutism in Old-Regime France* (Lanham, Md., 2007).

Revolution and the fall of the Jacobins, we might therefore ask, elicit a change of attitude towards luxury in particular and towards commerce more generally?

The Abbé Sieyès, principal ideologue and architect of the first stage of the Revolution, had been fully aware that the distinctive feature of modern society was that it rested upon the division of labour, an insight which he applied to his understanding of both politics and economics.[115] 'If', he wrote, 'every individual concerned himself with all the objects required for his own consumption, all individuals would be the same, and society would not depart from its state of infancy.'[116] This, he contended, was no longer the case as men now thought about production rather than happiness. Where Sieyès therefore diverged from the physiocratic school was in his conclusion that there was no fundamental difference in productive potential between agriculture and manufacturing and thus that the exclusive focus of the physiocrats upon the former was misplaced. From this it followed that the privileged position accorded to the aristocracy through the ownership of land had to be removed and that anti-commercial prejudices, most obviously associated with extravagance of the court and the idleness of the nobility, had to be eradicated.

Between the summer of 1789 and 1791 it was in this direction that France moved and, to that extent, the dominant tendency of the numerous reforms introduced in this period was broadly favourable to the further development of commerce and free trade. The ambition was not only to pay off France's enormous public debt but also to secure the economic regeneration of the country. To that end, the feudal regime, with its restrictions upon the free movement of goods and persons, was abolished. Property rather than privilege was established as the basis of the new order and came to define a person's status. The *loi Le Chapelier* of 1791 made illegal all forms of restrictive trade corporations. But, as events were to show, this did not mean that concerns about the potentially damaging consequences of gross inequality and unbridled luxury or about the need to balance wealth and virtue had been abandoned. Amidst fears of a complete economic breakdown, the radical demands of the Parisian populace and of the *enragés* saw to that.

As we already know, the advent of foreign war and internal revolt opened the door to a revival of the rhetoric of classical republicanism. With this came not only a return to the notion of the virtuous, frugal citizen-farmer of ancient Greece and Rome but also a victory for the claims of austerity and simplicity over those of ostentation and display. Moreover, in the face of food shortages and famine, the reintroduction of economic controls during 1793–4 amounted to 'the economy of the Terror'.[117] National price ceilings were introduced for grain and flour, and to these were later

[115] See William H. Sewell Jr, *A Rhetoric of Bourgeois Revolution: The Abbé Sieyès and What is the Third Estate?* (Durham, NC, and London, 1994). Sewell writes: 'Virtually all of Sieyès's political thought had an important economic dimension.... Sieyès rejected not only Rousseau's ideas about representation but the entire classical model of Greek and Roman political virtue on which it was based; he argued that material well-being, not political virtue, was the proper goal of a modern European State.' Ibid. 67.

[116] Roberto Zapperi (ed.), *Emmanuel-Joseph Sieyès: Écrits Politiques* (1985), 63.

[117] Judith A. Miller, *Mastering the Market: The State and the Grain Trade in Northern France, 1700–1860* (Cambridge, 1999), 155.

added price controls on all 'goods of first necessity' including such products as onions, soap, and paper. The General Maximum, introduced in September 1793, was, according to Colin Jones and Rebecca Spang, a 'shibboleth of overt consumer renunciation', providing 'a snapshot of what Revolutionary Government regarded as prime necessities'.[118] Envisaged was an alternative political economy based upon the satisfaction of needs rather than the production of luxuries. Its guiding spirit was to be fraternity rather than competition. Yet, by the same token, Jones and Spang argue, the General Maximun 'was a shimmeringly indeterminate document', revealing that '[d]espite their best attempts to look and sound like Athenians and Romans, the French found it altogether more difficult than their classical forbears to draw a hard-and-fast line betweens the realms of necessity and luxury'. Denouncing luxury, in other words, was easy but defining it proved well-nigh impossible, and constructing an economic policy upon the basis of its eradication quickly showed itself to be both catastrophic and repressive.

Thus, with the fall of the Jacobins, the General Maximum was abolished in December 1794 and an (often faltering) attempt was made to fashion something resembling a commercial republic more in tune with the demands and interests of the emerging industrial and mercantile elites. Yet it would be a mistake to believe that reflections on the nature of commercial activity were suddenly divested of moral and political concerns and thus that the question of luxury was now forgotten altogether.[119] Indeed, as Martin Staum has argued, 'concepts of public virtue remained indelibly linked to economic theory despite efforts to construct a value-neutral science based on private interest'.[120]

This can be shown by referring to the ideas of the best-known French economist of the time: Jean-Baptiste Say. He has usually been regarded as a classical political economist who uncritically embraced and popularized the ideas of Adam Smith. Pierre Manent, for example, states that his *Traité d'économie politique*, first published in 1803, 'constitutes the first great post-Smithian synthesis of economic liberalism'.[121] A somewhat different story might be told.

In 1800 Say published a curious text entitled *Olbie*.[122] It was an account of a utopian city recently established upon 'the ruins of an absolute monarchy' and was intended to answer a question that had previously fascinated the writers of the Enlightenment and that had now become especially pertinent in light of the events of the previous decade: by what means could morality be established among a people? The text itself covered a variety of issues. For example, Say argued that

---

[118] Colin Jones and Rebecca Spang, 'Sans-Culottes, *Sans Café, Sans Tabac*: Shifting Realms of Necessity and Luxury in Eighteenth-Century France', in Maxine Berg and Helen Clifford (eds.), *Consumers and Luxury: Consumer Culture in Europe, 1650–1850* (Manchester, 1999), 55.

[119] For a discussion of attempts to formulate a new republican political economy during Thermidor see James Livesey, *Making Democracy in the French Revolution* (Cambridge, Mass., 2001).

[120] See Martin S. Staum, *Minerva's Message: Stabilizing the French Revolution* (Montreal and Kingston, 1996), 192. See also Cheryl B. Welch, *Liberty and Utility: The French Idéologues and the Transformation of Liberalism* (New York, 1984), 70–96.

[121] Pierre Manent, *Les Libéraux* (1986), ii. 182.

[122] Jean-Baptiste Say, *Olbie, ou Essai sur les moyens de réformer les Moeurs d'une Nation* (1800).

lotteries should be banned because they not only encouraged 'avarice' and 'laziness' but also reinforced the belief that wealth depended upon chance rather than 'industrie'.[123] But, in essence, what Say described was a society characterized by 'modest comfort' rather than 'the excesses of wealth and of indigence'. 'The Olbiens', Say wrote, 'knew that the love of gain was a snare as dangerous as idleness. When this passion is very strong it becomes as exclusive as all the others; it extinguishes a mass of noble and disinterested sentiments which must be a part of the perfect human soul. It is thus that amongst certain peoples, or even amongst the habitants of certain towns, who are too much involved with commerce any idea, other than that of enriching oneself, is regarded as folly.'[124] Accordingly, in Say's account, the leaders of the Olbiens declared their opposition to displays of luxury, themselves adopting a 'system of simplicity' and forbidding their servants and soldiers from showing a 'stupid deference for luxurious livery'. As the taste for luxury diminished, the Olbiens came to consume nothing beyond what was necessary for their utility and comfort. Happiness grew at the same time as morals were reformed.[125]

In a note to this part of the text, Say clarified what he took to be the import of his argument. 'In criticizing luxury', he wrote, 'I would not insist on the foolish pretension of returning man to a savage state where there are no utensils but fingers and teeth.' The use of everything that was conducive to well-being in 'rich and industrious nations' should be allowed but, he continued, 'I do not hesitate to pronounce that luxury is harmful to states, large and small, and that the country where there is least would be the richest and the most happy.'[126] For that reason Say denied two of the main claims made in defence of luxury. The production of luxury did not provide jobs. There were, he countered, 'never fewer unemployed hands than in regions where morals are simple and where, by consequence, few luxuries are produced'.[127] Nor did luxury keep people alive. It was, Say argued, 'only in a country where there is no luxury, or very little, that one sees everyone well-dressed, well-housed, well-nourished, and content'.[128] It was in line with this argument that copious praise was heaped upon Lycurgus and the institutions of Sparta, whilst the fates of Carthage, Venice, and the Dutch Republic were cited as examples of the dire consequences which followed from the exclusive concentration upon the pursuit of wealth.

Conventional wisdom has had it that the transition from *Olbie* to the *Traité d'économie politique*, published only three years later, represented a shift from a republican political economy to a *laissez-faire* liberalism based on the inviolability of private property and minimum state activity. This account has been contested by Richard Whatmore.[129] While Whatmore has not wished to deny that innovations occurred in Say's thinking—Say, for example, no longer believed that a republican

---

[123] Ibid. 34–5.   [124] Ibid. 29.   [125] Ibid. 42–4.
[126] Ibid. 123.   [127] Ibid. 125–6.   [128] Ibid. 126.
[129] See Richard Whatmore, *Republicanism and the French Revolution: An Intellectual Biography of Jean-Baptiste Say* (Oxford, 2000). See also Evelyn L. Forget, *The Social Economics of Jean-Baptiste Say* (London, 1999). Forget's text includes a tr. of Say's *Olbie*: see pp. 196–241.

constitution was necessary for the inculcation of industrious manners nor did he retain his faith in legislation as a form of moral catechism—he nevertheless holds to the view that Say remained deeply concerned about the deleterious consequences of commerce as described by Adam Smith—not least what he took to be the impoverishment of the general population which would follow from the overzealous introduction of the division of labour—and for all his emphasis upon the importance of productive capital as the source of a nation's wealth he continued to disparage the unbridled pursuit of needless luxury.

Specifically, we should note that in his lengthy *Discours Préliminaire* (an astonishing text which not only proclaimed the autonomy of economic science but also reviewed all previous economic doctrines) Say dismissed the maxim that 'a state is enriched by luxury', further contending that its application in the France of the 1720s had led to bankruptcy. 'Moderation and economy', he commented, 'became terms of ridicule.'[130] This anti-luxury theme was then developed in the main body of the text. In line with his preference for frugality over excess and avarice, Say began by arguing that '[t]hose who say that money is only good to be spent and that products are only made to be consumed are badly mistaken if by this they mean solely expenditure and consumption devoted to securing pleasure'.[131] According to Say, luxury was a form of ostentation designed primarily to dazzle and impress others. Most importantly, it was a form of 'unproductive consumption', and as such directed resources away from 'reproductive expenditure'. There was no merit in consuming everything one could, Say concluded, only in consuming what was reasonable.

This was no minor matter, as it related to one of the central conclusions reached by Say. What later became known as Say's Law stipulated that total demand in an economy could not exceed or fall below total supply in that economy. As he himself expressed it, 'products are paid for by products', and not by consumption. Into what kind of error, he asked therefore, 'have fallen those who, seeing generally that production always equals consumption (because it is necessary that what is consumed should have been produced), have mistaken the effect for the cause, have conjectured that unproductive consumption alone brings about reproduction, that saving is directly contrary to public prosperity and that the most useful citizen is the one who spends the most.'[132] If this truth was demonstrated by economic theory, it was likewise proven by history. Poverty, Say wrote, 'always follows in the wake of luxury'. Do not be fooled, he counselled: a country in decline gives for a time 'the image of opulence', but it can never last and inevitably comes to an end. 'Those people', Say concluded, 'who, through their great power or talents, seek to spread the taste for luxury, therefore, conspire against the happiness of nations.'[133] For Say, the challenge was to find a means of reconciling the virtues of frugality and industry with commerce.

That Say's concerns about luxury were no isolated preoccupation can be easily shown by reference to the work of the most important of the political theorists

---

[130] *Traité d'Economie Politique*, in *Collection des Principaux Economistes* (Osnabrück, 1966), ix. 22–3.
[131] Ibid. 454.   [132] Ibid. 459.   [133] Ibid. 462.

associated with the French *Idéologues*, Antoine-Louis-Claude Destutt de Tracy. Destutt de Tracy discussed luxury at length in two of his most important texts: his *Commentaire sur l'Esprit des lois de Montesquieu* and the *Traité d'économie politique*.[134] There were many intriguing elements to his argument. First, Destutt de Tracy provided an account of the origin of private property that was the very antithesis of that provided by Rousseau. The concepts *yours* and *mine* were never invented because they derived from the faculty of our will. Second, the will was defined in terms of the desire to maximize pleasure and to minimize pain, thus placing us under a duty to satisfy our needs 'without any extraneous consideration'. Nevertheless Destutt de Tracy stood back from concluding that all consumption was inherently good, and he did so because the force of his argument was to be repeatedly directed against those he disparaged as *les oisifs*. 'Consumption', he wrote, 'varies greatly according to the type of consumer as well as according to the nature of the things consumed'.[135]

Accordingly, Destutt de Tracy's fulminations against luxury bore a marked resemblance to the criticisms pronounced by Say. Luxury consisted essentially in 'non-productive expenditures'. It was wrong to believe that the increase of luxury would enrich a nation. It did not favour commerce and encourage industry by quickening the circulation of money. Rather it changed the nature of that circulation and 'made it less useful'. It created only 'a fleeting pleasure'. Only if the alternative was to bury one's money in the ground did it make sense to spend it in this way. 'I believe myself entitled to conclude', Destutt de Tracy wrote, 'that, in economic terms, luxury is always an evil, a continuous cause of misery and weakness. Its true consequence is continuously to destroy, through the excessive consumption of some, the product of the work and industry of others.'[136]

If Say's argument stopped at this point, Destutt de Tracy pressed on, further contending that luxury was 'an even greater evil' from a moral point of view. It thrived on vanity and encouraged frivolity. In women it led to depravity and in men to avarice, and in both 'to a lack of delicacy and probity'. And it produced 'these sad effects, not only amongst those who enjoyed it, but also upon all those who admired it and who served to provide it'. Moreover, Destutt de Tracy found himself agreeing with Montesquieu's original contention that luxury was appropriate to monarchies, adding that representative governments had no need to pander to 'the natural tendency of man to give himself up to superfluous expenditure'. Did this mean, therefore, that governments, in whose interest it was to combat the advance of luxury, should resort to sumptuary laws? Not only, Destutt de Tracy replied, were they an abuse of authority and an attack on property, but they served no purpose

> when the spirit of vanity is not incessantly excited by all institutions; when the misery and ignorance of the lowest class are not so great as to encourage a stupid admiration for ostentation; when the opportunities to make fast and excessive fortunes are rare; when wealth is dispersed promptly through the equal division of inheritance; when

---

[134] *Commentaire sur l'Esprit des lois de Montesquieu* (1819) and *Traité d'économie politique* (1823), 232–65.

[135] Ibid. 243.

[136] Destutt de Tracy, *Commentaire*, 96–7.

finally everything leads us in another direction and towards real pleasures; in a word, when society is well-ordered.

There, he concluded, were 'the true means to combat luxury'.[137]

It has been suggested that the concept of luxury ceased to be a central concept of economic analysis in the nineteenth century. In his otherwise admirable book, Philippe Perrot repeats the earlier claim of Serge Latouche that the concept did not figure in any of the four major dictionaries of political economy published in France during the nineteenth century.[138] This is simply incorrect. There is an entry on luxury in Charles Ganilh's *Dictionnaire analytique d'économie politique* of 1826[139] and in Sandelin's *Répertoire général d'économie politique ancienne et moderne* of 1847.[140] The same entry by Courcelle-Seneuil figured in both the Coquelin and Guillaumin dictionary of 1852 and the dictionary edited by Léon Say and Joseph Chailley of 1892. Moreover, only the entry penned by Ganilh disclosed an indifference to the social and psychological consequences of luxury. Sandelin concluded that luxury went hand in hand with the 'depravity' of morals, whilst Courcelle-Seneuil wrote that, '[w]ith regard to luxury, the teachings of political economy fully confirm those of morality'.[141] It would be wrong therefore to conclude that, as the French economy took its first significant steps towards industrialization, the moral critique of luxury disappeared altogether from view.

Unsurprisingly, it was evident in much of the literature of Utopian socialism, where there was frequently displayed the hope that the workers would avoid a taste for opulence and ostentation and would limit their consumption to the satisfaction of 'real' needs. This was certainly the view of no less a figure than Pierre-Joseph Proudhon (who contended that the errors of socialism, be it 'epicurean or ascetic', derived from 'a false conception of value') as it was also that of Étienne Cabet. It was similarly to be found in the work of the most prominent legitimist political economist of the day, Alban de Villeneuve-Bargemont, most notably in his *Economie politique chrétienne, ou Recherches sur la Nature et les Causes du Paupérisme en France et en Europe et sur les Moyens de le soulager et de le prévenir*.[142] Other examples could be cited with relative ease.

Of greater significance was the fact that the moral critique of luxury continued to be articulated by nineteenth-century republicans. We can see this quite clearly by returning our attention to Renouvier's *Manuel Républicain de l'Homme et du*

---

[137] Destutt de Tracy, *Commentaire*, 112.

[138] See Perrot, *Le Luxe*, 38, and Serge Latouche, 'Luxe et économie', *Revue de MAUSS*, 16 (1985), 71–2.

[139] (1826), 270–80.

[140] (The Hague, 1847), iv. 400–3.

[141] Charles Coquelin and Gilbert-Urbain Guillaumin, *Dictionnaire de l'Économie Politique* (Paris, 1852), ii. 109–12, and Léon Say and Joseph Chailley, *Nouveaux Dictionnaire de l'Économie Politique* (Paris, 1892), ii. 191–4. Courcelle-Seneuil was a leading member of the so-called *laissez-faire ultras* or Paris group. The above-cited dictionaries also had entries on sumptuary law and discussions of luxury in relation to taxation.

[142] (1834). See also Villeneuve-Bargemont's *Histoire de l'Économie Politique ou Études Historiques, Philosophiques et Religieuse sur l'Économie Politique* (1841), 2 vols.

Citoyen.[143] As we have seen, Renouvier sought to define the rights and liberties to be enjoyed by the citizen of the Republic. Towards the end of his text, and after having discussed the importance of the sentiment of fraternity, he turned his thoughts to the desirability or otherwise of luxury.[144] You speak, Renouvier had his student interlocutor remark, of the 'levelling of conditions' but in such circumstances, he inquires, what would become of luxury and those who lived off its production? Was it not the case, he goes on to ask, that great wealth 'spent ostentatiously serves at least to maintain workers'? Renouvier's reply was to accept that at present the luxury of the rich provided a livelihood for the poor, but he then added that the poor would only die of hunger if the abolition of luxury was not accompanied by an acknowledgement of the right to work. Accompanied by such a reform, the worker would pass from the production of luxury goods to the production of something of use and of practical value. In addition, the 'idler' who had previously paid for luxury would now turn his reduced resources to the production of something useful. Was luxury to be abolished altogether? There was, Renouvier contended (thereby echoing the very arguments deployed in its favour at the height of the 1789 Revolution),[145] a place for 'collective luxury' in the shape of libraries, theatres, museums, and so on, all of which could be regarded as expressions of fraternity. There was even a place for luxury in the hands of private individuals; but such luxury was scandalous when so many people were denied the necessities of life. 'In a Republic', Renouvier wrote, 'where the solidarity between men is recognized, I find it repugnant that luxury should spread before ease of circumstance has been attained and that the caprices of men should be satisfied whilst the needs of others cry out before Providence.'[146] To this was then added two familiar refrains. He trembled, Renouvier declared, when he thought of those nations—in particular of England—whose wealth and prosperity consisted in the perfect comfort of a few thousand families whose actions condemned millions to live on bare necessities. Second, the greater majority of rich people were 'enervated' by luxury, 'debased' by dissolute living, and 'consumed' by boredom. However, this was 'just punishment' for those who had sought 'the refinement' of their lives through 'the exploitation of their brothers'. It was only in 'an age of corruption', Renouvier declared, that such behaviour was not condemned. 'Nothing is beautiful, nothing is noble', he remarked, 'that is not also useful.'

Arguments against luxury, forcibly articulated in the eighteenth century, clearly retained much of their vitality and vigour amongst republican opinion. Not only this but, as Renouvier's text testifies, they occupied an important position in the ferment of ideas that followed the fall of the July Monarchy and the establishment of the Second Republic. To extend this argument further we would need to look more closely at the study of political economy as it developed in the latter half of the nineteenth century. As fascinating and as tempting as this

---

[143] (1904).
[144] Ibid. 265–80.
[145] See Perrot, *Le Luxe*, 80.
[146] Renouvier, *Manuel Républicain*, 269.

would be, it is unfortunately not possible here. What can be established, however, is that the early decades of the Third Republic saw something akin to the democratization of consumption—exemplified above all by the opening of the first of Paris's great department stores—and that, in this context, there were some who were prepared to reconceptualize luxury as the search for comfort and convenience rather than a taste for selfish indulgence and ostentation. In this less aristocratic and less harmful form, luxury could be defended as a stimulus to manufacturing and the arts and, as the economist Paul Leroy-Beaulieu argued in 1894, as 'one of the principal agents of human progress'.[147] Nevertheless, it was not only conservative traditionalists who continued to worry about the dangers of material prosperity.[148] Republicans too remained deeply troubled at the thought of a market where the rules of social justice did not apply and where conspicuous and unregulated consumption was considered to be the norm. The analysis of the condition of *anomie* provided by Émile Durkheim would be a case in point. If this anxiety did not necessarily entail an attempted revival and recall of the virtues of austerity and self-denial, it did encourage the search for a new moral principle capable of placing restraints upon the workings of a market society. The doctrine of *solidarité*, discussed at the end of the previous chapter, performed this function admirably.[149] By way of conclusion, therefore, we might care to reflect upon the enduring quality of Rousseauian arguments against luxury (and by extension, of republican hostility to the commercial model embodied by England). That this was so tells us much about the difficulties faced by those who sought to see France embrace the values and practices of a commercial society.

[147] 'Le Luxe: La fonction de la richesse', *Revue des Deux Mondes,* 126 (1894), 72–100, 547–73. In its attempt to summarize all the arguments for and against luxury, the article by Leroy-Beaulieu recalls the earlier essay of Saint-Lambert.

[148] See Victoria E. Thompson, *The Virtuous Marketplace: Women and Men, Money and Politics in Paris, 1830–1870* (Baltimore, Md., 2000).

[149] See Rosalind H. Williams, *Dream Worlds: Mass Consumption in Late Nineteenth-Century France* (Berkeley and Los Angeles, Calif., 1982).

4

Commerce, Usurpation, and Democracy

I

'Voltaire discovered England; Voltaire discovered commerce': thus writes Daniel Roche at the beginning of his analysis of what he terms 'the kingdom of exchange'.[1] What this discovery meant for Voltaire was enthusiastically expressed in his *Lettres philosophiques*, published in 1734.[2] 'Commerce', Voltaire wrote, 'which has enriched the citizens of England, has contributed to making them free, and this liberty has extended commerce in its turn'.[3] Not only this but 'an Englishman, being a free man, goes to heaven by the route that he chooses'.[4] This was evidenced by the London Stock Exchange. 'There', he wrote, 'the Jew, the Mohammedan and the Christian deal with each other as if they were of the same religion, and give the name of infidel only to those who go bankrupt; the Presbyterian trusts the Anabaptist, and the Anglican accepts the promise of the Quaker. Upon departing from these peaceful and free exchanges, some go to the synagogue whilst others go for a drink.'[5] Trade and religious toleration went hand in hand, each mutually strengthening the other.

It was this combination, Voltaire concluded, which had allowed the English to become 'masters of the seas', but he also wanted us to understand that it was the commercial spirit which more broadly explained the character of English society and government. If in ancient Rome, Voltaire argued, the consequence of civil war had been slavery, in England it was liberty, and this was so because

> the English nation is the only one on earth which has succeeded in controlling the power of kings by resisting them and which, by dint of continuous effort, finally established a form of sound government where the prince, possessing the power necessary to do good, has his hands tied when it is a question of doing bad, where the nobility have authority without being insolent and without having vassals, where the people participate in government without producing confusion.[6]

This led Voltaire to reflect upon the comparative merits and utility of the 'powdered' aristocrat 'who knows precisely at what time the king rises and at what hour he goes to bed' and the trader who 'enriches his country, sends orders to the island

---

[1] Daniel Roche, *France in the Enlightenment* (Cambridge, Mass., 1998), 140.
[2] Voltaire, *Lettres philosophiques* (1986).
[3] Ibid. 75.   [4] Ibid. 54.   [5] Ibid. 60–1.   [6] Ibid. 66.

of Surate and to Cairo from his office, and contributes to the happiness of the world'.[7] Accordingly, when Voltaire discussed the great figures of English life, he focused upon Francis Bacon, John Locke, Isaac Newton, and William Shakespeare, reflecting at the same time upon the number of aristocrats in England who were well-known writers and who took pride from 'their works rather than their name'.

Voltaire offered neither a systematic treatise on England nor on the nature of commerce but his brief sketches nevertheless gave prominence to a set of themes which were to grow in importance as the eighteenth century developed. In particular, by associating commerce with liberty and also with England he not only provided, for those who wished to hear it, a telling critique of French society and manners— deemed still to be in the grip of religious fanaticism and arbitrary power—but also the contours of an alternative vision or model by the side of which France could be both judged and reformed.

The starting point of this debate was an interpretation of the English Revolution of 1688. Pierre Jurieu and Bossuet had clashed swords on this, the former strongly supporting the cause of William of Orange and the benefits that his reign was bringing to the English people.[8] Here the Glorious Revolution was accredited with two principal achievements. First was the recognition that a particular set of institutional arrangements was conducive—indeed indispensable—for the preservation of political liberty. This set of arrangements was the separation and balance of powers. Second was religious toleration. The importance of the last went far beyond that of a purely religious controversy. Implicit in the recognition of religious diversity was the acceptance that the extent of government action ought to be limited, that it should be defined by law, and, consequently, that it did not extend over the entire range of an individual's activities. The corollary was that there were a whole range of duties and actions which were best left either to individuals or to groups of individuals. Of these activities, one of the most important was trade.

Both Anglophilia and Anglophobia flourished in eighteenth-century France and continued to do so until well into the nineteenth century.[9] Typical of the spirit and tone of the latter was Joseph Fiévée's, *Lettres sur l'Angleterre et Réflexions sur la philosophie du XVIIIe siècle*, published in 1802, the year Britain and France signed the Treaty of Amiens. 'In England', he began, 'the words *peace* and *commerce* are what the words *peace* and *glory* are in France.'[10] In England everything—dress, manners, the arts—was cheap and vulgar and there was little evidence of good taste. 'The English', Fiévée remarked, 'are the least civilized nation in Europe', and this, he avowed,

---

[7] Voltaire, *Lettres philosophiques* (1986), 76.

[8] Pierre Jurieu, 'Justification du Prince d'Orange et de la Nation Anglaise', *Lettres pastorales XVI– XVII–XVIII* (Caen, 1991), 409–32.

[9] See Theodore Zeldin, 'English Ideals in French Politics during the Nineteenth Century', *Historical Journal*, 1 (1959), 40–58; Frances Acomb, *Anglophobia in France 1763–89* (New York, 1980); and Josephine Grieder, *Anglomania in France, 1740–1789: Fact, Fiction and Political Discourse* (Geneva, 1985).

[10] Fiévée, *Lettres sur l'Angleterre* (1802), 48.

followed from 'the great regard which they have for money'.[11] It also helped to explain why the English male did not enjoy the company of women. Similarly, Fiévée set little store by England's much-vaunted religious toleration. If England was a country where 'all religious extravagances are permitted', to be a Catholic was 'to be much less than a man'. As for the supposed liberty which flowed from the English system of government, Fiévée saw only corruption and oppression. 'In England', he commented, 'there are three types of election; those that you buy, those that you give away, and those that are contested by the use of reputation and money.'[12] Worse still was the 'agitation of the rabble'.

Why did it matter that the beneficial consequences of England's commerce and constitutional settlement should be contested? First, it was Fiévée's view that the *philosophes*, inspired by a hatred of their own country, had embraced 'anglomania', and that this had been one of the causes of the Revolution of 1789. Next, he believed that it was simply mistaken for one country to try to imitate another, and that this was especially so in the case of England and France where their guiding ethos— commerce for one, and glory for the other—were so diametrically opposed. 'The English', Fiévée concluded, 'like all peoples, are what their position, the centuries, and events have decided that they should be. To resemble them would require two impossible things: first, to cease to be ourselves, then to become them.'[13]

There was some justification in Fiévée's complaints. Throughout the eighteenth century the *philosophes* frequently cited England, its institutions, and its history, to illustrate what, in their opinion, were defects in France and had done so to a receptive public. To that extent, the Anglophiles came to be seen as dangerous subversives intent on destroying the fabric of French society and culture. There was, then, a serious political point to questioning whether England quite lived up to the glowing picture of it being purveyed, possibly out of ignorance or malice, by its admirers. Clearly, much of this discussion—as Fiévée himself recognized—was grounded in the long-standing economic, dynastic, and military rivalry which existed between the two countries but, that aside, there was some merit in posing the question of whether one country could usefully copy another. This was to be a question repeatedly asked, even by England's most enthusiastic admirers.

Such was the general awareness of France's decline relative to Britain that a wholesale rejection of the English example was comparatively rare. Once the animosity engendered by the Seven Years War had subsided there was a resurgence of Anglophilia in the highest government circles, most notably in the policies advocated by Jacques Necker, recalled to ministerial office in 1788.[14] As we have seen, defenders of moderate reform in 1789 came to see the English model of limited monarchy—made known to them principally through Jean Delolme's

[11] Ibid. 193.
[12] Ibid. 128.
[13] Ibid. 232.
[14] See Jacques Necker, *Du pouvoir exécutif dans les grands États* (1802). Necker returned to these questions in *Dernières vues de politique et de finance, offertes à la Nation Française* (1802), 266–363, specifically exploring the comparison between 'une Monarchie héréditaire et tempérée', based upon the English 'model', and a 'République une et indivisible'.

La Constitution de l'Angleterre of 1771—as a means of providing good government, extending the liberties of individuals, and of preserving public order. Their short-lived political supremacy handed power back to the Anglophobes, reaching its zenith with the ascent of the Jacobins.

Given their predilection to equate wealth with corruption, there was little to indicate that Robespierre and his colleagues would view England with anything but profound contempt or as being incapable of displaying the qualities required of republican virtue.[15] Indeed, in Jacobin discourse England was frequently cast as the new Carthage, as a maritime and trading power lacking the capacity for virtue displayed by both classical Rome and contemporary France.[16] This sentiment only intensified as Robespierre's obsession with internal opposition was extended to include 'the English faction'. France, he believed, was 'infested with the agents of England'. 'I hate the English as a people', Robespierre declared, and did so for the simple reason that there was nothing more despicable than a nation of slaves prepared to live under the rule of tyrants and despots.[17] England was no more than a 'contemptible meteor' which would disappear before the 'republican star'. France, and not an 'odious' and 'proud' England, was 'the last hope of the friends of humanity'.

The debate over England continued after the Restoration of the monarchy in 1814. On both sides of the argument there was agreement on one thing at least: England was the country of aristocracy, and thus of inequality. For example, in 1825 Auguste de Staël, son of Germaine de Staël, published his *Lettres sur l'Angleterre* and there listed the following aristocratic features of English life: 'The unequal division of property, primogeniture, an hereditary peerage, electoral influence, the distinction of ranks, honorific prerogatives, bodies possessing privileges'.[18] For his part, Benjamin Constant described England as 'a vast, opulent and vigorous aristocracy'.

The precise character of this aristocracy also received much attention, but the view of England's admirers was that its aristocracy was open to all talents and that their privileges were acknowledged by the English people as being indispensable to the preservation of English liberty. 'There has never existed in the world', wrote Charles de Montalembert, 'a government where the access to power, influence and prestige has been as easy and as assured as in England'. Similarly, for Montalembert England's inheritance laws were at once 'the consequence and guarantee' of its liberty.[19] For such enthusiasts, the challenge for France was that of recreating a new aristocracy upon similar lines and of appropriating the principal advantages of the English system.

For England's critics, by contrast, the influence of its aristocracy was something to be regretted and the political, economic, and social inequalities flowing from it

---

[15] See Sophie Wahnich, *L'Impossible Citoyen: L'Étranger dans le discours de la Révolution française* (1997), 243–346.
[16] See Norman Hampson, *The Perfidy of Albion: French Perceptions of England during the French Revolution* (Houndmills, 1998).
[17] *Œuvres de Maximilien Robespierre*, x. *Discours 27 juillet 1793–27 juillet 1794* (1967), 348–50.
[18] Auguste de Staël-Holstein, *Lettres sur l'Angleterre* (1825), 151–2.
[19] Charles de Montalembert, *De l'Avenir politique de l'Angleterre* (1857).

were at once a crime and a source of weakness. Moreover, with the advent of Britain's industrial revolution, the theme of aristocracy was transposed to this new setting. In Flora Tristan's *Promenades de Londres*, first published in 1842, we read, for example, that 'the greater proportion of workers lack clothing, a bed, furniture, a fire, and sufficient food'.[20] The cause of this parlous condition was the English aristocracy. 'Do you understand', she asked her readers, 'how a handful of aristocrats, lords, baronets, bishops, landed proprietors, and all manner of sinecurists, how this handful of privileged people can coerce, torture and starve a nation of twenty six million people?'[21] In England, she continued, the people suffered under the yoke of the 'pitiless egoism, revolting hypocrisy, and monstrous excess of this English oligarchy'. It was 'the most barbarous and the most frightful of all tyrannies'.[22] Tristan was by no means alone in travelling across the Channel in order to discover the secrets of the new industrial system that was there emerging. Equally representative of this strand of thought was Eugène Buret's *De la misère des classes laborieuses en Angleterre et en France*.[23] What Buret saw was a country that combined extreme opulence with profound poverty, 'the liberty of the rich and the strong' by the side of 'the servitude of the poor and the weak'.[24] 'France', he wrote, 'is poor, but England is miserable.' France was wrong to envy England's wealth and power, as it was on a road that would lead either to 'inevitable ruin or to the most radical and perhaps most terrible of revolutions'.[25] In general the diagnosis was a far from positive one. For many of the visitors to Britain's new industrial cities the arrival of the machine age was synonymous with poverty, criminality, and prostitution.

The surprise is that versions of these very criticisms were to be found in the writings of authors who might otherwise have been imagined to be broadly favourable to the English model. For example, Jean-Baptiste Say, author of *De l'Angleterre et les Anglais* of 1816, was far from convinced of the supposed merits of English commercial power or that this power would endure. As a consequence of the excessive taxation and borrowing required to defeat Napoleon Bonaparte, he contended, the cost of British industrial and agricultural products was exorbitant, such that even a decent hard-working family was frequently obliged to resort to public charity. To survive, all but the very rich were condemned to arduous toil and competition with their fellows. In such a situation, the rich thought only of getting richer, and so much so that Say feared that the country of Bacon, Newton, and Locke was taking rapid steps towards barbarism. 'The greatest disgrace in France', Say wrote, 'is to lack courage; in England it is to lack guineas.'[26] Corrupted by its politicians and debased by its material and social inequality, England was no model for France.[27]

---

[20] Flora Tristan, *Promenades dans Londres, ou L'aristocratie et les prolétaires anglais* (1978), 112.
[21] Ibid. 47.
[22] Ibid. 312.
[23] Eugène Buret, *De la misère des classes laborieuses en Angleterre et en France* (1840), i, p. ii.
[24] Ibid. 19.
[25] Ibid. ii. 475.
[26] Say, *De l'Angleterre* (1816), 22.
[27] See Jean-Paul Bertaud, Alan Forrest, and Annie Jourdan, *Napoléon, le monde et les Anglais* (2004), 90–101.

But this increasingly became a difficult position to sustain. In the guise of the new doctrine of 'industrialism', liberal economists in France became strong advocates of the wealth-creating power of commerce.[28] The key to wealth, they perceived, was through capital accumulation and in this a central role was allotted to the entrepreneur, to the market, and to free trade. No economy gave better proof of this than that of England. Moreover, given that France had again been subject to military defeat at the hands of England, that under the Empire she had once more found herself in the grip of arbitrary power, and that in 1815, 1830, and 1848 France was required to find another set of governmental institutions, it was not to be unexpected that a good number of French writers should for a further time cast an envious and inquiring eye towards the other side of the Channel.

II

To properly understand this disposition we should return to the eighteenth century and in particular to Montesquieu. He was not the first to use the term 'despotism' in France.[29] It had been widely used by aristocratic as well as Protestant opponents of Louis XIV. As a system of government rather than as a description of a form of personal rule it had been given wide currency by Pierre Bayle and others such as Fénelon and Boulainvilliers, to the point that even before Montesquieu was to place the concept of despotism at the heart of *De l'Esprit des lois* there existed a broad understanding of despotism as a form of arbitrary rule by a single sovereign power limited neither by law nor by secondary powers. Despotism was further associated with other features of the Sun King's reign: the centralization of power, religious intolerance, the pursuit of military glory, and financial corruption and mismanagement. To this Montesquieu was to add the description of despotism as rule by fear.

Montesquieu offered three criteria by which political regimes could be defined: who held sovereign power, by what method sovereign power was exercised, and by what principle the regime was set in motion. He accordingly stipulated that there were three types of government: republican, monarchical, and despotic; and then defined the principle determining the working of each in the following way: 'the nature of republican government is that the people as a body, or certain families, have the sovereign power; the nature of monarchical government is that the prince has the sovereign power, but that he exercises it according to established laws; the nature of despotic government is that one alone governs according to his wills and caprices'.[30] The despot, in short, had no rules by which he was bound and he was strong because he gloried in scorning life, being free to take life away as he chose. Honour, therefore, was unknown in despotic states, leaving the despot only with

---

[28] Martin S. Staum, 'French Lecturers in Political Economy, 1815–1848: Varieties of Liberalism', *History of Political Economy*, 30 (1998), 95–120.

[29] See Sharon Krause, 'Despotism in the Spirit of the Laws', in David D Carrithers, Michael A. Mosher, and Paul A. Rahe (eds.), *Montesquieu's Science of Politics: Essays on the Spirit of the Laws* (Lanham, Md., 2001), 231–72.

[30] *The Spirit of the Laws* (1989), 21.

rule by fear. It was thus in the nature of despotic government that it required 'extreme obedience' and that the people were to be made 'timid' and 'ignorant'. Politics likewise became devoid of substance. There was little public business, Montesquieu wrote, and government was reduced to 'the preservation of the prince, or rather the preservation of the palace in which he is enclosed'. Men acted only with the comforts of life in view and expected to be rewarded for everything they did. As Montesquieu observed, 'the worst Roman Emperors were those who gave the most'.[31] However, the goal of despotic government, for all its reliance upon caprice and fear, was nothing more than order and tranquillity, the reducing of all citizens to a servitude where all showed 'passive obedience' and where each 'blindly submits to the absolute will of the sovereign'. Everyone was equal, but this was because everyone counted for nothing and lived isolated from one another. What is more, the despot's subjects lived in a state of destitution and they did so because the laws of commerce scarcely applied. Embezzlement, Montesquieu recounted, was the normal condition under despotic rule.

Montesquieu summarized this deplorable state of human existence in one short observation. 'When the savages of Louisiana want fruit', he wrote, 'they cut down the tree and gather the fruit. There you have despotic government.'[32] What he meant by this was that despotic government was government determined by instinctive and irrational appetites and actions. It destroyed the very thing sustaining its life. It was government that lacked the all-important ingredient of moderation and where power was not counter-balanced. In institutional terms it was a situation where the instruments of government were not divided up between the executive, legislative, and judicial branches. Among the Turks, Montesquieu wrote, 'where the three powers are united in the person of the sultan, an atrocious despotism reigns'.[33]

From this Montesquieu concluded that 'political liberty is found only in moderate governments'.[34] This in turn begged the question of what was meant by political liberty. For Montesquieu it was defined in terms of the absence of fear and, its corollary, an individual's sense of personal security guaranteed by law. '[I]n a society where there are laws', Montesquieu wrote, 'liberty can consist only in having the power to do what one should want to do and in no way being constrained to do what one should not want to do.' 'Liberty', he continued, 'is the right to do everything that the laws permit.'[35] The worst situation was one where the enjoyment of liberty depended upon the caprice of the legislator or upon the arbitrary power of the despot. Unpromisingly, Montesquieu believed that there was something natural about despotism—hence his view that it arose more often in warm climates—and that there was no guarantee that liberty and moderation would ultimately prevail.

As Montesquieu famously contended, there was only one nation 'whose political constitution has political liberty for its direct purpose' and that nation was England.[36] Much has been written about Montesquieu's discussion of the

---

[31] Ibid. 68. [32] Ibid. 59. [33] Ibid. 157.
[34] Ibid. 155. [35] Ibid. [36] Ibid. 156.

English constitution, and in particular on the subject of whether he was providing a description of how the English constitution actually worked or an ideal type of the 'constitution of liberty' with England as its source.[37] Montesquieu himself appeared to suggest that it did not matter whether the English actually enjoyed the liberty he was describing: it was sufficient 'to say that it is established by their laws'. Whatever the truth of the matter, Montesquieu outlined what he took to be the tripartite division of the executive, legislative, and judicial branches of government and saw England as a system of mixed government in which power was shared between monarch, Lords, and Commons. Furthermore he recognized that such a system of division and balance was indispensable for the preservation of liberty. Thus, the essence of good government was a situation where power counter-balanced itself and could not be abused.

More difficult to assess was what Montesquieu thought of the French monarchy. Where Montesquieu cited a regime as an example of arbitrary despotism his standard instance was that of the Ottoman Empire. Monarchy itself, along with republics, was one of the two types of political regime which he identified as having potentially beneficial consequences. Monarchies, he wrote, do not have 'liberty for their direct purpose . . . they aim only for the glory of the citizens, the state, and the prince. But this glory results in a spirit of liberty that can, in these states, produce equally great things and can perhaps contribute as much to happiness as to liberty itself.'[38] Nor did he believe anything other than that executive power should be in the hands of a monarch. However, monarchies could degenerate into despotism. They did so not only when the three branches of government fell into the same hands but also when subordinate and intermediate institutions were weakened or, in the worst case, eradicated. As a member of the 'nobility of the robe' and of the provincial *parlement* of Bordeaux, Montesquieu's personal sympathies were clear enough. Indeed, as a means of restraining royal power, he was not averse to defending the practice of the buying of public offices.

One possible antidote to the slide towards despotism was religion, but this, Montesquieu recognized, could be used to induce passivity. Another was commerce. By commerce, Montesquieu here had in mind not merely the exchange of goods but also the creation of new patterns of social intercourse. 'It is an almost general rule', Montesquieu wrote, 'that everywhere there are gentle mores, there is commerce and that everywhere there is commerce, there are gentle mores'.[39] Our moral practices and habits, in other words, become less 'ferocious' as a result of our contacts with other people and through our greater familiarity with their ways. In particular, 'the natural effect' of commerce is to lead to peace: 'two nations that trade with each other become reciprocally dependent; if one has an interest in buying, the other has an interest in selling, and all unions are founded on mutual

[37] See e.g. R. Shackleton, *Montesquieu: A Critical Biography* (Oxford, 1961), 284–301; M. F. T. H. Fletcher, *Montesquieu and English Politics (1750–1800)* (Philadelphia, 1989), 107–51; M. J. C. Vile, *Constitutionalism and the Separation of Powers* (Oxford, 1967), 76–97; Melvin Richter, *The Political Theory of Montesquieu* (Cambridge, 1977), 84–97; and Paul Rahe, *Montesquieu and the Logic of Liberty* (2009).
[38] *Spirit of the Laws*, 166.   [39] Ibid. 338.

needs'.[40] Additionally, there existed a relationship between forms of government and commerce. As a general rule, Montesquieu wrote, 'in a nation that is in servitude, one works more to preserve than to acquire; in a free nation, one works more to acquire than to preserve'.[41] It was here that England again figured positively in Montesquieu's account. Other countries had put political interests before commercial interests. In England, it was always the reverse. The English were 'the people in the world who have best known how to take advantage of each of these three great things at the same time: religion, commerce, and liberty'.[42]

This did not mean that France should rush unreservedly towards an imitation of English *mœurs* and institutions. One of the most striking conclusions of *De l'Esprit des lois* was an awareness of the limitations attached to the activity of politics. Laws, Montesquieu believed, along with climate, religion, morals, manners, and examples drawn from the past, were the factors which 'governed men' and together they formed 'a general spirit'. The wise legislator was one who followed 'the spirit of the nation'. To that extent, government should be a reflection of society rather than a vehicle for securing the transformation of society. Faced therefore with the centuries-long deviation of royal power towards despotism, Montesquieu was left with little alternative but to conjure up the possibility of a return to a pre-feudal and 'gothic' past where the monarch made no decisions without first consulting the representatives of the people.

De l'Esprit des lois was not a book from which one could easily draw hard and fast conclusions. Nevertheless, despite the preoccupation with locating all societies within their diverse natural and historical conditions, there was no ambiguity in Montesquieu's condemnation of despotism in whatever form it took. Happy then, in Montesquieu's eyes, were all those fortunate enough to experience what was delightfully termed 'la douceur du gouvernement'. The best of situations seemed indubitably to be that where 'moderate' government was combined with the enjoyment of a 'moderate' liberty. This led to the conclusion that liberty was most readily preserved through the contrived balance of both governmental institutions and competing social interests.

But would this precarious equilibrium be overturned by the activity of commerce, the dynamic effects of which Montesquieu had identified so accurately?[43] Much has been made of Montesquieu's 'esprit conservateur'. Within his writings the maintenance of stability attained almost as much importance as the dispersal of political power. For this reason he opposed the emergence of a 'noblesse commmerçante' and believed that governments should regulate who could take part in commercial activities. Ultimately, however, such restrictions upon commercial activity proved untenable and with the collapse of the feudal order there occurred not only a reconfiguration of what Montesquieu would have regarded as the general spirit of society but also one potentially undermining the mainsprings of liberty. Once this had been perceived to have occurred, those who came increasingly to

---

[40] Ibid.   [41] Ibid. 341.   [42] Ibid. 343.
[43] Roger Boesche, 'Fearing Monarchs and Merchants: Montesquieu's Two Theories of Despotism', *Western Political Quarterly*, 43 (1990), 741–61.

regard themselves as liberals had the task of forging a new doctrine which would graft the fundamental insights of Montesquieu concerning the nature of liberty and its preservation onto a society dominated by new social classes, new political institutions, as well as by the pursuit of affluence. This was to prove to be no easy task.

During the Revolution Montesquieu was read consistently (and correctly) as a fierce critic of all forms of despotism. It was also the case that the tripartite division of governmental functions outlined by Montesquieu acted as a consistent point of reference in the constitutional debates that took place after 1789. Nearly everyone agreed that despotism could only be avoided if these three functions were not placed in the hands of either a single individual or institution and it was this that explained the preoccupation with ensuring that the legislative and executive functions in particular should remain separate. Not surprisingly, it was the *monarchiens* who were to prove to be the most enthusiastic and faithful advocates of Montesquieu's constitutional recommendations. As the Revolution progressed, and as attention turned away from the goal of constructing a balanced constitution towards that of using the State as a moral agent, Montesquieu continued to fade from view. Most importantly, the idea figuring at the very heart of Montesquieu's thought—'the need for power to check power through the arrangements of things'—was consistently ignored. Alongside demands for unity of political action, the moderation associated with a system of balances and manufactured equilibrium had little charm or attraction.

It was precisely this sentiment that underscored Napoleon Bonaparte's seizure of power on the 18 Brumaire.[44] What, more broadly, might be said of the character and significance of this new regime? At the heart of what became Bonapartist ideology was the aspiration to bring the Revolution to a close while preserving what were taken to be its achievements.[45] This was secured by a series of concessions towards those who had been most adversely affected by the Revolution. If this largely concerned measures to assuage the Catholic Church and the aristocracy (for example, allowing Christians to worship on Sundays and ending the commemoration of the execution of Louis XVI) it also meant that slavery, having been abolished in 1794, was re-established in French colonies in 1802. By the same token, there was to be no going back upon the abolition of the privileges associated with the *ancien régime*. Recognizing civil equality, the Revolution was to be stabilized upon a conservative basis. What followed were a series of wide-ranging administrative, financial, judicial, and educational reforms, many of which still operate in contemporary France. To take but two examples: the legal code was systematically overhauled between 1804 and1810, whilst the educational system was reformed with a view to providing a new elite equipped to serve the State. So too the *préfet*, symbol of the State's presence and authority beyond the capital, was brought into

---

[44] See Patrice Gueniffey, *Le Dix-Huit Brumaire* (2008).
[45] The term 'Bonapartism' was first used in 1816: see Melvin Richter, 'Towards a Concept of Political Illegitimacy: Bonapartist Dictatorship and Democratic Legitimacy', *Political Theory*, 10 (1982), 185–214.

existence. This was accompanied by a further reinforcement of administrative centralization.[46]

It was this feature of the Empire that was to become one of the abiding obsessions of its later liberal critics. Spreading its tentacles outwards from the Ministry of the Interior in Paris, the State's administrative apparatus came to be seen as an all-powerful mechanism of control, intruding into every aspect of local life. The reality, according to many of those charged with exercising these functions, was less interventionist and far more attuned to the needs of local communities, but the prefectoral system was seen to be an integral part of what was an authoritarian and centralized regime.

This was not to be the only feature of Napoleon's rule that was to meet with criticism. No sooner had power been seized than attempts to stifle opposition were made. Parliamentary dissidents and the press found themselves muzzled. After the proclamation of the Empire the regime moved ineluctably towards a personalization of power and the restoration of monarchical practices. If individual liberties were repeatedly sacrificed in the name of order, the propagation of a *culte impérial* glorified the achievements of both the Empire (replete with Roman trappings) and the emperor himself. The luxurious splendour of the royal court was re-established and, in 1808, a new nobility of the Empire was created, Napoleon ennobling as many as 3,600 hereditary *chevaliers*, *barons*, and *comtes*. Three of his brothers became kings whilst many of his victorious marshals were made princes and dukes. Much of what remained of the old aristocracy came back to France and with this homecoming also came a revival of the sumptuous entertainments of the past, regicides and the illustrious families of the Faubourg Saint-Germain dancing side by side. It was, as Isser Woloch has commented, 'monarchy in a new key'.[47] As dissatisfaction mounted, the press found itself under strict censorship, the vast majority of newspapers being forcibly closed. Only four Parisian titles remained in 1814. The theatre was similarly silenced, the censors going to great lengths to remove even the most indirect criticism of the imperial regime.[48]

Above all, the Empire came to be identified with the army and the activity of war. Napoleon engaged in military campaigns of a previously unknown scale, requiring the regular conscription of huge numbers of French males. The army assembled to invade Russia was 450,000 strong (approximately only 20,000 returned)[49] whilst around 2 million French citizens served in the *Grande Armée* between 1800 and 1814. As conquest turned into defeat, France came increasingly to resemble a militarized society, where the exercise of arbitrary power was the norm.

In April 1814 Napoleon was forced to abdicate. Encircled by its foreign enemies, domestic support for the Empire simply drained away. Eleven months later, he

---

[46] See Louis Bergeron, *L'Épisode napoléonien*, i. *Aspects intérieurs 1799–1815* (1972) and Jacques-Olivier Boudon, *Le Consulat et l'Empire* (1997).
[47] See Isser Woloch, *Napoleon and his Collaborators: The Making of a Dictatorship* (New York, 2001), 105.
[48] Ibid. 205–13.
[49] See Adam Zamoyski, *1812: Napoleon's Fatal March on Moscow* (London, 2004).

returned from exile in Elba, thus inaugurating his second reign of 'A Hundred Days'. In so doing, he had his erstwhile opponent, Benjamin Constant, write a new constitution.[50] In June 1815 defeat at Waterloo by Wellington brought this brief episode, and the First Empire, finally to an end.

Several years later Benjamin Constant went to considerable lengths to explain why he had rallied to a man he had 'for so long attacked' and why he had agreed to pen the *Acte additionnel aux constitutions de l'Empire*.[51] The context, he argued, was not one of his own making. There had been no conspiracy to bring back Napoleon. But he had had no desire to see France subject to foreign invasion or for her to fall into the hands of the forces of 'counter-revolution'. 'Thus', Constant wrote, 'we need to recognize that when Napoleon landed on the coast of France the result of this event could have been military and absolute government, that it was the *Acte additionnel* that placed an obstacle in the way of this outcome and that those who participated in drawing it up played a role in saving France from the caprice of despotism and the power of the sword.'[52] Constant also argued that, although 'imperfect', his constitution was in no sense 'inferior to any of those which seemed destined to replace it'.[53] On this, at least, he was probably right. The text itself was a compromise between Napoleon and Constant and rested upon the pretext that the former was turning his back upon his military ambitions in Europe.

Nevertheless, it set out clear principles of parliamentary and representative government within the framework of the Empire. Most importantly, section VI of the document virtually amounted to a declaration of rights, affirming equality before the law; protection from arbitrary arrest; liberty of religious practice and of the press; restrictions upon the proclamation of a 'state of siege'; and the prohibition of both the restoration of the Bourbon monarchy and of the reintroduction of 'feudal and seigneurial rights'. As such, Constant believed, his actions had been in line with the dominant preoccupation of his entire life: the desire 'to see constitutional liberty peaceably established among us'.[54]

On this occasion—as with so many others—Constant was to be thwarted in his ambitions. The 'Benjamine', as his constitution came to be known, operated for a mere two months, being jettisoned unceremoniously with the return to Paris of Louis XVIII in June 1815. For Constant it was an embarrassing interlude and one of the more curious episodes of a life rich in incident and surprise. A lack of strategic judgement, if not of principle, had dangerously undermined his status as the most eloquent and forceful critic of the Empire. It is, however, the views expressed by Constant in this role that most merit our attention.

[50] See Jacques Godechot, *Les Constitutions de la France depuis 1789* (1995), 225–39. In the words of André Jardin, it was 'the most elegant in its form of all our constitutional texts': Jardin, *Histoire du Libéralisme politique: De la crise de l'absolutisme à la constitution de 1875* (1985), 223.

[51] Benjamin Constant, *Mémoires sur les Cent-Jours* (1829). The text was originally published in two parts between 1820 and 1822. Only a few weeks earlier, Constant had compared Napoleon to Genghis Khan and Attila. See 'Journal de Paris, 19 mars 1815', in Ephraïm Harpaz (ed.) *Benjamin Constant: Receuil d'articles 1795–1817* (1978), 149–52.

[52] Constant, *Mémoires*, part 2, 70.

[53] Ibid. 64.

[54] Constant, *Mémoires*, part 1, 9.

We know relatively little of Constant's initial reaction to the Revolution, in part because between 1787 and 1794 he was employed as a Gentleman of the Chamber in the provincial German court of Brunswick. All the same, it appears that Constant saw himself as a supporter of the Revolution, and so much so that he voiced approval for Robespierre in private correspondence.[55] Upon his return to his native Switzerland he met Germaine de Staël, daughter of Jacques Necker, and wife of the Swedish ambassador to Paris.[56] Not long afterwards, they were to become lovers and, although often tempestuous, their friendship survived until Madame de Staël's death in 1817.[57] The two of them arrived in Paris in May 1795 and in the next two years Constant commenced the publication of the set of brilliant pamphlets—*De la Force du Gouvernement actuel de la France et de la nécessité de s'y rallier, Des Réactions politiques* and *Des Effets de la Terreur*—which served to define his pro-republican but anti-Jacobin stance.

Interestingly, it was at this early stage that Constant dismissed the argument that republics were only appropriate to small states.[58] Constant, therefore, supported the Directory as the regime most likely to 'terminate' the Revolution and to 'strengthen' the Republic, and did so to the extent of not opposing the removal from the legislative assembly of right-wing deputies in the *coup* of 18 Fructidor.[59] With the advent of the Consulate, Sieyès facilitated Constant's election to the Tribunate, one of the three chambers that operated under the constitution of the year VIII. As early as January 1800—and to Bonaparte's intense displeasure—Constant opposed plans to reduce the Tribunate's opportunities to discuss legislative proposals and again the following year denounced the introduction of special legal tribunals which, in his view, were in breach of the constitution. A project supposedly 'directed against a few brigands', Constant announced, 'would threaten all citizens' with arbitrary power. In 1802 Napoleon had Constant—along with Jean-Baptiste Say, Daunou, and others—expelled from the Tribunate. With this Constant commenced a decade and more of itinerant exile.

There is general agreement that Constant's political writings reached their full maturity around 1806, the year in which he began writing his *Principes de politiques applicables à tous les gouvernements*, the first version of which was published only in 1815. For our immediate purposes we should first focus on his most powerful diatribe against Napoleon Bonaparte: *De l'esprit de conquête et de l'usurpation.*[60]

[55] See K. Steven Vincent, 'Benjamin Constant, the French Revolution, and the Origins of French Romantic Liberalism', *French Historical Studies*, 23 (2000), 607–37. See also Kurt Kloocke, *Benjamin Constant: Une biographie intellectuelle* (Geneva, 1984); Dennis Wood, *Benjamin Constant: A Biography* (London, 1993) and Helena Rosenblatt (ed.), *The Cambridge Companion to Constant* (Cambridge, 2009).

[56] See Renee Winegarten, *Germaine de Staël and Benjamin Constant: A Dual Biography* (New Haven, Conn., 2008).

[57] For Constant's assessment of her personality and intellectual achievements see 'De Madame de Staël et des ses ouvrages', in Benjamin Constant, *Portraits, Mémoires, Souvenirs* (1992), 212–54.

[58] See *De la Force du Gouvernement*. See also Constant, *Fragments d'un ouvrage abandonné sur la possibilité d'une constitution républicaine dans un grand pays* (1991).

[59] The elections of April 1797 were a crushing defeat for the Directory, leading to a fear of a possible monarchical restoration. The response of the Directory was to annul the greater number of these elections.

[60] Constant, *De la liberté chez les modernes* (1980), 103–261.

'We have finally reached', Constant announced at the beginning of the text, 'the age of commerce, an age which necessarily replaces that of war.'[61] This familiar argument led him next to suggest that, for modern nations, war had lost both its attraction and its utility. From this it followed that 'any government wishing to drive a European people to war and conquest would commit a gross and disastrous anachronism'.[62] What form would this take? Constant first offered a description of what he termed 'a military race acting only out of self-interest'. 'Four hundred thousand well-trained, well-armed egoists', Constant wrote, 'would know that their destiny was either to inflict or to suffer death.'[63] Once in place, this army would have to be kept at work and new enemies would have to be found for it to fight. The system of conquest was thus self-perpetuating. Moreover, of necessity it would spread to the civilian population. Opposition would be seen as disorder, reasoning as a form of rebellion. And so 'the rest of the nation' would find itself called upon to display 'passive obedience'.[64] The result would be moral degradation and an ever-growing ignorance. As for the conquered peoples themselves, they would be forced to suffer a fate never inflicted upon the vanquished in times of antiquity: the imposition of a uniformity which touched 'the most intimate aspects of their existence'. 'Today', Constant wrote, 'the admiration for uniformity . . . is received as a religious dogma': it was 'the immediate and inseparable consequence of the spirit of conquest'.[65]

Constant reached a similar conclusion with regard to usurpation. It was impossible, he announced, for usurpation to endure, so removed was it from the spirit of the modern age. Not even force—'the last resort' of regular governments but the 'norm to usurpers'—could keep it in place indefinitely. One battle lost—the reference was to Napoleon's crushing defeat at Leipzig in 1813—had been sufficient to put it to flight across Europe. Nevertheless, it was to this condition that France had been reduced under Bonaparte. Usurpation too, as Constant made clear, was an anachronism. But he was also aware that he was describing something that was new.[66] Usurpation was but a novel form of government displaying its own destructive pathologies. To further make the point, Constant provided a sustained comparison between monarchy and usurpation, two forms of government in which power was in the hands of one man, but which were, in his opinion, very different from each other despite the 'deceptive resemblance'.

The example of monarchy chosen by Constant was that of England. There, he wrote, it can be seen that 'the rights of all citizens are safe from attack; that popular elections keep the body politic alive. . . . that freedom of the press is respected; that talent is assured of its triumph; and that, in individuals of all classes, there is the proud, calm security of the man embraced by the law of his country'.[67] This, by contrast, was Constant's vivid account of what was to be expected under the regime

---

[61] Constant, *De la liberté chez les modernes* (1980), 118.
[62] Ibid. 120.   [63] Ibid. 123.   [64] Ibid. 133.   [65] Ibid. 148.
[66] Richter, 'Towards a Concept of Political Legitimacy', 188, makes the point that usurpation had been 'a common word in the moral and political discourse of the old regime'. After 1789 it was used by royalist writers against the republic.
[67] Constant, *De la liberté*, 163.

of a usurper.[68] Usurpation was a system which nothing could modify or soften and which had 'the individuality of the usurper' stamped upon it. From all persons it exacted 'an immediate abdication in favour of a single individual'. Obliged always to justify his elevation, the usurper could never lapse into inaction and was routinely required to resort to treachery, violence, and perjury. Principles were invoked, only for them to be trampled upon. Greed was awakened and injustice emboldened. Illegality, Constant went on, haunted the usurper 'like a ghost', and so 'in vain' he sought refuge in 'ostentation and in victory'. For want of legitimacy, he surrounded himself with guards, engaged in 'incessant warfare' and was forced to 'abase' and 'insult' all those around him.

Constant ended his description by drawing attention to what, in his opinion, was the most decisive innovation introduced by usurpation, an innovation that not only served to differentiate it from earlier forms of despotism, but that made the latter preferable to the former.[69] Usurpation, Constant wrote, parodied and counterfeited liberty. It demanded the assent and approbation of its subjects and, through persecution, exacted signs of consent. Despotism, he explained, 'rules by means of silence, and leaves man with the right to be silent; usurpation condemns him to speak; it pursues him to the intimate sanctuary of his thoughts and, forcing him to lie to his own conscience, denies him the last consolation of the oppressed'.[70]

How had it been possible for this descent into a new, and more extensive, form of arbitrary government to occur? It arose, Constant stated unequivocally, as a consequence of a revolution that had fundamentally misunderstood the nature of liberty in modern commercial society. This was how Constant phrased the argument for which he was later to be best known.[71] 'The liberty which was offered to men at the end of the last century', he wrote, 'was borrowed from the ancient republics.'[72] That conception of liberty, Constant continued, consisted 'in active participation in the collective power rather than in the peaceful enjoyment of individual independence'. The ancients, in brief, gained their greatest enjoyment from public life and found little pleasure in their private existence; consequently they had been prepared to sacrifice 'individual liberty to political liberty'. By contrast, Constant affirmed, 'almost all the pleasures of the moderns lie in their private life'. Public matters were of only passing interest. Individuals wished to be left in 'perfect independence in all that concerns their occupations, their undertakings, their sphere of activity, their fantasies'. This, he concluded, was a form of civil liberty virtually unknown to the ancients.

The move from one form of liberty to the other, in Constant's view, had not been without its losses. Our pleasures were less vivid and immediate. We were incapable of lasting emotion. Our enthusiasm was tempered by reflection and experience. Nonetheless, Constant's argument was that we could not 'turn free men into Spartans'. This, he believed, had been the important truth overlooked by those at the end of the previous century who had seen themselves as 'charged with

---

[68] Ibid. 164–71.   [69] Ibid. 172–4.   [70] Ibid. 174.   [71] Ibid. 182–5.
[72] The same argument was advanced by Madame de Staël in her text of 1796, *Circonstances actuelles qui peuvent terminer la révolution* (Geneva, 1979).

the regeneration of the human race'. These reformers, Constant wrote, had mistakenly imagined 'that everything should give way before collective authority and
that all restrictions of individual rights would be compensated by participation in
the social power'.[73] It was in the name of liberty, Constant wrote, that the French,
'a people grown old in pleasure', had been given 'prisons, scaffolds, and countless
prosecutions'.

Constant drew several conclusions from this experience.[74] First, Napoleon was
guiltier than were the barbarous conquerors of the past. Unlike them, 'he had
chosen barbarism'. Next, usurpation had to be understood as a system, the blame
for what had occurred being attributable to usurpation itself, rather than to an
'exceptional individual, made for evil, and committing crimes neither out of
necessity nor self-interest'. Finally, Constant, now writing in the context of Restoration France, was led to recognize two forms of political legitimacy: the one,
'positive', derived from free election; the other, 'tacit', derived from hereditary
possession. The first, Constant wrote, 'is more seductive in theory' but it had the
drawback that it could be counterfeited: as it had been in England by Cromwell and
in France by Bonaparte.

The next move was to sketch out a form of government which would be
legitimate and which could not be counterfeited. This Constant attempted most
systematically in his *Principes de politique*, first published in 1815.[75] At the heart
of his response was the conviction that the task would be accomplished not
by attacking the holders of power but rather by attacking power itself, by placing
guaranteed restrictions upon the possible abuse of power, by limiting not a
particular form of sovereignty but sovereignty itself. No monarch, Constant
wrote, even if his claim to legitimacy derived from 'the assent of the people',
possessed 'a power without limits'. Similarly, the sovereignty of the people should
be 'circumscribed within the limits traced by justice and by the rights of individuals'. No authority, whatever its source, could call these rights into question.
More precisely, the limitation of sovereignty could be made into a reality 'through
the distribution and balance of powers'.[76]

As Constant sought to give institutional form to these basic principles, he turned
unfailingly towards England as an example. 'Since it is always useful to move away
from abstractions and turn to facts', he wrote, 'we shall refer to the English
constitution.'[77] The particular strength of a constitutional monarchy, Constant
therefore argued, was not that it was separated into three branches, as Montesquieu
had believed, but into five branches: royal power, executive power, the power that
represented permanence (i.e. the hereditary assembly), the power that represented
opinion (i.e. the elected assembly), and judicial power. Constant's innovation here
was to make the distinction between 'royal power', which he described as a 'neutral
power', and 'executive power', which he described as a active power. If one looked
at the English system of government, Constant argued, one would see not only that

---

[73] Constant, *De la liberté*, 189.
[74] Ibid. 253–61. This part of the text was added to the 4th edn.
[75] Ibid. 263–427.   [76] Ibid. 269–78.   [77] Ibid. 281.

laws were made with the consent of both assemblies, that executive acts needed the signature of a minister, and that judgments were made by independent courts of law, but also that the monarch exercised the essential function of ensuring that the whole system worked in harmony. The function of 'royal power' as neutral power was that of putting an end to any 'dangerous conflict' that might take place between the other powers. If the actions of the executive were unsound, the monarch could dismiss his ministers; should the hereditary chamber be unduly troublesome, the monarch could simply create new peers; and so on. 'The royal power', Constant wrote, 'is in the middle, yet above the four others, a superior and at the same time intermediate authority, with no interest in disturbing the balance, but on the contrary having a strong interest in maintaining it.'[78] Accordingly, Constant accredited the English monarch not only with the function of preserving the constitution but also of acting as the guarantor of all political liberties. The monarch performed this role through his capacity to ensure that all authority at any one time did not reside in one of the active powers. 'In a free country', Constant concluded, 'the king is a being apart, superior to differences of opinion, having no other interest than the maintenance of order and liberty.'[79]

Constant perceived other distinct advantages to this system of government, all of which, he believed, aided the preservation of liberty. The first derived from the practice of ministerial responsibility.[80] Constant spent considerable time outlining the manner in which this operated within the English system. The key issue was whether a minister's responsibility was penal or political, Constant recognizing that within the English system a minister's responsibility was increasingly seen to be political. This meant that ministers were no longer seen solely as the monarch's functionaries and therefore that ministers could be removed from power as a result of a loss of political support. This not only made the transfer of power all the easier to achieve but also led to the development of an 'animated sentiment of public life'. Through the watchfulness of parliamentary representatives and the openness of their debates, there would be engendered 'a spirit of examination, an habitual interest in the maintenance of the constitution of the State, a constant participation in public affairs'. Protection against the arbitrary abuse of power, in short, would be enhanced through 'a lively sense of public life'.[81]

Constant identified four other major guarantees of liberty within a system of constitutional monarchy drawing upon the English model. The first derived from one aspect of the separation of powers: namely, the independence of the judiciary. Constant not only strongly recommended the practice of the non-removability of judges but also the English jury system, both of which he felt were indispensable for the preservation of judicial independence. In response to the claim that juries could not be trusted to carry out their duties properly, Constant was brutally to the point. 'In England', he wrote, 'I have seen a jury find a young girl guilty of stealing muslin to the value of thirteen shillings. They knew that the sentence would be death.'[82]

---

[78] Ibid. 280.   [79] Ibid. 282.   [80] Ibid. 332–49.
[81] Ibid. 346.   [82] Ibid. 420.

The second guarantee derived from freedom of the press. In Constant's opinion, liberty of the press was essential if the government of the day was to be subject to informed criticism and publicity. Censorship, he believed, tended to do more harm than good, as liberty of the press and veracity went hand in hand. England was here cited as 'la terre classique' of freedom of the press.[83]

Third, Constant believed that constitutional monarchy provided the means of reducing the role of the army to that of its one, proper function: repelling foreign invaders. Internal dissent and lawlessness could be dealt with by 'salaried officers'. They would content themselves with 'pursuing' and 'supervising' rather than 'fighting' and 'conquering', posing no threat to either the authority of the State or the 'imprescriptible rights' of the citizen.

The final guarantee sprang from the independence of municipal and local authorities. In this we touch upon one of the central themes of French liberalism in the nineteenth century: the preservation of local independence as a means of restricting the power of despotic, central government. This argument was an updated supplement to Montesquieu's defence of the rights of the provincial nobility. The French liberals as a whole became obsessed by what they saw as the systematic destruction of all intermediary powers and the consequent subjection of an undifferentiated and amorphous population at the hands of a highly organized, centralized bureaucratic power. Constant, for example, spoke of 'individuals, lost in an unnatural isolation, strangers to the place of their birth, without any contact with the past, living only in a hurried present, scattered like atoms on a vast plain'.[84]

Constant voiced a series of largely theoretical justifications of local liberty and of what he did not hesitate to describe as federalism.[85] In France, he commented, local power had always been regarded as a 'dependent branch of executive power', with the result that laws were badly implemented and partial interests were poorly protected. It was only proper, Constant argued by way of response, that issues of a purely local interest should be decided at local level. The various authorities—*commune, arrondissement*, and national government—should only act within their proper sphere of competence. Such a system was not only conducive to the preservation of liberty but also to the most efficient use of resources. '[J]ust as in individual life that part which in no way threatens the social interest must remain free', Constant remarked, 'similarly in the life of groups, all that does not damage the whole collectivity must enjoy the same liberty.'[86] This system would have the added, and very important, advantage of fostering sentiments of local attachment and 'communal honour'. Such attachments, in Constant's view, drew upon feelings which were 'disinterested, noble and pious'.

Towards the end of the *Principes de politique* Constant made the following, acute observation: all of the constitutions which had been given to France had guaranteed the liberty of the individual but all of them had violated this liberty. Declarations of principles, in other words, were not enough. Positive safeguards, powerful enough to protect the interests of the oppressed, were required. This was the case, he went

---

[83] Constant, *De la liberté*, 389.   [84] Ibid. 366.   [85] Ibid. 361–6.   [86] Ibid. 365.

on, because 'political institutions are simply contracts; and it is in the nature of contracts to establish fixed limits'.[87] Thus, arbitrariness was incompatible with the existence of any government considered as a set of political institutions: it undermined their very foundations.

This was the message that Constant believed that Bonaparte had been ready to hear and which he tried to give constitutional embodiment in the *Acte additionnel.* With Louis XVIII's return, Constant was again forced into exile, returning to Paris at the end of 1816. After this, and until the end of his life in 1830, he embarked upon a new phase of his career, as both a journalist (writing voluminously for both the *Mercure de France* and the *Minerve Français*)[88] and a parliamentary deputy. He quickly adapted the fundamentals of his thought to the new circumstances of the restored monarchy—later he was to write that 'I have always believed, and this belief has been the rule of my conduct, that as far as government is concerned, we must set out from the point where we are'[89]—and sought to defend the guarantees of individual liberty provided by the new constitutional settlement. In *De la Doctrine politique qui peut réunir les parties en France*,[90] for example, he counselled the dominant royalist party against seeking to overturn what he termed 'the moral interests of the revolution'—'equality of citizens before the law, liberty of conscience, security of the person, the responsible independence of the press'—whilst as a member of the parliamentary opposition he proved to be an indefatigable defender of constitutional liberties.

In 1822 Constant published his *Commentaire sur l'ouvrage de Filangieri*,[91] a work which restated many of his by-now standard arguments linking the age of commerce with the need for constitutional government. When offered legislative improvement by government, he argued, the people should demand 'constitutional institutions'. In conclusion he argued that 'the functions of government are negative: it should oppress evil and leave good to operate by itself'. The general motto of all governments should be 'laissez passer et laissez faire'. Finally, the publication of *Mélanges de littérature et de politique* shortly before his death provided Constant with the opportunity to summarize what he took to be the overall significance of his work. 'For over forty years', Constant wrote, 'I have defended the same principle: liberty in everything; in religion, in philosophy, in literature, in industry, in politics, and by liberty I mean the triumph of individuality, as much over authority which would wish to govern through despotism as over the masses who claim the right to enslave the minority.'[92] Constant was in little doubt that it was towards this end that society was moving.[93]

This, of course, had been the theme of Constant's most famous text, *De la liberté des anciens comparée à celle des modernes*, first given as a lecture before the Athénée

---

[87] Ibid. 410.
[88] See Ephraïm Harpaz (ed.), *Constant: Receuil d'articles*, 2 vols. (Geneva, 1972).
[89] Constant, *Mémoires*, part 1, p. 61.
[90] Constant, *De la Doctrine politique qui peut réunir les parties en France* (1816).
[91] Constant, *Commentaire sur l'ouvrage de Filangieri* (1822–4).
[92] Constant, *Mélanges de littérature et de politique* (1829), p. v.
[93] See here 'De la perfectibilité de l'espèce humaine', 387–415.

Royal in Paris in 1819.[94] 'Since we live in modern times', Constant told his audience, 'I want a liberty suited to modern times.' As the aim of the moderns was 'the enjoyment of security in private pleasures', it followed that liberty should be defined in terms of 'the guarantees accorded by institutions to these pleasures'. Specifically, liberty consisted of

> the right to be subjected only to the laws, and to be neither arrested, detained, put to death or maltreated in any way by the arbitrary will of one or more individuals. It is the right of everyone to express their opinion, choose a profession and practice it, to dispose of property, and even to abuse it; to come and go without permission, and without having to account for their motives or undertakings. It is everyone's right to associate with other individuals, either to discuss their interests, or to profess the religion which they and their associates prefer, or even simply to occupy their days and hours in a way which is most compatible with their interests or whims.[95]

This contrasted with the liberty of the ancients under which, according to Constant, 'all private actions were submitted to severe surveillance'.

It is in this light that Constant's great lecture has been understood. He has been seen to espouse a purely negative conception of liberty. As ever, Constant's thinking merits a more complex reading. 'From the fact that modern liberty differs from ancient liberty', Constant explained, 'it follows that it is threatened by a different sort of danger.' That danger was none other than 'that, absorbed in the enjoyment of our private independence, and in pursuit of our particular interests, we should surrender our right to share in political power'. The temptation, in other words, was that we would turn our backs completely upon what Constant saw as the 'active and constant participation in public power' exercised by the ancients, thereby reducing our relationship with government to that of obeying and paying. This, Constant forcefully observed, would be a mistake, for the simple reason that happiness alone was not our goal. It is, he remarked, 'to self-development that our destiny calls us' and it was through the exercise of political liberty that this could best be attained. 'Political liberty', Constant declared, 'by submitting to all the citizens, without exception, the care and assessment of their most sacred interests, enlarges their spirit, ennobles their thoughts, and establishes among them a kind of intellectual equality which forms the glory and the power of a people'. The ambition, therefore, was not to enjoy one or other form of liberty but rather 'to learn to combine the two together'.

III

When, therefore, Constant provided his definition of the liberty of the moderns he did not stop at the idea that it amounted to our ability freely to pursue our whims and interests. Rather, he concluded with the suggestion that it consisted of 'everyone's right to exercise some influence on the administration of the government,

---

[94] See Constant, *De la liberté*, 493–515.   [95] Ibid. 494–5.

either by electing all or particular officials, or through representations, petitions, demands which the authorities are more or less compelled to take into consideration'.[96] The pressing problem was to create a political system that would make this possible, whilst at the same time avoiding a return to the excesses of popular sovereignty. In Constant's case, he again turned to England by way of example, arguing in favour of both a hereditary chamber and an elected lower house. Citing the House of Lords, Constant asserted that an hereditary chamber was compatible with the existence of 'civil and political liberty' and that it acted as a vital 'intermediary' body between monarch and the representatives of the people. Constant's views on the elected chamber were equally straightforward. He rejected the French system of electoral colleges in favour of the English practice of direct election based upon a stringent property qualification. Defending the latter, he articulated what was to be one of the key themes underpinning liberal discourse in the first half of the nineteenth century: enlightenment and 'rectitude of judgement' derived from leisure, and leisure was only possible through the possession of property: hence 'property alone makes men capable of exercising political rights'.[97] Just as importantly, Constant recognized the logic underpinning representative government. 'What', he remarked, 'is general representation but the representation of all partial interests which must reach a compromise on the objects they have in common'.[98] It was, in other words, private and sectional interests that formed the body politic.

Here was a perspective on politics that had been roundly condemned and rejected by France's practitioners of revolutionary politics.[99] The passion for national unity and for the overcoming of divisions, evident in the rhetoric of Sieyès onwards, made it almost impossible to conceive of divergences of opinion or examples of dissent as being anything other than the consequence of the existence of 'faction' and thus as being illegitimate. Similarly, the years of the Empire had scarcely been characterized by the toleration of voices opposed to the sovereign will of the Emperor. It was therefore only with the Restoration of the Bourbon monarchy in 1814 that France took a tentative step towards the creation of a system of representative government embracing both the existence of political parties and the practices of constitutional opposition. This experience, resting as it did upon a series of uneasy compromises made evident at the outset when Louis XVIII graciously 'granted' his people a new constitutional charter 'by the free exercise of our royal authority', proved to be an unhappy one, ending ignominiously with the Revolution of 1830. It did nevertheless provide an apprenticeship of sorts in the arts and principles of parliamentary government.

The foundational text of the Restoration was the Charte of 1814.[100] Dated the nineteenth year of Louis XVIII's reign, the clear intention was to reaffirm the continuity of French history across the divide of the Revolution. However, the rhetorical baggage of monarchical absolutism was accompanied by an acceptance of

---

[96] Ibid. 495.   [97] Ibid. 316.   [98] Ibid. 306.
[99] See Pierre Rosanvallon, *La Démocratie inachevée* (2000), 41–91.
[100] See Pierre Rosanvallon, *La Monarchie impossible: Les Chartes de 1814 et de 1830* (1994).

certain limitations to the monarch's power. Recognized was equality before the law and freedom of religious conscience. Greater liberty was accorded to the press. Powers to effect arbitrary arrest were diminished. In addition, although cast as ancient institutions, the Charte recognized the existence of two parliamentary chambers, one of which, the Chamber of Deputies, was elected upon the basis of a restricted property franchise. Parliament was to meet regularly and at prescribed intervals. No law could be enacted without its consent. Moreover, Louis XVIII certainly intended to reign as a constitutional monarch and, despite his own prejudices and the considerable powers invested in his person, largely remained true to his word.[101]

That said, the existence of the restored monarchy was never more than precarious and fragile. The Ultras, as the hard-line supporters of royal power became known, fought long and hard over the next two decades to strengthen the position of the throne, and were especially influential after the assassination of the king's nephew, the Duc de Berri, in 1820. Following the dismissal from the government of the king's favourite, the moderate Decazes, a series of measures were passed which restricted individual rights and the freedom of the press. Electoral reform, through the so-called Law of the Double Vote, shifted power back towards the owners of landed property.[102] With the ascent to the throne of a receptive Charles X in 1824, the Ultras appeared, momentarily, to have got their way, the government of Villèle passing legislation intended to protect the position of both Church and aristocracy. As opposition to Charles X's rule grew in intensity, the appointment of the Polignac ministry in 1829 amounted to a declaration of war against liberal and popular opinion. A year later the Bourbons sailed into exile for good.

Yet the principles underpinning the Charte were far from clear and were, accordingly, open to a variety of interpretations. There were those, following the opinions expressed by the Comte de Montlosier in his widely read *De la Monarchie française depuis son établissement jusqu'à nos jours*, who were prepared to see the Restoration in terms of an unadulterated return to the pre-revolutionary past. 'A King, a Senate, a Chamber of Representatives', Montlosier proclaimed in his addendum entitled 'Du Retour de la Maison du Bourbon', 'it is in this way that the French monarchy existed under Philip-Augustus and under Charlemagne; it is in this way that it existed in the forests of Germania'.[103] Others, equally enthusiastic about the royalist cause, were ready to endorse a more accommodating vision of the type of politics required in the France of the Restoration. Of these the most influential, and always the most eloquent, was François-René de Chateaubriand.

An early admirer of Louis XVIII's 'unfailing serenity', Chateaubriand saw that the restored monarchy offered France the possibility of peace, calm, and prosperity. Moreover, he saw that the Charte was not some 'exotic plant' imported into a

---

[101] See Isabelle Backouche, *La Monarchie parlementaire 1815–1848* (2000). See Philip Mansel, *Louis XVIII* (London, 2005). Mansel is of the view that, for all his faults, Louis XVIII realized that France needed 'peace, rest and forgetfulness'.
[102] See A. B. Spitzer, 'Restoration Political Theory and the Law of the Double Vote', *Journal of Modern History*, 54 (1982), 746–65.
[103] Cte de Montlosier, *De la Monarchie française* (1814), iii. 405.

foreign and hostile environment but 'a peace treaty signed between two parties which had divided the French', a treaty where each side—liberals and royalists—had given up something for 'the glory of the homeland'. If the new constitutional arrangements were not perfect—after all, the French could not achieve in six months what it had taken the English centuries to accomplish—the new government ruled in the interests of all, including those of the most numerous class.[104]

Chateaubriand's *De la monarchie selon la Charte*,[105] first published in 1816, gave a detailed exposition of the principles of what he did not hesitate to describe as 'representative monarchy'. Starting from the assumption that it was not possible to return to the *ancien régime* and that a return to Bonapartist despotism was to be avoided, the Charte, on this view, offered the only practical alternative for the monarchy. Chateaubriand therefore sketched out a plan for representative government, with ministers responsible before parliament and dependent upon the support of majority opinion. Within this schema, the monarch was to reign but not to govern, thus preserving the inviolability and sanctity of the throne.

But it was the advocates of the growing body of liberal opinion who did most, in both theory and in practice, to establish the foundations of a representative system. The key figures in the period between 1815 and 1848 were those who constituted the group known as the Doctrinaires.[106] Described in this way (by their opponents) because of their apparent attachment to 'principles' and 'doctrines', the membership of this imposing coterie included such eminent figures as Pierre-Paul Royer-Collard, François Guizot, Charles de Rémusat,[107] Prosper de Barante,[108] and Victor de Broglie. Others, only slightly less distinguished, were to be found among their number. Never a completely coherent or unified group, their basic position was that of seeking to secure what they regarded as the proper application of the Charte—a stance which ironically disposed them to allow the monarch greater discretion in the use of his power than envisaged by Chateaubriand—whilst ensuring that this was done in a liberal spirit.

This position was clearly disclosed in the parliamentary speeches of Royer-Collard.[109] Upon his first election as a deputy in April 1797, he declared to his electors that his principles were those of everyone who 'hoped and wished to see the return of order, of justice and of liberty, the restitution of morality upon long-established foundations, the definitive and absolute expulsion of the

---

[104] Chateaubriand, *Réflexions Politiques sur quelques écrits du jour et sur les intérêts de tous les Français* (1814), in *Chateaubriand: Grands Écrits politiques*, ed. Jean-Paul Clément (1993), i. 151–275.

[105] Chateaubriand, *De la monarchie selon la Charte* (1816), *Grands Écrits politiques*, ii. 319–522.

[106] See Aurelian Craiutu, *Liberalism under Siege: The Political Thought of the French Doctrinaires* (Lanham, Md., 2003).

[107] See Rémusat, *Politique libérale ou Fragments pour servir à la defense de la révolution française* (1860) and Darío Roldán (ed), *La Pensée politique doctrinaire sous la restauration: Charles de Rémusat:—Textes choisis* (2003). See also Dario Roldán, *Charles de Rémusat: certitudes et impasses du libéralisme doctrinaire* (1999).

[108] See Antoine Denis, *Amable-Guillaume-Prosper Brugière, Baron de Barante (1782–1866): Homme politique, diplomate et historien* (2000).

[109] See Prosper de Barante, *La Vie politique de M. Royer-Collard: Ses Discours et ses Écrits*, 2 vols. (1861). This text contains a commentary by Barante plus extensive selections from the speeches and writings of Royer-Collard.

revolutionary monster'.[110] In his subsequent career he did not waiver from these original convictions. With the Restoration, therefore, he did not hesitate to describe the monarchy as the form of government that most 'suited' France. This, he affirmed, was not just a political truth but one derived from sentiment as well as from experience. He thus concluded that the king should have the power necessary to govern and that to deprive the king of the power of initiative, to make his government dependent upon the support of a parliamentary majority, would be 'to strike royalty at the heart'.[111] Allied to these conclusions were a set of views about the nature of representation and a profound mistrust of elections as a process of selection. To elect a deputy, Royer-Collard believed, was not a right but a function, and one that had to be performed with independence and discernment. Once elected, the deputy was in no sense delegated to represent either the will or opinions of his electors.

The first thing to note is that Royer-Collard openly distanced himself from the British model of parliamentary government.[112] This argument was deployed to refute the demand of the Ultras that the electoral law should be changed so as allow the re-election of all deputies once very five years. Royer-Collard defended the system introduced by the Charte whereby one-fifth of the deputies sought re-election each year and he did so on the grounds that France could not and should not emulate English parliamentary practices. He listed three specific reasons for this. First, France had no tradition of fixed and stable parliamentary majorities. The spirit of party, he intimated, was alien to the French character, which prided itself upon independence and a refusal to prejudge an issue before the arguments had been heard and presented. Next, ministers would not have the means to cultivate such a majority. Corruption was anathema to 'French character and national scrupulousness'. Finally, no such fixed majority support would be required because, unlike in England, the monarch governed independently of the parliamentary chamber. The day, he predicted, when the government was dependent for its existence upon the 'majority of the Chamber' would be not only the day that marked the end of the Charte but also the day when 'nous sommes en république'.[113]

But these arguments were only a preface to a more complete theory of representation outlined by Royer-Collard in his parliamentary addresses. Recognizing that the Charte was silent on a number of important questions, he raised the issue of whether the vote should be seen as 'a fact created by the Charte relative to the Chamber or a right anterior to the one or the other'.[114] Was voting simply 'the most convenient way' of selecting the members of a parliamentary assembly or 'the exercise of a national right, a popular right, inherent to the very nature of political societies'?[115] On this, Royer-Collard argued, would depend whether the Charte received a monarchical or republican reading. Next, however, had to be considered the difficulty of what was constituted by and through the process of election.

---

[110] See Prosper de Barante, *La Vie politique de M. Royer-Collard: Ses Discours et ses Ecrits*, 2 vols. (1861). This text contains a commentary by Barante plus extensive selections from the speeches and writings of Royer-Collard, i. 26.

[111] Ibid. 217.   [112] Ibid.   [113] Ibid. 213–17.

[114] Ibid. 225.   [115] Ibid. 224

Royer-Collard's response was to suggest that representation had to be understood at best as a 'metaphor'. In order for the idea of representation to make any real sense, he contended, it was necessary that the representative bore a true resemblance to the person represented, and for this to be the case the representative had to do precisely what the represented would do. It followed that 'political representation presupposed a binding mandate' and that it was only in this strict sense that the Chamber of Deputies could be considered to be representative. Thus conceived, the will of the nation would be 'continuously expressed'. But few, if any, governments, Royer-Collard responded, could meet these conditions and when, as in France under the Charte, the number of electors was limited and no binding mandate existed to speak of, representation amounted to no more than 'a chimera, a lie'. Indeed, Royer-Collard argued, as conceived by the Charte the Chamber of Deputies constituted a 'power' and not a form of representation. It was therefore 'false in principle and impossible in fact that the opinion of the Chamber should always and necessarily be the opinion of the nation'. 'Interests', he proclaimed, 'are a far surer gauge of opinion than opinion can be of interests.'[116]

What purpose, then, did an elected assembly serve?[117] Royer-Collard immediately dismissed three arguments supposedly in its favour. Elections were not necessary to secure the existence of a second chamber. Elections were no better guarantee of independence than the hereditary principle. Elections were not the only means of ensuring that a chamber was peopled by honest and capable men. 'There is', he told his fellow deputies,

> an elected Chamber in the interests of the nation, in order that its views and needs should be known and its rights respected and so that political liberty can come to the aid of civil liberty, of which it is the sole effective guarantee. There is an elected Chamber in the interests of the government, in order that confidence, which is the principle of elections, extends to it and encourages a more ready and voluntary obedience. Finally, there is an elected Chamber in the interests of both nation and government, in order that serious errors and grave injustices, which are the motors of civil discord and revolutions, do not accumulate within the social body, and so that society as a whole, with all its known or unknown tribulations, should constantly resound within government and constantly secure its attention, thus ensuring that government, forewarned of the dangers, should be vigilant, prudent, and provident.[118]

As such, an elected chamber served as the best means of both protecting the hereditary monarchy and of averting revolution.

What was completely missing in this argument was any reference to either the sovereignty of the people or the equality of political rights. On this account, the elected deputy was no more a representative of the people than was a peer of the realm. The deputy had a function to perform, that of deliberating freely and without the restraints of party upon the interests of the country, and it was for this reason that Royer-Collard had no difficulty reconciling himself to the limited franchise endorsed by the Charte. 'According to the principles of our government', he announced, 'a higher [financial] contribution does not in itself confer any personal pre-eminence or privilege but it is

---

[116] Ibid. 229.   [117] Ibid. 274–86.   [118] Ibid. 278–9.

required for certain functions as a necessary guarantee of independence and enlightenment.'[119] 'Aptitude' and 'capacity' were associated with 'personal wealth' and therefore all those able to make the financial contribution required for eligibility to vote were deemed to be 'equally capable'. Similarly, Royer-Collard did not see an elected chamber as an especially appropriate vehicle to secure the protection of what he termed 'national liberties'. Such a role, he contended, resided in the government as a whole and among all its constituent parts: the monarchy, the hereditary chamber, and the elected chamber. Indeed, on this view, any strengthening of the political importance of the elected chamber would weaken these protections, as France's recent experience had revealed. 'The Revolution', Royer-Collard declared, was 'nothing else but the doctrine of representation in action'.[120]

These views were expressed by Royer-Collard in the early years of the Restoration, and were put under severe strain by a succession of ultra-conservative governments that seemed to wish to operate in opposition to the perceived interests of society and in violation of the principles laid down by the Charte. Nevertheless, if Royer-Collard's rhetoric was to change over time, the basic philosophy remained intact. This was the manner in which Royer-Collard sought to defend a parliamentary chamber composed of the hereditary peerage after the revolution of 1830. Against the sovereignty of the people, he counterpoised 'the sovereignty of reason, the sole legitimate legislator of humanity'. He further argued that society should not be seen as 'the numerical assemblage of individuals and of wills' but as being composed of 'legitimate interests'. To that extent, the peerage was a proper part of the system of representative government, because it was an expression of 'a social fact: namely, the social inequality resulting from different kinds of superiority: glory, services rendered to the State, property or wealth'. Royer-Collard then added that this amounted not to a representation of inequality for its own sake but rather to a mechanism that served 'the protection of society as a whole'. If this institutional device were taken away, France would be left with nothing but a form of democracy resting upon the sovereignty of the people and, as history had shown, this would lead to 'anarchy, tyranny, misery, bankruptcy, and finally despotism'. The stark conclusion was that democracy could not produce 'prudent' government, and therefore that 'political equality' was not 'the just and necessary consequence of civil equality'.[121]

The message, repeated time after time by Royer-Collard in his solemn speeches before the parliamentary chamber, was that the Revolution would only be brought to an end if politics could leave passion behind and enter a new age of reason. This, he believed, entailed the institutionalization of stable, constitutional government, resting upon the incorporation of those who represented the general interests of society. On pragmatic grounds alone, a limited franchise appeared to be the best means of avoiding tyranny and disorder. From this, however, we get little clue as to whom the Doctrinaires believed were best placed to represent the general

---

[119] See Prosper de Barante, *La Vie politique de M. Royer-Collard: Ses Discours et ses Ecrits*, 2 vols. (1861). This text contains a commentary by Barante plus extensive selections from the speeches and writings of Royer-Collard, 410.

[120] Ibid. 231.

[121] *Opinion de M. Royer-Collard sur l'hérédité de la Pairie, 4 Octobre 1831* (1831).

interests of society. To find out the answer, there is no surer guide than the writings of one of the towering figures of French politics in the first half of the nineteenth century: François Guizot.

The ideas of Guizot were briefly examined in the last chapter. There we saw that, in opposition to the contract theories of Rousseau, he had sought to establish that reason, rather than the will of the individual citizen, was the true source of legitimate power. For over five decades, this was the theme that informed his writings and his extensive political career: Guizot was Minister of Education between 1832 and 1837, Foreign Minister between 1840 and 1847, and Premier in 1848. Arguably, however, it was the short period between the restoration of the monarchy and the early years of the 1820s that was most decisive for his intellectual development. Responding to events as they unfolded, it was in these years that he published *Du gouvernement représentatif en France, en 1816*, *Du gouvernement de la France, depuis la Restauration et du ministère actuel*, and *Des moyens de gouvernement et d'opposition dans l'état actuel de la France*. Between 1820 and 1822 he also delivered the series of lectures that, three decades later, were published in two volumes as *Histoire des origines du gouvernement représentatif en Europe*.

Guizot was born in Nîmes to a prosperous Protestant family.[122] His father had been executed during the Terror. After a period of exile in Switzerland, Guizot arrived in Paris in 1805, and there began a brilliant academic career, matched by a rapid entry into liberal circles. In 1814 he participated in the formulation of the Charte and then, unlike Benjamin Constant, again went into exile with the return of Napoleon Bonaparte. For the next five years he operated on the margins of government, seeking like his friend Royer-Collard to secure a liberal reading of the Charte. With the assassination of the Duc de Berri he was effectively forced into opposition. Faced with this turn of events and with the threat of counter-revolution, he determined upon outlining the principles of a form of government he thought appropriate to modern society.

The starting point was an analysis and interpretation of the Revolution of 1789. The Revolution, Guizot argued controversially, 'was a war, a real war, such as the world had previously known between foreign peoples'.[123] For more than thirteen centuries, he argued, France had been divided between 'a defeated people' and a 'victorious people'. Her history had been the history of this struggle. The result of the Revolution, he asserted, was beyond doubt that the former defeated people had become the victorious people. To that extent, the Revolution was a form of retribution, an act of revenge by a majority which had been for so long oppressed by a dominant minority. It was, however, precisely the numerical superiority of the victors that had led the 'theoreticians of the revolution' to imagine, incorrectly, that this thereby presaged the establishment of the sovereignty of the people as the new principle of government. This was not so, Guizot replied, for the good reason that

---

[122] See Gabriel de Broglie, *Guizot* (1990) and Laurent Theis, *François Guizot* (2008).

[123] François Guizot, *Du gouvernement de la France depuis la Restauration et du ministère actuel* (1820), 1.

what had occurred was the straightforward victory of 'one portion of the people over another'. It was precisely this victory that the Charte had acknowledged.

The political dilemma that now faced France, Guizot argued in 1820, was whether she was to be governed in concert with these 'new interests' and to their 'profit' or whether she was to be ruled 'under the influence' of the old interests associated with the aristocracy and the clergy. In broad outline, Guizot believed that, before 1820, the governments of the Restoration had taken 'the new France as their ally' and that, after the arrival in power of the Villèle ministry, they had sided with the anachronistic and dangerous forces of counter-revolution. Consequently, Guizot spent the 1820s arguing against the foolishness of this strategy, believing that it would only serve to continue France's political instability. At the same time, he identified the need for a 'national party' that could rally and organize the forces of the 'new France' in the parliamentary chamber. In so doing, he sketched out what he saw as a 'new means of government' resting upon 'constitutional equality and legal liberty'.[124]

Guizot did this principally in *Des moyens de gouvernement et d'opposition dans l'état actuel de la France*.[125] He there questioned the principle of the sovereignty of the people, accepting nonetheless that during the Revolution it had served as a 'cri de guerre' and as the precursor of 'a great social metamorphosis'. Removed from its revolutionary context, he argued, it could properly be understood as a principle that defined 'government in terms of the general interest rather than government in the name of this or that private interest'. Thus reconceptualized, it could be allied to a recognition of the 'dominant interests' and 'legitimate needs' of the new society, and as such was better understood as 'the sovereignty of justice, of reason, of right'.[126] So too he questioned whether the Revolution's hostility to aristocracy and privilege had endured. The 'new France', Guizot accepted, had feared nothing more than 'the old French aristocracy', to the point that the 'doctrine of equality' had become 'a confused dogma' leading its proponents 'to pursue a fantasy'. With time, however, and as 'the inferior classes' had obtained their goals, the anger had subsided and 'the idea of equality had appeared in a more tranquil and pure form, always carrying the same name but no longer challenging all superiorities with the same threats, no longer provoking the same furious passions'.[127]

The demand for equality, Guizot therefore argued, could be reduced to the following terms: 'citizens should depend upon their own merits and upon their own strengths; through their own efforts, everyone should become what they can become, meeting no institutional obstacles that prevent them from rising (if they are capable of it) nor support that places them permanently in a superior position (if they are not able to hold their own)'.[128] The love of equality, in summary, should have no other principle than 'the need to rise in society, the most powerful of the needs of our nature'. Guizot's programme, then, was a plea for a civil and legal equality that would allow all those with ability and determination to make the

---

[124] See Craiutu, *Liberalism under Siege*, 155–84.
[125] Guizot, *Des moyens de gouvernement et d'opposition dans l'état actuel de la France* (1821).
[126] Ibid. 142–9.   [127] Ibid. 157.   [128] Ibid. 156–7.

most of their talents, free from external hindrance. What was being envisaged was the emergence of a 'true, natural aristocracy' appropriate to a 'new order' characterized by social mobility.[129] It was a liberal vision precisely because it opposed despotism in all its forms, be it popular, Bonapartist, or monarchical.

Certain important consequences followed from these conclusions. It meant that the function of a representative system of government was not to conjure up the will of the majority through a complex, but flawed, numerical arithmetic but rather to guarantee that 'power' passed into the hands of these 'new superiorities'.[130] Therefore, one of the tasks of government was to seek actively to bring these new capacities and new interests into its ranks. This in turn led Guizot to conceptualize government as 'the head of society' and to envisage that it could rightly concern itself 'with everything that is the object of public interest or that occasions general movement'.[131] This argument also obliged Guizot to reflect upon the mechanisms that would ensure that these new 'superiorities' remained worthy of their place in government. To that end, he envisaged an elaborate system of public transparency built around 'parliamentary chambers, the disclosure of their debates, elections, liberty of the press, and trial by jury'.

It was in Guizot's lectures at the Sorbonne that he gave his fullest exposition of the electoral and parliamentary systems he thought most appropriate to achieve these goals.[132] The point of reference was medieval England. Developing his anti-Rousseauian argument that government was legitimate if it rested upon the claims of 'eternal reason' rather than upon the individual wills of its subjects, Guizot contended that the function of representative government was to bring together all the 'scattered and incomplete fragments' of reason dispersed among the individuals who composed society. It was in this way that 'public reason' would be extracted from the 'bosom of society'.

Part of the charm of the medieval English system, according to Guizot, was that it had evolved almost naturally out of a vibrant pattern of social self-regulation, and it was thus 'the extension and development of existing liberties'. Who, then, were its electors and how did they exercise their rights? 'The true, the sole general principle made manifest in the distribution of electoral rights as it then existed in England', Guizot avowed, 'is this: that right is derived from and belongs to capacity.'[133] The possessors of these rights, he went on, included 'all men invested with real independence, free to dispose of their person and wealth'. These were primarily to be found among freeholders, the clergy, and the burgesses of the larger towns. Beyond these classes existed only those 'labouring on subordinate and precarious property', those reduced to 'servile dependence and brutal ignorance', all of whom could quite justly be excluded from the franchise on the grounds that they lacked the 'material and moral' conditions providing the 'degree of

---

[129] Ibid. 161.   [130] Ibid. 165.

[131] Ibid. 175. See Lucien Jaume, *L'Individu effacé: Ou le paradoxe du libéralisme français* (1997), 119–69.

[132] *Histoire des origines du gouvernement représentatif en Europe,* 2 vols. (1851).

[133] Ibid. ii. 227.

independence and intellectual development which enables a man freely and reasonably to accomplish the political act he is required to perform'.[134] Consequently,
Guizot argued, the medieval English electoral system 'summoned every capable
citizen' and among those deemed to be eligible 'no inequality was established'.

By what external signs could the capacity to participate in elections be ascer-
tained? Guizot's key point was that this question could not and should not be
answered in a definitive fashion, as the indicators of electoral capacity were neither
fixed nor permanent. Again, this observation was illustrated by reference to the
English example. It was very probable, Guizot contended, that in fourteenth-
century England 'all political capacity was almost entirely contained in the classes'
accorded the vote. Since then, however, 'the changes which have occurred in the
condition of property and industry' had been such as to reduce the 'exactness'
between capacity and eligibility. 'The law', Guizot explained to his audience, 'in
its description of the external characteristics of electoral capacity, no longer corre-
sponds really and truly with social facts', and thus 'a principle, equitable at first, has
ceased to be so'. This was the case because the category of freeholder was no longer
sufficient to embrace all those 'capable of exercising political rights'.

These reflections upon the pre-1832 English electoral system allowed Guizot to
reach three important conclusions. The principle that attached electoral rights to
capacity was 'universal in its nature'. Next, the conditions of electoral capacity are
'essentially variable' and would differ according to time, place, the internal situation
of society, and the level of 'public intelligence'. Finally, the laws defining electoral
eligibility should never be 'utterly immutable' and should respond to 'new capacities' as they formed and declared themselves in society.[135]

The next stage in Guizot's account concerned the proceedings and form of
election. Returning to his major theme, he asserted that 'the object of election is
evidently to obtain the most capable and the best accredited men in the country'.[136]
Electors needed to choose wisely. However, according to Guizot, elections were
'sudden acts' that left 'little room for deliberation' and that were 'open to the passions
of the moment'. To rectify this potential problem, Guizot's recommendations were
two-fold. First, the unit of election should be comprised of those who had 'long been
united by common interests' and who were 'accustomed to conduct their affairs
amongst themselves'. Political rights, to that extent, needed to be connected to local
rights. Second, the election itself should take place in the 'habitual sphere' where
the electors passed their lives. In other words, electoral boundaries should be drawn
in such a way as to allow 'respect for natural influences and relations'. Generally
speaking, Guizot concluded, the English system of division into counties had
'attained this two-fold objective'.

What was required of the electors once they had been assembled? Without going
into the precise details, Guizot argued that elections should be based upon a direct,
rather than an indirect, suffrage and that there should be public voting. He also
believed that the electors should avoid what he termed 'the despotism of party

---

[134] *Histoire des origines du gouvernement représentatif en Europe*, 2 vols. (1851), 228.
[135] Ibid. 234–7.   [136] Ibid. 241.

spirit'.[137] Every election was the result of influences but the 'soundness of election' depended upon the elector being subject to a variety of conflicting influences. Through informed deliberation and debate, election would 'bring publicly into proximity and contact the chief interests and various opinions which divide society', in the knowledge that this would produce outcomes 'most suitable for the country in general'. The end result of this process of 'rational and sincere' election, therefore, was 'the triumph of the true majority', 'the minority being constantly listened to with respect'. 'To summarize', Guizot concluded,

> one discovers in the electoral system of fourteenth-century England nearly all the fundamental principles of a free and reasonable electoral system: the bestowal of electoral rights based upon capacity, the close connection of electoral rights with other rights, regard to natural influences and relations, the absence of all arbitrary and factitious combinations in the formation and proceedings of electoral assemblies, prudent limitation in the number to be chosen by each assembly, direct election, and open voting.

Guizot did recognize however that this system, 'at least in part', had been corrupted over time and now required 'correction'.[138]

The final element of Guizot's account concerned the division of legislative power into two chambers. In medieval England, he argued, this separation had been a reflection of the immense inequality of power and wealth existing in society. Gradually the House of Lords had converted itself into 'a national institution' willing to address and defend the 'interests of all'.[139] A 'personal power' had been transformed into 'public power', allowing it to transcend narrow self-interest. Upon this evidence, Guizot defended the mechanism of two chambers on the grounds that it prevented the descent into 'absolute' and 'tyrannical' power. From this there followed a version of the separation of powers argument. The 'principle of representative government', Guizot stated, was 'the destruction of all absolute power on earth'. This was achieved by allowing individual citizens to criticize government, by allowing for the independent existence of such secondary powers as municipal and judicial authorities, and, most importantly, by 'organizing the central power itself in such a way as to make it very difficult for it to usurp rightful omnipotence'.[140] It was in the very nature of a power that had no equal that it would 'soon become absolute'. The 'secret of liberty' was to ensure that this was never the case.

It was only the final remarks of the last of Guizot's lectures that revealed the wider significance of these conclusions. From the latter half of the fifteenth century, Guizot argued, the intimate and continuous relations that had existed between royal power, the aristocracy, and Commons in England began to break down. As a consequence, government fell into the hands of a 'high aristocracy, who were divided and distracted by their intestine quarrels'. England quickly descended into a state of violence and disorder, and neither aristocracy nor Commons remained inclined to struggle against royal authority. Out of this arose the despotic power of Henry VIII and, later, Elizabeth I. 'More than a century', Guizot argued,

---

[137] Ibid. 248.   [138] Ibid. 264.   [139] Ibid. 298–9.   [140] Ibid. 307–8.

'was necessary to enable the English Commons—invigorated and strengthened from a material point of view by long years of order and prosperity and from a moral point of view by the reformation of religion—to acquire sufficient social importance and intellectual elevation to place themselves in turn at the head of the resistance against despotism, and to draw the ancient aristocracy in their train.'[141] It was only after fifty years of political revolution and conflict that representative government was finally established in England. The lesson for France could not have been clearer.[142]

The 1820s appeared to show that this was a lesson that could not be easily learnt. Charles X in particular revealed himself to be singularly unwilling to contemplate any compromise with the 'new France' invoked by Guizot. In May 1830 the monarch dissolved the parliamentary chamber and, when the results of the subsequent elections were not to his liking, he tried to repeat the manœuvre. By royal ordinance Charles X suspended freedom of the press and changed the electoral system. Two days later, on 27 July, protests and popular disturbances began, and within three days Charles X was reduced to humiliating abdication and exile. This is how one of the central actors in the drama, Adolphe Thiers, described the spirit and demands of the protests that brought about the end of the Bourbon monarchy. France, he argued, wanted, 'a representative monarchy, a king, two chambers; a majority whose wishes were respected; and in order for this to be the case: a new dynasty'.[143] The *Trois Glorieuses*, as the three days of popular insurrection overthrowing the Bourbon monarchy became known, had therefore neither changed French society nor changed 'the eternal laws of politics': they had simply realized the promise of the monarchy of 1814 by instituting a regime that was 'liberal and popular'. On this view—a view shared by Guizot[144]—the Revolution of 1789 had been brought to a close. 1830 was the French 1688.

The revisions introduced to the Charte by Louis-Philippe's July Monarchy can be quickly summarized.[145] The preamble to the original charter, which had insisted that the monarch was the sole source of sovereignty, was scrapped. The king, although head of state, could neither 'suspend the laws or prevent their execution'. Roman Catholicism ceased to be the religion of the State. Article 7 reaffirmed freedom of the press, and added that censorship could not be re-established. Greater restriction was placed upon the use of royal ordinances. The right of legislative initiative was to be shared by the monarch and the two parliamentary chambers. Most significant were the changes relating to the Chamber of Deputies. The parliamentary mandate was reduced from seven to five years. The age of eligibility for election to the chamber was reduced from 40 to 30, and for electors from 30 to 25. The tricolour flag was to replace the white flag of the House of Bourbon as the national emblem. A year later, it was decreed that membership of the Chambers of Peers would no longer be

---

[141] *Histoire des origines du gouvernement représentatif en Europe*, 2 vols. (1851), 429–31.
[142] Guizot pursued the same line of argument in his *Essais sur l'histoire de France* (1823).
[143] Adolphe Thiers, *La Monarchie de 1830* (1830), 13.
[144] See Guizot, *Mémoires* (1859), ii. 1–34.
[145] See Munro Price, *The Perilous Crown: France between Revolutions 1814–1848* (London, 2007).

upon a hereditary basis. Taken together, these reforms amounted to a small but significant shift of power away from the aristocracy towards the emerging class of bourgeois *notables* around whom Guizot hoped to build the durability and security of the new regime.

Despite Guizot's statements to the contrary,[146] this aspiration turned out to be something of a colossal failure. What was meant to be a new France based upon the moderate principles of *juste milieu* finished up looking like a corrupt and conservative system operating in the interests of the upper bourgeoisie alone. If the primary preoccupation of the regime appeared to be that of preserving order, Guizot himself unfairly (and inaccurately) became known for one piece of advice he gave to his fellow citizens: 'Get Rich'. In point of fact, Guizot was just as concerned to see the moral elevation of the French population as he was to see their material advancement. It was this concern that had informed the comprehensive educational reforms he introduced between 1832 and 1837. The law of 1833 implemented universal primary education, thereby doubling the number of pupils to almost 2.5 million. These, and other similar, reforms had the pragmatic purpose of seeking to create and strengthen national unity in post-revolutionary France. However, as Pierre Rosanvallon has noted,[147] Guizot's principal weakness derived from an inability to attribute popular protest and dissatisfaction to anything other than 'the simple manifestation of moral disorder'. Thus, when the economy started to run into serious trouble in 1847 and opposition began to mount, he showed himself to be incapable of responding to a situation that defied his understanding. In particular, he consistently opposed the demand to extend the franchise beyond its 260,000 electors. As that campaign mounted. with a series of what became illegal 'banquets', Guizot's unpopularity increased. On 23 February 1848 the king removed him from his position as the head of government. A day later Louis-Philippe himself abdicated in favour of his grandson, the Comte de Paris, and left for England in the guise of Mr Smith. On the next day the advent of the Second Republic was proclaimed from the Hôtel de Ville in Paris.

It was at this point that the increasing impoverishment of Guizot's thought became most visible. In 1849 he published *De la Démocratie en France*.[148] Written in exile in London, it was nothing if not polemical and rancorous in tone. What, however, is most striking was Guizot's refusal to contemplate any compromise with the spirit of a more extensive democracy. The text began with the assertion that France's 'greatest weakness', from which all her other ills derived, was that of 'idolâtrie démocratique'. It was this that undermined and destroyed France's governments as well as her liberties, her happiness, and her dignity. Democracy's 'empire' was such that it had become the 'sovereign, universal word', appropriated by all parties as their talisman and thus as a justification for 'social war'. Everywhere, Guizot contended, the individual liberties of citizens faced the 'volonté unique'

---

[146] In his *Mémoires*, Guizot argued that the system introduced by the Charte in 1814 and reformed in 1830 had given France 'thirty years of free and regular government'.

[147] Rosanvallon, *Le Moment Guizot*, 305.

[148] Guizot, *De la Démocratie en France* (Brussels, 1849).

embodied by the numerical majority of the nation. The inevitable result would be 'revolutionary despotism'. 'It is this idea', Guizot wrote, 'that has to be eradicated.'[149] And so, recognizing the immense appeal and vitality of this idea, Guizot was left only with the option of seeking to rally 'all the conservative forces of social order' to hold back the advancing tide. 'Not being able to suppress [democracy], it must be contained and controlled.'[150] Unless this could be done, he believed, France would be lost.

IV

Reading these lines it is hard not to recall the celebrated introduction provided by Alexis de Tocqueville to his *De la Démocratie en Amérique*.[151] Democracy was seen by Tocqueville as 'the rapidly rising power in Europe'. Due to political failure, it had been abandoned to its wildest instincts and was now slavishly worshipped as 'the idol of strength'. Democracy, therefore, needed to be educated and to be made fit to govern. But it was there that the similarities ended. A consistent thread running through Guizot's entire work was the contention that some form of inequality was an inevitable aspect of all societies and that to ignore this was to commit oneself to acts of unpardonable political folly. Tocqueville took an opposing view: for him, the gradual development of the principle of equality and its expression in the form of an equality of conditions was the fundamental and irresistible fact of our history. As a tendency it was universal and lasting, and it eluded all human interference. It was, indeed, a 'providential fact' and to attempt to check its progress was 'to resist the will of God'.

This conclusion had been confirmed by what Tocqueville had seen on his visit to America.[152] 'It appears to me beyond a doubt', he wrote, 'that, sooner or later, we shall arrive, like the Americans, at an almost complete equality of conditions.'[153] And for Tocqueville, this meant democracy, as both a political *and* a social principle, as a principle of both government and civil society.[154] 'I confess', Tocqueville commented, that 'in America I saw more than America; I sought there the image of democracy itself, with its inclinations, its character, its prejudices and its passions'.[155] What was more, America appeared to have achieved this 'great social revolution' with 'ease and simplicity'. There, democracy seemed to have 'nearly reached its natural limits'.[156] Tocqueville quickly added that he did not believe that it would necessarily be the case

[149] Guizot, *De la Démocratie en France* (Brussels, 1849), 8.
[150] Ibid. 115.
[151] Alexis de Tocqueville, *De la Démocratie en Amérique*, in *Œuvres complètes* (1951), i/1. 1–14.
[152] See James T. Schleiffer, *The Making of Tocqueville's 'Democracy in America'* (Chapel Hill, NC, 1980).
[153] *De la Démocratie*, i/1. 11.
[154] See Pierre Manent, *Tocqueville and the Nature of Democracy* (Lanham, Md., 1996).
[155] *De la Démocratie*, i/1. 12.
[156] For three recent commentaries see Cheryl Welch, *De Tocqueville* (Oxford, 2001); Sheldon Wolin, *Tocqueville between Two Worlds: The Making of a Political and Theoretical Life* (Princeton, NJ, 2001); and Lucien Jaume, *Tocqueville: Les Sources aristocratiques de la liberté* (2008).

that France would draw the same political conclusions from the equality of conditions. However, as the 'generating cause' operating in both countries was the same, he did consider that in the American example there could be found 'instruction from which we might profit'. 'A new science of politics', he proclaimed, 'is needed for a new world.'[157]

Yet the essential problem that Tocqueville believed was now confronting France was not one that he had been the first to disclose.[158] In the introduction to *De la Démocratie en Amérique*, Tocqueville painted a vivid picture of the condition of France. Distinctions of rank were disappearing. Property was divided and power was shared by the many. The spell of royalty had been broken. The individual powers which were able to struggle against tyranny had been destroyed. Government alone had inherited all the privileges formerly possessed by families, guilds, and individuals. The oppressive and conservative power of a small number had been succeeded by the weakness of the whole community. 'We have', he concluded, 'abandoned what advantages the old state of affairs afforded, without receiving anything of use from our present condition; we have destroyed an aristocracy but, having stopped complacently among the ruins of the former edifice, we seem to want to remain there forever.'[159] There was little here with which the Doctrinaires and many royalists would have disagreed. The mark of Tocqueville's originality was that he provided a new response, if not a new diagnosis, and one that was far more open to the possibilities offered by democracy.[160]

Prosper de Barante,[161] for example, had already provided a lucid account of the crushing of the *communes* in France by centralized, monarchical power. The consequence of this had been both the loss of local liberties and the moral and intellectual impoverishment of the country. The 'free and regular management of local affairs', he argued, gave citizens strength and wisdom, destroyed 'isolation' and 'apathy', taught them to know and love public order, and, just as importantly, not 'to tremble docilely' before men of power.[162] Restoring that system to vigour, he argued, would rest upon 'two elements': 'the spirit of association between citizens, which is the spirit of the *communes*, and the employment of social superiors for the general interest, which is the sole just and reasonable principle of aristocracy'.[163] It was when writers like Barante (not to mention Royer-Collard and Guizot and less-known writers such as Charles Cottu and Vincent de Vaublanc) came to reflect upon the practicalities of this strategy that they hit upon a major problem. In France, not only did such an aristocracy scarcely exist but its claims to superiority and to embody the general interest were not recognized by the population at large: hence the repeated calls for a new aristocracy and for one that would readily accept its social responsibilities.

---

[157] *De la Démocratie*, i/1. 11.
[158] See Annelien de Dijn, *French Political Thought from Montesquieu to Tocqueville: Liberty in a Levelled Society?* (Cambridge, 2008).
[159] Tocqueville, *De la Démocratie*, i/1. 8–9.
[160] Although Tocqueville was not an 'epigone' of the *Doctrinaires*, we know that he attended Guizot's lectures between 1828 and 1830: Mélonio, *Tocqueville et les Français* (1993), 23.
[161] *Des Communes et de l'Aristocratie* (1821).
[162] Ibid. 18–19.   [163] Ibid. 22.

Barante, in particular, tended to look somewhat longingly across the Channel to an England which, in contrast to France, appeared to 'administer itself'.[164] On this view, England alone appeared to have preserved and widened its aristocracy and this, combined with a decentralization of administration that effectively consigned the running of English society to this aristocratic class, had served both to enhance England's wealth and energy and to protect its political life and liberties. The question was not only whether the English system of 'self-government' could be transposed on to France (which even most French liberals doubted) but whether this was an accurate picture of English society or of the position and character of its aristocracy. Tocqueville's conclusions about democracy in America rested upon a significant revision of this picture.

Tocqueville visited America in the spring of 1831, returning to France in February 1832.[165] The first volume of *De la Démocratie en Amérique* appeared in 1835. In 1833 and again in 1835 he made extended visits to England, travelling widely (visiting industrial cities such as Birmingham for the first time) and meeting a variety of influential people in British society.[166] As a young man he had shared the fascination of the liberals for English history (accepting the legitimacy of the comparison between 1640 and 1789)[167] and now found himself in an England still agitated by the momentous events surrounding the 1832 Reform Act. His accounts were full of fascinating detail and revealed someone intent on trying to understand a society in the process of transition. Not the least of his interesting observations was his reversal of the equation established by Montesquieu to the effect that it was the spirit of commerce that gave birth to liberty. Tocqueville inverted the formula, arguing rather that it was 'liberty which gave birth to commerce'.[168] He similarly established a fundamental distinction between the characters of the English and French aristocracies on the evidence provided by the meaning of the words 'gentleman' and *gentilhomme*.[169] Although having the same origin, the English version denoted any well-bred person, whatever their birth, whilst the French was reserved for the nobility by birth. In short, the English aristocracy was open to all those with the ability to ascend into it and it was this that accounted for its continued strength and vigour.

Nevertheless, Tocqueville firmly believed that the English aristocracy was exposed to dangers to which it would eventually succumb. When he had arrived in England, Tocqueville wrote in September 1833, he had seen that the country 'was assuredly in a state of revolution, because the aristocratic principle, which is the dominant principle of its constitution, daily loses its force'.[170] This, he argued, had

---

[164] *Des Communes et de l'Aristocratie* (1821), 72.

[165] See André Jardin, *Tocqueville* (Baltimore, Md., 1998) and Hugh Brogan, *Alexis de Tocqueville: Prophet of Democracy in the Age of Revolution* (London, 2006).

[166] Alexis de Tocqueville, *Voyages en Angleterre et en Irelande* (1967). See Seymour Drescher, *Tocqueville and England* (Cambridge, Mass., 1964).

[167] Mélonio, *Tocqueville et les Français*, 25.

[168] Tocqueville, *Voyages*, 203–7.

[169] Ibid. 108. Tocqueville was later to rework this observation in *L'Ancien Régime et la Révolution*. The same distinction had earlier been made by Auguste de Staël: see *Lettres sur l'Angleterre*, 167–8.

[170] Tocqueville, *Voyages*, 107.

a number of causes but the most important flowed from 'the general movement imprinted upon the human spirit'. Democracy, he observed, was like a rising sea. It withdrew, only to come back with greater strength, always gaining ground. The immediate future of European society was therefore a democratic one. Of this, Tocqueville believed, there could be no doubt. Thus, in England the people were beginning to think that they too should have a share in power and, more numerous by the day, they were making increasingly strident protests. Every day a new aristocratic principle came under attack. 'Thus', Tocqueville concluded, 'the irresistible march of events leads to the gradual development of the democratic principle.'[171]

Tocqueville ended his account of his 1833 visit to England with a powerful metaphorical image. He compared the situation of England with that of the fishermen of Carrick Horn on the Atlantic coast of Ireland who caught their fish from a rope bridge suspended over the sea. In all probability they would survive this hazardous task but if, by chance, they were hit by an unexpected storm or showed a lack of dexterity, they would fall inevitably into the abyss. 'At this precise moment', Tocqueville wrote, 'the English people strongly resemble the fishermen of Carrick Horn.'[172] The stark conclusion was that Europe could not look to the aristocratic principle in the future.

When Tocqueville, with his colleague and friend Gustave de Beaumont, departed for America, their task was to carry out an inquiry into the American penitentiary system.[173] Yet a letter sent by both of them to Jared Sparks, dated 12 September 1831, made clear that their interests early turned to broader subjects. Listed were a set of detailed questions concerning practical matters (schools, roads, etc.) relating to the relationship of local to central government. Three months later, Tocqueville confided to Sparks that he attached great importance to 'studying the principles, forms and means of *local* government activity, of which for so long in France we have sensed the need and sought the model'.[174] It was by no means obvious, however, that Tocqueville should turn to America for lessons.[175] The early romanticism that had associated the new republic with a simple, virtuous and pastoral life had quickly dissipated, giving way to a nightmarish vision of brutish ignorance and squalor. Tocqueville's analysis, in short, went against the dominant current of French opinion.[176] This is not to say, as was later claimed, that Tocqueville painted a picture of 'l'Amérique en sucre'. Even at this stage of his reflections upon American life, he recognized its deficiencies and saw momentous problems ahead for the Union. For example, he saw that democracy in America did not produce good leaders and that those who rose to power were either mediocre or

[171] Ibid. 109.
[172] Ibid. 119.
[173] See Roger Boesche, *Tocqueville's Road Map* (Lanham, Md., 2006), 149–68.
[174] Tocqueville, *Œuvres complètes*, vii. *Correspondance Etrangère d'Alexis de Tocqueville* (1986), 29–39.
[175] See René Rémond, *Les États-Unis devant l'opinion française 1815–1852* (1962) and Philippe Roger, *L'Ennemi américain: Généalogie de l'antiaméricanisme français* (2003).
[176] See my 'French Visions of America: From Tocqueville to the Civil War', in Aurelian Craiutu and Jeffrey C. Isaacs (eds.), *America through European Ideas* (Pennsylvania, 2009), 161–84.

incompetent. Democratic government did not always display 'soundness of judgement' and promoted 'the feeling of envy in the human heart'. The American people were surrounded by 'flatterers'. Most importantly, in the long, final chapter of the first volume of *De la Démocratie en Amérique* Tocqueville showed a clear awareness of the unenviable and seemingly ineradicable plight of America's native and black populations.

However, Tocqueville believed that in America he had discerned a system of government and society that, for all its defects, deserved our admiration. What clearly served to distinguish America from other nations was that 'the principle of the sovereignty of the people was neither hidden nor barren'. It was recognized by the nation's customs and proclaimed by its laws. It expanded freely to touch all aspects of life. '[T]here', Tocqueville wrote, 'society acts by itself and on itself'.[177] The sovereignty of the people was therefore no 'isolated doctrine' of little relevance to either ideas or practices. Thus, in contradiction to European perceptions, what was understood by democratic and republican government in America was the 'slow and quiet action of society ', founded upon the 'enlightened will of the people'. It was 'conciliatory' government, resting upon 'peaceable' citizens, judged to be moderate and responsible, and who sincerely desired 'the welfare of their country'. So, Tocqueville recognized, the people in a very real sense were the ones who 'reign'. They chose the executive and the legislative power, and provided the jurors who sat in the courts. More than this, it was 'evident that the opinions, prejudices, interests, and even the passions of the people, can find no lasting obstacles that prevent them from making themselves felt in the daily direction of society'. It could, then, strictly be said that the 'people govern in the United States'.[178]

The tone in which this was written was one of profound wonder. Tocqueville seemed at times in awe of the sheer vigour and energy of the American people and of their democracy. Everything, he proclaimed, is extraordinary in America. He foresaw the emergence of America as a major commercial power. Likewise, he seemed charmed by the picture of the democratic individual living in conditions of equality. The laws generally promoted the welfare of the greatest possible number. Americans were characterized by public spirit, taking an active and zealous interest in the affairs of their township and county. The individual rights of citizens were protected and there was respect for the law. Yet *De la Démocratie en Amérique* has to be read as an extended comparison, both implicit and explicit, between democratic and aristocratic societies. What were missing in the former were precisely the barriers to tyranny and despotism provided in the latter by the mechanisms of privilege and patronage. It was thus, with astonishing prescience, that Tocqueville disclosed the dual character of democracy, that he saw its potential to unleash a new kind of tyranny: the tyranny of the majority.[179]

The unlimited power of the majority in America took various forms. It in part arose from the assumption that the interests of the many were to be preferred to the

---

[177] Tocqueville, *De la Démocratie*, i/1. 56.
[178] Ibid. 177.   [179] Ibid. 261–4.

interests of the few. It also followed from the belief that the people had the right to do anything they wished. It manifested itself in a 'legal despotism' that favoured 'the arbitrary power of the magistrate'. Most importantly, it existed as a 'moral power' exercised over opinion. 'I know of no other country', Tocqueville wrote, 'in which there is such little independence of mind and real freedom of discussion as in America.'[180] Once decided upon and irrevocably pronounced, the opinion of the majority induced a submissive silence, friends and opponents uniting in assenting to its correctness. It was a tyranny, Tocqueville remarked, that left the body alone and that enslaved the soul. No absolute government, no despotism of the old order, had had the possibility of such untrammelled power. What was more, this potential for tyranny arose directly from the condition of democratic equality.

Here lay the greatest danger facing the American republic. Nevertheless, Tocqueville was confident that the deleterious consequences of the power of the majority could be alleviated. To an extent this derived from the singular good fortune enjoyed by the Americans of living upon a 'boundless continent' that afforded them great material prosperity. More important, as Pierre Manent observes, were the 'artifices by which democracy arrives at gaining control *over itself*'.[181] First among these was the federal system of government, which served to deprive the majority of the 'most perfect' instrument of tyranny. Central government had been able to increase neither its power nor prerogatives. Next came the absence of a centralized administration, and with that the townships and municipal bodies which not only checked the 'tide of popular determination' but also gave the people 'a taste for freedom and the art of being free'. The third counterweight to democracy came in the shape of judicial power and the character of the legal profession. In such a society the latter constituted something of a natural aristocracy and the only one with which, without violence, democracy could be combined. As a general rule, the members of the legal profession were the friends of order and the opponents of innovation, and because of this they had a tendency 'to neutralize the vices inherent in popular government'. Moreover, in America, the legal profession had the all-important power of being able to declare laws to be unconstitutional.

More than this, democracy in America was preserved from the tyranny of the majority by 'the manners and customs of the people'. This had many dimensions, but Tocqueville primarily focused upon the extensive impact of religion upon American life.[182] What Tocqueville perceived clearly were the beneficial consequences of religion as a social force, irrespective of its doctrinal elements. Religion acted so as to elevate the aspirations of the majority, thereby making them more aware of the significance of human liberty. Secondly, religion diminished the element of caprice, of arbitrariness, that could inform the motives of the democratic majority. '[W]hile the law permits Americans to do everything', Tocqueville

---

[180] Ibid. 266.
[181] Manent, *Tocqueville and the Nature of Democracy*, 26.
[182] See Agnès Antoine, *L'Impensé de la démocratie: Tocqueville, la citoyenneté, et la religion* (2003).

remarked, 'religion prevents them from conceiving everything and forbids them to dare everything.'[183]

Tocqueville ended these reflections upon the factors that maintained democracy in America with a consideration of their relevance to Europe.[184] The most important dimension of these remarks followed from his conclusion that anyone in France who wished to revive the monarchies of either Henri IV or Louis XIV must be afflicted by mental blindness. Given the present condition of society there was but the choice between 'democratic liberty or the tyranny of the Caesars'. If this was our fate, should we not, he asked, incline towards the former rather than submit to the latter? Again, Tocqueville did not contend that France should copy the American example but he did believe that, unless France could succeed in gradually introducing democratic institutions and in securing 'the peaceable dominion of the majority', then sooner or later it would 'fall under the unlimited power of one man'.

To recall: these lines were published in 1835. Five years later, and to much less acclaim, the second volume of *De la Démocratie en Amérique* was published. Increasingly aware of the enthusiasm of Americans for physical well-being, Tocqueville now perceived that 'self-interest rightly understood' was one of the guiding principles of American society.[185] Individualism—the 'calm and considered feeling which disposes each citizen to isolate himself from the mass of his fellows and withdraw into the circle of his family and friends'—was the chief vice of democratic man.[186] It sapped 'public virtues' and in time produced outright 'selfishness'. Nevertheless it was through the art of association—'Americans of all ages, all conditions, and all persuasions', Tocqueville wrote, 'constantly unite'[187]—that America had combated individualism. Association, he admitted, did not call forth heroic virtues but it did serve to form 'a multitude of citizens who are orderly, temperate, moderate, farsighted, masters of themselves'.[188] Underlying this was an awareness that despotism prospered in a situation characterized by the social isolation of men.

This is a dimension of Tocqueville's argument that has tended to be overlooked. Towards the end of the second volume of *De la Démocratie en Amérique* Tocqueville remarked that 'the type of oppression with which democratic peoples are threatened will be different from anything there has been in the world before. Our contemporaries would find no image of it in their memories.'[189] As he could not name it, Tocqueville continued, he must define it. His description was as follows: 'In past centuries, there has never been a sovereign so absolute and so powerful that, without the aid of secondary powers, it undertook to administer every part of a great empire. There were none who ever tried to subject all their subjects indiscriminately to the details of a uniform rule.' Had they done so, 'inadequate education, an imperfect administrative machinery, and above all the obstacles raised by unequal conditions would soon have put an end to such a grandiose design'.[190]

---

[183] Tocqueville, *De la Démocratie*, i/1. 306.
[184] Ibid. 326–30.   [185] Ibid. i/2. 127–30.   [186] Ibid. 105.
[187] Ibid. 113.   [188] Ibid. 129.   [189] Ibid. 324.   [190] Ibid. 322.

Despotism in the past, then, 'was violent but its extent was restricted'. Now, however, the State possessed the capacity to administer the entire country and, furthermore, did so in a society characterized by near equality. Therefore, as Tocqueville wrote, 'if a despotism should be established among the democratic nations of our day, it would have different characteristics. It would be more widespread and milder, and it would degrade men rather than torment them.'[191] This 'immense tutelary power' would provide for our safety, secure our happiness, and provide for our needs. Rather than destroy and tyrannize, it would hinder, restrain, enervate, stifle, and stultify, and so much so that, in the end, each nation would be 'no more than a flock of timid and hard-working animals with the government as its shepherd'.[192]

Here was a form of despotism that had been unfamiliar to both Montesquieu and Constant. Moreover, one of the principal sources of this new kind of despotism had arguably been overlooked by Tocqueville himself in the first volume of his study of America.[193] At its outset, the main thrust of Tocqueville's argument had been that the equality of conditions favoured the centralization of power, and from this much by way of despotism sprang. This, he now saw, was not the whole picture. 'In the modern nations of Europe', Tocqueville wrote in 1840, 'there is one great cause . . . which constantly contributes to extending the action of the sovereign and to increasing its prerogatives. . . . This cause is the development of industry, which is favoured by the progress of equality.'[194] By bringing a multitude of people together in the same place, new relations between men were created: 'The industrial class, more than other classes, needs to be regulated, supervised, and restrained, and it naturally follows that the functions of government grow with it.'[195] Not only this, but as nations industrialized they felt the need for roads, canals, ports, and 'other semi-public works'. In such circumstances, not only did the government become the leading industrialist but it tended also to be the master of all others. Governments thus came to appropriate the greater part of the produce of industry and to employ enormous numbers of people. State control became ever more intrusive and minute and, little by little, all initiative was taken away from the private individual and handed over to a government that constantly extended its reach and functions.

We might conclude this discussion of *De la Démocratie en Amérique* with two observations from Tocqueville. The first is his comment that, for all the faults of the system of soft despotism, it was still 'infinitely preferable to [a constitution] which, after having concentrated all powers, would hand them over to one irresponsible man or body of men'.[196] The worst of all despotisms remained that of arbitrary and indiscriminate rule by fear. Second, Tocqueville commented that 'in the dawning centuries of democracy, individual independence and local liberties will always be

---

[191] Ibid. 323.   [192] Ibid. 325.
[193] See Boesche, *Tocqueville's Road Map*, 59–84, 189–210.
[194] Tocqueville, *De la Démocratie*, i/2. 315.
[195] Ibid. 315–16.   [196] Ibid. 325.

a product of art'.[197] In short, whether the equality of conditions would lead to servitude or liberty depended upon the actions of men themselves.

In 1839 Tocqueville entered parliament, where he remained until 1851, sitting on the centre-left of the parliamentary chamber. In 1841, at the tender age of 36, he was elected to the Académie Française. That same year, he visited the French colony of Algeria, and although he criticized military practices, stoutly defended the French imperial project.[198] In 1844–5 he, along with several friends, edited the daily newspaper, *Le Commerce*, a short-lived experiment that brought little success or prestige.[199] In political terms he found himself increasingly disenchanted with the policies pursued by the governments of the July Monarchy, and even less impressed by what he saw as a decline in the standards of public life.[200] Although opposed to the Revolution of 1848, Tocqueville believed initially that the new regime would give 'more liberty to individuals'. He persisted in stating that France had something to learn from American constitutional forms.[201] What followed dashed these illusions. Having been first removed from government, with the *coup d'état* of 2 December 1851 Tocqueville was briefly imprisoned. After this he retired from public life. In the few years remaining to him Tocqueville wrote, but did not complete, *L'Ancien Régime et la Révolution*.

A letter written to one of his many American correspondents reveals how quickly Tocqueville discerned the nature of the regime headed by Louis Napoleon. All of those, he commented, 'who have received a liberal education and who have involved themselves either directly or indirectly in public affairs understand and clearly see that in the name of the sovereignty of the nation all public liberties have been destroyed, that the appearance of a popular election has served to establish a despotism which is more absolute than any of those which have appeared in France before'.[202] Tocqueville did not waiver from this view, although presumably he took no pleasure in seeing his prediction come true.

The 1850s were bleak years for Tocqueville, his failing health accompanied by mounting political pessimism. More generally, this decade and the one following proved to be extremely difficult for those who entertained liberal opinions and for those who viewed France's willing embrace of Bonapartist despotism with dismay. Tocqueville's own political evolution was symptomatic of this. At this point we will leave aside his justly famous analysis of the nature of French society and

---

[197] Tocqueville, *De la Démocratie*, 303.

[198] See Seymour Drescher, *Dilemmas of Democracy, Tocqueville and Moderation* (1968), 151–95, and Jennifer Pitts (ed.), *Alexis de Tocqueville: Writings on Empire and Slavery* (Baltimore. Md., 2003).

[199] The prospectus published by the new editors indicated that they would support 'political liberty and equality before the law' as well as constitutional government: see '[Manifeste pour la nouvelle équipe] du Commerce', *Œuvres complètes*, iii/2. *Écrits et discours politiques* (1985), 122–5.

[200] See Alexis de Tocqueville, *Souvenirs* (1999).

[201] Tocqueville, *Œuvres complètes*, iii/3. *Écrits et discours politiques* (1990), 55–166. In a letter to George Bancroft, dated 15 June 1849, Tocqueville explained that he had accepted a ministerial position because he sought to 're-establish order' and to strengthen 'the moderate and constitutional republic': *Œuvres complètes*, vii. *Correspondance étrangère d'Alexis de Tocqueville: Amérique, Europe continentale* (1986), 125–6.

[202] Ibid. 144.

government prior to the Revolution of 1789, but we should note that it was in this text that Tocqueville gave his clearest statement of what he understood by liberty. Freedom, he wrote, 'is the pleasure of being able to speak, act and breathe without constraint, under the government of God and the laws alone'. Next, liberty was to be valued only as an end in itself. 'Whoever seeks for anything from freedom but itself', Tocqueville observed, 'is made for slavery.'[203] Nor was liberty to be confused with what Tocqueville termed 'a narrow individualism'. This he described as 'the desire to enrich oneself at any price, the preference for business, the love of profit, the search for material pleasure and comfort'.[204] Under the *ancien régime*, he observed, there existed 'an unusual kind of freedom'. People managed to keep 'their soul free in the midst of the most extreme subjection'. France had not yet become 'the deaf place where we live today'.[205] Only liberty, he concluded, could bring citizens out of their isolation; only freedom could 'substitute higher and stronger passions for the love of well-being'.[206]

Tocqueville's fascination with America did not diminish.[207] He was, he told one of his American correspondents, 'half Yankee'. Nevertheless, as his numerous letters reveal, he came to have serious doubts about the society he had once so strongly praised and recommended. Writing a week after the proclamation of the Second Empire, Tocqueville wrote to Jared Sparks that America had nothing to fear but its own excesses—the abuse of democracy, the spirit of adventure and conquest, an exaggerated pride in its strength, the impetuosity of youth—and he therefore strongly recommended the virtues of moderation. But in subsequent years he saw mounting levels of political corruption, increasing mob violence and lawlessness, the first signs of a reckless imperialism, and declining morals and customs. In part he attributed these regrettable developments to the growing levels of immigration from outside the English race and thus to the relative decline of those whom he always regarded as the 'Anglo-Americans'. He also started to appreciate that American capitalism, with its adventurous, gambler spirit, was underpinning the foundations of American democracy. Driven forward by men with 'the instincts of a savage', he could not imagine where it might lead if such people were to gain the upper hand in public affairs. All those institutions and practices that had characterized American democracy, the artifices that had sustained and nourished it, appeared to be losing their force.

The election to the presidency of James Buchanan in 1856 only confirmed this impression. What Tocqueville now perceived was that, in all probability, slavery was to be extended to new states as America moved westwards. The entire prospect filled him with horror and despair. Such a development would be 'a crime against humanity'. He saw too that the future of the Union could no longer be taken for granted. Writing in 1856, Tocqueville announced sadly that America risked

---

[203] Tocqueville, *Œuvres complètes*, ii/1. *L'Ancien Régime et la Révolution* (1952), 217.
[204] Ibid. 74.
[205] Ibid. 168–77.
[206] Ibid. 75.
[207] See Aurelian Craiutu and Jeremy Jennings (eds.), *Tocqueville on America after 1840: Letters and Other Writings* (Cambridge, 2009).

disappointing the hopes of millions of people for a better future, because it offered in reality the disquieting spectacle of an unstable regime led by incompetent and dishonest leaders, relying on corrupt institutions, and incapable of controlling the spirit of excess. 'Viewed from this side of the ocean', he told Theodore Sedgwick in 1856, 'you have become the *puer robustus* of Hobbes.'[208] The country Tocqueville had once seen as a stable and mature democracy, he now regarded as a child who responded only to the blandishments of the stick and the carrot.

It is thus interesting to note that *L'Ancien Régime et la Révolution*, first published in 1856, can be read as a sustained comparison between England and France and one where England was consistently regarded as the preferred example. In stark contrast to the relentless growth and centralization of the French state, Tocqueville argued, England was a country where judicial guarantees and local independence had been preserved. After the rise of Louis Napoleon and the advent of the Second Empire, in other words, England again appeared to be the location of political liberty.

Nor was Tocqueville to be the only liberal to share in this rekindling of enthusiasm for England and the wisdom of its constitutional principles. Michel Chevalier, in a review of Walter Bagehot's *The English Constitution*, praised the English constitution as being 'among the most beautiful products of our civilization' and then proceeded to offer the standard panegyric in praise of English self-government and liberty.[209] More enthusiastic still was the account provided by Charles de Montalembert, one of the leading proponents of liberal Catholicism, in his *De l'Avenir politique de l'Angleterre*,[210] a work greatly admired by Tocqueville. Montalembert's central claim was that England, almost alone, seemed able to hold back the twin perils of autocracy and anarchy. England, he remarked, had 'the sole durable, intelligent aristocracy that exists in Europe'.[211] These comments were all the more remarkable given that at this moment England was the subject of sustained criticism from all sides. As a result of the military and administrative disasters of the Crimean War, Montalembert acknowledged, a growing number of people were predicting the collapse of England.[212]

Yet the most extended and detailed recommendation of the English model can be found in Anatole Prévost-Paradol's *La France nouvelle*, first published in 1868. The title alone gave some indication of Prévost-Paradol's purpose. His subject was 'the political and administrative reform of France'. To secure that end he sketched out a system of government that, in its adumbration of all the essential elements of the English constitution, represented the culmination of liberal admiration of England. Recommended to his French readers were the separation of powers, freedom of the press, the jury system, religious toleration, the preservation of local liberties and self-government, a two-chamber system (one hereditary, one popular), a system of election that would protect minorities as well as recognize

---

[208] See Aurelian Craiutu and Jeremy Jennings (eds.), *Tocqueville on America after 1840: Letters and Other Writings* (Cambridge, 2009), 183.

[209] 'La Constitution de l'Angleterre', *Revue des Deux Mondes*, 72 (1867), 529–55.

[210] Charles de Montalembert, *De l'Avenir politique de l'Angleterre* (1860).

[211] Ibid. 97.

[212] See Charles de Rémusat, 'La Réforme administrative en Angleterre', *Revue des Deux Mondes*, 12 (1855), 241–84.

talent and ability, ministerial responsibility and cabinet government, and finally a constitutional monarch or head of state armed with the power of dissolution. All of these were wheeled out one after the other by way of example and contrasted with France's 'inexperience of parliamentary practices and lack of familiarity with free institutions'. But why did Prévost-Paradol imagine that it was necessary to contemplate such extensive borrowing?

The answer was contained in the opening discussion of the nature of democracy. If it was true, Prévost-Paradol argued, that all societies were moving towards democracy, sooner or later they would aspire to have a democratic political system. The natural tendency of all such democratic government was to become corrupt and to dissolve into anarchy. The disorder within the State would then become such that, out of this intolerable situation, would arise 'democratic despotism'. This, in turn, would justify its existence on the grounds that it could 'assure the maintenance of public order and the salvation of society'. Its goal would become that of satisfying the demands of the 'multitude' for 'well-being' and this would be attained by sacrificing individual liberties. 'Thus charged', Prévost-Paradol wrote,

> with an unlimited mandate and invested, through the laws, with an immense power over men and by the popular imagination with an immense power over things, with the aim of ensuring the general happiness democratic despotism advances with an irresistible force and an insolent pomp, until the inevitable day when, stunned by its own success and seized by a form of drunkenness, it comes up against some pathetic obstacle and collapses into a form of anarchy worse than that which served as its cradle.[213]

With such unremitting pessimism did one of France's leading liberals contemplate the advent of democracy over thirty years after the publication of the first volume of *De la Démocratie en Amérique*.

Even in the difficult political climate of the 1860s the voice of liberalism could still be heard (and often with great vigour). A work such as Odilon Barrot's *De la Centralisation et de ses effets*, published in 1861, continued to voice traditional liberal concerns about an overmighty state and did so by making explicit reference to the ideas of Montesquieu. Similar claims against administrative centralization were made by Jules Simon, through an immensely sophisticated argument grounded upon philosophical first principles and a close analysis of French history. Simon's ambition was to restate the conditions and guarantees of political liberty. Intriguingly, Simon contended that the Revolution of 1789 had 'slipped' rapidly down the slope from 'wise liberty to excessive liberty', leading to anarchy and despotism.[214]

Most impressive of all was Édouard Laboulaye.[215] Not only did he edit and republish Constant's major political writings,[216] but he reworked the latter's

---

[213] Prévost-Paradol, *La France nouvelle* (1869), 35–6.
[214] Jules Simon, *La Liberté* (1859). Simon's criticisms of centralization drew upon a reading of Tocqueville.
[215] See Walter D. Gray, *Interpreting American Democracy in France: The Career of Edouard Laboulaye, 1811–1883* (Newark, NJ, 1994).
[216] *Cours de politique constitutionnelle ou collection des ouvrages publiés sur le gouvernement représentatif par Benjamin Constant avec une introduction et note par M. Edouard Laboulaye*, 2 vols. (1861).

distinction between ancient and modern liberty as part of a self-conscious liberal tradition that ran from the *monarchiens* to Tocqueville.[217] In the same year that he published *L'Etat et ses limites*, he also published *Le Parti liberal, son programme, son avenir*, and in so doing set out a liberal agenda for a 'new generation' freed from the 'illusions and disappointments' of the past. His text, he announced, was a 'programme for modern democracy'. Accordingly, Laboulaye defended an extensive array of what he termed 'social liberties', beginning with religious liberty (he advocated the separation of Church and State), liberty of education, and liberty of association, combined with the traditional liberal advocacy of municipal liberty. With regard to political liberties, Laboulaye recommended not only freedom of the press and an independent judiciary but also 'national representation' and 'an extended electoral suffrage'. In the aftermath of the elections of 1863, in which liberal opinion appeared to be making advances, it seemed to Laboulaye that it was in this direction that France was moving.

V

If Prévost-Paradol's *La France nouvelle* remains known today it is for two reasons. The first is that its author, having thrown in his lot with the liberal Empire of Émile Ollivier, committed suicide upon his arrival in New York when he heard of the imminent outbreak of the Franco-Prussian war. The second is because the book contained the following memorable phrase: 'The French Revolution established a society: it still seeks a government.'[218] This, in a very real sense, had been the refrain of all liberals throughout the nineteenth century. They had sought to bring the political turmoil of the Revolution to an end and to build a regime based upon order, property, and the recognition of individual liberties. They were repeatedly thwarted in these ends, in part due to their own political ineptitude, but also by the combined forces of Bonapartism, republicanism, and monarchical reaction. As Pierre Rosanvallon has commented, '[t]he central question in France has always been that of knowing *who* is the holder of power rather than that of specifying what form this power should take'.[219] If this is true, then the liberals were arguably asking the wrong questions and providing answers that few people wished to hear. Rosanvallon similarly speaks of 'the want of moderation which characterizes a culture in which the sense of compromise and of concession is weak'.[220] Again, the liberal enthusiasm for a *juste milieu*, for constructing a political balance that would embrace all the social forces that made up the new France, held little appeal in such an environment. A harsher response is to suggest, as Sudhir Hazareesingh has done, that the political project of liberalism was 'inadequately attuned to the

---

[217] Edouard Laboulaye, 'La Liberté antique et la Liberté moderne' and 'Alexis de Tocqueville' in *L'Etat et ses limites* (1863), 103–201.
[218] Prévost-Paradol, *La France nouvelle*, 296.
[219] Rosanvallon, *La Monarchie impossible* (1994), 170.
[220] Ibid. 179.

imperatives of its time'. On this account, the rising democratic demands associated with radical republicanism 'triggered a number of recurring tensions among different liberal goals and principles'. Appeals to consensus failed to convince a public opinion that was increasingly polarized.[221] More tellingly still, Hazareesingh's contention is that the liberal conception of citizenship was 'riddled with contradictions'. The advocacy of communal liberties and autonomous citizens looked flimsy and insubstantial when placed by the side of 'an entrenched suspicion of universal suffrage, a sense of confidence in the natural superiority of bourgeois rule, and a defence of traditional social institutions'.[222]

This analysis undoubtedly contains a grain of truth. As we have seen, in the nineteenth century liberalism was not democratic. But nor, for that matter, was democracy liberal. And this should not be forgotten. To their immense credit, the French liberals, probably before anyone else, realized that democracy could spawn an entirely new type of despotism. In its mild form, it could take the shape of Tocqueville's tyranny of the majority; less benignly, it could appear as the Bonapartist usurpation described by Constant or the 'democratic despotism' of the Second Empire described by Prévost-Paradol. In either shape, the liberals were surely right to discern the danger, and right too to seek to find ways to alleviate it.

The irony is that, for all their political failure to carry the electorate with them, it can plausibly be argued that liberal opinion had a deep impact upon the formation of the Third Republic in its early years. This claim would not receive universal assent. However, it can be given substance in two ways. The first is to follow Pierre Rosanvallon and to acknowledge that the *pères fondateurs* of the Third Republic were deeply imbued with the liberal suspicion of a wayward universal suffrage. A 'democratic elitism', Rosanvallon claims, was 'one of the central elements of their political vision'. He quotes Jules Grévy, for example, to the effect that the purpose of representative government was 'to substitute the ignorance of the greatest number by the enlightenment of the elite of our citizens'. The castigation of 'parliamentary anarchy' by Grévy and many others, Rosanvallon argues, reflected the 'secret' desire to see a parliamentary assembly peopled with only 'wise men'. Most tellingly of all, Rosanvallon cites Jules Ferry in order to show that his goal was 'to place the Republic above universal suffrage', to protect it from the passions of society.[223]

Second, there was little in the actual institutional arrangements of the Third Republic that the liberals would have found uncongenial. Certainly this would have been the view of many radical republicans, who (as we have seen) felt deeply betrayed by the compromises entailed in the outcome. But we can surmise that a good few liberals saw the positive benefits of the new constitutional arrangements. For example, this would be the conclusion reached from reading *Vues sur le gouvernement de la France*, by Alfred, Duc de Broglie. Broglie's analysis reworked

---

[221] Hazareesingh, *From Subject to Citizen: The Second Empire and the Emergence of Modern French Democracy* (Princeton, NJ, 1998), 229.

[222] Ibid. 230.

[223] Rosanvallon, *La Démocratie inachévée* (2000), 235–41.

the standard account of how the destructive tendencies of republican democracy had led to Bonapartist dictatorship and the loss of liberty, but it concluded with the argument that only two types of government were now possible for France: a republic informed by constitutional monarchy or a constitutional monarchy informed by the republic. 'Every other Republic', he wrote, 'is the Convention; every other monarchy is the Empire.'[224] A similar argument was advanced by the young liberal Ernest Duvergier de Hauranne in his call for the acceptance of 'a conservative republic'. Accepting that a republic was inevitable, he argued that the 'moderate republicans' and 'conservative liberals' wanted practically the same thing and that, in the institutions of the Third Republic, France now had a system of representative government that combined liberty with order.[225]

Yet, all was clearly not well in the liberal garden. This chapter began with an invocation of the praise lavished upon England as the country of commerce and liberty. The liberals, most notably Constant, developed this theme in order to suggest that a new type of liberty was appropriate to the modern age. Whatever their complexion, all liberals in France accepted some version of this argument. To a greater or lesser degree, they were all prone to Anglophilia. But, with few exceptions, they seemed particularly blind to the fact that it was the changes wrought upon society by the advance of commerce that were to be deeply problematic and that in these circumstances the constitutional palliatives which they were recommending were likely to have little effect or appeal. If, to the evident dismay of the liberals, the workers and the peasantry persisted in wanting 'well-being' rather than 'liberty', this had much to do with the fact that they were hungry and poorly housed and felt themselves to be exploited. Faced with these demands, as was revealed by their response to the labour unrest of 1848, the liberals showed no desire to give up their free-market assumptions. Adolphe Blanqui, for example, insisted that the government should not supply the workers with work, should not help them when they were ill, nor provide for their security in old age. Regulations on minimum wages and maximum hours were deemed to be excessive interference in the workings of the market and thus detrimental to the interests of the workers themselves.[226] The same message received its most forceful and articulate expression in the writings of Frédéric Bastiat.[227]

By way of conclusion, therefore, we might return our attention to those writers who were prepared to challenge not just the virtues of commerce but also the paradigmatic status of English society and government. As we saw in our earlier discussion of Eugène Buret and Flora Tristan, there were many cases of this but undoubtedly one of the most sustained examples was *De la décadence de l'Angleterre*,

[224] (1870), p. lxxii.
[225] Ernest Duvergier de Hauranne, *La République conservatrice* (1873). Duvergier de Hauranne had clearly been influenced (like Tocqueville before him) by his visit to America: see *Huit Mois en Amérique* (1866).
[226] Adolphe Blanqui, *Des Classes ouvrières en France pendant l'année 1848* (1849). See also Michel Chevalier, *Question des travailleurs* (1848).
[227] In addition to the *Œuvres complètes de Frédéric Bastiat*, 6 vols. (1862), see two republications of Bastiat's work: *Sophismes économiques* (2005) and *Pamphlets* (2009).

first published in 1850, and written by the radical writer and parliamentary deputy Alexandre Ledru-Rollin.[228] Turning his back on the 'exaggerations of anglomania', Ledru-Rollin asserted that England was one enormous aristocracy, 'the aristocracy of the crown, the aristocracy of land, the aristocracy of business', and that England's famous liberties gave the people nothing. All aspects of English society came in for this treatment, but by far the greater part of Ledru-Rollin's text was taken up with an account of the conditions of the working class. In a series of sketches of the lives of the various occupational groups, he painted a heart-felt picture of the poverty and degradation resulting from the relentless competition associated with the industrial system. Behind the official prosperity, he argued, lay a universal misery and imminent bankruptcy. England, in sum, was a country that had been destroyed and enslaved by the greed of its aristocratic classes. With patriotic fervour, he thus announced that England's 'half principles of civil, commercial, political and religious liberty' had to be rejected by France, the 'daughter of Rousseau', and that such a rejection would amount to nothing less than the destruction of England itself. The two nations, he proclaimed, were 'going in diametrically opposed directions'. France was rushing towards 'the future of equality' whilst England fortified itself 'more than ever in the privileges of the past'. France, he therefore proclaimed, should stay true to her particular genius and call for 'social justice on earth, the justice of brothers'.[229]

That these were widely held sentiments can be shown by referring to the *Grand Dictionnaire Universel* of 1867. The so-called *Dictionnaire Larousse* had a substantial entry on England, running to fifteen pages. It began with a largely factual account of England's geography, history, and culture, but at the end Larousse took the liberty of adding an imaginary and intriguing discussion between the two archetypal figures of France and England, Jacques Bonhomme and John Bull. To aid his readers, Larousse kindly explained the context in which this discussion was taking place.

'Two entirely opposed currents of opinion about England are evident in France', Larousse wrote: 'One is very sympathetic to the laws and the constitution of England; the other, which has its source in long-standing national enmity, sees in the Englishman only a rival, an enemy that has to be fought to the bitter end.' Jacques Bonhomme, Larousse explained, 'is afflicted with an incurable anglophobia'. Thus, if he had Jacques Bonhomme accept that England possessed a certain amount of power and material wealth, John Bull was quickly informed that the English were 'one of the most wretched people on earth; despite your hard work you languish in poverty and abjection. . . . Your women throw themselves in their thousands into prostitution and your men are stupefied by hard liquor.' In no other country was the struggle for life so hard and defeat so tragic. The causes of this miserable existence were well-known. England's government was a 'veritable oligarchy' and a prey to a 'devouring aristocracy'. In the name of a respect for the law, injustice and arbitrary government were inflicted upon the poor. Liberty existed

---

[228] 2 vols. (1850).   [229] Ibid. ii. 272.

only for the upper classes. In sum, English civilization had remained impervious to demands for the moral and physical emancipation of the lower classes. 'The France of 1793', Jacques Bonhomme concluded, 'denounced your nation to the world as the modern Carthage and the enemy of humanity. The illusions of Montesquieu, of the *philosophes* and of the constitutional school vanished at that point. From cruel experience we had come to appreciate the lack of sincerity to be found in your liberalism.' A very good case could be made for arguing that, over the long term, the rhetorical force of these sentiments was to have far more appeal than liberal calls to commerce, moderation, and individual liberty.

5

Universalism, the Nation, and Defeat

I

Prévost-Paradol concluded *La France nouvelle* with an essay on geopolitics.[1] None of the maladies afflicting France, he ventured, were necessarily fatal but it would take a near superhuman effort for France to retain the position of eminence she had occupied over recent centuries. The context for this remark was Prussia's crushing victory over Austria at the battle of Sadowa in 1866 and France's failure to respond to Prussia's imposition of its hegemony over the other members of the German confederation.

Two aspects of Prévost-Paradol's argument stand out. The first was the contention that France had been mistaken in building her foreign policy around the principle of nationalities. This principle, Prévost-Paradol explained, laid down 'identity of race and language and the consent of the population' as the conditions necessary to legitimize the annexation of a territory.[2] Neither, he argued, could serve France's interests, but they could allow Prussia to forge the union of a single state composed of 51 million inhabitants. In the unlikely event of success against Prussia, he therefore suggested, it would be best for France to put this 'famous principle' to one side and to base her claims simply upon the rights of the victor. Next, Prévost-Paradol saw all too plainly what the outcome of defeat by Prussia would be. France, he surmised, would not be removed from the map—a general attachment to the idea of a balance of power in Europe would ensure this—nor would she necessarily lose Alsace and Lorraine, but she would lose 'the means of opposing this dismemberment on the day that our triumphant rival would judge it to be practicable and useful to its interests, and this day would not be long in coming'.[3] It was not impossible, Prévost-Paradol wrote, that war would be avoided, but, he avowed, France and Prussia had the look of two steam trains heading at full speed towards each other. The image was to prove to be all too accurate.

This was only part of the gloomy scenario facing France. Beyond Europe's borders, Prévost-Paradol continued, '[t]wo rival powers, but which from the point of view of race, language, manners and laws amount to one power, England

[1] Prévost-Paradol, *La France nouvelle* (1869).
[2] Ibid. 380.   [3] Ibid. 383.

and the United States, dominate the remainder of the planet'.[4] Here once more France' recent history had been one of woeful decline and ineptitude and it was this that led Prévost-Paradol to predict that the dominance of the 'Anglo-Saxon race' would only grow in the future, leaving the European powers (including a united Germany) with a few unimportant colonial outposts. From this Prévost-Paradol reached two important conclusions. If France were to survive in anything like a meaningful form 'the number of French people must increase sufficiently rapidly in order to maintain a level of equilibrium between our power and that of the other great nations on the earth'.[5] Next, France had to make the most of 'the supreme opportunity' provided by Algeria. There, he argued, was a colony that was fertile, not too far away from 'la mère patrie' and easy to defend. In addition, from this base colonization could be extended into Morocco and Tunisia so as to construct 'a Mediterranean Empire' appropriate to France's pride and stature. Only two obstacles, Prévost-Paradol believed, stood in the way of this plan: France's continuing uncertainty about what type of regime to construct in Algeria, and 'the Arab people'. 'It is time', Prévost-Paradol responded unambiguously, 'to establish laws in Africa conceived with regard to the extension of French colonization . . . this is French territory which as soon as possible must be peopled, possessed, and cultivated by the French'.[6]

Within two years of these lines being written, France's armies had been routed by those of Prussia and the eastern provinces of Alsace and Lorraine had been lost. Later, and by way of compensation for her national humiliation, France duly set out to construct her Mediterranean Empire, a strategy that was to have immense long-term costs and consequences. After the Franco-Prussian war there could be no denying the stark realities that Prévost-Paradol had only been able to guess at, and in these troubled circumstances, as Prévost-Paradol had already recommended, the validity and utility of the principle of nationalities had to be reconsidered. Just as striking was the pessimistic tone struck by Prévost-Paradol. Where once, he suggested, the question would have been whether France could hold her own against the combined forces of the European states, it now seemed doubtful that she could even stand up to Prussia alone. The 'glorious name of old France' seemed but a bitter memory.

The contrast with the mood of the previous century could not have been more marked. As Colin Jones has written, '[i]n many senses, the eighteenth century was France's century'.[7] The country bounced back from the gruelling wars that had characterized the final years of Louis XIV's reign and was able 'to imprint its influence on every aspect of eighteenth-century European life'. France had the largest population of any of the great powers and experienced long-term economic growth and improving living standards. Paris remained at the epicentre of the intellectual world and the eighteenth century was an age when Europe spoke French.[8] It was not only the language of international diplomacy but also the language of civilization, of the

---

[4] Prévost-Paradol, *La France nouvelle* (1869), 397.   [5] Ibid. 413.   [6] Ibid. 418.
[7] *The Great Nation: France from Louis XV to Napoleon* (London: 2003), p. xiii.
[8] Marc Fumaroli, *Quand l'Europe parlait Français* (2001).

arts, and of the republic of letters. To speak French, in this sense, was to be a party to the aspirations of humanity as a whole. As Jones himself acknowledges, this did not mean that France was a country without weaknesses. The monarchical system did not adapt and gradually imploded, before going bankrupt. There were significant losses of overseas territory, especially after the Seven Years War, when France was ignominiously booted out of both India and North America by the British. However, revenge was swiftly exacted through French support of the American colonists. Most importantly, despite the upheaval and turmoil produced by the Revolution, at the end of the century France had succeeded in greatly extending her borders. In short, what in retrospect looked like Britain's inevitable rise to become the world's dominant power in the nineteenth century did not look quite so certain from the vantage point of the windmill placed on the top of the hill at Valmy at the moment when France's revolutionary army put to rout their Prussian opponents on 12 September 1792.

There could be no better description of the manner in which France was constructed as a territory than that provided by Daniel Nordman.[9] His is an account that recognizes the importance of properly understanding the historic meaning of such words as 'frontier' and 'limit' as a necessary prelude to grasping the intricate processes through which France progressively extended her borders and removed the foreign enclaves that existed within them. It was largely during the reign of Louis XIV, and specifically after the Treaty of Munster in 1648, that France's territory became fixed. Sovereignty over Alsace was confirmed by treaty in 1648 and again by the treaty of Ryswick in 1697 (thereby establishing the Rhine as the frontier between France and the Holy Roman Empire), over Artois and Roussillon through the Treaty of the Pyrenees in 1659, over the Franche-Comté in 1678, and over Strasbourg in 1681. These extensions to French territory were usually the outcome of successful military campaigns. The pattern of acquisition changed significantly in the eighteenth century, when the most noteworthy additions were Lorraine in 1766 and Corsica in 1768. Through painstakingly detailed investigation, servants of the monarchy sought to establish sovereign claim upon often quite small areas of territory in cases where sovereignty was either indeterminate or contested. Relying usually upon either legal or historic evidence, the enterprise was carried out in a spirit of conciliation and exchange. Thus, despite politically useful myths to the contrary, the borders of France were relatively well defined and beyond dispute when the Revolution got under way in 1789.

Two points stand out from this analysis. The first is that, although there was a long-standing sense of the physical limits of France—a sense that at its most rudimentary rested upon a classical understanding of the territory of the Gauls as covering that of present-day France, Belgium, and northern Italy—the actual concept of 'natural frontiers' did not make its appearance until the early nineteenth century. Just as significantly, the concept of 'linguistic frontier' did not manifest itself until much later, probably around the time of the Second Empire. Indeed, the

---

[9] *Frontières de France: De l'espace au territoire XVIe–XIXe siècle* (1998).

language of the inhabitants was virtually absent from earlier territorial considerations, and did not figure significantly during the period of the Revolution. Nor indeed could it, as linguistic maps of Europe were at best sketchy and of little practical, political use. So too it was only during the period of the First Empire that systematic efforts were made to provide a linguistic map of France. The fact was, however, that from the beginning of the nineteenth century language became increasingly associated with nationality.

As Claude Nicolet has remarked, in a French context the word 'Nation' must be placed amongst the category of 'mots voyageurs', words central to political discourse whose sense has changed significantly with passage of time.[10] In the eighteenth century it had at best an indeterminate meaning. Prior to the Revolution of 1789 a person possessed not French nationality but 'the quality of being French' and this was determined not by place of birth but by the bond of parentage.[11] Thus Mirabeau, for example, could speak of 'la nation provençale', whilst Robespierre in Arras could publish an appeal to 'la nation artésienne', thereby maintaining its use as a term to describe a collection of individuals held together by a set of common interests. Voltaire and Montesquieu used the term in a purely descriptive, sociological fashion, as denoting a set of people held together by shared experiences and customs; whilst Rousseau, once again ahead of the game, could speak of all peoples as possessing 'a national character'.[12] For Rousseau, the existence of the nation preceded that of the State but it would be through the State that the sense of being a member of the nation would be strengthened and put to good use.[13]

It was outside the confines of discussions among the *philosophes* that the word came to take definitive shape. There is much that could, and arguably should, be said about the general manner in which over time the nation replaced God as the source of all legitimate authority. With God, although not yet dead, now deemed to be absent from human affairs, there was a felt-need for a new organizational principle capable of generating loyalty among individual members of the community and for some this dubious role fell to the nation. So much we will take as given by way of general background to the emergence of nationalism as an ideology, preferring rather to focus upon the specific context in which the word 'nation' came to prominence in eighteenth-century France.

The first thing to note is that the monarchy itself played an important role in fostering national sentiment. There has been a long-established view that prior to the French Revolution wars did not arouse strong national emotions. However, David Bell has shown that the literature of the Seven Years War, far from portraying

[10] *L'Idée républicaine en France* (1982), 16–18.
[11] Patrick Weil, *How to be French: Nationality in the Making since 1789* (Durham, NC, 2008), 11–13.
[12] See Robert Shaver, 'Paris and Patriotism', *History of Political Thought*, 12 (1991), 627–46.
[13] See Michel Delon, 'Nation', in Pascal Ory (ed.), *Nouvelle histoire des idées politiques* (1987), 127–35; Maurice Cranston, 'Sovereignty of the Nation', in Colin Lucas (ed.), *The Political Culture of the French Revolution* (Oxford, 1988), 97–104; Pierre Nora, 'Nation', in François Furet and Mona Ozouf (eds.), *Dictionnaire critique de la Révolution française* (1988), 801–11; J.-R. Suratteau, 'Nation/Nationalité', in Albert Soboul (ed.), *Dictionnaire historique de la Révolution française* (1989), 781–3.

the conflict between Britain and France as a duel between two royal houses or between two different religions, presented it as 'a battle between irreconcilable nations'. '[S]upporters of the French crown', he writes, 'sought to mobilize the nation as a whole against an enemy nation'. We cannot fully know the extent to which this induced spontaneous expressions of patriotic enthusiasm but we can accept Bell's conclusion that through such propaganda the French came increasingly to see themselves as a nation and one 'which could mobilize itself, instead of simply flocking behind a king'.[14]

More influential still was what Bell characterizes as 'the politics of patriotism'.[15] On this account there were three decisive moments in the development of national sentiment: the regency of Philippe d'Orléans (1715–22); the *parlementaire* crisis in the years 1748–54; and, finally, the so-called Maupeou revolution of 1771. By 1760, Bell argues, the concept of the nation had become central to French political culture, but political competition still existed between rival claims to have originally embodied the nation, to be its modern descendants, and to speak in its name. The contenders are well known: the monarch (clothed increasingly in patriotic garb); the aristocracy (never slow to articulate the view that it was from them, and in the distant Frankish past, that kings derived their original legitimacy); and the *parlements* (once recalled by Turgot, more than ever determined to cast themselves in the role of the patriot party). Yet in each case the language spoken revealed a desire to return to earlier, less troubled, legal arrangements and to put an end to the growing political clamour. This could not be done, and increasingly therefore the concept of the nation acted as a vehicle for political claims and as a source of legitimacy. As Bell makes abundantly clear, the key moment came in September 1788 when the *parlement* of Paris ruled that the Estates-General should meet in its traditional form, the three Estates sitting and voting separately. With this, aristocracy joined royal despotism as the enemy, and a new definition of the nation had quickly to be found.

This definition was provided with breathtaking audacity by the Abbé Sieyès.[16] Henceforth, the Third Estate was taken to be 'a complete nation', with the aristocracy in particular cast out unceremoniously and without regret from the body politic. Next, the representatives of the Third Estate formalized their political ascendancy not merely by redescribing themselves as 'the representatives of the French people' but also by declaring themselves to be members of the National Assembly. The nation thus had been given unambiguous political expression and henceforth it was acknowledged that 'the principle of all sovereignty resides in the nation'.

---

[14] David A. Bell, *The Cult of the Nation: Inventing Nationalism 1680–1800* (Cambridge, Mass., 2001), 78–106.

[15] Ibid. 50–77.

[16] See above p. 75. See also Charles-Philippe-Toussaint Guiraudet, *Qu'est-ce que la nation et qu'est-ce que la France?* (1991). The emphasis in the text fell on overcoming the 'imagined divisions' which separated the French as individuals from one another.

In this way were disclosed two ideas of immense significance and importance.[17] The first was that the nation was a self-conscious political construct, the fruit and product of an immense act of (revolutionary) will. The second, and one soon to be made graphically explicit, was that nations possessed the right to self-determination. The latter in particular denoted a complete break with traditional international practices, although it had been presaged by the slightly earlier American example. Both were made manifest at the Fête de la Fédération, celebrated on the Champ de Mars a year to the day after the storming of the Bastille and orchestrated in such a way as to shroud the nation in a mystical halo. As Pierre Nora has written, '[t]he festival expressed the disappearance of internal frontiers, the abolition of regional disparities, the excitement associated with an act of mutual consent submitting a united France to an authority freely accepted'.[18] Just as dramatically, these same ideas were applied to those parts of the territory that had been annexed to France under the monarchy. In the so-called *serment de Strasbourg* the delegates of the national guards of Alsace, Lorraine, and Franche-Comté affirmed the determination of these territories and their inhabitants to be a part of the French nation. In similar vein, in May 1790 it was declared that 'the French nation renounces the intention to undertake any war whose goal is that of conquest and it will never employ its arms against the liberty of a people'.

One of the most striking aspects of the Revolution of 1789 was that from the outset its participants believed that their actions were of international significance and that what was at stake was a set of universal values. One example of this universalistic mentality was the assumption that France was not born to follow the example of others but was rather the example that should be followed. As Tocqueville was later to comment: 'It was not a question of taking lessons, but of furnishing new examples.'[19] Another feature was the manner in which it was assumed that the truths being proclaimed were applicable to the whole of humankind. To cite Tocqueville again: 'there was no Frenchman who did not believe he had in his hands, not the destiny of his country, but the very future of the species'.[20] Seen from the political hothouses of Paris, the whole world was watching and listening as revolutionary events unfolded. So too, a reborn French nation, shorn of privilege, was thought capable of infinite enlargement and of embracing the inhabitants of the earth. France was 'la patrie de l'humanité'.

Given this, there are few more fascinating tales than the manner in which the universalistic aspirations of the Revolution were replaced by the denunciation of the foreigner and by what Mona Ozouf has termed a 'fraternité xenophobe'.[21] If, at the outset, all those who accepted the principles of the Revolution were

---

[17] See Jacques Godechot, *La Grande Nation: L'Expansion révolutionnaire de la France dans le monde de 1789 à 1799* (1956).

[18] Nora, 'Nation', 806.

[19] Alexis de Tocqueville, *The Old Regime and the Revolution* (Chicago, 2001), ii. 67.

[20] Ibid.

[21] Mona Ozouf, 'L'Idée républicain et l'interprétation du passé national', *Annales*, 53 (1998), 1074–87. See also Sophie Wahnich, *L'Impossible citoyen: L'Étranger dans le discours de la Révolution française* (1997).

welcomed as citizens, the rhetoric of fraternity and hospitality quickly changed into that of enmity as these very same foreigners—seven of whom, including Joseph Priestley and Thomas Paine, were elected to the Convention—were recast as traitors and false friends. In part this can be explained by the yawning gap that existed between the dream of national unity and the reality of a deeply divided and heterogeneous country. The foreigner was no more—and no less—an object of suspicion than the aristocrat and the priest. Next, the very logic of universalism played its part. To harbour doubts about the claims of French liberty was to place oneself in the position of being an enemy of the French nation and therefore, by extension, of humanity. The foreigner could thus very easily be equated with tyranny. To this could then be added the demands of political necessity. From 1792 onwards France, and the Revolution, was at war with her neighbours and this perilous situation, in an atmosphere where rumours of plots and conspiracies were rife, called for no half measures.

Most importantly, the retreat from the idealistic posture of universal embrace followed inevitably from the realization that the nation as envisaged by the revolutionaries had still to be made. From Sieyès onwards, the very definition of the nation had a logic of inclusion and exclusion written into it and the boundaries of the nation were drawn within and not beyond French territory. But it was undoubtedly the discourse of political virtue voiced so enthusiastically by the Jacobins that did most to separate the foreigner from the erstwhile country of humanity. If Louis XVI, in the words of Saint-Just, could be cast (fatally) as 'a foreigner living among us',[22] the same could be said all too easily of the non-French nationals who became the subject of relentless rebuke and attack in Robespierre's speeches. As Sophie Wahnich comments: for the Jacobins, 'the victory of liberty would be signified by the perfect transparency of the public space . . . the struggle engaged upon was a struggle against all forms of opacity which might act as an obstacle to the actions of revolutionary government'.[23] The foreigner was necessarily opaque, the mask-wearer *par excellence*, and therefore, unwittingly or not, a traitor, a plotter, and an enemy of the *patrie*.[24] As will be readily surmised, of these foreign enemies the English were given pride of place as the enemies of the entire human race (a sentiment later continued by Jules Michelet amongst many others). Echoing the royalist propaganda of the Seven Years War almost word for word, 'the people of this debased island' were again compared to the brigands and thieves of Carthage.

Why France, having made known its pacific intentions, actually went to war is a question not easily answered. The Girondins seem mistakenly to have believed that this was their best way of keeping hold of the reins of power. Robespierre for one opposed this policy, fearing that it would lead to military despotism and the

---

[22] 'Discours sur le jugement de Louis XVI', in Saint-Just, *Œuvres complètes* (2004), 475–84.

[23] Wahnich, *L'Impossible citoyen*, 155.

[24] The concept of *patrie* is closely related to that of nation. It was, if anything, even vaguer in meaning, both before and during the Revolution. In the Furet and Ozouf *Dictionnaire critique de la Révolution* there is no separate entry for *patrie*.

overthrow of the constitution.[25] Military success, however, brought its own problems. What was to be done with the newly conquered territories? If the annexations of Nice, Avignon, and even Savoy (each of which formally requested incorporation into France) were relatively straightforward, the same could not be said of Belgium. Here there was deep unease and indecision, not least amongst the members of the Convention. Help however was at hand from the exiled Prussian noble and (soon to be guillotined) apostle of universal fraternity, Anacharsis Cloots, who justified the annexation of the left bank of the Rhine on the grounds that 'this river is the natural boundary of the Gauls'. It was this theme that was taken up and given clear expression in the famous remarks of Danton before the Convention on 30 January 1793. The limits of the French republic, he announced, were 'indicated by nature. We will reach them at the four corners of the horizon: at the Rhine, the Oceans and the Alps.'[26] Two weeks later Carnot added the Pyrenees to the list. Was this a novel doctrine or was it, as the nineteenth-century historians Augustin Thierry and Henri Martin were to argue, a reworking of the traditional policy of the French monarchy from Richelieu onwards?[27] It matters relatively little because, whatever the truth of the matter, it was now accepted that the principle of geographical determinism could supplement or even supersede that of the right to self-determination.

Appeals to local consent continued to be made and were duly met by the minority determined to lend their support to the principles of the Revolution, but henceforth the notion that peoples were being liberated from oppression served only as a fiction and a pretext for national self-interest. What, moreover, was to be done when French arms brought victories beyond even these natural boundaries? Could these territories too not be brought within the confines of the universal republic or did such geographical expansion (as the frequently cited example of classical Rome appeared to show) entail the grave risk of subverting the Republic itself? Prudence alone dictated that the first course should not be followed, and thus, under the guise of respect for the sovereignty of other peoples, an additional variety of annexation was invented: that of 'sister republics'.[28] All countries conquered by France were to be given new republican constitutions, and were in effect to exist as French protectorates.[29] This was the fate that first befell Holland in 1795 and much of the Italian peninsula in the next two to three years. 'The system of "sister republics"', Jacques Godechot writes, 'had the advantage, not merely of flattering the national pride as well as the revolutionary pride of the French by extending the influence of the new France, but it afforded undeniable strategic benefits . . . and economic advantages.'[30]

[25] See Robespierre, Œuvres complètes, iv. Le Défenseur de la Constitution (1939).

[26] Quoted in Wahnich, L'Impossible citoyen, 340.

[27] See Daniel Nordman, 'La Frontière', in Vincent Duclert and Christophe Prochasson (eds.), Dictionnaire critique de la République (2002), 499–505.

[28] See Jean-Louis Harouel, Les Républiques sœurs (1997).

[29] See Lucien Jaume (ed.), Les Déclarations des droits de l'homme (1989), 313–18.

[30] Godechot, La Grande nation, 83.

The last remnants of universalistic fervour were removed following the fall of the Jacobins and the installation of the Thermidorian republic. This continued under the Directory, when for the first time the notion of the 'constitutional limits' of France was invoked in order to justify French expansion beyond its pre-revolutionary borders. Indeed, to the objectives of attaining natural frontiers and establishing sister republics, the Directory added one new priority: economic and maritime expansion in the Mediterranean. This was a policy that would shortly see the departure of Napoleon Bonaparte for Egypt.

Bonaparte's oriental adventure was very far from being a complete success but one crushing military victory at Aboukir over disorganized Ottoman opponents and some astute propaganda turned it into a personal triumph for the young general. It was soldiers, rather than civilians, who were now the heroes of the new Republic. From 1792 onwards, in fact, the *levée en masse*, conscription by another name, had produced an army numbering as many as 800,000 men and this not only turned the aristocratic army of the past into an anachronism, but also changed the very way that war was fought, putting the entire resources of the nation at the army's disposal. From this it appeared to follow naturally that, when politicians proved themselves incapable of managing affairs, recourse should be made to one of those who had led the national army to glory. In this way the First Republic came to an end.

Gone now was to be any reference to the right of nations to self-determination. Far from granting them independence, whenever practicable, Napoleon integrated conquered territories into metropolitan France, producing at its most extensive in 1811 a France consisting of 130 *départements*, stretching from the mouth of the Elbe and Flanders in the north and to Rome and Tuscany in the south. Where integration was not feasible, Napoleon set up what amounted to vassal states, frequently headed by some undistinguished member of his own extended family graced with a royal title. The purpose of the Napoleonic *imperium* was to serve one nation and one person. Napoleon did not abandon all reference to national and patriotic sentiment however. He skilfully exploited the military successes of his army—*la Grande Armée*—to bolster support, but over time the vast cost in human and physical resources engendered sentiments of sullen resistance and indifference, especially amongst the peasantry (whose male offspring bore the brunt of the carnage). Only briefly in 1814 was anything like a resurgence of military patriotism witnessed. If, later, this gave rise to the mythological patriotism associated with the figure of Nicolas Chauvin,[31] the consequences of defeat could not have been starker. By the treaty of Paris in 1814 France returned to its borders of 1792. Following defeat at Waterloo, she returned to her borders of 1790. The restored European order of the Holy Alliance was to rest upon the principles of legitimacy and stability.

---

[31] See Gérard de Puymège, 'Le soldat Chauvin', in Nora, *Les Lieux de mémoire* (1997), ii. 1699–1728.

II

There were powerful currents of thought in France prepared to turn their backs
on the nationalist inheritance of the French Revolution. Benjamin Constant for
one saw that the doctrine of natural frontiers would be such as to condemn
Europe to permanent war. He also saw—here developing his theme of the
distinction between the liberty of the ancients and the moderns—that in a
commercial age the relationship of the individual to the *patrie* was undergoing
a fundamental change. In the past, he wrote, 'the fatherland represented what
was dearest to a man; to lose his fatherland was to lose his children, his friends, all
the objects of his affection'. But now, he contended, 'what we love in a country is
our possessions, the safety of our person and of those close to us, the careers of
our children, the progress resulting from our industry . . . in a word, the countless
forms of happiness that flow from our interests and tastes'. If our own *patrie*
could not provide these benefits, Constant argued, we could easily move to one
of the many 'civilized and hospitable nations' that surrounded us. What is more,
Constant was clear that no government should have 'either the right or the
power' to prevent us from doing so.[32]

It would be a mistake to believe that the glorification of the French nation ever
attained anything like unanimous assent. The voice of theocratic reaction had little
difficulty in dismissing the unjustified pretensions of the people to constitute the
nation. In Joseph de Maistre's view, what characterized a nation was the 'general
soul' or moral unity given to it directly by God and this was not something that
could find expression through what was taken (in error) to be the popular will.
'What is a nation?' Maistre asked. 'It is the sovereign and the aristocracy. One must
weigh voices, not count them.'[33] Similarly, Auguste Comte, when he came to
provide a detailed specification of the political organization of the envisaged
positivist society, predicted the eventual break-up of France into 'seventeen independent republics' and saw a future in which the family, the city, and humanity,
bound together by the positivist Church, would leave no place for the nation-state.
Countries the size of Tuscany, Holland, and Belgium, Comte believed, would
become the norm.[34]

Comte expressed these views in the early 1850s, and in doing so courted
unpopularity by being among the few to oppose the cause of Italian unification.
A decade later, the ever-controversial Pierre-Joseph Proudhon did not hesitate to
adopt the same stance, castigating Mazzini for pursuing a policy that would
threaten peace in Europe without adding to liberty. 'Unification in Italy', Proudhon contended, 'is the same as the indivisible republic of Robespierre, no more
than the corner stone of despotism and bourgeois exploitation.'[35] Attacking what

---

[32] Benjamin Constant, *Commentaire sur l'ouvrage de Filangieri* (1822–4) (2004), 149–50.
[33] Joseph de Maistre, *Œuvres* (2007), 1234–5.
[34] See Auguste Comte, *Système de politique positive* (1852), ii. 263–338.
[35] 'La Fédération et l'Unité en Italie' (1862), in *Du Principe Fédératif: Œuvres complètes de P-J.
Proudhon* (1959), 106.

he saw as the dangerous fallacies of 'la topographie politique',[36] Proudhon not only disputed the logic of the natural frontiers argument—nations were often built around rather than separated by such rivers as the Rhine, for example—but went on to characterize nation-states in general as wasteful, regressive, bureaucratic, a threat to peace, and arbitrary in their manner of operation. 'The Frenchman', he continued, 'is a figment of the imagination: he does not exist', France being 'composed of at least twenty distinct nations'.[37] Entities such as France, therefore, had to be seen as 'abstract' and 'artificial' constructions designed solely to secure the centralization of power. Proudhon's proposed alternative thus broke with the tradition of centuries of French state-building: France was to be split up into a set of loose, self-governing federations. 'In the Confederation', he stated, 'the units which comprise the political bodies . . . are groups, constituted a priori by nature, and whose average size will not be greater than that of a population drawn from a territory of no more than several hundred square miles.'[38] In the interests of peace and 'self-government', the same principle was to be applied across Europe as a whole. Proudhon also opposed the claims of Polish nationalism.

However, there were those for whom almost nothing—not even the descent into Terror and the rise to power of Napoleon Bonaparte—could diminish their preoccupation with the nation, the left bank of the Rhine, and the need to liberate oppressed peoples everywhere. Indeed, the humiliating peace treaties imposed upon a defeated France and the return to the throne of what was sometimes deprecatingly referred to as the 'royauté cosaque' were sufficient to rekindle nationalist fervour amongst a new generation, born with the century, and for whom the collective trauma was not the Revolution but the collapse of the Empire.[39] For these young men, blessed with the exuberance of youth (as well as a certain gravity and high moral tone), the desire to free France from the humiliating clutches of the Holy Alliance was of necessity combined with the wish to see Europe's established monarchical order overturned.

This mood was captured in Edgar Quinet's essay *1815 et 1840*.[40] As Quinet was later to write, 'I set myself the task of relating, from a personal point of view, the moral history of the generation to which I belonged.'[41] The moment at which the text itself was written—the latter of the two dates—was not without significance. In that year, Adolphe Thiers, recalled to head the government, was embroiled in a serious diplomatic crisis with England over Egypt, which threatened war.[42]

---

[36] 'France et Rhin' (1867), ibid. 558. The texts that make up this collection were probably written between 1859 and 1861.

[37] Ibid. 594.

[38] 'Du Principe Fédératif et de la Nécessité de Reconstituer le Parti de la Révolution' (1863), ibid. 546.

[39] Alan B. Spitzer, *The French Generation of 1820* (Princeton, NJ, 1983), 10. See also Jean-Claude Caron, *Générations Romantiques: Les Étudiants de Paris et le Quartier Latin* (1991). Caron speaks of the students of this period as being 'more patriotic than Bonapartist'.

[40] See Paul Bénichou, *Le Temps des prophètes: Doctrines de l'âge romantique* (1977), 454–96.

[41] Edgar Quinet, *Œuvres complètes de Edgar Quinet: Histoire de mes idées* (1858), pp. iii–iv.

[42] On 10 July 1840 Britain concluded a treaty with Russia, Prussia, and Austrian requiring France's protégé, the Pasha of Egypt, to withdraw from Syria. France did not learn of this treaty until 26 July, after which there was a general outcry for war.

This itself had hastened the decision to encircle Paris with military fortifications. At the same time the triumphal return of the Emperor Napoleon's remains to the French capital was being carefully orchestrated, an event only made possible as a consequence of Napoleon's earlier reincarnation as both romantic hero and saviour of the *patrie*.[43]

The scene was set by a preface dated 15 November 1840.[44] Quinet began by asking the Germans to recognize that the interests, the ideas, and even the enemy of France and Germany were the same, and thus that Germany should wish that France should not die. Germany, he therefore argued, should turn its attention away from the Rhine—which was to be shared with France—towards the Danube. If not, he concluded, it would be to Russia's advantage.[45] However, what Quinet found most difficult to forgive was that those who had governed France since the Restoration had been more troubled by the 'noise of the street' than they had been by the position and fate of France in Europe. France, in effect, has turned away from her wounds, as was evidenced by the passion for utopian thinking. '[T]he character of the greater part of the new doctrines', Quinet commented, 'is that of the absence of national sentiment. Instead of France, they all embrace the human race.'[46] Everyone had become cosmopolitan out of necessity.

It was after these preliminaries that Quinet developed the substance of his argument. The Revolution, he argued, had lasted for thirty years but it had only been in 1815 that it had 'handed over its sword'.[47] What followed had been a catastrophe. 'If', Quinet wrote, 'the French Revolution was defeated in 1815, the international order, based upon the treaties of Vienna, was the legal, concrete and permanent sign of this defeat. Subjected to treaties written with the blood of Waterloo, in the eyes of the world, we are still legally the defeated of Waterloo.'[48] Worse still, since then France had been 'complicit' in her ruin and had appeared to accept her 'enslavement'. The Revolution of 1830, Quinet argued, had given hope to some that things would change but 'this large wounded body was only able to raise itself to its knees'.

The result was that a country believing itself to be free was 'enclosed in a circle of iron'. It lived in a web of lies and hypocrisy. France assured the foreign powers that the country was resigned to the situation, whilst she told the people that the country had been liberated from external threat. As long as France acknowledged this defeat, the foreign powers were prepared to extend her chains, but as soon as France showed signs of real life and determination 'the dependence to which she has been reduced, and that she has accepted, was harshly felt'.[49] This situation, Quinet affirmed, could only lead France to the 'abyss'. She therefore had to have the courage to resist or else accept that she would cease to exist. And to resist meant

---

[43] See Jean Tulard, 'Le retour des cendres', in Nora, *Les Lieux*, ii. 1729–52. See also Natalie Petiteau, *Napoléon: de la mythologie à l'histoire* (1999), 57–105.

[44] Edgar Quinet, *1815 et 1840* (1840).

[45] See Quinet, *De l'Allemagne et la Révolution* (1832).

[46] Quinet, *1815 et 1840*, 25.

[47] Ibid. 26.   [48] Ibid. 27–8.   [49] Ibid. 40.

that the treaties which had followed Waterloo had to be overturned—by war if necessary.

What was evident in this text was a deep sense of national shame and dishonour. This was combined with a powerful resentment directed against the politicians who appeared to have accepted the abject enslavement and humiliation imposed upon France by the victorious powers in the wake of Waterloo. If we are to believe Quinet, these sentiments were shared by his generation. What this text did not explain, however, was the manner in which the architect of this disgrace—Napoleon—was reintegrated into the patriotic vision. How was it possible that the man who had so recklessly squandered the lives of so many Frenchmen could be viewed as the nation's saviour?[50]

Here again Quinet can act as our guide. In 1858 he published an intellectual biography entitled *Histoire de mes idées*.[51] Written in a tone of genuine modesty, much of it concerned Quinet's early years and recounted his life in a countryside untouched by considerations of the Revolution. As a child, Quinet told his readers, he had not known who the Girondins and the Jacobins were. Nevertheless, 'the events which changed the face of the world' eventually reached his isolated village. It was 'by chance', he recalled, that one of the children of his own age told him of the burning of Moscow. Subsequently, there occurred the invasion of the Prussians and the beginning of 'the bereavement of France, the deep sense of her fall'. A decisive moment in Quinet's intellectual development, however, came with the return of Napoleon from Elba. Prior to this 'the legend of the Empire' had only had an 'impersonal' existence for him: henceforth it had a real physical form and was called Napoleon. His abiding sentiment after the defeat at Waterloo was that of 'treason', only to be followed by a sense of shame with the second invasion of France. From this point onwards, Quinet argued, the 'temperament' of France changed, as indeed did his own character. He was, he wrote, surrounded by a 'profound sadness'. Everything he had idolized was suddenly denied and slandered. All that he had considered honourable and virtuous was viewed as infamy and a crime. Moreover, this was true not only of himself but of an entire nation which was forced to abandon its 'past education' and to construct 'another nature'. Such were the emotional and psychological outcomes of 'the cataclysm' of 1815.

In these dire circumstances what happened to the legend of Napoleon? 'Like everything else', Quinet wrote, 'this legend suffered a great eclipse in the first years which followed 1815. . . . It was forbidden to speak of it; forced to be silent, one found oneself forgetting.'[52] It was then that Quinet felt 'a violent interior struggle'. How, he asked, could 'my religion for Napoleon' be reconciled with the 'ferment of liberal ideas that were coming at me from all sides and that I had firmly decided not to give up?'[53] Need he make a choice between Napoleon and liberty? At first Quinet believed not, but little by little he thought more about liberty and less about Napoleon. But this changed with Napoleon's death in 1821. Napoleon came back,

---

[50] See Sudhir Hazareesingh, *The Legend of Napoleon* (London, 2004).
[51] See *Œuvres complètes de Edgar Quinet*, 89–270.
[52] Ibid. 210.   [53] Ibid. 212.

Quinet recorded, 'to haunt my mind, no longer as my Emperor and as my absolute master, but as a spectre that death had almost entirely changed'.[54] Quinet therefore conjured up the final one hundred days of Napoleon's reign as proof that at the end Napoleon had embraced the liberal ideas that he had formerly rejected. 'This is how', Quinet explained, 'I was able to accommodate what had appeared to me to be irreconcilable, my worship of Napoleon with my thirst for liberty. It was not we who went to Napoleon but Napoleon who came back to us.'[55]

Seen from this perspective, Napoleon's ambitions could be allied to the struggles for national liberation and emancipation emerging right across Europe. So also the story of his life could be retold and refashioned as one dedicated to the cause of the French nation. And this was how Napoleon was increasingly seen, the image of the Corsican brigand and adventurer quickly fading from view. Following his death, intimate accounts of his final years in exile appeared in print, each confirming the portrait of a man (and harshly treated prisoner) selflessly dedicated to high and noble ideals. Poets and novelists continued the trend, exalting Napoleon's exploits and praising his almost superhuman genius. Thus romanticized, all ordinary mortals could only suffer in comparison. By the same token, the mediocre might be elevated by the Emperor's presence. Louis-Philippe and the politicians of the July Monarchy proved themselves not slow to appreciate this. In 1833 Napoleon's statue was placed on the top of the column in the place Vendôme and three years later the building of the Arc de Triomphe was completed. This was followed by the return of the Emperor's ashes in 1840.

It would be wrong to believe that this reappraisal of Napoleon received a universal welcome. There were many legitimists and republicans in particular who felt deep unease at what was occurring and who were (rightly) troubled by the possible future political consequences. Nevertheless, as Quinet's account revealed, this reworking of the Napoleonic myth was integral to the manner in which his generation came to terms with the defeat and national humiliation that accompanied the return of the Bourbon monarchy. More intriguing still was the facility with which this generation believed that the aspirations embodied in both liberalism and nationalism could be combined.

No one better expressed these sentiments than Armand Carrel. Through both his writings and his actions he provided a vivid, not to say romantic, illustration of the hopes and ideals of his age.[56] Born in Rouen in 1800, Carrel was educated at the military academy of Saint-Cyr before entering the army in 1821. His political sympathies were quickly disclosed through membership of the most notorious of the secret societies of the Restoration period: the Carbonari. Inspired by the original Neapolitan model, the French version attracted as many as 30,000 adherents, organized on military lines but with no recognizable programme beyond that of the desire to remove the Bourbon monarchy.[57] The movement's not unexpected

---

[54] See *Œuvres complètes de Edgar Quinet*, 213.   [55] Ibid.

[56] See James S. Allen, 'Y-a-t-il eu en France une "génération romantique de 1830"?', *Romantisme*, 28–9 (1980), 103–8.

[57] Alan B. Spitzer, *Old Hatreds and Young Hopes* (Cambridge, Mass., 1971).

failure led Carrel to resign from the army in 1823, only for him soon afterwards to depart for Spain in order to take up arms in support of the liberal cause and against the French army sent to defend Ferdinand VII. His regiment of volunteers was named after Napoleon II and fought in the uniform of the Imperial army. Captured and imprisoned, upon his release Carrel secured employment as secretary to the historian Augustin Thierry. There followed, in rapid succession, the publication (as part of a series of national histories) of his *Résumé de l'histoire de l'Ecosse*[58] and his *Résumé de l'histoire des Grecs modernes*,[59] the creation of *La Revue Américaine* (which ran from July 1826 to June 1827), participation in some of the most distinguished journals of the epoch—*Le Constitutionnel, Le Globe, La Revue Française* as well as the Saint-Simonian *Le Producteur*—and, in 1827, the appearance of his *Histoire de la Contre-Révolution en Angleterre*.[60] January 1830 saw the publication of the first issue of *Le National*, of which Carrel remained the editor until his death in a duel in 1836.

Carrel's preoccupation with the nation and the oppression of nationalities was evident from the outset. His history of Scotland, for example, provided him not only with ample evidence of the intolerable injustices inflicted upon a subject population but also with series of events which could be genuinely portrayed as a national uprising against foreign domination. The 'audacious expedition' of Charles Edward Stuart was not an attempt to reclaim the monarchy for Catholic absolutism but rather 'the last effort of a population armed for independence and implacable in its hatred of England'. Likewise, his outline of Greek history revealed both a people struggling to free itself from slavery and a nation whose hopes for independence had been sacrificed to the principles of stability proclaimed by the Holy Alliance. 'The Greek revolution', Carrel proclaimed, was 'a new and sad proof of the relative strength of governments and nations'.

Equally visible was an attachment to liberal principles of constitutional government designed to limit the absolute power of monarchs. Reflecting upon the civil war in Spain and what he saw as 'a hatred of French domination', he concluded that if, in the first instance, Spain's liberal constitution of 1812 had been perceived by the people only as 'an instrument of resistance against foreign usurpation', they had later come to understand that 'the constitution and Ferdinand could not coexist'.[61] In far greater detail, he argued that the experience of 'counter-revolution', the attempt by James II to impose his will upon the nation, 'had taught the English people that its liberties were at variance with a royalty lacking consent and that in order to preserve royalty to any advantage it was necessary to regenerate it, to separate it from the principle of legitimacy'.[62] The 'enlightened' section of the English population, Carrel believed, had come to accept that, if monarchy was necessary in a country divided into classes, it should not be in a position to

---

[58] *Résumé de l'histoire de l'Ecosse* (1825).
[59] *Résumé de l'histoire des Grecs modernes* (1825).
[60] *Histoire de la Contre-Révolution en Angleterre* (1827).
[61] 'De l'Espagne et de sa Révolution' in *Œuvres littéraires et économiques d'Armand Carrel* (1854), 113–37. First publ. in *La Revue Française* (Mar. 1828).
[62] Carrel, *Histoire de la Contre-Révolution*, 4.

withdraw 'national liberties' at will. Carrel also felt that a reformed monarchy resting upon the consent of the nation was in accord with the 'new interests' that had emerged within English society. It was this characteristically liberal theme that he deployed elsewhere in his writings in the 1820s to demonstrate what he took to be the connection between trade and national renaissance.

The title and content of one article, 'Du commerce de la grèce moderne, consideré dans son influence sur la régénération politique de cette nation', is sufficient to illustrate this point.[63] The recent struggle for national independence in Greece, Carrel argued, had its source in the commercial expansion of the Greek economy. 'A certain degree of prosperity' had in turn produced a desire for a 'liberal education', confirming the 'intellectual superiority' of the Greeks over their Turkish masters. 'It is certain', Carrel wrote, that the 'enlightened, well-off, industrious class created by business within the Greek nation has constantly tended . . . to upset the balance that, since the conquest, existed between the means of oppression of the conquerors and the means of resistance of the subjugated'.[64] It was but a short step from 'affluence' to 'emancipation'. However, as befitted a government driven by 'a superstitious and ferocious egoism', the Turks had taken the alternative of extermination and terror rather than that of liberation.

The specifically domestic implications of this argument were spelt out in Carrel's response to Stendhal's charge, in *D'un nouveau complot contre les industriels*, that Saint-Simonianism was nothing else but a glorification of businessmen and of vulgar materialism.[65] 'The workers are for us', Carrel wrote in *Le Producteur*, 'not a class within society but society itself' and it was through their useful work that 'old Europe' was to be reformed. The future, he acknowledged, would in all probability be less prolific in 'transcendental virtues' but so too it would be less characterized by vice and corruption. The enlightenment and well-being that would arise out of 'the application of the skills that each one of us has received' would ensure that 'public virtues' would flourish where now only 'private' ones existed. The sciences, arts, and industry, would become a new 'Panthéon national': it was in this sense, and not in Stendhal's deprecating sense, that society would be 'materialized'.

As we saw in the previous chapter, the stress upon the relationship between commerce or 'industrie' and the emergence of new and advanced political forms was a theme commonly to be found in the writings of French liberals at this time. On this account, constitutional and limited government was appropriate to all modern peoples intent upon the pursuit of material ease through industry. By the same token, the activity of war had become a deadly anachronism. Carrel, for all his immense admiration for Constant and their shared assumptions about the beneficial influence of commerce,[66] disagreed both with the interpretation of recent French history that this implied and with the view that the uniform tendency

---

[63] *Œuvres littéraires et économiques*, 67–96. First publ. in *Le Producteur* (Oct.–Nov. 1825).

[64] Ibid. 92.

[65] Carrel, 'A Propos d'une brochure', in *Œuvres littéraires et économiques*, 93–6. First publ. in *Le Producteur* (Dec. 1825).

[66] See the obituary notice written by Carrel for *Le National*, in *Œuvres politiques et littéraires d'Armand Carrel* (1857), i. 424–6. Constant was described as 'a great defender of liberty'.

of modern society was or should be towards peace. When this is understood, we move closer to understanding what made Carrel, unlike Constant, a liberal and a nationalist.

For liberals of Constant's generation the tumultuous events of 1789–1815 were not only ones that had had to be personally lived through but they had also vividly demonstrated how legitimate demands for political equality could be subverted first into a reign of terror and then into an authoritarian military regime. From this experience derived a general reluctance to draw any positive lessons from the experience of these twenty-six years. The mood in liberal circles was to start to change in the 1820s when a new generation of historians began to produce the first full-length, relatively unpolemical accounts of the revolutionary period.[67] First Adolphe Thiers (born 1797) with his ten-volume *Histoire de la Révolution française* (published 1823–7) and then Auguste Mignet (born 1798) with his more modest two-volume *Histoire de la Révolution française depuis 1789 jusqu'en 1814* (published in 1824) described in detail, and despite their obvious mutual detestation of Robespierrre and the Jacobins, a process of revolution that, taken as a whole and regardless of its inevitable excesses, had nevertheless transformed France from top to bottom and brought it to the dawn of a new era.[68] It was this innovative assessment of the Revolution and its outcome that made its mark upon Carrel. The work of Thiers, he wrote, 'is the first where this magnificent and terrible epoch is described with an appropriate breadth and impartiality',[69] whilst that of Mignet invited people 'to return to the truth of the Revolution, to recall the eternal justice of its claims, to admire its invincible perseverance in its struggles, to understand it in each of the necessities imposed by the alternative of conquering or being destroyed'.[70] Of Napoleon Bonaparte, Carrel accepted that the consequence of his rise to power had been to extinguish liberty 'as if the word had never been pronounced and the Bastille never taken', but here he was prepared to accept that 'the man of war does not appear to merit the reproaches directed at the man of politics'. In the same article Carrel commented that a society in 'perpetual peace' would fall into 'decay'. 'Look', he remarked by way of justification, 'at the state of France at the end of the eighteenth century. Without doubt a war should be just but grounded in justice and following a long interval of peace it can reinvigorate the morals and character of nations.'[71] Carrel, then, was prepared to locate his liberalism within the traditions of the Revolution and to embrace its glorious military achievements.

---

[67] See Olivier Bétourné and Aglaia I. Hartog, *Penser l'histoire de la Révolution: Deux siècles de passion française* (1989), 35–56.

[68] See Yvonne Knibiehler, 'Une révolution "nécessaire": Thiers, Mignet et l'école fataliste', *Romantisme*, 28–9 (1980), 279–88.

[69] 'Histoire de la Révolution française de M. A. Thiers', *Œuvres littéraires et économiques*, 104. First publ. in *Le Constitutionel* (Jan. 1826).

[70] Ibid. 108–9.

[71] 'Mémoires sur les campagnes des armées de Rhin et de Rhin et Moselle', *Œuvres littéraires et économiques*, 174–207.

All of this figured by way of preparation for Carrel's greatest and most significant undertaking: the editing, at first with Adolphe Thiers and François Mignet and then alone, of *Le National*. Financed by the banker Jacques Laffitte with Talleyrand's moral support, the first issue appeared on 3 January 1830. Its audience, we are told, was largely composed of middle-class patriots, students, soldiers, and the occasional artisan. Whilst never attaining anything like a mass circulation—estimates put its circulation at between 2,000 and 4,000—*Le National* was, in a sense, *the* paper of the July Revolution. Not only did its young editors help to launch the protests that led ultimately to the downfall of the Bourbon monarchy but, as events unfolded, the offices of *Le National* became the unofficial headquarters of the opposition.[72]

Thiers immediately made clear his and the journal's position. The Charte of 1814, daily flouted by Charles X, had to be fully respected and if implemented would produce a system of constitutional and representative government broadly similar to the English model. As the months proceeded, to this was added fierce criticism of the Polignac ministry, support for the 221 deputies who in March 1830 voted against the government, and finally, with what were seen as the efforts of the forces of counter-revolution to shackle the press, the call for Louis-Philippe to occupy the throne.

Carrel played a part in each of these campaigns, producing a series of brilliant articles attacking 'le parti prétendu monarchique' and 'le parti royaliste'. From the outset he was a supporter of the July Monarchy but he, unlike Thiers, remained outside government, proclaiming that *Le National* would 'never become a ministerial broadsheet'. What followed, therefore, were hectic years of journalistic activity, court appearances, and vigorous campaigning in defence of the principles of 1830. For Carrel, the July Revolution had been, above all, the work of the people and it was to them that the victory was due. Moreover, Carrel was convinced that the July Revolution could not possibly degenerate in the same manner as the great revolution of 1789. This was because the people were 'much less ignorant and much more moral' than had previously been the case and, more significantly, because 1789 and 1830 were different events with different scenarios. If both had been victories over the same principle—divine or absolute monarchy—then the scale of opposition that had been faced bore no comparison. The first had confronted not just the monarchy, but also a powerful nobility and the clergy, as well as the armies of Europe, and it was for this reason that the 'power and the passions of the multitude' had needed to be unleashed. In 1830, by contrast, 'the monarchy, through a change of dynasty, became the accomplice of the revolution, whilst as a result of the principle of equality before the law the interests of the privileged classes were at one with the interests of the nation'. Thus there would be no emigration, no new Coblenz, 'no absolutist crusade against France'.[73]

Nevertheless, the mistake, in Carrel's view, was to imagine that all that had occurred was that one government had replaced another. It was the whole system of

---

[72] See J. P. T. Bury and Robert Tombs, *Thiers* (London, 1986), 18–39.
[73] *Œuvres politiques et littéraires d'Armand Carrel*, i. 227–33.

Charles X that had been removed and with that came the realization that France could no longer 'be governed by the sword'. The restored Bourbon monarchs had never been able to accept that the liberties and rights contained in the Charte had not been granted to France by the monarchy but had been gained by 'our arms and our civilization'. 1830 made it indisputably clear that the monarchy owed its existence to an act of 'the national will'. 'It is the people', Carrel wrote, 'who are in possession of the original sovereignty and royalty which exists by virtue of a concession.'[74] Seen in this light, the Orleanist regime of Louis-Philippe was to be 'a popular monarchy surrounded by republican institutions'.[75]

The fact was that the July Monarchy was not to go in this direction. As Carrel quickly realized, the intention of Louis-Philippe's ministers, especially Guizot, was to make a return to the Charte of 1814, minus only the principle of divine right. France was not to have Carrel's formula but rather 'a monarchy surrounded by constitutional institutions'. It was this realization that pushed Carrel into the ranks of the opposition and then, as we shall see, on to an endorsement of republicanism. In the first instance, however, the source of Carrel's displeasure was what he contemptuously referred to as the party of 'peace at any price' and the government's adamant refusal to carry the principles of the Revolution to the rest of Europe.[76] The specific issue was how France was to respond to the popular uprisings in Belgium and Poland: the broader question concerned the relevance of revolutionary nationalism.

A foretaste of how Carrel was to respond to the European revolutions of 1830 was provided immediately prior to the fall of the Bourbon dynasty. In June 1830, Charles X, desperately courting popularity, dispatched French troops to Algeria on the somewhat spurious grounds that the Dey of Algiers had been providing sanctuary for Mediterranean pirates. Liberals, including Thiers in *Le National*, at first denounced the expedition, perceiving its ultimate domestic purpose and fearing war with England, only for them to find the idea of a French colony to be irresistible. Carrel was no exception to this rule. Discounting fears that a victorious army—the 'national' army—would be used by the counter-revolutionaries to crush opposition in France, what he saw and what he believed that the rest of Europe would see in the 'African campaign' was 'the France that the Revolution had made', a France of immense resources, a young army, and a revolutionary spirit.[77]

After the July Revolution, Carrel's basic position was that the international order of Europe could not be allowed to date from the Treaty of Vienna and from

---

[74] Ibid. ii. 95. Carrel made it clear as early as Feb. 1830 that his interpretation of the sovereignty of the people was not to be understood as a Rousseauian vision of direct democracy.

[75] Ibid. ii. 107–14.

[76] Louis-Philippe, as well as his ambassador to England, Talleyrand, quickly appreciated that peace could only be preserved if France did not seek to use the Belgian revolt against the Netherlands as an excuse to annex the Belgian provinces. The Treaty of London established Belgium as an independent and neutral power. Talleyrand was less successful in the case of Poland where his proposals for an independent Poland were firmly rejected by the other Great Powers. In Sept. 1831 the Russians retook Warsaw.

[77] Carrel, *Œuvres politiques et littéraires*, i. 46–51, 89–96, 121–6.

France's defeat at Waterloo. 'The expulsion of the Bourbons, who signed the infamous treaties of 1814', he wrote, 'entails the revision of these treaties. It is a duty for us to ask for, to demand their immediate revision.'[78] The new regime, in other words, was not bound by the arrangements that had been imposed upon France in a situation of abject humiliation and which had been agreed to by rulers imposed upon a hostile population. 'Never', Carrel complained, 'will a more inhumane cunning better calculate all the conditions of a permanent degradation of a nation without allies.'[79] To submit to these conditions, as the new government appeared ready to do, was therefore to accept that France was to be placed amongst the 'second rank' and that she was forever to be subject to the dictates of the Holy Alliance. 'If they could divide us up', Carrel wrote, 'they would do it; if we could not defend Paris, they would raze it to the ground . . . they only want us as ruined, enchained, humbled supplicants.'[80] In short, the European powers would go to war to keep France within the boundaries of the post-Napoleonic settlement.

1830 was thus as much a rejection of the dominance of the Holy Alliance as it was of the principles of the Restoration. To that end, Carrel was prepared to reject nothing of the previous 'forty years' of French history: Valmy, Austerlitz, Waterloo, 'the battle outside Algiers under the white flag', were all part of a past in which the France that had not emigrated and that had remained true to itself had stood up against Europe. Carrel therefore had no time for those who believed that, at best, France could fight a defensive war from within the borders of 1814. 'The Revolution', he declared, 'can only defend itself through attack. This was the instinctive French cry in 1792 and still this time there is only salvation for us if we strike the first blows.'[81] Diplomacy would settle nothing and thus the responsibility of the new government was to impose a recognition of the changed balance of forces now operating in Europe upon France's enemies.

True to the messianism of the revolutionary tradition, Carrel believed that, of all the modern nations, it was France that was most blessed with ideas, activity, and intelligence, and to this was to be added an unequalled geographical position, excellent military institutions, and 'the staunchest and most extensive warlike spirit'. France's course of action would of necessity be that of 'a nation which wishes the liberty of others as a guarantee of its own liberty' and therefore her actions would rekindle 'the hopes of European liberty'. Thus, from the outset Carrel not only supported the Belgian uprising against the Dutch but also advocated French military intervention in what he saw as a 'neighbouring revolution', equally intent upon removing 'the odious yoke' imposed by the Congress of Vienna. 'Belgium', he wrote, 'is on our doorstep: its revolution and ours are interdependent.'[82]

But there was more to Carrel's enthusiasm for the Belgian struggle than the recognition that the Belgians faced the same opponents as the French. At its most immediate level, Belgian independence could be justified in terms of the right of every nation to self-determination.[83] To this consideration Carrel appended a less

---

[78] Carrel, *Œuvres politiques et littéraires*, ii. 186.   [79] Ibid. i. 397.
[80] Ibid. ii. 159–65.   [81] Ibid. i. 388–94.   [82] Ibid. ii. 199–204.   [83] Ibid. i. 340.

altruistic preoccupation born out of the Revolution of 1789. For Carrel, France's 'incomparable situation' derived from her position between what he described as 'two seas and its impregnable natural frontiers'.[84] One of these frontiers was 'the barrier of the Rhine'. The questions that Carrel set before the Belgians as a consequence were quite simple: 'are you a distinct people capable of ensuring that its existence will be respected? You have neighbours: do you have frontiers?'[85] Carrel's answer was that it was highly unlikely that Belgium could secure its national and territorial independence and therefore that its 'honour and security' would best be safeguarded by sharing in 'our riches, our name, our civilization, our future, our certain predominance in Europe'.[86] His preferred option, then, was the 'reunification' of Belgium and France.

Carrel accepted that this was an improbable outcome and that the Belgians were wary of France's intentions but as the months passed he became increasingly concerned that the government of the day had not even the courage to ensure the establishment of an independent Belgium capable of defending itself. 'We have renounced', he wrote in April 1831, 'the task of protecting our natural borders.'[87] Some consolation was forthcoming when French troops were sent into Belgium to drive out the invading Dutch army but again Carrel was to complain that the justification provided was unduly apologetic. Invasion, he stated bluntly, was in 'the interest of the revolution'; it served to protect French territory from surprise attack; and it supported a 'sister revolution'; but to argue, as had been done, that France was defending the Belgian King Leopold I was 'ridiculous'.[88]

Moreover, the dishonour done to France by this policy of inaction was compounded by similar responses to the other popular uprisings that spread across Europe in the months following the July Revolution. Carrel advocated assistance for Italian claims against Austria and fought a lengthy journalistic campaign in support of Poland's fight to recover its 'liberty and national existence'.[89] The Poles, he argued, were the French of the North. Their cause was France's cause. The two nations were 'brothers in arms'. Poland's struggle against Russia, Austria, and Prussia struck at the very heart of the Holy Alliance. Furthermore, Poland had natural borders, the Dnieper and the Dwina, and, like all other nations, had the right to free itself from foreign oppression. To have abandoned Poland, Carrel believed, was 'a national crime'.[90]

Carrel's overall conclusion was that the monarchical powers, having turned back the revolutionary tide in Belgium, Italy, and Poland, would be content to let France die of starvation. This in turn led to the articulation of a stridently nationalist message. 'The country before everything', he declared, 'the defence of the soil, the purity of the soil, because the foreigner cannot take a step on it without defiling it; the unity, the integrity of the soil before everything else.'[91] To that end, new

---

[84] Ibid. 321.   [85] Ibid. ii. 30–2.   [86] Ibid. 32.
[87] Ibid. 201.   [88] Ibid. 340–4.
[89] Carrel's articles on Poland from *Le National* were repr. with a preface by Ladislas Mickiewicz: see *Les Articles d'Armand Carrel pour la Pologne* (1862).
[90] Carrel, *Œuvres politiques et littéraires*, i. 417–24, 426–30; ii. 49–57, 153–65, 403–25.
[91] Ibid. ii. 429.

policies and a new government were required and from July 1831 Carrel took up the call for the formation of 'a ministry of the left'. It was at this point, as Carrel began the relatively short journey that was to lead to his conversion to republican-ism, that a more general distancing of nationalism from liberalism could be discerned.

Writing in November 1832 Carrel commented that, at its inception, the writers of *Le National* had believed that the end of the 'legitimist' regime would be brought about by a 'French 1688'. In line with this perspective, Carrel had initially acknowledged the parallel, only for him soon afterwards to argue that nothing more than superficial agreement was possible between the governmental principles of France and England. Then, as his opposition to Guizot intensified, he poured scorn upon those who wished to imitate the English model.[92] At first, his central point was that England and France were different countries with markedly different histories. Crucially, in England the aristocracy had thrown in its lot with the people (thereby producing the renowned three-way balance of power); in France, by contrast, the aristocracy in 1789 had fled, becoming 'Austrian, Prussian, English, out of hatred for their French name'. Thus, to replicate the English model was to side with the representatives of anti-France and of anti-democratic sentiment. Pressed further, Carrel went on to comment that, if the Revolution of 1830 had been the defeat of a dynasty that had opposed the principles of 1789, it likewise represented a rejection of 'the constitutional monarchy based upon the English system'.[93] Yet, as Carrel's displeasure with the government of Casimir-Périer intensified, he concluded that an 'elected monarchy' was no better than a 'legitimist monarchy'. It was just as 'irresponsible', just as capable of abusing power and of thwarting the wishes of an elected chamber. 'The private interests of the elected monarchy', he wrote, 'have greater affinity with the doctrines of the Holy Alliance than they do with the principles of liberty, civilization, and social amelioration.' In article after article he pointed out the colossal cost and waste entailed by the Orleanist monarchy and then, with almost obsessive detail, followed and criticized the plans to fortify Paris. The intention, he argued, was not to defend the capital from foreign aggression but to protect the monarchy from the populace. Finally, in an article entitled 'Identité de la Contre-Révolution et du Principe Monarchique',[94] he reached the conclusion that the July Monarchy was as much on the side of counter-revolution as had been the regime of Charles X.

Faced with what he continued to regard as the 'provisional' nature of Louis-Philippe's reign—'La Révolution de 1830 est-elle totalement détruite?' demanded the title of one of his best articles in *Le National*—from June 1832 onwards Carrel was unequivocal in his support of what he characterized as 'the government of the country by the country' but which more specifically he identified as the Republic.[95] The Republic alone, he wrote in March 1833, is 'the government of the nation by the nation, the government of France by herself, and France will not be terrified of herself, will not loathe herself, will not be frightened of her own shadow'.[96] It was,

---

[92] Carrel, *Œuvres politiques et littéraires*, 114–23.   [93] Ibid. 110, 292–301, 379–87.
[94] Ibid. 485–97.   [95] Ibid. 123–30, 180–205, 311–12.   [96] Ibid. 382.

in sum, the most complete expression of representative government and of the duty of government 'to conform like a slave to the wishes of the real majority'. The Republic was, moreover, a system of government compatible with the order, prosperity, and glory of the country.

To the charge that France and her people did not have the virtues required for living in a republic, Carrel had two answers. First, it was rather the case that France no longer had all the vices necessary to sustain a monarchy. Second, the combination of a vigorous, serious-minded young generation and a proletariat daily giving proof of its maturity and moderation was sufficient to ensure that a new republic would not degenerate into another Committee of Public Safety. Therefore, if Carrel saw no affinities between his position and those of 'Robespierre, leader of the triumvirate of the Terror', he did see parallels between his views and that of 'Robespierre, the theoretician'. They shared, he wrote in what was his most elaborate statement of general policy, *Extrait du Dossier d'un prévenu de complicité morale*,[97] 'the same goal, the same wish, the same end: the more equal distribution of property, the more complete triumph of the political equality, the moral regeneration of the rich and the poor, social reform as the end, political reform as the means'.[98] How, then, could the descent of the Robespierrean project into terror be explained? According to Carrel, it derived from the fact that the people had been reduced to a 'passive nation', to the status of 'inactive citizens'. The Revolution had served only 'bourgeois interests', thereby encouraging the people to believe that their aims could only be attained through 'the dictatorship of a minority'.

Much of what Carrel wrote in the few years of life that remained to him seemed designed to avoid a recurrence of this tragedy. Scattered among the articles dealing with his numerous court appearances, his (ultimately fatal) squabbles with his fellow journalists, and his ceaseless campaign to defend freedom of the press, were those that spoke passionately of the plight of the urban poor and of their disillusionment with the Orleanist regime. 'We explain the lack of hope of the people of Lyons by their misery', he wrote, 'their misery by the bad laws which favour unproductive property and put the burden of taxation upon a man that eighteen hours work a day scarcely nourishes.'[99] The people were condemned to live and die like abandoned beings. A nation united before 1830 in its opposition to the Bourbon monarchy had been divided into 'people and bourgeois . . . property owner and proletarian, middle class and lower class' and all in the interest of preserving the government of a minority.

It was, therefore, with some difficulty that Carrel responded to Alexis de Tocqueville's proposition (outlined in *De la Démocratie an Amérique*) that the future rested with the Anglo-Americans and the Russians, with its clear implication that the French nation had entered a period of 'decadence'. Carrel had for some time been aware of what he described as 'the ambition of the Russian colossus' in the Black Sea and he had always been an admirer of the American system of government, but on this issue he was convinced that Tocqueville was mistaken. For

---

[97] *Extrait du Dossier d'un prévenu de complicité morale* (1835).
[98] Ibid. 59.   [99] *Œuvres politiques et littéraires*, iii. 84.

France, he wrote, 'the present epoch is certainly dismal' but this did not mean that she had reached the 'natural' limits of her development or that these had been traced by chance by 'the finger of the victorious coalition upon the table of the Congress of Vienna in 1815' For those who had celebrated after Waterloo, he argued, this might have seemed the case but, he continued, they had been disabused of this idea by the July Revolution, an event of greater significance than 'even the fall of Napoleon since it had reconciled liberty and the tricolour flag'. Therefore, Carrel concluded with undiminished fervour, 'in ten years from now one will see the French nation . . . prove again that she is the queen of modern nations. No, Europe will not be Cossack and if it becomes republican, that is free, this will not be because of the American Union: France is there: she has not abdicated her role.'[100]

Thus in Armand Carrel we have an example of a nationalist and of what in the France of his day was regarded as a liberal. He saw the connection between commerce and liberty. He believed in representative and responsible government and in such eminently liberal causes as the independence of the judiciary and freedom of the press; but all of this was inseparable from a desire to see France freed from the ignominious position imposed upon her by the post-Napoleonic peace settlement and a support for other nations oppressed by the monarchical European order. Quickly, as he responded to what he saw as the failure of the Orleanist regime to live up to the principles of the July Revolution, he distanced himself from those like Guizot who sought to copy the English constitution, and turned his back upon the philosophy of the *juste milieu*. Most importantly, he believed that the Revolution had to be carried beyond the borders of France and that France was the natural leader of oppressed nations across Europe. Military intervention in support of popular insurrections in Poland and elsewhere amounted to an almost sacred obligation. From 1831 onwards, therefore, as he realized that France was not to pursue this warlike strategy, Carrel moved ever closer to what eventually became an open endorsement of republicanism and with that came even an acknowledgement of the wisdom of Robespierre.

III

Carrel was by no means alone in voicing these sentiments.[101] A broad spectrum of opinion, especially on the left, was united by its patriotism and by the belief that revolution and war went hand in hand. 1830 was not to be merely a matter of constitutional reform and of dynastic change but also an opportunity, as Philippe Darriulat has written, 'to re-establish national glory, to restore France to the rank that the Revolution had given her amongst the nations and peoples of Europe'.[102] The heroic military campaigns of the past were to be relived and consequently there

---

[100] *Œuvres politiques et littéraires*, iv. 273–8.
[101] See Philippe Darriulat, *Les Patriotes: La Gauche républicaine et la nation 1830–1870* (2001), 13–52.
[102] Ibid. 14.

was widespread support for the view that Belgium should be annexed and Poland given succour.

Of the two it was undoubtedly the cause of Poland that aroused the greater enthusiasm. This derived largely from the participation of Polish troops in Napoleon's Imperial army and from a widespread hatred of a barbarous Russia and its fearsome Cossacks. Only the legitimist press showed itself immune from an eagerness to intervene militarily.[103] However, it was Poland, far more than Belgium, which came to highlight the divisions between those who wished to carry the Revolution across Europe and those who were accused of wanting peace at any price. To the chagrin of its opponents, the government, erring on the side of prudence, felt able to offer only diplomatic intervention, a policy that induced a crescendo of criticism with the fall of Warsaw to the Russian army and called forth the charge that France had simply abandoned Poland to its fate.

Nowhere was this sense of outrage more intensely felt than among those who gravitated around Felicité de Lamennais and his journal, *L'Avenir*. It was precisely the tragic outcome of the Polish insurrection that was decisive in determining Lamennais's rupture with the Roman Catholic Church and no one—not even Carrel—did more to voice their support of the Polish cause than the authors of *L'Avenir*.[104] 'Sleep, my Poland', wrote Lamennais after the fall of Warsaw in the autumn of 1831, 'sleep in peace, in what people call your tomb but which I know to be your cradle'.[105] However, as with Carrel, Lamennais's preoccupation with those nations seeking to rid themselves of their oppressors had much deeper roots than the Polish tragedy and what he saw as the betrayal of its heroic people. Above all else, Lamennais was concerned to regenerate Catholicism and thus, in a variety of very different guises, he could be seen defending the claims of ultramontanism against the pretensions of Gallicanism and the ecclesiastical prerogatives of the French crown.

It was not until 1829 that Lamennais's work took a decidedly liberal turn and then in *Des Progrès de la révolution et de la guerre contre l'Eglise* he came down clearly in favour of liberty of the press, liberty of conscience, and liberty of education.[106] Catholicism, he now claimed, offered 'the union of order and liberty'. After the July Revolution, and under the banner of *Dieu et la liberté*, to this Lamennais added calls for the extension of the suffrage, liberty of association, and the abolition of 'the baneful system of centralization'.[107] Lamennais also demanded the separation of Church and State.[108] The liberty of peoples, he argued, had as its necessary prior condition the liberty of the Church.[109] Beneath this lay something even more fundamental. If, in theological terms, Lamennais's liberal Catholicism found

[103] See Michel Fridieff, 'L'Opinion publique française devant l'insurrection polonaise de 1830–1831', *Revue internationale d'histoire politique et constitutionnelle*, 2 (1952), 111–21, 205–14, 280–304.

[104] Louis Le Guillou, 'La Pologne et les mennaisiens en 1830', in Daniel Beauvois, *Pologne: L'Insurrection de 1830–1831, sa réception en Europe* (Lille, 1982), 101–11.

[105] 'A la Pologne' in *Œuvres Complètes de F. de La Mennais* (1836–7), xi. 231–6. See also 'Prise de Varsovie', ibid. x. 380–1.

[106] *Œuvres Complètes de F. de La Mennais*, ix. 1–198.

[107] 'Des doctrines de l'Avenir', ibid. x. 196–205.

[108] 'De la séparation de l'Église et de l'État', ibid. 149–59.

[109] 'De la position de l'Église en France', ibid. 223.

justification in the doctrine of *sensus communis*, in political terms it amounted to a refusal to abandon 'peoples to the arbitrary wills of kings'. The people did not exist to serve those in power: rather power was there to serve the people. It was from this that derived Lamennais's profound admiration for the struggle for emancipation enjoined by the Catholic communities of Belgium, Poland, and Ireland. Thus, for Lamennais (as for Carrel), 1830 meant not just the end of the Bourbon monarchy but also a challenge to the entire European order established by the Holy Alliance and the opportunity for each nation to recover its rights. In part, this optimistic assessment of the future rested upon a recognition of the moderation and unanimity of the French people in July 1830 but it also drew upon what was lauded as the devotion and sacrifice of the oppressed Catholic nations of Europe. 'I tell you', Lamennais wrote in June 1831, 'Jesus Christ is there.'[110]

Only bitter disappointment was to follow. If Lamennais thought that the Revolution of 1830 was inevitable, he also believed that it was to mark 'the dawn of a new era'. The new regime, in his view, had singularly failed to appreciate the significance of these events and had failed to understand the demands for liberty they entailed. A king had been substituted for a king, a dynasty for a dynasty. It was nothing but a 'palace revolution', with all democratic aspirations quickly quashed and forgotten. The same lack of radical intent and resolve applied to foreign policy, where everything had been done to assure Europe's monarchical regimes that the July Revolution posed no threat to the established order. From this had followed the disgraceful betrayal of Belgium and the abandonment of a 'heroic and generous Poland'. Dishonour abroad and a disregard for liberty at home was the result.[111]

Where Lamennais and his fellow writers of *L'Avenir* differed from Carrel and *Le National* was that their disappointment extended to include dissatisfaction with the response of the Catholic Church to the revolutions and uprisings of 1830. To their dismay, the Church had sided with the temporal powers, be they Catholic or not, and had abandoned 'the cause of peoples'. It had thereby contributed to the victory of the 'princes' over those forces that had stood for emancipation. Poland had been allowed to succumb to the 'evil spirit of the north'; in Italy, the Church had been 'totally enslaved'; whilst in Ireland (described by Lamennais as 'this noble land of faith and liberty')[112] the people had been ordered to submit to British power. The Church, in short, had distanced itself (perhaps fatally) from the people and from their aspirations for national liberation.[113]

The response of the Church to these charges was swift and unforgiving. The liberal Catholic programme in its entirety was condemned in the encyclical *Mirari vos* in August 1832.[114] Although never formally excommunicated, Lamennais steadily drifted away from the Church, devoting the remainder of his days to the cause of the people as a democrat, republican, and socialist.[115] For its part, the

---

[110] 'De l'Avenir de la société', ibid. 326.
[111] 'Du Système suivi par les ministres depuis la révolution de juillet', ibid. 351–60.
[112] 'Ce que sera le catholicisme dans la société nouvelle', ibid. 346.
[113] 'Préface', ibid., pp. i–cxxii.
[114] For Lamennais's defence see 'Affaires de Rome', ibid., vol. xii.
[115] See Lamennais, *Du Passé et de l'Avenir du Peuple* (1868).

Church maintained its attachment to the unity of throne and altar for some years to come.

1830 and its immediate aftermath, therefore, constituted something of a high-water mark in nationalist sentiment. A nation reborn and one freed from its Bourbon past was to redraw the map of Europe and to lend succour to those peoples who shared the universal aspiration to emancipation. In the process what amounted to a theory of just war came to be articulated.[116] Intervention in the internal affairs of another country, on this view, was perfectly legitimate if its goal was that of removing a tyrant or despotic regime and if it set an enslaved people free. Coincidentally, a France reduced to abject humiliation would rise up from her knees and take her rightful place as Europe's leading nation.

The July Monarchy, however, pursued an altogether different course, preferring stability to war, and, as far as possible, alliance with England. The latter was the cornerstone of the policy pursued by Guizot as Minister of Foreign Affairs after the departure of Adolphe Thiers in 1840. It survived a minor skirmish over Tahiti in 1844 and then was sorely tested by mutual intrigues over the marriage of the young Isabella II, Queen of Spain. When Lord Palmerston returned to the Foreign Office in 1846, whatever superficial *entente* there had been between the two countries was quietly put to one side and Franco-British relations again went into decline. Palmerston's bellicose protestations about French policy in Spain not only served to further discredit the by-now-tarnished regime headed by King Louis-Philippe but also gave an added fillip to an already vigorous Anglophobia.

It was in these years of widespread resentment at the absence of a glorious foreign policy that the most eloquent expression of a doctrine which combined an ardent embrace of France as both a nation and as a vehicle of the hopes of humanity received its fullest and most coherent exposition. Jules Michelet, in the words of Paul Viallaneix, was 'the secular Lamennais of Romanticism'.[117] Sparked in his youth and given intellectual force through his reading of the eighteenth-century Neapolitan philosopher Giambattista Vico, Michelet's belief in the personality of the French people and in the special destiny accorded to France was brought vividly to life, as he himself explained, by the 'three glorious' days of July 1830. If Vico had taught him that humanity made its own history,[118] then the Revolution of 1830 had provided the 'the first example of a revolution without heroes, without proper names'. No one had prepared or led it, and afterwards all that was visible was the 'unity' of millions of people ready 'to die for an idea'. Here, Michelet believed, was proof of 'the work of human liberty'.[119]

---

[116] Karma Nabulsi, '"La Guerre Sainte": Debates about Just War among Republicans in the Nineteenth Century', in Sudhir Hazareesingh (ed.), *The Jacobin Legacy in Modern France* (Oxford, 2002), 21–44.

[117] See Paul Viallaneix, *La Voie royale : Essai sur l'idée de peuple dans l'œuvre de Michelet* (1959); Viallaneix, *Michelet, les travaux et les jours 1798–1874* (1998); Eric Fauquet, *Michelet ou la gloire du professeur d'histoire* (1990), and Paule Petitier, *Jules Michelet, L'Homme histoire* (2006).

[118] See Jules Michelet, 'Discours sur le système et la vie de Vico' (1827), in Marcel Gauchet (ed.), *Philosophie des sciences historiques* (2002), 225–60.

[119] Jules Michelet, 'Introduction à l'histoire universelle' (1831), *Œuvres complètes de Michelet* (1972), ii, *1828–1831*, 254–5.

Seen through these Vichian lenses, history was a process by which humanity, by dint of incessant struggle, escaped the world of fatality and of nature. Furthermore, this process had attained its apogee in the history of France. A recurrent theme in Michelet's writings, this evocation of the exemplarity of the French experience was most vividly expressed in a chapter entitled 'Tableau de France' hidden within his lengthy account of the history of the middle ages.[120] The special genius of France, according to this interpretation, lay in her unity and diversity and in her capacity for interaction and assimilation. 'It is', Michelet wrote, 'a wonderful spectacle to regard this vast and powerful organism, where the varied parts are so skilfully related, contrasted, and connected, combining the strong with the weak, the negative with the positive.'[121] France, however, had to be seen as a whole and when she was the impression was one of unity and of a single personality. Here Michelet made uncritical reference to the long process of centralization and unification begun under the monarchy, commenting that 'in this way was formed the general, universal spirit of the country'. With each day, he remarked, 'the local spirit' was overcome and the influence of the 'soil, of climate, of race' gave way before that of 'social and political action'. History had prevailed over geography. Men had escaped 'the tyranny of material circumstances'. In this 'marvellous transformation', Michelet continued, 'spirit has triumphed over matter, the general over the particular, the idea over the real'.[122]

Attention might be drawn to three important elements of this transformative process. The first is the weight that Michelet attached to the French language. 'The history of France', he wrote, 'begins with the French language. Language is the principal sign of a nationality.'[123] The 'continuous infiltration' of the French language over the entire territory was an integral part of the overcoming of local particularisms and of the intimate fusion of races that constituted the identity of the nation. France, on Michelet's view, accordingly stopped at the border between Lorraine and Alsace. Next, Michelet was in no doubt that 'the war of wars' that had opposed England and France had been of 'immense service' in confirming and strengthening French nationality. It was, he wrote, 'through seeing the English close up that [the provinces] became conscious that they were a part of France'.[124] Thirdly, Michelet did not hesitate to describe Paris as 'the great and complete symbol of the country'. An entity which resulted from the complete annihilation of local and provincial sentiment, Michelet ventured, might be regarded as being 'entirely negative', but in the case of Paris it was precisely from the negation of such local particularities that derived the qualities of 'generality' and 'receptivity' towards the universal that in turn denoted the 'superiority' of the Ile-de-France over the regions and of France herself over Europe.[125]

France, according to Michelet, had therefore been able to 'neutralize' and 'convert' those parts of her territory that had been originally English, German, or Spanish and, in so doing, she had produced an 'intimate fusion' of civilizations

---

[120] 'Tableau de France' in Michelet, *Œuvres complètes*, iv. *Histoire de France*, 331–84.
[121] Ibid. 381.   [122] Ibid. 384.   [123] Ibid. 331.
[124] Ibid. 377.   [125] Ibid. 381.

and races. Hence, she was the most 'artificial', 'human', and 'free' of countries. France as such existed as 'an abstract unity' and it was precisely because of this level of abstraction that she could be conceived as 'the universal *patrie* and as the city of Providence'.[126] Accordingly Michelet was able to begin his *Introduction à l'histoire universelle* with the lavish claims that France was 'the pilot of the vessel of humanity' and that his introduction to universal history might just as well have been entitled an introduction to the history of France.[127]

Yet, as Michelet accepted, France had failed to live up to the promise announced by 'the brilliant morning of July', and it was therefore in a mood of profound pessimism that Michelet penned his classic essay, *Le Peuple*, published in 1846. 'I see France' he wrote in the preface dedicated to Edgar Quinet, 'sinking hour by hour...our country is disappearing.' The central theme of *Le Peuple* was a straightforward one. The text began with a long discussion of the aspirations and sentiments of the different classes and groups which made up French society: the peasant, the factory worker, the artisan, the manufacturer, the shopkeeper, the government official, and the wealthy bourgeois. Michelet's conclusion was that each class, in its own particular way, existed in a state of bondage. For example, the factory worker, despite his relative affluence, lived in a world of 'fate and necessity'. Dominated by the machine he was reduced to 'physical weakness and mental impotence'. Likewise, the peasant, for all that he possessed and loved his land, was ground down by poverty and consumed by hatred of his neighbours and the world. As alone on his property as on a desert island, Michelet wrote, he had become 'a savage'. The total effect of this situation of generalized bondage, Michelet argued, was that the French people hated and despised one another. The rich hated and no longer knew the poor; the poor despised and did not trust the rich. France, in sum, was afflicted by an 'evil', an evil which Michelet identified as 'the chill and paralysis of the heart' and which, he believed, manifested itself as 'unsociableness'.

Where was the remedy to be found? Michelet's short answer was that, if the evil lay in the heart, it was here also that the solution was to be found. The French had to remember that they were 'brothers after all'. They had difficulty doing this, Michelet contended, because France had become overrefined, overcultivated, and, as a consequence, the emotions of the French and their capacity for love, as well as for action, had been dwarfed and stultified. 'The separation of men and classes', Michelet wrote, 'is due principally to the absurd opposition between instinct and reflection that has been established in our time.' What was needed was a return to instincts and with that an escape from what Michelet described as 'this bastard hotchpotch'.

It was precisely at this point that Michelet's prose was at its most lyrical. The best example that he could find of man in his uncorrupted and instinctive state was in the shape of the child. 'The child', he wrote, 'is the people themselves in their native truth before they were deformed; it is the people without vulgarity, rudeness or

---

[126] Ibid. 384.   [127] 'Introduction à l'histoire universelle', 227.

envy.' The child, put simply, was the 'interpreter of the people', the purest expression of what was 'young and primitive' in the people, an expression of 'the people innocent'. What of the people themselves? 'Son of the people', Michelet wrote, 'I have lived with them, I know them', and what he knew was that, although disfigured, their degeneration was only 'superficial'. The foundations were intact. This race, he told his readers, still has wine in its blood and 'is capable of action and is ever ready to act'. The people, in brief, maintained the virtues of innocence, compassion, self-sacrifice, love, and faith. They possessed the qualities of simplicity, the capacity to see what their more sophisticated fellows were blind to, an instinct which allowed them to sympathize with life. This led to the final, curious element of this part of Michelet's argument. The simplicity of the people, he argued, drew them close to 'the man of genius', that rare person who combined 'the instinct of the simple and the reflection of the wise', the merits of both the child and adult, the barbarian and the civilized. The people exist, Michelet contended, 'in their highest power only in the man of genius; in him resides their great soul'.

It is the concluding, third part of Michelet's *Le Peuple* that takes us to the heart of his nationalism. The regeneration of the French nation would not be achieved by a return to instinct alone. A faith was also required, because only 'a God, an altar' could engender sacrifice. The problem was that we had lost our gods, and thus required a new faith. This faith was to be France herself. It was to be through France, and not as isolated individuals, that 'the soul of the people' was to realize its nature. From this Michelet was able to provide a description of France, and of France alone, as the inheritor of the traditions of Greece and Rome, and as the country which had realized what Christianity had promised: brotherly equality. France embodied 'the salvation of the world', whilst 'its own interest and its own destiny' was identical with that of 'humanity'. Such a conclusion, Michelet remarked, was 'not fanaticism' but a 'short summary of a considered judgement based upon long study'. In particular, this view rested upon Michelet's identification of the Revolution of 1789 with the advent of the age of Justice, Right and Fraternity.[128]

For Michelet it was no idle coincidence that France had proclaimed her 'lofty and original revelation' at the very moment when the 'conflicting' Frances existing within her bosom were being suppressed and her provincialisms were disappearing. France was herself, and in the very instant that she proclaimed 'the future common rights of the entire world' was never more distinguishable from other nations. This in turn led to a broader conclusion: nationalities were not on the point of disappearing. On the contrary, Michelet announced, 'I see them every day developing profound moral characteristics and becoming individuals instead of collections of men.'

There were several interesting dimensions to this claim. We have seen that Michelet accredited the long war against England with a key role in the formation of French national self-consciousness. France came to know herself through her enemy. In similar vein, Michelet now scorned all those who believed that France

---

[128] Michelet's interpretation of the Revolution will be explored in the next chapter.

should copy or imitate English arts, fashion, literature, and, worse still, political institutions. To do so, Michelet argued, was to invite France 'to march against her history and her nature', to counsel that France should model herself upon 'anti-France'.

That England explained France but by opposition was a theme very evident in Michelet's *Introduction à l'histoire universelle*, and was used not only to demonstrate that the two nations possessed different moral characteristics but also to lend further support to the claim that France had a special destiny. At bottom, Michelet shared the prevailing republican view that England was a country dominated by the aristocracy. In his particular case he stressed that '[t]he land of France belongs to fifteen or twenty million peasants who cultivate it', whilst in England it was held by a few thousand individuals who had it farmed for them. 'What a serious moral difference', he remarked. Moreover, if Michelet recognized that it had been the 'heroism' of the English aristocracy that had begun the long march towards 'modern liberty', he was unambiguously of the view that heroism was not to be confused with liberty. 'In England', Michelet wrote, 'dominated as it is by Germanic and feudal elements, it is old, barbaric heroism, aristocracy, liberty through privilege that triumphs. Liberty without equality, unjust and impious liberty, is nothing else than the absence of sociability in society. France wants liberty through equality. . . . Liberty in France is just and holy.' It was around this ideal, this vision of liberty combined with equality, that France, a country made for action and not for conquest, would construct a future not only for herself but for the entire 'human race'.[129] France, Michelet concluded eloquently, was 'a religion'.

Eric Hobsbawm has argued that the liberal nationalism associated with mid-nineteenth-century Europe rested upon two important assumptions: the principle of nationalities applied in practice only to nations of a certain geographical size and self-determination was relevant only to nations that could be considered to be both culturally and economically viable.[130] Applied to the nationalism of Michelet, this characterization arguably misses its mark. For Michelet, the very idea of a nation implied not homogeneity but a plurality of different cultures living harmoniously side by side around a common point of unity. The particular genius of the French nation lay in its capacity to absorb and to assimilate these cultures (as well as races) and to do so in a manner that enhanced, rather than diminished, their vitality. Thus, the creation of the French nation had been a spontaneous and voluntary process, and one devoid of either economic imperatives or cultural expansionism. More than this, France was also adjudged to possess the capacity to absorb the best of what other nations and peoples had to offer, thereby making the French nation in aspiration the most human and universal of all nationalities. Fraternity both within and beyond the nation was the common theme.

Accordingly, for Michelet, the worst moments of France's history were those characterized by bitter division, and this, it seemed, was increasingly the case under the July Monarchy. It was therefore with immense relief and enthusiasm that

---

[129] 'Introduction à l'histoire universelle', 253.
[130] *Nations and Nationalism since 1870* (Cambridge, 1999).

Michelet, like so many of his fellow citizens, greeted the revolution of 1848.[131] Reinstated to his teaching post at the Collège de France, he again proclaimed his faith in the ability of France to lead the other nations of Europe towards emancipation and towards a future characterized by liberty and justice. He was not to be alone.[132] However, the Republic, with first Alphonse de Lamartine and later Alexis de Tocqueville as its Minister of Foreign Affairs, showed itself to be distinctly disinclined to carry its principles abroad by force of arms (or, for that matter, to issue a direct challenge to the much-hated treaties of 1815), preferring rather to affirm France's right to defend her own territory whilst offering only moral support to other nations seeking to pursue a similar path.[133]

It was in the wake of the disillusionment that followed the bloody repression of the popular protests of the 'June days' and the gradual reassertion of monarchical and counter-revolutionary power across Europe that Michelet envisaged the publication of a further volume asserting the primacy of the nation. Intended as an act of recompense for the betrayal inflicted upon the heroic and oppressed peoples abandoned by the Republic, the primary focus of *Légendes démocratiques du Nord* fell upon the struggles for national emancipation in eastern and south-eastern Europe.[134] As with Carrel and Lamennais, the tragic fate of Poland occupied centre stage, and again it was assumed that Poland and France were joined together by a singular bond of shared experiences and sentiments. Michelet's message was unmistakable. Europe, he announced, 'is not in any way a chance grouping, a simple juxtaposition of peoples; it is a melodious instrument, a lyre, where each nationality is a note and represents a key. There is nothing arbitrary about it; each one is necessary in itself and necessary in relation to the others. To remove one alone would be to modify the whole, to reduce this array of nations to impossibility, dissonance, and silence.'[135] To seek to destroy one of these nations was therefore to act against 'the sublime harmony designed by Providence'.

It was also an act of folly. Nations, according to Michelet, were indestructible. Despite every attempt to suppress their existence, they reappeared, reinvigorated by their travails. And this was the lesson to be drawn from the repeated attempts of a barbarous Russia to annihilate 'the France of the North'. Paradoxically, Michelet affirmed, Polish nationhood had been reaffirmed by Russian oppression, and it was Russia itself that had been immeasurably weakened, descending 'into degradation, into moral asphyxia'. The truth therefore was that it was to the Polish people that Russia would owe its own 'resurrection'. No greater calling was bestowed upon 'poor Poland' than the 'salvation' of 'this drunken and mad giant'.

---

[131] See Vialleneix, *Michelet, les travaux et les jours*, 322–35.

[132] See Darriulat, *Les Patriotes*, 182–92.

[133] On 6 Mar. 1848 Lamartine had issued a *Manifeste aux Puissances*, indicating that France no longer accepted the treaties of 1815 as binding and offering support to 'oppressed nationalities'. Lamartine subsequently went out of his way to assure the rival powers that France's intentions were pacific.

[134] *Œuvres complètes de Michelet*, xvi. 99–323.

[135] Ibid. 137.

Michelet's zeal for the cause of Poland was not without reservation. He was troubled in particular by the desire of many Polish nationalists to ally the fate of the Polish nation to that of the Catholic Church. In Ireland, Spain, Italy, and France herself, Michelet contended, Catholicism had had a sterilizing and neutralizing effect, sapping the vitality of each nation. Poland in turn had been weakened by the intrusion of the Church (and especially by the 'invasion' of the Jesuits), becoming separated from its Orthodox neighbours. In this, therefore, he did not share the views of Lamennais. Nevertheless, Michelet did not wish to suggest that the Poles should abjure their faith. This, he knew, was not possible. Rather, he wished only that their faith should be extended and broadened. He was thus able to return to one of his favourite themes and again to underline what he took to be the emancipatory and morally uplifting qualities of his own conception of the nation. The religion of the world, Michelet proclaimed, was no longer an egoistic faith, where salvation was secured in isolation. Our own salvation was only secured through the salvation of everyone else, was only to be obtained through what Michelet termed 'the fraternal embrace of humanity by humanity'.[136]

IV

Michelet republished *Légendes démocratiques du Nord* in 1863, the year in which Poland again unsuccessfully rose in revolt against Tsarist Russia. If anything his distaste for the Russian 'monster' had only intensified over time, although this did not prevent him from recognizing the 'magnanimity' of Alexander Herzen and the 'heroism' of Mikhail Bakunin.[137] Something had changed however. Upon this occasion, Russian repression had formal Prussian support, Bismarck having signed an agreement with the Tsar in February 1863 specifying that an uprising in the Polish provinces of Prussia would be met by similar repression. The following year Prussia went to war successfully with Denmark over the contested duchies of Schleswig and Holstein. Two years later Prussia defeated Austria, leaving the way open for the establishment of the North German Confederation in 1867 and further Prussian expansion. In a few short years Bismarck had overturned the European balance of power and France, under the incompetent and vainglorious guidance of Napoleon III, found herself facing a politically unified and increasingly aggressive Germany. Three years later, under the pretext of a dispute about the succession to the Spanish throne, Prussia and France went to war. The French army was decisively defeated; and (in an act calculated to inflict maximum humiliation) the second German Reich was proclaimed in the hall of mirrors of the Palace of Versailles. The latter event, the Goncourt brothers confided to their diary, marked 'the end of the greatness of France'.[138]

If the loss of French pre-eminence in continental Europe dramatically overturned the fragile military and diplomatic equilibrium that had existed since 1815,

---

[136] Ibid. 186.   [137] Ibid. 134.
[138] *Pages from the Goncourt Journal* (Harmondsworth, 1984), 183.

it had been an outcome long foretold by pessimists such as Prévost-Paradol. The experience of the Second Empire had forced republicans to rethink their very idea of the nation and to recognize that the nation could as well be embodied in an autocrat as in the people. The military successes in the Crimea (1854–5) and Italy (1859) allowed both Napoleon III and the army to bask in the afterglow of national triumph. In such a bellicose atmosphere, the romantic messianism associated with the likes of Michelet and Ledru-Rollin continued to find a voice but did so in an atmosphere increasingly drawn towards anti-militarism and a more overt endorsement of internationalism. As Napoleon III's foreign and colonial adventures grew in recklessness, so opponents of the regime came more and more to cast themselves as the party of peace. Even the myth of Napoleon Bonaparte now began to lose its appeal.

The less bellicose and overtly anti-militarist mood of the period was clearly captured and expressed in the writings and actions of Jules Barni. From his exile in Switzerland, Barni acted as president of the Ligue Internationale pour la Paix et la Liberté, an organization which he helped to launch in 1867. This was no minor interest, as the final section of *La morale dans la démocratie*, published the following year,[139] demonstrated. There Barni showed himself to be totally opposed to the republican 'just war' tradition, preferring rather to explore how peaceful relations among states could best be achieved.[140] Accordingly, Barni was quick to reject all the arguments then advanced in defence of war and conquest: those that justified war in terms of the advance of civilization, the claims of nationality, and the recognition of natural borders. Frequently contradicting each other, even when taken together they could not absolve an 'unjust' act.[141] 'What', Barni asked, 'is a state, a people, a nation? Not a herd of animals but an association of men, of free beings, forming a kind of *moral person*. . . . We must therefore grant to states the same rights that we grant to individuals and apply the same moral rules to them as those which govern the relationship between persons.'[142] It followed that no state had the right to get involved in the internal affairs of another and that one of the first rules of international morality was the 'principle of non-intervention'. Until such time as states moved out of the state of nature and war could definitively be abolished, the best that could be hoped for was that we could 'moralize and humanize' war. To that end Barni recommended a set of preliminary conditions including the abolition of standing armies. The ultimate goal—as befitted a convinced Kantian—was 'a federation of free states designed to guarantee the rights of each nation and to resolve the differences between them by means of binding arbitration'.[143] Underpinning all of this was Barni's unshakable conviction that the principal threat to peace came from the militarism and despotism he associated with 'Caesarism', and therefore from the absence of free, republican systems of

[139] Jules Barni, *La Morale dans la démocratie* (1868), 218–66.
[140] Sudhir Hazareesingh, *Intellectual Founders of the Republic: Five Studies in Nineteenth-Century French Political Thought* (Oxford, 2001), 246–56.
[141] Barni, *La Morale dans la démocratie*, 220–4.
[142] Ibid. 219.
[143] Ibid. 255.

government. 'Let us work', he told delegates to the 1867 Geneva congress of the Ligue Internationale pour la Paix et la Liberté, 'to oppose the republican spirit to the Caesarian spirit, the civic spirit to the militaristic spirit, the spirit of federation to the spirit of centralization, in brief, the spirit of liberty and peace to the spirit of despotism and war'.[144]

The events of 1870–1 sorely tested the anti-militarism and internationalism of men like Barni. If, as Karma Nabulsi has shown,[145] there was plenty of evidence to suggest that 'a republican culture of war was still operating at the outbreak of the Franco-Prussian war', it was equally the case that expressions of anti-German patriotism were not slow to be voiced. As Léon Gambetta, Minister of the Interior in the newly formed provisional government, toured the country seeking to rally a people's army to defend the Republic, even old cynics such as Gustave Flaubert could not resist the occasional, heartfelt chauvinistic outburst.[146] Barni himself returned to France with the fall of the Second Empire and immediately offered his services to the Government of National Defence.

To this powerful intellectual challenge was added the emotional trauma associated with the establishment and subsequent violent repression of the Paris Commune. For seventy-three days, between 18 March and 28 May 1871, the administration of Paris was in the hands of the people, in open defiance of the government located in Versailles. Few, if any, writers of distinction or renown lent their support to its cause, most showing themselves deeply troubled by the brutal anticlericalism and artistic vandalism of the Parisian mob. Concerns about religious freedom and the fate of the Venus de Milo were, however, dwarfed by the shock and apprehension that accompanied the deaths of approximately 20,000 Parisians, killed or executed by government troops as they recaptured the capital during 'la semaine sanglante' that brought the Commune to an end. Thousands more were arrested, many being deported to far-off New Caledonia. To national humiliation was added a sense of bereavement and shame.

Following the Treaty of Frankfurt, signed on 21 May 1871, France therefore faced not one but two questions of central importance. She again needed to decide what form of political regime should be put in place. Secondly, France had to find a way of responding to Prussian military supremacy whilst rehabilitating herself in the eyes of the international community. For many, the answers to the two questions were intimately related.

Michelet, nearing the end of his life, continued to strike a tone of hope and defiance.[147] If Prussia owed its victory not to the heroism of its troops but to espionage and 'the triumph of the machine', so also it derived from the 'rottenness' of the Second Empire. Was Napoleon III even French? Michelet asked. Yet the 'soul' of France was 'invincible' and her 'renaissance' would save Europe. It was out of the trials of military resistance, Michelet contended, that France would overcome

---

[144] Ibid. 260.
[145] Nabulsi, 'La Guerre Sainte', 38.
[146] See Michel Winock, *Les Voix de la liberté: Les Écrivains engagés au XIXe siècle* (2001), 492–6.
[147] See *La France devant l'Europe, Œuvres complètes de Michelet*, xx. *1867–1871*, 601–712.

her divisions and again take her place as Europe's leader in the fight against 'Prusso-Russian militarism'. With her 'moral unity' still intact, France would quickly restore her 'material unity'.

The response of Edgar Quinet was altogether more thought-provoking and profound.[148] Like Michelet, Quinet had but a few years to live and it is hard not to be moved by the passion he brought to the task of sketching out the conditions through which France could be regenerated. At their heart lay the necessity of confirming the existence of the Republic and therefore the need to break with the backward-looking, reactionary doctrines of the past. These doctrines, with 'their aversion to modern liberty', represented 'the remains and the ashes of everything which is dead in the human spirit'.[149] Thus there could be no talk of a republic reconciled to the monarchy, of a republic without republicans. To abandon the Republic would be for France to turn its back to the light and to descend into chaos. In practical terms, this meant: the reform of the army and the re-establishment of its links with the nation; the reorganization of the educational system with a view to reawakening the 'spirit of liberty'; the separation of Church and State; and consequently the eradication of the baneful influence of theocracy. To this Quinet added the reform of the diplomatic service (which had been blind to the rise of Prussia), of the judiciary (which was still imprinted with the 'decrepit spirit of the past'), and of the education of France's political leaders (so as to forge closer links with the aspirations of the people). These changes, plus other measures such as the return of the government to Paris, would, in Quinet's opinion, lead to an artistic and intellectual revival, and would thus allow France to escape from the 'Prussian spectre'. 'It is unquestionable', Quinet wrote, 'that a nation, even one bowed by defeat, can quickly raise itself, regenerate itself and surprise the world.'[150]

To that extent, Quinet concluded, France had to take the battle to Prussia on the 'field of civilization'.[151] All enduring victories, he argued, had had 'the fusion of human races' as a consequence but this had not been so with the victory of Prussia.[152] 'The Germans', Quinet wrote, 'boast of extinguishing the Latin race' to the advantage of 'the Teutonic race'. They thought of themselves only as Germans and were driven by hatred and 'the egoism of race'. It was therefore a 'barbarous victory' and one that was antithetical to civilization. Herein lay 'the superiority of France', a country bringing together 'many different races of men, the Gallic, the Latin, the Iberian and the German'.[153] Herein too lay the particular offence that arose from the forced annexation of Alsace and Lorraine. An integral part of the spirit of France—the German race—had been torn away. Behind this however lay a deeper awareness of the strategic significance of this loss. Alsace and Lorraine, Quinet wrote, were 'not just two provinces; they are the two highways of France, the two ramparts'. Annexed to Germany, it meant that France was open to the enemy, that he was always ready and able to march on Paris, that he had 'France

---

[148] See Edgar Quinet, *La République, conditions de la régénération de la France* (1873). See also *L'Esprit Nouveau* (1879; 1st publ. 1874).
[149] Quinet, *La République*, 138.   [150] Ibid. 120.   [151] Ibid. 93.
[152] Ibid. 248–51.   [153] Ibid. 250.

by the throat'. This, Quinet declared, was not peace but rather 'permanent war under the guise of peace'.[154]

Quinet was not prepared to accept that France had come to the end of her history with the defeats at Metz and Sedan. Peoples were slow to mature and to achieve their full greatness and by these criteria France as a nation 'had a brilliant future before her'. Above all, France must not become the feudal vassal of Prussia, meekly paying her war indemnity 'in the manner of the enslaved peoples of antiquity'. That fate, and the further dismemberment which would follow, could only be avoided through the Republic, the one regime that could, in Quinet's opinion, 'unite all of the French into the same body'.[155]

Yet the annexation of Alsace and Lorraine was like an open wound, a constant affront not just to French dignity but to the very conception of France that had been built up over the preceding eighty years or more. On this view, France was an artificial construct and it was out of this very artificiality that had arisen her special genius: the ability to bring different nations and cultures together into a harmonious totality that opened itself up to the noblest aspirations of humanity. It was precisely this idea that Michelet restated in 1869 when, after a lifetime of study spent recovering the history of France, he distanced his account from that provided by his distinguished predecessor Augustin Thierry with its reliance upon the unchanging character of races. 'France', Michelet wrote, 'has made France, and the fatal element of race seems to me to be of secondary importance. She is the product of her liberty. In human progress the essential part falls to the active force that one calls man. *Man is his own Prometheus.*'[156] A year later it was arguably the ideological antithesis of this sentiment that was triumphant on the battlefield.

The task of working through the political and intellectual implications of France's defeat was to preoccupy French writers for decades to come. A sense of the challenge it represented can nonetheless be glimpsed by looking at one of the first, and also best-known, responses to the claims of German nationalism. In 1870 Numa-Denis Fustel de Coulanges, one of the most distinguished French historians of the second half of the nineteenth century, published a short pamphlet entitled *L'Alsace, est-elle Allemande ou Française?*[157] It was a direct response to the arguments put forward to justify German annexation by Theodore Mommsen, a fellow historian at the University of Berlin. According to Mommsen, Alsace was German because its people spoke German and because they belonged to the German race. Fustel de Coulanges disputed the validity of these arguments on a series of grounds, not the least of them being that they could justify Prussian expansion into Holland, Austria, Switzerland, and eastward into Russia. At the heart of his reply, however, was the contention that 'neither race nor language constituted nationality'.[158] 'What distinguishes nations', Fustel de Coulanges went on, 'is neither race nor language. Men feel in their heart that they belong to the same people when they

---

[154] Ibid. 290–4. [155] Ibid. 277.

[156] Michelet, 'Préface de 1869', *Histoire de France: Le Moyen Âge* (1981), 17.

[157] Numa-Denis Fustel de Coulanges, *L'Alsace, est-elle Allemande ou Française?* (1870).

[158] Ibid. 8.

share a common stock of ideas, of interests, of affections, of memories and of hopes.'[159] One's homeland was the place that one loved and by this criterion Alsace, irrespective of race and language, was French. And it had been so since 1789. 'From that moment onwards', Fustel de Coulanges argued, 'Alsace has followed our fortunes: she has lived our life.' In its heart and mind Alsace was 'one of the most French of provinces' and of this no better proof had been given than by the way that Alsace had bravely defended itself against Prussian aggression. To speak of nationality in terms of race and language, therefore, was to look to the past. 'Our principle', Fustel de Coulanges concluded, 'is that a population can only be governed by the institutions which it freely accepts and that it must only form part of a state through its own will and consent.'[160] France's sole motive in wishing to keep Alsace French was that this was what the people of Alsace themselves wanted.

Fustel de Coulanges by no means had the last word on the subject. Within a matter of a few years a doctrine that had initially bathed in the waters of national unity, natural frontiers, and sister republics and which had consistently portrayed France as the embodiment of a universal idea, had been subverted by the very ideas that Fustel de Coulanges had challenged. After 1870 the talk was of 'revenge' and of the recovery of the 'lost provinces' and with that the path was open to Vacher de Lapouge's measurement of human skulls to prove that 'race and nation are everything' and, later, Maurice Barrès's cult of 'la Terre et les Morts' and the 'integral nationalism' of Charles Maurras. Moreover, it was to be in this guise, as a reactionary, anti-parliamentary, and anti-liberal doctrine, that nationalism was largely to figure in subsequent French political thinking.

But did this trajectory represent as fundamental a change in the character of French nationalism as this might suggest? According to Raoul Girardet, it did not.[161] If he accepts that between the nationalism of someone like Armand Carrel and the right-wing nationalism of the late nineteenth century there existed 'irreducible oppositions of ideological motivation and historical reference',[162] Girardet nevertheless contends that on several substantive points they were in agreement. Each proclaimed the cult of the army and of military glory. They both articulated a conception of national grandeur built around a vision of a glorious French past and a providential future. Most importantly, they shared what he terms a 'dynamic of refusal'. 'Under the Restoration, under the July Monarchy, and almost constantly since 1883', Girardet writes, 'the spokesmen of French nationalism have not ceased to accuse those in power of pursuing a foreign policy of weakness and faintheartedness, of scorning and humiliating French pride, of betraying the overriding interests of the homeland.'[163] This was certainly true of men like Carrel and Quinet. Their nationalism was rooted in a deep sense of the permanent humiliation and

---

[159] Numa-Denis Fustel de Coulanges, *L'Alsace, est-elle Allemande ou Française?* (1870), 10.
[160] Ibid. 15.
[161] Raoul Girardet, 'Pour une introduction à l'histoire du nationalisme français', *Revue Française de Science Politique*, 8 (1958), 505–28, and Girardet (ed) *Le Nationalisme français* (1983).
[162] Girardet, 'Pour une introduction', 515.
[163] Ibid. 519.

abasement of a defeated France and the need for this to be reversed by a call to arms. Similarly, their hostility to the restored Bourbon monarchy derived from the conviction that Louis XVIII and Charles X were the supreme symbols of that humiliation and it was this that drew them into the ranks of the liberal opposition. The diplomatic and military defeats of Napoleon III only served to confirm this perspective.

Other long-term continuities can be discerned. The revolutionary tradition in France, replete with its messianic message, made much not just of the idea of national unity but also of the virtue of assimilation: the aspirations of the Revolution, and through it of France, were universal and could embrace not only the entire French nation but could also be extended indefinitely to include all of humankind. Yet, according to Bernard Manin, 'French republican culture has essentially been a culture of exclusion'.[164] The most dramatic illustration of this was undoubtedly the Terror but, as Manin points out, 'an analogous vision of exclusion can be found in the writings of Sieyès'. The members of the privileged orders were deemed to have nothing in common with the Third Estate. Hence the privileged orders could legitimately be excluded from all consideration and deliberation. Their flight into exile was subsequently taken as proof of their 'anti-national' credentials and was sufficient to convince the revolutionaries that they faced a handful of foreign enemies possessing only tenuous links with the national community.

From this was derived the *mythe de l'adversaire* and the vision of *le peuple*, united and in harmony, pitted against *les gros*.[165] If, initially, it was the monarchy, aristocracy, and the Church which fell into the latter category, republican ideology had little difficulty converting its enemies into the capitalists and the bourgeoisie, Sieyès's minority of 200,000 aristocrats and priests being replaced by the financial feudalism of the '200 families', the émigrés of Coblenz giving way to a *bourgeoisie apatride*, a *bourgeoisie antinationale*.[166] For their part, the nationalists of the right had little difficulty replicating these xenophobic conspiracy theories, the targets of their hatred being Jews, Freemasons, and Protestants. As Pierre Birnbaum has written: 'even if the nationalisms of the right and the left diverge upon certain crucial points they merge together in the common defence of the French nation, partially occupied and threatened by the foreigner'.[167]

In both cases this vision of the people confronting a handful of opponents deemed by definition to be non-members of the national community was at best an absurd caricature of French society, but in purely political terms it was a vision that proved to be remarkably effective and enduring. Few political movements were to prosper without recourse to the language of *union nationale* and *rassemblement*, even though the nature and character of that coming together was subject to bitter

---

[164] Bernard Manin, 'Pourquoi la République?', *Intervention*, 10 (1984), 10.

[165] See Pierre Birnbaum, *Le Peuple et les Gros: Histoire d'un mythe* (1979).

[166] See Alain Bergounioux and Bernard Manin, 'L'Exclu de la nation: La Gauche française et son mythe de l'adversaire', *Le Débat*, 5 (1980), 45–53.

[167] Birnbaum, *Le Peuple et les Gros*, 20.

dispute. Somehow or other, it was agreed, the integrity of the French people and of France herself had to be reasserted and re-established.

In a later chapter we will return to this theme but here we might conclude by reflecting upon two of the very different ways in which the preoccupation with re-establishing the integrity of the French nation found its way into the broader culture of everyday life during the Third Republic. One would be the *tour de France*, the cycle race first staged in 1903.[168] Although in origin a commercial venture designed to boost newspaper circulation, sport (and physical exercise in general) was closely linked to the theme of national renaissance and revival. More than this, from the outset the *tour* not only celebrated the history of France but self-consciously exploited the physical beauty of France, paying particular attention to natural frontiers and to the mountain ranges of the Alps and Pyrenees especially. Between 1906 and 1910 it even managed to penetrate into the two provinces lost to Prussia in 1870, where, it was reported, crowds sang *La Marseillaise* as the cyclists passed by. It is no idle coincidence that the longest *tour* of all took place in 1919. At over 5,380 kilometres it wound its way across the battlefields of northern France and around the newly reclaimed borders of Alsace and Lorraine.[169]

The other example would be *Le Tour de la France par Deux Enfants*, first published in 1877. This was the tale of two young boys forced to leave their native Lorraine (then under Prussian occupation) and who travel the length and breadth of France, in the process discovering both the variety and the unity of their homeland. The author, whose identity was long hidden, was Augustine Fouillée, wife of the philosopher Alfred Fouillée, and her work reflected the solidarist ideas developed by her husband. Lauded, therefore, were the values of hard work, perseverance, frugality, honesty, the home, and respect for the law as the expression of the national will. But, above all, there was love of country and of France herself. The happiest of countries, Augustine Fouillée's young readers were told, was one where people were always ready to help each other and where there was agreement and union amongst the inhabitants. Their journey at an end, and having at last seen the wonders of Paris (including its zoo), the text concluded with a chapter entitled 'J'aime la France'. Amidst the ruins of war and at last reunited with their family, the two boys set about the rebuilding of France. In ten years *Le Tour de la France par Deux Enfants* sold over 3 million copies. By 1901 this figure had reached 6 million.[170]

---

[168] See Georges Vigarello, 'Le Tour de France', in Nora, *Les Lieux*, iii. 3801–33.

[169] See Richard Holt, *Sport and Society in Modern France* (London, 1981), 96–102. Graham Robb has commented that: 'The Tour de France gave millions of people their first true sense of the shape and size of France, but it also proved beyond doubt that the land of a thousand little *pays* was still alive': *The Discovery of France* (London, 2007), 344.

[170] See Jacques and Mona Ozouf, 'Le Tour de la France par Deux Enfants: Le petit livre rouge de la République', in Nora, *Les Lieux*, i. 291–321. The 2nd edn., publ. after the separation of Church and State in 1905, was more secular in tone and concluded with a eulogy in honour of Louis Pasteur and the wonders of industrial and technological progress.

6

History, Revolution, and Terror

I

In the first half of 1791 there took place an exchange of letters between Edmund Burke and Claude-François de Rivarol.[1] At first glance, their publication looked unpromising, as the Parisian editor was obliged to announce that the first of Rivarol's letters could not be published because its author had not retained a copy of it. However, there can be no doubt as to the interest of this brief exchange for, if Burke was now hailed as the author of the celebrated *Reflections on the Revolution in France*, Rivarol's brother, Antoine, was unquestionably the most brilliant and the most defamatory of all of France's counter-revolutionary journalists, as well as being the editor of the *Journal national politique*. Indeed Burke was not slow to praise Antoine de Rivarol. Having indicated that his *Reflections* were intended to serve the interests of 'this kingdom and of mankind', he next confessed that he had read the *Journal national politique* too late for it to have informed his own account. Yet, he averred, there was 'a strong coincidence in our way of thinking', adding that 'I should rather have chosen to enrich my pamphlet with quotations from thence, than have ventured to express my thoughts in which we agreed, in worse words of my own.'[2] Rivarol's annals, Burke continued, 'may rank with those of Tacitus'.

For the most part, Burke's reply to Claude-François de Rivarol addressed recent events in the Low Countries and the question of how the Emperor Leopold II might set about restoring his authority. 'A wise prince', Burke responded, 'studies the genius of his people' and will not seek to contradict its mores. Nor will he take away its privileges. He will act according to the circumstances and for as long as he follows 'the practical principles of a practical policy' he will be the happy prince of a happy people. He should ignore the chatter and rebukes voiced by those Burke referred to, with contempt, as 'the magpies and jays' of philosophy. These conclusions were confirmed by recent experience in France. In general, Burke continued, a politics based upon civil discord was perilous for the prince and fatal for his subjects. The maintenance and permanence of

---

[1] *Lettre de M. Burke sur les Affaires de France et des Pays-Bas; adressée à M. Le Vicomte de Rivarol* (1791). Burke's letter, written in English, can be found in *The Correspondence of Edmund Burke*, ed. Alfred Cobban and Robert A. Smith (Cambridge, 1967), vi. 265–70.

[2] Ibid. 265.

orders and a genuine understanding between all the parties that made up government offered the best chance of peace and tranquillity. Corporations with a permanent existence and hereditary nobles were the protectors of monarchical succession. Yet, in post-1789 France, the monarchy alone rested upon the hereditary principle. All other institutions were elective. And thus the monarchy existed in blatant contradiction to all the sentiments and ideas of the people. In brief, the intricate web of self-regulating institutions and practices, around which ties of duty, friendship, loyalty, and reciprocity had been enacted and formed, had been ruthlessly stripped away, leaving the hereditary monarchy exposed and ready to fall. The monarchy of France, Burke concluded, was 'a solitary, unsupported, anomalous thing'.

The final aspect of Burke's reply concerned Rivarol's poem, *Les Chartreux*. Burke did not agree with what he took to be Rivarol's view that the only love worth its name was that professed by Phædre and Myrrhas or by 'ancient or modern Eloyses'.[3] 'I do not want', Burke announced, 'women to pursue their lovers into convents of Carthusiens, nor follow them in disguise to camps and slaughterhouses.' Beneath this plea for a moderation of the passions, however, lay a deeper point, and one relating directly to the fate of contemporary France. It was, Burke observed, in the nature of poets to choose subjects intended to 'excite the high relish arising from the mixed sensations which will arise in that anxious embarrassment of the mind' found where 'vices and virtues meet near their confines'. In Paris, he sensed that philosophers shared the instincts of the poets, that they sought only 'to flatter and to excite the passions'. What, Burke commented, might be allowed in a poet could not be indulged in philosophers. Through a mixture of hatred and scorn, they had succeeded in exploding what Burke termed 'that class of virtues which restrain the appetite'. In their place had been substituted a virtue called humanity or benevolence. By this expedient, Burke observed, the morality of the philosophers had no idea of restraint or of 'any settled principle of any kind'. 'When', he concluded, 'their disciples are thus left free, and guided only by present feeling, they are no longer to be depended upon for good or evil. The men who to-day snatch the worst criminals from justice will murder the most innocent persons tomorrow.'

Rivarol largely agreed with Burke's analysis of the best course of action to be taken both in France and in the Low Countries. 'The odious and disruptive sect' of the *philosophes*, he conceded, was best dealt with by 'firm and wise' government than by 'bayonets'. A sound administration of the finances—as, he admitted, had not been the case in France—would take away the pretexts for their complaints and deprive them of a receptive audience, leaving them with nothing better to do than drown themselves in metaphysics and their love of the universe. The thousand-headed hydra of democracy must not be replaced by the hydra of aristocracy intent on devouring the people. On the moral to be drawn from the experience of the two lovers, Rivarol reaffirmed his view that there was no merit in solitude. It was in

---

[3] Presumably one of these was Rousseau's *Nouvelle Héloise*.

the midst of society that 'gentle sympathy' was nurtured and bore fruit, where relationships and lines of affection united the human race in an 'immense marriage' of the heart. 'I have also noticed', Rivarol remarked, 'that the most dreadful man is the man without family, and I have also noticed that, in the national assembly, the most criminal sedition monger was either a bachelor or a bad husband, which amounts to the same thing.' The *philosophes*, on this view, were all monks: they had neither affections, nor fathers, nor children.

As previously observed, in the ideas of Antoine de Rivarol (and, as we now see, of his less famous brother) can be distinguished prefigurations of what were to become central themes raised by theorists of counter-revolution in France from the early 1790s onwards. From this perspective, there was much to be admired in Burke's account of the Revolution. Above all, he had perceived the frightening originality of the events that were unfolding and, from the outset, had seen the spirit of innovation and of philosophy that would drive the Revolution forward towards its cataclysmic and destructive conclusion.

Yet, for all the popularity and commercial success of Burke's account, there were limits to the admiration felt by the French counter-revolutionaries for Burke, limits that were to become most obvious in the writings of Joseph de Maistre and Louis de Bonald. Despite their agreement on the pernicious influence of the atheistic and fanatical *philosophe* sect, they did not share Burke's appreciation of traditional English liberties nor his attachment to representative institutions. Least of all were they prepared to accept the exemplary character and role that Burke attributed to English history. This position was to be held by France as the eldest daughter of the Church. So Burke was largely to fade from view in subsequent counter-revolutionary histories. Indeed, Burke was to be absent from most French histories of the Revolution written in the nineteenth and twentieth centuries.[4] The prevailing view was simply that Burke had misunderstood the nature of the French Revolution. Jules Michelet, for example, referred to 'his infamous book, wild with rage, full of lies and cheap insults'.[5] Although more measured in tone, Alexis de Tocqueville was of a similar opinion. Burke, he believed, had been mesmerized by events and, as a consequence, had failed to see what was before his very eyes. The monarchy had sealed its own fate. Thus, Burke's unapologetic defence of the old order, of its institutions and its manners, could have no purchase upon a French society long accustomed to the uniformity and administrative centralization of the absolute monarchy.[6]

Nevertheless, Burke himself (and not without good cause) clearly felt that his views chimed with those of some of the Revolution's very first opponents in France. In May 1797, for example, he wrote a short letter to the exiled Abbé Augustin

---

[4] Furet, 'Burke ou la fin d'une seule histoire de l'Europe', in Furet, *La Révolution française* (2007), 902.
[5] *Histoire de la Révolution française* (1979), i. 341–2.
[6] See Robert T. Gannett, jun., *Tocqueville Unveiled: The Historian and his Sources for the Old Regime and the Revolution* (Chicago, 2003), 57–77.

Barruel.[7] 'I cannot easily express to you', Burke commented, 'how much I am instructed and delighted by the first Volume of your History of Jacobinism. The whole of the wonderful narrative is supported by documents and proofs with the most juridical regularity and exactness.' It was admirable in every way, Burke continued, and, to the extent that he could judge French style, 'the language is of the first water'. He also testified from personal experience to the veracity of Barruel's argument, reporting that he had known 'five of your principal conspirators'.

Born in 1741, Barruel was a Jesuit priest and was now serving as chaplain to the Princess de Conti in England. He had left France in 1792, shortly before the September massacres, having denounced the Revolution as early as 1789 in a text entitled *Le Patriote véridique, ou Discours sur les vrais causes de la Révolution actuelle*. Whilst in England he had collected material for his *Histoire du clergé pendant la Révolution française*, and there attacked the Civil Constitution of the Clergy as being blasphemous and heretical and as a prelude to the 'persecution, massacres and deportation of the French clergy'. In both works could be discerned the lineaments of an explanation of the Revolution which he was to develop at greater length in the book referred to by Burke, his *Mémoires pour servir à l'histoire du jacobinisme*.[8] the Revolution was the product of a conspiracy led by the *philosophes* against both throne and altar.[9]

The opening paragraphs clearly stated Barruel's thesis and purpose. It was an error, he contended, to believe that the Revolution was the result of a set of unforeseen and unpredictable circumstances. Rather, 'supported by facts and armed with proofs', he believed that it could be shown that 'everything in this French Revolution, including its most heinous crimes, was planned, premeditated, coordinated, resolved, decided upon. Everything was the result of the darkest villainy, since everything had been prepared and led by men who for long had hatched conspiracies in secret societies and who knew how to choose and hasten those moments most propitious for plots'.[10] Circumstances had provided a pretext, as 'the great cause' of the Revolution, of its crimes and atrocities, was to be found in 'plots hatched well beforehand'. Barruel's intention, therefore, was to unmask this conspiracy. In broad outline, he believed that it had come in three forms. First, long before the Revolution, had been the conspiracy of the philosophers against God and against Christianity in all its forms. It had been a conspiracy led by the 'sophists of unbelief and impiety'. Next had come a conspiracy led by 'the sophists of rebellion' directed against all kings. Finally, there had emerged a conspiracy of anarchy combined against all religion and all government, against society, and against property. It was, Barruel concluded, 'this coalition of the adepts of *impiety*,

---

[7] *The Correspondence of Edmund Burke*, ed. R. B. McDowell and John A. Woods (Cambridge, 1970), ix. 319–20.

[8] Barruel's text was originally publ. in London and Hamburg; references are to the 1973 edn., 2 vols.

[9] See e.g. *Le Patriote véridique* (1789), 20–1 and *Histoire du clergé* (London, 1793), 3. For a refutation of Barruel's position see J. J. Mounier, *De l'Influence attribuée aux Philosophes, aux Francs-maçons et aux Illuminés sur la Révolution de France* (Tubingen, 1801).

[10] Barruel, *Mémoires*, i. 42.

of the adepts of *rebellion*, of the adepts of *anarchy*, which had formed the Jacobin clubs'.[11]

The details of Barruel's account of this philosophical conspiracy are intriguing. For the *philosophes* to attain their ends, it had been necessary for public opinion to be corrupted: only then could the altar fall beneath the axe. This had been achieved in a series of stages. It began with 'the most infallible of means': the *Encyclopédie*. Then came the eradication of the Jesuits and, after this, of all religious orders. There next emerged 'Voltaire's colony', the group of like-minded people who had congregated around Voltaire in exile. More influential still had been the corruption of France's literary establishment, paving the way for a 'general apostasy'. This was followed by a 'flood of anti-Christian books' and the successful attempt to hide the conspiracy in the 'name of toleration'. Liberty of the press, Barruel contended, was especially dangerous in France, as even the simplest bourgeois wished to have his library. In consequence there appeared a new generation equipped only to mouth the platitudes of Voltaire and Rousseau and ready to articulate their enthusiasm for revolution. 'Men of letters without religion', Barruel observed, 'are the most depraved and dangerous group of citizens.'[12]

To impiety towards religion was adjoined the spirit of rebellion towards the king. Here, somewhat unusually, Barruel laid much of the blame at the feet of Montesquieu. It had been Montesquieu who had taught the French that the guiding principle of republics was virtue and that monarchies were despotic and arbitrary. Similarly, he had encouraged the French to admire the constitution of England and to see France's own government as a 'painful and shameful slavery'. His greatest error, however, was to fail to see that, if the principle of representation could lead in one country to liberty, in another—as the calling of the Estates-General had demonstrated—it could produce anarchy and despotism. 'It is to Montesquieu', Barruel concluded, 'that the French owe the entire system based upon the necessity of dividing up the sceptre of the king, of making the monarch dependent upon the multitude' and therefore of turning Louis XVI into 'un roi de théâtre'. Rousseau, by doing away with Montesquieu's aristocratic intermediaries and by proclaiming the people to be both sovereign and infallible, had only completed the process, breaking 'absolutely' the sceptre of kings, nobles, and the rich.[13] If, Barruel believed, the consequences of these doctrines were obvious to anyone who took the trouble to look, it had taken the conspiracy of the *philosophes* and their followers to put them into practice.

The final, key ingredient of Barruel's account focused upon the Freemasons, the friends and allies of the philosophical sect. With the Revolution of 1789, the Freemasons had poured out of their lodges and into the revolutionary sections and committees, determined to deliver the world from the 'twin plagues' of religious credulity and political tyranny. Yet, it had taken the emergence of the Jacobins—'this monstrous association' always insatiable for blood—to bring the conspiracy to its conclusion and to proclaim its zeal to change the face of the entire

---

[11] Ibid. 47.   [12] Ibid. 217.
[13] In *Histoire du clergé*, 139, Barruel refers to Rousseau as 'the Hercules of the sophists'.

universe. From this, Barruel believed, the following lesson should be learnt: the French Revolution was nothing but the product of a 'fixed, steadfast, and unshakable determination to everywhere overturn altar, throne, and society'.[14]

A second, important theme underpinned Barruel's account. Even as the Revolution got under way there were those prepared to see France's misfortunes as the work of a vengeful God and as the punishment of a sinful people.[15] Barruel shared this providential perspective. For all that he recounted in vivid detail the murder and imprisonment of refractory priests, he readily recognized that the Church had become subject to abuse and corruption[16] and that it had shown itself incapable of preventing the decline of public morals and of turning back the tide of impious philosophy. The Church too had its traitors, idlers, intriguers, and hypocrites, and for this France was being punished by an angry God. Deployed by Barruel (and others) as a prophetic warning of the calamities to come if France continued her sinful ways, divine retribution came subsequently to occupy a central place in explanations of the terrible events that had taken place.

No one gave clearer voice to this fundamental part of the rhetoric of counter-revolution than Joseph de Maistre. He was born in 1753 in Savoy, then part of the kingdom of Piedmont-Sardinia. Despite professing a devout Catholic faith, for many years he was a Freemason and initially welcomed the Revolution in France as a partisan of moderate reform. He supported the campaign for the calling of the Estates-General but from the summer of 1789 came to have growing doubts about the course taken by events in what he described as the 'warm mud' of Paris. Certainly, the invasion (and subsequent annexation) of Savoy by France in September 1792 convinced him of the need to rally to the royalist cause and it was from his exile in Switzerland that, with consummate rigour, he began to articulate the principles of monarchical and religious restoration. Nevertheless, in his first published writings he did not explore the possibilities of a providential explanation of the Revolution. In his *Lettres d'un royaliste savoisien à ses compatriots*,[17] for example, he was content to suggest that the Revolution was not only 'a unique event' but that it was a consequence of the 'rottenness' of the monarchy and a mistaken 'universal enchantment' with the possibility of the regeneration of society. However, by the time Maistre published *Considérations sur la France* in 1797, he made no attempt to explain the Revolution in terms of political, social, or economic causes. 'Never', he averred, 'has the Divinity shown itself so clearly in any human event.'[18] The moral to be learnt was a simple one: since France had 'used her influence to contradict her vocation and to demoralize Europe, we should not be surprised if she is brought back to her mission by terrible means'.[19]

---

[14] Barruel, *Mémoires*, ii. 526.
[15] Darrin M. McMahon, *Enemies of the Enlightenment: The French Counter-Enlightenment and the Making of Modernity* (Oxford, 2001), 56–8.
[16] See Barruel, *Le Patriote véridique*, 37–89.
[17] (Lyons and Paris, 1872): 1st publ. in 1793.
[18] Maistre, *Considérations sur la France* (1980), 34.
[19] Ibid.

The opening sentence proclaimed a clear doctrine of political theodicy. 'We are all', Maistre announced, 'attached to the throne of the Supreme Being by a supple chain which restrains us without enslaving us.'[20] Men acted voluntarily and necessarily at the same time and nothing they did could disturb the 'general plans' of a God whose power was exercised effortlessly and irresistibly. Thus the most striking thing about the Revolution was that it was not men who led the Revolution but 'the Revolution that uses men'. Each of the 'rascals' and 'detestable tyrants' who sought to direct its path were merely its 'simple instruments', men swept to power by what Maistre called the 'revolutionary chariot', only to be discarded 'ignobly' once they had 'completed the measure of crime necessary to that phase of the Revolution'. Remarkably, Maistre extended this argument even to include the Jacobins, who alone had been able to save France from dismemberment and annihilation by her enemies. 'All life, all wealth, all power', Maistre exclaimed, 'was in the hands of the revolutionary authority, and this monstrous power, drunk with blood and success, the most frightful phenomenon that has ever been seen and the like of which will never be seen again, was both a horrible punishment for the French and the sole means of saving France.'[21]

At no point did Maistre seek to diminish the extent of the sacrificial punishment that would be entailed by 'this horrible effusion of human blood'. All those who willed the Revolution would justly become its victims and few were those who had not '*willed*' all the follies, all the injustices, all the outrages that led up to the catastrophe [of Louis XVI's execution] of 21 January [1793]'.[22] Never before had so many people shared in such a sinful deed and each drop of blood would be repaid in torrents. 'Perhaps four million Frenchmen', Maistre wrote, 'will pay with their heads for this great national crime of an anti-religious and anti-social insurrection crowned by a regicide.'[23] Few would be innocent victims.

Despite its 'satanic' and 'diabolical' character, order could be discerned in the disorder of the Revolution. With France's enemies defeated and peace returned, the monarchy would be restored and the king would reascend to his throne 'with all his pomp and power'. Purified by the travails of injustice and tyranny, the clergy would be regenerated and freed from the temptations of luxury and moral laxity. Moreover, it was with absolute certainty that Maistre asserted that the Republic could not last, as divine sanction alone could establish durable institutions. Thus, if France had nothing to fear from counter-revolution—the king's most pressing interest would be to 'unite justice and mercy'—so also it was inevitable, as 'all the monsters born of the Revolution have, apparently, laboured only for the monarchy'.[24] Maistre's view, therefore, was that the Revolution was 'one of the most astonishing spectacles that humanity has ever seen'. Through it would be secured the redemption not only of France but of European civilization more generally.

Legitimist opinion was never in total agreement about the causes and character of the Revolution. Nor did legitimists necessarily agree about the political implications of this satanic event. Not all royalists were prepared to lay all the blame upon

---

[20] Ibid. 31. [21] Ibid. 39. [22] Ibid. 36.
[23] Ibid. 37. [24] Ibid. 39.

the *philosophes* and many were not convinced of either the desirability or
practicality of a restored theocratic state and society. One such was François-
René de Chateaubriand.[25] Chateaubriand's reaction to the unfolding of revolutionary events was vividly recounted in his justly famous *Mémoires d'outre-tombe*.
A native of Saint-Malo, it was from Brittany that, not without an element of
sympathy, he witnessed the first stirrings of discontent, only later to return to Paris
and there observe the storming of the Bastille and other equally horrific 'cannibal
feasts'. These events, he recalled, 'changed my political frame of mind'.[26] He soon
departed to America and upon his return in January 1792 quickly perceived that
'the sovereign people' was becoming a universal tyrant, a 'universal Tiberius'. Paris
in 1792, he wrote, 'no longer had the same physiognomy as in 1789 and 1790; this
was no longer the Revolution at its birth but a people marching drunkenly to its
destiny'.[27] Variety of dress, he noticed, was a thing of the past. He joined the
émigré army of the princes in Coblenz and later, having been seriously injured in
battle, went into exile in England. It was there that he wrote and published his first
book: the *Essai historique, politique, et moral sur les révolutions considerées dans leur
rapports avec la Révolution française.*[28]

Dedicated 'to all the parties', it was a book that pleased almost no one, least of all
his family. Chateaubriand himself felt that it 'offered a compendium of his
existence as poet, moralist, writer, and politician'.[29] It was quite definitely not a
book with a clear, ordered structure, but its central premise was simple enough: the
course of the French Revolution could best be understood if one studied all the
other revolutions that had taken place in the world. By revolution, Chateaubriand
explained at the outset, he understood 'a total change in the government of a
people, be it monarchical to republican or republican to monarchical',[30] and by this
definition it was possible to identify five revolutions in antiquity and seven in
modern Europe. Thus Chateaubriand's argument proceeded by way of constant
comparison between the ancient and modern worlds but still, he admitted, he had
difficulty grasping 'the efficient cause of all revolutions'. This had its source, he
believed, in that 'vague restlessness' and dissatisfaction with our lot which itself
'perhaps' derived from our consciousness of another life or even 'our secret aspiration towards divinity'. Whatever its origin, Chateaubriand declared, it existed
among all peoples. Moreover, it received 'striking confirmation' when the causes
of the Revolution in France were examined.[31]

Everywhere that a small group of people held power and wealth for a long time,
Chateaubriand explained, there would be corruption. Every man had his vices, plus
the vices of those who had preceded him. This was true of the court of France,
where 'a weak king' had been easily misled by 'incapable and wicked ministers' and

---

[25] See Jean-Paul Clement, *Chateaubriand: Biographie morale et intellectuelle* (1998) and Marc
Fumaroli, *Chateaubriand, Poésie et Terreur* (2003).
[26] Chateaubriand, *Mémoires d'outre tombe* (1973), i. 220.
[27] Ibid. 344–5.
[28] *Essai historique, politique, et moral sur les révolutions considerées dans leur rapports avec la Révolution
française* (1797): references to *Œuvres complètes de Chateaubriand* (1861), i.
[29] Ibid. 442.   [30] Ibid. 275.   [31] Ibid. 461.

their 'host of half-starved servants, lackeys, flatterers, actors, and mistresses'. The 'follies' and 'imbecilities' of government had in turn engendered moral disorder in society. In this situation of baneful emptiness and isolation where France enjoyed only the appearance of wealth, was it any surprise, Chateaubriand ventured, that the French were prepared 'to embrace the first phantom which showed them a new universe'? And so it was, as corruption devoured the State and as society fell into 'general dissolution', that 'a race of men' suddenly rose up and announced the hour of Sparta and Athens. 'The total overturning that the French and, above all, the Jacobins had sought to bring about in the morals of the nation', Chateaubriand wrote, 'was only an imitation of what Lycurgus did in his homeland.'[32] The ambition had been to attain a purity of morals as a prelude to the inauguration of democracy and to that end France had been 'flooded in blood, covered in ruins, her king led to the scaffold, her ministers proscribed or murdered'.[33]

Chateaubriand did not doubt that the *philosophes* were here at fault. Their methods and their aims were those of destruction. They displayed a 'rage' against established political institutions and undermined religious faith, putting nothing in their place but a 'torrent of new ideas' preaching innovation and change.[34] However, it was central to Chateaubriand's argument that, if the *philosophes* had been a cause of the Revolution, they had not been the sole cause. 'The French Revolution', he wrote, 'did not come from this or that man, from this or that book.'[35] Rather, it had been inevitable, arising from the march of civilization towards both enlightenment and corruption. That explained the 'incomprehensible combination of crimes grafted onto a philosophical trunk'.

The mistake, then, had been to believe that everything could become virtuous because the corrupt French had wished it so, to imagine that a country of 25 million inhabitants could imitate an ancient realm. To act as if republics could be created anywhere, regardless of the obstacles, Chateaubriand wrote, was both absurd and wicked. What political recommendations followed from this? Chateaubriand was honest enough to admit that he did not properly know. All governments were an evil, he observed, but from this we should not conclude that they should all be destroyed. 'Since it is our lot only to be slaves', Chateaubriand argued, 'let us endure our chains without complaint.'[36] No matter what was published to the contrary, it was always better to be ruled by one of our 'rich and enlightened compatriots' than by the 'ignorant multitude'. Happiness, in short, would return to France only when she had been returned to the monarchy.[37]

Would this fill the 'interior void' and 'unknown desire' that so tormented us and drove our discontent? Ultimately, it was Chateaubriand's view that all political, indeed all human, institutions were a mass of putrefied corruption and that all the trappings of art and civilization were as nothing compared to the simplicity and

---

[32] Ibid. 301.   [33] Ibid. 364.   [34] Ibid. 548.
[35] Ibid. 548 n. 2.   [36] Ibid. 466.
[37] When the *Essai historique* was republ. in 1826, Chateaubriand nuanced this position, explaining that he had only in the mind the model of ancient republics and that 'the discovery of the representative republic had completely changed the question'.

beauty of nature. Only this could quell our spiritual hunger and only through
nature would we be truly free. Such a liberty, he told his readers, could be painted
only with difficulty, but it could be glimpsed if they were to spend a night with him
amongst 'the savages of Canada' before the falls of Niagara. 'Freed from the
tyrannical yoke of society, I there understood', he wrote, 'the spell of the independence of nature which far surpasses all the pleasures of which a civil man can have
an idea.'[38] Five years later, and to instant acclaim, Chateaubriand was to provide a
more sophisticated and compelling response to his own 'doubt and sorrow' in the
form of *Le Génie du Christianisme*.

   Following the fall of the Directory, Chateaubriand returned to France in
May 1800, initially enjoying a good relationship with Napoleon Bonaparte.
But following the unlawful arrest and execution of the Duc d'Enghien, ordered
by Napoleon in 1804, he joined the opposition to imperial despotism and quickly
found himself exiled from Paris. He continued to write and was elected to the
Académie Française.[39] In 1814 he penned a damning portrait of Napoleon and
the First Empire and not only welcomed the return of Louis XVIII but also the
parliamentary monarchy instituted by the Charte. To that extent, Chateaubriand
shared much with Germaine de Staël. Yet, as François Furet has written, the two
'were not breathing the same air'.[40] If both wished to secure the Bourbon monarchy
upon a solid foundation and if both knew that this could only be done by resolving
the question of the heritage of the revolutionary past, they belonged to two separate
and deeply antagonistic worlds: those of ultra-royalism and of liberalism. If Chateaubriand felt a mournful nostalgia for the past, Madame de Staël had no cause to regret
its passing. His Revolution was not hers, as the *Considérations sur les principaux
évènemens de la Révolution française* made abundantly clear.

   As we know, Germaine de Staël was the daughter of Louis XVI's much-abused
finance minister, Jacques Necker.[41] She was Swiss and she was Protestant.[42]
She also witnessed the opening events of the French Revolution at first hand, her
salon in the rue de Bac subsequently becoming a meeting place for political
moderates. Exile to England soon followed and when, later, she came to doubt
that the Directory would be able to provide the stable republic required by France,
she rallied to the Consulate headed by Napoleon Bonaparte. Much has been
written about Madame de Staël's personal relationship with Napoleon—much of
it entirely speculative—but there can be no doubt that their political positions
quickly diverged and that the emperor increasingly found her to be an irritating
and troublesome presence. As a consequence she spent the greater part of the years
of the First Empire either in hiding, at her Swiss family home in Coppet, or

---

[38] *Œuvres complètes de Chateaubriand* (1861), i, 622.
[39] Chateaubriand did not take up his seat until after the Restoration.
[40] Furet, *Revolutionary France, 1770–1880* (Oxford, 1992), 286.
[41] See Jean-Denis Bredin, *Une singulière famille: Jacques Necker, Suzanne Necker et Germaine de
Staël* (1999).
[42] See J. Christopher Herold, *Mistress to an Age: A Life of Madame de Staël* (New York: 1958) and
Maria Fairweather, *Madame de Staël* (London: 2005).

travelling across Europe with a variety of distinguished intellectual and emotional companions.[43]

Despite this life spent in almost permanent exile, Madame de Staël's literary output was never less than brilliantly original and influential. In 1800 she published *De la Littérature considérée dans ses rapports avec les institutions sociales*, a groundbreaking work whose purpose was 'to examine the influence of religion, custom, and law upon literature, and the influence of literature upon religion, custom, and law'. This was followed by two novels, *Delphine* in 1802 and *Corinne* in 1807: both enjoyed enormous international success. Then, in 1810 came the publication of *De l'Allemagne*. Ostensibly the study of the spirit and character of a people, it was immediately seized and then pulped upon Napoleon's direct orders, the implicit criticism of the latter's person and regime being all too clear.[44]

Banished from France, it was in Sweden in 1813 that Madame de Staël began the writing of *Considérations sur les principaux évènemens de la Révolution française*.[45] It existed only in manuscript at the time of her death in 1817 and was published a year later. The first edition of 60,000 copies sold out almost immediately. In truth, *Considérations sur les principaux évènemens de la Révolution française* amounted to three, if not four, books in one. Since the death of her father in 1804 it had been Madame de Staël's intention to write an account (and defence) of his political career. In the process of writing, this became a description of the principal events of the Revolution itself and of the manner in which the Terror emerged. To this was added a paean to England and English liberty. Finally, in the wake of the emperor's defeat, there was added an anti-Napoleon tract.

If royalist accounts of the Revolution had already established that it was evidence of the workings of divine providence, Madame de Staël similarly believed, although for very different reasons, that the Revolution was inevitable. 'Those who consider it an accidental event', she wrote in her opening paragraph, 'have not turned their attention either to the past or to the future. They have mistaken the actors for the play; and, in order to satisfy their passions, they have attributed to transient individuals what it took centuries to prepare.'[46] To justify this assertion, she deployed a three-stage interpretation of European history since the fall of the Roman Empire. The first epoch was feudalism; the second was monarchical despotism; the third was the age of representative government. Thus far, Madame de Staël argued, only England had properly reached this 'final perfecting of the social order' but, with the gradual spread of intellectual enlightenment and commerce, all of Europe was following the path indicated by the English and French Revolutions.

None of this was to suggest that such progress could not be interrupted by lapses into arbitrary government and tyranny. Indeed, it was precisely this that had

---

[43] See Germaine de Staël, *Dix années d'exil* (1996).

[44] Selections from *De la Littérature* and *De l'Allemagne* can be found in Morroe Berger (ed.), *Germaine de Staël: Politics, Literature and National Character* (New Brunswick, NJ, 2000).

[45] For an English edn. see Germaine de Staël, *Considerations on the Principal Events of the French Revolution* (Indianapolis, 2008).

[46] *Considérations sur la Révolution française* (1983), 63.

occurred in France. As Madame de Staël sought to remind her readers, 'it is liberty that is old and despotism which is modern'.[47] The four 'best' kings of France—St Louis, Charles V, Louis XII, and 'above all' Henri IV—had striven to establish the rule of law, religious toleration, and the rudiments of a representative system but this had been subverted from the time of Cardinal Richelieu in the seventeenth century onwards. From that moment, the government of France had been characterized by corruption, intrigue, vanity, privilege, and despotism, and so much so that the private virtues of Louis XVI and Marie-Antoinette had been hidden beneath 'the vast collection of abuses by which they were surrounded'.

It was this parlous situation that Jacques Necker had been called upon to rectify. The clear and unambiguous message of Madame de Staël's text was that, if her father's advice had been followed, administrative order and financial stability would have been restored to France and thus the horrors of the Revolution and the ensuing European war would have been avoided. However, this was not to be so and, as a consequence, moderation was replaced by 'the spirit of faction' and 'the fever of revolution'.

Yet Madame de Staël was prepared to accept that, in its early work, the National Assembly did much to earn the gratitude of the nation. It established religious toleration and freedom of the press. It reformed the judicial system and introduced trial by jury. It abolished the privileges of caste and suppressed unfair taxes. It created provincial assemblies and removed restraints on industry and trade. In short, it cleared away many of the abuses associated with arbitrary power. With regard to the institutions it created, however, the National Assembly committed 'the most serious errors'.

The most grievous of these was to have considered executive power as being inimical to liberty. This explained why the king had been stripped of his prerogatives and why he had been reduced to a 'public functionary'. From a fear of supporting conspiracy followed a refusal to contemplate the usefulness of a second chamber. The result was an 'ill-fated constitution', 'good in its foundation' but 'bad in its superstructure', and one incapable of protecting 'the blessings of civil liberty'.[48] How could this be explained? According to Madame de Staël, the National Assembly had been seized by 'philosophical enthusiasm', by a passion for abstract thinking at the expense of practical common sense. The deputies had shown themselves to be vain and cowardly, devoid of a sense of public duty. Consequently, they had been mistaken in 1791 to believe that the Revolution was finished and that liberty had been established. Rather, an abyss was about to open up beneath their feet.

The logic of the next stage of the Revolution was all too clear. Arbitrary power was given new strength by the Revolution itself. The revolutionaries, in serving the people, sacrificed the happiness of each in the name of the common interest and the demands of equality. 'To the animosity against the nobles and the priests', Madame de Staël wrote, 'succeeded a feeling of irritation against the landowners, next,

---

[47] *Considérations sur la Révolution française* (1983), 70.   [48] Ibid. 249.

against talents, then even against personal beauty; finally against whatever was to be found of greatness or generosity in human nature.'[49] Persecution led to the need for further persecution, the Terror driven forward by a monstrous frenzy of political fanaticism that, in taking away all restraints from the people, placed them in a position to commit every crime. It was a mistake, she believed, to imagine that the Jacobins had reduced government to a state of anarchy. 'Never', Madame de Staël observed, 'has a stronger authority reigned over France, but it was a strange sort of power; springing from popular fanaticism it inspired dread in the very persons who commanded in its name, for they always feared being proscribed in turn by men who would go further than they in the daring boldness of persecution.'[50] Not even Robespierre—whom Madame de Staël portrayed as a hypocrite interested only in power—felt entirely secure. It was 'the most horrible period' in French history.

How had such violent behaviour been possible? How could the people of France have been so depraved? The answer, in Madame de Staël's opinion, was to be found in centuries of superstition and arbitrary power. The French were what bad government had made them. They had acquired few ideas of justice and still believed that an enemy was not entitled to the protection of the law. Nevertheless, she argued, all countries and all peoples, including France and the French, were fit for liberty, and all, she believed, would attain it in their own way.

This was where England figured in Madame de Staël's argument, for, as she wrote, 'we cannot believe that Providence should have placed this fine monument of social order so near to France merely to inspire in us the regret of never being able to equal it'.[51] If she added little to the familiar litany of praise for English institutions and morals, the depth of Madame de Staël's admiration for England needs to be recognized. It drew upon her father's Anglophilia, her visits to England, her reading, and her conversations with many English friends. Above all, she believed that England's power, prosperity, and tranquillity derived from its long-established freedoms, its commercial spirit, its Protestantism, and its political institutions. Needless to say, she turned a blind eye to many, although not all, of England's faults, singling out for praise the rule of law, a decentralized administration, an exemplary public spirit, and a vigorous, open aristocracy. Her point was that the England of today could be the France of tomorrow.

Yet France had not pursued the course taken by England and, as a consequence, she languished in a state of despotism. For Madame de Staël, Napoleon Bonaparte had arisen naturally and almost inevitably out of the chaos of the Revolution. The two principal causes of his power, she observed, were that he had given France military glory rather than liberty and had restored order without attacking selfish passions. From personal experience she knew that he was no ordinary man, that he had a desire to astonish the human race, but not content with being a master he had

---

[49] Ibid. 303.
[50] Ibid. 305.
[51] Ibid. 530. See Robert Escarpit, *L'Angleterre dans l'œuvre de Madame de Staël* (1954) and V. de Pange, 'Le Rêve anglais de Madame de Staël', in Colloque de Coppet, *Madame de Staël et l'Europe* (1970), 173–92.

wished to be a tyrant. In words that echoed those of Montesquieu, she described a regime based upon corruption and immorality, where the will of a single man decided everything, where all liberties were suppressed, where opponents were banished without trial, and which daily displayed contempt for humanity. Napoleon's despotism was one of conquest and of continuous wars. No one dared to tell him the truth.

Madame de Staël recorded that she met the emperor's fall with mixed emotions. It seemed, she wrote, as if Burke's prediction had been accomplished: France had fallen into the abyss. However, she was not eager to see a return of the Bourbon monarchy. Nor, unlike Benjamin Constant, was she fooled by the returning Napoleon's conversion to constitutional government. The friends of liberty, she observed, needed to separate their cause entirely from his and should never confuse the principles of the Revolution with those of imperial government. Indeed, this stance embodied the fundamental political message of her text: liberty could only ever be attained through liberty and never through coercion. And nothing but liberty could arouse the soul and ennoble our character. This was a lesson that French liberals were to seek to build upon during the nineteenth century.

In historiographical terms, Madame de Staël's legacy was no less important. Not only was she the first to examine the course and aftermath of the Revolution in any detail, but her lasting contribution lay in her characterization of the Revolution as the culmination of a thousand-year struggle for liberty by the people of France. Moreover, that this aspiration had been betrayed by the leaders of the Revolution did not, for her, diminish the achievement of overturning centuries of injustice and oppression. She thereby established the distinction between 1789 and 1793. The Terror was not the logical consequence of the principles of 1789 and Napoleon was not the necessary solution.

Published in the early years of the Restoration period, *Considérations sur les principaux évènemens de la Révolution française* evoked a series of immediate and varied responses.[52] Many simply asserted that Madame de Staël's affection for her father had blinded her to the true nature of the Revolution. Others saw her book as anti-French and unpatriotic. Three commentaries merit particular attention. The first was penned by royalist Louis de Bonald.[53] It disputed the virtues attributed to Jacques Necker. It denied that the Revolution had been inevitable and that its cause lay in the misery of the people. It challenged the description of absolute monarchy as arbitrary government, contending that France had had a constitution and that it had resided in her 'religion, royalty, and justice'.[54] It contradicted the claim that England was a free polity, placing little or no value in its much-vaunted liberties such as freedom of the press or trial by jury and characterizing the English as

---

[52] See G. E. Gwynne, *Madame de Staël et la Révolution française* (1969), 262–71, and Ezio Cappadocia, 'The Liberals and Madame de Staël in 1818', in Richard Herr and Harold T. Parker (eds.), *Ideas in History: Essays Presented to Louis Gottschalk by his Former Students* (Durham, NC, 1965), 182–97.

[53] *Observations sur l'ouvrage de Mme la Baronne de Staël, ayant pour titre: Considérations sur les principaux évenéments de la révolution française* (1818).

[54] Ibid. 37.

'morose, irritable, unhappy, selfish'.[55] It suggested that liberals such as Madame de Staël despised Napoleon not because he had oppressed France but because he had oppressed the Revolution. Finally, it argued that the veracity of Madame de Staël's entire account was undermined by her Protestantism. The royalist and theocratic reply, in short, remained that the Revolution was misconceived from the outset and that its 'inevitable' and 'natural' quality was crime.[56] In the decades that followed, conservative writers were to seek to remind the French of this reality.[57]

The second commentary, published in 1818, amounted to a two-volume, chapter-by-chapter, refutation of Madame de Staël's argument running to over 900 pages. Its author was Jacques-Charles Bailleul.[58] He was a former Girondin and member of the Convention who had narrowly escaped death thanks to the fall of Robespierre. He too had fallen foul of Napoleon Bonaparte. Yet he viewed the Revolution in an entirely different light from Madame de Staël. Naturally, Bailleul disparaged Madame de Staël's eulogy of her father and was thoroughly dismissive of her praise of England, suggesting that it was the French and not the English who were made for liberty. More substantively, Bailleul characterized the period of French history from Richelieu onwards not in terms of a loss of liberty but as the time when it was possible to speak of the deliverance of the people, the setting free of the nation. By the nation, Bailleul clearly intended the Third Estate and thus, on this account, 1789 was the moment when, for the first time, the nation came fully into existence, when, equal before the same laws, Gascons and Normans became French. Crucially, he then suggested that the derailing of the Revolution arose not from anything intrinsic to the Revolution itself but as a consequence of the actions of an 'antinational party' composed of the forces of privilege and, all importantly, from the exigencies of a foreign-imposed war. In other words, it was the opponents of the Revolution who were responsible for the chaos and external threats that made resort to Terror into a political and military necessity. 'The Jacobin party', Bailleul wrote, 'did not wish to exercise despotism; it wished only to defend the homeland and liberty.'[59] Robespierre was not a hypocrite but a principled man seeking to bring about the reign of virtue. Forced by events to push the logic of virtue to its extreme, he became a 'monster' and France under the Jacobins lapsed into arbitrary government, but the fault for this lay unambiguously with the 'conspiracy of the privileged'. In brief, it was circumstances, rather than revolutionary doctrine, that explained the Terror. Here were powerful arguments that later historians of the Revolution were to deploy with great effectiveness.

A far kinder assessment of Madame de Staël's achievement came from Benjamin Constant.[60] Her book, he wrote, was more than a simple apology for Jacques

---

[55] Ibid. 26.   [56] Ibid. 129–31.

[57] See Stanley Mellon, *The Political Uses of History* (Stanford, Calif., 1958), 58–100.

[58] *Examen Critique des Considérations de Mme la Baronne de Staël sur les principaux événements de la Révolution française*, 2 vols. (1822).

[59] Ibid. ii. 215.

[60] 'Considérations sur les principaux événements de la Révolution française', in Ephraïm Harpaz (ed.), *Benjamin Constant: Receuil d'Articles. Le Mercure de France et la Rénommée* (1972), i. 407–12, 450–9, 469–78.

Necker. In it, he continued, were to be observed all the principles that had inspired Madame de Staël throughout her life: an attachment to liberty, a profound sense of the dignity of the human race, a respect for the application of morality to politics, and, he insisted, a love of France. Moreover, it was 'the best history of our revolution that has appeared so far'.

Liberalism in Restoration France was an amorphous doctrine.[61] All the same, the liberals had three main political tasks: to preserve the civil acquisitions of 1789, to deny their responsibility for the Terror, and to outline a political programme for power. As Stanley Mellon observed: 'The Revolution was lurking beneath every political issue: it had to be explained and defended, right up to the day that the revolution of 1830 successfully enshrined it.'[62] Madame de Staël provided some of the armoury required for these tasks but more would be needed if liberals were to win their bitter political battles with their royalist opponents. In the first instance, a response had to be made to the thesis expounded by the Comte de Montlosier in his *De la monarchie française.*[63]

Montlosier's text had a curious history, the count having been asked by Napoleon Bonaparte to write a history of France which would establish the legitimacy of the Empire by establishing its continuity with the monarchy of the *ancien régime.* When no such book was forthcoming, it was sent back to its author, only to be published in 1814, at the very moment when the restored Bourbon monarchy itself was impatient to re-establish its own historical credentials. At the core of Montlosier's account was a reworking of what had become a familiar theme of eighteenth-century polemic: namely, that the history of France could be summarized as a struggle between two races, the Franks and the Gauls.[64] In its most famous formulation, Henri de Boulainvilliers had retold the history of the victory of the noble Franks over the Gauls in order, first, to celebrate an ideal of feudal liberty and, second, to reassert the ancient right of the Franks to participate in government. On this account, by excluding the nobility, the rise of royal absolutism had destroyed feudal liberty. Just as importantly, Boulainvilliers affirmed that the subject Gauls had been excluded from government. Montlosier recast this argument in terms of the gradual under-mining of aristocracy of the Franks by the Gauls of the Third Estate, a process which culminated in the Revolution of 1789. Read in the context of the Restoration, Montlosier not only seemed to be suggesting that the struggle between these two races was never ending but also that the returning émigré aristocracy had good grounds for affirming its supremacy anew. For those of a liberal disposition wishing to establish that the Charte granted to the French people in 1814 had an altogether

[61] See Laurence Jacobs, 'Le Moment Libéral: The Distinctive Character of Restoration Liberalism', *Historical Journal,* 31 (1988), 479–92.

[62] Mellon, *Political Uses,* 193.

[63] See Furet, *Revolutionary France,* 307–8, and Sarah Maza, *The Myth of the French Bourgeoisie* (Cambridge, Mass., 2003), 150–2. The argument developed in the next section of the text draws upon Shirley M. Gruner, 'Political Historiography in Restoration France', *History and Theory,* 8 (1969), 346–65.

[64] See Claude Nicolet, *La Fabrique d'une nation: La France entre Rome et les Germains* (2006), 107–37.

different message, the stakes could hardly have been higher. They had to show that history was on the side of the Third Estate. In brief, the bourgeoisie needed to get a history, and it needed to get one quickly.

By general agreement this history was largely provided by Augustin Thierry in his *Lettres sur l'histoire de France* of 1820[65] and by François Guizot in his *Essais sur l'histoire de France* of 1823. Although different in tone and substance, each turned Montlosier's argument on its head in order not only to describe the Third Estate as the driving force of French history, but also to portray its role in a positive light. The claim was that the facts of French history had been 'perverted' by a series of 'arbitrary' accounts intended to reduce 'a free people' to mere 'subjects standing before a master who alone speaks and who no one could contradict'. It was not in the recent past, Thierry countered, but seven hundred years before that France had first seen men deploy their courage and their convictions 'to create for themselves and for their children an existence that was at once free and benign'. This, he affirmed, could be clearly seen among those former serfs who had 'built the walls and the civilization of the ancient Gallic cities'. According to Thierry, therefore, the 'difficult' but 'glorious' task of writing a 'truthful history' of France would restore 'the most numerous and most forgotten part of the nation' to its rightful place.[66] If Thierry was only ever to remain a historian, dedicating his life to writing the history of the oppressed French 'nation', Guizot was to deploy these historical insights to defend and to further the interests of the 'new France'. In parallel to this, and with similar motives and inspiration, Auguste Mignet and Adolphe Thiers wrote and published histories of the French Revolution.

Both histories were largely narrative in form and were meticulous in their attention to detail. Each author placed his account in the broad sweep of French history and was comprehensive in his analysis of the events and personalities of the period, although Thiers, unlike Mignet, ended his narration with Napoleon Bonaparte's overthrow of the Directory in November 1799.[67] Both sought to write histories for a general public and both succeeded in reaching what was, by nineteenth-century standards, a vast readership.[68] Likewise, Mignet and Thiers sought to place themselves above the fray, putting passions and hatreds to one side, Thiers in particular alerting his readers to the fact that his aim had been to grasp 'the deep designs of Providence in these great events'.[69] The ambition was to make the Revolution intelligible. Yet, for all the appearance of impartiality and detachment, the two men, both schooled in the liberal journalism of the 1820s,[70] believed that there were important lessons to be learnt from the history of the Revolution.

---

[65] See Lionel Gossman, *Between History and Literature* (Cambridge, Mass., 1990), 83–151.

[66] 'Première lettre sur l'histoire de France', *Dix Ans d'Études Historiques* (1846), 257–62. This text was 1st publ. in *Le Courrier français* in July 1820 and republ. in the 1st edn. of the *Lettres sur l'Histoire de France* in 1827.

[67] Thiers was subsequently to remedy this omission by writing his *Histoire du Consulat et de l'Empire*, vol. i of which appeared in 1845; 20 vols. appeared in all.

[68] It is estimated that by 1833 Thiers's history had sold 150,000 volumes.

[69] *Histoire de la Révolution française* (1823–7), x. 530.

[70] Mignet wrote for *Le Courrier français*; Thiers wrote for *Le Constitutionnel*.

From the very first sentence of his *Histoire de la Révolution française,* Mignet made his intentions absolutely clear. 'I am going to trace', he announced, 'the history of the French Revolution, which in Europe began the era of new societies in the same way as the English Revolution began the era of new governments. This revolution did not only modify political power: it changed the entire interior constitution of the nation.'[71] France, he specified, had been a country where royal power knew no limits and which had been given over to arbitrary government and privilege. In place of this abusive regime, Mignet continued, 'the revolution substituted one which better conformed to justice and which was more appropriate to the age'.[72] It had replaced arbitrary rule by law and privilege by equality; it had freed men from the distinctions of class, land from the barriers of provinces, trade from the restrictions of corporations, and agriculture from feudalism; the whole had been reduced to one state, to one law, and to one people.

To attain these great reforms, the Revolution had had many obstacles to overcome and it was this that had produced its 'fleeting excesses'. Forced to fight its enemies, it had not known how to measure its efforts or moderate its victory. Internal resistance had produced 'the sovereignty of the multitude' and external aggression had generated 'military domination'. However, 'despite the anarchy and despite the despotism, the end has been obtained: the old society has been destroyed during the Revolution and the new one has been founded under the Empire'.[73] To this Mignet then added the observation that, when a reform was necessary and the moment to realize it had arrived, nothing could prevent it. Thus, in retracing the events of the Revolution from the opening of the Estates-General to the fall of Napoleon in 1814, it had to be recognized that each phase was 'almost obligatory', that, given its causes and the passions it had aroused, the Revolution had to follow this specific path and produce this particular outcome.

Next, Mignet sketched out a history of France that broke decisively with that of Frankish conquest. At its origin, he specified, the crown was elective; the nation was sovereign; and the king was nothing but a military leader. The nation exercised both legislative and judicial power. Nevertheless, in the feudal period this 'royal democracy' gave way to a 'royal aristocracy'. The monarch became hereditary and the people were deprived of their sovereignty. Over time power became concentrated in the hands of one person. 'During several centuries of continuous exertion', Mignet wrote, 'the kings of France reduced the feudal edifice to ruins and lifted themselves up on the debris.'[74] Under Louis XIV, the 'absolute monarchy' was established definitively and from that point onwards France lived under a regime that was more arbitrary than it was despotic. Yet, little by little, the nation in the form of the Third Estate began to reassert itself and to defend its own interests. With each day it grew in strength, in wealth, and in enlightenment, to the extent that it was 'destined to combat and to dispossess' the crown. At this point there also emerged the new phenomenon of public opinion, increasingly critical and intolerant of governmental abuses. 'The century of reforms', Mignet wrote, 'was prepared

---

[71] Mignet, *Histoire de la Révolution française, depuis 1789 jusqu'en 1814* (1824), 1–2.
[72] Ibid. 2.   [73] Ibid. 3.   [74] Ibid. 5.

by the century of philosophy'.[75] Such was the state of affairs when Louis XVI ascended to the throne and, despite his good intentions, there had been nothing he could do to improve the situation. 'The Estates-General', Mignet concluded, 'could only decree a revolution which had already been accomplished.'[76]

Such was the eloquence of Mignet's account of the Revolution that it would be tempting to relate it in detail. For our purposes, however, it is sufficient to focus on its major themes. Mignet, like Thiers, saw Louis XVI as a well-intentioned but irresolute monarch, dominated by incompetent and unscrupulous courtiers. It was his alliance with the clergy and the nobility against the Third Estate that first pushed events in a radical direction, the Revolution gathering pace over the summer of 1789 such that by the night of 4 August the monarchy had lost all 'moral' and 'material' influence. The people had become 'the masters of society'. Moreover, the divisions between those who wanted a 'constitutional revolution' and those eager to foster a 'republican revolution' were already visible. These tensions were played out in the debates of the National Assembly but, as its members grappled with the complicated issue of providing France with a new constitution, the forces of counter-revolution were preparing civil and foreign war. Therefore, if the imposing Fête de la Fédération held to mark the first anniversary of the storming of the Bastille was one of the most joyous and magnificent days of the Revolution, it could only suspend the hostilities arising from the abolition of the nobility and the Civil Constitution of the Clergy. Nevertheless, the Constitution of 1791 was a constitution in tune with 'the ideas and situation' of France. It was 'the work of the middle class'. It represented the end point of a journey that had seen France endure the feudalism of aristocracy and the absolute power of monarchy, finally to arrive at a situation where the source, if not the exercise, of power rested with the people. All citizens possessed equal rights and all could aspire to participate in government. To that extent, it had established 'genuine equality'.[77]

If this constitution was to perish, Mignet argued, it was not because of its own defects. Placed between the aristocracy and the multitude, it was attacked from both sides. Yet the multitude would never have become the 'sovereign' power without civil war and without the foreign coalition against France. As a consequence, the multitude made its own revolution, and was to do so in much the same way as the middle class had done before it. The storming of the Tuileries on 10 August 1792 and the subsequent fall of the monarchy would be its 14 July 1789. But, Mignet affirmed, 'without the emigration there would not have been a republic'.[78]

On this view, the 10 August amounted to an insurrection of the multitude against the bourgeoisie and it was now that the 'dictatorial and arbitrary' phase of the Revolution began. If the goal pursued had been liberty, henceforth it was to be 'public safety'.[79] The Girondins, Mignet contended, had been forced by circumstances to be republicans. The Jacobins, on the other hand, 'wanted a republic with the people'. To them, the most extreme form of democracy seemed the best form of

[75] Ibid. 15.   [76] Ibid. 34.   [77] Ibid. 195–6.
[78] Ibid. 198.   [79] Ibid. 270.

government. Thus, in the shape of the constitution of 1793, they 'established the pure regime of the multitude'. But they also established 'a terrible power' that would devour itself, where death became the only means of government and the republic was delivered up to 'daily and systematic executions'. With each step, the spilling of blood became greater and the system of tyranny more violent.[80]

According to Mignet, Robespierre's fall was inevitable and with his fall the ascending revolutionary movement came to an end. Like Thiers, Mignet detested Robespierre. He had all the personal qualities required for tyranny and was supported by an 'immense and fanatical sect'. Yet Mignet, like Joseph de Maistre before him,[81] acknowledged that the Jacobins had saved France and had saved the Revolution. Liberty might have been abandoned but the salvation of the country had been secured. With the organization of military victory, the task of the Jacobins was accomplished. Their own success made them superfluous. Dictatorship could come to an end.

Mignet's account of what followed was premised upon the claim that the Revolution had had two distinct goals: the setting up of a 'free constitution' and the attainment of 'a more perfected society'.[82] The first six years of the Revolution—until the Constitution of Year III in 1795—had focused upon the first of these but each attempt to forge a new constitutional settlement, either on the part of the aristocracy, the bourgeoisie, or the multitude, had failed because each class had sought to secure power exclusively for itself. After the 'agitation' and 'destruction' of the first years, the second stage of the Revolution sought 'order' and 'rest'. This period, Mignet contended, could itself be split into two: from the Directory to the Consulate and from the Consulate through to the end of the Empire. In the first, the Revolution had sought to produce 'a people of workers', in the second 'a people of soldiers'. At this point, we were far removed from the France of 14 July and 10 August, from the morality and liberty of the former and the language and fanaticism of the latter.

Mignet therefore next described the moment in 1795 when people withdrew into a world of private pleasure, of luxury, of lavish balls and intimate salons, and where government sought to facilitate commerce and material abundance. But as the authority of the Directory diminished, it increasingly relied upon repressive measures and became dependent upon the support of the army. And so Napoleon Bonaparte came to be seen as the only person who could save *la patrie*. His *coup d'état* of the 18 Brumaire, accomplished in November 1799, was, according to Mignet, the final desecration of liberty and the beginning of the domination of 'brutal force'.[83] Napoleon's intentions quickly became clear. He sought to reconstitute the clergy, establish a new military order, create an administrative caste loyal to the State, and silence opposition. Such, in only two years, was 'the frightening progress of privilege and absolute power'.[84] Over time, the exercise of power became more arbitrary and society became more aristocratic. All interests were

---

[80] Mignet, *Histoire de la Révolution française, depuis 1789 jusqu'en 1814* (1824), 437–8.
[81] Mignet specifically quoted Maistre's *Considérations sur la France*: ibid. 270–1.
[82] Ibid. 552–3.   [83] Ibid. 635.   [84] Ibid. 666.

arranged hierarchically under one leader. It was military defeat and exhaustion that brought the vast edifice of the Empire to its knees and 'the most gigantic being of modern times' to his end. War, Mignet observed, was Napoleon's passion, domination his goal. As such, he had aroused universal enmity and his fall proved 'the extent to which in our day despotism is impossible'.[85]

Nevertheless, Mignet acknowledged the achievements of Napoleon. If he had enslaved France, he had pushed European civilization forward, shaking its old foundations. More intriguingly, Mignet ended his account with an explicit comparison between Napoleon and Oliver Cromwell. Both embodied government by the army, but Cromwell had had only to face internal enemies. Again therefore Mignet was able to underline the central role played by foreign intervention in determining the course of the Revolution in France. Napoleon had secured an easy dominance over the people and it had been this that had allowed him to deploy his immense power to secure his grandiose ends. At best Cromwell had been able to neutralize his opponents. Napoleon fell due to a general European uprising, Cromwell to internal conspiracy. Such, Mignet concluded, 'is the fate of all powers which, born out of liberty, are not founded upon it'.[86]

Adolphe Thiers's *Histoire de la Révolution française* comprises ten weighty volumes, each devoted to recounting the phases of the Revolution in minute detail. Supporting evidence is marshalled with impressive thoroughness. Few incidents or personalities escape its penetrating gaze. Acknowledging the immensity of his task, at times Thiers despaired of being able 'to say everything, to judge everything, to paint everything'.[87] However, if the different nuances of interpretation are significant, it is a tale told in a very similar vein to that by Mignet. Again, the Revolution was located within the broad sweep of French history and again the conclusion was that the corruption, injustice, and inequalities of the *ancien régime* were such that 'sooner or later' the Revolution was certain to occur.[88] It took only 'a chance combination of various circumstances' to set it going. Like Mignet, Thiers captured brilliantly the speed with which events unfolded in the summer of 1789, recording each momentous step and decision, each tactical error made by the Louis XVI and his supporters, each expression of popular agitation. In the aftermath of the storming of the Bastille, he ventured, the Revolution could have been considered to have achieved its purpose: the nation, by now in control of legislative and public power, 'could henceforth put into effect everything that was useful for its interests'.[89] He scarcely mentions the Déclaration des Droits de l'Homme et du Citoyen: the next momentous step came with the abolition of the feudal order on 4 August.[90] This, in Thiers's view, was 'the most important reform of the Revolution'.[91] He saw the immense emotional appeal for its participants of the Fête de la Fédération but, again like Mignet, recognized that it was no more than a brief pause in hostilities. The king's flight and capture at Varennes destroyed the last vestiges of respect for the monarchy.

---

[85] Ibid. 721. [86] Ibid. 724. [87] Thiers, *Histoire de la Révolution française*, iv, p. x.
[88] Ibid. i. 40. [89] Ibid. 119. [90] Ibid. 142–3. [91] Ibid. 148.

Above all, Thiers celebrated the work of the National Assembly.[92] Perhaps for the first time, he argued, an assembly had brought together all the enlightened men of the nation, men united in the desire to realize the wishes of philosophy. Convinced of its rights, it had prevailed heroically over its enemies 'by the simple expression of its will'. In this lay the first and most noble act of the Revolution. Never, Thiers contended, 'had a nation acted with more justice or more danger'. However, the fundamental error of the National Assembly was to believe that the king would resign himself to his loss of sovereignty and that the people, recently awakened, would be content with only a share of it. Herein, Thiers conjectured, was to be found a tension and dynamic that would drive the Revolution forward towards its final resolution.

To understand this, Thiers argued, it was sufficient to reflect upon the differences between revolutions that had occurred among subject and free peoples. In Rome and Athens, the nation and their leaders had argued about who held authority. In modern societies, by contrast, the first signs of awakening were evident in 'the most enlightened classes', only for it progressively to spread throughout the entire population. Soon satisfied with the share of power they had obtained, the enlightened classes sought to bring the revolution to an end, but they could not do so and were ceaselessly harried by those who followed them. For the latter, those who had preceded them were the enemy. 'The simple bourgeois', Thiers explained, 'is called an aristocrat by the manual worker and is pursued as such.'[93]

The National Assembly, being the first to challenge an all-powerful authority, being wise enough to recognize what was owed to those who had had everything and to those who had had nothing, had wished to leave to the former some of its power and provide the latter with learning and rights. Yet, from the one they encountered resentment, from the other ambition; as a consequence, 'a war of extermination' was set in motion. The members of the National Assembly were, thus, 'the first men of good will who, shaking off slavery, attempted to found a just order ... but who succumbed through wanting to commit a few to concede something and others not to want everything'.[94]

The stage was now set for the descent of France into 'murderous war'. A revolution that pitted the base of society against the upper classes was driven by envy and violent passions; and, in the case of Robespierre, by a combination of purity, vanity, and 'habitual egoism'. As for Marat, Thiers described a fanatic gripped by hatred and obsession, intent on destruction and extermination.[95] The result, vividly described over several volumes, was a society where the prison and the scaffold were a daily reality; where one feared to express an opinion or to see one's friends and family; where merchants were forced to sell goods at 'fictitious prices'; where to display wealth or luxury was dangerous; and where women and the old were denied the right to practise their religion. 'Never', Thiers wrote, 'did power more violently overturn the habits of a people.'[96] Nonetheless, Thiers gave full vent

---

[92] Thiers, *Histoire de la Révolution française*, ii. 3–12.
[93] Ibid. 7–8.   [94] Ibid. 8.   [95] Ibid. 217–21.   [96] Ibid. v. 471.

to the argument that 'destiny' had given the Jacobins and their supporters 'a unique and terrible mission': that of 'defending the revolution against Europe and the Vendée'. 'Sublime and atrocious' at one and the same time, of their 'bloody dictatorship' only 'the glory of defence' would remain.[97]

The 'happy catastrophe' of Robespierre's fall and execution brought the 'ascending march' of the Revolution to an end. What followed, in the form of the Directory, was a regime which sought to restore order and prosperity and to combine this with continued military success. No more glowing account of its achievements could have been provided. By the summer of 1796, and following one of the 'most beautiful and extraordinary' military campaigns in history, France was 'at the height of her power'. She was 'resplendent in her immortal glory'. The storms of the Revolution appeared to have calmed. Commerce and agriculture were flourishing. All voices were free to be heard. A government, 'composed of the bourgeoisie, our equals', ruled the republic with 'moderation'. Let us not forget, Thiers wrote, these 'immortal days of liberty, greatness, and hope'.[98] The decline which followed was attributed to continued internal opposition and the plotting of the European powers. The repression of the royalists in September 1797, achieved through the *coup d'état* of 18 Fructidor, was viewed by Thiers as 'a sad but inevitable necessity'. Legality was an illusion in times of revolution.[99] But, little by little, the regime became 'decayed' and 'worn-out'. The government was disorganized; factions were ungovernable; everywhere there were signs of social collapse and brigandry; military defeat occurred against the Austrians and in Italy. In these circumstances, the Republic again seemed in mortal danger. To save the situation a 'force' was required and that force could only be found in the army. A sword was necessary.[100] It was to belong to Napoleon Bonaparte. The Revolution, therefore, having been in turn monarchical, republican, and democratic in character, finished up by being military and this was so because, 'in the midst of this perpetual struggle with Europe', it needed to establish itself on a 'solid and strong' foundation.[101]

What sense could be made of this turbulent decade? Were the republicans right to deplore the immolation of liberty by one of the heroes born of the Revolution? According to Thiers, the Revolution, 'which was to give us liberty, and which prepared everything for us to have it one day, was not itself and could not be liberty'.[102] Rather, it was 'a great struggle against the old order of things'. Having defeated that order in France, it was necessary to defeat it in Europe but such a 'violent struggle' was not compatible with either the forms or spirit of liberty. Thus, if during the period of the National Assembly there had been a brief period of liberty, all too quickly it had been replaced by 'passions and heroism'. With

---

[97] Ibid. iv. 5. Thiers did not spare his readers the details of the 'murderous' repression that took place. See his account of the infamous *noyades* in Nantes: ibid. vi. 399–402.

[98] Ibid. viii. 572–4.

[99] Ibid. ix. 333.

[100] Ibid. x. 409–10.

[101] Ibid. 527.

[102] Ibid.

victories won and danger receding, Thiers argued, liberty had returned under the Directory, but war with Europe could only be suspended temporarily. The *coup d'état* of 18 Brumaire had therefore been 'necessary'. Napoleon's 'mysterious task', of which he was the 'involuntary agent', was not to pursue the cause of liberty—as it could not be pursued in the circumstances—but to continue the Revolution 'under monarchical forms'. He had done this by mixing his 'plebeian' blood with the oldest blood of European monarchy. He had blended the peoples of Europe together and had carried French laws to Germany, Italy, and Spain. Everywhere he had contradicted and shaken what had existed before. In this way, Thiers pronounced in conclusion, 'the new society was consolidated under the protection of his sword such that liberty would come one day. It has not come, it will come.'[103]

In summary, Mignet and Thiers were successful in formulating what might be termed a liberal catechism of the Revolution. Seen from this perspective, the Revolution was not accidental, but inevitable, with roots deep in French history. It was not a conspiracy but had popular support. Its causes were political, rather than social and economic. At the outset the Revolution had possessed a purity of intention but this had been undermined by the emigration of the aristocracy, foreign intervention, and the passions of the people. Circumstances explained the resort to terror and the existence of Jacobin dictatorship. Despite its crimes, the Revolution established the foundations of a new society upon the ruins of the *ancien régime* and the conditions in which liberty, if not actually realized, could one day be attained. To that end, any future liberal revolution had to avoid involvement in a foreign war, as it had been war above all that had unleashed the popular passions that had ultimately produced despotism.[104]

Nevertheless, Mignet and Thiers provided an interpretation of the Revolution that was not without ambiguity or even, as Linda Orr has suggested, a 'basic schizophrenia'.[105] If the notion of inevitability could serve to vindicate the Revolution, it was not at all clear—beyond some vague idea of the movement of civilization—what the determining factors in this history were. Next, while both authors were without hesitation in their condemnation of despotism, their critique was undoubtedly weakened by an enthusiasm for national glory and an admiration for the military achievements of the 1790s and the Empire. It is interesting to note that Thiers later felt the need to refute the criticism that, by fostering the image of Napoleon's greatness, he had contributed to the 1851 *coup d'état* by Louis Napoleon.[106] More fundamentally, to the horror of their conservative opponents, Mignet and Thiers appeared to be suggesting that the crimes of the Revolution could be justified in terms of its positive achievements. Just as importantly, to judge that the Revolution would come to an end with the victory of the bourgeois representatives of the Third Estate was to imagine and hope that the people

[103] Thiers, *Histoire de la Révolution française*, 530.

[104] This view was restated by Thiers following the revolution of 1830 when he affirmed that it was in the interest of the revolution to want peace: see Thiers, *La Monarchie de 1830* (1831), 101.

[105] Linda Orr, *Headless History: Nineteenth-Century French Historiography of the Revolution* (Ithaca, NY, 1990), 19.

[106] See J. P. T. Bury and R. P. Tombs, *Thiers 1797–1877: A Political Life* (London, 1986), 151.

would acquiesce to their exclusion from the political processes of the new order. This was to prove recklessly optimistic.

All the same, it was to the creation of such an order that Mignet and Thiers were to devote their political energies over the next decade, the two friends from the south of France playing a leading role in the agitation that led to the final departure of the Bourbon monarchy in July 1830. The central political objective was now to transform the relegitimated ideas of 1789 into a set of stable and regular representative institutions. In those circumstances, as Guizot rallied the liberal cause to the defence of moderate constitutional government and the new regime turned its back on the populist uprisings across Europe, royalist attempts to discredit the Revolution appeared to have been largely vanquished. However, as François Furet has observed, 'the opponents of the new Orleanist regime suddenly began to fly the banner of 1793: they clamoured for the Republic and the Montagnard Constitution, not for the bastard regime offered by the Constituent Assembly'. In short, the battle grounds of the historiography of the Revolution were about to be redrawn.

II

Much of this new historiography was socialist in inspiration. The 'dominant idea', according to Michel Winock, was that 'after the defeat of the Jacobins, the bourgeoisie had profited from the Revolution; and therefore that it was necessary to reclaim it for the people, in the name of equality and fraternity'.[107] What the liberals had both excused and deplored in the Revolution was now to be celebrated and praised. No longer was the grand narrative of the Revolution to be the struggle between the aristocracy and the Third Estate but that between the bourgeoisie and the people. The tyrant Robespierre was to be recast as the very incarnation of the Revolution's emancipatory message of earthly salvation. Rather than bringing the Revolution to a close, the goal was to reverse its betrayal and to allow it to be seen as a prefiguration of a new social order. Bourgeois sensibilities were to give way before proletarian messianism.

Broadly representative of this new interpretation of the Revolution was the monumental forty-volume *Histoire parlementaire de la Révolution française*, written and compiled by Philippe Buchez and his friend Pierre Roux and published in instalments between 1834 and 1839.[108] Unlike many nineteenth-century histories, it is not one that has withstood the test of time, but, in its day, it was both widely consulted and deeply influential.[109] For the most part, each volume consisted of primary documents gleaned from official reports, parliamentary sessions, brochures, newspapers, and so on, but interspersed among these was a running

---

[107] Michel Winock, *Les Voix de la Liberté: Les Écrivains engagés au XIXe siècle* (2001), 287.

[108] Buchez had earlier set out the philosophical and religious basis of his ideas in his *Introduction à la science de l'histoire* (1833). At the end of the 1820s he had broken with the Saint-Simonian movement and at this point had abandoned science for religion.

[109] Buchez and Roux imagined that their collection of material might act as a 'guide for future historians': *Histoire parlementaire de la Révolution française*, xvii. 186.

interpretative commentary. In addition, the early volumes provided a preface loosely summarizing the broader philosophical and religious themes underpinning the argument. What makes this account especially intriguing was the ambition to wed the Revolution to Catholicism, Jacobinism to religion.[110] The 'beginning and the end of the Revolution', Buchez and Roux declared, 'are contained in these words: liberty, equality, fraternity, or, in other words, in this goal: the realization in society of Christian morality'.[111]

This was made evident in the very first sentence. 'The French Revolution', it declared, 'is the most advanced and final outcome of modern civilization, and the whole of modern civilization derives from the Gospels'. This was a fact both 'irrefutable' and 'incontestable'.[112] The error, Buchez and Roux claimed, was to have continued to see the Revolution as an accident, as the product of financial insolvency, governmental mistakes, aristocratic insolence, royal scandal, and personal ambition. Indeed, they went so far as to suggest that 'this profound ignorance of the goal of humanity' was not only the cause of all the Revolution's misfortunes but also why, in 1833, it could still be dismissed only as disorder rather than as the foundation of right. But, they next argued, to be perceived in this way the Revolution had to be located upon a 'Christian soil'. Then it would be seen that the 'axioms' of the Revolution were 'laws long taught, long pursued, and approaching realization'. To claim, therefore, that the people had given themselves over to revolution in order to secure material well-being was to insult those 'dead martyrs' who had 'sacrificed themselves' to 'the great ideas of equality and fraternity'. It was also to fail to understand that it had taken fourteen centuries of constant effort to produce 'this proud nation' which, of itself and without a leader, had risen up as one. Thus, Buchez and Roux affirmed in their introduction, 'the revolutionary idea has a history which is that of the world, and where we learn, at the same time, why each people occupies the place it does and why our nation is the first among modern nations'.[113]

Like their predecessors, Buchez and Roux prefaced their history with a précis of French history. Resting firmly upon the conviction that France was not the result of Frankish conquest, they unhesitatingly asserted that the French nation emerged as a consequence of the desire to protect the Gauls and to defend and strengthen Catholicism. The whole of European history, they claimed, could be understood in just two words: France and the Church. With this historical preface to the Revolution completed, Buchez and Roux lost no time in setting out their argument. From the summer of 1789, 'the bourgeoisie sought to confiscate the Revolution for its own benefit'.[114] To protect its newly acquired dominance it wished to stop the Revolution. It became reactionary. It pursued its particular interest rather than the general interest. It placed egoism and 'the system of

---

[110] Buchez and Roux were extremely hostile to Protestantism, regarding it as entirely opposed to the spirit of the Revolution. Considerable venom was directed against the Protestant Guizot. They were similarly hostile to the philosophy associated with Victor Cousin and Eclecticism. The Girondins were also tarred with the brush of Eclecticism: Buchez and Roux, *Histoire parlementaire*, xxviii, pp. v–xv.

[111] Ibid. ii, p. v.   [112] Ibid. i. 1.
[113] Ibid. 5.   [114] Ibid. ii, p. ii.

individualism' before the happiness of future generations. This was no more evident than in the Déclaration des Droits de l'Homme et du Citoyen. This 'negative' document placed individual rights before duties and imagined that the whole nation was composed of property owners. It was similarly evident in the distinction established between 'passive' and 'active' citizens. The members of the National Assembly believed that the best government was an 'impassive spectator' protecting individual interests. They spoke only of man and never of France or the nation. They saw the Revolution as an 'obstacle' and acted without any sense of the future. Accordingly, the bourgeoisie made every effort to contain popular discontent. All the later misfortunes of the Revolution, Buchez and Roux argued, had their origin in the errors of this assembly.[115]

It followed that the impetus and initiative driving the Revolution forward had come not from the National Assembly but from the masses.[116] It was among the masses that was to be found 'certainty in the fraternity of men'. It was here that lay the 'true doctrine' of the Revolution, here that the obligations of duty preceded the rights of men, here that was displayed a spontaneous love of the homeland. In contrast to the Protestant and bourgeois doctrine of the sovereignty of individual reason, it was here too that the doctrines of the sovereignty of the people and of universal fraternity were found. The people did not calculate their interest. They had acted, and in so doing they had saved France.

From this perspective, terror could be described as 'an exceptional means, invoked in certain circumstances against a defined enemy' and as such could be justified according to the end pursued. Faced with 'evil' and 'anti-social interests', it was at times 'obligatory'.[117] Buchez and Roux thus displayed no sympathy towards the Girondins, as not the least of their faults had been a failure properly to organize the defence of France.[118] But their antipathy towards Brissot and his colleagues went much deeper. 'In the Girondin system', they wrote, 'everything begins with the individual and everything ends with the individual.'[119] For them, society was only a mechanism, where liberty was understood as the right to exercise our natural faculties and where equality amounted to the equal right to exercise this right. In sum, the Girondins stood for a philosophy of 'absolute individualism'.

This, in the eyes of Buchez and Roux, was the very antithesis of what was found among the Jacobins. Starting from a belief in God and the immortality of the soul, the Jacobins saw personal self-sacrifice and devotion to duty as the basis of the new social order. To this they had added the sentiment of universal fraternity. If the Girondins were federalists lacking in 'good faith', the Jacobins were the 'national party' totally committed to the 'salvation of France'. Writing of Saint-Just, this was

---

[115] Ibid. xii, p. xiv.

[116] Buchez and Roux referred to Joseph de Maistre's comment that it was not men who led the Revolution but the Revolution that led men: ibid. iv, p. ii.

[117] Ibid. xx, pp. v–xv. Buchez and Roux were at pains to deny the charge that they believed that the end justified the means: ibid. xxv, pp. v–xv.

[118] Ibid. xxviii. 145–6.

[119] Ibid. xxvi, p. vi.

how they explained the contrast: 'To the liberty that proceeds from natural right, he opposed as alone being acceptable the liberty of innocence and virtue; to mutual defence, to the passive interest of men . . . that the Girondin constitution declared to be the sole object of social security, he opposed the active interest of the greatest number.'[120] Nor did Buchez and Roux seek to diminish the enormity of the struggle engaged upon by the Jacobins. It was 'a war of extermination between the principle of modern civilization represented by France and that of the former civilization represented by the absolute powers of continental Europe'.[121] It was a battle between the world of the fall and slavery and that of redemption and liberty. In those circumstances, they ventured, it was not prisons and the scaffold that were 'odious' but 'indifference'.[122] According to Buchez and Roux, for Robespierre and the Jacobins revolutionary government denoted 'the absolute reign of morality'.[123] If there had been excesses, these were to be attributed to selfish, unprincipled rogues like Danton or atheists such as Hébert and his supporters. It was they, and not Robespierre, who had turned the law of 22 Prairial into 'the instrument of an atrocious despotism'.[124] When Robespierre failed to protect the Republic from the 'most bloodthirsty and the most corrupt' members of the Convention, the door was opened to reaction and counter-revolution. After Thermidor, the army alone remained devoted to the Republic. Exhausted, the people wanted rest and security: from the Revolution they now cherished only military glory. Accordingly, 'without resistance' they gave themselves up to the promises of a man who claimed to understand them but who, in turn, would betray the Revolution and France. The Restoration was nothing but 'an act of egoism'.

Reading the final volumes of Buchez and Roux's collection it is difficult to fathom what sense they could possibly have made of the years between 1795 and Napoleon's final defeat in 1815. Certainly this period received far less space and attention in their narrative than the period from 1789 to Thermidor. How, from their perspective of messianic expectation and possibility, could the Revolution have initially faltered and then failed so badly? Their answer was that, if the 'destructive' phase of the Revolution had been completed, it had not gone on to establish new forms of social organization. This was largely explained in terms of the absence of sound morality and belief among its participants, who, on this view, were consumed by doubt and 'hypocritical egoism'. Likewise, the crimes of the Revolution had their deeper cause in what Buchez and Roux repeatedly castigated as the materialism of the eighteenth century. The mistake of men like Robespierre was not to have proclaimed loudly the Christian origin of the beliefs they held. As a consequence, many fine principles were announced but they were easily abused and overturned. In the final analysis, however, the fundamental error had been to attempt to rebuild society upon the doctrines of the rights of man and individual interest, both of which only served to separate men from one another. The diagnosis for France's future, therefore, was that a 'true social life' could only rest

---

[120] Buchez and Roux, *Histoire parlementaire*, p. xiv. See also 310–15.
[121] Ibid. xxviii. 143.   [122] Ibid. xxix. 4.   [123] Ibid. xxx. 130.   [124] Ibid. xxxiii. 5.

upon the spirit of sacrifice and duty and that, as a Catholic nation, her goal must be 'to realize the ethics of Jesus Christ'.[125]

Few things could have been further from the thoughts of the governments of the July Monarchy. Largely indifferent to religious matters as well as to the condition of the people, for them the development of the economy and the expansion of banking and industry was a far greater priority. They consistently repressed popular dissent and defended the interests of wealthy property owners. And so, as opposition to the regime mounted and its unpopularity increased, the reappraisal of the Revolution continued apace.

In 1836 Armand Marrast and Jacques-François Dupont published their celebration of the great days of the Revolution, *Fastes de la Révolution française*. Two years later came Albert Laponneraye's overtly anti-Girondin and pro-Jacobin *Histoire de la Révolution française, depuis 1789 jusqu'en 1814*, with the 'virtuous' and 'exalted democrat' Robespierre as its undisputed hero.[126] The following year, the fiftieth anniversary of the beginning of the Revolution, Étienne Cabet commenced the publication of his four-volume *Histoire populaire de la Révolution française*. Again the Girondins were condemned as men without morals and principles and the Jacobins praised for their disinterested commitment to the people and to the values of justice and fraternity. This was followed in 1845 by Edgar Quinet's *Le Christianisme et la Révolution* where the message, although hostile to Buchez and Roux's Catholic neo-Jacobinism, was once more that the Revolution was the embodiment of what was best in Christianity. Only two years later, three of the most important histories of the Revolution appeared within months of each other: the first parts of Louis Blanc's *Histoire de la Révolution française*,[127] Jules Michelet's book of the same title, and the eight volumes of Alphonse de Lamartine's *Histoire des Girondins*. Despite its self-evident weaknesses as a work of history, it was Lamartine's poetical tale, 'full of blood and tears', which immediately proved to be most popular with the reading public.[128] Who, after all, could be unmoved by such rhetorical flourishes as the following: 'After five years, the Revolution was no more than a vast cemetery. Upon the tomb of each of its victims is written an exemplifying word: On one, *philosophy*, on another, *eloquence*; on this one, *genius*, on that one, *courage*; here, *crime*, there, *virtue*. But on every one is written: Died for the future and an artisan of humanity.'[129] The history of the Revolution, Lamartine concluded, was glorious and sad, full of sorrow but above all full of hope. Its 'immortal principles' transcended its blood-soaked reality.

---

[125] Ibid. xl, pp. iii–xv.

[126] In 1840 Laponneraye also produced a 3-vol. edn. of Robespierre's speeches.

[127] Blanc's 13-vol. history was written for the most part in exile in London and was completed in 1862.

[128] Subsequently Lamartine's history has been regarded as the most ephemeral of these three works, Norman Hampson going so far as to write that it could be disregarded as 'something of a potboiler': see Hampson, 'The French Revolution and its Historians', in Geoffrey Best (ed.), *The Permanent Revolution: The French Revolution and its Legacy 1789–1989* (London, 1988), 216.

[129] *Histoire des Girondins*, viii. 381–2.

The same year Alphonse Esquiros, author in 1840 of *L'Évangile du Peuple*, published his lyrical *Histoire des Montagnards*.[130] It can be read as a compendium of the new orthodoxy. The Revolution was the Gospel, armed by human reason and the sentiment of right. To fight against the Revolution was to fight against God. The people were the heart and soul of the Revolution. In the hands of the Jacobins, the Revolution had taken on a character that nothing could efface. It had 'helped the poor, the weak, the oppressed, and the child'.[131] Robespierre and the Jacobins were absolved of their crimes by a 'purity of motives'. The Girondins were 'the pagans' of the Revolution, selfish, immoral, and unprincipled.[132] Providence had called upon the French people to fulfil 'a great mission'. France was a 'sacrificial nation, a Christ nation: she lived and died for the salvation of the world'.[133] The Revolution marked the dawn of a new age.

III

In producing what was undoubtedly the most influential of all nineteenth-century histories of the Revolution, Jules Michelet both embraced and challenged this orthodoxy. When Michelet began writing his history in 1846 he was already one of the great figures of the French academic world, having been elected to a chair at the Collège de France in 1838. The first volume of his celebrated *Histoire de France* had appeared in 1833 and by 1843, when he put this project to one side, seven volumes (covering the period up to the reign of Louis XI) had been published. Volume iv, published in 1840, with its portrait of a Jeanne d'Arc inspired by her love of the people and by a fervent patriotism, had met with almost universal acclaim.[134] Yet Michelet had become an increasingly controversial figure, largely because of his undisguised antipathy towards the Roman Catholic Church and his determination to keep the University free from its influence. Taking the battle to the enemy, in 1843 he published *Des Jésuites* and then, two years later, *Du Prêtre, de la Femme et de la Famille*.[135] 'Our wives and our daughters', Michelet declared, 'are brought up and ruled by our enemies.' Both volumes were attacked by the Catholic press but both sold fabulously well (by 1844 *Des Jésuites* was into its sixth edition) and attendance at Michelet's lectures, briefly suspended by Guizot, became a way for radical students to voice their opposition to an increasingly beleaguered July Monarchy.

---

[130] See Anthony Zielonka, *Alphonse Esquiros (1812–1876): A Study of his Work* (Geneva, 1985).
[131] Esquiros, *Histoire des Montagnards* (1847), i. 3.
[132] Ibid. ii. 336.
[133] Ibid. i. 77.
[134] See 'La Pucelle d'Orléans', in Michelet, *Le Moyen Âge* (1981), 740–56.
[135] The themes of these two works reappear in Michelet's *Histoire de la Révolution française*. For example, whilst Michelet recognized that Louis XVI showed himself to be a good man, he could not refrain from saying that he remained a liar to the last because he had been a pupil of the Jesuits. He similarly attributed counter-revolutionary sentiment to the alliance existing between priests and women.

We have a reasonably clear idea of the sources employed by Michelet to write his history of the Revolution.[136] As attested by his diaries, he made assiduous use of the French National Archives (where he was head of the Historical Section) and, despite his antipathy towards the views of its authors, drew extensively upon the primary material assembled by Buchez and Roux. He consulted newspapers (especially *Le Moniteur*) and read the memoirs of participants. But this scarcely begins to capture what Michelet understood by history. For Michelet, the historian recreated and re-enacted the past. He placed himself within the action of events as they unfolded, straining to recapture the emotions of those involved. His style therefore was dramatic, declamatory, exclamatory, and exhortatory. But, just as importantly, Michelet also drew upon his own youth and life experience for inspiration. 'I commune with myself', he wrote.[137] This was especially so with regard to the people. 'To know the life of the people and their toil and sufferings', Michelet wrote, 'I had only to consult my memory.'[138] For Michelet, the people were not only the principal actors in his account but also, 'from the first to last page', its collective hero.[139]

'I define the Revolution', Michelet proclaimed, 'The advent of the Law, the resurrection of Right, and the reaction of Justice'.[140] This did not mean, he immediately avowed, that the Revolution was the realization of Christianity. Rather, it was, 'at one and same time, its heir and adversary'.[141] They shared the sentiment of human fraternity but the Revolution, unlike Christianity, 'founds fraternity on the love of man for man, on mutual duty, on right and justice'.[142] For Christianity, salvation was a gift and relied upon faith alone; for the Revolution, it was the work of justice itself. Moreover, the reality of Christianity had been 'a vast sea of blood' and the *ancien régime*, the monarchy of king and priest, nothing else but 'tyranny in the name of grace'.[143] So, as 'the dogma of royal incarnation perished forever'[144] and as the Bastille fell, a new doctrine, with causes deep and profound, was brought forth by the Revolution: the rights of man. 'The approaching dawn', Michelet wrote, 'was that of liberty.'[145]

In what followed Michelet was always at pains to relieve the people of any responsibility for the acts of violence and savagery that came increasingly to characterize the Revolution. Those 'sanguinary deeds' had as their perpetrators only 'an infinitely small number of men'.[146] Rather, Michelet's emphasis fell upon what he described as 'the epoch of unanimity, the holy epoch when the whole nation, free from distinctions of party and scarcely knowing opposition between classes, marched together under the flag of fraternity'.[147] This 'humane and benevolent' phase of the Revolution, on Michelet's account, attained its apotheosis with the first Fête de la Fédération on 14 July 1790. 'I do not believe', Michelet wrote, 'that at any time the heart of man was more generous or full.'[148] What was

---

[136] See Eric Fauquet, *Michelet ou la gloire du professeur d'histoire* (1990), 224–316; Paul Viallaneix, *Michelet, les travaux et les jours 1798–1874* (1998), 299–326; and Paule Petitier, *Jules Michelet: L'Homme histoire* (2006), 201–53.

[137] *Histoire de la Révolution française*, i. 31.   [138] *Le Peuple*, 58.

[139] *Histoire de la Révolution française*, ii. 897.   [140] Ibid. i. 51.

[141] Ibid. 54.   [142] Ibid. 55.   [143] Ibid. 93.   [144] Ibid. 75.

[145] Ibid. 198.   [146] Ibid. 37.   [147] Ibid. 38.   [148] Ibid. 330.

here most evident was what Michelet described as 'the spontaneous organization of France', the overcoming of the distinctions and barriers of geography, race, wealth, language, and religion that had formerly divided the French from one another.[149] 'To attain unity', Michelet wrote, 'nothing was able to prove an obstacle, no sacrifice was too dear.'[150] Such was the power of love. Was this a miracle? Yes, Michelet replied, and 'the greatest and the simplest of miracles', the renunciation of 'senseless animosities' and a return to 'sociability'.[151] So too it was but 'the natural and necessary application of the very principle of the Revolution': justice.[152]

Yet Michelet knew as much as anyone else that the Revolution had not delivered on this initial promise and that he had to explain the failure of the new religion of fraternity. Not for the first or the last time, ambiguity appeared in the account provided. It began in the first chapter that followed the three devoted to the Fête de la Fédération. The unity there displayed, Michelet wrote, had been sincere but momentary and had not been strong enough to prevent the reappearance of class divisions and differences of opinion. The bourgeoisie 'trembled' before the Revolution it had made and, standing back from its work, was soon consumed by hatred and fear. As this 'internal obstacle' to the Revolution took shape, there emerged the external obstacles fuelled by the hypocrisy and 'unshakable hatred' of the clergy and the English. 'The bourgeoisie', Michelet commented, 'drank the English opium, with all its ingredients of egoism, well-being, comfort, and liberty without sacrifice.'[153] It was then that Michelet introduced the Jacobins into his account, describing what he termed 'a revolutionary clergy' with Robespierre as its leader.[154] 'Mutual surveillance, public censure, and even secret denunciation' were what they taught and practised, their vision of society modelled upon the 'illustrious examples of Antiquity' and 'the monastic cities of the Middle Ages'. For these bitter and distrustful men everyone appeared as a suspect.

Over the next several hundred pages, Michelet explored the dynamics of this situation, the great Jacobin 'machine' thriving on public apathy and indifference and progressively substituting the spirit of conspiracy for that of fraternity.[155] He castigated the clergy and their counter-revolutionary allies. He condemned the duplicity of traitors such as Charles-François Dumouriez[156] and deplored the endless infighting among the factions that vied with each other for leadership of the Revolution. He likewise scorned the lack of principle and vanity of the Girondins, deriding them as 'the protective mask' of royalism.[157] The Terror was nothing but a 'judicial dictatorship' inspired by fanaticism and sectarianism. Unusually, but intentionally, Michelet ended his account with the fall of Robespierre. After Thermidor, there was nothing left of the Revolution.[158]

---

[149] *Histoire de la Révolution française*, 318.
[150] Ibid. 326.   [151] Ibid. 325.   [152] Ibid. 336.
[153] Ibid. 356.   [154] Ibid. 393.   [155] Ibid., ii. 127–8.
[156] Ibid. 335–48. After having led the French army to victory at Valmy and Jemmapes, Dumouriez went over to the Austrians.
[157] Ibid. 143–8.
[158] Michelet was to explore this period of French history in his *Histoire du dix-neuvième siècle* (see *Œuvres complètes*, xxi. *1872–1874* (1982)), starting his history of the 19th cent. with the fall of

Michelet's Revolution, therefore, was the Revolution of 1789. For him, the stirring events that followed the calling of the Estates-General denoted a radical rupture with the past and the advent of a new age. He gloried in the Revolution's universal message of justice and peace, believing that for the first time law and religion had been brought together as one.[159] He recognized the uniqueness of the event and saw it as being embedded in the history and destiny of France. He never ceased to praise the heroism and generosity of the people, always comparing their behaviour favourably with that of their leaders. To that end, Michelet's Revolution was not, unlike that of Mignet and Thiers, a history of the rise of the bourgeoisie. Nor was it infused with the liberal Anglophilia associated with Guizot's popular notion that 1789 was a French 1640 and, therefore, that the Revolution of 1830 was a replay of England's Glorious Revolution of 1688. In contradistinction to Buchez and many others, he saw the Revolution not as a rebirth of the true spirit of Christianity but as marking its end, as the effacement of a doctrine that espoused 'the unjust transmission of evil by original sin'.[160] Michelet's Revolution took inspiration from Voltaire and Rousseau, not from the Bible. Likewise, if Michelet accepted that the Jacobins had saved France from external invasion, he was not prepared, as Mignet and Louis Blanc had been, to attribute the Terror to circumstances alone. It had been tyranny and Michelet could not refrain from observing that many royalists had a weakness and sneaking admiration for Robespierre.

Michelet defined his own position as 'Montagnard but not Jacobin'.[161] He would, he told his readers, have voted against the Girondins but he would have opposed the 'inquisitorial spirit' and 'violent Machiavellianism' of the Jacobin club. If, beyond the people themselves, he had any heroes they were Danton and Camille Desmoulins.[162] Yet Michelet believed that the violent efforts that the Revolution had made to save itself had subsequently been mistaken 'by a forgetful generation' for the Revolution itself. So unknown was its origin and nature that the 'the profoundly peaceful and benevolent character' of the Revolution now seemed a paradox. None remained upon the altar of the Revolution but Robespierre and Saint-Just and, for as long as this remained the case, Michelet concluded, the message of the Revolution would not be heard and absolute governments could sleep easily. The world would only be won over by 'the fraternity of love, and not that of the guillotine'.[163]

Michelet began writing his *Histoire de la Révolution française* under the July Monarchy and completed it in August 1853 under the Second Empire. In the mean time, in April 1852, he had been removed from his post at the Collège de France by the new Minister of Public Education. The same fate befell his close

---

Robespierre. As he commented: 'At this moment history seems to fall into a chasm'. History was now reduced to that of one man, Napoleon, and to 'pure biography': ibid. 218–19.

[159] *Histoire de la Révolution française*, ii. 172–3.
[160] Ibid. i. 36.
[161] Ibid. ii. 404.
[162] Desmoulins was a talented journalist and member of the Convention. He was executed, along with Danton, on 5 Apr. 1794.
[163] Ibid. i. 34.

friend Edgar Quinet.[164] During the Second Republic Quinet had served as a parliamentary deputy and he was now to begin a period of lengthy exile in Belgium and Switzerland.[165] Side by side, both men had waged a common struggle against the power of the Roman Catholic Church, each devoting a course of lectures to the Jesuits.[166] In Quinet's case, he followed this with a second volume in 1844 devoted to a doctrine closely associated with the Jesuits: Ultramontanism.[167] In the introduction to the latter, Quinet indicated his preference for what he called 'a religion of sincerity'. A similar battle cry was heard one year later when Quinet published his magisterial *Le Christianisme et la Révolution française*, except that this time he began by voicing his disapproval of the dominant philosophy of the age: the Eclecticism associated with Victor Cousin.[168] It was, Quinet announced, a philosophy that no longer even believed in itself and denoted nothing else than 'spiritual and moral bankruptcy'.[169] If then, as he proclaimed, the 'philosophy of the Restoration was dead', from what sources could the discouraged generation of the July Monarchy derive moral and intellectual succour?

To answer that question Quinet delved deep into the history of the Christian Church, uncovering a set of beliefs and practices that were far removed from those of its modern equivalent. The early Christians were not constrained by a body of fixed and rigid dogma—all was 'inspiration, fervour, spontaneity, movement'—and the Christian fathers had believed that the spirit of God was to be found in all of us. They similarly thought that the ideals of Christianity were realizable here on earth. However, overlaid upon this early faith had been doctrines that had undermined the emancipatory potential of the Christian religion. The distinction between the City of God and the City of Man entailed the indefinite postponement of a terrestrial paradise. The doctrine of predestination took away any notion of man's 'moral liberty'. Bossuet's conception of a Christian sovereign relieved the monarch of any concern for his people. The Crusades turned war into a form of hatred and extermination. Quinet's list was extensive but each item was designed to show that Christianity had been betrayed by the Catholic Church. Conversely, Quinet was prepared to draw inspiration from those heretics and dissenters who had sought to return to the words of Christ himself and running through his lectures was the constant invocation to his audience that they should aspire to do the same. 'Our task, and that of those who come after us', he wrote, 'will be to show that the people of God are not only in Judea, that they live among us, that the city

---

[164] See Hermione Quinet, *Cinquante Ans d'amitié: Michelet-Quinet (1825–1875)* (1899). See also Edgar Quinet, *Lettres d'éxil à Michelet et à divers amis*, 2 vols. (1885).

[165] On Quinet see Winock, *Les Voix de la Liberté*, 450–62, Furet, *La Gauche et la révolution au XIXe siècle* (1986) and Ceri Crossley, *Edgar Quinet (1803–1875): A Study in Romantic Thought* (Lexington, Ky., 1983).

[166] The courses of both men were printed in the same volume: *Des Jésuites* (1843). Quinet's text appears at pp. 107–249.

[167] *L'Ultramontanisme ou l'église romaine et la société moderne* (1844). As opposed to Gallicanism, Ultramontanism stressed the authority of the Pope over the Catholic Church in France.

[168] On Cousin and Eclecticism see pp. 320–3 below.

[169] Quinet, *Le Christianisme et la Révolution française* (1845), 41.

of God is not in ruins, that each day it continues to grow in the midst of us and through us.'[170]

Yet Quinet also believed that the true spirit of Christianity found expression outside the Church. It existed within the French people and defined the character of the French Revolution. The Revolution, he argued, drew upon the hope that the message of the Gospel could be realized in this world and that it was not consigned to the 'city of the dead'.[171] In this Quinet was scarcely original: the assumption of a similarity between the Christian and the revolutionary idea had become something of a commonplace. It was what came next in Quinet's argument that was new.

'Alone of modern nations', Quinet asserted, 'France carried out a political and social revolution before completing its religious revolution.' From this, he continued, arose all that was 'original, monstrous, gigantic, and implacable in this history'.[172] A revolution that began by wishing to reconcile Church and State finished up by setting them at war with each other but, although seemingly banished, the intolerant spirit of Catholicism had remained at the heart of things. Quickly one church was replaced by another, replete with its own ceremonies, rituals, and images. A new state religion was created with Robespierre cast not only as dictator but also as the new pope. Why, Quinet asked, was Danton sent to the scaffold if not for lack of faith, 'to be an epicurean became a crime of heresy'.[173]

In brief, the argument was that the Revolution had not freed itself from the exclusive and absolutist temper of the Church and therefore that the least dissent was viewed as 'inexpiable schism'. 'The sentimental logic of Rousseau', Quinet wrote, took 'as its instrument the axe of Saint Bartholomew'.[174] The result was violence and a disregard for individual conscience. If Quinet admired the heroic efforts of the Convention to secure the defence of France, he saw the Terror and the cult of the Supreme Being as nothing but manifestations of a new state religion. He also believed that the armies of the Revolution were new crusaders, their task being the 'moral elevation of their adversaries' and 'friendship between peoples'.[175] The defeat of Napoleon at Waterloo, by contrast, was the Golgotha of the modern age, an act of Providence that had left France for dead.[176]

Manifestly, Quinet was not writing a history of the Revolution. His concern was to explore its temperament and spirit, to trace its lineage and affiliations. The failure of the Revolution, in his view, resulted from the prior absence of a genuine religious revolution but this did not prevent him from maintaining that, 'in many regards', the ideal of the Revolution came closer to that of Christianity than did anything then being preached by the Church.[177] The significance of this should not be lost upon us. First, it meant that, in Quinet's eyes, Catholicism could no longer be considered 'the national religion of our country'. Next, by drawing out the absolutist tendencies of both the Revolution and the Church, he distanced himself from interpretations of the Revolution and of Jacobinism as forerunners of

[170] Ibid. 127–8. [171] Ibid. 113–14. [172] Ibid. 334.
[173] Ibid. 348. [174] Ibid. 349. [175] Ibid. 202–3.
[176] Ibid. 383. [177] Ibid. 402.

Christian socialism. This was so because, although no Protestant,[178] at the heart of Quinet's conception of Christianity was the sanctity of the individual conscience. Quinet unambiguously placed the rights of the individual before the demands of association.[179] Finally, although *Le Christianisme et la Révolution française* was dedicated to Michelet, what separated the two men was all too clear. Both endorsed the exemplary and universal character of French history and of the Revolution itself; but for Michelet the Revolution terminated the history of Christianity whilst, for Quinet, what was best in the Revolution recaptured and gave life to Christianity's original message.

The political conclusion that Quinet sought to convey was summarized in the fourteenth of his lectures. The 'ideal of the future', he announced, 'must contain and reconcile the moral advance of the Constituent Assembly without its illusions, the energy of the Convention without its cruelty, and the splendour of Napoleon without his despotism'.[180] In line with this clarion call Quinet actively embraced the new Second Republic,[181] but he quickly came to view the resurgence of neo-Jacobinism with apprehension. The election of Louis Napoleon as president diminished his hopes further and following the *coup d'état* of December 1851 he, like many fellow republicans, was forced to flee the country. In his often lonely exile his obsession now became that of reversing the dishonour inflicted upon his country and of understanding the failure of democracy in France.[182] This, for example, was evident in such diverse works as his verse drama *Les Esclaves* (1853) and his anti-Napoleonic *Histoire de la campagne de 1815* (1862). However, it was most clearly and controversially visible in *La Révolution*, first published in 1865.[183]

In contrast to the earlier *Le Christianisme et la Révolution française*, this was a full-blown history of the Revolution, taking its reader from the collapse of the *ancien régime* to the rise to power of Napoleon Bonaparte: but, in essence, it built upon the themes of the earlier volume. The question posed was the following: why had so many immense efforts and sacrifices produced such meagre results?[184] The answer again was that France, unlike England, had not preceded its political revolution with a religious revolution.[185] 'With regard to the moral order', Quinet wrote, 'the success of this Revolution was absolutely impossible, since its leaders, while completely overturning the Middle Ages, preserved the ideal of the Middle Ages with regard to ideas.' 'In the midst of massive upheaval', he went on, 'everything changed except the mind of man, which was systematically left a captive of the past.'[186] From its very first step, therefore, the Revolution revealed that it had feet of clay.

---

[178] Quinet's mother was a Protestant and he himself acknowledged the beneficial consequences of the Reformation.

[179] Ibid. 406.

[180] Ibid. 385.

[181] See the speech made by Quinet on 8 Mar. 1848 before the students of the Sorbonne: Hermione Quinet, *Cinquante Ans d'amitié*, 158–60.

[182] See e.g. Edgar Quinet, *Le Réveil d'un grand peuple* (1869).

[183] Quinet, *La Révolution* (1865; references to the 1987 edn.).

[184] Ibid. 65.   [185] Ibid. 168.   [186] Ibid. 186.

What followed was a very different account of the Revolution from anything that had been penned before. Quinet's view was that the people had risen up in rebellion against what he termed the 'byzantine and imperial' traditions of the absolutist monarchy but that these had been preserved by the Revolution. 'The classical, official, disciplined, literary republic of Robespierre', Quinet wrote, 'could understand nothing of this popular movement, since no model for it could be found in either Rousseau or Lycurgus.'[187] So, Quinet disapproved of the Revolution's destruction of provincial liberties, arguing that this had left the entire country at the mercy of the capital.[188] This led ineluctably to the central question explored by Quinet: what was the nature of the Terror and how could it be explained? His answer provoked the eruption of one of the most bitter controversies among republicans during the nineteenth century.

Quinet's political sympathies clearly lay with the Girondins.[189] 'Because they wanted to arrive at liberty through liberty', he wrote, 'they rejected the heritage of old France in its entirety.'[190] With their arrest, he postulated, it was resolved that henceforth the 'regeneration of France' would not be attained by a new route but 'by the method of the *ancien régime*: tyranny'. 'To abolish liberty under the pretext that it would be established much later', Quinet wrote, 'is the guiding thread of French history. It was also that of the Revolution.'[191] The Jacobins, on this view, set out to force the people to be free and, to that end, all opposition, all dissent, all disagreement, became a crime punishable by death. They believed that there was virtue in the spilling of an enemy's blood and that a golden age would arise from the scaffold. But only the goal pursued by the Jacobins was new. 'As for the means of constraint and authority', Quinet argued, 'it is what we have always had for centuries.'[192] So, circumstances did not explain the Terror, nor could success legitimize it. The Terror was rooted in historical precedent and was but 'the fatal legacy' of France's absolutist tradition and, as such, was a product of the Revolution itself. In no other revolution, Quinet contended, had leaders acted in a manner so contrary to the goals they pursued.

According to Quinet, therefore, the Terror had its initial cause in the 'irreconcilable' clash between old and new France. This sentiment of 'absolute incompatibility' pushed people towards a state of frenzy, leading both sides to intensify and heighten their actions. Threatened and provoked, with each day the Revolution gained in audacity, engendering 'a state of exaltation' among the French nation. Robespierre and his colleagues simply changed what was a passing 'accident' into 'a permanent state of affairs'. Coldly and impassively, they transformed a condition of anger and despair into a principle and system of government and turned spontaneous fury into a cold and calculated instrument of salvation. The whole edifice rested upon another 'sad' legacy of earlier oppression: contempt for the individual.[193] Moreover, the exercise of absolute power during the Revolution had exactly the

---

[187] Ibid. 475.   [188] Ibid. 140.   [189] Ibid. 426–8.
[190] Ibid. 373.   [191] Ibid. 389.   [192] Ibid. 373.
[193] Ibid. 497–501.

same impact as it had had under the monarchy. Fear corrupted and abased people. Night descended upon their intellects.

Quinet's conclusion was that in each of the barbarities of 1793 could be seen a reappearance of the mentality of the Middle Ages. Salvation, according to this logic, would be attained if only a few perfidious and malign individuals were eradicated and this was as true for the Revolution as it had been when Louis XIV had sent out troops against the Huguenots. Similarly, Quinet saw that, if it was easy to inaugurate government by terror, it was immeasurably more difficult to bring it to an end. Driven forward by the illusion of necessity it would march on until only the executioners themselves remained. The circle would then be closed and we would have returned to our point of departure: servitude.[194]

This, in Quinet's view, was precisely what had occurred. In 1789, the French had risen up against three forms of oppression: absolute power, Roman Catholicism, and administrative centralization. Once the storm had passed, all three reappeared: absolute power with Napoleon as First Consul; Roman Catholicism with the signing of the Concordat in 1801; and administrative centralization in the shape of the Napoleonic state. Rephrased by Quinet in the idiom of nineteenth-century French historiography, this meant that, if the French Revolution had freed the nation from its original conquest by the Franks, the Gauls remained enslaved to the Romans and to the Caesarean traditions of emperor and pope.[195]

What sense could be made of this 'bloody labyrinth'? The Revolution, Quinet concluded, had bequeathed a 'disastrous heritage' to France and to French democracy. At its heart was a belief in 'the necessity of dictatorship' as the indispensable step towards the establishment of liberty. The revolutionaries, he observed, were past masters in the art of death. The result was that all that remained of the Revolution was 'an ideal, a flag and a few words about justice which float above the abyss'.[196] Whoever wished to live freely therefore had to renounce the joys of exacting vengeance and to dare to acknowledge that the proper response to tyranny was not more tyranny. Yet, as Quinet sadly recognized, whether openly or in disguise, 'this has not ceased to reappear as the supreme expedient'.[197]

It was a mark of the originality and power of Quinet's *La Révolution* that, not only did its first edition sell out in six days, but that it was met by howls of protest from those associated with the 'democratic party'.[198] The tone of these protests was best captured in the series of articles written by Alphonse Peyrat, editor of *L'Avenir national*. Quinet's two volumes, Peyrat argued, were a 'satire' of the Revolution: they were 'anti-historical and anti-revolutionary', a mixture of prejudice and philosophical pretension, bizarre comparisons and surprising banalities. Taken as a whole, they dishonoured the Revolution. More substantially, Peyrat unapologetically reaffirmed the pro-Jacobin orthodoxy. The Jacobins had not sought to raise terror into a system of government. Dictatorship had been imposed upon the Revolution by necessity and circumstance. Through their prodigious efforts,

---

[194] Quinet, *La Révolution* (1865; references to the 1987 edn.), 534.
[195] Ibid. 729.   [196] Ibid. 730.   [197] Ibid. 599.
[198] Key texts are republ. in Furet, *La Gauche et la révolution au XIXe siècle*, 134–383.

the Jacobins had saved the Revolution. For good measure, Peyrat condemned the Girondins for being a bunch of unprincipled chancers and pointed out that Quinet's book had been taken up by royalists.[199]

The polemic rumbled on over the winter of 1865, with liberals and moderate republicans, including Jules Ferry and Emile Ollivier, voicing their support for Quinet. But it came to a head in February 1866 when the exiled Louis Blanc published a long article in *Le Temps* effectively charging Quinet with giving succour to the forces of counter-revolution.[200] After 'eighteen years of research, study and meditation',[201] Blanc had finished his own twelve-volume history of the Revolution in 1862 and could not but take offence at what he saw as a summary dismissal of all that he had long believed in and cherished. Above all, he took exception to Quinet's allegation that the Jacobins had raised terror into a system of government. 'The Terror', he responded, 'was not a *system*; it was something very different, an immense misfortune born out of extraordinary dangers.'[202] Nor was it true that the Terror had its origins in the minds of a few individuals. 'Prepared by centuries of oppression, provoked by frightful attacks and spurred on by the dangers of a titanic struggle', Blanc continued, 'the Terror came out of the bowels of history.'[203] No one had wanted dictatorship less than Robespierre. Moreover, the killing had not stopped with his fall. It had simply been replaced by the 'white Terror'.

Blanc's argument was that the 'idea of dictatorship' was 'directly opposed to the spirit of the Revolution'. 'Let us not say', he concluded, 'that the results were disproportionate to the sacrifices made when the results were the intellectual conquests that have made us what we are and a France saved.'[204] At first Quinet did not respond. Then, for the fifth edition of *La Révolution* published in 1867, he wrote a lengthy new preface, lambasting his detractors for presuming to dictate what could be said about the Revolution and contrasting this with his own 'scientific' method.[205] On the substantive point of disagreement he was not prepared to compromise. It was not necessity that had produced 'the system' of the Terror but 'false ideas'.[206] Furthermore, critics such as Blanc failed to appreciate what was distinctive about the violence of the Terror. 'Do you not see', he asked, 'that one of the special characteristics of the French Revolution is that the revolutionaries were put to death by revolutionaries, the Jacobins by Jacobins, the Montagnards by Montagnards?'[207] To accept the logic of the Terror was to accept the logic of 'eradication' and such a logic, Quinet affirmed, was 'illogical, illusory and necessarily sterile'. From this, he wrote, 'I have been able to conclude that there was a complete incompatibility between the means of 93 and the end pursued, between the barbarities of the Jacobins and the philosophy of the eighteenth century, between theory and practice.'[208]

One casualty of the publication of Quinet's *La Révolution* was his close friendship with Michelet. This might appear odd, given that Michelet had shown little

[199] Ibid. 139–230. These essays were subsequently republ. in Peyrat, *La Révolution et le livre de M. Quinet* (1866).
[200] Furet, *La Gauche et la révolution*, 289–305.   [201] Ibid. 289.
[202] Ibid. 291.   [203] Ibid. 293.   [204] Ibid. 305.   [205] Ibid. 308–37.
[206] Ibid. 332.   [207] Ibid. 327.   [208] Ibid. 321.

sympathy for the priestly Robespierre and even less liking for the Jacobin 'machine'. Indeed, for the 1869 edition of his *Histoire de la Révolution française* he added a new preface to volume v entitled simply 'The Tyrant'.[209] Similarly, in his preface to the 1868 edition he directed his fire primarily at Louis Blanc, referring to him as 'half-Christian in the manner of Rousseau and Robespierre'.[210] Yet Michelet had counselled against mistaking the Terror for the Revolution, never quite stating the dichotomy between 1789 and 1793 in such stark terms, and he had no respect whatsoever for the Girondins. Importantly, Michelet and Quinet differed fundamentally about the place and role of religion in the Revolution. Hurt pride and professional jealousy also played a part. If only briefly, everyone was reading Quinet and Michelet was out of the limelight. Whatever the cause, the two men were never to regain the intellectual intimacy they had shared in the past.

IV

In 1862 Quinet took up his copy of Alexis de Tocqueville's *L'Ancien Régime et la Révolution* for a second time and began to annotate it line by line.[211] Despite their political and personal differences, the two men shared one central intellectual preoccupation. Both believed passionately in liberty and both understood that the durability of French traditions of despotism worked against its realization. If this meant that each of them was resolute in his opposition to the Second Empire, it likewise demanded an explanation of the causes of what was indubitably the failure of the Revolution to effect a real break with the past. Tocqueville's answer to this conundrum might have had less rhetorical force than that provided by Quinet but it was no less compelling and many have subsequently found it to be extremely convincing. When published in 1856 *L'Ancien Régime et la Révolution* proved to be at least as successful with the reading public as *De la Démocratie en Amérique* had been and, to Tocqueville's evident delight, quickly went through several editions. It was however a text suffused with pessimism.

The precise moment at which Tocqueville resolved to write a study of the Revolution can be dated to December 1850 when he was in Sorrento recuperating from a bout of illness, but it took him several more years before he decided upon the form and content of his inquiry.[212] As his correspondence with Gustave de Beaumont reveals, it was only at the point of publication and after much discussion

---

[209] Michelet, *Histoire de la Révolution française*, ii. 349–65.
[210] Ibid. i. 47.
[211] See Furet, *La Gauche et la révolution*, 41–58.
[212] On the writing of *L'Ancien Régime et la Révolution* see Gannett, *Tocqueville Unveiled*. Among the other texts that might be consulted see François Furet and Françoise Mélonio, 'Introduction', to Alexis de Tocqueville, *The Old Regime and the Revolution*, i. *The Complete Text* (Chicago: 1998), 1–79; André Jardin, *Tocqueville: A Biography* (Baltimore, Md., 1998), 481–507; Robert T. Gannett, jun., 'The Shifting Puzzles of Tocqueville's *the Old Regime and the Revolution*', in Cheryl Welch (ed.), *The Cambridge Companion to Tocqueville* (Cambridge, 2006), 188–215; Brogan, *Alexis de Tocqueville* (2006), 525–84.

that an appropriate title was decided upon.[213] These hesitations are easy to understand. Unlike Michelet and Quinet, Tocqueville was a man who had spent most of his adult life as a politician and journalist. If he had attended the famous lectures on European civilization given by Guizot in the 1820s and now counted François Mignet among his personal acquaintances, he was not an academic historian and therefore was initially uncertain about both his subject matter and methods of investigation. The end product did not take a narrative form and it dispensed with the conventional chronology of events, focusing rather upon the prehistory of the Revolution and what Tocqueville saw as its long-term causes. A never-to-be completed sequel was to be devoted to the Revolution proper. The final text drew upon extensive archival work, for the most part carried out in Tours (where Tocqueville was again in need of a period of convalescence), and it was here that he became convinced that the centralized administrative machinery associated with Napoleon was 'purely the old regime preserved'.[214] Tocqueville also made an extended trip to Germany in 1854 in search of still-existing feudal traditions analogous to those of pre-1789 France. In addition, he read memoirs of the period and consulted diplomatic documents.

Tocqueville's argument also built upon insights developed in two earlier texts: an essay detailing the social and political condition of France prior to 1789 published in John Stuart Mill's *London and Westminster Review* in 1836[215] and the reception speech he made before the Académie Française in April 1842.[216] In the first, Tocqueville described a France that was increasingly homogeneous and characterized by social equality and one where the central power of the State was stronger than anywhere else in the world. The Revolution, he argued, had only served to augment the equality of conditions and further to strengthen state power. In the second, and despite the formality of the occasion, Tocqueville castigated Napoleon for creating 'the most perfected despotism', commenting that 'the eighteenth century and the Revolution, at the same time that they introduced new elements of liberty into the world, secretly sowed in the new society dangerous seeds from which absolute power could grow'.[217]

The result of this long and arduous process of deliberation and research was a work divided clearly into three sections and held together by an argument that was deceptively simple. That argument was succinctly set out in the Foreword and then developed in book 1. The opening lines of the second paragraph read as follows: 'in

---

[213] Alexis de Tocqueville, *Œuvres complètes*, viii/3. *Correspondance d'Alexis de Tocqueville et de Gustave de Beaumont* (1967), 370, 372–3, 379, 384.

[214] See Gannett, *Tocqueville Unveiled*, 79–98. Tocqueville first observed that the French system of administrative centralization was not born with the French Revolution but only perfected by it as early as 1835: see *Œuvres complètes*, i/1. *De la Démocratie en Amérique* (1961), 447.

[215] Alexis de Tocqueville, 'Political and Social Condition of France', *London and Westminster Review*, 8 (Apr. 1836), 137–69. See also 'État social et politique de France avant et depuis 1789', in *Œuvres complètes*, ii/1. *L'Ancien Régime et la Révolution* (1952), 31–66.

[216] 'Discours de M. de Tocqueville prononcé dans la séance publique du 21 avril 1842 en venant prendre séance à la place de M. le Comte de Cessac", in *Œuvres complètes*, xvi. *Mélanges* (1989), 251–69.

[217] Ibid. 259.

1789 the French made the greatest effort ever undertaken by any people to break with their past and to put an abyss between what they had been and what they wished to become. To this end, they took all manner of precautions to bring nothing of the past into the new order.'[218] Yet, Tocqueville continued, the French were far less successful in this than they had believed. Despite themselves and unintentionally, 'they retained from the old regime most of the feelings, habits, and even ideas which helped them make the Revolution that destroyed it'.[219] The new society was built upon the debris and wreckage of the past. From this Tocqueville drew two conclusions. The first was that properly to understand the Revolution one had to interrogate a France that no longer existed. The second was that no fundamental break had taken place in 1789. What the Revolution destroyed was everything in the old order that derived from aristocratic and feudal institutions but beneath the seemingly chaotic surface a clear pattern of continuity could be discerned. 'I will show', Tocqueville wrote, 'how a stronger government, much more absolute than that which the Revolution had overthrown, arose and concentrated all power in itself, suppressed all freedoms so dearly bought, and put vain images in their place.'[220]

The central empirical claim underpinning this interpretation of the Revolution was sketched in book 2 and was summarized by Tocqueville in the title he gave to one of its chapters: 'How Administrative Centralization is an Institution of the *Ancien Régime* and not the Work of either the Revolution or the Empire, as is said'.[221] In brief, Tocqueville's argument was that, despite appearances of diversity and confusion to the contrary, it had been the French monarchy that had built a vast centralized bureaucracy with tentacles spreading throughout the kingdom and intruding into all aspects of daily life. In summary, Tocqueville wrote, there existed 'a single body, located at the centre of the kingdom, which regulated public administration throughout the entire country; the same minister directing almost all internal affairs; in each province, a single official in charge of all the details; no secondary administrative bodies or bodies able to act without prior authorization to do so; exceptional courts which judged matters relating to the administration and its officers'.[222] If its procedures were less regular and its machinery less efficient than what now existed, nothing of importance had since been added or subtracted from it. 'It has been sufficient', Tocqueville commented, 'to pull down all that had been erected around it for it to appear as we now see it.'[223]

The consequences for the condition of French society, according to Tocqueville, had been profound. Government exercised a quasi-paternal tutelage over the population. Municipal government had declined into petty oligarchy. The administration resented all independent bodies and distrusted any display of initiative from private citizens. Paris had achieved absolute predominance over the country. More troubling still were the pathologies that had arisen from the vast gulf existing between the government and individual citizen. Having taken the place of divine

---

[218] *Œuvres complètes*, ii/1. *L'Ancien Régime et la Révolution*, 69.
[219] Ibid.   [220] Ibid. 72.   [221] Ibid. 107.
[222] Ibid. 127.   [223] Ibid.

providence, it was but natural that everyone should turn to government when in need. 'No one imagined', Tocqueville argued, 'that an important matter could be brought to a successful conclusion without the intervention of the State.'[224] If the eradication of local and regional differences and of distinctions between classes meant that individuals more and more resembled each other, the process of centralization also ensured that they were more than ever separated from one another. People were indifferent to the fate of others and mutual suspicion reigned. What mattered most were the petty privileges and prerogatives marking them out, however flimsily, from their rivals. But, Tocqueville observed, 'everyone was ready to merge into the same mass, provided that no one remained apart and no one rose above the common level'.[225] When, at last, they had come together in 1789 their first thought was to tear each other apart.

The final component of this noxious state of mind was the existence of an 'unusual kind of freedom'. It would be wrong to believe, Tocqueville commented, that the *ancien régime* was a time of 'servility and subservience'. The 'art' of silencing dissent was far less perfected than it had later become. To that extent there was more freedom than now existed—the soul was kept free—but 'it was a kind of freedom that was irregular and intermittent, always constrained within the limits of a class, always linked to the idea of exception and privilege'.[226] If it served a function in preparing the French to overthrow despotism, 'it perhaps made them less suited than any other people to establish in its place the free and peaceable empire of law'.[227] When taken together, Tocqueville seemed to suggest, the combined weight of these factors was such as to indicate that the outcome of the Revolution was predetermined. We should not be surprised, he speculated, by the ease with which centralization had been re-established at the beginning of the nineteenth century: 'The men of 89 had toppled the building but its foundations had remained in the very souls of its destroyers and upon these foundations it was possible to raise it up anew and to build it more solidly than ever before.'[228]

All that remained to be done was to assess the immediate causes and precise character of the Revolution. Here Tocqueville returned his readers to one of the original questions that had informed analyses of the Revolution: what had been the role played by men of letters? In Tocqueville's opinion, it had been a very significant one. Despite their disagreements, Tocqueville argued, the political programmes of the writers of the eighteenth century all agreed on the need to replace the old order with one grounded upon a set of simple and general principles derived from reason and natural law. Given the injustice and absurdities of the world they saw around them, Tocqueville conceded, it could hardly have been otherwise. However, Tocqueville next postulated that this predilection for abstract theories and generalizations was a reflection of their social and political marginality. They simply lacked experience of the real world and, as a consequence, failed to appreciate the obstacles that stood in the way of even the most laudable and seemingly straightforward reforms. The same ignorance of the everyday realities

---

[224] Ibid. 135.   [225] Ibid. 158.   [226] Ibid. 176.
[227] Ibid. 177.   [228] Ibid. 138.

of politics among the French in general provided a wider public receptive to these ideas, with the result that the entire nation ended up adopting the attitudes and tastes of the men of letters. 'Little by little', Tocqueville observed, 'there was built up an imaginary society in which everything appeared simple and coordinated, uniform, equitable and in accordance with reason.'[229] Moreover, it was precisely this fondness for abstract theory and ingenious preconceived institutions that had inspired the Revolution to believe that society could be reordered from top to bottom following the rules of logic.

To this 'frightening sight' needed to be added two further dimensions of the thinking of the men of letters. The first was the widespread and virulent anti-religious sentiment that came to prevail in France. Nowhere else had irreligion become such 'a general, ardent, intolerant, and oppressive passion'.[230] To those who deified reason an institution for which tradition was fundamental could only be worthy of contempt. In Tocqueville's opinion, 'the universal discredit' suffered by religion was to shape the character of the Revolution in a decisive and prepon-derant way. The result of overthrowing religious institutions and government at the same time, Tocqueville argued, was that 'the human mind entirely lost its direction; it no longer knew what to hold on to nor where to stop'.[231] As a consequence, a new species of revolutionary appeared who took audacity to the point of madness and, lacking scruples, hesitated before no innovation. These 'new beings', Tocque-ville commented, were not 'ephemeral creations of the moment': they had perpe-tuated themselves and were still with us.

Tocqueville's next allegation was that the men of letters had taught the French to prize reform before freedom. This claim rested upon the unusual argument that the most substantial reforms of the Revolution had been announced in the writings of the physiocrats. Why Tocqueville sought to argue this becomes clear when we see that, in his view, the physiocrats were not only completely contemptuous of the past but were also of the opinion that 'it was not a question of destroying absolute power but of converting it' to a more appropriate use.[232] It was the function of the State to reform and transform both society and the nation and to achieve that end they set little store upon political liberty. For that reason, the French came to embrace a set of ideas that were antithetical to free institutions such that, when at last a love of freedom awoke among them, they found that they had accepted 'as an ideal society a people without any other aristocracy than that of public function-aries, with a single and all-powerful administration directing affairs of State and acting as the guardian of all individuals'.[233] It was this attempt to superimpose liberty upon the institutions of a servile state, Tocqueville concluded, that ex-plained why, for the last sixty years, so many vain attempts to establish free government had been followed by disastrous revolutions. Fatigued, the French were now content to live as equals.

---

[229] *Œuvres complètes*, ii/1. *L'Ancien Régime et la Révolution*, 199.
[230] Ibid. 202.   [231] Ibid. 208.
[232] Ibid. 212.   [233] Ibid. 216.

How, finally, were these ideas turned into action? Tocqueville highlighted three factors. First, and contrary to what had been imagined, the very prosperity of Louis XVI's reign hastened revolution by raising expectations. Second, well-intentioned and disinterested efforts to improve the welfare of the people only served to fuel their resentment and increase their desires. Third, the monarchy itself employed practices that were 'hostile to the individual, contrary to private rights, and friendly to violence'.[234] 'The *ancien régime*', Tocqueville commented, 'provided the Revolution with many of its methods: the latter only added the savagery of its spirit.'[235] When, therefore, administrative reform was introduced, this set in motion a process that led to 'the greatest upheaval and the most frightening confusion there ever was'.[236]

Thus the Revolution was inevitable and so, Tocqueville suggested, was the contrast between theory and practice, good intentions and violent acts, which marked its course. However, what Tocqueville chose to highlight by way of conclusion was that the eighteenth century had given rise to two ruling passions. The first, with deeper roots and of longer standing, was an intense hatred of inequality. The second, of more recent origin, was a zeal for liberty. In 1789, these two passions coalesced, the French believing that they could be equal in their freedom. Free institutions existed alongside democratic institutions, and 'centralization fell with absolute government'.[237] Yet, with the passing of the 'vigorous generation' that had begun the Revolution, the love of liberty subsided amidst 'anarchy and popular dictatorship' and the taste for equality prevailed. And so 'from the very bowels of a nation that had just overthrown the monarchy suddenly emerged a power more extensive, more detailed, and more absolute than that exercised by any of our kings'.[238] From this point onwards, Tocqueville concluded, the French had limited themselves to 'placing the head of Liberty upon a servile body'.[239]

Contained within *L'Ancien Régime et la Révolution* was a passionate plea for individual liberty as an end in itself. Yet this very same book served as an explanation of the failure of liberty to secure a solid foundation and sustained existence in France. Seen thus, the anomaly in Tocqueville's account was the moment of 'greatness' and 'virility', the 'time of immortal memory' as he described it, when the call for liberty, long submerged beneath despotism, all-too-briefly made its voice heard above the clamour for vengeance. It was a moment that almost defied explanation, such was the weight that Tocqueville attributed to the prevailing tradition of centralization and its eradication of countervailing trends. This perhaps explains the peculiar passage at the very end of the book where Tocqueville spoke of the unique character of the French people. No nation was so full of contrasts, so changeable, so routine-bound, and so capable of coming above or below the 'common norms of humanity'. France alone, Tocqueville wrote, 'could give birth to a revolution so sudden, so radical, so impetuous in its course and yet so full of reverses, contradictory facts and contrary examples'.[240] But the reality, as he himself acknowledged, was that, for all its frequent revival in new and unexpected forms, the desire for liberty quickly succumbed before a love of equality that remained

---

[234] Ibid. 232.   [235] Ibid. 235.   [236] Ibid. 243.
[237] Ibid. 248.   [238] Ibid.   [239] Ibid.   [240] Ibid. 250.

constant. Such, at least, was how it appeared to Tocqueville from deep within the Second Empire of Napoleon III.

Tocqueville, like so many of his fellow historians, could not resist asserting the unique and exceptional character of the Revolution. He was, on the other hand, immune from the commonly held faith in the virtues of the people and plainly saw little evidence of the Revolution as the dawn of a new religion of justice and fraternity. Indeed, with the notable exception of the summer of 1789, Tocqueville appears to have discerned few signs of political innovation among the momentous events that shook France to her very foundations. However, Tocqueville was to be by no means alone in stressing the theme of continuity. As we have seen, Quinet, under the influence of Tocqueville, was to rework the idea in order to suggest that the Revolution marked a revival of monarchical absolutism. Another person to develop this theme was the diplomatic historian Albert Sorel. [241] 'The fact is', Sorel wrote, almost three decades later, 'that the Revolution did not, as has too often been said, break the chain of French history.'[242] Although probably the most remarkable of episodes, it was nonetheless only 'one episode' in that history. Indeed, Sorel ended the introduction to his *L'Europe et la Révolution française* by emphasizing that this was the very point of his eight-volume study. 'I should consider my work not to have been useless', he observed, 'if I had attained the following result: to have shown the French Revolution, which to some has appeared as the subversion and to others as the regeneration of the old European world, to be the natural and necessary consequence of the history of Europe and to have established that this Revolution produced no consequence, not even the most surprising, that does not flow from this history and is not explicable by the precedents of the *ancien régime*.'[243]

With regard to the internal dynamics of the Revolution, Sorel's argument built upon a set of insights gleaned from Tocqueville. In 1789, he believed, everything was ready for revolution. The *ancien régime* was in decay; the government was bankrupt and powerless; men of letters displayed a mixture of fanaticism and doctrinal infatuation; and 'a wild frenzy was brewing among the masses'. Above all, Sorel wrote, 'the spirit of the Third Estate was that of the lawyers'.[244] It was they who were to turn the ideas of the *philosophes* into legislation and by choosing its representatives from among this group 'the people were appropriating and continuing the traditions of the crown'.[245] True to these traditions, if sovereignty passed from the monarch to the people, the lawyers attributed to the new sovereign all the qualities of the old one. 'At bottom', Sorel commented, 'things returned to the point from which they had started.'[246] The State remained what it had always

---

[241] On Albert Sorel, see *L'Europe et la Révolution française: Discours prononcés le 29 mars 1905 à la fête en l'honneur de M. Albert Sorel* (1905). Of particular interest are the texts by Emile Boutmy and Gabriel Hanotaux: ibid. 23–61.

[242] *L'Europe et la Révolution française* (1885), i. 238.

[243] Ibid. 8.

[244] Ibid. 221.

[245] Ibid.

[246] Ibid. 222.

been and 'the spirit of the old government reappeared in the very institutions intended to destroy it'.[247] Thus, the National Assembly 'promptly' set about concentrating all power in its own hands; and when, through 'force of circumstances', abstract ideals were abandoned, 'traditional forms of behaviour and ideas prevailed'. None were on the side of liberty and they provided countless precedents for despotism. 'Thus', Sorel wrote, 'in the guise of expedients all the procedures of the *ancien régime* insinuated themselves into the Revolution.'[248] Once returned, they remained uncontested, and power came to be concentrated in ever fewer hands, from a Committee of twelve to a Directory of five, from a Consulate of three to an Empire of one.

Sorel gave many examples of the continuities in practice that this entailed. Two might be cited here. The first concerned the Revolution's treatment of the Church. Despite the appearance of innovation the Revolution 'quite simply applied to the clergy and to recalcitrant Catholics measures which the monarchy had employed against heretics'.[249] Revolutionary legislation merely copied the edicts of Louis XIV against the Protestants. The second example related to the Terror. It could not be said that the abuses and excesses of the *ancien régime* produced the Terror but they did 'all derive from the same source'. The 'terrorists' had had no intention of avenging the victims of Louis XIV but 'the same fanaticism produced the same results'. 'Considered in this way', Sorel wrote, 'the Terror is stripped of the sophistical prestige with which its retrospective apologists have tried to surround it. The only striking thing that remains is the extent of its plagiarism.'[250]

Given that the *ancien régime* had no pretensions to liberty and that the Revolution had so readily aped its customs and practices, it would have been 'truly extraordinary', Sorel concluded, if the Revolution had marked the 'triumph of liberty'. The cause for regret was that, if the *ancien régime* had been 'self-consistent' in its despotism, the 'terrorists' had been 'humanitarian and sentimental' in theory and 'barbarous' in practice.[251] It was this contradiction that the world had seen.

However, Sorel's exploration of the theme of continuity merits particular attention because his primary focus was upon foreign policy. His fundamental point was that 'for external as well as internal affairs there had existed permanent historical necessities' and that these had been played out during the Revolution.[252] This argument was developed by Sorel in the first of his eight volumes and then summarized in a conclusion which, in his words, provided 'the basic structure of this history'.[253] Sorel's thesis was that French foreign policy was determined by geography and, therefore, by the need to establish secure frontiers. This was a constant from the Capetian monarchs onwards and it produced what Sorel termed the 'classic system' of French diplomacy. Its essential principle was moderation and compromise and a recognition that in foreign undertakings there were certain limits beyond which it was unwise to go and which would not be tolerated by her neighbours. Henri IV and Richelieu were the primary exemplars of this tradition. Alongside this, on the other hand, were a set of contrary instincts, described by

---

[247] Ibid. 223.   [248] Ibid. 225.   [249] Ibid. 230.   [250] Ibid. 232–3.
[251] Ibid. 233.   [252] Ibid. 242.   [253] Ibid. 537–52.

Sorel as 'gusts of romantic ambition, an intoxication with conquest and a capricious taste for glory and adventure'.[254] This 'craving for the impossible' was best exemplified (with disastrous results) by the military excesses of Louis XIV. Sorel's point was that these two instincts had coexisted over the centuries and that the Revolution brought each of them into operation in turn.

In essence, Sorel's claim was the National Assembly of 1789 sought to continue the policies of moderation and that there was nothing in the new political principles of the Revolution that was not compatible with peace across Europe. The Revolution had renounced the right of conquest for the reasons which 'self-interest rightly understood, prudence and reflection had suggested to the most far-seeing diplomats of the *ancien régime*'.[255] Moreover, if 'honestly applied', the 'one basic principle of the Revolution', sovereignty of the people, would have prevented 'all the abuses of conquest'. Every nation would have had the right to determine its own fate.

Sorel next suggested, however, that neither France nor Europe were ready for such a radical reform of political habits and thus 'the spirit of proselytism quickly came to dominate the Revolution; the idea of conquest continued to prevail in Europe; and a bitter war followed'.[256] By the time that peace again became possible in 1795 those who now ruled had 'transferred to the people all the qualities that their predecessors had attributed to the majesty of the king: they incited them to pursue glory, urged them to war, and founded on their passions the power they exercised in their name'.[257] In short, by embarking upon a war of conquest the Revolution deviated from 'the true French tradition' and recklessly endangered France's permanent interests. If this signified that the revolutionaries were following 'impulses as old as French history', it also meant that the Republic was handed over to the generals and that France committed herself to an expansion that she was incapable of supporting. As Sorel concluded, the result could only ever have been self-destruction. The sole remedy, therefore, was for France 'to revive the policies drawn up by the wisest of her ministers on the eve of the Revolution' and it was this that had been done 'after twenty-two years of relentless struggle' and when France had been 'defeated by the enemies allied against her'.

Many nineteenth-century histories of the Revolution devoted considerable space to the wars engaged upon by the Republic and the Empire. In these accounts, the achievement of military glory frequently figured as a compensation for domestic failure and the abandonment of revolutionary ideals. To an extent, Sorel mirrored this perspective, stating that it was in war that the Revolution 'secured its most astonishing achievements'. But, he added, 'this was its greatness and its ruin'.[258] In the main body of his history, therefore, Sorel displayed no sympathy for the view that the Terror had saved France from her external enemies nor did he countenance a justification of revolutionary war as a means of defeating counter-revolutionary forces. Rather, what he emphasized repeatedly was that the vices of the Revolution were a legacy of the past. So, for Sorel, it was not only the internal causes leading to the degeneration of France into 'bloody anarchy' that had existed before 1789: the

---

[254] *L'Europe et la Révolution française* (1885), 242–3.
[255] Ibid. 318.   [256] Ibid. 318–19.   [257] Ibid. 319.   [258] Ibid. 242.

same was true of the tendency to despotism and conquest in foreign affairs. 'The Revolution of 1789', Sorel wrote, 'was easily reconcilable with policy of Henri IV and Richelieu but not that of Louis XIV.' Such, however, had been the 'strange destiny' of the Revolution.[259]

Albert Sorel had been exceptionally well placed to undertake his study of the international dimensions of the Revolution. From 1866 to 1875 he had held an appointment in the Ministry of Foreign Affairs, after which he obtained a teaching post at the newly established École Libre des Sciences Politiques. Early in his academic career he wrote several works of diplomatic history, most notably studies of the partition of Poland and of the Franco-Prussian war, before embarking upon his history of the Revolution, a task completed only in 1904. Sorel also wrote book-length studies of both Montesquieu and Madame de Staël. The political views he espoused, as might be surmised, were those of a conservative and moderate republicanism, and as such mirrored those of his academic colleagues in Paris.

That same institution, founded by Émile Boutmy, also remained deeply indebted to the influence of Alexis de Tocqueville. This merits comment because in this period both Tocqueville's work and his reputation were quickly consigned to oblivion.[260] In truth, this fate befell *De la Démocratie en Amérique* long before it did *L'Ancien Régime et la Révolution*, but the institutionalization of the study of the Revolution—symbolized through the creation of a chair in the history of Revolution at the Sorbonne in 1891 and the founding of the Société de l'Histoire de la Révolution française—engendered a method of inquiry and perspective widely at odds with that exemplified by Tocqueville. University lecture courses on the Revolution were now deemed permissible because the Third Republic believed itself to have been established upon sound institutional and political foundations. Moreover, as Françoise Mélonio remarks, 'teaching revolutionary history was part of a republican strategy to give the Republic the halo of a glorious birth'.[261] Michelet, and not Tocqueville, was to provide the republican textbook.[262]

V

The first holder of the chair in the history of the Revolution was Alphonse Aulard and it was to be him, more than any one else, who provided the Third Republic with the history it required. To achieve that end, however, he had to remove the towering figure of Hippolyte Taine from the field of revolutionary historiography. Taine was the author of the monumental *Les Origines de la France contemporaine*. Its eleven volumes were subdivided into three parts. Two volumes devoted to *L'Ancien Régime* appeared in 1875. This was followed by six volumes on *La*

---

[259] Ibid. 552.
[260] Mélonio, 'Introduction' 149–88.
[261] Ibid. 171.
[262] For the centenary celebrations in 1889 a government subsidy was provided to republish Michelet's history of the Revolution. On the emergence of this distinctively Third Republic analysis of the Revolution see Paul Farmer, *France Reviews its Revolutionary Origins* (1944), 37–45.

Révolution, published in 1878–84 and three concluding volumes, *La France mo-derne*, in 1891 and 1893. At the very moment of the Third Republic's triumph, Taine painted an unforgettable picture of the Revolution as nothing else but bloodthirsty anarchy and horror.

As the controversy surrounding the publication of Quinet's *La Révolution* indicates, the 1860s saw no diminution in the importance attached to rival interpretations of the Revolution. The year of the publication of Quinet's history also saw the appearance of the first volume of Ernest Hamel's *Histoire de Robespierre d'après des papiers de famille, les sources originales et des documents entièrement inédits.*[263] Claiming to be guided by a spirit of 'impartiality' and to be the first study that provided a 'day-by-day' account of Robespierre's life, its conclusion was that posterity would one day place Robespierre 'amongst the martyrs of humanity'. In marked contrast, the middle years of the decade saw the publication of the first volumes of Mortimer-Ternaux's anti-revolutionary *Histoire de la Terreur*[264] and of Jules Sauzay's heartfelt account of the Revolution's attack upon the Church, *Histoire de la Persécution Révolutionnaire dans le département du Doubs de 1789 à 1801.*[265] Both were to be read by Taine. Then, in the aftermath of military defeat and humiliation, came the Paris Commune, an event which, for some (including Taine), bore a very unwelcome resemblance to the events of 1793. What this violent and destructive episode revealed, Henri Wallon wrote in *La Terreur, Études critiques sur l'histoire* (1873), was that the Terror required only a propitious moment to make its return and that the 'sinister' people associated with it were not 'phantasms of the past'. Émile Montégut, writing in the prestigious *Revue des Deux Mondes*,[266] argued that the Commune demonstrated that 'the bankruptcy of the French Revolution' was 'an irrevocable and established fact'. Taine was to be of a very similar opinion.

Any hope that the debate might diminish in intensity was dispelled as France began its preparations for the commemoration of the centenary of 1789. If the central parts of Taine's history were now in print, the period 1886–90 saw the publication of over 100 new books on the Revolution.[267] Dated 1 January, the first to appear in 1889 was a work by the Bishop of Angers which, having dissected the errors of revolutionary ideology, denounced the Revolution as 'the most disastrous event in our national history'.[268] By way of response, a veritable deluge of articles, brochures, reviews, biographies, and books sought to popularize the official message that, despite regrettable excesses, the achievements of the Revolution were to be celebrated and its heritage defended. Nevertheless, there was some very thin ice to

---

[263] (1865). The next 2 vols. were publ. in 1866 and 1867.
[264] 7 vols. (1862–91). The message was that France had been saved *despite* the Terror.
[265] 6 vols. (1867–73).
[266] 'Où en est la Révolution française: simples notes sur la situation actuelle', *Revue des Deux Mondes*, 41 (5 Aug. 1871), 872–98.
[267] For reviews of a selection of the books publ. during 1889 see 'Bibliographie du centenaire', *La Réforme sociale et le Centenaire de la Révolution* (1889), 173–85.
[268] Mgr Charles Freppel, *La Révolution française à propos du centenaire de 1789* (1889), 139. Some nine years earlier Mgr Freppel had written a preface to a remarkable book by P. Ubald de Chanday, *Les Trois Frances* (1880). The France of the Revolution was categorized as 'la France satanique'.

be skated over[269] and, regardless of the statues unveiled, dinners enjoyed, ceremonies held, and an Eiffel Tower built, the experience was by no means an unalloyed success. The admirers of the *revanchist* General Boulanger could not be dissuaded from describing the Republic as a 'Bastille parlementaire' that needed to be stormed anew and the emerging socialist press complained repeatedly about a Revolution betrayed by the bourgeoisie.[270]

Nor did calm return with the ending of the centenary. On 24 January 1891 the Comédie-Française, the very pinnacle of the French theatrical establishment, gave its first performance of a play by Victorien Sardou titled *Thermidor*. It told a simple but controversial tale. The action took place on the eve of the fall of Robespierre and brought together two old friends, Labussière and Martial Hugon, the former recounting how, as a minor official in the *bureau des détenus*, he had sought to save those who were innocent from execution. Recently returned from the front, Martial was seeking to find his lover. As the action unfolds we see that neither man can save her from the guillotine. Martial dies in the process and Labussière is reduced to despair. At the heart of the play is a conversation between the two men that reveals the gulf separating sincere and courageous republicans prepared to defend their country from the Parisian and Jacobin world of denunciations, suspicion, and cruelty. The question posed was whether such a world was worth fighting for?

For his pains Sardou was roundly denounced as a reactionary who had written a reactionary play.[271] However, the most significant (and subsequently famous) response came only five days later when the radical parliamentary deputy Georges Clemenceau stood before the parliamentary Chamber of Deputies and there denounced those on the right who, in his view, sought to mutilate the legacy of the Revolution. 'Messieurs', he proclaimed, 'whether we wish it or not, whether it pleases or shocks us, the French Revolution is a block, a block from which nothing can be severed because historical truth does not permit it.'[272] In brief, to support the Third Republic was to accept the Revolution, to endorse the principles of 1789, *and* to sanction the Terror. To do otherwise was to support the Revolution's enemies and to challenge the republican message that the Revolution constituted the founding moment of modern France. In that same year, Taine expressed the contrary view that it was Napoleon Bonaparte who had made modern France.[273]

Hippolyte Taine was one of the great literary figures of the second half of the nineteenth century.[274] Born in 1828, in the years before the Paris Commune he

---

[269] It proved difficult to come to an agreement about which dates were to be celebrated.

[270] See Marc Angenot, *Le Centenaire de la révolution: 1889* (1989) and Pascal Ory, 'Le Centenaire de la Révolution française', in Pierre Nora (ed.), *Les Lieux de mémoire* (1984), i. 465–92.

[271] See e.g. Edmond Bourgeois, *Thermidor: Réponse à la pièce de Victorien Sardou* (1891). For a contrary view see Ernest Desmarest, *Thermidor et la pièce de M. Sardou* (1891). Sardou's play was quickly removed from the stage.

[272] Quoted in Bétourné and Hartig, *Penser l'histoire de la Révolution* (1989), 94 n. 1.

[273] Taine, *Les Origines de la France contemporaine* (1900–2), i. 4.

[274] Given the precipitous decline in Taine's reputation relatively little recent scholarship has been devoted to him: however, see Susanna Barrows, 'Hippolyte Taine and the Spectre of the Commune', *Distorting Mirrors: Visions of the Crowd in Late Nineteenth-Century France* (New Haven, Conn., 1981), 73–92, and Eric Gasparini, *La Pensée politique d'Hippolyte Taine: Entre traditionalisme et libéralisme* (Aix-en-Provence, 1993).

published works on English literature,[275] Italian, Flemish, and Greek art, French
philosophy,[276] and human psychology.[277] For good measure, he also published a
novel and accounts of his travels. Elected a member of the Académie Française,
Taine was appointed professor of aesthetics at the École des Beaux-Arts. Like
Tocqueville, Taine turned late to the writing of history and he too failed to
complete the masterpiece that, for good or ill, was to define his reputation.[278]
Like Tocqueville, he studied the past primarily to understand the present and its
many discontents.

No republican, Taine greeted the Franco-Prussian war with ill-disguised fore-
boding. This turned to horror and despair with the inauguration of the Paris
Commune on 17 March 1871. 'I am very sad and very discouraged', he wrote to
his mother four days later; 'the future looks very black, but what is worse, it is
impossible to know what lays hidden beneath this darkness'.[279] Not long afterwards he concluded that it was to be 'a return to barbarism and the dangers of
primitive anarchy', describing Paris as 'a pandemonium'.[280] In May 1871 Taine
left for England and it was in the Oxford University library that he learnt of the
fighting in Paris. The defeated Communards, he wrote to his wife, were miserable
wretches, savage wolves, brigands who placed themselves beyond the pale of
humanity.[281] No sooner was he back in Paris than he began the long and laborious
research for *Les Origines de la France contemporaine*, convinced that to comprehend
the current disorder it was necessary to return to the crisis of the *ancien régime* and
to the Revolution. This was the issue that was to preoccupy him for the best part of
the next twenty years until his death in 1893.

Taine had made his reputation through the application of scientific method to
fields previously dominated by the traditions of classical studies. His most famous
statement of this commitment came in the introduction to his *Histoire de la
littérature anglaise* of 1863.[282] He there argued that, in the course of the previous
century, the writing of history had been revolutionized, first through the extension
of historical imagination,[283] and then through the use of observation and experiment to understand the inner psychology of human beings. According to this
methodology, the actions of individuals or groups of persons were as amenable to
causal explanation as any event in the natural world. As Taine famously remarked:
'No matter if the facts be physical or moral: they all have their causes; there is a
cause for ambition, for courage, for truth, as there is for digestion, for muscular
movement, for animal heat. Vice and virtue are products just like vitriol and

---

[275] *Histoire de la littérature anglaise*, 4 vols. (1863–4).
[276] *Les Philosophes français du XXe siècle* (1857).
[277] *De l'Intelligence*, 2 vols. (1870).
[278] Alfred Cobban said of Taine that he was 'perhaps the greatest of bad historians': 'Hippolyte
Taine, Historian of the French Revolution', *History*, 53 (1968), 331.
[279] *H. Taine: Sa vie et correspondance* (1905), iii. 68.
[280] Ibid. 75.
[281] Ibid. 128–9.
[282] *Histoire de la littérature anglaise*, i, pp. i–xlviii. See also the Preface to Taine's *Essais de Critique et
d'Histoire* (1858), pp. i–xv.
[283] By way of example, Taine cited Lessing, Walter Scott, Chateaubriand, Thierry, and Michelet.

sugar.'[284] Taine further specified that the three primary determinants of human behaviour were 'la race, le milieu, le moment'[285] and that these provided the key to an understanding of the mental habits of a people. The writing of history, therefore, was not primarily narration but a form of applied psychology.[286]

Upon their appearance in 1875, the first volumes of *Les Origines de la France contemporaine* greatly displeased monarchist opinion for there was described a venal Church, an ornamental nobility, and a vain and arbitrary monarchy. They also provided a portrayal of a people brutalized by misery and ignorance, prone to displays of blind rage, and of limited political capacity. 'Every object', Taine wrote, 'appears to them in a false light. They are like children who, at every turn of the road, see in each tree or bush, some frightful apparition.'[287] However, those same volumes also began the description of a 'spirit and doctrine' which Taine took to be distinctively French and which, in his view, provided the ideological driving force of the Revolution. While the *esprit classique* that had underpinned French civilization had been held in check by religious belief and by the authority of the monarchy, Taine argued, it had produced such wonders as the gardens of Versailles, but, set free from these restraints, as the eighteenth century progressed it had generated an entirely abstract and rational conception of man and, from this, a vision of politics based upon mathematical models. The philosophy of the eighteenth century, Taine wrote, resembled a religion: it had 'the same impetus of faith, hope, and enthusiasm, the same spirit of propaganda and domination, the same severity and intolerance, the same ambition to recast man and to remodel all human life according to a preconceived plan'.[288]

Taine's rejoinder to this simplified logic, to what he termed 'la raison raison-nante', was to outline an entirely different vision of the human condition. 'Not only', Taine wrote, 'is reason not natural to man or universal in humanity, but in the conduct of man its influence is small.'[289] In most cases, our actions were guided by 'physical temperament, bodily needs, animal instinct, hereditary prejudice, imagination' and, above all, 'personal self-interest'.[290] Nor was it correct to imagine that people were naturally good. In human beings there was 'an enduring substra-tum of brutality and ferocity, of violent and destructive instincts'.[291] Given the paucity of resources provided by an 'intractable earth', our constant preoccupation was 'to acquire, to amass, to possess'. Finally, our fertile minds were such as to turn our incessant dreams into 'monstrous chimeras' and to exaggerate our 'fears, hopes, and desires'. From this arose, 'especially if he were French', sudden outbursts of emotion, irresistible passions, epidemics of credulity and suspicion, enthusiasm and panic.[292] These, Taine argued, were the 'brute forces which governed human life'. In normal circumstances they remained hidden but the truth was that, like a flood, the havoc and destruction they caused were only restrained by an equal force. 'To control and limit their blows', Taine wrote, 'various mechanisms are employed: a

---

[284] *Histoire de la littérature anglaise*, i, p. xv.   [285] Ibid., pp. xxii–xxiii.
[286] Ibid., p. xliii.   [287] *Origines de la France contemporaine*, ii. 277.
[288] Ibid. 2.   [289] Ibid. 59.   [290] Ibid. 60.
[291] Ibid.   [292] Ibid. 61.

pre-established constitution, the division of powers, a code of laws, tribunals and legal formalities. Behind all these wheels of government always appears the final appeal, the efficient instrument, namely the gendarme armed against the savage, the brigand, the madman that each of us conceals, asleep or enchained, but always alive, in the recesses of his own breast.'[293]

The problem with the 'new theory', Taine continued, was that all its principles and precepts were directed against the gendarme. In the name of the sovereignty of the people, government was deprived of all authority, initiative, and power. Yet, by the same token, it also led to 'the unlimited dictatorship of the State'.[294] A new contract, agreed upon by perfectly free and equal individuals, was deemed to supersede all other contracts and all other claims to rights—be they those of property, family, or Church—were as naught before the new State. In the 'democratic convent' modelled on Sparta and Rome, 'the individual is nothing'.[295] What would this mean when theory was put into practice? 'The dogma of the sovereignty of the people, when interpreted by the crowd', Taine wrote, 'will produce perfect anarchy, until such point when, interpreted by its leaders, it will produce a perfect despotism.'[296] This, in Taine's view, was exactly what had occurred in the Revolution.

In the most marvellously expressive prose, Taine described the descent of France into 'spontaneous anarchy'. What began in 1789 was the very dissolution of society. The craving for bread degenerated into murder and incendiarism, the people acting like a 'blind colossus'. As the fermentation increased, the agitators sat in permanent session, the 'dictatorship of the mob' striking out at anything that resisted it. The dregs of society came to the surface. 'Like a tame elephant which suddenly becomes wild again', Taine wrote, 'in a flourish the people throw off their ordinary keeper and the new guides that it tolerates perched on its neck are there simply for show; henceforth, it will move along as it pleases, freed from their control, and guided by its own feelings, instincts, and appetites.'[297] The storming of the Bastille was nothing else but an example of how popular insurrection turned frenzy into ferocity. Scarcely had the gates been entered than the work of destruction began. 'Suddenly', Taine announced, 'we see spring forth the barbarian, still worse, the primitive animal, the grinning, sanguinary and lustful ape, who chuckles while he kills and gambols over the ruins he has created.'[298] Such, Taine wrote, was the 'actual government' to which France had been given up.

For page upon page, chapter upon chapter, Taine continued in similar vein, the tone only changing when he described how the National Assembly, operating like 'an academy of utopians' rather than a 'legislature of practitioners',[299] began the process of turning spontaneous anarchy into 'legal anarchy'.[300] With great obstinacy it had refused to consider the 'real man' before its very eyes and had persisted in writing a constitution for 'the abstract beings found in books'. It was 'a masterpiece of speculative reason and of practical unreason'.[301] Meanwhile, the people set about

---

[293] *Origines de la France contemporaine*, 62.
[294] Ibid. 65.   [295] Ibid. 68.   [296] Ibid. 65.   [297] Ibid. iii. 61.
[298] Ibid. 84.   [299] Ibid. iv. 44.   [300] Ibid. 47.   [301] Ibid.

'the voluntary destruction of property'. It was this passion, Taine wrote, that gave the Revolution its 'enduring energy, its primary impulse'.[302]

It was from this 'social decomposition' that the Jacobins emerged and, like 'mushrooms out of compost', began the conquest of power. Their programme, Taine recognized, amounted to the regeneration of society and of man. The vehicle of this 'liberating operation' was to be 'an omnipotent State' exercising unlimited jurisdiction. No freedom was to be left to the individual. Again the quality of Taine's prose is masterful. 'Nothing', Taine wrote, 'is now clearer than the object of government: it is to subject the wicked to the good, or, which is briefer, to suppress the wicked. To this end let us employ confiscation, imprisonment, deportation, drowning and the guillotine. Against traitors, all means are permitted and meritorious; the Jacobin has canonized his murders and now he kills out of philanthropy.'[303] The Jacobins massacred, he observed, 'with the same impunity and as methodically as cleaning the streets or killing stray dogs'.[304]

It was, however, in his psychological portraits of those whom he believed to have led the Revolution—Marat 'the lunatic', Danton 'the barbarian', and Robespierre 'the incurable, insignificant rhetorician'—that Taine excelled himself. Of the three, Taine wrote, Marat was 'the most monstrous'. He displayed 'furious exaltation, constant excitement, feverish activity, an inexhaustible propensity for writing, that automatism of the mind and tetanus of the will under the constraint and rule of a fixed idea and, in addition to this, the usual physical symptoms such as sleeplessness, a livid tint, bad blood, foulness of person and dress'. In short, Marat was subject to 'homicidal mania'.[305] There was, Taine conceded, 'nothing of the madman about Danton'. Nonetheless, he possessed 'the air of an exterminator'. It was Danton who was the first to understand that the ultimate object of the Revolution was 'the dictatorship of the violent minority' and that its means were those of 'popular brutality'.[306] As for Robespierre, he was a pedant and a prig. 'No mind, in its mediocrity and incompetence', Taine wrote, 'so well harmonizes with the spirit of the times.' The very reverse of a statesman, Robespierre 'soars in empty space, surrounded by abstractions'.[307] In his 'elaborate eloquence' there was nothing but 'the recipes of a worn-out art, Greek and Roman commonplaces'. It was only natural that he should see himself as being persecuted and as a martyr. This, Taine concluded, 'is the exterior of the Revolution, a specious mask, and this, what was hidden beneath it, a hideous face; under the nominal guise of a humanitarian theory it covers the effective dictatorship of evil and base passions; in its true representative, as in itself, we everywhere see ferocity surface from philanthropy and from the pedant appears the executioner'.[308] In sum, the Jacobins were madmen and fanatics and the Revolution was an episode of collective insanity.

The Jacobin Republic, Taine wrote, came to an end not only because of its murders but, above all, because it was not 'born viable'. It had within itself 'a principle of dissolution, an innate and mortal poison'. It lacked, Taine argued, the essential principle required for the maintenance of all political societies: 'the respect

---

[302] Ibid. 173.   [303] Ibid. v. 37.   [304] Ibid. vi. 7.
[305] Ibid. vii. 198.   [306] Ibid. 225.   [307] Ibid. 233.   [308] Ibid. 272.

of its members for each other'.[309] The habits of trust and confidence between governed and governors did not exist. As a consequence, the social body disintegrated and 'and among the millions of disaggregated atoms there remains not one nucleus of spontaneous cohesion and stable coordination'.[310] In such circumstances, 'civil France' could not reconstruct itself. The same, however, was not true of 'military France'. Here, Taine wrote, 'men have put each other to the test; they are devoted to each other, subordinates to leaders, leaders to subordinates, and all to one great work'.[311] They had everything that was lacking in revolutionary institutions. 'Let a famous general appear', therefore, and he will be followed and when, 'to his own advantage', he acts to save the Republic 'the whole of civil France will welcome its liberator, its protector, its restorer'.[312] To that end, the 'master' chose despotism and all his great works—the civil code, the university, the Concordat, the centralized administration—tended towards the omnipotence of the State and the omnipresence of government. Never, Taine remarked, had finer and more symmetrical barracks been built and none were more adapted to narrow egoism and the lowest elements of human nature. 'In this philosophical barracks', Taine concluded, 'we have lived for eighty years.'[313]

Between 1905 and 1907 Alphonse Aulard took time out from his own historical researches to give two sets of lectures at the Sorbonne devoted (in a spirit of 'impartiality') to demolishing the reputation of Hippolyte Taine as a serious historian of the Revolution.[314] The catalogue of deficiencies detailed by Aulard ranged *inter alia* from factual errors, inadequate sources, negligence, undue haste, unproven assertions, unsubstantiated generalizations, and an uncritical judgement bordering on naivety.[315] Taine, Aulard wrote, showed himself 'little capable of reviewing a text, little capable of providing a true idea of its content, and little capable of methodological exactitude'.[316] But Aulard's complaints amounted to more than the charge of professional incompetence. At bottom, as must surely have been clear to his audience, Aulard took exception to what he termed 'the politico-historical theory' underpinning Taine's vast enterprise. Taine's intention, Aulard argued, had been 'to drive into the mind of the reader the idea that a Revolution, inspired by bad philosophy, could only be calamitous'.[317] Follow tradition and innovate less was its 'conservative conclusion'.

In Aulard's opinion, Taine had failed completely to understand the purposes and goals of the Jacobins,[318] reducing all their actions to pillage and murder inspired by revolutionary utopianism and a retrogressive conception of the State. By way of conclusion, therefore, Aulard did not pull his punches. 'The whole of the Terror', he declared, 'can be explained (I do not say: can be justified) by the circumstances of civil and foreign war in which France then found itself. Taine does not speak of

---

[309] *Origines de la France contemporaine*, 424.   [310] Ibid. 427.
[311] Ibid.   [312] Ibid. 429.   [313] Ibid. 431.
[314] *Taine, Historien de la Révolution Française* (1907).
[315] For a summary of these deficiencies, ibid. 63.
[316] Ibid. 26.
[317] Ibid. 113.
[318] Aulard took particular exception to Taine's description of the Jacobins as crocodiles: ibid. 207.

these circumstances or makes only passing allusion to them.'[319] The means of violence employed by the Montagnards, Aulard continued, were attributed by Taine to philosophical fanaticism alone. He revealed their rage without explaining their anger and thus portrayed it as a form of madness. Consequently, if Taine had intended to renew the history of the Revolution, he had succeeded in adding nothing to what had already been said in the past by 'royalist pamphleteers'. 'When all is said and done', Aulard ended, 'this book and its general conclusions seem almost useless as history.'[320] At best, it served to enlighten us on the intellectual biography of Taine himself and on that of some of his disciples. Thus damned with faint praise, what did Aulard intend to put in its place?

An important early clue was visible in a short study he published in 1884 devoted to the guillotined Georges Danton.[321] For Aulard, Danton was the true hero of the Revolution. Not only was he a good man—against Danton's detractors, Aulard painted a picture of someone who was honest, loyal to his friends, incapable of hatred, and devoted to both his widowed mother and wife—but he was also the person who saved France from her enemies and who, 'through his wisdom and good practical sense', defended a vision of the Republic as a system of government most likely to reconcile order and progress. Without Danton, Aulard commented, 'France, delivered up to anarchy, would not have been able to defend herself against Europe and the Revolution would have been choked in blood'.[322] Had not Robespierre's jealousy of Danton turned to hatred, Aulard argued, France would have been saved from Bonaparte and the return of the Bourbons. Nor would the advent of a 'well-ordered Republic' have been delayed for seventy-five years.

Aulard's *Histoire politique de la Révolution française*[323] was, as its title suggests, a book that left the military, financial, and diplomatic history of the Revolution to one side. 'Every attempt at writing history', he observed, 'is necessarily an abstraction.'[324] It was also, for the most part, chronological in form, recounting the complex events of the time with great clarity, pace, and verve. In Aulard's own opinion, his book had no 'historical thesis' and no 'preconceived idea' to sustain.[325] His was to be an 'objective' narration of the facts. Yet the reader had not to look far to discover either the overall theme or the explicit political message. 'I wish to write', Aulard announced, 'the political history of the Revolution from the point of view of the origin and development of democracy and of the republic.'[326] Having completed his task, he then felt able to assert that 'the facts brought together in this book remove any equivocal meaning from the words: French Revolution'.[327] No longer would it be possible to confuse the principles of the Revolution and the actions conforming to those principles with the period of the Revolution itself and all the actions performed during that time. This 'abusive manner of speaking' had been such as to allow many people to see the Revolution as being in the grip of a 'capricious, sanguinary, and violent' power. 'Now, I think', Aulard wrote, 'the

---

[319] Ibid. 326. [320] Ibid. 330. [321] *Danton* (1884).
[322] Ibid. 54. [323] (1901). [324] Ibid., p. viii.
[325] Ibid. 780. [326] Ibid., p. v. [327] Ibid. 782.

meaning is clearer: the Revolution consists in the Declaration of rights drafted in 1789 and completed in 1793, and in the attempts made to realise this declaration: the counter-revolution consists in the attempts made to prevent the French from acting in accordance with the principles of the Declaration of rights.'[328] The two most important of these principles, Aulard further specified, were those of equality of rights and of national sovereignty. Democracy was the 'logical consequence' of the first and the Republic was the logical consequence of the second.[329] Subsequent French history was an attempt to secure their full realization.

There is little need to set out anything more than the broad outlines of Aulard's narrative. Crucially, he believed that 'on the eve of the Revolution no one dreamt of establishing a republic in France'.[330] There was, in other words, no republican party and no philosophers' plot. So, instead of democracy, the 'men of 1789 established a bourgeois government based upon a property qualification' and instead of a republic they set up a constitutional monarchy.[331] Aulard suggested that much the same state of mind persisted right up to the moment of the king's flight to Varennes in June 1792, the majority of democrats 'considering it a dangerous folly to propose a republic given the ignorance and obliviousness of the masses'.[332] After the king's abortive flight, both 'logic and the future' were on the side of the republic. Given that it had proved impossible to reform the old state of affairs, a sudden and violent revolution was now inevitable. To this was added 'the complexity of circumstances'. 'These conditions of internal and external war', Aulard affirmed, 'imprinted upon the development and application of the principles of 1789 a quality of feverish haste, of improvisation, of contradiction, of violence, and of weakness, especially from 1792 onwards.'[333] The revolutionaries were obliged to legislate for peace in a time of war, for a democratic republic from within a military camp. There could be neither unity of plan nor continuity of method.

Accordingly, Aulard went to great lengths to emphasize that the revolutionary government associated with the Terror 'formed itself empirically, from day to day, out of elements imposed upon it by the successive necessities of national defence and of a people at war against Europe'.[334] The Terror was an 'expedient of war' and one that was always envisaged to be temporary and provisional. As such, it was incorrect to speak of either a 'system' or a 'reign' of terror. For the revolutionaries, Aulard insisted, the Terror amounted to the 'opposite of their dreams and ideals' and was only resorted to in order to secure 'the final triumph of the principles of 1789'.[335]

Aulard, therefore, did not seek to deny that the revolutionary government brought to a close with Robespierre's fall constituted a 'tyrannical dictatorship', but, in his opinion, this experience was an aberration that did nothing to diminish the Revolution's fundamental message of government through law and liberty. Moreover, the full significance of this moment was not properly captured in its

---

[328] Aulard, *Histoire politique*, 78.
[329] Ibid. 5.   [330] Ibid. 28.   [331] Ibid., p. v.
[332] Ibid. 112.   [333] Ibid., p. vi.   [334] Ibid. 357–8.   [335] Ibid. 367.

designation as a provisional expedient. Certain of the measures taken by the revolutionary government, although entirely fortuitous, bore, in Aulard's phrase, 'the mark of preoccupations concerning the future'.[336] This was true of the declaration that the means of subsistence were to be held in common. It was true of the cult of the Supreme Being which, according to Aulard, was 'an attempt to establish one of the essential foundations of the future State'.[337] It was also true of schemes for a national education system. 'This government according to circumstance', Aulard concluded, 'contains the germs and outlines of institutions, the points of departure for new and renovated theories, an element of the France of the future.'[338]

The same theme was evident in the few concluding remarks with which Aulard closed his narrative. The French Revolution, he argued, was not the work of a few distinguished individuals or of a superior generation: it was 'a political, social, and rational ideal which the French have attempted partially to realize'. If the march towards the attainment of that ideal had been, at times, arrested, suspended, abolished, and reversed, it was because the French people had proved 'insufficiently educated to exercise its sovereignty'. To educate the people, therefore, was the true political task of the republicans.

The contrast between Taine and Aulard could not have been starker. The Revolution as pathological crisis and as spontaneous anarchy was countered by a description of 1789 as defence of the nation and as an immanent social and democratic republic. It was, moreover, a contrast broadly representative of tensions and disagreements that had run right through the nineteenth century and one that was heavy with political implications. In this case, conservative liberalism was pitched against moderate republicanism, but, in essence, the questions being fought over remained those of whether the achievements of the Revolution justified its crimes and whether the Revolution was the harbinger of a new society of liberty or a fundamentally evil and destructive event. Was there, for historians at least, a way out of this impasse? One man, Augustin Cochin, believed that there was and to that end in 1909 he published a brilliant essay entitled *La Crise de l'histoire révolutionnaire: Taine et M. Aulard*.[339] In part it was Cochin's purpose to defend Taine against Aulard's criticisms of poor scholarship (both, in Cochin's opinion, were equally culpable) but the broader, and far more important, ambition was to enable revolutionary historiography to transcend this polemic.

The 'problem', as Cochin termed it,[340] had its origin in the fact that, to date, all historians of the Revolution had worked with an idealized conception of the people, portraying them as one enormous allegorical and anonymous figure. Yet, in his view, this ideal form only existed in the imaginations of the 'initiated', in the consciences of those shaped through what Cochin called the philosophical societies

---

[336] Ibid. 368.   [337] Ibid. 367.   [338] Ibid. 368.

[339] According to François Furet, Cochin is 'probably the most neglected historian of the French Revolution': 'Augustin Cochin: the theory of Jacobinism', in *Interpreting the French Revolution*, 164. See also Fred E. Schrader, *Augustin Cochin et la République Française* (1992). Cochin was killed at the front in 1916. Much of his work was publ. after his death.

[340] Cochin, *La Crise de l'histoire révolutionnaire: Taine et M. Aulard* (1909), 1–8.

or 'sociétés de pensée'. From within this perspective, the Revolution amounted to the emancipation and then victory of the 'God-people' as the 'true sovereign', and it was this belief in a pure or direct democracy, Cochin contended, that provided the Revolution's internal and irresistible dynamic. 'So simple in theory', Cochin wrote, 'pure democracy is less so in fact', and this was so because the people could neither administer nor govern on every detail: therefore, some form of administrative and representative machinery was required. If, then, they were to remain the governors, the people had to have the means of watching over and controlling their administrators and deputies 'without cease'. This, Cochin argued, was the role of 'popular societies' such as the Jacobin club. They were the eyes of the people: 'their function is surveillance, and their means, terror'.[341] In the name of the people these clubs exercised a power that was without limit or appeal. Everything done in the name of the people was legitimate. From this, Cochin argued, arose a 'new morality which asked not if an act was good or not, but if it was revolutionary or not, whether it conformed to the active and present will of god'.[342] For this reason, it made no sense to talk of terrorist 'excesses': rather 'the first illegal act of the Revolution is the 9th Thermidor'.[343]

It was this argument that allowed Cochin to dismiss Aulard's attribution of the Terror to external circumstances as being unfounded. Cochin accepted that certain external circumstances influenced the Revolution but denied that these circumstances acted in such a way as to define its essential characteristics. It was from the principles of pure democracy and not from the circumstances of war that 'proceeded the most frightening attributes of the new rule'.[344] 'What we affirm', Cochin wrote, 'is that the very idea of law, of a revolutionary act defined in the precise terms of 93—that is to say, of legitimate acts which violate all the rules of law and of the most elementary morality—would not have been born without the principle of direct sovereignty and the regime which flows from it.'[345]

Cochin saw the origin of the thesis (articulated, as he acknowledged, from Barruel onwards)[346] that the Revolution was the result of a conspiracy as laying in the great gap that came to exist between 'the People Sovereign and the people', between the 'purified and enclosed' world of 'the Jacobin nobility' and the majority. Robespierre, Cochin recalled, believed that virtue only existed among the minority. Yet, Cochin observed, if the Revolution was a tyranny, it was also a Revolution without tyrants, a dictatorship without dictators, and this was so because no one individual or group of individuals ever came properly to control or understand the Revolution. The Jacobins, he wrote, ruled 'by virtue of an impersonal force which they served without understanding and which destroyed them as effortlessly as it had raised them up'.[347] Seen from this perspective, Taine's mistake had been to try to explain Jacobinism in terms of a collection of individual psychological traits and to see the Revolution through the lenses of its participants,

---

[341] Cochin, *La Crise de l'histoire révolutionnaire: Taine et M. Aulard* (1909), 35.
[342] Ibid. 39.   [343] Ibid. 41.   [344] Ibid. 37.
[345] Ibid. 41.   [346] Ibid. 48.   [347] Ibid. 51.

as the result of conscious intentions. With the new age, Cochin wrote, we entered a world of 'unconscious forces'.

A new method was required, therefore, and Cochin believed that he had found it in the sociological programme recently set out by Émile Durkheim. 'According to M. Durkheim', Cochin commented, 'the psychological school, when it wishes to explain social facts, attributes too much weight to *intentions* and not enough to situations.' It saw 'only the calculations of men' where it should see 'the slow and deep operation of institutions and human relations'.[348] In other words, the Jacobins were not the products of contingent circumstances or of a few months of anarchy. Rather, Jacobinism was the developed form of a particular type of philosophical society that had come into existence in the latter half of the eighteenth century and that had propagated a particular form of 'social opinion' focused upon an abstract form of social equality. Viewed incorrectly, as was later to be done by Aulard,[349] Cochin's analysis looked like a restatement of the Revolution as conspiracy thesis, but this was the exact opposite of what he wanted to argue. For Cochin, the Revolution was not the result of conscious intrigue but the unconscious outcome of an impersonal 'social machine' or apparatus.

How, therefore, could the crisis of revolutionary historiography be brought to a close? First, historians had to forego 'indignation' and embrace 'explanation'. As Cochin observed, the last three months of the Terror might not have been the most odious and unhappy in French history but they were the 'most interesting': 'there was then attempted a moral, political, and social experiment that was truly unique'.[350] Next, historians had to abandon the 'revolutionary fetish' for the people, and should relegate it to 'the museum of religious myths'.[351] When this had been done, Cochin believed, historians would be able to comprehend why the Revolution was so innovative, why it constituted such a radical break with the past, and why it possessed an internal dynamic that proved so irresistible. And, if they did so, they would come to see that what they were dealing with was the birth of modern democratic politics. It was, however, to be some years before Cochin's advice was acted upon. As we shall see, the impact of the Bolshevik Revolution of 1917 in France was sufficient to ensure many more years of indignation and revolutionary fetishism.

---

[348] Ibid. 58.   [349] See Furet, 'Augustin Cochin', 168.
[350] Cochin, *La Crise*, 99.   [351] Ibid. 100.

7

Religion, Enlightenment, and Reaction

I

In 1925 Alphonse Aulard published *Le Christianisme et la Révolution française.*
In tone and approach, it bore the hallmarks of his earlier work on the Revolution.[1]
'My endeavour', he wrote, 'has been to be impartial.' Yet the historian's 'tale' he was
to tell was nothing less than that of the attempted 'de-Christianization' of France.
'I am startled', Aulard added, 'by the ease with which the people of France in 1794
began to abandon their customary forms of worship.'[2]

On the eve of the Revolution, Aulard recalled, France was a country which—
with the exception of a few Protestants and Jews—enjoyed religious unity
and where Christianity seemed to be flourishing. Her monarchs did not hesitate
to style themselves 'the most Christian' of kings and her people were happy to
be members of a nation which, in the papacy's eyes, was 'the eldest daughter of
the Church'. 'The Gallican Church', Aulard wrote, shone 'with the splendour of an
unrivalled power.'[3] Undoubtedly, there existed—as there had always existed—
'a small minority of unbelievers', and to this was to be added a larger number of
people 'indifferent' to religion, but 'no one dreamt in 1789 of de-Christianizing
France'.[4]

Four years later, according to Aulard, this was exactly what was being contemplated. By then, the Revolution had been drawn into conflict with the
Church; the idea of a secular state was gaining ground; and refractory priests
who refused to endorse the new Civil Constitution of the Clergy were feared as
counter-revolutionaries. After the uprising in the Vendée—'a crime against the
patrie', Aulard avowed[5]—moves against the Christian religion became more
general. The republican calendar was introduced. Churches were closed and
turned into Temples of Reason. Undertaken 'in an atmosphere of militant joy',
the culmination of this process of 'destruction and replacement' was attained, in

---

[1] In addition to *Histoire politique de la Révolution française*, see *Le Culte de la Raison et le Culte de
l'Être suprême* (1892).
[2] Ibid. 10.
[3] Aulard, *Le Christianisme et la Révolution française*, 17.
[4] Ibid. 28.
[5] Ibid. 88.

Aulard's words, with the inauguration of Robespierre's 'great political-religious project': the cult of the Supreme Being.[6]

Why was there no sustained opposition to such acts of impiety? Aulard advanced three facts by way of explanation. First, the French peasant was fundamentally 'indifferent' to religion. His Christianity was superficial, something superimposed upon older, pagan rituals.[7] Next, the urban middle classes were 'largely imbued with the natural religion of Voltaire and Rousseau'.[8] Finally, and most importantly, de-Christianization was 'a means or expedient of national defence, of defending the Revolution'.[9] 'Whether under the name of the Supreme Being or that of Reason', Aulard wrote, 'it was the *patrie* that was worshipped more and more.'[10]

With France saved and the nation's independence secured, the fire of anti-Christian sentiment diminished. After 1795, Aulard observed, there was a revival in Catholic worship and churches were restored to the faithful. Nevertheless, under the Directory the work of secularization went on, most notably with the introduction of legislation in 1795 separating Church and State. Through public instruction founded upon rational principles and through civic festivals, the hold of revealed religion over the people was to be progressively eliminated. Whether just or unjust in its treatment of the Catholic Church, Aulard argued, this had been a system that had worked. Placed 'beneath the superior independence of the State', no religion occupied a dominant position and no sect could become tyrannical. There existed 'a kind of religious equilibrium'.[11] It was this 'political-religious regime', Aulard concluded, that Napoleon Bonaparte had destroyed in 1801 when he had signed the Concordat with Pope Pius VII. The *laïcité* of the State was abandoned and the dominant position of the Catholic Church was re-established. Napoleon had done this not out of piety but for political ends. 'He thought', Aulard wrote, 'that he would dominate the pope and, through the pope, the consciences of mankind.'[12]

Two things stand out in Aulard's account. The first is the manner in which its argument complemented that provided in his *Histoire politique de la Révolution française*. In the same way that the Terror had been attributed to the imperious necessity of circumstances, so the struggle against France's inherited religion had been largely driven by the sentiment of the Church's betrayal of the nation. There had been no preconceived plan to destroy the Church or philosophers' plot to turn the French nation into Protestants or atheists. If the Revolution had attacked Christianity it had had little to do with the influence of Voltairean scepticism and more to do with the fact that Catholic priests were conspiring with the external enemy. This view ignored the fact that, from the moment the National Assembly

[6] Ibid. 122. See Timothy Tackett, 'The French Revolution and Religion to 1794', in Stewart J. Brown and Timothy Tackett (eds.), *The Cambridge History of Christianity*, vii. *Enlightenment, Reawakening and Revolution 1660–1815* (Cambridge, 2006), 536–55.

[7] Aulard, *Le Christianisme*, 113.

[8] Ibid. 114.

[9] Ibid. 115.

[10] Ibid. 123.

[11] Ibid. 138.

[12] Ibid. 151. See Suzanne Desan, 'The French Revolution and Religion, 1795–1815', in Brown and Tackett, *Cambridge History of Christianity*, vii. 556–74.

decreed the confiscation and sale of Church property in November 1789, it embarked upon a course of action that would lead to the reconstruction of the ecclesiastical system and, therefore, conflict with the Holy See. It likewise provided no explanation of the sheer ferocity of popular violence directed against the clergy, many of whom were imprisoned, driven into exile, or forced to renounce their priestly calling.

The second point relates to the broader historiography of the Revolution. As we have seen, throughout the nineteenth century there had been no agreement as to whether the Revolution had presaged the final realization or ruin of Christianity. There was, in fact, much truth in Aulard's description of the position of the Church in pre-revolutionary France. Since Louis XIV's revocation of the Edict of Nantes in 1685, it had enjoyed a legal monopoly of the right of worship.[13] The Church possessed immense power and wealth. The clergy were a privileged class. Yet the Church—even in its post-Tridentine form[14]—lacked spiritual vitality. Its bishops cared little for the religious welfare of their flocks. Its parish priests, often impoverished, were largely ignorant of matters theological. Many of its monasteries were closed or empty. If the people remained attached to the rituals of the Church, they observed them with less frequency and their faith was frequently lukewarm. Factors such as these led Aulard to the conclusion that Christianity was not 'indestructibly embedded in the consciences of the French'.[15] It is in this light, therefore, that Aulard's favourable comments on the religious policies of the Directory have to be interpreted.

With the separation of Church and State in 1795, religion became a purely private affair. To that extent, the Revolution, when not deflected from its original purpose by dire necessity, denoted neither the realization nor the ruin of Christianity but rather its removal from the public realm. Moreover, this was precisely the religious settlement arrived at by the Third Republic when, following the Dreyfus Affair, in 1905 it re-established the separation of Church and State.[16] By such a separation, it was imagined, the bitter polemic that, for over a century, had pitted philosophy against religion, science against faith, would be brought to an end. Certainly, in the years following the Revolution no such stable solution had been found. Indeed, the question more often posed was whether there could be a revival of Catholic thought and, if not, whether a new religion could be established and put in its place. Few were those who doubted the social utility of religion.

Let us next accept that a case can be made for saying that the Revolution of 1789 had its own religious origins.[17] As Dale Van Kley has observed: much followed

[13] The Edict of Nantes, promulgated in 1598, had granted freedom of public worship to Protestants.

[14] The Council of Trent (1545–63) defined the doctrines that were to inspire the Catholic Counter-Reformation.

[15] Aulard, *Le Christianisme*, 10.

[16] See Dominique de Villepin (ed.), *1905, la séparation des Églises et de l'État* (2004) and Jacqueline Lalouette, *La Séparation des Églises et de l'État: Genèse et développement d'une idée 1789–1905* (2005).

[17] See Dale K. Van Kley, *The Religious Origins of the French Revolution: From Calvin to the Civil Constitution 1560–1791* (New Haven, Conn., 1996).

from the French monarchy's puzzling decision not to side with the Protestant Reformation.[18] In particular, the threat of internal disorder was met not only by the bureaucratization of the monarchy but also by its divinization, with Bodin's secular version of absolutism—rooted in a conception of the indivisibility of sovereignty—being complemented by Bishop Bossuet's affirmation that the majesty of God was most clearly visible in kings.[19] To attempt anything against the person of a king, Bossuet declared, was sacrilege. In this way, the mortal monarch acquired the quality of quasi-divinity whilst the monarchy as an institution was adorned with the trappings of religious sanctity: thus strengthened, the crown could be rendered immune from the perils of Protestant dissent.[20]

Protestant dissent had indeed posed a formidable challenge to royal supremacy. From the mid-sixteenth century onwards, Huguenot writers developed a radical constitutionalist theory that not only emphasized the legal limits on absolutism but also came to relocate the original source of sovereignty among the people themselves. In so doing, as Quentin Skinner has argued, they were to perform 'the epoch-making move' of transforming a purely religious theory of resistance into a political theory of revolution. On this view, there existed the moral right (as opposed to religious duty) to resist any ruler who did not honour the obligation to pursue the welfare of his people.[21] After the massacre of St Bartholomew in 1572 (when as many as two thousand Protestants were murdered in Paris) such 'monarchomach' principles were deployed to justify outright rebellion and civil war. This was a battle that French Calvinists were destined to lose and one that allowed proponents of absolutism to claim, with some justification, that royal authority alone could protect France from the decline into anarchy, but the subversive potential of Calvinist political theory, much of it developed in exile in the Netherlands, remained intact until the end of the *ancien régime*.

For its part, the French state continued to persecute Protestants and what it regarded as Protestant tendencies within the Catholic Church, most notably Jansenism.[22] The doctrinal controversy that separated Jansenism with its austere Augustinian theology from the humanistic optimism of the Jesuits constituted one

---

[18] Ibid. 15.

[19] See *Politics Drawn from the Very Words of Holy Scripture* (Cambridge, 1990), 160. For the broader context see William Farr Church, *Constitutional Thought in Sixteenth-Century France: A Study in the Evolution of Ideas* (Cambridge, Mass., 1941) and Quentin Skinner, *The Foundations of Modern Political Thought*, ii. *The Age of Reformation* (Cambridge, 1978), 239–301.

[20] See Jean-Frédéric Schaub, *La France espagnole: Les Racines hispaniques de l'absolutisme français* (2003). Schaub shows that the French monarchy, in driving out Protestants from France, sought to emulate the example of Spain's expulsion of Muslims and Jews.

[21] Skinner, *Foundations*, 335.

[22] See William Doyle, *Jansenism* (Houndmills, 2000) and Catherine Maire, *De la cause de Dieu à la cause de la Nation: Le Jansénisme au XVIIIe siècle* (1998). See also Maire (ed.), *Jansénisme et Révolution* (1990) and Maire, 'Port Royal: The Jansenist Schism', in Pierre Nora (ed.), *Realms of Memory*, i. *Conflicts and Divisions* (New York, 1996), 301–51. The classic study is by Lucien Goldmann, *The Hidden God: A Study of Tragic Vision in the Pensées of Pascal and the Tragedies of Racine* (London, 1964). For a brilliant discussion of the theological issues at stake see Leszek Kolakowski, *God Owes Us Nothing: A Brief Remark on Pascal's Religion and on the Spirit of Jansenism* (Chicago, 1995). Jansenism took its name from Cornelius Jansenius (1585–1638), Bishop of Ypres, whose study of the thought of St Augustine was published posthumously in 1640.

of the great religious quarrels of the seventeenth and eighteenth centuries.[23] Much of the serious polemic focused upon discussion of the 'Five Propositions' deemed by their opponents to be at the heart of Jansenist doctrine, but, in essence, what was at stake was a divergence over the extent to which Christianity had to make concessions to worldliness. For the Jesuits, the emphasis placed by Jansenists upon divine grace and moral rigour smacked of Protestant heresy whilst, for the Jansenists, the defence of human free will associated with Jesuit Pelagianism and Molinism was a pretext for confessional and spiritual laxity.[24] By 1669 the Jesuits appeared victorious and the supporters of Jansenism had been largely reduced to silence and submission. Moreover, any potential political challenge posed by Jansenism to the claims of divine right monarchy had failed to materialize.

This might have remained the case had the State and the Church not persisted in the persecution of what survived of the Jansenist community. In 1709 its spiritual home, the monastery of Port Royal outside Paris, was closed down. Two years later the buildings were demolished in order to prevent them from becoming a site of pilgrimage. Then, in 1713, Pope Clement XI published the papal bull *Unigenitus* condemning 101 Jansenist propositions deemed to be false and heretical. This proved to be a major miscalculation and something of a pyrrhic victory. *Unigenitus* quickly became a metaphor for absolutism and a regalvanized Jansenist movement found growing support amongst both clergy and laity alike. Matters came to a head between 1730 and 1733 when Cardinal Fleury, Louis XV's first minister, determined to put an end to dissent once and for all by having it declared that *Unigenitus* had the status of a 'law of Church and State'.

How might these theological disputes have contributed to the origins of the Revolution of 1789? First, under the weight of persecution the Jansenist cause converged with that of the *Parlements* in their opposition to the arbitrary power and unlimited authority of royal absolutism and ecclesiastical hierarchy.[25] Next, the continuous replaying of these Jansenist controversies throughout the eighteenth century severely undermined the legislative and religious symbols of absolutism, thereby, it is argued, contributing to the 'desacralization' of the monarchy and its ultimate delegitimation.[26] Finally, in the wake of the so-called Maupeou revolution

---

[23] See Dale K. Van Kley, 'Jansenism and the International Suppression of the Jesuits', in Brown and Tackett, *Cambridge History of Christianity*, vii. 302–28, and Kley, *The Jansenists and the Expulsion of the Jesuits from France, 1757–1765* (New Haven, Conn., 1975).

[24] The most famous Jansenist attack upon this aspect of Jesuit practice—known as casuistry—was Blaise Pascal's *Lettres provinciales* of 1656. Pascal's text highlighted what he regarded as the theological frivolity and hypocrisy of the Jesuits.

[25] See Julian Swann, *Politics and the Parlement of Paris under Louis XV, 1754–1774* (Cambridge, 1995). If Swann accepts that a 'coterie' of Jansenist magistrates exercised influence within the *Parlement* of Paris, he nevertheless suggests that 'it is important not to allow the Jansenist tale to wag the *parlementaire* dog': p. 38.

[26] See Kley, *Religious Origins*, and Jeffrey Merrick, *The Desacralization of the French Monarchy in the Eighteenth Century* (Baton Rouge, La., 1990). Merrick argues that 'These conflicts, more than the Enlightenment, undermined the judicial fictions that bound the *ancien régime* together': p.49.The counter-argument affirms that the desacralization of the monarchy was far less profound and widespread than this might suggest: see Roger Chartier, *Les Origines culturelles de la Révolution française* (1990), 138–66, and Timothy Tackett, *Becoming a Revolutionary: The Deputies of the*

of 1771 designed to emasculate the *Parlements*, Jansenists rallied to the cause of popular representation and, in so doing, contributed to the elaboration of the ideology of national sovereignty and citizens' rights that was to emerge on the eve of the Revolution.[27] Accepted with qualification, each of these arguments lends support to Roger Chartier's conclusion that Jansenism 'drew upon religion to build a radical critique of both ecclesiastical and ministerial despotism that, in certain places at least, most notably Paris, accustomed people to distrust established authorities'.[28]

Not surprisingly, there were those who suspected the Jansenists of preparing the way for the Revolution and, at worst, of actually instigating it.[29] These are exaggerated claims, not least because they rest upon a misplaced characterization of Jansenism as an occult party or sect intent upon the destruction of religion. Nevertheless, a case can be made in defence of the argument that Jansenism did have a direct, if not decisive, influence upon the course of the Revolution. A considerable number of the clergy elected to represent their Estate in 1789 had Jansenist sympathies. One of these was the Abbé Grégoire, subsequently to achieve fame as the advocate of the 'regeneration' of the Jews and an opponent of slavery.[30] More significantly, and of grave consequence, the Jansenist contingent played a key role in driving through the legislation that established the Civil Constitution of the Clergy.[31] As William Doyle has written of the latter: 'Its hostility to the pope, subjection of bishops to election, and emphasis on the active role of the lay faithful, as well as a number of (now) lesser matters like the prohibition of formularies, were clearly of Jansenist inspiration.'[32] Of course, the Revolution quickly outpaced its Jansenist supporters and it soon became apparent that many were far from happy to contemplate the consequences of their own actions. In effect, therefore, the Revolution killed off what remained of Jansenism and if, in subsequent years, it survived this was largely to be in the form of a spiritual ancestry dear to later

---

French National Assembly and the Emergence of a Revolutionary Culture (1789–1790) (Princeton, NJ, 1996), 102 and 304.

[27] Doyle, *Jansenism*, 83. See also Kley, 'The Jansenist Constitutional Legacy in the French Prerevolution', in Keith Michael Baker (ed.), *The French Revolution and the Creation of Modern Political Culture*, i. *The Political Culture of the Old Regime* (Oxford, 1987), 169–201; Kley, 'Du parti janséniste au parti patriote (1770–1775)', and Shanti-Marie Singham, 'Vox populi vox Dei: Les Jansénistes pendant la révolution Maupeou', in Maire, *Jansénisme et Révolution*, 115–30, 183–93.

[28] Chartier, *Les Origines culturelles*, 208. See also Jonathan Israel, *Enlightenment Contested: Philosophy, Modernity and the Emancipation of Man 1670–1752* (Oxford, 2006), 699–712. Israel, ibid. 710, quotes Diderot to the effect that the Jansenists did more to diminish respect for the Church and raise the prestige of philosophy than the *philosophes* did in the forty years prior to the publication of the first volume of the *Encyclopédie*.

[29] See Marcel Gauchet, 'La Question du Jansénisme dans l'historiographie de la Révolution', in Maire, *Jansénisme et Révolution*, 15–23.

[30] See Rita Hermon-Belot, *L'Abbé Grégoire, la politique et la verité* (2000); J. D. and R. H. Popkin (eds.), *The Abbé Grégoire and his World* (Dordrecht, 2000) and Alyssa Goldstein Sepinwall, *The Abbé Grégoire and the French Revolution: The Making of Modern Universalism* (Berkeley and Los Angeles, Calif., 2005).

[31] See Tackett, *Becoming a Revolutionary* , 290–1; Kley, *Religious Origins*, 353–60; and Maire, 'Port Royal: The Jansenist Schism', 333–4.

[32] Doyle, *Jansenism*, 83.

republicans. The point, however, is that, for all that the Revolution came to constitute a fundamental challenge to the Church and to Christianity more generally, it is a mistake to conceive the relationship between the Revolution and Catholicism exclusively in terms of mutual antagonism.

It is similarly a mistake to believe that Christianity was in principle hostile to science and that Catholicism in France remained untouched by the intellectual developments of the early modern period. If Jonathan Israel has insisted upon the need to pluralize our conception of the Enlightenment—from the very outset, he has argued, there were two enlightenments, one radical and one moderate main-stream[33]—then Helena Rosenblatt has suggested that we should be prepared to contemplate the existence of a Christian Enlightenment.[34] There is evidence, she asserts, of a common commitment among those she describes as Enlightened Christians to embrace reasonableness, toleration, a relatively optimistic view of human nature, and a positive attitude towards reform and progress. These same people, she adds, 'sought ways to reconcile their faith with the new sciences emerging in Europe'.[35]

French Catholicism, as unlikely as it might seem, was no exception. Here too members of the Catholic community were receptive to science, shunned blind dogma, and defended religion in terms of its social usefulness. When, from the mid-eighteenth century onwards, Christians in France faced a growing challenge from deism and atheism some responded by adopting another vocabulary integral to the Enlightenment, that of sentiment and sensibility. Thus, to see France and her religious history in terms of a stark and irreconcilable division between secular *philosophes* and religious *anti-philosophes* is a gross over-simplification. As Rosenblatt concludes: 'the boundaries between Enlightenment and counter-Enlightenment were, in fact, often blurred'.[36]

The fact of the matter was, however, that from Voltaire onwards many of the French *philosophes* specialized in a particularly virulent and vitriolic form of anti-clerical and anti-religious polemic. In large part, this arose from the association of the Church with absolutism and with intolerance, an association given vivid substance by Louis XIV's revocation of the Edict of Nantes and the subsequent departure into exile of over 200,000 French Protestants. The Church was an arm of the State and few opportunities, if any, were missed to publicize the persecutions and punishments meted out by organized religion. Held in particular opprobrium was a corrupt and self-seeking priesthood intent on keeping the faithful in a condition of credulous superstition and fear. Yet, even among the *philosophes*, the

---

[33] Israel, *Enlightenment Contested*, 11. Israel's thesis is an explicit rejection of Peter Gay's earlier claim that 'there was only one Enlightenment': see Gay, *The Enlightenment: An Interpretation*, i. *The Rise of Modern Paganism* (1973), 3. See also Margaret C. Jacob, *The Radical Enlightenment: Pantheists, Freemasons and Republicans* (London, 1981).

[34] Rosenblatt. 'The Christian Enlightenment', in Brown and Tackett, *Cambridge History of Christianity*, vii. 283–301. See also Ann Thomson, *Bodies of Thought: Science, Religion and the Soul in the Early Enlightenment* (Oxford, 2008).

[35] Rosenblatt, 'The Christian Enlightenment', 284.

[36] Ibid. 290.

prevailing opinion was that religious faith, purged of idolatrous disfigurations, could be sustained by reason

There is little need here to explore the details of this immense controversy, despite the obvious temptations provided by the work of the great teacher of doubt, the sometime Protestant Pierre Bayle.[37] Suffice it to say that mainstream opinion was disinclined to accept Bayle's contention that atheism was no greater evil than idolatry and that a society of atheists could be well-ordered and durable. Montesquieu was a case in point. For all its naturalistic premises, *De l'Esprit des lois* affirmed that the Christian religion played a central role in preserving morality and maintaining the stability of society.[38] 'He who has no religion at all', Montesquieu wrote, 'is that terrible animal who feels his liberty only when it claws and devours.'[39] Voltaire, perhaps surprisingly, was another. His *Essai sur les moeurs* of 1745 denied that morality had been made known to us through either scriptural revelation or miraculous means but nevertheless concluded that it was divinely ordained. He wrote, for example, of the 'fatal and invincible destiny by which the Supreme Being enchains all the events of the universe'.[40] The slightly earlier *Elements de la philosophie de Newton* accepted the Newtonian 'argument from design' postulating the existence of a benign Deity who had created the world in accordance with mathematical principles. In brief, many *philosophes*, if they broke with Christian orthodoxy, were happy to embrace a form of deism and, as such, were prepared to believe that reason disclosed the mind of the Creator and that this Creator had instilled in our own minds knowledge of both his attributes and the fundamental principles of ethical life. Indeed, they tended to believe that, once religion had been stripped of the fraudulent accretions of the past, its essential and beneficent truths would again become visible.

Nevertheless, as the century wore on, the expression of irreligious and materialist sentiments became increasingly common, many writers going beyond deism to voice a radical scepticism about the existence of God. These included such influential figures as Diderot, La Mettrie, Helvétius, and the baron d'Holbach. La Mettrie's notorious *L'Homme machine* of 1747, for example, simply maintained that all our ideas and sentiments resulted from the self-motivated movement of matter. Accordingly, there was no substantial difference between men and animals and it was a mistake to talk of the immateriality of the soul. For his part, Helvétius argued in *De l'Esprit* of 1758 that man was primarily motivated by a desire to avoid pain and seek pleasure. The supreme law of his nature was that of self-interest. These atheistic conclusions were bolstered by the discoveries of natural scientists such as Buffon which challenged the biblical chronology described in the book of

[37] Bayle (1647–1706) was of the contrary view, maintaining that faith stood alone unaided by reason. Bayle's masterwork was his *Dictionnaire historique et critique* of 1697. Selections can be found in English translation in Bayle, *Political Writings* (Cambridge, 2000).

[38] Montesquieu, *The Spirit of the Laws* (Cambridge, 1989). See books 24 and 25, where Montesquieu not only refutes what he terms 'Bayle's paradox' but also establishes the superiority of Christianity over Islam.

[39] Ibid. 460.

[40] Voltaire, *Essai sur les mœurs et l'esprit des nations* (1963), i. 832.

Genesis. All the evidence suggested that human life evolved first in the sea. And so, over time, enlightened opinion increasingly dispensed with the notion of a distant but purposeful deity and came to adopt what was often a thinly disguised atheistic monism. Armed with a sensationalist epistemology introduced by Condillac, the *parti philosophique* (as it came to be known by mid-century) dismissed divine revelation and commandment as a guide to morality and set about the difficult task of providing a purely secular and non-transcendental basis to ethics. No longer was society to be held together by the threat of divine punishment and retribution.

The chosen vehicle for this campaign was to be the *Encyclopédie*, seventeen volumes of which were published between 1751 and 1772. Its ambition, in the words of its editor, Denis Diderot, was nothing less than to assemble all 'the knowledge scattered across the earth' in order that 'our descendants, in becoming better informed, may be at the same time more virtuous and content'. Such a project, Diderot avowed, could only be undertaken in 'a philosophic age' and by 'a society of men of letters' joined together in the name of 'the general interests of humanity'. Everything was to be examined and investigated, without hesitation or exception, free from the yoke of authority and precedent.[41] From this vast enterprise was to be excluded any reliance upon organized religion and a providential God. Whether Diderot and his collaborators merited Rousseau's description of them as 'ardent missionaries of atheism' is not clear, but when religion did find a place in the *Encyclopédie*, it was largely intended to expose outworn and ridiculous opinions. The entry on cannibalism, for example, cross-referenced the reader to articles on the Eucharist and Holy Communion. The article on consecrated bread estimated the huge cost of providing wafers for the celebration of the sacraments and suggested that the money would be better spent in feeding the poor.[42] Consequently, the philosophic spirit came to be seen as a concerted and relentless assault upon Christian values and the Holy Church. And, to the extent that the Revolution came to be seen as the vehicle and expression of a godless philosophy, it too was imagined to be anti-Christian.[43]

No one gave clearer or stronger voice to the possibilities of a radiant future without the Christian religion than the ill-fated Marie-Jean-Nicolas Caritat de Condorcet.[44] As he hid beneath the shadow of the guillotine, Condorcet sketched out a plan for the indefinite progress of mankind of unrivalled optimism. The purpose of his *Esquisse d'un tableau historique des progrès de l'esprit humain*, he declared, was to show that 'Nature has set no term to the perfection of the human faculties; that the perfectibility of man is truly infinite; and that the progress of this perfectibility. . . . has no other limit that the duration of the globe upon which

[41] Diderot, 'Encyclopédie', in John Hope Mason and Robert Wokler (eds.), *Denis Diderot: Political Writings* (Cambridge, 1992), 21–7.

[42] See Joseph Edmund Barker, *Diderot's Treatment of the Christian Religion in the Encyclopédie* (New York, 1941).

[43] See Nigel Aston, *Religion and the Revolution in France 1780–1804* (Houndmills, 2000), 81–99.

[44] See Keith Michael Baker, *Condorcet: From Natural Philosophy to Social Mathematics* (Chicago, 1975).

nature has cast us.'[45] Whilst this progress might vary in speed, it could never be permanently reversed. Moreover, the progress of knowledge was indissolubly linked to that of liberty, virtue, and the rights of man.

Within this ten-stage chronology of human development, organized religion unambiguously figured as one of those 'widespread errors which have somewhat retarded or suspended the progress of reason and which have, as often as political events, even caused man to fall back into ignorance'.[46] The art of deceiving men, Condorcet suggested, was established early and there soon emerged a class of men expert in the mysteries of religion and the practices of superstition. They sought truth in order to propagate error. They exploited the vices of ordinary language to play upon the meanings of words and to confuse. Christianity was no exception to this rule. Its triumph, Condorcet wrote, 'was the signal for the complete decadence of philosophy and the sciences'.[47] The human mind went into dramatic decline. 'Man's only achievements', he added, 'were theological day-dreams and supersti-tious impostures; his only morality was religious intolerance.'[48]

Yet, Condorcet argued, the priests were powerless to prevent the spread of the spirit of liberty and of free inquiry. Little by little, and in face of relentless persecution meted out by 'armies of fanatics', the human mind gradually recovered its strength and energy. The moral depravity and scandalous greed of the priests could no longer be hidden beneath the mask of hypocrisy. Over time, 'men of good sense' came to see that all religions were incapable of combating the vices and passions of mankind. The practice of writing in Latin declined and the use of the vernacular spread, further reducing the domination of the priests. Philosophy and science now shook off the yoke of authority and reason moved towards its 'moment of liberation'. The key figures here for Condorcet were Bacon, Galileo, and Descartes. They demonstrated that, if 'the human mind was not yet free, it was formed to be so'.[49] Next came the discovery that man was 'a sentient being, capable of reasoning and acquiring moral ideas'.[50] From this, it had been possible to 'deduce' the true rights of man and to conclude that 'the maintenance of these rights was the sole object for which men came together in political societies'.[51] The world could no longer be divided into those born to obey and those born to rule.

It was at this moment that John Locke made his decisive contribution to the progress of human knowledge. 'At last', Condorcet wrote, 'Locke seized the thread by which [philosophy] was to be guided: he showed that an exact and precise analysis of ideas, by reducing them step by step to other ideas of more immediate origin or of simpler composition, was the only means of avoiding being lost in the chaos of incomplete, incoherent and indeterminate notions which chance has presented to us randomly and which we have accepted unthinkingly.'[52] Locke, in short, was the first philosopher to establish the nature of the truths we could come to know and the objects that we could comprehend, and his method was quickly adopted by all philosophers. Not only this, but this same method destroyed the

---

[45] Condorcet, *Esquisse d'un tableau historique des progrès de l'esprit humain* (1795), 4.
[46] Ibid. 15.   [47] Ibid. 136.   [48] Ibid. 144.   [49] Ibid. 231.
[50] Ibid. 240.   [51] Ibid.   [52] Ibid. 249–50.

prejudices of the masses and taught them that they were not forever condemned to accept their opinions from others. There emerged then a new philosophy, transported across Europe by 'the almost universal French language', and which became a 'common faith' guiding public opinion. Preached by a 'solid phalanx' of philosophers united against all forms of error and tyranny, at its core was a belief in 'reason, toleration, and humanity'.[53] Such, Condorcet proclaimed, was the new philosophy and such, he implied, was the philosophy that was to inspire the French Revolution. A great revolution, he believed, was simply inevitable.

Whatever the explanation, Condorcet's optimism proved unfounded and the policies pursued by the Revolution towards the Church proved to be an abject failure as well as a political disaster.[54] After an initial move towards religious toleration, the attempt to institute the Civil Constitution of the Clergy led not only to schism with the papacy but also proved to be the point at which Louis XVI resolved that no further compromises could be made. The effect was to divide the country and to radicalize the Revolution, leading ultimately to what amounted to a veritable war against Christianity and those who stubbornly persisted in the maintenance of their faith.[55] With the fall of the Jacobins, the campaign of de-Christianization eased but the hostility remained. Indeed, it continued under the Directory, where the Thermidorian leaders showed no enthusiasm to repeal existing legislation directed against the Church or to allow the public expression of religious worship. In line with the policy of neutrality in religious matters so admired by Aulard, state funding of the Church was withdrawn. The armies of the Directory carried these reforms with them across Europe, looting churches as they went and banning the celebration of religious ceremonies. After the fall of Rome in 1798, Pope Pius VI was imprisoned in Valance (where he remained until his death a year later). Yet, as Aulard had also observed, the period of the Directory saw a marked religious revival, and one fuelled by popular sentiment. Priests came back to France and the laity (often unaided by the clergy) did their utmost to resurrect the frequently archaic religious practices and public rituals of the *ancien régime*. Pilgrimages and the celebration of saints' day festivals made their return.[56]

Faced with this unexpected resurgence and convinced of a continuing incompatibility between Catholicism and the Revolution, the leaders of the Directory renewed their efforts to instil a republican culture among the French population. Civic education was to be fostered by a new set of republican festivals, the *culte décadaire*, replete with its own secular catechisms and covering everything from birth and marriage to the seasons and the founding moments of the Republic.[57] The government also promoted a new religion: theophilanthropy. Described by

---

[53] Condorcet, *Esquisse d'un tableau historique des progrès de l'esprit humain* (1795), 259.
[54] See John McManners, *The French Revolution and the Church* (London, 1969).
[55] See Aston, *Religion and the Revolution*, 122–276.
[56] See Suzanne Desan, *Reclaiming the Sacred: Lay Religion and Popular Politics in Revolutionary France* (Ithaca, NY, 1990); Desan, 'The French Revolution and Religion, 1795–1815', in Brown and Tackett, *Cambridge History of Christianity*, vii. 556–64; and Aston, *Religion and the Revolution*, 279–315.
[57] See Mona Ozouf, *Festivals and the French Revolution* (Cambridge, Mass., 1988), 106–283.

Nigel Aston as 'the crankiest religious manifestation of the 1790s',[58] this amounted to an eclectic mix of moral teachings drawn from the world's religions and the histories of ancient republics served up as a reconstituted, lukewarm deism.[59] The doctrine of original sin was explicitly denied and its creed was to be one of extreme simplicity: there was to be no dressing up in priestly costumes and temples were to be austere. Above all, the purpose of theophilanthropy was to enhance the civic commitment of the population. Apart from a few misguided writers and poets, few people took it (or the new festivals) seriously, although many people were no doubt either bemused or annoyed by official attempts to ban fish markets on Fridays.

Of far greater significance was the establishment in 1795 of the Institut National des Sciences et des Arts. If the name had been invented by Talleyrand, the pedagogical blueprint for this project had been set out by the Marquis de Condorcet in 1792. Intended to replace the learned academies of the *ancien régime*, all of which had been abolished in 1793, the second of its three classes was designated as the 'Classe des Sciences morales et politiques'. The first and third classes were to be devoted to the physical and mathematical sciences and to literature and the fine arts respectively. The second class was itself subdivided into six sections: the analysis of sensations and ideas; ethics; social science and legislation; political economy; history; and geography. The establishment of the Institut was directly linked to plans to found a national scheme of public and secular education.

If members of the *Idéologue* circle did not constitute the majority of the second class, they certainly were a vocal minority, being both disproportionately active in its deliberations and providing its most coherent intellectual programme.[60] No one more than they could claim to be the intellectual descendants of Helvétius, Condillac, and Condorcet and no one displayed a greater commitment to the development of a science of morals than the two most prominent members of the circle, Destutt de Tracy and Pierre Cabanis.[61] The moralist and the doctor, Cabanis ventured in his *Rapports du physique et du moral de l'homme*,[62] had an equal interest in the study of man as a physical mechanism. Physical sensitivity, he concluded, was the source of all the ideas and habits that made up the mental and moral existence of man.

As we have seen, the primary purpose of *idéologie* was to purge our moral and political concepts of the unsound and disordered accretions of the past, a task achieved through the decomposition of complex ideas into their simplest elements. The intellectual possibilities and practical applications of this new analytical science appeared almost limitless.[63] Its end result would be the perfection and the

---

[58] Aston, *Religion and the Revolution*, 280.

[59] The best study remains Albert Mathiez, *La Théophilanthropie et le Culte Décadaire 1796–1801: Essai sur l'histoire religieuse de la Révolution* (1904).

[60] See Martin S. Staum, *Minerva's Message: Stabilizing the French Revolution* (Montreal and Kingston, 1996), 33–55.

[61] See Martin S. Staum, *Cabanis: Enlightenment and Medical Philosophy in the French Revolution* (Princeton, NJ, 1980).

[62] Cabanis, *Rapports du physique et du moral de l'homme* (1830), i. 5–20. This work consisted of twelve memoirs written between 1796 and 1802.

[63] See Cabanis, *Du Degré de certitude de la médecine* (1798), 2–8.

happiness of man. This was so because the moral and political sciences could achieve the same level of certainty as the physical sciences and, upon this basis, society could be reformed without fear of descent into anarchy. Beginning with an analysis of the self and our sensations, *idéologie*, as set out by Destutt de Tracy himself, would first explore grammar (the science of communicating ideas), then logic (the science of discovering new truths), before moving on to investigate education, morality, and, ultimately, politics. From the perspective of a unified scientific method, therefore, it was *idéologie*, and not religion or the accidental opinions of an earlier age, which would be our infallible guide. Philosophers and physicians, and not priests or misguided moralists, would be the superintendents of our behaviour and beliefs. In line with their conclusions and advice, legislators and governments would take the leading role in shaping and improving human conduct and manners and in this way the conflicting interests of the individuals who made up society would be brought into harmony. The State, and not the Church, would be our moral educator and there would be no need to have recourse to divine inspiration or sanction.

In summary, the *Idéologues* placed their full weight behind attempts to discredit Christian metaphysics and used the considerable institutional power at their disposal to propagate a secular moral science and ethics. If this was true of their activities within the Institut, it was similarly so of the most important journal in which they published, the *Décade philosophique*.[64] Whilst the articles it published displayed a limited sympathy towards Protestantism and Jansenism, Catholicism was characterized as being intrinsically intolerant and obscurantist. Its pages were never anything less than intransigently anticlerical. Moreover, the journal held Christianity as a whole responsible for preventing the advance of the human spirit by filling people's heads with irrational fears and absurd beliefs. Humanity had to be cured of this malady.

Yet the abiding preoccupation of the *Idéologues* was to stabilize the Republic and to bring the revolutionary turmoil of the 1790s to a close. Their philosophy reflected their disillusionment. To that end, *idéologie* was arguably designed to replace what they saw as a discredited Church and thus to replicate the stabilizing function of religion. As the late Robert Wokler argued,[65] *idéologie* exuded a distrust of politics and placed what faith it had in the development of a new social science to cure the ills of the nation. Order would be secured through the inculcation of a morality of prudent and tempered self-interest, implanted in the minds of the people via a set of moralizing public institutions. Social hygiene was to be the maxim.

This, like so much else at the time, proved to be a chimera. If the members of the *Idéologue* circle offered their services to Napoleon Bonaparte, he made clear his

---

[64] See Joanna Kitchin, *Un journal 'philosophique': La Décade (1794–1807)* (1965), 139–77, and Marc Regaldo, *Un milieu intellectuel: La Décade philosophique (1794–1807)*, 5 vols. (1976). Kitchin refers to *La Décade* as the 'organ of the *Idéologues*': *Un journal 'philosophique'*, p. vii. McManners, *French Revolution*, 135, refers to *La Décade* as 'their mouth-piece'.

[65] 'Ideology and the origins of social science', in Mark Goldie and Robert Wokler (eds.), *The Cambridge History of Eighteenth-Century Political Thought* (Cambridge, 2006), 688–709.

opinion of the Classe des Sciences morales et politiques by closing it down in January 1803, the First Consul quickly concluding that they were a disruptive and unwelcome presence. Although no believer, he readily perceived that the Church was a far more efficient institution of social control than a coterie of 'twelve or fifteen obscure metaphysicians'.[66] As Napoleon told the assembled clergy of Milan in June 1800: 'No society can exist without morality. But there is no good morality without religion. Religion alone therefore can give the State firm and lasting support.'[67] The Concordat of 1801 and the presence of Pope Pius VII at his coronation as emperor served Napoleon's purpose admirably and certainly far better than any *Idéologue*-inspired Council of Public Instruction might have done. When this strategy faltered, he persuaded the Church to canonize a St Napoleon and conveniently arranged for the celebration to coincide with the Feast of the Assumption, thereby obliging the faithful to worship the Virgin Mary and the emperor at one and the same time.[68] Nevertheless, the preoccupation with developing and establishing a secular, non-theistic morality endured throughout the nineteenth century. So too did the perceived need to moralize the people in a post-revolutionary society. The curious thing is that the arguments advanced by believers and non-believers often sounded strangely alike.

II

One group that might have been expected to welcome the Revolution were French Protestants. Calvinists in the south and Lutherans in Alsace, they comprised about 700,000 adherents in total. Although the harsh persecutions of the reigns of Louis XIV and XV had largely subsided—the last Protestants were freed from the galley ships of Toulon in 1775—they continued to suffer legal disabilities until the promulgation of the Edict of Non-Catholics in 1788. Moreover, if doctrinal debate mattered little to the vast majority of Protestant believers—most of whom lived in small, isolated rural communities—at an elite level there was undoubtedly a coincidence of interest allying Protestant pleas for toleration and the concerns of the *philosophes*.

Protestants (along with Jews) were therefore amongst the first beneficiaries of the Revolution's reforms, all legal distinctions between Protestants and Catholics being abolished before the end of 1789. Two Protestants, the pastor Rabaut de Saint-Étienne and the future leader of the *Feuillants*, Antoine-Pierre Barnave,[69] achieved early prominence in Parisian politics and others came to the fore at a provincial level. Many Protestants welcomed the inauguration of the Republic in 1792 but, to

---

[66] This was the derogatory phrase used to describe the *Idéologues* in an article publ. in the *Journal de Paris*. The article was inspired by Napoleon.

[67] Quoted in Bernard Reardon, *Liberalism and Tradition: Aspects of Catholic Thought in Nineteenth-Century France* (Cambridge, 1975), 2.

[68] See Sudhir Hazareesingh, *The Saint Napoleon: Celebrations of Sovereignty in Nineteenth-Century France* (Cambridge, Mass., 2004).

[69] Both were executed in 1793.

the extent that they supported the Girondins and the federalist cause, they quickly fell foul of Jacobin repression (one of the victims being the father of François Guizot). Nor could they entirely escape the excesses of the campaign of de-Christianization: recently opened Protestant temples were forced to close and pastors, often under threat of imprisonment, were obliged to abandon their ministry. Nevertheless, despite the considerable damage inflicted upon the Protestant community, the Republic displayed less fervour in eradicating Protestantism than it did in attempting to destroy the very last remnants of Catholicism. In acknowledgement of this fact, Catholics were subsequently to extract their (sometimes bloody) revenge. After 1795, a much-weakened Protestant congregation sought to reconstitute the fabric of its religious life as best it could, and with varying levels of success. Protestants benefited from the separation of Church and State instituted by the Directory and they continued to enjoy the right of religious observance even after Napoleon had signed the Concordat with the papacy. The restored monarchy of Louis XVIII and Charles X likewise did not take away this right. The July Monarchy proved especially sympathetic towards Protestants.[70]

One Protestant who had risen to prominence under the *ancien régime* was Jacques Necker, Louis XVI's finance minister.[71] Out of power between 1784 and 1788, he had spent much of his time musing over the decline of morality in French society and, by way of response, published *De l'importance de la morale et des opinions religieuses* at the very moment when preparations began for the summoning of the Estates-General.[72] In the words of George Armstrong Kelly, it was 'an extremely long and windy work' but also one of 'remarkable interest'.[73] Two themes are prominent. The first was Necker's unambiguous recognition of the social utility of religion and that the general influence of religious morality was on the decline. Moreover, he doubted that the 'cold lessons' of political philosophy would serve as an adequate replacement. 'We are delivering ourselves up to an illusion', he wrote, 'if we hope to establish morality upon the connection between individual interest and the public interest, and if we imagine that the authority of social laws can do without the support of religion.'[74] A 'political catechism' would have little purchase upon the behaviour of the people. Good laws alone, in other words, were not sufficient. The second theme had a more distinctively Protestant flavour. Religious opinions and sentiments, in Necker's view, enlarged and deepened our moral inclinations. They freed us from the tyranny of our passions and distanced us from our immediate, temporal interests. Religion instilled us with 'benevolent virtues', and, above all, with the virtue of charity. There was, Necker believed, nothing good, beautiful, or dignified about a condition of irreligion. The

---

[70] See Burdette C. Poland, *French Protestantism and the French Revolution: A Study of Church and State, Thought and Religion, 1685–1815* (Princeton, NJ, 1957).

[71] See Henri Grange, *Les Idées de Necker* (1974), 53–9, 514–614.

[72] Necker, *De l'importance de la morale et des opinions religieuses* (1788).

[73] Armstrong Kelly, *The Humane Comedy: Constant, Tocqueville, and French Liberalism* (Cambridge, 1992), 95.

[74] Necker, *De l'importance*, 21.

behaviour of a 'virtuous atheist', he maintained, merely reflected 'the indirect influence of religious opinions'.[75]

All the evidence suggests that Necker's own experiences in the Revolution did little to change these convictions. In 1800 he published his three-volume *Cours de morale religieuse*.[76] The topics addressed ranged from divine providence and the immortality of the soul to conjugal duty and the general principles of morality. Nothing, he there reaffirmed, was more important to nations than the alliance between morality and religion. And the best of religions was one that was 'simple, reasonable, and pure' and free of 'fanatical intolerance' and superstition. Only such a religion, 'majestic in its simplicity', would provide us with the 'wisdom' and 'dignity' required to make proper use of our liberty. Religion fostered the spirit of moderation.

We could speculate at some length about the influence such Calvinist piety had upon Necker's daughter, Germaine de Staël. By all accounts she received a solid religious education from her parents and one which, if light on dogma, emphasized the reasonableness of Christianity.[77] Like her father, she came to believe in the social benefits of religion. Indeed, she developed this argument further by suggesting that nowhere was this more so than in a republic. Writing in *Des Circonstances actuelles qui peuvent terminer la Révolution*,[78] she bewailed the 'demoralization' of France under the Republic—everyone, she stated, was motivated by self-interest and the love of money—and asserted that only a morality supported by religion could provide a 'complete code' covering all our actions as well as 'a code which unites men by way of a kind of covenant of souls, the indispensable preliminary to any social contract'. Religion alone, she argued, could endow us with a sense of personal dignity, an awareness of the perfectibility of the human spirit, and a love of virtue. In the same text, Madame de Staël completely dismissed the idea that religion was only necessary for the ignorant masses. 'Nothing', she wrote, 'seems more to be detested than this assertion.'[79]

Similarly, she never tired of announcing the merits of Protestantism over Catholicism. 'The Reformation', she wrote in *De la Littérature considérée dans ses rapports avec les institutions sociales*, 'is the period of history that most effectively served the perfectibility of the human species. The Protestant religion contains within itself no active germ of superstition and gives to virtue every support that can be gained from sensible opinions. In those countries where the Protestant religion is professed, it does nothing to prevent philosophical research and efficaciously maintains the purity of morals.'[80] Luther, she was later to write, recalled religion to the land of thought.[81] Just as importantly, Madame de Staël realized that the

[75] Ibid. 78.

[76] Necker, *Cours de morale religieuse*, 3 vols. (Geneva, 1800). See esp. vol. i, pp. i–xliv.

[77] See Rosenblatt, *Liberal Values*, 34–5.

[78] Written in 1798, this text was publ. posthumously.

[79] Germaine de Staël, *Des Circonstances actuelles qui peuvent terminer la Révolution* (1906), 212–29.

[80] Staël-Holstein, *De la Littérature considérée dans ses rapports avec les institutions sociales* (1800), i. 311.

[81] Germaine de Staël, *De l'Allemagne* (1968), ii. 245.

advocates of revolution had made the mistake of believing that only an atheist could love liberty and that aristocratic privilege and the absolute power of the throne were integral to religious belief. It was Christianity, she countered, that had 'brought liberty to this earth, justice to the oppressed, respect for the unfortunate, and finally equality before God, of which equality before the law is only an imperfect reflection'.[82] If, as she willingly conceded, the light of reason was necessary to free us from our prejudices, then, by the same token, it was 'in the soul that the principles of liberty are grounded'.[83]

Yet Madame de Staël's religious sensibilities were nothing if not complex. Her original Calvinism had overlaid upon it elements of Rousseauian deism and, after the turn of the century, Kantianism[84] and, later still, aesthetic mysticism. 'Religious emotions, more than all others together,' she wrote, 'awaken in us the feeling of the infinite.'[85] The universe, she was also to write, resembled a poem rather than a machine. It is not, therefore, without some justification that Madame de Staël has been seen as one of the founders of European Romanticism. However, it was these religious views—those of a 'good Calvinist', as she once described herself[86]—that not only underpinned her criticisms of the political fanaticism of the Terror, but also informed her censure of the Republic and her disparagement of Bonaparte. She had only disdain for Napoleon's attempt to reinstate the dominant position of the Catholic Church.

Germaine de Staël's most sustained engagement with matters relating to religion is found in what was arguably her most important work, *De l'Allemagne*. The text was begun in exile in Weimar in 1808, where she had been reading Schiller and Fichte and conversing at length with such friends as Auguste von Schlegel. Through this she became persuaded that Germany was the very antithesis of France, that the genius and erudition of the Germans was the very opposite of the superficiality and mediocrity of the French. Their literature and philosophy were untouched by the spirit of materialism and concerned themselves with the most hidden mysteries of our being. 'The German moralists', she wrote, 'have raised up sentiment and enthusiasm from the contempt of a tyrannical reason.'[87] To that extent, it struck her that the Germanic nations were 'naturally religious' and 'metaphysical'. More-over, theirs was a religion of inner conviction rather than fanaticism, of contempla-tion and meditation rather than dogmatism. The Catholic religion in Germany, she conceded, was more tolerant than in any other country.[88] By way of contrast, she made perfectly explicit her criticism of the French philosophy of the eighteenth century. If 'the new German philosophy' respected religion and affirmed the moral dignity of man, the French variety rested upon a 'scoffing scepticism' that was, in

---

[82] Germaine de Staël, *Considérations sur la Révolution française* (1983), 604.

[83] Ibid. 605.

[84] An important influence was Charles de Villers. In 1804 he had publ. *Essai sur l'esprit et l'influence de la Réformation de Luther.*

[85] Staël, *De l'Allemagne*, ii. 238.

[86] Staël, *Des Circonstances*, 220.

[87] Staël, *De l'Allemagne*, ii. 200.

[88] Ibid. 255.

her opinion, 'destructive of every belief of the heart'. It was, she remarked more than once, a 'degrading doctrine' based upon a mixture of 'frivolity' of the mind and 'dogmatic incredulity'.[89]

This was no minor theme but one that Madame de Staël developed at considerable length. The strength of German philosophy, she believed, flowed from its willingness to reflect upon the nature of the soul and upon the source of our moral faculties. This was completely lacking in France. Building upon the sensationalist epistemology of John Locke, Madame de Staël argued, the French writers of the eighteenth century from Condillac to Helvétius and d'Holbach had developed an experimental metaphysics that had come to assume that the entire development of our moral being derived directly from external objects. If the first steps taken by Locke and Condillac had been innocent— neither had appreciated the dangers attaching to their ideas with regard to our conception of personal identity—the end result had been 'the annihilation of the Deity in the universe and of free will in men'.[90] Within such a materialist system, there could be no place for the immortality of the soul and the sentiment of duty. 'No sensation', Madame de Staël observed, 'reveals immortality in death to us.'[91] Nor could it find a place for profound meditation and exalted sentiment for, by reducing all ideas to our sensations, it could at best provide 'specious arguments' for selfishness. The only morality that could follow from such a sensationalist epistemology, in her view, was one of self-interest and self-love. Relations between individuals could not but be based upon prudent calculation and could not rest upon sympathy and generosity.[92]

The same, Madame de Staël argued, applied to public morals, where the principles of justice, fidelity, and equity all too easily gave way before those of advantage, national interest, and self-preservation. 'When once it has been said that morals ought to be sacrificed to the national interest', she concluded, 'we are very liable to contract the sense of the word nation from day to day, and to make it signify at first our supporters, then our friends, and then our family, which is only a polite way of saying ourselves.'[93] Although never mentioned by name, the target here was as much the *Idéologues* as it was Napoleon Bonaparte. If the emperor had reduced the French to abject servitude, Destutt de Tracy and his colleagues, as the survivors of eighteenth-century materialism, were responsible for the deplorable state of French morals. Notions of self-sacrifice, duty, and the general good had all but vanished.

The explicitly political dimensions of these arguments were forcefully developed by Germaine de Staël's fellow Swiss Protestant, Benjamin Constant. This aspect of Constant's thought has been best explored in recent work by Helena Rosenblatt.[94] Not only has she drawn our attention to the importance of Constant's lifelong

---

[89] Ibid. 113–17.   [90] Ibid. 109.   [91] Ibid. 110.
[92] Ibid. 181–6.   [93] Ibid. 194.
[94] See Rosenblatt, *Liberal Values*. See also Giovanni Paoletti, *Benjamin Constant et les Anciens: Politique, religion, histoire* (2006).

fascination with religion and his enduring interest in the new Protestant theology coming out of Germany at the time, but she has also suggested that Constant's contemporaries understood that his Protestantism was integral to his liberalism.[95] Here we might briefly focus upon the preface to *De la Religion*, for it is arguably in this text (published in 1824) that Constant most strongly challenged the worth of self-interest as a guide to our actions.[96] Casting his mind back over the last twenty years Constant saw a depressing catalogue of what he described as human indifference, servility, calculation, prudence, and 'moral arithmetic'. The effect of this, Constant continued, had been to drive men within themselves, for them to be consumed by a narrow egoism, and thus for all of us to become isolated one from another. In these circumstances liberty could no more be enjoyed than it could be established or preserved.

In consequence Constant distinguished between two broad moral systems: one where personal well-being was our goal and self-interest our guide; another, where we were driven by a sense of self-abnegation and personal sacrifice.[97] For Constant, the second of these constituted the essence of what he regarded as an indestructible and indefinable inner religious sentiment. Not only did this inform our capacity for disinterested actions—thereby making us worthy of our freedom—but it also gave us a glimpse of our capacity to attain to a level of human perfection. That Constant believed in the reality of the latter as an unfolding and progressive movement of humankind towards a condition of moral and intellectual maturity is beyond dispute.[98] Our progress towards that end could be impeded, and sometimes temporarily reversed, but it could never be thwarted, not even by the most barbarous of tyrants. By the same token, it demonstrated conclusively that, in a modern society, commerce alone was not a sufficient guarantee of the existence of liberty, and that liberty itself was grounded upon and was sustained by religious sentiment.

The guiding threads of this argument were, first, that religion was not a fixed and immutable thing (the power of the priesthood, Constant recognized, depended on the immutability of doctrine) and, secondly, that religious sentiment was both inherent to human beings and the most pure of our passions. Everything that was noble and most beautiful in us derived from it. Through it we broke out of the narrow circle of our interests and opened ourselves up to others in a spirit of generosity and sympathy. Yet, as Constant repeatedly avowed, religion had been distorted and denatured. 'Man', Constant wrote, 'has been pursued into this last refuge, this intimate sanctuary of his existence. In the hands of government, religion has been transformed into a menacing institution.'[99] It had been twisted into an instrument of oppression and into a social institution designed to repress the people. For Constant the conclusions to be drawn were clear. True religion

---

[95] Rosenblatt, *Liberal Values*, 2.
[96] Benjamin Constant, *De la Religion* (Arles, 1999), 25–34.
[97] Ibid. 33.
[98] See Benjamin Constant, 'De la perfectibilité de l'espèce humaine', in *De la liberté chez les Modernes* (1980), 580–95 and 'Du développement progressif des idées religieuses', ibid. 523–42.
[99] Constant, *Principles of Politics Applicable to All Governments* (Indianapolis, 2003), 134.

served no utilitarian ends. It was not 'a supplement to the gallows or the wheel'.[100] Whenever governments interfered in matters relating to religion it did harm, and it should therefore leave it alone. There should be no state religion. Neither the spirit of inquiry nor the proliferation of sects was antithetical to the flourishing of religion. Indeed, they ensured that religion kept its vitality and did not descend into ossified dogma. The preferred policy therefore was to be religious pluralism and freedom of conscience.[101]

In the years that followed the writing and the publication of these texts, Constant continued both to restate his defence of modern liberty and to restate the importance of our religious sentiments. He did so, for example, in a speech to the Athénée royal in December 1825 entitled 'La Tendance générale des esprits dans le dix-neuvième siècle'[102] and again in a long review of Charles Dunoyer's *L'Industrie et la Morale considerées dans leur rapport avec la liberté*.[103] What is intriguing about Constant's latter text, however, is that it provided a glimpse of what he imagined might be a new form of religious despotism. In a postscript, he turned his fire against what he termed 'an industrial papacy' and which he clearly associated with the new positivist doctrines of Saint-Simon and his disciples.[104] In contrast to the *individualisme* developed by Dunoyer,[105] Constant argued, this 'new sect' saw all diversity of thought and activity as an expression of anarchy. Terrified that not all people thought the same (or the same as their leaders), they invoked a spiritual authority designed to reconstitute a broken intellectual unity and harmony. Under the guise of coordinating our thoughts and actions, they sought, in Constant's opinion, 'to organize tyranny' and to impose 'a new yoke', to bring an end to what they saw as the spiritual disorganization of society. Constant's response was to suggest that this supposed 'moral anarchy' was nothing other than 'the natural, desirable, happy state of a society in which each person, according to his own understanding, tastes, intellectual disposition, believes or examines, preserves or improves, in a word, makes a free and independent use of his faculties'. Moreover, Constant was in little doubt that it was towards this end that society was moving. Nevertheless, in these few remarks on Saint-Simonianism and its quest to establish a new theocracy, he had identified what would become a growing trend in nineteenth-century France and the potential breeding ground for a new type of despotism.[106]

---

[100] Ibid. 141.
[101] Ibid. 129–46. Similar views can be found in book 1 of *De la Religion*, 39–97, in the *Commentaire sur l'ouvrage de Filangieri* (2004), 290–315, and in articles published by Constant in such journals as *Le Mercure*, *La Minerve*, *La Renommée* and the *Courrier Français*: see Ephraim Harpaz (ed.), *Benjamin Constant: Recueil d'articles*, 2 vols. (Geneva, 1972); *Receuil d'articles 1825–1829* (1992); *Receuil d'articles 1829–1830* (1992).
[102] *Revue Encyclopédique*, 28 (1825), 661–74.
[103] Ibid. 29 (1826), 416–35.
[104] Ibid. 432–5.
[105] See Charles Dunoyer, 'Notice historique sur l'industrialisme', *Œuvres de Charles Dunoyer* (1870), ii. 173–99.
[106] It was Constant's fellow liberal, Élie Halévy, who insisted upon the connexion between Saint-Simonianism and Bonapartist 'Caesarism': see Élie Halévy, *L'Ère des tyrannies* (1938), 213, 219.

The years of the Restoration were difficult ones for French Protestants. Although the Revolution and the Empire had left Catholicism in a parlous state—the Church was short of both priests and money—it was re-established as the state religion and Louis XVIII quickly displayed his intention to restore the unity of throne and altar. The teaching of the Catholic religion in the primary school curriculum and a return to an unadulterated Christian calendar were among the many gestures intended to secure a revival of Catholic faith and to re-Christianize France. Catholic intransigence only intensified further in the 1820s after the assassination of the Duc de Berri and the ascent to the throne of the devout Charles X. In 1825 a new Law of Sacrilege stipulated that the crime of blasphemy was punishable by death. Protestants had good cause to be worried by these measures as renewed enthusiasm for Catholicism was often accompanied by a reactionary politics which specifically identified Protestantism as being among the nation's ills. There were many calls to put an end to religious liberty. Protestants responded to these pressures by launching such journals as the *Archives du christianisme* and the *Revue protestante*. They likewise established various voluntary associations to defend Protestant values and sought to create links with like-minded Catholics. It was, therefore, with some relief that Protestants greeted the Revolution of 1830 and the calmer, less religiously orthodox, atmosphere of the July Monarchy.[107]

No one gave better voice to the possibilities that this novel situation might offer Protestantism than François Guizot. Remarkably, during the 1820s the historian of representative government had found time to write a series of essays on such diverse religious topics as the immortality of the soul and the meaning of faith and he continued these interests into the 1830s and beyond.[108] In 1838, now temporarily free of ministerial responsibilities, he penned two texts that addressed the relationship between religion and politics, both of extraordinary quality and insight and both intent upon effecting a new religious settlement under the Orleanist monarchy of Louis-Philippe.

The first, *De la Religion dans les Sociétés Modernes*,[109] developed the argument that, as 'there is an intimate connection between man's earthly ideas and his religious ideas, between his temporal desires and his eternal desires',[110] it was necessary that there should exist an 'entente and a harmony' between politics and religion. This was especially true of a society such as that of contemporary France where the 'docteurs populaires' had told everyone that they had a right to be happy and a right to everything they desired. 'The more the social movement becomes animated and widespread', Guizot observed, 'the less politics will suffice to guide a troubled humanity.'[111] Yet such an argument, Guizot acknowledged, faced two

---

[107] For an account of the development of Catholic and Protestant opinion see the remarkable essay by François Guizot, 'Le Réveil Chrétien en France au XIXe siècle', *Méditations sur l'État Actuel de la Religion Chrétienne* (1866), ii. 1–200.

[108] See Guizot, *Méditations et Études Morales* (1852), 87–210. Guizot's later religious writings can be found in the 3-vol. *Méditations sur l'État Actuel de la Religion Chrétienne*.

[109] Guizot, *Méditations et Études Morales*, 25–52.

[110] Ibid. 32.

[111] Ibid.

obstacles. First, there were 'clever men' who had seen religion as 'a means of order and of social control' and who denied its 'intrinsic value' for the individual. Second, 'great religious minds' had regarded the world as 'evil incarnate', as a barrier to the accomplishment of 'our moral destiny'. Religious belief existed only in opposition to human society. Both views, in Guizot's estimation, were wrong and dangerous. To the first, he responded that religious beliefs derived from what was 'most precious, most compelling and most noble in man' and that a politics which did not recognize this would be ultimately 'futile'. To the second, he replied that the world was not a place of proscription and perdition where men lived in exile but rather that it was in this world and through their social existence that men lived out and advanced their 'destiny'. It was, Guizot continued, to the glory of Christianity that it had understood that, if the fundamental purpose of religion was 'the regeneration and salvation of souls', then, by the same token, men should engage with this world and seek to improve it. Of late, however, religion and society, in Guizot's view, had ceased to understand each other and to develop in parallel. The 'ideas, sentiments, and interests' that prevailed in the temporal world were in disharmony with those relating to 'eternal life' and we were all the poorer and the less secure as a consequence. The challenging task ahead, therefore, was 'to draw together the Christian spirit and the spirit of the century, the old religion and the new society'.[112]

To that end, Guizot concluded his essay by drawing the reader's attention to efforts, both Catholic and Protestant, to effect reconciliation between these two worlds and to do so in conditions of mutual respect and shared liberty. 'The religious spirit', he wrote, 'has returned to the world to conquer it but not to usurp it.'[113] It was upon this premise that Guizot built the argument of his second text, *Du Catholicisme, du Protestantisme et de la Philosophie*.[114] 'I am convinced', he began, 'that, in the new society, in the France of the Charte, Catholicism, Protestantism and philosophy can live in peace together,... not only materially, but morally.... and voluntarily.'[115] The greatest challenge to this thesis, Guizot willingly accepted, came from the Catholic Church. The solution, however, lay in the neutrality of the State in religious matters and in the recognition of its 'incompetence' in matters of faith and dogma. The Church had nothing to fear from the new civil authority and could preserve its claims to infallibility in spiritual matters. All it had to do in return was to accept the central principle of France's constitutional regime, namely, that 'all human power is fallible and should be controlled and limited'.[116] In simple terms, this meant that the Catholic Church had to acknowledge the legitimacy of freedom of conscience. As for Protestantism, Guizot readily recognized that it was often seen as being on the side of revolution, as being 'incompatible with social order, religious peace, and monarchy'. This was a mistake for, despite the fact that liberty of thought had always been at the heart of Protestantism, 'never has a religious society been more disposed to show deference and respect towards the civil power'.[117] Nor was it

[112] Ibid. 38–9.   [113] Ibid. 51.   [114] Ibid. 53–86.
[115] Ibid. 56.   [116] Ibid. 66.   [117] Ibid. 75.

conceivable that France would be converted to Protestantism. Catholics and Protestants, therefore, should rather fight together against their common enemies of impiety and immorality and, in doing so, 'revive religious life'. 'Harmony in liberty', Guizot wrote, 'is the Christian spirit; it is charity combined with fervour'.[118] Accordingly, it was to the benefit of both religions and of society in general that the State should accord equal protection to all creeds and forms of worship.

The same principles of mutual respect and toleration applied to philosophy. Guizot's argument here was that, if the philosophical enterprise itself remained unchanged, it now better understood that philosophy alone was not sufficient to secure the conditions in which society and morality could thrive. For all philosophy's victory over its old adversaries, it had ceased to be 'utopian' and saw that its impiety and religious indifference were in need of correction. Consequently, he continued, 'philosophy is ready to become once again seriously and sincerely religious'.[119] In sum, Catholicism, Protestantism, and philosophy would come to constitute a new spiritual alliance and from this the 'spiritual order' would recover 'its activity and its brilliance'.

The connection between these opinions and Guizot's better-known political views was a tight one. Most obviously, in much the same way that Guizot wished to see the political order of the new France characterized by a *juste milieu*, so too he sought to encourage the emergence of spiritual consensus built around moderate, non-dogmatic religious beliefs. The ambition was to harness our striving for the eternal not only to enrich our souls but also to consolidate the principles and practices of constitutional monarchy.

In the second of his essays, Guizot did not specify the philosophy that he had in mind to contribute to this task. However, it was without doubt the Eclecticism of Victor Cousin. Cousin was a truly remarkable presence in French intellectual life, exercising immense influence over a whole 'regiment' of young disciples.[120] In addition to holding a chair in philosophy at the Sorbonne (from the tender age of 23), he became a member of the Institut de France and the Académie Française as well a peer of France, sitting in the upper house of the French parliament. More than this, under the July Monarchy it was Cousin who effectively controlled the curriculum of the French university system and the nation's *lycées*. It was, for example, Cousin who in 1840 introduced the now-famous *agrégation* in philosophy, a qualification he oversaw from his lofty position as director of the École Normale Supérieure. It is only a slight exaggeration to suggest that his thought represented the official philosophy of the July Monarchy.[121]

Eclecticism, as its name implies, drew upon a distinct conception of philosophical methodology. Through a study of the history of philosophy, it aimed to combine what it regarded as 'the true and essential elements' of all philosophical

---

[118] Guizot, *Méditations et Études Morales*, 83.
[119] Ibid. 85.
[120] See Goldstein, *The Post-Revolutionary Self: Politics and the Psyche, 1750–1850* (Cambridge, Mass., 2005); Armstrong Kelly, *The Humane Comedy*, 134–80; and Jules Simon, *Victor Cousin* (London, 1888).
[121] See Taine, *Les Philosophes Français du XIXe siècle* (1857), 299.

knowledge. Through this, Cousin contended, it generated 'the decomposition of all systems by the fire and steel of criticism' and 'their reconstruction in a new system which is the complete representation of consciousness in history'.[122] In essence, however, Eclecticism denoted a wholesale reaction against the sensationalist episte- mology of the eighteenth century.[123] Cousin arrived at this position by a somewhat circuitous route—his early influences included the voluntarism of Maine de Biran,[124] the commonsense philosophy of Thomas Reid and the Scottish school,[125] the classes of his first professor, the Doctrinaire Pierre-Paul Royer-Collard,[126] and, most important of all, the German philosophy of Kant, Hegel, and Schelling[127]— but in doing so he moved decisively against the psychological model of the self derived from Locke and Condillac and what remained of *idéologie*.[128] The outcome was not only to open up the possibility of new speculative and metaphysical considerations but was also to let God back into philosophy, albeit a God that was far from satisfying the requirements of Catholic orthodoxy. Cousin, as his former pupil Jules Simon wrote, 'admitted the infinite'.[129] He also admitted the eternal. So, to his own satisfaction at least, Cousin was able to reconcile the demands of faith and of reason and, in so doing, to affirm the instinctive convic- tions of religious belief. From what we know, he also managed to convince much of his sizeable audience.

Eclecticism was forged in opposition to the theocratic logic of the Restoration (Cousin was twice suspended from his teaching post at the Sorbonne during the 1820s) and, perhaps not unsurprisingly, it lost most of its critical edge once its institutional hegemony had been established.[130] The simplest (and crudest) char- acterization of Eclecticism in power is that it provided a philosophy for the newly dominant bourgeoisie. As Cousin himself observed at the close of one of his most famous pieces of writing, the preface to the 1833 edition of his *Fragmens philoso- phiques*, 'My political faith is in entire accordance with my philosophical faith.'[131] To be sure, the limited political pronouncements made by Cousin prior to and after the 1848 Revolution made unambiguously clear his attachment to both the principles of constitutional monarchy and those of the French Revolution.[132]

---

[122] Cousin, *Fragmens philosophiques* (1833), p. liv.

[123] See Philibert Damiron, *Mémoires pour server à l'histoire de la philosophie au XVIIIe siècle*, 2 vols. (1858).

[124] See Maine de Biran, 'Comparison des trois points de vue de Th. Reid, Condillac et M. de Tracy sur l'idée de l'existence ou le jugement d'extériorité', in Stéphane Douailler, Roger-Pol Droit, and Patrice Vermeren (eds.), *Philosophie, France, XIXe siècle: Écrits et opuscules* (1994), 29–35.

[125] See Théodore Jouffroy, 'De la philosophie et du sens commun', ibid. 60–75.

[126] See Royer-Collard, 'Cours de troisième année 1813–1814', ibid. 36–59.

[127] Cousin visited Germany in 1817 and 1818 and then again in 1824.

[128] See Cousin, *Cours de la philosophie morale au dix-huitième siècle, professé à la Faculté des Lettres, en 1819 et 1820*, 4 vols. (1837–42).

[129] Simon, *Victor Cousin*, 59.

[130] See Paul Bénichou, *Le Sacre de l'écrivain 1750–1830: Essai sur l'avènement d'un pouvoir spirituel laïque dans la France moderne* (1996), 245–63.

[131] Cousin, *Fragmens philosophiques*, p. lx.

[132] Cousin, *Cours de la philosophie morale au dix-huitième siècle, professé à la Faculté des Lettres, en 1819 et 1820*, i. 325–47; *Justice et charité* (1848); and *Des Principes de la Révolution française et du Gouvernement représentatif* (1864).

'In sum', Cousin wrote, 'the three great principles that for me represent the genius of the French Revolution are national sovereignty, justice or the emancipation of the individual, and civil charity or the gradual lessening of ignorance, poverty, and vice.'[133] However, for Cousin, this did not entail the establishment of a republic but rather the need for a government that was stable, durable, and moderate. 'The Republic', Cousin wrote, 'is the sinister face of the Revolution.'[134] 'Pure democracy' gave power not to the 'intelligent and enlightened' part of the nation but to the 'ignorant mass'. Constitutional monarchy, by contrast, was 'the revolution organized' and, in Cousin's opinion, the regime most appropriate to the France and the Europe of the nineteenth century.

The more serious part of the charge against Eclecticism is that its proponents self-consciously set out to fashion a philosophy with appeal to an educated minority and one which (it goes without saying) defended the interests of property owners. This is not without a grain of truth. Eclecticism saw property as a right, inherent in our personality and not dependent upon work.[135] It stipulated that one of our fundamental duties was to respect the liberty of others. Moreover, in attributing an educational function to the State—government, Cousin wrote, had an obligation to develop and protect the 'moral life' of the individual[136]—it gave considerable weight to the moral instruction of the poor and, in doing so, assumed that this largely Christian education would inculcate a set of conservative values. The moral law taught us not only to will what was good but also that universal happiness on earth was a chimera.[137]

But seen exclusively in this light much of what amounted to the immense appeal and attraction of Eclecticism to its original, mostly young, and often wildly enthusiastic, audience escapes our understanding.[138] What Cousin offered was a creed that denied that philosophy led inevitably to scepticism and atheism. Rather, it was 'the view of the soul'.[139] As such, Eclecticism distanced religion from sterile dogma and ceremony and opened up the possibility of a renewal of our sense of 'the true, the beautiful, and the good'.[140] It was this that Guizot, for long a colleague and friend of Cousin, had fully appreciated and had set before his readers in 1838.

For Eclecticism's opponents, its message was a very different and much less inspiring one. The traditionalist school associated with legitimist Catholicism not

---

[133] Cousin, *Des Principes*, pp. xxii–xxiii.

[134] Ibid., p. xxxiii.

[135] Cousin, *Justice et charité*, 27–35.

[136] Ibid. 48.

[137] Cousin, 'De la loi morale et de la liberté', *Fragmens philosophiques*, 209–16.

[138] See Alan B. Spitzer, *The French Generation of 1820* (Princeton, NJ, 1987), 71–96. Spitzer writes that the whole point of Cousin's lectures was to 'provide the answer to the question of not only what to believe but how to live'.

[139] Cousin, 'De la loi morale et de la liberté', 210.

[140] See *Du Vrai, du Beau, et du Bien* (1858). In the author's preface to the 1853 edn., Cousin said of Eclecticism that 'it teaches the spirituality of the soul, the liberty and responsibility of human actions, moral obligation, disinterested virtue, the dignity of justice, the beauty of charity; and beyond the limits of the world it shows a God, author and model of humanity, who, after having evidently made man for an excellent end, will not abandon him in the mysterious development of his destiny': ibid., pp. vii–viii.

only believed that Eclecticism wanted to dispense with the supernatural entirely but also that its ultimate ambition was to supplant the Catholic Church. From this counter-revolutionary position, Eclecticism looked like one more step towards a secular world. The left, in search of spiritual regeneration through a rejuvenated and purified Christianity,[141] was similarly dismissive of a doctrine that offered little to satisfy popular passions and little prospect of the appearance of a new Messiah. The Christian socialist Pierre Leroux, for example, offered a detailed refutation of Eclecticism, criticizing what he took to be its psychology, ontology, methodology, and conception of philosophy.[142] This 'false' and 'Machiavellian' philosophy, he wrote, had shrouded society and government in 'lethargy and a feeble torpor'. It was a doctrine for those content with the present and who denied the possibility of progress. 'As for us', Leroux concluded, 'this present has nothing which pleases us. Therefore let the dead bury the dead, as Jesus said, and let us, as Saint Paul said, turn our thoughts towards the city of the future.'[143] For his part, Hippolyte Taine, writing in the 1850s when Cousin's celebrity and power had all but evaporated, attributed the success of Eclecticism to what had been a fashionable desire to subordinate science to morality and a taste for abstract ideas. It amounted, he wrote, to no more than 'a pile of inaccurate sentences, unsatisfactory arguments, and obvious ambiguities'. As a doctrine, he continued, it was powerless, forgotten, and moribund.[144] In these criticisms lay Eclecticism's fate. It simply wilted under the combined assault of revelation, utopianism, and science. The July Monarchy fared little better.

III

Viewed from the vantage point of its close, the nineteenth century was one of scientific progress and technological advance. Street lighting, electric tramways, the department store, and the Paris Métro provided daily evidence of a society rushing headlong towards modernity. Yet it was also a century of persistent and resurgent religiosity. Eugen Weber, for example, records that in the mid-1870s, 35,387,703 of the 36,000,000 people in France were listed in the official census as Catholics. There was still one priest for every 639 inhabitants. The rural masses continued to venerate local saints and religious shrines in great numbers and did so in a world that was 'eager for miracles'.[145] After a vision of the Virgin Mary appeared to a

[141] See Edward Berenson, *Populist Religion and Left-Wing Politics in France, 1830–1852* (Princeton, NJ, 1984), 36–73, and 'A New Religion of the Left: Christianity and Social Revolution in France, 1815–1848', in François Furet and Mona Ozouf (eds.), *The French Revolution and the Creation of Modern Political Culture*, iii. *The Transformation of Political Culture 1789–1848* (Oxford, 1989), 543–60.

[142] Pierre Leroux, *Réfutation de l'Éclectisme ou se trouve exposée la vraie définition de la philosophie* (1839).

[143] Ibid. 276.

[144] Taine, *Les Philosophes Français*, 283–307.

[145] Eugen Weber, *Peasants into Frenchmen: The Modernisation of Rural France 1870–1914* (London, 1976), 339.

peasant girl, Bernadette Soubirous, at Lourdes in 1858, thousands upon thousands of believers made the pilgrimage to the holy site every year (a journey made all the easier by the existence of the railways and all the more accessible by adverts in the popular press). Remarkable cures of the lame and infirm were regularly witnessed, thus giving further vitality to Marian piety.[146] The national search for renewal after the military defeat of 1870 was accompanied by a widespread call among the devout for the expiation of the nation's sins and a renewal of France's broken covenant with the Church, a sentiment given lasting expression through the construction of the Sacré-Cœur Basilica on the hillside of Montmartre above Paris. Everything was done to ensure the Basilica's completion before the Republic commenced the celebrations of the centenary of the Revolution.[147] Throughout the entire century, the Church fought long and hard to restrict state control over the education system, a battle it pursued not only from the pulpit but through the *parti catholique* in parliament and the powerful Catholic press (most notably, *L'Univers,* edited by Louis Veuillot, and the monthly journal, *Le Correspondant*). Moreover, it was only in 1892—in his encyclical *Au milieu des solicitudes*—that Pope Leo XIII urged French Catholics to rally to the Republic. Prior to this the Church hierarchy had unhesitatingly and unfailingly sided with the causes of political reaction and the enemies of liberalism. Popular anticlericalism developed a language all of its own to characterize and stigmatize such anti-republican behaviour.[148]

It was the publication of Chateaubriand's *Le Génie du Christianisme* in 1802 that provided the first significant sign of Catholic revival.[149] As he was later to comment in his memoirs:

It was amid the remains of our temples that I published *Le Génie du Christianisme*. The faithful felt themselves saved; there was then a need for a faith, a hunger for religious consolation, which sprang from the denial of these consolations over many years.... People were rushing into the house of God in the same way as they entered a doctor's at the outbreak of a contagious disease. The victims of our troubles (and how many they were) sought salvation at the altar, like the shipwrecked clinging to a rock for safety.

'The idea of God and the immortality of the soul', he continued, 'reclaimed their dominion.'[150] As a work of theology, the quality of Chateaubriand's text may be judged by his concluding argument. 'Christianity is perfect; men are imperfect. A perfect outcome cannot follow from an imperfect principle. Therefore Christianity does not come from men. If it does not come from men, it can only come from God. If it comes from God, men can only know it by revelation. Therefore

[146] See Ruth Harris, *Lourdes: Body and Spirit in the Secular Age* (London, 1999).
[147] See Raymond A. Jones, 'Monument as Ex-Voto, Monument as Historiography: The Basilica of Sacré-Cœur', *French Historical Studies*, 18 (1993), 482–502.
[148] See Jacqueline Lalouette, *La République anticléricale* (2002), 301–412.
[149] See James F. McMillan, 'Catholic Christianity in France from Restoration to the Separation of Church and State, 1815–1905', in Sheridan Gilley and Brian Stanley (eds.), *The Cambridge History of Christianity*, viii. *World Christianities c.1815–c.1914* (Cambridge, 2006), 219.
[150] Chateaubriand, *Mémoires d'outre-tombe* (1973), i. 527–9.

Christianity is a revealed religion.'[151] Arguments of a similar style and dubious quality were used to sustain the accuracy of biblical chronology. These defects, however, did little to diminish the rapture induced among its readers.

Subtitled 'The Beauties of the Christian Religion', Chateaubriand's text started from the premise that there was nothing beautiful, sweet, or great in the world that was not also mysterious and from this it set out to prove that,

> of all religions, the Christian religion is the most poetic, the most humane, the most favourable to liberty and to the arts and literature . . . that there is nothing more divine than its morality, nothing more attractive and splendid than its tenets, its doctrines and its forms of worship; that it encourages genius, refines taste, develops the virtuous passions, imparts vigour to thought, presents noble forms to the writer and perfect models to the artist.[152]

The ambition, in other words, was to refute all those from Voltaire onwards who had claimed incorrectly that Christianity was born out of barbarism and that it held men in a condition of savagery, darkness, and slavery; and thus to show the contribution of Christianity to everything that was most sublime, inspiring, and valuable in Western civilization. This Chateaubriand achieved with both eloquence and erudition. Having safely navigated around the mysteries and sacraments of Christian doctrine, the text warmed to its task, exploring first 'the Poetry of Christianity' and then 'Fine Arts and Literature'. Sculpture, drama, sacred music, painting, and the Gothic cathedrals were all deployed *inter alia* to provide what amounted to a Christian apologetic as aesthetics. In similar vein, the concluding section evoked the beauties of the liturgy and the emotional power of the church bell and country cemetery. Chateaubriand, then, appealed not to the reason of his readers but to their hearts, to their feelings, and to their deepest sensibilities.

Not everyone was convinced or swayed—least of all, the house journal of the *Idéologues*, the *Décade philosophique*, where it was severely treated by Pierre-Louis Ginguené as a text defending counter-revolution and superstition[153]—but its influence among literary circles and the broader public spread far and wide and did so for much of the first half of the nineteenth century. Above all, Chateaubriand gave Catholics cause to be proud of their faith, restoring its credibility and prestige, and in so doing he revealed the spiritual poverty and sterility of the atheism bequeathed by the eighteenth century. The latter, he wrote, offered us only suffering, death, the coffin, and nothingness.[154]

In Chateaubriand's hands, Catholicism not only became attractive but almost fashionable. His evocative and rich prose struck a chord with a France disillusioned by the violence and chaos of the Revolution and a country grown sceptical of the claims of reason. The mood had changed and, capturing the moment, Chateaubriand conjured up the romance of the past and the possibilities of a new age of imagination and sentiment. The publication of *Le Génie du Christianisme*, Barbey d'Aurevilly was to write in 1851, 'had something of the supernatural and the astral

---

[151] Chateaubriand, *Le Génie du Christianisme* (1966), ii. 256.   [152] Ibid. i. 57.
[153] See Kitchin, *Un journal 'philosophique'*, 174–7.   [154] Ibid. 214.

about it'.[155] Yet Chateaubriand's poignant apology for Christianity was not the only manifestation of a resurgent Catholicism present at the time. By its side was to be found a darker and more apocalyptic expression of Catholic faith and one which, in its total opposition to the Enlightenment and all its supposed ills, set itself resolutely against the moral decay of post-revolutionary society.

Antoine Compagnon has described some of the essential features of this mentality in a work appropriately entitled *Les antimodernes*.[156] The discourse of antimodernity, he argues, was counter-revolutionary, against the *philosophes*, pessimistic about the possibilities of man and society, believed in one version or other of the doctrine of original sin, embraced an aesthetics of the sublime, and, last but not least, adopted a tone of vituperation and vengeance. The specific characteristics of this frame of mind typical of the early nineteenth century have likewise been sketched by Darrin McMahon.[157] After 1800, McMahon records, the defenders of the *philosophes* were subject to a 'powerful new onslaught' and this from authors who had but recently been forced 'to conduct their campaigns in exile, in hiding, and in fear of revolutionary reprisals'.[158] For these writers, Christianity was not merely socially necessary and useful but also true. It was a repository of certainty in a world of scepticism and doubt. Articles in such periodicals as the *Journal des débats* and the *Mercure* argued against toleration and for the rigorous censorship of religious opinion. In similar vein, anti-*philosophe* polemic praised the patriarchal family and denounced divorce, believing that parricide went hand in hand with regicide. History, on this view, showed the limits to human perfection and demonstrated the need for strong social and political institutions to control the wayward behaviour of ordinary mortals. Prejudice, custom, and tradition were to be valued, as were France's ancient monarchy and institutions. Finally, the anti-*philosophes* were in near-unanimous agreement that France had been at its greatest, most polished, and most devout, under the reign of Louis XIV and that since then the country had passed 'into utter depravity'.[159] The political agenda spawned by such tirades against the present was clear enough. France, these 'prophets of the past' believed,[160] would not make a return to social harmony and order until such time as religious orthodoxy had been re-established and the unity of throne and altar had been restored.

It would be wrong to overstate the level of doctrinal unity that existed among this diverse and, for the most part, little-known group of writers. Theological divisions in particular were never far from the surface and it would be a mistake to think in terms of an organized movement or party galvanized around an exclusive opposition to the *siècle des lumières*. Likewise, many of the strident criticisms of the corrosive and contagious effects of the philosophic spirit that were articulated in

[155] Jules Barbey d'Aurevilly, *Les Prophètes du passé* (1860), 110.
[156] Compagnon, *Les Antimodernes de Joseph de Maistre à Roland Barthes* (2005).
[157] Darrin M. McMahon, *Enemies of the Enlightenment: The French Counter-Enlightenment and the Making of Modernity* (Oxford, 2001), 122–52.
[158] Ibid. 122–3.
[159] Ibid. 147.
[160] This is the title of the work by Barbey d'Aurevilly cited above.

the wake of the Revolution were in circulation (sometimes albeit in embryonic form) before 1789. However, the Revolution itself, holding aloft the very possibility of the annihilation of the Catholic religion, served to radicalize these earlier pronouncements and to give them greater urgency and force. To that extent, the Revolution appeared to validate the dire warnings of disaster that the defenders of the Church had made repeatedly under the *ancien régime*. After the Revolution, therefore, with the worst fears of anti-*philosophe* opinion realized, the battle was truly enjoined. In the previous chapter we saw one example of this bitter enmity: the *philosophes* stood accused of leading a revolutionary conspiracy to destroy both Christianity and the monarchy. *Philosophie* and the *philosophes* were now to be subjected to relentless and destructive criticism before the jury of public opinion that they themselves had worked to create. Central to this was an attempted refutation of everything that the Enlightenment was taken to stand for.

We have already had reason to examine the ideas of Joseph de Maistre. He has featured as an opponent of the doctrine of rights, as an acerbic critic of Rousseau and of social contract theory, and as an advocate of the satanic quality of the Revolution. Now he is to figure as the staunch defender of religion, papal authority, and the public executioner.[161] Maistre, we might recall, was firmly of the opinion that it was the philosophers of the Enlightenment who had produced the revolutionary monster that had devastated France and Europe. In addition to this, he had a series of substantive objections to the *philosophisme* of his eighteenth-century enemy.[162] These objections informed all his mature writings and took three primary forms. First, Maistre rejected what he took to be the Enlightenment's theory of knowledge. In particular, he rejected the view that there were no such things as innate ideas. Next, he dismissed the paradigmatic status accorded to natural science. Finally, he denounced (and ridiculed) the Enlightenment's enthusiasm for a priori and abstract reasoning. Taken together, they amounted to one overall criticism: the Enlightenment displayed a misplaced pride and trust in the power of man's unaided intellect. 'Philosophy', Maistre countered, 'is nothing but human reason acting alone, and human reason reduced to its own resources is nothing but a brute whose power is restricted to destroying.'[163] It amounted, he wrote in May 1809, to an 'insurrection against God'.[164] Elsewhere, in the later *Les Soirées de Saint-Petersbourg*, he spoke of philosophy as 'theophobia' and as 'a system of practical atheism'.[165] In his view, we were witnessing a fight to the death between Christianity and the cult of philosophy.

---

[161] See Jesse Goldhammer, 'Joseph de Maistre and the Politics of Conservative Regeneration', *The Headless Republic: Sacrificial Violence in Modern French Thought* (Ithaca, NY, and London, 2005), 71–111.

[162] When Maistre spoke of *philosophisme* rather than *philosophie*, he was intentionally designating a form of false philosophy that relied upon the misuse of reason. The term was very current in the latter half of the 18th cent.

[163] *De la Souveraineté du peuple* (1992), 132–3.

[164] 'Essai sur le Principe générateur des constitutions politiques et des autres institutions humaines', in Pierre Glaudes (ed.), *Joseph de Maistre: Œuvres* (2007), 399.

[165] 'Les Soirées de Saint-Petersbourg ou Entretiens sur le gouvernement temporal de la Providence', ibid. 59.

Maistre did not read Locke's *Essay on the Human Understanding* until 1806.[166] Having read it, he quickly concluded that 'contempt for Locke is the beginning of wisdom'.[167] His philosophy was as false as it was dangerous. Maistre's argument against Locke and Lockean epistemology may be briefly summarized as follows.[168] Locke was a superficial and mediocre thinker. He was 'incapacity demonstrated'. His work was frequently characterized by 'grossness' of expression, as, for example, when he described the memory as a box where ideas were stored until needed or the human intellect as a dark room with several windows to let in the light.[169] Most of all, what Locke said was either straightforwardly banal or plain wrong. This, Maistre maintained, was true of Locke's central proposition: that all our ideas came from either the senses or from reflection. 'Torturing the truth', Maistre argued, Locke was forced to accept that 'general ideas' were 'inventions or CREATURES of the human mind', for 'according to the doctrine of this great philosopher, man *makes* general ideas *with* simple ideas, just as he *makes* boats *with* planks'.[170] The fallacy in Locke's argument was all too evident. Every idea, Maistre argued, that did not originate either in the mind's interaction with external objects or the consideration of itself by the mind must derive from the substance of the mind. From this, Maistre declared jubilantly, it followed that 'there are ideas that are innate and prior to all experience'.[171] Consequently, Locke's entire argument stood exposed as 'splendid nonsense'.

Maistre's own references to innate ideas displayed a significant (and perhaps understandable) element of uncertainty and hesitation. 'Whether universal ideas are innate in us, or whether we derive them from God, or whatever you like', Maistre argued defensively, 'is not important.'[172] What mattered was that we recognized that Locke's epistemology contained 'the gravest and vilest of errors'. To deny the existence of innate ideas was not only to deny the spiritual essence of man but also to deny the very possibility of morality. Man, Maistre insisted, carried within him certain common moral opinions or eternal verities. '*I ought to do it*' was, Maistre contended, an 'innate idea whose nature is independent of every error of application'. If this assumption were not accepted, he concluded, it would be impossible to conceive of 'the unity of the human species'.[173]

Having thus dismissed Locke's theory of knowledge and pointed out its dangers when placed in the hands of its 'venomous' French adherents, Maistre was next in a position to challenge what he saw as the false and mistaken conception of science so dear to the eighteenth century. Upon this occasion his ire was directed against yet another illustrious exemplar of English empiricism: Francis Bacon. The *Examen de la Philosophie de Bacon ou l'on traite différentes questions de la philosophie rationnelle* was written between 1814 and 1816 (although not published until 1836) and followed the publication of Bacon's complete works in French at the turn of the

---

[166] See Richard A. Lebrun, 'Maistrian Epistemology', in Lebrun (ed.), *Maistre Studies* (Lanham, Md., 1988), 209. See also E. D. Watt, '"Locked In": De Maistre's Critique of French Lockeanism', *Journal of the History of Ideas*, 32 (1971), 129–32.
[167] Maistre, 'Les Soirées de Saint-Petersbourg', 640.
[168] Ibid. 601–48.   [169] Ibid. 612.   [170] Ibid. 623.
[171] Ibid. 624.   [172] Ibid. 511.   [173] Ibid. 626–7.

century. It amounted to a 700-page, two-volume refutation and dismissal of everything Bacon ever wrote or said.[174] His philosophy, Maistre stated, was 'a continuous aberration'. Bacon 'was mistaken about logic, about metaphysics, about physics, about natural history, about astronomy, about mathematics, about chemistry, about medicine and, finally, about everything relating to the vast area of natural philosophy on which he dared to speak'.[175] Specifically, Maistre denied that science had had need of a new method and that Bacon had invented one.[176] Indeed, Maistre went so far as to argue that Bacon's *novum organum* was 'directly contrary to the advancement of the sciences'.[177] 'Nothing can excuse him', Maistre wrote, 'for having written, with the pretension of being a legislator, whole volumes upon things about which he did not have the least idea.'[178]

The more substantive criticism was that Bacon's 'false, vile, and corrupting theories' rested upon the assumption that the natural sciences (and 'experimental physics' in particular) were the only valid or 'real' forms of knowledge. Not only was this to seek to dislodge theology and metaphysics from the pre-eminent position they had traditionally occupied but, more gravely still, it postulated the separation of science from religion. It was in this sense, Maistre argued, that 'every line of Bacon leads to materialism'.[179] Nowhere was this more evident, in Maistre's opinion, than when Bacon spoke of the soul, but the same applied to his account of the origin of spontaneous motion. God was simply removed from the explanation provided. 'Bacon's central principle', Maistre wrote, 'is that God can be compared to nothing, if one speaks without resort to metaphor, and nothing being able to be known except by comparison, God is absolutely inaccessible to reason, and by consequence cannot be perceived in the universe.'[180] 'It would have been rather difficult', Maistre continued, 'to drive God out from everywhere but it is already something to enclose him firmly within the Bible: it only remains to burn the book.'[181]

By way of rejoinder, Maistre argued that science was good only when it was 'restrained within a certain circle'. Separated from theology, it was dangerous; subordinated to theology, it would be 'perfected' and given more 'strength and breadth'. This was so, Maistre argued, 'because religion, by purifying and exalting the human mind, renders it more able to make discoveries, because it ceaselessly combats those vices which are the principal enemy of truth'.[182] The same rule applied to all other manifestations of the human spirit, be it architecture, music, painting, drama, or sculpture. It was not true, Maistre countered, that the Roman Catholic Church had hindered scientific advance. It was, however, only right that it should challenge untruth. It was Maistre's opinion that, had Pope Leo X stifled Protestantism at its birth, Europe would have been spared many of its worst

---

[174] See *Examen de la Philosophie de Bacon ou l'on traite différentes questions de la philosophie rationnelle*, 2 vols. (Lyons, 1845). In English see *An Examination of the Philosophy of Bacon wherein Different Questions of Rational Philosophy are Treated* (Montreal and Kingston, 1998).
[175] Maistre, *Examen*, ii. 372–3.   [176] Ibid. i. 72.
[177] Ibid. 83.   [178] Ibid. 260.   [179] Ibid. ii. 33.
[180] Ibid. 14.   [181] Ibid.   [182] Ibid. 290.

disasters, including 'the French Revolution, the incontestable daughter of the revolution of the sixteenth century'.[183]

In summary, Maistre's argument was that the philosophy of the eighteenth century had been uniquely negative and worthless precisely because of its 'anti-religious spirit'. It had worked tirelessly to unburden men of everything they knew and to leave them with 'only physics'. It had sought 'to isolate man, to render him proud, egotistical, and pernicious to himself and to others'.[184] Bacon, Maistre concluded, was 'the father of these deadly maxims'. He had given 'the worst counsel to men'. Those 'conspirators' who had chosen him as their 'oracle', Maistre speculated, 'no doubt knew what they were doing'.[185] Maistre could at least reassure himself with the thought that they had received the punishment they deserved.

If natural science had limited merit as a source of knowledge, where else might man look? Maistre rarely made reference to either of the two obvious candidates: natural law and biblical revelation. Yet he clearly believed that the dictates of God's will could be known.[186] Accordingly, Maistre identified four alternative sources of knowledge. The first, and most important, was the knowledge generated by the traditional beliefs and customs of a society. These, in a very real sense, embodied not only the wisdom of past generations but also the voice of God. Moreover, they needed to be adopted 'without examination'. At a man's birth, Maistre wrote, 'his cradle should be surrounded by dogmas, and when his reason awakes all his opinions should be given to him . . . Nothing is more vital to him than preju-dices.'[187] Related to this was language. Each language, Maistre argued, mirrored 'the spiritual realities' of its birth and to that extent it was language that evidenced the 'general soul' and 'true moral unity' that made up each nation.[188] Maistre had only contempt for modern notions of a 'philosophical language'. Next was the knowledge that arose from the 'inner sentiments' of the heart. 'The upright man', Maistre observed, 'is very commonly alerted, by an inner sentiment, to the falsity or truth of certain propositions before any examination, often without even having made the studies necessary to be in a position to examine them with full knowledge of the case.'[189] This 'secret instinct', Maistre believed, was 'almost infallible in questions of theoretical philosophy, morality, metaphysics, and natural theology'. Finally, Maistre had recourse to the concept of 'the true elect'. Vaguely reminiscent of Rousseau's lawgiver, these were men invested by God with 'extraordinary power, often unrecognized by their contemporaries, and perhaps to themselves'. They acted from inspiration and, if ever they took up their pen, it was to command. Through their 'infallible instinct' they were able to 'divine' the 'hidden forces and qualities' that formed the character of a nation.[190] It was in these four ways,

---

[183] Maistre, *Examen*, ii. 372–3.   [184] Ibid. 269.   [185] Ibid. 272.
[186] Richard A. Lebrun, 'Maistre and Natural Law', in Lebrun (ed.), *Maistre Studies*, 193–206.
[187] Maistre, *De la Souveraineté du peuple*, 147.
[188] Maistre, 'Les Soirées de Saint-Petersbourg', 497–507; *De la Souveraineté du peuple*, 106.
[189] Maistre, 'Les Soirées de Saint-Petersbourg', 461.
[190] Maistre, *De la Souveraineté du peuple*, 122.

therefore, that a people, if it should so wish, was able to apprehend the purposes of God.

Maistre's next target was the abstract reasoning he associated with the Enlightenment's projects for social and political reform. Constitutions, Maistre argued, were not made by man alone or 'as a watchmaker makes a watch'.[191] This was so for the fundamental reason that, if man was capable of modifying things, he was capable of creating nothing. If a man could plant a seed or cultivate a tree, Maistre argued, it could never be imagined that he could make a tree.[192] Where men did deliberate rationally upon a constitution they could at best produce a naïve simplification of what was required, a 'pure abstraction' that was ill-suited to the complexities of a nation's character and situation. The inevitable outcome would be civil disorder and anarchy and a form of government that could not last. Moreover, such a product of abstract deliberation would not possess the power to bind men and to guarantee their loyalty and obedience.

One example of these difficulties provided by Maistre related to what he called 'the theory of names'.[193] Starting from the assumption that God alone had the right to bestow a name, Maistre concluded that, if an institution had a name imposed upon it by a deliberative assembly, 'both the name and the thing will disappear in a short time'. A name needed to 'germinate': otherwise it would not ring true. Speaking therefore of the decision to build a new American capital, Maistre concluded that 'it is a thousand to one that the town will not be built, or that it will not be called *Washington*, or that the Congress will not sit there'.[194] Indeed, Maistre went so far as to suggest that the very act of having to write something down was 'always a sign of weakness, ignorance, or danger' and that a law or institution possessed no real force.[195] Never, Maistre suggested, had statesmen in England gathered together and resolved a priori to create three powers and to balance them and yet, after several centuries, the English constitution displayed 'the most complex unity and the most delicate equilibrium of political forces the world has ever seen'. It was 'a work of circumstances' and those circumstances were 'infinite'[196]

A priori reasoning, therefore, could not produce institutions that would endure. On the contrary, a successful constitution could only ever be the work of God and one that was seen to enjoy divine sanction. 'The author of all things', Maistre wrote, 'has only two ways of giving a government to a people.' Either it grew 'imperceptibly like a plant' or the task was entrusted to one of the true elect. Whatever the case, it could never be the result of rational deliberation.[197] And so, Maistre argued, man

---

[191] Ibid.
[192] Maistre, 'Considérations sur la France', 232.
[193] Maistre, 'Essai sur le Principe générateur des constitutions politiques et des autres institutions humaines', 393–8.
[194] Maistre, 'Considérations sur la France', 242.
[195] Maistre, 'Essai sur le Principe générateur des constitutions politiques et des autres institutions humaines', 378.
[196] Ibid. 373.
[197] Maistre, *De la Souveraineté du peuple*, 122.

must always be brought back to history as the 'first and only teacher in politics'. Indeed, history was 'experimental politics' and was of infinitely more worth than 'a hundred books of speculative theories'.[198] Two immediate lessons could be learnt. The first was that 'in its laws and ancient customs each nation has everything it needs to be as happy as it can be'.[199] The second was that, as a republic of 24 million people had never been known before, its existence in the future was an impossibility.[200] Europe's sin, Maistre contended, was that it had closed its eyes to these, and other, 'great truths' and, as a consequence, it had suffered.

Maistre had not yet finished with the Enlightenment. *Philosophisme* was intimately linked to Protestantism and both, in his view, embodied 'the spirit of insurrection' that was destroying Europe.[201] In truth, it would be difficult to do justice to the vituperative ferocity of Maistre's polemic against Protestantism. He asserted that Protestantism was born 'rebellious' and fully armed. It was 'the son of pride and the father of anarchy'. It protested against everything and submitted to no authority. It was the enemy of all belief. Its very name was a crime. It was a 'deadly sore' that destroyed everything. It was dissolving the 'cement' that had bound European civilization together. More than this, Protestantism was not only a religious heresy but also a civil heresy, for the primary reason that it had freed people from 'the yoke of obedience'. It was, Maistre avowed, 'the mortal enemy of all sovereignty'. From all sides its apostles preached resistance to authority. There was consequently a direct line from Protestantism to Jansenism, to the *philosophes*, and on to the Revolution and Jacobinism. Protestantism, Maistre wrote, 'is not favourable to any government; it attacks them all; but as sovereignty only fully exists under monarchies, it particularly detests this form of government'.[202] It was, he concluded, the '*sans-culottisme* of religions'.[203]

Louis XIV had been right therefore to revoke the Edict of Nantes and everything now needed to be done, Maistre wrote in the late 1790s, to suffocate this 'great enemy'. In later years Maistre's public stance on Protestantism mellowed somewhat and, as he demonstrated in the concluding pages of *Du Pape*,[204] he even came to consider it likely that Protestants, and Anglicans in particular, might return to the Catholic Church. Nevertheless, the overall tenor of his argument was that, in marked contrast to Protestantism, Catholicism was a religion of obedience. Resting upon the 'infallibility' of the teaching provided by its clergy, it urged 'the abnegation of all individual reasoning' and 'unquestioning respect for authority'.[205] Never had it preached the doctrines of resistance and insurrection, always preferring martyrdom to rebellion. Rather, Catholicism was 'the most ardent friend, guardian, and defender of government'.[206]

---

[198] Maistre, *De la Souveraineté du peuple*, 186–7.   [199] Ibid. 260.
[200] Maistre, 'Considérations sur la France', 219–20.
[201] Maistre, 'Sur le protestantisme', in Glaudes (ed.), *Joseph de Maistre*, 311–30.
[202] Ibid. 326.
[203] Ibid. 330.
[204] Maistre, *Du Pape* (Antwerp, 1820), 483–515.
[205] Maistre, 'Sur le protestantisme', 312.
[206] Ibid. 324.

It was in this context that Maistre lauded what he described unhesitatingly as 'the monarchical supremacy of the Supreme Pontiff'.[207] The very idea of universality, he stated, presupposed that the Church was a monarchy and that the spiritual authority of the pope was infallible. In embracing this position, it is important to realize that Maistre was setting himself firmly and unequivocally against the doctrine known as Gallicanism.[208] At its simplest, Gallicanism denoted a tendency within the French Church to emphasize its relative independence from the Holy See. As it came to be defined in the seventeenth and eighteenth centuries, the articles of Gallicanism stipulated that monarchs, and sovereigns more generally, were not subject to ecclesiastical authority in temporal matters and therefore that the head of the Church could not free their subjects from any oath of allegiance or obedience. It also laid down that the primacy of the papacy in spiritual matters was limited either by the episcopate or, in its more radical version, by the entire body of the faithful. Both the Constitutional Church foisted upon France during the Revolution and the Napoleonic Concordat of 1801 drew heavily upon these traditions and they were again to prevail under the Restoration.

In Maistre's eyes, there was little to distinguish Gallicanism from Calvinism and Jansenism.[209] He regarded the Gallican Declaration of 1682, drawn up to settle the dispute between Louis XIV and Pope Innocent XI, as one of the most 'reprehensible' and 'pernicious' documents in ecclesiastical history, and in the process dismissed talk of 'the ancient tradition of the Gallican church' as 'a pure chimera'.[210] The so-called Gallican liberties enjoyed by the Church in France, in Maistre's view, were non-existent and, by subordinating the Church to the State, amounted to no more than the liberty not to be Catholic.[211] Accordingly, Maistre argued that the pope's authority was as absolute as that of any other sovereign and that the government of the Church could not be devolved to its ecumenical councils. This, he avowed, did not amount, as Protestants claimed, to a justification of despotism, but rather to a recognition that a 'periodic or intermittent sovereignty [was] a contradiction in terms'.[212] It did mean, however, that, when faced with 'the horrors of tyranny', the pope and the pope alone could act as a dispensing power. 'The Sovereign Pontiff', Maistre wrote, 'would do nothing contrary to divine law by releasing subjects from their oath of allegiance. He would simply claim that sovereignty is a divine and sacred authority which can be controlled only by another similarly divine authority, but of a superior order and one specially vested with this power in certain extraordinary situations.'[213] By the same token, there could be no general right of rebellion or resistance. Man, Maistre observed, 'in his capacity as a being at once moral and corrupt, of right understanding and perverse will, must necessarily be governed'.[214] It was no more possible to imagine a society without a sovereign than a hive of bees without a queen.

[207] Maistre, *Du Pape*, 34.
[208] In addition to *Du Pape*, see Maistre, *De l'Église Gallicane dans son rapport avec le souverain pontife* (Lyons, 1821).
[209] Ibid. 4–110. [210] Ibid. 138. [211] Ibid. 324.
[212] Maistre, *Du Pape*, 12. [213] Ibid. 168. [214] Ibid. 157.

It was this that the eighteenth century, 'with its intense and blind pride', had failed to understand. Man, tainted by original sin, was 'evil, horribly evil'. He was 'insatiable for power' and 'infinite in his desires'. All men were born despots and left to their own devices would sow chaos and anarchy round them. As such, evil existed on the earth and acted constantly in it, producing endless suffering. And it was because of this that God had granted to sovereigns 'the supreme prerogative of punishing crimes'. From this arose the 'necessary existence' of the executioner. This 'inexplicable being', Maistre wrote, was a species unto himself, a man who had put all pleasant and honourable occupations to one side and had chosen to torture and to put to death his fellow creatures. And yet, Maistre continued, 'all grandeur, all power, all subordination rests on the executioner: he is the horror and bond of human association. Remove this incomprehensible agent from the world and, at that very moment, order gives way to chaos, thrones topple and society disappears.'[215]

It was consequently without hesitation that Maistre advanced the cause of counter-revolution, arguing that the people themselves would be the principal beneficiaries of a return to the old order. Monarchy, he proclaimed, was the most ancient, the most universal, and the most natural form of government. Democracy, by contrast, was an association of men without sovereignty and, as such, was destined to perish. The idea of a whole people acting as sovereign and legislator defied belief. A restored monarchy alone would return France to a condition of order and tranquillity. The truth of the matter, however, was that, over time, even Maistre himself came to see that a return to the *ancien régime*, for all its desirability, was well-nigh impossible and that the change introduced into French society by the Revolution was irreversible.

Ultramontane opinions such as those of Maistre were always in a minority, and remained so under the Restoration. Gallican sentiments prevailed among both the clergy and the laity, and the government, through the Ministry of Ecclesiastical Affairs, continued to regulate the external aspects of religious life and practice. Yet the return of the monarchy did not put an end to these disputes and Maistre proved to be by no means alone in combining fideism and a rejection of eighteenth-century rationalism with royalism and a reassertion of papal authority. Another such was the passionate, tormented, and ill-fated Abbé Félicité de Lamennais.[216]

We catch a first glimpse of this stance in Lamennais's text of 1809, *Réflexions sur l'état de l'Église en France*,[217] written when its author was still in his mid-twenties. The blame for France's descent into a state of irreligion was placed firmly at the door of the Reformation and its descendants, the *philosophes* of the eighteenth century. By destroying the foundations of social and political order they had established anarchy as the principle of both Church and State. A belief in the sovereignty of the people had been combined with the affirmation of the right of

---

[215] Maistre, 'Les Soirées de Saint-Petersbourg', 471.

[216] See Alec R. Vidler, *Prophecy and Papacy: A Study of Lamennais, the Church and the Revolution* (London, 1954); Louis Le Guillou, *Lamennais* (Brussels, 1969); and Le Guillou, *L'Évolution de la pensée religieuse de Félicité de Lamennais* (1966).

[217] See Lamennais, 'Réflexions sur l'état de l'Église en France pendant le dix-huitième siècle, et sur sa situation actuelle', *Œuvres Complètes de F. de La Mennais* (1836–7), vi. 1–115.

private judgement in matters of belief. Pierre Bayle, the Jansensists, Voltaire, Diderot and his fellow writers of the *Encyclopédie*, and finally Rousseau, were attributed with the creation of 'a monstrous chaos of incoherent ideas'. And so, 'as error produces error and disorder leads to disorder', the men of letters extended their power over public opinion and the persecution of the Church began, leading eventually to 'the plan of destruction adopted by the legislators of 1789'. The end point was reached in 1793 when 'terror and death walked in silence from one end of France to the other'. Then, Lamennais contended, 'the designs and hopes of philosophy' were fully realized. In the name of liberty 25 million people were reduced to 'the most abject slavery'.[218]

In the second, concluding part of the text Lamennais outlined a set of proposals for the reinvigoration of the Church. These were far-ranging, and included organizational reform, the recruitment of more clergy, as well as the revitalization of Christian teaching amongst the laity. The ambition was 'to save religion, to save civilization, to save France'. It was here that a new enemy was identified: indifference. Described as 'the miserable and baneful consequence of materialist doctrines' which had taught us that only those things which we could see and touch were real, it was a manifestation of the complete disappearance of 'our moral sense'.[219] Never, Lamennais wrote, has man been subject to such wholesale degeneration. Here was the powerful and polemical theme that Lamennais would develop in his most brilliant work, the *Essai sur l'indifférence en matière de la religion* of 1817.

As Lamennais stated in this text: 'A fundamental error in religion is also a fundamental error in politics and vice versa'.[220] Therefore, an error which destroyed power in 'religious society' was equally destructive of power within 'political society' and this was 'proved incontrovertibly' by the French Revolution. Pre-revolutionary France, according to Lamennais, was a country ruled by an 'ancient race of kings' and was possessed of both a perfect constitution and wise laws. It flourished in peace with its neighbours and was admired as 'the queen of civilization'.[221] This was destroyed once man proclaimed himself to be sovereign, by virtue of which he rose up against God and against power, declaring himself to be free and equal in his relationship towards both. In the name of liberty, the constitution, the laws, and all political and religious institutions were overturned. In the name of equality, all hierarchy, along with all political and religious distinctions, was abolished. Not since the act of deicide committed by the Jews had such an enormous crime been perpetrated, Lamennais contended. When Louis XVI mounted upon the scaffold, it was not a simple mortal who had succumbed to the rage of evil but 'the living image of the Divinity' and with it the principle of order. Thus, 'upon the ruins of the throne and the altar, upon the remains of the priest and the sovereign, began the reign of force, the reign of hatred and of terror'.[222]

From this it was abundantly clear that Lamennais would not be reconciled to the political and religious compromises associated with the Restoration. This was most

---

[218] Ibid. 68.   [219] Ibid. 79.
[220] 'Essai sur l'indifférence en matière de la religion', ibid. i. 335.
[221] Ibid. 330.   [222] Ibid. 336.

apparent in *De la religion considérée dans ses rapports avec l'ordre politique et civile*, published in 1825.[223] The text itself was a powerful and relentless critique of Protestantism, the consequences of which were broadly taken to be the destruction of 'European unity' and the overturning of the system of 'public law' upon which European civilization had rested.[224] Beneath this lay an appreciation of the destructive power of Protestantism when seen as the supreme expression of liberty of conscience. 'The religion of the century', Lamennais wrote, 'is the right of everyone to *do as they please*; and this without limits or restrictions, and applied as much to our duties as to our beliefs.'[225] It represented the negation of all truth and thus not only of divine law but of all morality and of society as a whole.

However, the text began with the familiar comparison between England and France of the time. Given the impact of the Protestant religion upon English affairs Lamennais saw nothing to admire (or emulate) in the sorry tale that had led to the execution of Charles I. Yet Lamennais acknowledged that in France, unlike in England, all trace of aristocracy had been eradicated, with the result that France was 'an assemblage of thirty million individuals between whom the law recognized no distinctions except those of wealth'.[226] In political terms this meant that the two chambers instituted under the Charte did not represent, as in England, the interests of aristocratic and landed power but were rather part of what Lamennais described as 'a vast democracy'.

The consequences of this were dire in the extreme. Each form of government had its own distinctive character and that of democracy was 'perpetual mobility'. Everything was subject to rapid and frightening change at the behest of passion and opinion. Society was plunged into a state of 'general instability' and politics became nothing more than intrigue and the pursuit of office. It might one day come to the pass, Lamennais speculated, that the country would be handed over to the 'men of money' and perhaps even 'sold to a Jew'.

This was not all that was to be feared. The doctrine of the sovereignty of the people contained within it the 'principle of atheism'.[227] Lamennais consequently devoted the second chapter of *De la religion* to demonstrating not merely that the French Revolution was the supreme political expression of Protestantism but also that Catholicism could no longer be considered either the religion of the State or of French society. Christianity, he continued, was now seen as something merely to be administered by the State, and everything was being done to undermine the status of the Church as an institution that was 'one, universal, eternal, and holy'.[228] Once the infallibility of the pope was challenged, the infallibility of the Church could be challenged, and when this occurred it followed that there would be no Christianity and that the idea of religion itself would soon vanish. All that would remain was a 'national Church' with its 'Gallican liberties', liberties that, in Lamennais's view, were no more than a form of slavery.

It was in response to legislation of 1828 directed against religious congregations that Lamennais called for the Catholic Church to enjoy the liberties promised by

---

[223] See *Œuvres Complètes de F. de La Mennais*, vii.   [224] Ibid. 255.   [225] Ibid. 143.
[226] Ibid. 9–10.   [227] Ibid. 22.   [228] Ibid. 129.

the Charte to all other religions.[229] *Des Progrès de la révolution et de la guerre contre l'Église* began by stating that, in a society not possessing a common faith, government would be dictatorial and arbitrary.[230] The attraction of religion was that it submitted all, without exception, to an 'immutable law' where men 'in their minds have the same thoughts, in their hearts the same love, in their consciences the same duties'. There was no division between public and private morality. Things had started to go wrong, therefore, when the relationship between religion and politics broke down. Little by little, monarchs freed themselves from this jurisdiction, and so, in establishing the separation between the temporal and the spiritual, Louis XIV had made 'despotism the fundamental law of the State'. Correspondingly, the 'universal independence' of individual reason became the grounds upon which religious belief and morality were premised. Nothing was taken to be either absolutely true or absolutely false, with the result that the world was 'delivered up to an infinite number of permanently changing opinions'.[231]

Lamennais drew particular attention to one aspect of this new social and political order: individualism. It was but a reflection of the 'sovereignty of individual reason' in the spiritual sphere and of the 'sovereignty of each man' in the political sphere. It destroyed the very idea of obedience and duty, destroyed the legitimacy of power and of the law, with the result that 'domination' could have no other basis than 'force' and no other form but tyranny. Its ultimate consequence would be 'the total extinction of society and the death of the human race'.[232]

Having set his argument in this apocalyptic context, Lamennais next considered two doctrines that, in his view, flowed from the separation of government from Christianity: liberalism and Gallicanism.[233] Both were 'equally false, equally opposed to the fundamental laws of the social order'. The 'most general principle' of 'dogmatic liberalism', Lamennais contended, was the sovereignty and 'absolute independence' of individual reason, a principle that excluded all 'external authority' and therefore excluded all notion of 'divine and obligatory law'. Despite what liberalism might proclaim, it would lead to 'an inevitable slavery'. In response Lamennais provided his own definition of both liberalism and liberty. By liberty, he argued, was meant the 'legitimacy of power' and its accord with 'immutable justice'. Thus, in demanding liberty a properly conceived liberalism would demand 'order', and it would demand 'what no one had the right to refuse to men, what God himself had commanded them to want and to love'.[234] By way of proof Lamennais instanced the plight of the poor in Protestant countries. Without the benefits of a 'true Christianity' they were easily made subject to 'arbitrary power'. England, 'the classic land of liberty', had reduced a substantial portion of its population to the virtual slavery of 'industrial tyranny'.

---

[229] On the history of liberal Catholicism, a movement which can be dated from Lamennais's reaction to the ordinances of 1828, the classic text remains Georges Weill, *Histoire du Catholicisme libéral en France 1828–1908* (1909).

[230] 'Des Progrès de la révolution et de la guerre contre l'Église', *Œuvres Complètes de F. de La Mennais*, ix. 1–198.

[231] Ibid. 1–7.   [232] Ibid. 19.   [233] Ibid. 20–57.   [234] Ibid. 25.

Similar arguments were deployed against Gallicanism. The so-called liberties of the French Church were a cloak that hid the potential for 'despotism without any limits'. Here was a doctrine which accepted the basic premise that all power derived from God, only then to disregard it in an effort to demonstrate that kings were subject to no ecclesiastical authority in the temporal realm. From this, in Lamennais's opinion, Gallicanism drew two woeful conclusions. First, a government could be deemed legitimate if it was constituted according to 'the political laws of the country' and irrespective of whether it was 'tyrannical, heretical, a persecutor, or impious'. Next, whilst the sovereign as a person had the same duties towards others as everyone else, as sovereign the only rule which applied in the treatment of his subjects and other rulers was that of self-interest. Acting according to the laws of justice was an irrelevance.

Lamennais's conclusion therefore was that, in their different ways, both liberalism and Gallicanism destroyed 'the idea of power and of obedience'. 'Their common vice', he claimed, was to establish 'a deep, inevitable, and permanent slavery', where power operated arbitrarily and without limits.[235] If liberalism refused to recognize divine law, Gallicanism freed the sovereign from any obligation to obey it. Thus, there could be no repose for society if it were to remain under the influence of these 'two erroneous systems'. Rather, only Christianity could offer 'the union of order and liberty', because it alone conformed to the eternal laws of justice and possessed the capacity to constrain 'rebel wills to submit to this law'. At one and the same time Christianity would establish power upon 'a divine foundation' and 'protect peoples from the arbitrary power of kings'.[236] The salvation of the world, therefore, depended upon a return to 'true Christianity'.

It was only at this point of the argument, as Lamennais considered how such a return might be attained, that he embraced the recognizably liberal causes with which he was later associated. Upon this occasion, he did so for the straightforward reason that, in his view, it was the Catholic Church and its members who were most subject to oppression by the State. In the context of state regulation of Catholic schools, for example, his view was that 'never since the origin of the world has such a terrible despotism been visited upon the human race'.[237] The ultimate ambition of the civil authorities, he stated, was 'the abolition of Catholicism'. The Church therefore should withdraw from the State and recover its independence, thereby to prepare itself for the renewal of the social and spiritual order. 'We cannot repeat often enough', Lamennais wrote, 'that the most urgent duty of the clergy in the present circumstances is to separate itself completely from an atheistic political society.'[238]

The difficult question that remains is that of assessing the extent to which Lamennais's thinking evolved in a more conventionally liberal direction after the Revolution of 1830. Lamennais's famous, but short-lived, journal, *L'Avenir*, saw itself as proclaiming a 'true liberalism' where 'liberty must be equal for all or it is

---

[235] 'Des Progrès de la révolution et de la guerre contre l'Eglise', *Œuvres Complètes de F. de La Mennais*, 39.
[236] Ibid. 46.   [237] Ibid. 115.   [238] Ibid. 188.

secure for no one'.[239] In its pages, the extension of the suffrage was defended in terms of the need to implant the principle of election within the 'bosom of the masses'. Liberty of association was justified as a means of protection against arbitrary power and of facilitating the articulation of public opinion. The centralization of state power was described as 'a shameful leftover of imperial despotism' that was contrary to both nature and liberty.[240] The people did not exist to serve those in power: rather power was there to serve the people.

Crucially, however, Lamennais now believed that the Church had nothing to fear from the emergence of what he termed 'a truly enlightened and generous liberalism'.[241] Christianity, he continued, found the world enslaved and its 'political mission' therefore was to set it free. 'Through its emancipatory power', he proclaimed, the Church 'will deliver man from the yoke of man; through the principle of order which it embodies and through the charity of which it is the source, it will lead men, free in Jesus Christ, to the unity of the family and to the unity of the nation, in anticipation of the day which is approaching where it will constitute the nations themselves into one single, great nation.'[242] The role of the Church was thus not simply to free men but to bring them together, and to do so not through any political jurisdiction but through the power of love. Specifically Lamennais here mentioned the 'question of the poor', recognizing that unless there was 'a total change in the industrial system' there would be a 'general uprising of the poor against the rich'. In the new society of the future the priest would play a key role in ministering to 'the suffering part of humanity'.[243]

But those who collaborated in the writing of *L'Avenir* also saw themselves as 'sincere Catholics' and Lamennais did not hesitate to affirm that the doctrines of the Holy See were the 'pure expression of Christianity, to which the world owes everything in terms of civilization and liberty'.[244] 'In order to be free', he wrote, 'it is necessary first of all to love God; because if you love God you will do his will; and the will of God is that of justice and charity, without which there can be no liberty.'[245] The ambition, in other words, remained the institution of liberty and order as a necessary precondition for the return of society to spiritual health and stability. What changed was not Lamennais's understanding of liberty but his assessment of how it might be attained in what he saw as the increasingly oppressive and anti-Christian France of his day. Given that the theocratic argument demanding the subordination of the civil authority to the Church appeared less and less likely to carry the day, there was no alternative but to abandon the idea of a Christian polity. The *Mémoire*, written for Pope Gregory XVI in 1832 and intended to justify the position taken by *L'Avenir*, started from the premise that

---

[239] Lamennais, 'Articles publiés dans le journal *L'Avenir*', *Œuvres Complètes de F. de La Mennais*, x. 134.

[240] 'Des doctrines de *L'Avenir*', ibid. 196–205

[241] 'Réponse à la lettre du Père Ventura', ibid. 267.

[242] 'De l'Avenir de la société', ibid. 337.

[243] "Ce que sera le catholicisme dans la société nouvelle', ibid. 348–9.

[244] 'Des doctrines de *L'Avenir*', ibid. 197.

[245] 'Paroles d'un croyant', *Œuvres Complètes de F. de La Mennais*, xi. 83.

under the Restoration the Church was both oppressed by government and hated by the greater proportion of the population. In these circumstances, it argued, it was necessary to recognize 'in good faith' that the Catholic religion was compatible with the liberties of religion, education, and the press and that these 'various liberties' could alone protect the Church from a similar 'catastrophe' to that which had befallen Catholicism in England. Let us imagine, Lamennais asked, that the press was enchained by censorship, who would suffer? Only Catholics, was his answer.[246]

Lamennais presents us with a peculiar set of paradoxes that are not easily resolved. No one could doubt the sincerity of his faith and, unlike Maistre, he did not place the emphasis upon the utility and necessity of religion for the maintenance of social and political order; but why, given his deep attachment to the supremacy of the spiritual over the temporal order and his passionate defence of the Ultramontane cause, did he embark upon the fateful course of action that led him into irreconcilable conflict with the papacy? In his day, there were many who were prepared to attribute it to pride and ambition (not least his admirer Henri-Dominique Lacordaire as well as John Henry Newman in England). From what we have seen, however, the answer might lie in Lamennais's conviction that the separation of Church and State, combined with a recognition of certain core liberties, was the only means of saving the Church itself. On this view, the triumph of monarchical despotism would go hand in hand with the servitude of the papacy. Therefore, the future lay not in an alliance with kings but in the sustenance that would be derived from the community of the faithful (as the Irish in particular had shown). Love, humility, and the works of charity, and not Maistrean authority, was the essence of Lamennais's Catholicism.

As Lamennais was not able to prove his case to the satisfaction of his ecclesiastical superiors, his first response was submission to papal authority, followed by a gradual distancing from a faith he had so eloquently expressed in his *Paroles d'un croyant* of 1833. Lamennais was never formally excommunicated but over the next decade he steadily drifted away from the Church and, as he did so, the first serious attempt to reconcile the Church to modern society came to an end. He then openly embraced the 'cause of the people', arguing in such texts as *Du Passé et de l'Avenir du Peuple* and *De l'Esclavage moderne* that this was a 'holy cause' and one where the release of the poor from slavery and poverty was in line with God's will. The enslaved, he argued, consisted not merely of the propertyless proletariat but 'of the entire nation, with the exception of 200,000 members of the privileged classes under whose domination bend ignominiously 33 million French people, the true slaves of our day'.[247] In 1848 he rallied to the Republic, founding another short-lived journal, *Le Peuple Constituent*, and that same year was elected to parliament, where he sat on the extreme left. With Louis Napoleon's *coup d'état* of December 1851 he went into retirement, dying three years later in near obscurity.

---

[246] 'Paroles d'un croyant', *Œuvres Complètes de F. de La Mennais*, xii. 36–87.
[247] Lamennais, *Du Passé et de l'Avenir du Peuple* (1868), 141.

The influence of the charismatic and lyrical Lamennais was truly extensive, his seminary at La Chenaie in Brittany attracting many of the brightest Catholics of the day and adding greatly to the vigour of the Catholic revival in the 1820s. *L'Avenir*, in the words of Adrien Dansette, was 'the birth certificate of Catholic liberalism' and, if largely ignored by non-Catholics, secured a wide readership among young priests in particular and the laity.[248] Yet few, if any, of Lamennais's inner circle of firm supporters and disciples were prepared to follow him into the religious wilderness. Without him, therefore, liberal Ultramontane Catholics such as Père Lacordaire and Charles de Montalembert had to find and pursue a new course of action.[249] This they did largely through an extended campaign to secure religious freedom, and especially to break the State's monopoly of the education system. Success (of a limited kind) was achieved with the passing of the *loi Falloux* in 1850 which allowed the Church to have its own secondary schools but subject to state inspection and supervision. As political liberals, they sought to establish that there was no opposition in principle between Catholicism and liberty.

Two texts serve to illustrate this frame of mind in mid-century. The first, by the Abbé Félix Dupanloup, sometime Bishop of Orléans, was entitled *De la Pacification religieuse* and was published in 1845, a moment when debate about educational reform (and the Jesuits) was again at the top of the political agenda.[250] Dupanloup, a prelate of considerable intelligence and prominence, was no admirer of Lamennais but he had the foresight to recognize that a new situation required a rethinking of the old relationship between throne and altar. Much of Dupanloup's text was designed to refute the charge (articulated most forcefully at the time by Adolphe Thiers) that the Church remained opposed to 'the spirit of the Revolution'. He repeatedly denounced such calumnies directed against the clergy, affirming unambiguously that the Church proclaimed 'the generous spirit, the true spirit of the French Revolution, while deploring with M. Thiers its excesses and errors'.[251] The Church, in other words, was neither the enemy of liberty nor of the nation. It accepted the legitimacy of free institutions, liberty of conscience, political and civil liberty, liberty of education and opinion, equality before the law, and fair distribution of taxation. 'Liberty for all; peace as our goal; moderation, disinterestedness, and perseverance as our means; war as a painful last resort':[252] this was the programme that Dupanloup placed before his adversaries and, in doing so, he simply asked that these same people should be prepared to observe the same maxims and that they should not condemn the Church, in the name of 'a supposed liberty of conscience', to a vile and contemptuous servitude. We demand justice,

---

[248] Adrien Dansette, *Religious History of Modern France* (Edinburgh, 1961), i. 216.

[249] See José Cabanis, *Lacordaire et quelques autres: Politique et religion* (1982) and Edouard Lecanuet, *Montalembert*, 3 vols. (1902). See also Charles de Montalembert, *Memoir of the Abbé Lacordaire* (London, 1863) and M. M. C. Calthorp, 'Lacordaire and Montalembert' (London, 1915).

[250] Dupanloup, *De la Pacification religieuse: Quelle est l'origine des querelles actuelles? Quelle en peut être l'issue* (1845).

[251] Ibid. 264.

[252] Ibid. 17–18.

Dupanloup wrote, and 'we call for it in our own way, with charity in our hearts, with reason on our lips, and with the Gospel and the Charte in our hands'.[253]

The second text was written by one of Lamennais's early close associates, Charles de Montalembert, in September 1852, soon after the disintegration of the Second Republic and as Louis Napoleon tightened his grip on power.[254] *Des Intérêts catholiques au XIXe siècle* began from the supposition that the nineteenth century had seen a Europe-wide 'Catholic renaissance' and that this had been accompanied by the fall of its principal rivals: Protestantism, philosophy, 'Voltairean liberalism', and the forces of temporal power.[255] In such circumstances of triumph, did this mean that Catholics should 'deny reason and sacrifice liberty'?[256] Montalembert's answer was in the negative, for the reason that it was to liberty—'sincere and serious' liberty—that the Church was indebted for its 'wonderful and unexpected success'.[257] Indeed, Montalembert went further by arguing that, of all governments, it had been absolute government that had most exposed the Church to danger. In short, religion needed liberty as much as liberty needed religion. The worst and most intolerable of despotisms was that exercised with the sanction of religion. In the present circumstances, therefore, it was 'representative, constitutional, and parliamentary government' that was 'the only possible expression of political liberty'.[258] Despite its failings, this was the regime, Montalembert affirmed, that best served the interests of Catholics. The cause of absolutism therefore was a lost cause and liberty would not be stifled. 'I feel bound to say', he wrote, 'that the liberty which we have demanded during the last twenty years was not in any way a trap set for our enemies, but an act of good faith and of courage, not a matter of tactics but of principle.'[259]

Nevertheless, there were qualifications to Montalembert's enthusiasm for liberty and these were qualifications that revealed the political limitations of liberal Catholicism more generally. For Montalembert, liberty was only a relative and not an absolute good.[260] He believed in what he described as 'a well-regulated, restrained, orderly, tempered, *upright and moderate* liberty',[261] a liberty that was not hostile to authority or that served as a mask for revolution. The liberty he defended did not embrace either democracy or universal suffrage, both of which, he believed, destroyed liberty in the name of envy and equality. His was a liberty that was antithetical to socialism.

In point of fact, the *loi Falloux* of 1850 was greeted as an unholy compromise and great betrayal by many Catholics, not least by die-hard Ultramontanes who persisted in their demands for complete Church freedom. Henceforth, the divide between liberal and Ultramontane tendencies within the Church was only to grow, the latter group in particular becoming ever more intransigent, obscurantist, and legitimist in their views. Matters only worsened with the advent of

---

[253] Dupanloup, *De la Pacification religieuse: Quelle est l'origine des querelles actuelles? Quelle en peut être l'issue* (1845), 8.

[254] Montalembert, *Des Intérêts catholiques au XIXe siècle* (1852).

[255] Ibid. 71–5.   [256] Ibid. 77.   [257] Ibid. 83–4.

[258] Ibid. 133.   [259] Ibid. 235.   [260] Ibid. 86.   [261] Ibid. 85.

the Second Empire, the Church hierarchy unhesitatingly falling in behind the new regime and seeming to prosper as a result. Liberal Catholics did not give up without a fight and in August 1863, at the Catholic Congress of Malines in Belgium, Montalembert again returned to the fray, setting out a powerful programme built around the maxim of 'a free Church in a free State'.[262] The task ahead, Montalembert announced, was to reconcile Catholicism to democracy and to the conditions prevailing in modern society. The extension of civil and political liberties served the Church's interests. Its enemies were the same as those of liberal democracy: absolutism, centralization, and demagogy. The Church, then, asked for no privileges, for no protection from a theocratic State, for no revival of the old alliance between throne and altar. It simply asked for freedom, and for freedom for everyone. Breaking with the long-established doctrine of the Church, in his second lecture Montalembert went so far as to argue that liberty of thought should include the toleration of heresy and error.

For his pains Montalembert was reprimanded by the Church and did not appear at the next Malines conference the following year. Three months after that Congress, Pope Pius IX promulgated his encyclical *Quanta Cura*, to which was appended the *Syllabus Errorum* detailing the Holy See's objections to the secular state, freedom of conscience and religion, freedom of the press, popular sovereignty, and much else. Six years later, in 1870, the Vatican Council affirmed the doctrine of papal infallibility. The papacy, to all intents and purposes, had turned its back, rightly or wrongly, upon the modern world. Yet not even these measures could put an end to what was a genuine and profound disagreement about how the Christian religion could best be protected. On the one side stood the traditionalists, convinced of the incompatibility between faith and reason and that dogmatic intolerance required political and civil intolerance; on the other were the liberals, intent on remaining sincere and loyal Catholics, but determined to effect a reconciliation between the Church and modern society and learning. The Church in France had made a remarkable and unexpected recovery in the nineteenth century and now stood in a stronger position than might ever have been imagined, but the renewal of hostilities was not far away. The anticlerical Third Republic awaited.

---

[262] Montalembert, *L'Église libre dans l'État libre* (1863). An important part of the context here was a discussion of moves towards Italian unification. To Montalembert's displeasure Cavour took up his slogan.

8

Positivism, Science, and Philosophy

I

On 24 January 1861 an event took place in Paris that no other country could replicate and that also provided a fine illustration of the complicated arguments that had divided liberal opinion on religious matters during the first half of the nineteenth century. On that day Henri-Dominique Lacordaire, follower of the Ultramontane Lamennais, was received as one of the forty members of the Académie Française. The person he replaced was the Jansenist and Gallican Alexis de Tocqueville. The formal welcome to Lacordaire was given by the Protestant François Guizot.[1] As befitted the occasion and the demands of tradition, Lacordaire's speech in honour of Tocqueville was as generous as it was uncritical.[2] Coming from a priest, it made repeated mention of Tocqueville as a Christian, concluding that Tocqueville had seen the truth of Christianity and of 'an active, living, personal God', and had served both 'with no sense of shame'. 'It was death', Lacordaire announced to his fellow *immortels*, 'that brought him the gift of love. He received the God who visited him as an old friend and, touched to tears by his presence, at last free of the world, he forgot what he had been, his name, his services, his regrets, and his desires ... keeping in his soul only the virtues he had gained from his passage here on earth.'[3]

From what we know of Tocqueville's last, desperate days in Cannes this reassuring picture of a man secure in the bosom of the Church seems far from accurate. It also glosses over the complexities of Tocqueville's religious beliefs and makes no mention of his profound doubts on religious matters. In a (now well-known) letter to Madame Swetchine, a woman who had herself been instructed by Joseph de Maistre in Russia, he wrote that 'I believe firmly in another life, since God who is supremely just has given us the idea of it; in this other life, I believe in the remuneration of good and evil, since God has allowed us to distinguish between them and given us the freedom to choose; but beyond these clear ideas, everything beyond the bounds of this world seems to me to be surrounded by shadows which

---

[1] Lacordaire's election was secured through a coalition of Catholics (including Montalembert), Protestants, supporters of Eclecticism (Victor Cousin), and Voltaireans (in this case, Adolphe Thiers): see Tocqueville, *Œuvres complètes*, xvi. *Mélanges* (1989), 312 n. 1.

[2] 'Discours de M. Lacordaire', ibid. 312–31. See also 'Réponse de M.Guizot', ibid. 332–45.

[3] 'Discours de M. Lacordaire', 326.

terrify me.'[4] The cousin of the author of *Le Génie du Christianisme*, it is clear that Tocqueville lost the severe Augustinian faith imparted to him in his youth by the devoted Abbé Le Sueur and that, for all his lifelong reading of Pascal, he was never fully to recover from this early religious crisis. Yet Tocqueville remained convinced that religion was 'as natural to the human heart as hope itself'.[5] And, just as importantly, he understood that religion would not die with the advent of democracy. 'The philosophers of the eighteenth century', Tocqueville wrote, 'had a very simple explanation for the gradual weakening of beliefs. Religious zeal, they said, was bound to be extinguished as enlightenment and freedom spread. It is tiresome that the facts do not fit the theory at all.'[6] Disbelief, he argued, was the exception.

But what sort of religion was this to be?[7] One of the first things that the young Tocqueville had noticed was that 'Men of religion combat freedom, and the friends of freedom attack religion.'[8] This was perplexing because, as he had seen in America, Catholicism was no enemy of democracy. Indeed, one of the most surprising conclusions he reached during his visit was that Catholicism, rather than Protestantism, thrived in a democratic and republican environment.[9] More-over, he had seen that religion could perform the key function of regulating the 'overly ardent and overly exclusive taste for well-being that men feel in times of equality'.[10] Viewed 'from a purely human point of view', religion curbed the potential excesses associated with the materialism and individualism of democratic man.

Yet Tocqueville also saw that democracy would change the nature of religious experience, and specifically that the act of worship would be less bound by external forms and practices. Religion in the United States, he observed, 'presents ideas more clearly, simply, and generally to the human mind'.[11] This was a tendency with which Tocqueville had some sympathy and he saw that it was only to be expected in a mobile society that the 'external and secondary' dimensions of religious observance would themselves change. However, with equal conviction Tocqueville thought that 'men cannot do without dogmatic beliefs' and therefore that 'general ideas about God and human nature are, among all ideas, the ones it is most fitting to shield from the habitual action of individual reason and for which there is most to gain and least to lose in recognizing an authority'.[12] The danger was

---

[4] Tocqueville, letter of 26 Feb. 1857, in Olivier Zunz and Alan S. Kahan (eds.), *The Tocqueville Reader: A Life in Letters and Politics* (Oxford, 2002), 336.

[5] Tocqueville, *De la Démocratie en Amérique*, *Œuvres complètes* (1951), i/1. 310.

[6] Ibid. 308.

[7] See Agnès Antoine, *L'Impensé de la démocratie: Tocqueville, la citoyenneté et la religion* (2003). See also Joshua Mitchell, 'Tocqueville on Democratic Religious Experience', in Cheryl B. Welch (ed.), *The Cambridge Companion to Tocqueville* (Cambridge, 2006), 276–302; Agnès Antoine, 'Démocratie et religion: le point de vue tocquevillien', *Tocqueville Review*, 27/2 (2006), 121–32; Pierre Gilbert, 'Tocqueville et la religion: Entre réflexion politique et confidences épistolaires', *Tocqueville Review*, 27/2 (2006), 133–48; Frank M. Turner, 'Alexis de Tocqueville and John Stuart Mill on Religion', *Tocqueville Review*, 27/2 (2006), 149–72; and Larry Siedentop, *Tocqueville* (Oxford, 1994), 96–112.

[8] Tocqueville, *De la Démocratie*, 10.

[9] Ibid. i/2. 35–6.   [10] Ibid. 33.   [11] Ibid.   [12] Ibid. 28.

that, divested of its 'general and eternal truths', Christianity would be reduced to an unmediated personal religious experience. The outcome, as Tocqueville correctly sensed, would be pantheism.[13] Religion, as we now know to our cost, would amount to little more than tree hugging.

But Tocqueville had a further point of considerable significance to make. Men, he believed, required 'very fixed ideas' about God, their souls, and their general duties towards their Creator. Few were they, in his opinion, who could 'let their minds float at random between obedience and freedom'[14] and the consequence of complete religious independence was a generalized sentiment of doubt throughout society. With that came confusion and the sense that all actions were delivered up to chance. Men, Tocqueville wrote, were condemned to 'a sort of disorder and impotence'.[15]

It is possibly only a slight exaggeration to say that a large proportion of the literary and philosophical output of the French nineteenth century was a commentary upon and response to that feeling of disorder and impotence. As D. G. Charlton remarked some years ago,[16] the characteristic temperament of the age was one of 'honest unbelief', of religious sensibility estranged from Christian belief. This took a variety of forms, not the least being a profound distress and regret for lost faith, but included in these responses was the very frequent theme that, if it was no longer possible to accept the literal inerrancy of the Bible or the truth of Christian doctrines, a religious ethic of some kind was still indispensable to the well-being of society as a whole. The nineteenth century therefore saw a remarkable proliferation of alternative creeds (many both bizarre and exotic), each designed to offer a substitute for a discredited and outmoded Christianity. One of these was science itself, raised to the level of a guide to the future of humanity. Others took a more prophetic and messianic form. Quite commonly, however, there was a shared aspiration to put an end to the epistemological and metaphysical uncertainties associated with what continued to be seen by many as the destructive and sceptical philosophy of the eighteenth century. In its place there was to be provided a new intellectual synthesis appropriate to the conditions of the new century. The irony was that, not infrequently, these spiritual offerings came clothed in the regalia of the old religion. Ecclesiastical orthodoxy simply reappeared in novel (if less convincing and less aesthetically pleasing) garb.

A key early protagonist in these (and many other) developments was Claude-Henri de Rouvray, Comte de Saint-Simon.[17] Few men could have had as varied and as eventful life as Saint-Simon and few could have been as influential.[18] Having narrowly escaped both death and financial ruin during the Revolution, he published his first text, *Lettres d'un habitant de Genève à ses contemporains*, in 1802 and

---

[13] Tocqueville, *De la Démocratie*, 37–8.   [14] Ibid. 36.   [15] Ibid. 27.

[16] Charlton, *Secular Religions in France 1815–1870* (London, 1963), 1–12.

[17] See Frank E. Manuel, *The New World of Henri de Saint-Simon* (Cambridge, Mass., 1956); Manuel, *The Prophets of Paris* (Cambridge, Mass., 1962), 103–48; Jack Hayward, *After the French Revolution: Six Critics of Democracy and Nationalism* (Hemel Hempstead, 1991), 65–100.

[18] See Antoine Picon, *Les Saint-Simoniens: Raison, imaginaire et utopie* (2002) and Christophe Prochasson, *Saint-Simon ou l'Anti-Marx* (2005).

from then on he did not cease in his endeavours to establish a set of doctrines outlining the principles required to effect the complete reorganization of society and the creation of a new terrestrial morality. Moreover, as an admirer of Condorcet, Saint-Simon developed this analysis within the framework of an account of the development of the human mind.

History, Saint-Simon argued, could be divided into three distinct periods: the Greek and Roman; the Christian and medieval; and the scientific or 'positive'. At their height, each of these periods was characterized by a moral or intellectual system that bound society together as a unified whole and by a set of political institutions in conformity with existing ideas and circumstances. The Christian period, for example, had imagined that everything could be explained in terms of 'one universal and unique intelligence', had been held in concert by the 'passive link' of the Catholic religion and the 'active link' of the clergy, and had formed 'a confederate society united through common institutions and subject to a common government' under the direction of the papacy. As such, it had lived at peace with itself.

According to Saint-Simon, there were two principal phenomena that explained the disintegration of the social and political organization of the Christian period. The first was the emergence of science, which from the thirteenth century onwards began to dislodge theistic explanations of the world. Consequently, over time, it came to be seen that 'the relations between God and the universe were incomprehensible and unimportant'.[19] Nothing, it was now established, was to be accepted as true unless it was confirmed by reason and experience. The heroes of this process were the very same thinkers who had been lambasted by Maistre—Bacon, Descartes, Newton, and Locke—as it was they who had masterminded the 'scientific revolution' that had come to fruition with the Enlightenment. They had revealed 'the most essential faults' of the old 'religious system' and 'constructed the first scaffolding for the erection of the new system'.[20] Manifestly, Saint-Simon had considerable sympathy for this exercise—the philosophers of the eighteenth century had been right to overturn the 'edifice that the clergy had taken centuries to construct'[21]—but he also saw that, when developed with greater boldness by Condillac and Condorcet, the result had been to formulate a 'general anti-theology'. In summary, the Encyclopedists had succeeded in destroying the theological system but they had not been able to fashion a new system to replace the one they had torn down. 'The philosophy of the eighteenth century', Saint-Simon concluded, 'was critical and revolutionary; that of the nineteenth will be inventive and constructive.'[22]

The second phenomenon serving to undermine the feudal and Christian order was the emergence of industry and of an industrial class. Saint-Simon wrote at great

---

[19] 'Introduction aux Travaux scientifiques du XIXe siècle', *Œuvres de Claude-Henri de Saint-Simon* (1966), vi. 155.

[20] Ibid. 25.

[21] 'Saint-Simon à Chateaubriand', *Œuvres de Saint-Simon* (1868), ii. 216.

[22] 'Sur l'Encyclopédie', ibid. i. 92.

length upon this theme and many of his numerous (and often short-lived and unread) publishing initiatives were designed to convey the message that *les industriels*, as the most useful class in society, should assume its direction. This was the argument to be found in *Catéchisme des Industriels*, written in 1823.[23] Saint-Simon's point was that the aristocratic, military, and religious classes that had dominated feudal society had lost their *raison d'être*, for the simple reason that they no longer had any useful function to perform. Similarly, this was the force of the parable sketched out in the opening pages of *L'Organisateur*, where Saint-Simon asked his readers to contemplate the loss of 'all the great officers of the crown, all Ministers of State, all the Councillors of State, all chief magistrates, all its marshals, all its cardinals, archbishops, vicars-general, and canons'.[24] Apart from distress from a purely sentimental point of view, Saint-Simon suggested, no harm would be caused. Indeed, a hindrance to the progress of society would have been removed. *Les oisifs*, as Saint-Simon derogatively described them, were no more than parasites.

The first major political expression of this fundamental change in the structure of society, Saint-Simon argued, had been the English Civil War. It was, however, to France that 'the natural order of things and the advance of civilization' had reserved 'the glory of ending the great European Revolution'.[25] 'When the French Revolution broke out', Saint-Simon argued, 'it was no longer a matter of modifying the feudal and theological system which had already lost almost all its force. It was a question of organizing the industrial and scientific system summoned by the level of civilization to replace it.'[26] By rights, therefore, the industrialists and the scientists should have led the Revolution but this place had been occupied by lawyers who directed the Revolution 'with the doctrines of the metaphysicians'. The result was the occurrence of 'terrible atrocities' and the installation of 'an absolutely impracticable form of government'. The Revolution, Saint-Simon observed, 'placed power in different hands but it did not change the nature of power'.[27] From this flowed all its 'strange wanderings' and its final reconstitution of feudalism in the shape of a bourgeois king, Napoleon.

France and Europe more generally, therefore, existed in an unstable situation of transition. The process of social and political reorganization had not been completed and there remained a need to find a unified philosophical system capable of replacing Christianity. To resolve the first part of this problem, Saint-Simon recommended that, 'for the sake of the general good, domination should be proportionate to enlightenment'.[28] This was a proposition that he reworked on many occasions over a period of twenty years or more but, in broad outline, it tended to take the form that spiritual power should be in the hands of the *savants* or scientists and that temporal power should be in the hands of the industrialists or producers. Various improbable schemes, ranging from a Council of Newton

---

[23] 'Sur l'Encyclopédie', viii. 1–203.   [24] Ibid. iv. 20–1.
[25] 'Coup d'oeil sur l'histoire politique de l'industrie', ibid. iii. 147.
[26] 'Du Système industriel', ibid. v. 10.
[27] 'De l'Organisation sociale', ibid. x. 154.
[28] 'Lettre d'un habitant de Genève', ibid. i. 41.

composed of 'the twenty-one elect of humanity' to a larger Parliament of Improvement composed of 'forty-five men of genius', were drawn up to implement this formula, each one of them seeking, as far as possible, to transfer power to those with the capacity to secure the proper administration of public affairs. 'Governments', Saint-Simon declared in 1817, 'will no longer command men: their functions will be limited to ensuring that all useful work is not hindered.'[29]

But more than the social reorganization of society was required if the disorder made manifest in the Revolution was to be brought to a close. To put an end to philosophical and intellectual confusion, the sciences themselves had to be unified and given a systematic 'positive' foundation. What was needed was an overarching theory which, in replacing outmoded theistic explanations of the world, would effectively work as the equivalent of God. Somewhat improbably this role, as was made clear in the *Introduction aux Travaux scientifiques du dix-neuvième siècle* of 1807, fell to Newton's theory of 'universal gravitation', the 'single immutable law' from which it was possible to deduce the explanation of all phenomena.[30] Saint-Simon's broader point was that, if astronomy, physics, and chemistry had already attained the status of 'positive' science, it was no less important that the methods of scientific observation should be extended so as to embrace the study of man and of society.[31] Saint-Simon, therefore, unhesitatingly spoke of the 'science of man', believing that upon the basis of 'the positive organization of physiological theory' it would be possible to move the 'social' sciences beyond the 'conjectural' stage and thereby turn morals, politics, and philosophy into a 'positive science'.[32] To that end Saint-Simon contemplated the creation of a new *Encyclopédie des idées positives* appropriate to the scientific system and enlightenment of the nineteenth century.[33]

Of singular consequence for this entire argument was Saint-Simon's further contention that it was not only possible but also necessary that we should pass from a 'celestial' to a 'terrestrial' morality. Again this was a theme to which Saint-Simon returned on frequent occasions, often giving his argument significant changes of emphasis, but from his earliest writings it is clear that he believed strongly that morality could be refashioned according to what he described as 'purely human principles'. In its first formulation, for example, Saint-Simon envisaged the establishment of 'temples of Newton'.[34] The content of this terrestrial morality would be marked by a complete break from the Christian gospels. Gone would be the maxim that one should do unto others as you have them do unto you—such a principle, Saint-Simon observed, was only indirectly binding and imposed no obligation on the individual towards himself—and in its stead was to be the dictum that 'man must work'. It followed that the most moral persons were those engaged in science as their work was the most useful to humanity.[35]

[29] 'Lettres de Henri Saint-Simon à un Américain', ibid. ii. 168.
[30] See also 'Travail sur la gravitation universelle', ibid. xi. 214–310.
[31] 'Correspondance avec M. de Redern', ibid. i. 108–10.
[32] 'Mémoire sur la science de l'homme', ibid. xi. 25–30.
[33] 'Saint-Simon à Chateaubriand', 219.
[34] 'Lettre d'un habitant de Genève', 48–57.
[35] 'Introduction aux Travaux scientifiques du XIXe siècle', 176–8.

It followed equally that the propagation of this new morality would need to be in the hands of a new 'spiritual power'. Lay mathematicians and physicists would become the new clergy.

Saint-Simon was similarly convinced that this morality should and needed to be taught to all. He wrote:

> The philosophers of the eighteenth century succeeded in having it generally accepted that each person was free to profess his own religion and to teach his children the religion he preferred. The philosophers of the nineteenth century will make people aware of the necessity of submitting all children to the study of the same code of terrestrial morality, since the similarity of positive moral ideas is the only link which can unite men in society and, ultimately, an improvement in the social condition is nothing else than an improvement in the system of positive morality.[36]

There would be a 'national catechism' and only those with proven knowledge of it would be entitled to enjoy the rights of French citizenship. Taken as a whole, Saint-Simon believed, these moves towards the development of the doctrines and practices of a terrestrial morality amounted to the 'perfection' of what he continued to describe as 'the religious system'.

It is not clear at what point Saint-Simon began to appreciate the unsatisfactory nature of these arguments but in 1825, the very last year of his life, he broke decisively with his earlier secular pronouncements and declared himself the exponent of a 'New Christianity'.[37] 'Do you believe in God?' the Conservative asked in the opening sentence of Saint-Simon's imaginary (and unconvincing) dialogue. 'Yes, I believe in God', replied the Innovator. 'Do you believe that the Christian religion is of divine origin?': 'Yes, I believe it is', came the catechistic affirmation in reply. The 'sublime principle' of this divine doctrine, the Innovator continued, was that 'men ought to act towards each other as brethren' and, in accordance with this God-given rule, they 'ought to propose to themselves, as the end of all their labours and of all their actions, the most prompt and complete amelioration possible of the moral and physical condition of the most numerous class'.[38] This constituted the doctrinal heart of the New Christianity, although Saint-Simon did promise his readers that in subsequent (but never to be completed) dialogues he would 'propose a profession of faith for the New Christians', replete with its own morality, forms of worship, and dogma.[39] The New Christianity would have its clergy and they would have their leaders.

Crucially, the 'new church' would be purged of all 'existing heresies' and thus the greater part of Saint-Simon's text focused upon exposing what he considered to be the heresies associated with the Catholic and Protestant religions. Among these, the Inquisition and the Jesuits and, on the Protestant side, inadequate forms of worship figured prominently. Saint-Simon's ambition was to purify the Christian religion by divesting it of 'all its superstitions and its useless creeds and practices' and, in so doing, to return it to its 'original principle' made evident among 'the Christians of

---

[36] 'Lettre d'un habitant de Genève', 218 n. 1.
[37] 'Nouveau Christianisme', *Œuvres de Saint-Simon* (1868), vii. 99–192.
[38] Ibid. 109.   [39] Ibid. 186.

the primitive Church'.[40] When restored to its 'youth' a 'regenerated' Christianity would pronounce 'impious every doctrine having for its object to teach men any other means of obtaining life eternal than that of working with all their might to ameliorate the condition of their fellows'.[41] In a final rhetorical flourish, all princes were called upon to become 'good Christians' and to recognize that Christianity commanded them to 'increase the social happiness of the poor'.[42]

As a religion, the spiritual inadequacies of the new faith were all too evident. Devoid of any meaningful reference to the supernatural, what was being offered was a social philosophy dressed up as religious conviction. Indeed, in this guise Christianity was reduced to little more than a doctrine of social fraternity with the earthly preoccupation of physical well-being posited as its only end. Nevertheless, Saint-Simon, it can be assumed, believed that he had correctly gauged that the reorganization of society along the lines he had sketched in his earlier writings—with its stress upon the temporal power of *les industriels*—would not be attained unless it was accompanied by an equally strong emphasis upon the need for a spiritual rebirth across society as a whole. Such, undoubtedly, was the mood of the time, although what Saint-Simon had to offer bore little resemblance to either the spiritual intensity evoked by Lamennais or the dark pessimism of Maistre.

The final years of Saint-Simon's life were far from untroubled. In 1820, following the murder of the Duc de Berri, he was placed on trial on the pretext that his (by now well-known) parable had constituted an incitement to the crime. Only some very nimble legal footwork enabled him to escape imprisonment. Three years later, with his various projects having come to naught and suffering from depression, he unsuccessfully attempted suicide by shooting himself. Despite this, Saint-Simon continued to attract a sizeable number of young, able, and loyal followers, and it was to be they who, in the years immediately following Saint-Simon's death, were to develop the suggestive ideas found in the *Nouveau Christianisme* into a full-blown religious creed built around a Church (formally established on Christmas Day 1829) with its own rituals, colourful regalia, calendar, and intricate hierarchy of apostles, priests, missionaries, and disciples.[43]

'The children of Saint-Simon', as the members of the new Church habitually referred to each other, gave themselves 'the mission of progressively converting the world to this universal communion' and the improvement of the condition of the poorest and most numerous class now became unambiguously 'the will of God'.[44]

---

[40] Ibid. 163, 178–9.   [41] Ibid. 164.   [42] Ibid. 192.

[43] The first significant reformulation of Saint-Simonian doctrine came in the form of the collective text *Doctrine de Saint-Simon: Exposition Première Année 1828–1829* (1831). See Georges Weill, *L'École Saint-Simonienne: Son Histoire, son Influence jusqu'à nos jours* (1896); Sebastien Charléty, *Histoire du Saint-Simonisme 1825–1864* (1896) and Henry-René d'Allemagne, *Les Saint-Simoniens 1827–1837* (1930); in English see Robert E. Carlisle, *The Proffered Crown: Saint-Simonianism and the Doctrine of Hope* (Baltimore, Md., 1987). Allemagne's book contains reproductions of some wonderful archive material.

[44] A wide-ranging selection of Saint-Simonian texts, bound together in 2 vols., can be found at the library of the Musée social in Paris. Reading these texts is a challenging experience, as it is hard not to conclude that many of the meetings held by the Saint-Simonians were characterized by collective hysteria.

Prosper Enfantin[45] and Saint-Amand Bazard, the family's two holy Fathers, set about leading the faithful to a 'new life' where war, exploitation, and hatred would cease forever. Central to the new Church's doctrine, and the cause of repeated debate, was the proclamation of equality between men and women, between the proletarian and the victim of prostitution and adultery.[46] With this were soon to come schisms,[47] excommunications, and, most bizarre of all, the prolonged and unsuccessful search for a female Messiah. Enfantin, supreme pontiff of the movement following Bazard's embittered departure and now hailed by his remaining followers as 'the most moral man' of his time,[48] commenced a further reformulation of doctrine in a series of lofty pronouncements beginning in late November 1831. He now reworked the Christian concept of the Trinity into the central precept of the Saint-Simonian religion, claiming that, although unperceived, it had been present on every page of the *Nouveau Christianisme*.[49] The contraries of man and the world, he maintained, were united in God; the self and the non-self in the Infinite, to the point where all antagonism would be overcome.[50] 'Our apostolic work', Enfantin declared, 'consists principally in the Rehabilitation of the Flesh through the creation of a new cult, the organization of industry and the appeal to women.'[51] Matters came to a head when, in the spring of 1832, the Père Enfantin was placed on trial for offending public morality.[52] For Enfantin the religious and the erotic had become inextricably intertwined and his unconventional views on the sexual emancipation of women were causing increasing public controversy, as well as opposition from many adherents of the new religion.[53] Following Enfantin's release from prison, the community, having established itself in monastery-like seclusion at Ménilmontant on the eastern outskirts of Paris, was dissolved. Enfantin himself departed for Egypt, from where he returned in 1837, many of his remaining followers having died from the plague and with his efforts to build a barrage across the Nile a failure. The other Saint-Simonians, including such men as Michel

---

[45] Sebastien Charléty, *Enfantin* (1930); Henry-René d'Allemagne, *Prosper Enfantin et les Grands Entreprises du XIXe siècle* (1935).

[46] Jehan d'Ivray, *L'Aventure Saint-Simonienne et les Femmes* (1930); Michèle Riot-Sarcey, *De la liberté des femme: Lettres de dames au Globe (1831–1832)* (1992); Claire Goldberg Moses, *French Feminism in the Nineteenth Century* (Albany, NY, 1984), 41–60.

[47] See Armand Cuvillier, *Un schisme Saint-Simonien: Les Origines de l'École buchézienne* (1920). Buchez left the movement in 1829 but the most significant schism came in Nov. 1831 when Bazard and nineteen 'dissidents' left after a bitter dispute with Enfantin: see *Réunion Générale de la Famille: Séances des 19 et 21 novembre* (1831). Subsequent to this, Bazard's replacement in the hierarchy, Olinde Rodrigues, was also to depart in Feb. 1832. See the two texts cited by Rodrigues below. If Rodrigues accepted the legitimacy of divorce, he could not accept Enfantin's view that children should not know the name of their father.

[48] *Cérémonie du 27 novembre* (1831), 7. These were the words of Rodrigues.

[49] *Œuvres d'Enfantin*, 3 vols. (1868).

[50] Ibid. i. 15.

[51] Ibid. i. 136.

[52] See Marcel Pournin, *Le Procès des Saint-Simoniens* (1907).

[53] See e.g. two pamphlets written by Olinde Rodrigues, 'Aux Saint-Simoniens' (1832) and 'Bases de la loi morale proposées à l'acceptation des femmes' (1832). Enfantin was openly accused of immorality by other Saint-Simonians.

Chevalier,[54] went their various ways, contributing subsequently to the life of France in a quite remarkable fashion.

As a religion, Saint-Simonianism was still-born and such was the manifest absurdity of many of its rituals and beliefs that one cannot but be reminded of the earlier failure to establish the religion of theophilanthropy under the Directory. Here was a religion which mistook humourless solemnity for authentic spirituality and which, in Enfantin's hands, came dangerously close to being that of the sexual predator. With no meaningful concept of God, it provided an exemplary illustration of the pantheism that so disquieted Tocqueville. Yet it would be a mistake to regard the Saint-Simonian religion as nothing more than an amusing, if at times disconcerting, episode. This is so for the primary reason that it set a pattern for later social religions. This aspect of the question will be explored at greater length in the next chapter but here we might note the manner in which the 'new Christianity' sought to purge the old of its doctrinal impurities and erroneous beliefs whilst at the same time replicating the hierarchical and unitary model of the Catholic Church. Similarly, the new faith sought to re-establish social harmony and unity by putting an end to the philosophical doubt and uncertainty for so long denounced and abhorred by the Holy See. One sacerdotal caste was being called upon to replace another.

In his day, one of the best-known advocates of the need for a new religion was Pierre Leroux.[55] He had broken with the Saint-Simonians in opposition to Enfantin's more outlandish views but over the course of the next decade he developed a sophisticated and appealing doctrine that encompassed many of the dimensions of faith traditionally addressed by the established Church. His 'true definition of religion', set out in what was his most notable work, *De l'Humanité*,[56] sought to define both the deity and the immortality of our being. His central message was one of God's immanence in this world—'It is a God who is immanent in the universe, in humanity, and in each person that I worship', he wrote[57]—and from this he concluded that there was a 'harmony' and 'identity' between humanity and man.[58] As we perfected ourselves, so we perfected others. We became 'l'Homme humanité'. Leroux also shared the widely held view that some form of religion was necessary to ensure the stability of society, but unlike his Saint-Simonian brethren he did not believe that this entailed the creation of a new priestly caste. Rather, as his later writings were to reveal, he placed his hopes in the formation of a national church and in a religion without a theocracy.[59] Leroux considered freedom of religious conscience to be of only 'temporary value'.[60]

---

[54] See my 'Democracy before Tocqueville: Michel Chevalier's America', *Review of Politics*, 68 (2006), 398–427.

[55] See David Owen Evans, *Le Socialisme Romantique: Pierre Leroux et ses contemporains* (1948) and Bruno Viard (ed.), *À la source du socialisme français* (1997). The latter text contains an extensive selection of Leroux's writings.

[56] Pierre Leroux, *De l'Humanité*, 2 vols. (1840).

[57] Ibid. i, p. vii.

[58] Ibid. 247–67.

[59] *D'une Religion nationale, ou du culte* (1846).

[60] Ibid. 130. In this work Leroux addressed Bayle's hypothesis of the desirability of a society of atheists.

Leroux was not to be the only former Saint-Simonian who accepted the task of defining a religion of humanity. Nor, for all the admiration he evoked among his contemporaries,[61] was he to be the most celebrated of those who did so. Saint-Simon was fortunate to employ two young men of exceptional ability as his private secretary. The first was the future historian, Augustin Thierry; the second was Auguste Comte, the acknowledged founder of positivist sociology.[62] Comte joined Saint-Simon's service in 1817, having been expelled as a student from the École Polytechnique along with the rest of his year, and he remained there until 1824, seemingly content to be described as Saint-Simon's 'pupil'. In those early years it is virtually impossible to distinguish the ideas of Comte from those of Saint-Simon but gradually the disciple became tired of the demands and mounting jealousy of his master and an acrimonious separation became the inevitable outcome. Nevertheless, for the most part, Comte succeeded only in systemizing ideas found in inchoate form in Saint-Simon's richly variegated corpus. Indeed, Comte was systematic to a fault.

Comte's best-known idea, first glimpsed in Saint-Simon's *Mémoire sur la science de l'Homme* of 1813 but given its first full articulation by Comte in his *Système de politique positive* of 1824,[63] was that 'by the very nature of the human mind, each branch of our knowledge is necessarily subject in its course of development to pass successively through three different theoretical states: the theological or fictional state; the metaphysical or abstract state; the scientific or positive state'.[64] During the first stage, the human mind directed its search to the very nature of being, to first and final causes, and concluded that phenomena were 'products of the direct and continuous action of more or less numerous supernatural agents'.[65] During the second, transitional, stage the search to understand the nature of things continued but now explanation was attributed to such metaphysical entities as forces, properties, qualities, and powers imagined to be inherent in certain objects. By contrast, the third or final stage was, in Comte's opinion, 'the definitive mode of any science' and here the mind contented itself with relating observable phenomena to general laws. This was expressed by Comte as follows: 'in the positive state, the human mind, recognizing the impossibility of attaining absolute concepts, gives up the search for the origin and destiny of the universe and the inner causes of phenomena, and confines itself to the discovery, through reason and observation combined, of

---

[61] See the sketch of Leroux provided by George Sand in Viard, *A la source du socialisme français*, 304–5.

[62] See Mary Pickering, *Auguste Comte: An Intellectual Biography*, 3 vols. (Cambridge, 1993 and 2009). See also Henri Gouhier, *La Jeunesse d'Auguste Comte et la formation du positivisme*, 3 vols. (1933–41) and *La Vie d'Auguste Comte* (1965).

[63] The first version of this text was published as the third *cahier* of Saint-Simon's *Catéchisme des industriels*: see *Œuvres de Saint-Simon*, ix. 7–207. It was later republ. by Comte under the title of *Plan des travaux scientifiques nécessaires pour réorganiser la société*. In English see 'Plan of the Scientific Work Necessary for the Reorganization of Society', in H. S. Jones (ed.), *Auguste Comte: Early Political Writings* (Cambridge, 1998), 47–144.

[64] *Œuvres de Saint-Simon*, ix. 75.

[65] Stanislav Andreski (ed.), *The Essential Comte* (London, 1974), 20. This is a translation from Comte's slightly later work, the *Cours de Philosophie Positive*, begun in 1826.

the actual laws that govern the succession and similarity of phenomena'.[66] According to Comte, if all the branches of science passed through these three stages of
development, they did not do so at a uniform pace. The classification of the
sciences, he affirmed, was determined by their decreasing generality of validity
and the increasing complexity of their subject matter, and this produced an order
that corresponded to their historical emergence: mathematics had been followed, in
turn, by astronomy, physics, chemistry, and physiology. However, there was much
more to Comte's endeavour than an attempt to define and defend a conception of
positivist science that would, in his words, reduce 'the totality of acquired knowledge to one single body of homogeneous doctrine'.[67]

The second, and more important, task Comte set himself was to bring an end to
the historical legacy of instability and disorder bequeathed by the French Revolution. Here too Comte was working a rich vein already mined by Saint-Simon.[68]
'From a moral point of view', Comte wrote in 'Considérations philosophiques sur
les sciences et sur les savans' published in Saint-Simon's *Le Producteur*,[69] 'society is
today obviously in a state of true and profound anarchy'. This stemmed from the
absence of any dominant system capable of producing 'a single communion of
ideas'. From this, Comte continued, flowed unrestrained individuality, universal
excesses of egoism, the predominance of purely material considerations, and
corruption erected into a system of government. If this disorder were to persist,
Comte concluded, there could be 'no other outcome than the complete dissolution
of social relations'.[70] This was so, he further explained, because, while the social
system which corresponded to the theological and metaphysical stage of our mind
was disintegrating, the spiritual and temporal reorganization of society had yet to be
completed. We lived in the shadow of what remained of the theological and
military era. It was, Comte therefore wrote, 'the great and noble enterprise' of his
generation to put an end to this crisis by developing the 'organic doctrine' that
would determine the exclusive direction of all the details of society. This was to be
done not by taking the backward step of restoring theological philosophy to its
position of pre-eminence but by completing positive philosophy in such a way that
it would replace theology definitively and this itself was to be achieved by extending
scientific method to the study of society, by founding what Comte described as
'social physics'.[71]

Shortage of space (as well as the sheer tedium induced by Comte's repetitive and
dreary writing style) prevents a detailed examination of the methodological dimensions of this important argument. Central to it was the contention that social

[66] Andreski, *Essential Comte*, 20.
[67] Ibid. 39.
[68] See in particular Saint-Simon, *Considérations sur les mesures à prendre pour terminer la Révolution* (1820).
[69] *Le Producteur*, 1 (1825), 289–305, 348–73, 450–69; in English see 'Philosophical Considerations on the Sciences and the Scientists', in Jones, *Auguste Comte*, 145–86.
[70] *Le Producteur*, 1 (1825), 369–70. This argument was developed at greater length in 'Considérations sur le pouvoir spirituel', *Le Producteur*, 1 (1825), 607–14.
[71] Such, Comte announced, was the principal aim of his *Cours de Philosophie*: see Andreski, *Essential Comte*, 27.

phenomena were as susceptible to both observation and prediction as natural phenomena and that they could be investigated by means of what Comte called 'the historical operation'. 'The spirit of this science', he wrote, 'consists above all in seeing, through the detailed study of the past, the true explanation of the present and the general appearance of the future.'[72] Specifically, Comte argued that social physics could be subdivided into the twin sciences of social statics, the study of the conditions of existence of a society, and social dynamics, the study of the laws of movement of a society. Together they studied the coexistence and the succession of phenomena and in doing so disclosed not only the interdependence of all parts of the 'social organism' but also what Comte referred to as 'the positive theory of order . . . [and] of social progress'.[73]

What, at this early stage of his intellectual development, were the conclusions that Comte drew from these formulations? The most obvious was that the course of civilization was subject to 'a natural and constant law' and that this course was 'only modifiable, to a greater or lesser extent, in its speed, within certain limits, by a number of physical and moral causes which can themselves be estimated'.[74] The second was that, to date, the prevailing disposition of the theological and metaphysical school had been to 'conceive social phenomena as arbitrarily modifiable to an indefinite extent'.[75] From this had originated the harmful legislation and violent revolutions of the recent past. Next, only a 'positive politics' could enable the human race to 'escape from the condition of arbitrariness' and therefore it was an absolute imperative that politics should be elevated to the rank of the sciences of observation. Political science was to be a branch of physics.[76] Comte further concluded—again echoing the voice of his master—that this elevation of politics to a new rank could only be effected by the scientists because, within the new social system dominated by industry, they alone possessed the requisite capacity and theoretical authority. No less Saint-Simonian in tone was Comte's conclusion that, in an age of scientific politics, the government of things would replace that of men.[77]

These views were most thoroughly set out in Comte's magisterial *Cours de philosophie positive*, begun in 1826 and published in six volumes between 1830 and 1842.[78] It was this set of lectures that was to have an enormous influence both upon Comte's contemporaries and subsequent generations, and not only in France. The English writer George Henry Lewes, now probably best known as the paramour of novelist George Eliot, wrote of it in his *History of Philosophy* that 'A new era has dawned. For the first time in history an Explanation of the world, society, and man is presented which is thoroughly homogeneous, and, at the same time, thoroughly in accordance with accurate knowledge.'[79] John Stuart Mill, as testified in his *Auguste Comte and Positivism*, was similarly impressed. Yet these same writers had scarcely a good word for such subsequent Comtean publications

---

[72] *Le Producteur*, 1 (1825), 356.   [73] Andreski, *Essential Comte*, 148.
[74] *Œuvres de Saint-Simon*, ix. 109.   [75] Andreski, *Essential Comte*, 143.
[76] *Œuvres de Saint-Simon*, ix. 193.   [77] Ibid. 131.   [78] (1830–42).
[79] George Henry Lewes, *The History of Philosophy from Thales to Comte* (London, 1867), ii. 590.

as *Le Calendrier positiviste* (1849), the *Système de politique positiviste* (1851–4), and *Le Catéchisme positiviste* (1852). To quote Lewes again, he wrote that 'I have never been able to accept the later works as more than magnificent efforts to construct an Utopia.'[80] J. S. Mill was less charitable. Of the *Système de politique positiviste* he simply remarked that it was 'the completest system of spiritual and temporal despotism which has ever yet emanated from a human brain, unless that of possibly Ignatius Loyola'.[81] For many of his readers Comte's increasing preoccupation with the formulation of a religion of humanity seemed a betrayal of his earlier positivism and, moreover, something to be deplored.

Comte did not see it that way, preferring to emphasize 'the perfect harmony of the efforts that characterized my youth with the works accomplished by my maturity'.[82] The evidence suggests that he did so with some justification. In his earliest writings, Comte inveighed against 'the anarchic state of the intellect' and damned Protestantism's approval of the right of private judgement, commenting that 'there is no freedom of conscience in astronomy'.[83] In one of his most important texts of the period, *Considérations sur le pouvoir spirituel*,[84] he affirmed his faith in the necessity of a spiritual power and argued that its distinctive function was the 'government of opinion' and the 'direction of education'. To that end, its task was to develop the 'system of ideas and habits necessary to prepare individuals for the social order' and to secure 'the voluntary subordination of private interest to the common interest'. The extent and intensity of this spiritual power, Comte remarked, could be gauged by observing 'the Catholic clergy in the era of its greatest vigour and its most complete independence'.[85] Temporal power would be subordinated to spiritual power.

In the *Cours de Philosophie Positive* itself, the argument moved overtly at its conclusion from social physics to social ethics. Under the new philosophic regime there would exist both 'a complete mental coherence' and 'the scientific ascendancy of the social point of view'. 'When', Comte wrote, 'a true education has familiarized modern minds with the notions of solidarity and perpetuity that the positive contemplation of social evolution suggests in so many cases, then will be felt the essential moral superiority of a philosophy that binds each one of us to the whole existence of humanity.'[86] Positive morality, he continued, 'will tend to present each man's happiness as dependent on the extension of benevolent acts and sympathetic emotions to our species as a whole'.[87] More than this, in the work that Comte himself always regarded as his 'fundamental opuscule', the *Système de politique positive*, he openly conceded that the philosophical truth of positivism would never 'impassion the mass of men' unless it was presented 'as a vivid picture of the improvements' it would bring to 'the human condition'. This, he stated, was 'an order of works in which the imagination must play a predominant role'.[88]

---

[80] Ibid. 635.   [81] *Autobiography* (Oxford, 1969), 127.
[82] Quoted in 'Introduction', Jones, *Auguste Comte*, p. x.
[83] *Œuvres de Saint-Simon*, ix. 23–4.
[84] *Le Producteur*, 1 (1825), 596–616, 2 (1825), 314–29, 358–76.
[85] Ibid. 315.   [86] Andreski, *Auguste Comte*, 220.
[87] Ibid. 221.   [88] *Œuvres de Saint-Simon*, ix. 136–8.

At this stage Comte equated such works of the imagination with the fine arts and gave to artists the role of inducing 'the universal adoption' of the new system. There was no mention of a new religion or of a new clergy. However, if Comte's intention from the outset was to bring an end to the societal crisis made manifest in the French Revolution, so too it can be seen that his concerns were never exclusively philosophical and that he always had in mind the need for a spiritual reorganization of society as a whole. Why the emphasis within his work shifted—as it undoubtedly did and to the dismay and shock of some of his most loyal disciples—was the cause of considerable speculation. Much was made of Comte's fragile psychological condition,[89] especially after the death of Clotilde de Vaux (with whom he had fallen passionately in love in 1844).[90] But the fact of the matter was that, in developing his ideas in the direction of a religion of humanity, Comte was to a considerable degree following a path taken by many social reformers of his day.[91] As we have seen, Pierre Leroux was one case in point.

The fascinating details of the Comtean religion—itself recalling Robespierre's cult of the Supreme Being—have been well documented.[92] Nothing was left to chance. Each and every aspect of its ceremonies, sacraments, and organization was the subject of minute description. The positivist calendar alone—with each day and each of its thirteen months named not after a saint but a great figure of the past (Homer, Dante, Shakespeare, and so on), each month of twenty-eight days, 'a universal festival of the dead' to mark the last day of the year, and an additional festival in leap years—represented a considerable feat of intellectual ingenuity and one that received lengthy clarification from Comte himself.[93] There were to be festivals celebrating both the static and dynamic aspects of humanity.

For all their undoubted importance to Comte, these were not among the four essential features of the new religion.[94] The first was that it claimed to regulate all aspects of both our private and public existence and thus subordinated politics to morals. Second, the 'proven religion' of humanity—'the one true Great Being'—was taken to supersede the revealed religion of a Christian God and thus of the Catholic Church. It was 'the only complete, real and true religion'[95] because this 'new Great Being' was not 'a purely subjective abstraction' but the result of 'exact objective judgement'.[96] Third, the superiority of the positive morality was demonstrated by its substitution of the love of humanity for the love of God. 'To love

---

[89] See Émile Littré, *Auguste Comte et la philosophie positive* (1863), 580–91.

[90] See Comte, *Discours sur l'ensemble du postivisme* (1848), 261–3.

[91] See Edward Berenson, 'A New Religion of the Left: Christianity and Social Revolution in France, 1815–1848', in François Furet and Mona Ozouf (eds.), *The French Revolution and the Creation of Modern Political Culture*, iii. *The Transformation of Political Culture 1789–1848* (Oxford, 1989), 543–60.

[92] See Andrew Wernick, *Auguste Comte and the Religion of Humanity: The Post-Theistic Program of French Social Theory* (Cambridge, 2001). See also 'Auguste Comte and the Religion of Humanity', in Bernard M. G. Reardon, *Religion in the Age of Romanticism* (Cambridge, 1985), 207–36.

[93] Comte, *Le Calendrier positiviste ou système générale de commémoration publique* (1849).

[94] In addition to the texts already cited see *Discours sur l'ensemble du positivisme* (1848), 315–93.

[95] Ibid. 324.   [96] Ibid. 328.

Humanity', Comte wrote, 'truly constitutes all that is best in morality.'[97] Altruism would prevail over egoism, sociability over personality. 'Live for others' was positivism's golden rule. Finally, Comte attributed a central role in the new religion to women.[98] In part this disclosed an increasing disillusionment with the proletariat during the Second Republic, but more substantially it reflected his conviction that social regeneration would depend upon the subordination of masculine reason to feminine sentiment. The positivist religion, Comte wrote, was but 'a systematic consecration of what women feel instinctively'[99] and in conjugal love they provided a model of the 'universal love' to come.[100] Accordingly, women would act as the 'priestesses of Humanity'[101] and it was to be through 'the cult of women' that men would be prepared for the worship of humanity. The parallels with the Catholic cult of the Virgin Mary are self-evident.

Here was a religion that was to be 'thoroughly human' and which, for all its imitation of the organizational and doctrinal principles of the Catholic Church, was unambiguously intended to secure the 'irrevocable' elimination of Catholicism. But this religion, as much as Comte's overtly positivist sociology, was equally intended to bring the Revolution to a close. Under the guidance of the new religion, politics was to be transformed into the 'active worship' and 'service' of humanity.[102] Moreover, the most important part of this transformation was to be the 'substitution of duties for rights'. 'The word *right*', Comte wrote, 'should be as much excluded from the proper language of politics as should the word *cause* from the language of philosophy. Both are theological-metaphysical concepts; and the former is as immoral and anarchical as the latter is irrational and sophistical.'[103] In the positive state of the future, individual rights would disappear and everyone would have duties towards others. Whatever security the individual might require would be achieved through the general recognition of reciprocal obligations. Submission to government, Comte asserted, was not the foundation of virtue. Rather, 'true liberty' consisted in 'obedience to objective laws' capable of scientific demonstration.

Writing in the immediate aftermath of the Revolution of 1848, it was Comte's view that society was not yet ready to attain to the positivist state but he did nevertheless believe that the negative phase of the Revolution—characterized by the slogan of Liberty and Equality—was over and that the reconciliation of Order and Progress was now possible. Accordingly, he set out a provisional programme for the transitional period ahead which, with typical thoroughness, included detailed specifications for an occidental navy, international coinage, and a flag for the new western republic proclaiming 'universal love'. Comte, as he made expressly clear in his last major work, *Système de politique positive*, was convinced that the triumph of positivism would entail the decomposition of the nation-state, the idea of a polity

---

[97] Ibid. 352.   [98] See *Discours sur l'ensemble du positivisme*, 198–267.
[99] Ibid. 203.
[100] Comte believed that the family was to be the principal sphere of action for women. He likewise believed in monogamy and the indissolubility of marriage, even beyond death: ibid. 226–36.
[101] Ibid. 253.   [102] Ibid. 357.   [103] Ibid.

or political society being progressively evacuated of content. Likewise, Comte believed that his positivist religion would be universal and that, over time, it would come to unify not only France but the entire globe. It would first embrace the other monotheistic religions of the world, then the polytheistic creeds of the East, before finally replacing the fetishist faiths of Africa.

II

Most churches are subject to schisms and the Comtean religion was no exception. The first, and probably most significant, occurred as early as 1852 when Émile Littré, future editor of the *Dictionnaire de la langue française* and member of the Académie Française, found himself unable to follow his master's deduction of a positive politics from his earlier positive philosophy.[104] The flame of orthodoxy was kept alive under the leadership of Pierre Laffitte, but not even his undoubted abilities as a Comtean exegete could prevent further splits in the 1870s and 1880s.[105] However, both men merit our attention, if only briefly, because each, in their different ways, illustrates the political direction that positivism was to take in the final decades of the nineteenth century.[106]

Littré never disguised his immense debt to Comte—'the work of Comte transformed me', he wrote[107]—and thus the break was all the more painful.[108] Nevertheless, he was incapable of seeing Comte's later writings as anything other than a betrayal of the original positivist philosophy. The charge was sustained and wounding, and in essence amounted to the judgement that Comte 'changed his methodology', that as he developed the religion of humanity he passed from 'the objective method' to the 'subjective method', from the mind to the heart, from evidence to imagination, and with disastrous consequences.[109] The result, Littré stated unambiguously, was a 'return to the theological state'.[110] Yet it is clear that Littré's disquiet also arose from mounting political differences, especially after the demise of the Second Republic, an eventuality broadly welcomed by Comte.

The political trajectory followed by Littré is most clearly seen through the lens of the 1879 edition of his *Conservation, Révolution et Positivisme*.[111] In this text Littré republished a wide selection of his articles from the years 1849–51 but to each he

---

[104] These views were most clearly expressed in Littré, *Auguste Comte*, 517–681.

[105] See Emile Corra, *Pierre Laffitte: Successeur d'Auguste Comte* (1923).

[106] On positivism in France after Comte's death see W. M. Simon, *European Positivism in the Nineteenth Century: An Essay in Intellectual History* (Port Washington, NY, 1963), 19–171.

[107] Littré, *Auguste Comte*, 662–3.

[108] See Sudhir Hazareesingh, *Intellectual Founders of the Republic: Five Studies in Nineteenth-Century French Political Thought* (Oxford, 2001), 23–83. Specifically upon Littré's engagement with Comte see D. G. Charlton, *Positivist Thought in France during the Second Empire 1852–1870* (Oxford, 1959), 51–71.

[109] Littré, *Auguste Comte*, 527–37.

[110] Ibid. 570–9.

[111] The distance travelled can also be appreciated by looking at a document written by Littré, Laffitte, and Fabien Magnin, *Rapport à la société positiviste par la commission chargée d'examiner la nature et le plan du nouveau gouvernement révolutionnaire de la république française* (1848).

added a commentary from 1878. Time and time again, in a display of unflinching honesty, Littré admitted his earlier mistakes and naivety.[112] He had been wrong to believe that the separation of temporal and spiritual powers was anything more than a utopia.[113] He was mistaken in his appraisal of the political situation of the Second Republic, believing, like Comte, that the republic was now 'definitively established'.[114] As the violence and destruction of the Paris Commune had demonstrated, the 'pretension' to marry socialism to positive philosophy had been 'chimerical'.[115] It was out of 'puerile enthusiasm' and 'dogmatic blindness' that he had imagined that there would be only peace between European nations.[116] The most substantive set of errors, however, related to the provisions for revolutionary government set out in the heady days of 1848–9. Littré's proposals had envisaged, first, 'the continued preponderance of central power' in Paris in order that 'progressive tendencies' should predominate and 'material order' should be maintained; the 'strict limitation' of local power and a 'considerable reduction' in the attributes of the Chamber of Deputies; and, thirdly, 'the placing of power in the hands of eminent proletarians' and its removal from the 'incompetent' members of the 'classes supérieures'. An element of counter-balance to executive power was to be attained through freedom of speech and the press, the regular publication of government projects, and the existence of political 'clubs'. The duration of a government's mandate would not be set by a limited term but by the use that was made of it.[117] Thirty years later Littré recognized that he had been in error in believing, like Comte, that a period of transition to a positive political order had begun, that the proletariat were in a condition to wield power, and that the socialists were 'half-positivist'. 'These three factual errors' he wrote, 'removed any possible chance of the application of this project for revolutionary and transitional government, not to mention the obstacles that would have arisen from the opposition of the provinces to the domination of Paris, from the bourgeoisie to the preponderance of the proletariat and from the peasantry to the systems of the socialists and others.'[118]

In the interim France had seen the *coup d'état* of Louis Napoleon Bonaparte—'the 2nd December has been the ruin of France', Littré wrote[119]—the traumas of foreign occupation and the Paris Commune. For want of any other alternative, therefore, Littré was left with the conservative republic of Adolphe Thiers and the politics of opportunism.[120] Littré could not abandon his distaste for the

---

[112] See e.g. *Conservation, Révolution et Positivisme* (1879), 266–7.
[113] Ibid. 64–5.
[114] Ibid. 75.
[115] Ibid. 454.
[116] Ibid. 481–2.
[117] These views were most clearly expressed in an article entitled 'Révision de la Constitution', 237–45 and *Rapport à la société positiviste par la commission chargée d'examiner la nature et le plan du nouveau gouvernement révolutionnaire de la république française*.
[118] *Conservation, Révolution et Positivisme*, 248.
[119] Ibid. 142.
[120] See Littré's reflections on the early years of the Third Republic in *De l'Établissement de la Troisième République* (1880). See also Claude Nicolet, *L'Idée républicaine en France* (1994), 187–248

bloodletting of the Revolution,[121] nor could he overcome his deep antipathy towards the republican slogan of liberty, equality, and fraternity,[122] but he was now convinced that a moderate, parliamentary republic was the best guarantee of the Comtean maxims of order and progress,[123] that it alone could provide the mixture of 'wisely conservative' and 'widely progressive' measures that would make genuine improvements possible and secure the confidence and stability of the nation. 'Peaceable legality',[124] achieved through participation, representation, discussion, education, and gradual reform, was to be the watchword. The succinct and novel phrase Littré used to describe this regime when he became a Freemason in 1875 was 'the conspiracy of toleration'.[125]

What now remained of Littré's Comteanism, stripped as it was of the religious paraphernalia of his master's final years? The 'disciple' did not hesitate to provide an answer.[126] Above all, there endured a vehement opposition towards all theological and metaphysical conceptions of the world, combined with an unshakable commitment to the philosophy of positivism as a form of proven and provable scientific knowledge. So too Littré continued to believe in the terrestrial, although quite definitely not the religious, ideal of humanity and that it was through education, and not violence or revolution, that the regeneration of humanity would be secured.

Yet even here Littré gave positivism an unexpected (and not insignificant) twist. As the 1870s drew to a close (and to great controversy) Littré published an article entitled 'Le catholicisme selon le suffrage universel',[127] in which he insisted upon drawing a distinction between the Catholicism that was the moderate and lived religion of 'the great majority of the French' and that of clerical Ultramontanism and the Jesuits. The latter, he argued, was no less a threat to the former than the rabid anticlerical secularism that had had its origins in the eighteenth century. The political point he wanted to make was that the (Third) Republic would commit a major error if it chose needlessly to provoke and antagonize ordinary French Catholics, the Catholics of 'universal suffrage' who often voted for republican candidates, by immediately pushing for the separation of Church and State and by overturning the terms of the Napoleonic Concordat.[128]

---

and Theodore Zeldin, *Politics and Anger: France 1848–1945* (1979), 241–75. Zeldin brings out well the link between positivism and men such as Gambetta and Jules Ferry.

[121] *Conservation, Révolution et Positivisme*, 314.

[122] Ibid. 338–40.

[123] Ibid. 123.

[124] Ibid. 142.

[125] 'Discours de Réception dans la Franc-Maçonnerie', *Fragments de Philosophie Positive et de Sociologie contemporaine* (1876), 597.

[126] For the 1868 edn. of Comte's *Principes de Philosophie Positive* Littré provided a 'Préface d'un disciple'. For the 1877 edn., he provided a 'second preface' titled 'Étude sur les Progrès du Positivisme': see Comte, *Cours de Philosophie Positive* (1877), pp. vi–lxvii. The second text was publ. separately by Baillière in 1877.

[127] *De l'Établissement de la Troisième République*, 489–508.

[128] Ibid. 495.

Such a stance towards Catholicism, Littré maintained, did not denote either indifference towards or an underestimation of the threats posed to the existence of the Republic by the forces of clerical reaction but was rather to suggest that the way forward was through a combination of what he termed 'science and liberty' and not legal interdiction.[129] The Republic should trust to time and to the benefits of moral and educational suasion. To that extent, he argued, just as there should be no state religion, so there should be no state irreligion. In effect, this was to be the policy pursued by the Third Republic in its early years and these were the sentiments that informed the major educational reforms proposed by Jules Ferry, measures broadly supported by Littré from his position as a member of the upper house of the French parliament but opposed by orthodox positivist opinion.[130] It was only at the turn of the century that the Republic decided to declare war on the Church.

Our second central figure in the history of positivism, Pierre Laffitte, had only a marginally less impressive and influential career. He became interested in Comtean ideas in the early 1840s and in 1848 was a founder member of the Société positiviste. After Comte's death, he became the effective leader of the positivist movement and, despite considerable dissension and opposition,[131] remained so until his own death in 1897. In many respects he was the Engels of positivism,[132] further developing Comtean ideas through a truly impressive number of books, lectures (from 1892 he held the professorial chair in the *histoire générale des sciences* at the Collège de France) and, from 1878, as editor of *La Revue occidentale*.[133] Laffitte was less enthusiastic about the religion of humanity than many of Comte's orthodox disciples, but he, like other of his fellow positivists,[134] sought to make sense of Comte's remarks, enunciated most forcefully in his *Appel aux conservateurs* of 1855,[135] on the need for republican dictatorship. In doing so he provided the most authoritative positivist account of the Revolution of 1789.[136]

As might be expected, Laffitte located the Revolution within the broad sweep of European history and, to that extent, saw it as the inevitable outcome of the decomposition of the *ancien régime* and the progress of civilization. Nevertheless, it had failed in its 'abortive aspiration' to reconstruct the modern order. Laffitte's argument became more interesting when he suggested that this outcome might have been avoided had there come to the throne a monarch who would have transformed the 'retrograde dictatorship' of Louis XIV and Louis XV into 'a progressive dictatorship' governing with the support of 'elements of the new

---

[129] Ibid. 503.

[130] Orthodox positivist opinion saw religious liberty as the equivalent of Catholic domination.

[131] As an example of the sustained criticism Laffitte received see Jorge Lagarrigue, *Le Faux et le Vrai positivisme* (1892). Laffitte faced opposition from outside France, esp. England.

[132] For an example of how the ideas of Comte and Laffitte were merged together by other leading positivists see Jean-François Robinet, *La Philosophie Positiviste: Auguste Comte et M. Pierre Laffitte* (1885).

[133] See Laffitte, 'Nécessité de l'intervention du Positivisme dans l'Ensemble des Affaires Humaines', *Revue occidentale*, 1 (1878), 1–29, and *De la Morale positive* (1881).

[134] See Nicolet, *L'Idée républicaine*, 239–42.

[135] (Paris, 1855).

[136] *La Révolution Française (1789–1815)* (1880).

society, the industrialists, the philosophers, and the scientists'.[137] This had not occurred and thus the National Assembly, 'despite its ardent desire to secure the total regeneration of French society', was torn apart by its own contradictory policy of proclaiming the sovereignty of the nation whilst establishing a constitutional monarchy. This allowed Laffitte to justify both the insurrection against the monarchy of 10 August 1792—'a *coup d'état* or an insurrection', he argued, 'is legitimate when legality, being no longer in harmony with the spontaneous condition and natural development of society, threatens the public interest'[138]—and the execution of the king on the grounds that the new government had to demonstrate that it could break 'the prestige of theocracy' and that *raison d'état* had to prevail over the 'quibbles of jurisprudence'.[139] A similar argument applied to the putting to death of the Girondins who, had they remained in power, would have precipitated 'the triumph of federalism' and therefore the defeat of France at the hands of her enemies.[140] France had had to be defended against herself and this could only have been done through the imposition of 'an inflexible dictatorship' on the part of 'a minority' who alone understood the demands of 'necessity'.

Could the actions of this minority be described as having been illegitimate? Laffitte's reply was unequivocal. 'Legitimacy in politics', he wrote, 'derives no more from number than it does from birth, no more from popular sovereignty than it does from the divine right of kings.' Rather it existed when 'the conduct of those who govern' was in accord with 'the natural laws of social phenomena, with the force of circumstances and the universal order'.[141] Where people still went wrong, he insisted, was in 'their determination to retain and to apply democratic theory despite the lessons of history'.[142] Thus, in Laffitte's opinion, the reign of Terror was as inevitable as it was indispensable,[143] and he found himself agreeing with Joseph de Maistre's 'paradox' that only Jacobinism could have saved France.[144]

In line with Comte's own views, this argument disclosed the name of the real hero of the Revolution: Danton.[145] He, more than anyone else, had been able to 'raise himself above all the theoretical prejudices of his day to arrive at what was true, useful, and indispensable'.[146] Through instinct he had grasped the nature of the 'real legality' demanded by the terrible circumstances. Moreover, he had understood that revolutionary government should only have been 'provisional' and that it should have been brought to a close once the threat from France's external enemies had ceased. Accordingly, Laffitte had only praise for the achievements of 1793 but he also believed that, with the death of Danton, the Revolution had gone into decline. 'Suddenly', he wrote, 'France, via the confusion of the spiritual and the temporal, via legal deism, and via the divine right of a single individual, fell back into the theocracy of Rousseau: Robespierre prepared the way for Bonaparte.'[147] Napoleon, Laffitte continued, re-established the 'absolute

[137] *La Révolution Française (1789–1815)* (1880), 15.   [138] Ibid. 45.   [139] Ibid. 58.
[140] Ibid. 61.   [141] Ibid. 75.   [142] Ibid. 76.   [143] Ibid. 84.   [144] Ibid. 83.
[145] See Émile Antoine, 'La Théorie positiviste de la Révolution Française', *Revue occidentale*, 7 (1893), 253–90. This article was a response to criticisms made of Comte's account of the role of Danton by Alphonse Aulard.
[146] *La Révolution Française*, 85.   [147] Ibid. 141.

monarchy' and this 'criminal' and 'imbecilic' act had subsequently produced the Restoration and the July Monarchy, the most 'corrupt' of regimes. Since Napoleon, he concluded, France had oscillated between 'anarchy' and 'retrogression', throughout the course of which the positive principles required for social regeneration and a new industrial regime had gradually come into existence. After a century of turmoil, the 'organic' phase of the Revolution had begun.

Laffitte published *La Révolution Française* in 1880. Nine years later, with considerable enthusiasm,[148] the positivists joined the celebrations of the Revolution's centenary, most notably through a joint commemoration with their English colleagues marked by numerous speeches, a 'civic pilgrimage' to Versailles, the laying of wreaths, and a formal banquet attended, we are told, by over 100 guests.[149] All the familiar positivist themes made their appearance, not least the refrain that the Revolution had marked the beginning of the modern era and that positivism alone would be able to bring the revolutionary period to a close. 'The French Revolution', Laffitte announced at the former home of Auguste Comte, 'put forward an ideal which, in metaphysical form, prefigured the positive ideal which one day, and as a result of a slow process of evolution, will unite the whole of Humanity around a demonstrable faith.'[150] Despite the usual positivist disclaimers with regard to the rights of man and the merits of popular election,[151] there was general approval of the fact that the Republic was the 'normal' and 'definitively established' form of government in France—Laffitte characterized the Second Empire as an 'unfortunate but temporary aberration'[152]—and that 'a socially and territorially homogeneous' country was governed not only by a State that was 'strongly centralized' but one that made no reference either to kings or to God.[153] From a political point of view at least, the official representatives of the positivist movement in France, with Laffitte at their fore, seemed only too willing to embrace the cause of the Third Republic and to cast themselves as 'the sons and heirs of the Revolution'.[154] For the most part, their master's authoritarian proclivities had been quietly put to one side.

There was to be one further and improbable twist to the story of Comtean positivism at the *fin-de-siècle*. In 1891, a young Charles Maurras,[155] not yet the principal theoretician of the monarchist Action Française,[156] published an article entitled 'L'Evolution des idées sociales'.[157] To this point Maurras's interests had

---

[148] See Laffitte, 'Le Centenaire de 1789', *Revue occidentale*, 22 (1889), 241–70.
[149] 'Célébration positiviste du centenaire de la Révolution', *Revue occidentale*, 23 (1889), 353–441.
[150] Ibid. 422.
[151] Ibid. 429–30. See also Laffitte, 'De la Souveraineté', *Revue occidentale*, 23 (1889), 31–85.
[152] 'Célébration positiviste du centenaire de la Révolution', 442.
[153] Ibid. 432.
[154] Ibid. 363.
[155] See Pierre Boutang, *Maurras: La Destinée et l'œuvre* (1984) and Victor Nguyen, *Aux origines de l'Action Française* (1991). In what follows I am indebted to Michael Sutton's *Nationalism, Positivism and Catholicism: The Politics of Charles Maurras and French Catholics 1890–1914* (Cambridge, 1982).
[156] See William Curt Buthman, *The Rise of Integral Nationalism, with Special Reference to the Ideas and Activities of Charles Maurras* (New York, 1939); Eugen Weber, *Action Française* (Stanford, Calif., 1962); Edward Robert Tannenbaum, *The Action Française* (New York, 1962).
[157] *La Réforme sociale*, 21 (1891), 125–31, 200–98, 277–85.

been largely literary and aesthetic but, in writing for the leading publication of the school of conservative sociologist Frédéric Le Play,[158] he made one of his first forays into the world of politics. Written in three parts, this article was to disclose many of the themes that Maurras was to make familiar over the next fifty years and more. Above all, he lambasted 'the most famous revolutionary sophisms'—liberty, equality, and fraternity—and condemned the ravages of individualism upon French society. Nonetheless, Maurras, with cautious optimism, believed that he discerned a 'slow' and 'subterranean' evolution of ideas—dated from around 1857[159]—away from the naïve 'romantic' faith in 'l'État Dieu', the 'Revolution' and the 'People', towards social discipline and stability, hierarchy and continuity, and a sense of solidarity engendered by the family, 'le milieu social', and 'la patrie'. In this evolution, Maurras—no doubt to the surprise of the journal's largely Catholic readership—attributed a central role to none other than . . . Auguste Comte! 'The dominant trait of this philosophy', Maurras wrote, 'is its extraordinary lucid perception of all that is illogical and ridiculous in modern individualism; in contrast, it binds men to their fellows across time and space through the carnal embrace of race and blood as well as through respect for the law of continuity'.[160] To this Maurras added that 'even the most timorous Catholic could not take exception to the philosophy of Comte to the extent that it relates to earthly matters'.[161]

In the years that immediately followed—years that saw his conversion to monarchism following a visit to Athens to report on the Olympic Games in 1896—Maurras continued to explore the pertinence of Comte's ideas in a series of short, journalistic pieces and it was not therefore to be until 1902 that he published an essay specifically devoted to Comte himself.[162] When he eventually did so, there could be no doubting Maurras's immense admiration for the 'master'. 'I know of no other name', he wrote, 'that should be pronounced with a greater sense of gratitude.'[163]

Why was this so? At the heart of Maurras's thought lay the firm conviction that the nineteenth century had been an age of intellectual anarchy. No one, in his view, had better appreciated this than Comte and no one had made greater effort to restore order and hierarchy to our intellectual (and therefore moral) universe.[164] Moreover, Maurras saw that Comte had understood that, to be convinced of the discoveries of positivism, the people would need convictions, a faith, a dogma, and that this would demand 'an ensemble of daily practices' constituted by a religion. Nor did Maurras hesitate to describe the guiding article of faith of this new religion.

---

[158] See Michael Zachary Taylor, *Le Play, Engineer and Social Scientist* (London, 1970).
[159] 1857 was the year of Comte's death.
[160] 'L'Evolution des idées sociales', 128.
[161] Ibid.
[162] 'Auguste Comte', *Romantisme et Révolution: L'Œuvre de Charles Maurras* (1922), iii. 91–130. This volume contains the texts of *L'Avenir de l'Intelligence* (1905) and *Trois Idées Politiques* (1898). In addition, the introductory preface is a reworking of the earlier essay entitled 'Idées françaises et idées suisses' (1899).
[163] Ibid. 91.
[164] Ibid. 99–106.

'Catholic dogma', he wrote, 'places at its centre the greatest being that we are capable of conceiving ... the being of beings. ... Positivist dogma puts at the centre the greatest being capable of being known but known "positively", that is to say, without recourse to any theological or metaphysical process.' That great being was humanity.[165] The beneficial consequences that would flow from this new religion were, for Maurras, beyond doubt. From the moment of its inception, the positivist religion would impose 'a spontaneous respect for tradition' and 'the sentiment of the superiority of obedience and submission to that of rebellion'.[166]

It should be clear that Maurras's Comteanism drew little from such central positivist concepts as the law of the three stages and that, unlike many of Comte's admirers, he felt little embarrassment about the religious eccentricities of Comte's later years. Indeed, in marked contrast to Emile Littré, he seems to have thought that Comte's infatuation with Madame de Vaux only served to enliven and to enrich his philosophy.[167] The more substantive point is that Maurras worked this reading of Comte into the broader historical and political framework that came to underpin his arguments for a restoration of the French monarchy.

A clue to how this was done can be found in their mutual antipathy towards Protestantism. There were many facets to this argument but, at bottom, both Comte and Maurras were inclined to see a strong connection between the Protestant Reformation and the Revolution of 1789 and were encouraged to do so by their belief that the Protestant emphasis upon the individual conscience was fundamentally corrosive of all social bonds and social hierarchy.[168] To that extent, the Revolution was deemed to have had its origins in Wittemberg and Geneva and, more distantly still, in Jerusalem rather than Rome. In Maurras's case, this interpretation was strengthened by a particular vision of the French past as a vehicle for the transmission of what he termed the 'classical spirit'.[169] 'Old France', Maurras wrote, 'professed traditional Catholicism which, combining Jewish visions, Christian sentiment, and the discipline received from the Hellenic and Roman world, carries within it the natural order of humanity.'[170] The 'biblisme' of Protestantism, Maurras averred, had overturned this 'mental, moral, and aesthetic order'.[171]

For Maurras, the recent history of France was one of decline from its high point in the sixteenth and seventeenth centuries characterized by a monarchical state, a Catholic religion, and what he described as 'an aesthetics of harmony'.[172] After the introduction of Protestantism, the descent continued, perhaps inadvertently, as a consequence of the voyages of Voltaire and Montesquieu to England and their resulting corruption by the 'Hebraic and Germanic spirit'.[173] This had only served

---

[165] Ibid. 107.   [166] Ibid. 114.   [167] Ibid. 120–5.

[168] For Maurras it was an 'objective truth' that Protestantism had its roots in 'individual anarchy' and that the summit of its achievement would be 'the insurrection of citizens, the convulsion of society, and the anarchy of the State': 'La Politique Religieuse', *La Démocratie Religieuse: L'Œuvre de Charles Maurras* (1921), ii. 225.

[169] See the note appended by Maurras to 'Trois Idées Politiques: Chateaubriand, Michelet, Sainte-Beuve', ibid. 269–70.

[170] Ibid. 246.   [171] 'Préface de l'édition définitive', ibid. 4.

[172] 'Le Romantisme féminin', ibid. 192.   [173] 'Préface de l'édition définitive', 5.

to open up the way for the 'miserable Rousseau'. It is impossible to do justice to the venomous and vitriolic scorn heaped upon Rousseau by Maurras. 'Nourished upon the heart of the Bible', Rousseau was the arch-villain, the 'half-man' most responsible for spreading the folly, savagery, and ignorance which ultimately was to overwhelm France at the end of the eighteenth century.[174] Worse still, 'the mortal principles' brought forth by Rousseau's arrogance and rage had not only instilled a spirit of revolt among France's citizens and weakened the French state—Maurras's contempt for the 'principle of planetary fraternity' knew no bounds[175]—but they had lived on into the nineteenth century, fuelling the self-indulgent emotional sentimentalism of an effeminate and anarchic Romanticism in thrall to the misguided and misplaced passion for personal sincerity.[176] Chateaubriand—'a shame-faced Protestant dressed up in the purple of Rome', according to Maurras[177]—Lamennais, Michelet, and Victor Hugo, were among the culprits but, as a class, *les lettrés*, the professional men of letters, had ceased to defend either the national interest or the classical traditions of France.

At the end of *L'Avenir de l'Entelligence* Maurras sought to call this increasingly 'blind and irresolute' class to order, rallying them to 'the ship of counter-revolution', but for our purposes the most salient feature of Maurras's proposals for national renewal was his call for a necessary alliance between Atheists (by which he meant Positivists) and Catholics.[178] In effect, he was speaking to those who, like himself, had been 'born into the Catholic tradition' but who had become 'strangers to the Catholic faith', those who felt 'the rigorous need of the absence of God' but also 'the intellectual, moral, and political needs which are natural to all civilized men'.[179] These, Maurras stipulated, were the needs for order in one's thoughts, in one's life, and in the society in which one lived. If others such as Le Play, Taine, and Sainte-Beuve, the latter being the very embodiment of 'organizing empiricism',[180] had provided sustenance to these needs, it was the founder of positivism who could best satisfy them. Nevertheless, there was one crucial step in Maurras's argument that had yet to be taken. Maurras had little time for the wilder excesses of Comte's hopes for a new and peaceful international order—indeed, he suggested that, had Comte lived to witness Italian and German unification, the rise of the British Empire, and France's defeat in 1870, he would have abandoned these views—and he was therefore of the opinion that, for some considerable time to come, 'the *patrie* will represent humankind for any given group of men'.[181] For Maurras, it was one's country and not humanity that was our primary reality and to the extent that it united the dead of past generations with those still living and those yet unborn it was an object of religious veneration.[182]

---

[174] 'Préface de l'édition définitive', 5–10. For a selection of Maurras's writings on the French Revolution see *Réflexions sur la Révolution de 1789* (1948).
[175] 'Préface de l'édition définitive', 21 bis.
[176] 'Le Romantisme féminin', 185–203. This argument was developed in Pierre Lasserre, *Le Romantisme français: Essai sur la Révolution dans les sentiments et dans les idées au XIXe siècle* (1907).
[177] 'Trois Idées Politiques', 246.   [178] Ibid. 287–8.
[179] 'Auguste Comte', 95–6.   [180] 'Trois Idées Politiques', 255–63.
[181] 'Auguste Comte', 118.   [182] Ibid. 119.

The monarchist Action Française came into existence in 1899. In the feverish atmosphere created by the Dreyfus Affair and then, in 1905, by the separation of Church and State, it flourished and prospered as one of the principal anti-republican movements of the day, conveying its message through an impressive combination of sophisticated intellectual argument, strident anti-Semitic propaganda, and street fighting. There is little evidence to suggest that any but a few of its members were sympathetic to Maurras's calls for an alliance between Positivism and Catholicism—although when the Institut d'Action Française was founded in 1906 it did establish a Chaire Auguste Comte—but this did little to dissuade Maurras from developing further the doctrine of 'integral nationalism' or from imagining that Comte—'the builder anew of the *cité* and of the *patrie*, of authority and of hierarchy, the philosopher well-versed in the laws of social nature, the critic of modern forms of anarchy',[183] as Maurras described him in 1913—had an important role to play in fashioning this new doctrine. One aspect of this surfaced forcibly when Marc Sangnier, leader of the social Catholic movement associated with *Le Sillon*, was bold enough to suggest that, sooner or later, people would have to choose between 'Monarchical Positivism' and 'Social Christianity'.[184] Maurras's response was both to voice surprise and to counter that, 'for diverse reasons, and ones that are not at all irreconcilable, they hold to the same historical and political truths that they have observed or discovered together'.[185] 'I am Roman: I am human', he affirmed. These, in Maurras's view, were 'two identical propositions'.[186] The 'anarchist Christian called Marc Sangnier' was simply brushed aside as an irrelevance.

Where this was ultimately to lead Maurras was to the endorsement of a restored monarchy which, in his often repeated phrase, was to be 'traditional, hereditary, antiparliamentary, and decentralized'.[187] Maurras's argument was that the parliamentary Republic was a weak, unstable, and corrupt regime. It was in the grip of those he described as 'the four confederated Estates'—Jews, Protestants, Free-masons, and *métèques*—and thus was controlled by foreign and cosmopolitan interests. It was a prey to the forces of 'anti-France', the 'pays légal' of government being in fundamental contradiction with the 'pays réel' of those who did not live for politics. To reverse this decline, Maurras affirmed, a fundamental reform of the State was required and this was only possible through the restoration of the traditional Bourbon monarchy. The regime would be hereditary in the most obvious sense—the hazards of birth, Maurras argued, were far less of a lottery than elections[188]—and traditional because sovereignty would pass from 'an inert mass of individuals' back to the nation as 'personified and symbolized' in the king

---

[183] 'L'"Action Française" et la Religion Catholique', *La Démocratie Religieuse*, 504.

[184] See Sutton, *Nationalism, Positivism and Catholicism*, 77–8.

[185] 'Le Dilemme de Marc Sangnier', *La Démocratie Religieuse*, 35.

[186] Ibid. 26–7.

[187] This argument was most extensively set out in Maurras's *Enquête sur la Monarchie*, an inquiry publ. in the columns of *La Gazette de France* in 1900–1: see *Enquête sur la Monarchie: L'Œuvre de Charles Maurras* (1925), v. 1–463.

[188] 'Discours préliminaire', ibid., p. xcvi.

and his descendants.[189] It would be anti-parliamentary because politicians and political parties only served to divide and make use of the French people, to diminish and enslave the country, and decentralized because the enervating administration of the Jacobin and Bonapartist state would be removed and liberty restored to the intermediary bodies of the family, the commune, and the region as well as to professional and confessional associations.[190]

To arrive at this position, Maurras was required to provide a new synthesis of counter-revolutionary doctrine, drawing upon insights from Maistre, Bonald, and Taine as well as from more recent writers such as Fustel de Coulanges, Édouard Drumont, and Maurice Barrès, but, in doing so, he continued to give Comte pride of place at the centre of his reflections. Repeating his claim that, although divided in matters relating to the sky, Positivism and Catholicism often agreed about matters relating to the earth, Maurras wrote that Comte 'always considered Catholicism as a necessary ally of science against anarchy and barbarism'.[191] The Church and Positivism, he continued, 'tend to strengthen the family [and] tend to support political authorities as coming from God or as flowing from the best natural laws. The Church and Positivism are friends of tradition, of order, of the homeland and of civilization. In a word, the Church and Positivism have the same enemies in common. Moreover, there is not a French Positivist who forgets that, if the Capetians made France, the bishops and the clerics were the first people to cooperate with them.'[192] It is hard to believe that when General Louis André, ardent republican and admirer of Emile Littré, unveiled a statue of Auguste Comte on the Place de la Sorbonne in 1902 these opinions were shared by many of those present from the Société positiviste. Nevertheless, Maurras's views were far from being without a grain of truth.

III

'We would never have imagined', Maurras was later to write, 'giving the name of Renan to a Chair at the Institut d'Action Française because, for a very wide section of the public, Renan is synonymous with scandal and with insulting Catholics. It is not a matter of deciding whether he merits this reputation. It is simply a fact.'[193] For his part, Ernest Renan held a somewhat jaundiced view of Comte. 'I felt quite irritated', he commented, 'at the idea of Auguste Comte being dignified with the title of great man for having expressed in bad French what all scientific minds had done for the past hundred years as clearly as he had done.'[194]

What might Renan have done to scandalize so many Catholics? Renan was born in Brittany in 1823 and, as he recounted in his *Souvenirs d'Enfance et de Jeunesse*, his early years were deeply impregnated with the faith of the Catholic Church, and to

---

[189] 'Discours préliminaire', p. cxxx.   [190] 'Dictateur et Roi', ibid. 449–51.
[191] 'Une Campagne Royaliste au "Figaro" 1901–1902', 481.   [192] Ibid.
[193] 'L'"Action Française" et la Religion Catholique', 491–2.
[194] Renan, *Œuvres complètes* (1947–61), ii. 845.

such a point that he believed himself 'destined to become a priest'. But this changed dramatically when, in 1838, he entered the seminary of Saint-Nicholas de Chardonnet in Paris to begin his training for holy orders. 'This', he wrote, 'was the worst crisis of my life',[195] producing 'a complete transformation' in the manner in which he saw the world and a consequent 'diminution' of his Christianity.[196] A further four years at the seminary of Saint-Sulpice, where he learnt Hebrew and familiarized himself with the new critical methodology of German biblical scholarship, left him with insufficient faith to become a 'sincere priest'.[197] 'The close study that I made of the Bible', he wrote, 'whilst revealing historical and aesthetic treasures, also showed me that this book was no more exempt than any other old book from contradictions, mistakes and errors.'[198] Henceforth, for Renan, 'positive science' was to be the 'only source of truth'.[199]

In the years that followed, Renan went on to be one of the most important and famous scholars of his generation, becoming both professor of Hebrew at the Collège de France in 1862 and a member of the Académie Française in 1879. When he died in 1892 many of the great figures of the Republic turned out to mourn his passing. Yet his career was never far from controversy, not least because in the many books he published—for example, the seven-volume *Histoire des origines du christianisme* (1863–81) and the five-volume *Histoire du peuple d'Israël* (1887–93)[200]—he persisted in adopting a positivist standpoint and in denying all validity to the supernatural. This was nowhere more evident—and, indeed, nowhere more controversial—than in his *Vie de Jésus*, first published in 1863.[201] In quick succession it went through eleven editions, selling in enormous numbers and offending as many readers as it pleased.

The search for the historical Jesus had been a controversial subject ever since the publication of David Friedrich Strauss's *Leben Jesu* in 1835 (a work translated into French by Emile Littré in 1838) but Renan was arguably the first to attempt such a daring enterprise in France.[202] For all its undoubted scholarship and its detailed examination of the composition and status of the Gospels,[203] the book's theme was a simple one: Jesus was an extraordinary person—Renan spoke of a man of 'colossal proportions'—but he was not the son of God. In this story there were no miracles and no examples of divine intervention. Rather, Renan wrote a purely human biography of Christ as a man who had broken decisively with 'the Jewish faith'[204] and as such it is not difficult to understand why he managed to offend the theologically orthodox. However, Renan's message was an infinitely more sophisticated one than this reaction would allow: for, as he told the readers of his *Souvenirs*, if he had broken with the Church he had remained 'faithful to Christ'.[205] Jesus, in his view, 'will never be surpassed'.[206]

---

[195] Ibid. 808.   [196] Ibid. 818.   [197] Ibid. 819.
[198] Ibid. 866.   [199] Ibid. 845.   [200] See Renan, *Œuvres complètes*, vi.
[201] Ibid. iv. See Perrine Simon-Nahum, 'Le Scandale de la *Vie de Jésus* de Renan', *Mil Neuf Cent*, 25 (2007), 61–74.
[202] See Stephen Neill, *The Interpretation of the New Testament, 1861–1961* (Oxford, 1964).
[203] See Renan, *Œuvres complètes*, iv. 375–427.   [204] Ibid. 369.
[205] 'Souvenirs d'Enfance et de Jeunesse', ibid. ii. 876.   [206] Ibid. iv. 371.

Christ, Renan wrote, had lived in a world of 'uniform vulgarity', but in that world Jesus had embodied 'everything that is good and elevated in our nature'. He had not been without fault—'he had overcome the same passions as we struggle with'—but he had shown a perfect idealism, a purity of heart, a selfless dedication to the interest of humanity, and a scorn for 'the vanities of the world'. To that extent, Renan concluded, it was possible to regard the 'sublime person' of Christ as having been 'divine'. This was not because he was identical with the divine but for the reason that Jesus had enabled his species to take 'the greatest step towards the divine'.[207] His achievement, therefore, had been to evoke the boundless loyalty of his disciples and to sow among them the seed of a doctrine which, in their hands, would become not a dogma but a 'new spirit' in the world. The final lines of Renan's *Vie de Jésus* thus read as follows: 'His creed will be renewed without cease; his tale will bring forth tears without end; his sufferings will soften the best of hearts; and every century will proclaim that, among the sons of men, no one was born greater than Jesus.'[208]

Renan, then, was a man of decidedly divided allegiances, a man who felt deceived by the God of his youth but who loved him still.[209] The void left by this present state of unbelief had, however, to be filled and, to that end, the still-young Renan set out to turn science into a religion. This he did most forcefully in *L'Avenir de la science*, a text written at the end of the 1840s but not published until 1890. It was very much the work of a young man, betraying all the confidence of someone who believed that 'science alone can supply mankind with those vital truths without which life would be intolerable and society impossible'. To this he added that 'it is no exaggeration to say that science contains the future of humanity, that it alone can provide an explanation of its destiny and teach it the way to attain its end'.[210]

Such extravagant claims rested, first, upon a rejection of the validity of all metaphysics and of all references to the supernatural—'the task of modern criticism', Renan wrote, 'is to destroy every system of belief tainted by supernaturalism'[211]—and, second, upon an affirmation of the necessary autonomy of science and, therefore, its divorce from theology. More specifically, Renan equated science with philosophy and, in turn, philosophy with philology, defining the latter as 'the science of the products of the human mind'[212] and as 'the science of humanity'.[213] This is not the place to dwell upon either the strengths or inadequacies of Renan's argument, as of greater interest is his conclusion that, when applied to human life, this 'universal experimental method' would reveal that the world has a purpose and that this purpose was the development of mind or consciousness towards a point of perfection. Thus, 'the end of humanity' was to 'realize the highest human culture

---

207 'Souvenirs d'Enfance et de Jeunesse', 370.

208 Ibid. 371. The central weakness of this, and similar, attempts to domesticate Jesus was excellently summarized by Albert Schweitzer when he remarked that 'the mistake was to suppose that Jesus could mean more to our time by entering into it as a man like ourselves': *The Quest of the Historical Jesus* (London, 1954), 397.

209 This is the sentiment with which Renan closes *L'Avenir de la science*: see *Œuvres complètes*, iii. 1121.

210 Ibid. 756.   211 Ibid. 768.   212 Ibid. 839.   213 Ibid. 850.

possible', and this Renan identified as 'the most perfect religion'.[214] Here were the elements of a future religion and one which, in *L'Avenir de la science*, he categorized as being a form of 'pure humanism', as being 'the cult of everything that pertains to man, the whole of life sanctified and raised to a moral value'.[215]

Renan was at pains to specify that what he had in mind was markedly different in content from what, on the surface, looked to be similar pronouncements by Auguste Comte. The latter, he wrote, had failed 'to understand the infinite variety of the changing, capricious, varied, indefinable material that constitutes human nature'.[216] If human nature were such as he described it, Renan continued, 'every noble soul would hasten to commit suicide'.[217] In brief, Renan considered that his notion of intellectual culture was broad enough to embrace 'things of the heart and of the imagination',[218] that it was far removed from a dry and analytical scepticism—'we are the believers', he wrote[219]—and that it could find a place for both poetry and the contemplation of beauty.[220] Unlike Comte, in other words, Renan sought to overcome the tension between religion and science not by creating a fake and unconvincing imitation of Catholic organization and ritual but by imbuing science with religious sentiment and by inviting science to give a new religious purpose to life. Only science, Renan avowed, could solve our 'eternal problems'.[221] Its task was 'to make God perfect'.[222]

Over the next thirty years Renan continued to articulate versions of this position but he did so, it has been argued, with less and less conviction, such that he came to be seen as the very embodiment of intellectual cynicism and disenchantment, as a combination of pessimism and dilettantism.[223] This was nowhere more evident than in the political views he came to espouse, where scientism appeared to give way to a version of conservative authoritarianism. This can be explained in terms of Renan's reaction to the traumatic events of the Franco-Prussian war of 1870,[224] but, with equal plausibility, evidence of its origin can be found in the very text that had announced 'the scientific organization of humanity'.[225] The clue to this lies in Renan's then acceptance that 'a rational and pure religion is only accessible to a small minority'.[226] In the context of the Second Republic, he countered this by saying that morality could be summarized in the maxim 'to elevate the people'[227] and accordingly that government was under an obligation to enlighten the people, to rid us of barbarians. However, Renan was equally of the conviction that government could not be handed over to the forces of ignorance, that universal suffrage was legitimate only when 'everyone shall possess that share of intelligence without which one does not deserve to be regarded as a human being',[228] when the

---

[214] Ibid. 1018–19.   [215] Ibid. 809.   [216] Ibid. 847.
[217] Ibid. 848.   [218] Ibid. 780.   [219] Ibid. 778.
[220] Ibid. 809.   [221] Ibid. 814.   [222] Ibid. 757.
[223] See Bernard M. G. Reardon, *Religion in the Age of Romanticism* (Cambridge, 1985), 237–66; Charlton, *Positivist Thought*, 123–5; G. Armstrong Kelly, *The Humane Comedy* (Cambridge, 1992), 236–45.
[224] 'La Réforme intellectuelle et morale de la France', *Œuvres complètes*, i. 323–407.
[225] 'L'Avenir de la science', 757.   [226] Ibid. 983.
[227] Ibid. 999.   [228] Ibid. 999–1000.

majority 'represents the most enlightened reason and opinions'.[229] When this did not apply, he wrote, 'the ideal government would be a scientific government, where competent specialists would treat governmental questions as scientific ones and would seek their rational solution'.[230] There was, in other words, always something of the intellectual aristocrat about Renan.

It was in circumstances of acute national humiliation that Renan penned his long essay, *La Réforme intellectuelle et morale de la France*, and not surprisingly a sustained comparison between France and Prussia was at its heart.[231] 'In Prussia', Renan wrote, 'a privileged nobility, a peasantry living under a quasi-feudal regime, a military and national spirit . . . a hard life [and] a general level of poverty. . . . have preserved the conditions that constituted the might of nations'.[232] The victory of Prussia, he continued, was 'the victory of the disciplined man over the undisciplined, of the respectful, careful, attentive, and methodical man'. So too it was 'a victory of science and reason' and 'of the *ancien régime*, of the principle which denies the sovereignty of the people'.[233] In praising Prussia, then, Renan was praising what he saw as a monarchical, aristocratic, and semi-feudal regime, one untouched by the spirit of democracy and equality and one where moral discipline (including the virtue of chastity) and the military ethos had been retained. It was also a country that recognized the utility of science. As Renan observed, the Prussians had applied science to the 'art of killing'.

The contrast with France could not have been more marked. In broad outline, Renan's view was that France had been in decline since the Revolution of 1789. France, he wrote, 'committed suicide' on the day that it cut off the king's head.[234] In the interim, France had become completely demoralized and decadent. Her people were idle, ill-disciplined, self-interested, ignorant, materialistic, and lacked honesty. Her statesmen had proved themselves to be 'children'. Her administration was inefficient and her education system had been 'swallowed up by nothingness'.[235] The French masses were 'stupid and vulgar'. Worse still, France had become 'the most pacific country in the world', captivated only by the pursuit of wealth and the progress of industry.[236] France, he wrote, increasingly had the appearance of 'a second-rate America, mean and mediocre, perhaps more resembling Mexico or South America than the United States'.[237] France, in brief, had been 'enervated by democracy'.[238]

These were the fundamental causes of France's defeat and in response Renan proposed not merely a lengthy period of national penitence but also a set of remedies which effectively amounted to a ditching of democracy and the reconstitution of a 'developed and improved *ancien régime*'.[239] This fortuitous phrase enabled Renan to pass over the precise details of the monarchical system that he was recommending in order to focus upon the measures required to secure 'an era of renovation'. These fell into two broad categories: political and educational

[229] 'L'Avenir de la science', 1001.   [230] Ibid. 1007.
[231] 'La Réforme intellectuelle et morale de la France', 333–407.   [232] Ibid. 364.
[233] Ibid. 366.   [234] Ibid. 338.   [235] Ibid. 334.   [236] Ibid. 348.
[237] Ibid. 350.   [238] Ibid. 332.   [239] Ibid. 402.

reform. In political terms, the ambition was to replace a 'superficial democracy' with an arrangement capable of giving full recognition to the claims of 'natural superiority'. In essence, this entailed a two-tier system of parliamentary representation, with the lower house, nominally resting upon universal suffrage, so designed as to give predominance to electoral colleges composed of approximately 80,000 'local aristocrats, authorities, and notables' capable of acting as 'the guardians of morals and the overseers of public money', and an upper house 'representing the capacities, the specialisms, and diverse interests' of the social and occupational groups that made up France. If the latter was to be composed, for the most part, of hereditary and life members, for the former Renan recommended that the vote of a married man should count as double. Parliamentary sessions were not to be held in public so as improve the quality of debate and discourage demagoguery. Faithful to the liberal programme of the past, Renan also called for administrative decentralization and freedom of the press.

Renan also envisaged measures designed to strengthen the moral fibre of the French. These included compulsory military service for all and an active policy of colonization. 'The conquest of a country belonging to an inferior race by a superior race intent on establishing a government there', he wrote, 'has nothing shocking about it.'[240] However, Renan was convinced that France's 'inferiority' was above all an intellectual one and that this could only be reversed through a radical reform of the educational system. 'The lack of faith in science', he affirmed, 'is the most serious deficiency in France.'[241]

Renan's proposals covered all levels of education from the primary school upwards but the main focus of his attention fell upon the universities. At the secondary level, Renan suggested that the French tradition of inculcating literary and philosophical excellence should give way to the German pattern of technical and scientific education. This was to be accentuated further in the universities, Renan going so far as to counsel the closure of Paris's prestigious *grandes écoles* and their replacement by five or six universities on the German model. Thus reconstituted, the universities would become 'the nurseries of aristocrats' and their students would parade their knowledge of science as 'a title of nobility'. Nor did Renan seek to disguise what he hoped would be their anti-democratic ethos. Reflection, he wrote, 'teaches us that reason is not the expression of the ideas and views of the multitude but that it is the result of the perceptions of a very small number of privileged individuals'.[242] In accordance with these views, Renan recommended that the education of the masses could be safely left in the hands of the Church.

It was conclusions such as these that led critics to speak of Renan's scepticism and, even more bluntly, of his cynicism. Of greater interest is the fact that Renan seemed intent on further advancing the claims of science at the moment when many of those around him were beginning to distance themselves from the more extravagant ambitions of scientism. Stated at its simplest, positivism denoted a rejection of metaphysics and a belief that the adequacy of our knowledge was

---

[240] Ibid. 390.   [241] Ibid. 391.   [242] Ibid. 396.

extended as it approximated to the model established by the physical sciences. A science that had freed itself of metaphysical considerations would concern itself only with discovering reliable correlations between empirically observable phenomena. Any reference to transcendental entities was deemed to be illegitimate. The clearest statement of such a scientific methodology can be found in Claude Bernard's *Introduction à l'étude de la médecine expérimentale*, published in 1867.[243] Science was here described as an autonomous discipline, distinct and separate from philosophy, and Bernard did not hesitate from affirming the certainty and reality of scientific knowledge.

The astonishing advances in the physical and natural sciences during the nineteenth century were unquestionably such as to capture the public imagination and to encourage the conviction that the progress of science, when combined with technological innovation, offered the prospect of rapid and unlimited improvement in the physical and mental condition of the population at large. Science promised health, comfort, and prosperity; and—no less importantly—an end to ignorance. To a large extent, science delivered on those promises, contributing significantly to the attainment of better standards of living and increases in life expectancy witnessed in the early decades of the Third Republic. However, among many of France's cultural spokespersons faith in the beneficial and progressive capacities of science began to decline considerably as the century drew towards its end.

The response here took a variety of forms. Most commonly, the material prosperity and ease proffered by science was equated with the ascendancy of the bourgeoisie and, by extension, with a culture of philistinism and mediocrity. *Fin-de-siècle* France had no shortage of expressions of such cultural pessimism[244] but no better perhaps was it given voice than in the decadent aestheticism of the protagonist of Huysmans's famous novel of 1884, *A Rebours*.[245] The 'jolly bourgeois', according to the sublime Duc Jean Floressas des Esseintes, 'lorded it over the country, putting his trust in the power of his money and the contagiousness of his stupidity'. Could it be, he asked, 'that this slime would go on spreading until it covered with its pestilential filth this old world where now only seeds of iniquity sprang up and only harvests of shame were gathered?'[246] Arguably more profound was the damage done to the idea of progress by science itself. France in the early decades of the Third Republic was haunted by a sense of racial decline. This had many sources, but one of them was Arthur de Gobineau's *Essai sur l'Enégalité des races humaines*, published in four volumes between 1853 and 1855. Gobineau's text gave a scientific veneer to the claim that many of France's (and, more generally, European civilization's) ills derived ultimately from the miscegenation of the white race. His theory of racial determinism predicted an inevitable degeneration into

[243] See *Introduction à l'étude de la médecine expérimentale* (1966). On Bernard see Charlton, *Positivist Thought*, 72–85; Reino Virtanen, *Claude Bernard and his Place in the History of Ideas* (Lincoln, Neb., 1960); and Paul Q. Hirst, *Durkheim, Bernard and Epistemology* (London, 1975).

[244] K. W. Swart, *The Sense of Decadence in Nineteenth-Century France* (The Hague, 1964).

[245] See Winock, *Les Voix de la liberté*, 575–87.

[246] In translation see Joris-Karl Huysmans, *Against Nature* (Harmondsworth, 1973), 218–19. Huysmans was no minor figure: he was e.g. president of the Académie Goncourt.

mediocrity and, finally, nothingness, for which there was no cure. Ever the disillusioned elitist, Gobineau believed that the last stages of man's domination of the earth had already begun.

This sentiment of physical decay was accompanied by a broader sense of moral and societal decline, often attributed to the consequences of greater social mobility and urbanization. Among these supposed evils were crime, alcoholism, venereal disease, low birth rates, suicide, and mental illness. The huge literature on these problems generated by the French medical and hygiene professions only served to intensify public anxiety about the nation's declining vitality. It is no accident that these years saw the emergence of criminology as a distinct, if controversy-bound, discipline.[247] The same years also coincided with the development of what purported to be the science of crowd psychology and mass behaviour. In this burgeoning debate the crowd was always seen as being capricious, feminine, impulsive, destructive, and bordering on the bestial. Insatiable in its desires and a vehicle for the expression of a primitive and savage mentality, it was governed by instinct rather than by reason, acting in an almost hypnotic state. Inspired by Taine, given scientific validity by the likes of Gabriel Tarde, and popularized in particular by Gustave Le Bon,[248] whose *La Psychologie des foules* of 1895 was an instant bestseller, such theories generated a profound fear of social dissolution and disorder. The barbarians, it seemed, were waiting at the gates.[249]

It is difficult to pinpoint the precise moment when the mood began to change and the critical reaction against science set in, but it could already be felt by the 1870s. This was something of a Europe-wide phenomenon, a generation of European intellectuals casting off the 'spiritual yoke' of their predecessors, but it took a particularly aggressive and pervasive form in France. Nor was it a reaction limited only to the philosophical profession. To no insignificant degree, the cause can be located in a mounting antipathy towards the positivist pretensions of Comte, Renan, and Taine. Their aspirations to provide a new morality and social ethic had ultimately come to nothing, a fact abundantly illustrated by their own espousal of differing versions of anti-democratic and reactionary conservatism at the end of their careers. Moreover, it was one of the paradoxes of positivism that a doctrine which had begun by professing a belief in reason and science ended up as a thinly disguised form of anti-intellectualism, condemning society and those who comprised it to a form of scientific fatalism, the potentialities of human action being outweighed by an invasive social and psychological determinism. As the reign of science drew to a close, these presuppositions were countered by what D. M. Eastwood, in a remarkable book devoted to the revival of interest in Pascal during this period, described as 'an insurrection of personality'.[250]

---

[247] See Robert A. Nye, *Crime, Madness and Politics in Modern France: The Medical Concept of National Decline* (Princeton, NJ, 1984).

[248] See Benoit Marpeau, *Gustave Le Bon: Parcours d'un intellectuel, 1841–1931* (2000), 95–130.

[249] See Susanna Burrows, *Distorting Mirrors: Visions of the Crowd in Late Nineteenth-Century France* (New Haven, Conn., 1981) and Daniel Pick, *Faces of Degeneration: A European Disorder, 1848–1918* (Cambridge, 1989), 37–106.

[250] *The Revival of Pascal: A Study of his Relation to Modern French Thought* (Oxford, 1936), 17.

It was in this atmosphere of mounting pessimism and anxiety that the critical reaction against science gathered strength. It had many diverse and varied manifestations, by no means all of them limited to philosophical and theological speculation. It was evident, for example, in the move away from literary naturalism to the symbolist poetry of Mallarmé, Rimbaud, and Verlaine, in the vogue for the Russian novel, the cult of Wagnerism during the 1880s and 1890s, the enthusiasm for the writings of Friedrich Nietzsche among the intellectual avant-garde, and even the passing fashion for Buddhism and oriental mysticism.[251] For our purposes we need look no further than the celebrated article by Ferdinand Brunetière entitled 'Après une visite au Vatican', first published in January 1895.[252] For some years, far-sighted Catholics had been making headway in their search for a convincing response to the challenge of positivism but few could have expected that the most audacious rejoinder of all would come from the editor of the leading periodical of the day, the *Revue des Deux Mondes*.[253] Brunetière had made his name as a literary critic and such was his reputation that, in 1893, he was elected to the Académie Française. In the following year he was accorded an audience with Pope Leo XIII and it was upon his return from Rome that he penned the text with which talk of the 'failure' and 'bankruptcy' of science has since been notoriously linked.

Brunetière's central claim was that the physical and natural sciences had not delivered on their claim to rid life of 'mystery'. Not only had they not done so, he wrote, 'but today we can see that they will never throw light on it. They are powerless, I do not say to resolve but even to ask the questions which matter: those that touch upon the origin of man, his conduct, and his destiny.'[254] We were, he continued, surrounded and enveloped by the 'unknowable' and no laws of physics or physiology could facilitate its comprehension. A similar failure afflicted science with regard to questions of morality. 'If we were to ask Darwinism for lessons on behaviour', Brunetière argued, 'it would give us only loathsome ones.'[255] Morality, he affirmed, could not be separated from religion. In brief, he wrote, 'science has lost its prestige whilst religion has recovered some of its own'.[256] In point of fact, Brunetière's overall conclusion was more nuanced than this might lead us to believe: he called not for a complete rejection of science but for a recognition of the fact that, when properly conceived, science and religion spoke of different things. Each, in his view, had its own 'kingdom'.[257] In the clamour accorded to the reception of Brunetière's article, however, the subtleties of the message tended to be lost. What stuck in the public's mind was Brunetière's return to Catholicism.

It would be wrong to suggest that the end of the nineteenth century was marked by a wholesale rejection of science. This was far from being the case. Émile Zola

---

[251] See F. W. J. Hemmings, *Culture and Society in France 1848–1898: Dissidents and Philistines* (London, 1971), 209–53, and Christopher E. Forth, *Zarathustra in Paris: The Nietzsche Vogue in France 1891–1918* (DeKalb, Ill., 2001).
[252] 'Après une visite au Vatican', *Revue des Deux Mondes*, 127 (1895), 97–118.
[253] See Antoine Compagnon, *Connaissez-vous Brunetière? Enquête sur un antidreyfusard et ses amis* (1997).
[254] 'Après une visite au Vatican', 99.   [255] Ibid. 104.
[256] Ibid. 105.   [257] Ibid. 110–11.

continued to write 'experimental' novels directly inspired by the scientific methodology of Claude Bernard.[258] The mathematician and physicist Henri Poincaré, first in *La Science et l'Hypothèse*[259] and then in *La Valeur de la science*,[260] led the way in reformulating science as a series of conventional hypotheses, thereby establishing that scientific propositions were to be regarded as true to the extent that they were convenient, useful, or even possessed aesthetic appeal. It made no sense, Poincaré observed, to ask if one system of geometry was more true than another. Our choice was limited only by the necessity of avoiding contradiction. If Poincaré was less naïvely empiricist than many of his positivist predecessors, he nevertheless remained committed to the objectivity of science.[261]

Even more noteworthy were the continuing efforts to reconcile science and biblical criticism. This emerged in the form of the so-called Modernist controversy and was principally associated with the work of Alfred Loisy, formerly Professor of Holy Scripture at the Institut Catholique, France's premier Catholic University.[262] The context was again one of a perceived need for doctrinal reform, to adapt the Gospel, as Loisy put it, 'to the changing condition of humanity'.[263] To this was added a desire to find a coherent response to the influential writings of liberal Protestants such as Adolf Harnack in Germany and Auguste Sabatier in France, and so much so that Loisy's *L'Évangile et l'Église* amounted to an attempted detailed refutation of Harnack's *Das Wesen des Christentums*.[264] There is little need to dwell upon the details of what occurred and the issues that were at stake—at one level it could be read as yet another story of sincere and loyal Catholics finding themselves condemned at the hands of an uncomprehending papacy[265]—but, in essence, Loisy sought to recover the substantive content of Christianity through the abandonment of traditionalist assumptions of biblical inerrancy and the application of a critical historical methodology. In so doing, he believed himself able to show that there was no fundamental disjunction or discontinuity of principle or of practice between the Gospel and the Roman Church, that the Church, as he expressed it, was as necessary to the Gospel as the Gospel was to the Church.[266] In effect, the ambition was to turn historical science against the liberal Protestants, and thereby to beat them at their own game.

---

[258] See Zola, *Le Roman expérimental* (1880)   [259] (1902).   [260] (1905).

[261] Ideas similar to those of Poincaré were also developed by Pierre Duhem (1861–1916) and Édouard Le Roy (1870–1954). See Yenima Ben-Menahem, *Conventionalism: From Poincaré to Quine* (Cambridge, 2006).

[262] See Loisy, *L'Évangile et l'Église* (1902) and *Autour d'un petit livre* (1903). In French see Pierre Colin, *L'Audace et le soupcon: La Crise du modernisme dans le catholicisme français 1893–1914* (1997) and Yves Palau, 'Le Modernisme comme controverse', *Mil Neuf Cent*, 25 (2007), 75–90; in English see A. R. Vidler, *The Modernist Movement in the Roman Church* (Cambridge, 1934) and *A Variety of Catholic Modernists* (Cambridge, 1970), and B. M. G. Reardon, *Roman Catholic Modernism* (London, 1970).

[263] Loisy, *L'Évangile et l'Église*, 234.

[264] First publ. in 1900, Harnack's text appeared in French in 1902.

[265] The theses of modernism were formally condemned by Pope Pius X in the encyclical *Pascendi* of 1907.

[266] Loisy, *L'Évangile et l'Église*, 95.

The most striking illustration of the 'positivist remainder',[267] however, must be Émile Durkheim, founder of the modern discipline of sociology[268] and holder of the first chair of social science in France.[269] Throughout his career Durkheim made little effort to disguise his aversion to what he termed a 'renascent mysticism'[270] and he had little time for anything that fell short of the rigorous demands of scientific inquiry. He saw himself as living in a world threatened by the forces of irrationalism. 'Sociology', he wrote, 'does not need to choose between the great hypotheses that divide metaphysicians. . . . All that it asks is that the principle of causality be applied to social phenomena.'[271] If these methodological guidelines were set out in *Les Règles de la méthode sociologique*,[272] they were exemplified in Durkheim's detailed empirical studies of suicide[273] and the division of labour.[274]

Durkheim's guiding principle was that of the objective reality of social facts[275] and his subject was the nature of social solidarity. By extension, it was also Durkheim's opinion that the study of religion could be approached 'sociologically'.[276] This, it appears, came as something of a revelation to him in 1895 but from then on—as is testified by *Les Formes élémentaires de la vie religieuse*[277]—the sociology of religion became one of his central preoccupations. Durkheim's basic assumption was that 'all the essential elements of religious thought and life ought to be found, at least in germ, in the most primitive religions'[278] and it was this thesis that directed him towards the investigation of totemic religions (especially those of aboriginal Australia). More important from our perspective was Durkheim's conclusion that, when viewed sociologically, 'there are no religions that are false'. All were 'true in their own fashion' and 'all corresponded, although in different ways, to given conditions of human existence'.[279] For Durkheim, therefore, the crucial object of inquiry was not whether the explanations and justifications provided by the faithful of their beliefs and practices were correct or erroneous but what function was performed by religion. And here his answer did not waiver: if religion was itself socially determined, its function was to create and reinforce the ties which bound the individual to the society to which he or she belonged.[280] The challenge for the ardently republican Durkheim was to provide a scientifically grounded form of secular education and morality that, in replacing religion, would perform a similar function.[281]

---

[267] Hughes, *Consciousness and Society* (New York, 1958), 278.
[268] See Durkheim. 'La Sociologie', in *La Science française* (1915), i. 39–49.
[269] See Steven Lukes, *Emile Durkheim: His Life and Work* (London, 1973).
[270] *Les Règles de la méthode sociologique* (1895), p. viii.
[271] Ibid. 172–3.
[272] Ibid.
[273] *Le Suicide* (1897).
[274] *De la division du travail social: étude sur l'Organisation des sociétés supérieures* (1893).
[275] *Les Règles de la méthode sociologique*, 175.
[276] Quoted in Lukes, *Emile Durkheim*, 237.
[277] Durkheim, *Les Formes élémentaires de la vie religieuse* (1912).
[278] Ibid. 450.
[279] Ibid. 3.
[280] See Lukes, *Emile Durkheim*, 450–84.
[281] For a selection of Durkheim's writings on this subject see *Leçons de sociologie* (1997).

It was in the world of academic philosophy that the move away from positivism was most visible and noteworthy.[282] The discipline of philosophy was given a central place in the educational reforms of the Third Republic and it was in these years that the subject underwent significant professionalization. The *Revue philosophique de la France et de l'Étranger* was established by Théodule Ribot in 1876 and this was followed by the creation of Xavier Léon's *Revue de métaphysique et de morale* in 1893. The Société Française de Philosophie was founded in 1901. The state of the discipline was succinctly summarized when, later that decade, Émile Boutroux, a key figure in the French philosophical establishment, presented a paper entitled 'La Philosophie en France depuis 1867' to an international philosophy conference in Heidelberg.[283] The oddity of Boutroux's title is explained by the fact that it was his intention to update Félix Ravaisson's *La philosophie en France au XIXe siècle*, a work commissioned by the French government to coincide with the Universal Exhibition of 1867. In his survey of French philosophy since 1800 Ravaisson had painted a picture of a subject which had been dominated by the rival schools of Comtean Positivism and the Eclecticism of Victor Cousin, although he had also predicted accurately that the future would see moves towards the development of a spiritualist ontology. In contrast, Boutroux described a discipline characterized by increasing specialization and diversification but among the principal trends he identified was a revival of metaphysics. This took various forms, of which one of the most influential was a return to Kantianism, but its most original manifestation by far was the work of Henri Bergson.[284]

Bergson was educated at the École Normale Supérieure (the historic powerhouse of French philosophy) and after graduating in 1881 taught at a series of *lycées* in both Paris and the provinces before being elected to a chair at the Collège de France in 1900.[285] His weekly lectures there attracted large crowds and created something of a sensation, and not only among philosophers. Bergson's influence quickly spread into the worlds of literature, art, poetry, music, the theatre, and, in due course, politics.[286] His first book, *Essai sur les données immédiates de la conscience*, was published in 1889. This was followed, seven years later, by *Matière et mémoire* and then, in 1907, *L'Évolution créatrice*. It was the latter—with the concept of *élan vital* at its heart—that secured Bergson's international reputation,[287] even though it

---

[282] See Jean-Louis Fabiani, *Les Philosophes de la république* (1988); Gary Gutting, *French Philosophy in the Twentieth Century* (Cambridge, 2001), 3–25; Bernard Bourgeois, 'La Société des philosophes en France en 1900', in Frédéric Worms, *Le Moment 1900 en Philosophie* (Villeneuve d'Escq, 2004), 63–79; and François Azouvi, *La Gloire de Bergson: Essai sur le magistère philosophique* (2007), 19–58.

[283] The text was publ. in the *Revue de métaphysique et de morale*, 16 (1908), 683–716. It is repr. in Stéphane Douailler, Roger-Pol Droit, and Patrice Vermeren (eds.), *Philosophie, France, XIXe siècle: Écrits et opuscules* (1994), 912–60.

[284] See Worms, *Le Moment 1900*.

[285] See Philippe Soulez and Frédéric Worms, *Bergson* (1997).

[286] See Gaston Picard and Gustave-Louis Tautin, 'Enquête sur M. Henri Bergson et l'influence de sa pensée sur la sensibilité contemporaine', *La Grande Revue*, 83 (1914), 544–60, 744–60; 84 (1914), 110–28, 309–28, 513–28, and A. E. Pilkington, *Bergson and his Influence: A Reassessment* (Cambridge, 1976). See esp. Azouvi, *La Gloire*.

[287] Bergson was awarded the Nobel Prize for Literature in 1927.

was seen by some of his critics as marking a fundamental departure from his early work.[288]

Bergson's central idea was that time is real.[289] This argument had many dimensions, but one of the most important was the conclusion that philosophical arguments frequently rested upon a mistaken equation of the categories of space and time. Space, Bergson wanted to argue, could be divided into an infinite series of homogeneous and distinct entities whereas time or, more accurately, real time was characterized by what he termed *la durée* or duration: it was heterogeneous and continuous. 'The indivisible continuity of change', Bergson wrote, 'is precisely what constitutes true duration.'[290] At its simplest, Bergson believed that the analytical categories of the intellect were incapable of comprehending the reality of duration and that the only way of doing so, of grasping what he saw as the pure flow of consciousness, was through intuition. We call intuition, he wrote in 1903, 'the sympathy by which one is transported into the interior of an object in order to coincide with what is unique and consequently inexpressible in it'.[291] Intuition, Bergson argued, was capable of 'following reality in all its winding and of adopting the very movement of the inward life of things'.[292] In short, the intellect was characterized by a natural inability to comprehend life and therefore we had to abandon the rigid categories of language in order to comprehend the diversity, uniqueness, and multiplicity of the phenomena that made up the fluidity of experience. We had to give up 'the utilitarian habits of mind of everyday life'.[293] *L'Évolution créatrice* continued this theme but did so by generalizing Bergson's attack upon conceptual thinking so as to provide an explanation of the evolution of life in terms of a vital impulse or life drive that, in his words, 'carried life, by more and more complex forms, to higher and higher destinies'.[294]

The criticisms directed at the latter text for the most part focused upon the lack of explanatory force possessed by the concept of *élan vital*. For some, it appeared to be no more than an elaborate biological or occult fantasy. For others, it looked suspiciously like an attempt to smuggle God back into the evolutionary process through the back door. More damaging still was the argument that, in postulating the existence of a vital impulse, Bergson was himself attempting to reduce the rich complexity of life to one absolute principle and that, in doing so, he was abandoning the very epistemological and methodological pluralism that had drawn people to his philosophy in the first place. For this had been part of its immense appeal.

---

[288] See François Azouvi, 'Anatomie d'un succès philosophique: Les Effets de *L'Évolution créatrice*', *Le Débat*, 140 (2006), 153–71.

[289] See A. R. Lacey, *Bergson* (London, 1989) and Gutting, *French Philosophy*, 49–83. Those wishing to pursue this subject further should consult Frédéric Worms, *Bergson ou les deux sens de la vie* (2004) and the *Annales Bergsoniennes*, publ. from 2002 onwards.

[290] 'The Perception of Change', in Bergson, *The Creative Mind* (New York, 1968), 176. This was first presented as a lecture at the University of Oxford in 1911.

[291] 'Introduction to Metaphysics', in Bergson, *The Creative Mind*, 190. This essay was first publ. in the *Revue de métaphysique et de morale*.

[292] *The Creative Mind*, 224.

[293] Ibid. 195.

[294] Bergson, *Creative Evolution* (London, 1911), 107.

Bergsonisme appeared to be the very antithesis of a closed and systematic philosophy. For writers such as Charles Péguy it represented a decisive break with what he described as an *intellectualisme universel.*[295]

Tracing the ways in which Bergson's work influenced his contemporaries is outside our compass—there were many forms of *bergsonisme appliqué*—but one admirer of Bergson—Georges Sorel[296]—certainly merits our attention. Sorel was thoroughly familiar with Bergson's ideas, attending his Paris lectures every week.[297] He made an explicit appeal to Bergsonian epistemology and he self-consciously set out to transpose Bergson's ideas onto a social setting. He did not, as is often supposed, deploy Bergsonian ideas to develop a cult of the irrational nor did he make use of the concept of *élan vital* in his most infamous book, *Réflexions sur la violence.* In point of fact, Sorel was deeply critical of Bergson's attempt to provide explanations of social phenomena in terms of biological concepts.[298] Rather, over a period of many years he worked Bergson's ideas into the rich pattern of his thought, producing a highly original synthesis that, in one comprehensive theory, brought together ideas that had been central to debates about politics, religion, and science since the beginning of the nineteenth century.

There was nothing in Sorel's background that gave any indication of his later radicalism. He was born into a bourgeois family from the Cherbourg peninsula and educated at the best academic institutions that Paris could offer. The conservative historian Albert Sorel was one of his cousins. He spent his professional career as a government engineer, building bridges and roads for the Third Republic. But some time in the 1880s Sorel's prodigious intellect began to gnaw its way into a set of issues that were to remain with him until his death in 1922.

Sorel's first book, published in 1889, was on the trial of Socrates.[299] His sympathies were with Socrates's Athenian accusers. His second, published in the same year, was a work of biblical scholarship in which Sorel primarily focused his attention upon the question of the authenticity or otherwise of the Gospel according to St John. In doing so, Sorel was concerned to refute the claims of a whole school of thought which he characterized as 'modern positivism'.[300] This school, he argued, was unable to see religious thought as anything other than a manifestation of our intellect in its infancy and, accordingly, it saw the development of Christian thought in terms of 'a slow and obscure evolution' away from its primitive origins towards the creation of a more rational edifice. Biblical scholarship guided by these principles, Sorel believed, could only succeed in 'distorting the fundamental principle behind all religion',[301] and this was so, in his view, because there could

---

[295] 'Note sur M. Bergson et la philosophie bergsonienne', *La Grande Revue,* 84 (1914), 618. See also 'Note sur M. Bergson et la philosophie bergsonienne' and 'Note conjointe sur M. Descartes et la philosophie cartésienne', in Péguy, *Œuvres en prose 1909–1914* (1961), 1313–47, 1357–1554.

[296] See my *Georges Sorel: The Character and Development of his Thought* (London, 1985).

[297] See Pierre Andreu, *Georges Sorel: Entre le noir et le rouge* (1982), 239–68.

[298] See Sorel, *De l'utilité du pragmatisme* (1921).

[299] *Le Procès de Socrate* (1889).

[300] *Contribution à l'étude profane de la Bible* (1889), 1.

[301] Ibid.

be no religious faith without the existence of miracles. 'Every religion', he wrote, 'is based upon a spontaneous metaphysical creation, a *revelation*.'[302] It is this that explains why Sorel took the Gospel of John as the most authentic of the four and why he determined that it had been written prior to the others. 'If one admits the Fourth Gospel', Sorel wrote, 'there was no evolution: there was a revelation.' The positivist school, by contrast, universally assumed the Gospel of John to be bogus, the theme of the miraculous and of the divinity of Christ which pervaded it not being to its taste.

Such was the conclusion of Sorel's *Contribution à l'étude profane de la Bible* and it was in a similar vein that he was later to write his *Système historique de Renan*, the focus now shifting to criticism of Renan's attempt to provide 'a completely human biography of Christ'.[303] Sorel's argument was a long and complex one but, at its most immediate level, amounted to saying that Renan's rationalist presuppositions had simply prevented him from understanding both 'the true reality of Christianity' and its 'fundamental conceptions'.[304] For Renan the history of Christianity was nothing more than a history of 'illusions and accidents'.[305] Crucially, Sorel believed that the central tenets of Christianity—for example, the resurrection of Jesus— were immune from historical criticism. The more complex argument dismissed Renan's account of Christianity as a mere continuation of the Judaic tradition. 'One cannot insist too much', Sorel wrote, 'upon the newness of Christianity. It was neither a reform nor a perfecting of Judaism, nor a synthesis of Jewish monotheism and Greek polytheism: with it a truly new age began.'[306] Sorel's point here was that early Christianity had possessed something akin to a primitive ferocity; that it had expressed itself in the language of 'absolute revolt'; and thus that it had fostered a deep scission between itself and a degenerate civilization. The establishment of the Church, on this view, made sense as a means of preserving that separate identity and of preventing attempts to 'civilize Christian barbarism'.[307]

From these conclusions Sorel developed a series of important arguments but two need to be highlighted. The first was that if the Catholic Church wished to escape from the crisis within which it found itself—and Sorel did not dispute that, in the context of the anticlericalism associated with the Dreyfus Affair, the Church was in crisis[308]—it should seek to make a return to its *noyau fondamental*, to the heart of its original and divinely inspired doctrine. It was through a reorientation of its faith around the concept of the miraculous that the Church would overcome 'the spirit of doubt'. In this Sorel was explicit in his criticism not only of liberal Protestant theology—about which he had not a good word to say—but also the Catholic Modernism of Alfred Loisy. Significantly Sorel added that this return to what he also described as the 'instinctive, the passionate [and] the mythological' would only occur if resort were made to 'the most profound of our feelings, to that which above all is individual, to that which is not yet socialized in man'.[309] There was every

---

[302] *Contribution à l'étude profane de la Bible* (1889), 1.
[303] *Le Système historique de Renan* (1906), 12.
[304] Ibid. 66.   [305] Ibid. 70.   [306] Ibid. 459–60.   [307] Ibid. 207.
[308] Sorel, 'La Crise de la pensée catholique', *Revue de métaphysique et de morale*, 10 (1902), 523–51.
[309] Ibid. 550.

likelihood, Sorel indicated, that this transition would come not from within the Church itself but from tendencies inherent in contemporary thought. The reference to Bergson was oblique but unmistakable.

The second point of interest was that Sorel subsequently transposed the qualities he ascribed to early Christianity—its austere and heroic morality, its reliance upon instinct and mystical thought, its separation from society, its very newness and purity—onto the emerging French syndicalist movement. For Sorel, striking workers engaged in the class struggle were to possess all the qualities of the early Christian martyrs.

If Sorel was able to adopt this position with regard to the Catholic religion, it was because over time he had come to espouse a pluralistic conception of our forms of knowledge. A trained scientist, Sorel had initially accepted a realist conception of science and it was in this context that he had expressed his approval of the epistemological positions advanced by both Claude Bernard and Émile Durkheim.[310] However, through a reading of the eighteenth-century Neapolitan philosopher, Gianbattista Vico, Sorel had moved progressively towards a conventionalist reading of science, a position given clearest expression in his essay of 1905, *Les Préoccupations métaphysiques des physiciens modernes*.[311] This detailed essay considered the recent writings of Henri Poincaré and, in doing so, allowed Sorel to argue that experimental science worked upon what he called an 'artificial nature' and accordingly that it was a fundamental error to imagine that there existed an identity between science and what he termed 'natural nature'. As was the case with Poincaré, Sorel denied that this had subjectivist implications for science but crucially his argument entailed a rejection of all positivist claims to a unitary and universalistic body of knowledge. Such monist illusions failed to see that science and religion offered two equally valid ways of seeing the world. As scientific explanations were conventions or hypotheses that said nothing about the real world they could not claim to present scientific objections to Catholic faith. It was via a similar logic that Sorel, having first accepted the empirical veracity of Marx's laws of capitalist development, came to redefine the central tenets of Marxist socialism as 'social poetry' and then as 'social myth'.

Sorel's challenge to positivism went further than this however. As an assiduous reader of the works of Max Nordau, Théodule Ribot, and Gustave Le Bon, as well as John Henry Newman, Sorel had become acutely aware of the non-rational sources of human motivation. Individuals, he wrote, 'do nothing great without the help of warmly coloured and clearly defined images, which absorb the whole of our attention'.[312] It was the failure of the 'intellectualist philosophy'[313] (Sorel again had Renan in mind) to appreciate this which explained why it could not grasp that an individual, be he a Napoleonic soldier, a striking worker, or an early Christian,

---

[310] See e.g. 'Les Théories de M. Durkheim', *Le Devenir social*, 1 (1895), 1–26, 148–80.
[311] *Revue de métaphysique et de morale*, 13 (1905), 858–89.
[312] *Réflexions sur la violence* (1972), 184.
[313] Sorel frequently made contemptuous reference to the 'intellectualist philosophy' as the 'little science'.

might perform a selfless and heroic act. This led to the development of one of Sorel's most important ideas: the importance of myths. Myths, Sorel argued, were 'expressions of the will to act' and were the very antithesis of such intellectualist constructions as utopias.[314] This, as he wrote in his introduction to *Réflexions sur la violence*, could be explained by reference to the ideas of Bergson. Sorel argued that Bergson asks us to consider 'the inner depths of the mind and what happens during a creative moment'. Acting freely, we recovered ourselves, attaining the level of pure 'duration' that Bergson equated with 'integral knowledge'.[315] This new form of knowledge, as Sorel recognized, could be understood as intuition and it was precisely this variety of intuitive understanding that Sorel believed was encompassed by his category of myth.

Sorel had been moving towards this conclusion for some time, arguing in his essay *La Décomposition du marxisme* of 1908 that Marx had 'always described revolution in mythical form' but in the main body of *Réflexions sur la violence* it was the general strike that featured as a myth, precisely because, in Sorel's view, it provided an 'intuitive' understanding and picture of the essence of socialism. More than this, those who lived in the world of myths were 'secure from all refutation' and could not be discouraged. They attained an 'entirely epic state of mind', were capable of 'serious, formidable, and sublime work' and saw themselves as 'the army of truth fighting the army of evil'. Seen in this light, the revolution was 'a revolt, pure and simple', an expression of class war, in which the proletariat, in a display of 'black ingratitude', sought the 'total elimination' of its bourgeois and capitalist adversaries.

What was the purpose of this decisive and violent struggle? Crucially, Sorel dismissed what he saw as the nineteenth-century 'illusion of progress',[316] believing rather that French society was entering a period of decadence, of corruption, of moral frivolity, and of economic decline. He poured scorn upon the superficial and misguided optimism of his age, seeing the optimist in politics as an 'inconstant and even dangerous man' and preferring to embrace an undisguised pessimism. The latter, he avowed, was a doctrine 'without which nothing of greatness has been accomplished in the world' and which considered 'the march towards deliverance' as narrowly conditioned by the immense obstacles before us and by 'our natural weaknesses'.[317] Thus, when faced with what Sorel saw as the total ruin of institutions and of morals, it was to violence that socialism owed 'those high ethical ideals by means of which it brings salvation to the modern world'.[318] It might not, Sorel conceded, be the best means of securing immediate material advantages but it did nevertheless serve 'the immemorial interests of civilisation' and might yet save the world from barbarism.[319]

In brief, for Georges Sorel the triumphant bourgeoisie and democracy of the Third Republic were the heirs of the rationalism and scepticism of the Enlightenment

---

[314] *Reflexions sur la violence*, 38.
[315] Ibid. 34–5.   [316] See *Les Illusions du progrès* (1908).
[317] *Réflexions sur la violence*, 9–19.   [318] Ibid. 331.   [319] Ibid. 110.

and as such represented everything that was shallow, mediocre, corrupt, and lacking in moral seriousness. In their hands, science was reduced to little more than a subject of conversation in the *salons* of polite society and religion was treated as an object of ridicule. In such circumstances, the existence of a sublime ethics was not possible and politics became the domain of intellectuals who believed themselves capable of thinking for the people. The entire force of Sorel's mature writings was that a decisive and irrevocable break had to be made with such a decadent society. This involved him not in a dismissal of science as a valid form of knowledge or in a flight towards a blind irrationalism but in a rejection of the positivist designation of science as the sole mode of explanation applicable to all natural as well as social phenomena and in an acceptance of the reality and distinctiveness of religious faith. In ethical terms, as Sorel made clear, it amounted to a denunciation of the casuistry of the Jesuits and their bourgeois descendants and a return to the moral rigour and severity of Pascal and Jansenism, replete with an emphasis upon original sin. To that extent, the wheel has come full circle and we find ourselves again in a world where an austere Augustinianism finds itself face to face with the Voltairean spirit, the important difference being that it was no longer a question of Catholicism versus Protestantism or of the Enlightenment against the Church but of the proletariat against the bourgeoisie. It is to this struggle that we will now turn our attention.

9

Insurrection, Utopianism, and Socialism

I

As Auguste Comte's own writings testify, he was deeply concerned that the material and spiritual condition of working people should be subject to improvement. The entire third section of the *Discours sur l'Ensemble du positivisme* was devoted to a discussion of the place of the proletarian within positivism. Moreover, in Fabien Magnin, converted to positivism in the 1840s and subsequently an executor of Comte's will, positivism had its first proletarian disciple.[1] An early illustration of positivist interest in the condition of labour can be found in the *Rapport à la société positiviste par la commission chargée d'examiner la question du travail*, published in June 1848 with a preface by Comte himself.[2] After Comte's death, Magnin continued to spread the gospel of *le positivisme ouvrier*. In 1863 he established the Cercle des prolétaires positivistes, which formally affiliated to the (socialist) First International in 1870. With the advent of the Third Republic and the slow re-emergence of the workers' movement after the Paris Commune, the positivists continued to press their case, a process culminating in the publication in 1876 of *Le Positivisme au congrès ouvrier*. For its time, this represented the most complete expression of the positivist strategy for proletarian emancipation. In their preface, Magnin, Émile Laporte, and Isidore Finance specifically denied that positivism was 'an oppressive doctrine' which sought 'to condemn the proletariat without hope to a social hell under the double exploitation of the capitalists and the priests'.[3] Indeed, the proletarian positivists talked of the need to develop 'a rational, scientific, positive socialism' and sought to replace an economic system characterized by exploitation and selfish individualism. They also shared a belief in the autonomy of the working class. Participation in parliamentary politics would deprive the proletariat of its best elements.

---

[1] See 'Notice sur la vie et l'œuvre de Fabien Magnin', in Fabien Magnin, *Études sociales* (1913), pp. v–xxxvii. See also 'Discours de M. A. Keufer sur la tombe de M. F. Magnin', *Revue occidentale*, 23 (1889), 408–14.

[2] Magnin, Jacquemin, and Belpaume, *Rapport à la société positiviste* (1848). Comte's preface affirmed his belief in the need for a 'new spiritual authority' capable of acting as 'a neutral arbiter' in industrial conflicts. This text was repr. in Magnin, *Études sociales*, 1–12.

[3] Magnin, *Le Positivisme au congrès ouvrier* (1876), 13.

The positivists therefore were of the view that they disagreed with the mainstream of the socialist movement—described by the positivists themselves as 'metaphysical socialism'—only about means and not ends. This was only partly true. The disagreement on means was unequivocal. 'We prefer', Magnin and his colleagues wrote, 'peaceful, enduring, slow but sure changes to dangerous agitation.'[4] Education, not violence, was what was required. Similarly, they believed that the State should be reformed rather than abolished.[5]

However, what truly separated the positivists from the increasingly radical opinions of the workers' movement in France was their view that classes would continue to exist in the future society. Faithful to the dictates of Comte's original pronouncements, the positivists held to the belief that the resolution of the social problem did not demand a transfer of wealth or the abolition of property but rather the establishment of 'a set of reciprocal duties between industrial leaders and their employees'.[6] If this meant that, at the Congress of Marseilles in 1879, the positivists voted against the collectivist resolutions that received majority support, it also entailed support for the Third Republic as the regime best suited to make possible the advances required towards a positivist society. In line with this, the positivists were prepared to participate in the activities of the State and from the 1890s onwards were to be found in influential positions in such consultative bodies as the Conseil Supérieure du Travail and the Office du Travail. Designed to facilitate mutual understanding between workers, employers, and the State, these institutions were the physical embodiment of the solidarist aspiration towards social and economic peace.

One of the leading figures in the Conseil Supérieure du Travail was the positivist Auguste Keufer, general-secretary of the print workers union, the Fédération du Livre, from 1884 until 1920.[7] Drawn to the labour movement by a distaste for the impurities of political activity—in 1906 Keufer voted for the Charte d'Amiens distancing the French trade union movement from political parties—and the desire to improve the material and mental condition of the working class, he consistently endorsed a reformist strategy placing the attainment of immediate and piecemeal goals before the achievement of revolutionary ends. Negotiation, compromise, and dialogue, rather than strike action and industrial sabotage, were his preferred courses of action. A change of heart amongst industrialists was deemed to be more beneficial than the enforced expropriation of their wealth.

It was this stance that brought Keufer repeatedly into conflict with the revolutionary leadership of the Confédération Générale du Travail (CGT) after the turn of the twentieth century. However, it was Keufer's approach that was to prevail with the outbreak of the First World War—when the vast majority of the labour movement supported the French war effort to the bitter end—and this approach also that the CGT was to endorse in 1918 in the shape of a 'minimum programme' of desired reforms. Nevertheless, two years later at the Congress of Tours, the

---

[4] Ibid. 17.   [5] Ibid. 82.   [6] Ibid. 149.
[7] See my *Syndicalism in France* (London, 1990), 119–32. Keufer was both President of the Cercle des prolétaires positivistes and vice-President of the Société Positiviste Internationale.

French socialist movement split, and the French Communist Party (PCF) came into existence. The following year, at Saint-Etienne, the trade union movement split along the same lines, the newly created Confédération Générale du Travail Unifié (CGTU) aligning itself with Moscow's International of Red Trade Unions, the Profintern. The cold and iron-like grip of Bolshevism was about to seize hold of the French left.[8]

II

That the French left remains wedded to a conception of the Revolution of 1789 as an anticipation of later movements towards greater social and economic equality is beyond dispute. Likewise it is clear that this reverence for the Great Revolution as a formative and defining example of what revolution can be taken to mean is not of recent origin.[9] If the terms 'socialist' and socialism' did not come into usage in France until around 1830, the actual distinction between 'left' and 'right' had its origin in the seating arrangements of the National Assembly. At the outset, to be on the left was to be in favour of reform and to be against the arbitrary power of the crown, but such was the dynamic internal to the Revolution that this position was quickly outdistanced by those calling for an end to monarchy and the introduction of universal suffrage. As popular protest continued to push the Revolution in an ever-more radical direction, so the political map of left opinion was redrawn on a regular basis, the *sans-culottes* of Paris ruthlessly determining the fate of their erstwhile representatives. In those circumstances, it was the Jacobins who not only succeeded in establishing themselves as the authentic voice of the people's demands for social justice but who were also to define a distinctive and enduring conception of the ends and means of revolutionary activity. It was to be upon this experience that the various branches of what came to constitute the left in France were to reflect for decades to come, the cult of the revolutionary tradition becoming part of the mental universe of broad sections of left-wing opinion.[10] It was, moreover, an experience that was never to secure universal approval.

The Jacobins came to be seen by their nineteenth-century admirers as democrats and republicans and as fervent defenders both of the nation and of international solidarity with the oppressed. Collectively and individually they set an example of heroic and selfless devotion to the cause of the people. More than this, they established a paradigm for the seizure and use of power in the name of the revolution. According to this model, a dedicated and virtuous minority was to lay hold of the central levers of power in Paris and, once secured, revolutionary government was to be installed with the express purpose of defeating the forces of counter-revolution. If power was to be exercised in the name of the masses, the

---

[8]   Robert Wohl, *French Communism in the Making 1914–1924* (Stanford, Calif., 1966).
[9]   In 1893 the anarchist thinker Kropotkin published an account of the Revolution entitled *La Grande Révolution*.
[10]   Patrick H. Hutton, *The Cult of the Revolutionary Tradition* (Berkeley, Calif., 1981).

people were called upon to be ever-vigilant, to watch over their parliamentary representatives, to remain present upon the public stage, and, at the least sign of betrayal, to rise up in armed insurrection. Yet, as even their most enthusiastic admirers acknowledged, the Jacobins were not socialists. If their cause was that of the regeneration of humanity and the privileged were their enemies, they were supporters of private property and favoured moral equality over material equality. Nowhere was this more evident than in the summary punishment meted out to the faction constituted by the Hébertists. Jacques-René Hébert and his followers were not only atheists (anathema to Robespierre) but also advocates of an 'agrarian law' modelled on that of ancient Rome and designed to bring about a wholesale redistribution of wealth. On the instructions of the Committee of Public Safety they were executed on 24 March 1794. In contrast, the Jacobin vision was one of a moralized capitalism, free of speculation, monopoly, and undue opulence, and peopled by hard-working and frugal property owners and artisans.

With the removal of the Jacobins from power, it became clear to what remained of the radical supporters of the *sans-culottes* that the Revolution had stalled and that all efforts to ameliorate the conditions of the poor were to be abandoned. Now, and in the shape of the Conspiration pour l'Égalité led by François-Noël (Gracchus) Babeuf, France was to witness the birth of her first recognizably communist movement. The key document was Sylvain Maréchal's *Manifeste des Egaux*, the programmatic statement that set out the goals of Babeuf and his fellow conspirators. Its central argument was that the French Revolution was 'only the harbinger of a greater and more solemn revolution'.[11] Thus conceived, the goal of the revolution was to destroy inequality and re-establish the happiness and well-being of all. To that end, the manifesto proclaimed, the only choice was between 'real equality and death'. Let us be finished, it went on, with 'the revolting distinctions between rich and poor, the great and the small, masters and servants, the governors and the governed'. There must be an end to private property: 'the earth belongs to no one'. The 'common good' and the 'community of goods' were to be the guiding principles of the new society.

Needless to say, Babeuf's conspiracy came to nothing, a police spy having kept the government of the Directory informed of their every move. The leaders were arrested on 10 May 1796 and Babeuf, after a trial in which he proclaimed that 'property is the source of all the evils upon this earth',[12] was subsequently executed in May 1797. It was a glorious fate, he told his accusers, 'to die for the cause of virtue'. Others of the conspirators, including Filippo Buonarroti, were deported. But despite this ignominious defeat a set of principles had been set out that was to inspire many a later socialist in their quest to establish a republic of equals. The immediate consequence, however, was to drive egalitarian demands underground and to encourage a seemingly inexhaustible enthusiasm for secret organizations and societies among those intent upon securing radical social change. The latter flourished in particular under the Restoration but none was able to mastermind

[11] See Philippe Buonarroti, *Conspiration pour l'Égalité, dite de Babeuf* (Brussels, 1828), ii. 130–6.
[12] Ibid. i. 53.

anything but the most abortive and futile of uprisings. All the same, the principles of Babouvism came to the surface yet again when in 1828, and to great effect, the now-aged exile Buonarroti published his history of Babeuf's conspiracy.

When retold in this sanitized version, the Revolution had been a struggle between the 'order of egoism and of aristocracy' and the promoters of 'the order of equality', between avarice and ignorance and the 'sublime cause' of 'the imprescribable rights of humanity'. For all its misplaced recognition of the right to property, the democratic constitution of 1793, with its acknowledgement of the sovereignty of the people, had been the Revolution's high point, the very 'palladium of French liberty'. It had also held out the prospect of greater economic equality. The constitution of 1795, in contrast, was an instrument of tyranny and violence, an act of treason and counter-revolution: and, with just cause, it had been this corrupt and illegal regime that Babeuf and his fellow conspirators had sought to overthrow. What followed from the pen of Buonarroti was, first, an account of the manner in which the insurrection was to be carried out and, second, a description of 'the system of equality'.

Conceived in the subterranean worlds of the prison cell and the Directoire secret de salut public, the plan had been to place an agent in each of the (then) twelve *arrondissements* of Paris and to supplement these with others among the military units located in and around the capital. At a precisely coordinated moment and upon the orders of its central command, this clandestine organization was to draw upon the discontent of the masses and instigate a popular insurrection. 'From this way of thinking', Buonarroti commented, 'was born the project of replacing the existing government with a revolutionary and provisional authority constituted in such a manner as to protect forever the people from the influence of the enemies of equality and to provide them with the unity of will necessary to secure republican institutions.'[13] To this Buonarroti added his own opinion that the 'experience of the French Revolution' had demonstrated that 'in order to establish equality in a corrupt nation one had need of a strong and irresistible authority' placed in the hands of those who were 'wise and strongly committed to revolution'.[14] No sooner would the insurrection have commenced than the first measures designed to establish 'the new social order' would have been introduced. The possessions of the enemies of the people were to be redistributed immediately and the poor would be housed and fed at the expense of the republic. After this, a set of 'transitional institutions' were to be put in place with the express intention of creating 'an unrestricted equality' and of founding 'the greatest possible happiness for all'.

Buonarroti's description of this process of transition was detailed in the extreme. Top of the list were measures to secure the complete abolition of private property and the equal distribution of wealth. To these was added an obligation upon everyone to work equally for the prosperity and maintenance of society as a whole. Labour was to be the constituent activity of the new order. Much followed from this. Work was to be a function regulated by law and citizens were to be

[13] See Philippe Buonarroti, *Conspiration pour l'Egalité, dite de Babeuf* (Brussels, 1828), 133.
[14] Ibid. 134 n. 1, 139 n. 1.

distributed to particular occupations according to the needs of the nation. All external trade was to be subject to the direction of the republic. The 'surplus' of the population, no longer required to serve the rich and perform the old functions of government, would move from the capital and the large cities, the countryside as a consequence being 'imperceptibly' covered by villages built in 'the most healthy and convenient locations'. Houses, furniture, and clothing would be simple and clean. 'It is essential to the happiness of individuals and to the preservation of public order', Buonarroti wrote, 'that in his compatriots the citizen habitually finds only those who are his equals and his brothers and that he nowhere comes across the least sign of superiority, however superficial.'[15] Public buildings, and especially those dedicated to the exercise of popular sovereignty, were however to be 'magnificent' in design.

The political structures of the new society were to be similarly reformed. Once the insurrectionary committee had decided that temporary dictatorship had served its purpose, the people were to be called upon constantly to exercise their sovereignty and all those who had served the requisite time in 'military camps' were to play their role as citizens. An intricate system of legislative and consultative assemblies would be introduced but few laws, it was envisaged, would be required by a people without property, vices, crimes, money, or need for taxes. Thus, for the most part, the assemblies of the people would concern themselves with instituting the festivals and ceremonies needed to encourage civic duty and to 'repress the secret desires of egoism'. Education, taking account of the 'natural division' between the sexes, would 'change the face of the nation', instilling a love of country, of liberty, and of equality; freedom of the press would exist but would not extend to the right to question 'the sacred principles of equality and of the sovereignty of the people'. In similar vein, it would be decreed that equality alone met with the approval of the divine power. It goes without saying that a simplicity of morals would be required of everyone and that everything was to be done to discourage a liking for frivolity and the superfluous. Taken as a whole, the project was no better summarized than by Buonarroti's observation that 'the masterwork of politics lies in the modification of the human heart through education, example, reasoning, opinion, and encouragement in such a way that no other desires are formed than those which tend to make society more free, happier, and stronger. When a nation has reached this point ... the most onerous duties are observed with pleasure; laws are obeyed freely; the limits imposed upon natural independence are seen as benefits; reasonable proposals meet with no opposition; and a unity of interest, will and action exists within the body politic.'[16]

There was much in this argument that presaged the calamities of the future, not least the misguided assumption that revolutionary dictatorship would be only temporary and the belief that the liberty of the individual could be so easily and readily subsumed without loss under the wishes of a unanimous collectivity. Nevertheless, by effectively ignoring the differences that had separated the Jacobins

---

[15] Ibid. 225.   [16] Ibid. 228-9.

from Babeuf and his supporters, Buonarroti established that, if the Revolution of 1789 had not been socialist, it had given birth to a set of egalitarian aspirations and had provided an experience of revolution that could be drawn upon by adherents of a nascent socialist movement in the years to come. The nineteenth century was to provide no shortage of such enthusiasts.

Of one thing there can be no doubt: conceptions of property were transformed during the Revolution.[17] No longer was ownership to be tied to privilege but to labour. Similarly, the spirit and practices of corporation that had so defined the economy of the *ancien régime* were consigned to the past, making way for the emergence of something resembling a market economy. In those circumstances, France took its first, hesitant steps towards industrialization and, in place of the craft workshop and the artisan, there gradually emerged the factory and the proletarian. If this pattern of industrial development was not uniform either across the country or over time, it was extensive, especially in such sectors as textiles and mining. The organized labour movement, on the other hand, remained little developed during the years of the Restoration, with the result that expressions of popular protest and disaffection were not only spasmodic but also pre-industrial in style and content (the bread riot posing far more of a threat to public order than strike action). Consequently, in the early decades of the century socialist ideas tended to emerge outside and separate from those workers' organizations that had come into existence, and to that extent they reflected a different set of concerns and preoccupations. The ambition was first and foremost to capture the apparatus of the State.[18]

This was best exemplified by the inheritors of the Babouvist tradition, and most notably by the person of Auguste Blanqui. Blanqui's life was one of agitation, conspiracy, trials, and lengthy imprisonment, his career as a dedicated revolutionary stretching from the early 1830s until his death in 1881. If he himself became a legend and an object of intense reverence, no one did more to perpetuate and glorify the revolutionary memories of the past or to consolidate them into a living tradition of opposition to the established order. To that end, Blanqui never wavered in his conviction that, to achieve the goal of emancipation, the people would have need of 'a revolutionary authority' led by a minority of committed revolutionaries. Partial reforms and the ballot box were an irrelevance beside the imperative of forcibly seizing control of the State at the earliest possible opportunity. To his credit, Blanqui repeatedly attempted to put these ideas into practice, but to no avail and at great personal cost: nevertheless, among his admirers, faith in the tactics of insurrection lived on through the Revolution of 1848, the Paris Commune, and, although much diminished, into the early years of the Third Republic.

One writer on the left who, on the face of things, never shared this vision of conspiratorial politics was Étienne Cabet. Rather than the insurrectionary and

---

[17] See William H. Sewell, jun., *Work and Revolution in France: The Language of Labor from the Old Regime to 1848* (Cambridge, 1980).

[18] *Marxism and the French Left: Studies on Labour and Politics in France 1830–1981* (Oxford, 1986), 58.

violent seizure of power, his preferred course of action was the setting up of model communities based upon principles sketched out in his famous *Voyage en Icarie* as well as in other writings from the late 1830s onward. This he attempted first in Texas and then Nauvoo, Illinois, with little success in either case.[19] The 'interest of the people', Cabet wrote, prevents us from wanting revolution. This was so because the first signs of revolt would be crushed by the State at a heavy cost to the people themselves. Even if the revolution were successful and managed to defeat 'the foreign coalition' intent upon its destruction, the beneficiaries would not be the people but the bourgeoisie. The people, Cabet explained, were not sufficiently well educated or sure of their rights to prevent their victory being 'stolen' from them. In addition, the destruction of commerce and industry arising from 'a great catastrophe' of this kind would leave the 'unfortunate proletarian' in a worse material condition than before. 'How', Cabet asked, 'from an old society, with its prejudices, customs and innumerable obstacles, could we ever hope to enter a new society?' In America, by contrast, 'from the very first, there would be the most beautiful roads, the most perfect towns and villages, the most magnificent work-shops, perfection in housing, furniture, clothing, food, hygiene, and education, in a word, in everything!'[20] In brief, for Cabet, emigration to an unpopulated and virgin territory appeared a far better strategy than riots, conspiracies, and the machinations of secret societies. This was even more firmly his view after the failure of the Revolution of 1848.

Yet all was not entirely as it might have seemed, for Cabet too was not untouched by the weight of Jacobinism and the revolutionary tradition. Drawn to the world of radical secret societies during the 1820s, Cabet had taken to the streets in July 1830 and had initially lent his support to the new regime of Louis-Philippe.[21] Elected to parliament, he was quickly disillusioned by what he was to describe as a 'disappear-ing revolution'[22] and in 1833 launched his own radical newspaper, *Le Populaire*. By the standards of its day, this proved to be a great success, circulation quickly reaching 12,000. Its existence was short-lived. Support for the right of association brought prosecution and, faced with the prospect of two years' imprisonment, Cabet chose exile in England. It was there that he wrote his four-volume *Histoire Populaire de la Révolution Française de 1789 à 1830*.[23]

Written expressly as a refutation of the monumental history recently provided by Adolphe Thiers, Cabet had no doubt that the Revolution of 1789 was 'the greatest event of modern times'[24] and that, when 'exposed in all its truth', it provided 'the most complete practical course in politics and philosophy'.[25] Like so many of his

---

[19] See *Prospectus: Grande Émigration au Texas en Amérique pour réaliser la Communauté d'Icarie* (Paris, 1847).
[20] *Réalisation d'Icarie* (1847), 33.
[21] See e.g. Cabet, *Correspondance avec sa Majesté Louis-Philippe 1er* (Dijon, 1830).
[22] *Révolution de 1830 et situation présente (Novembre 1833) expliquées et éclairées par les révolutions de 1789, 1792, 1799 et 1804 et par la Restauration* (1833), i. 157.
[23] Cabet, *Histoire Populaire de la Révolution Française de 1789 à 1830*, 4 vols. (1839–40).
[24] Ibid. i. 145.
[25] Ibid., p. v.

contemporaries, he also believed that it could only be understood if it were located in the long sweep of French history from its very origins onwards. The first men, Cabet affirmed in Rousseauian tones, were born free and equal in rights. Only later did political society and government begin to emerge and when they did so governments were either 'popular or democratic or republican'. Monarchy appeared only later still and initially had been either 'elective, personal, temporary, or for life'. It was therefore solely through 'usurpation' that monarchies had been able to become 'hereditary and permanent, aristocratic and patrimonial, irresponsible and despotic'.[26] It was from that point onwards, and not before, that society had been divided into 'a conquering aristocracy' which owned everything and a people reduced to either serfdom or slavery. The course of French (and, more generally, of European) history had thus been one of progressive and mounting insurgence against oppression, reaching its culmination in the writings of the eighteenth-century *philosophes*—Rousseau, Cabet wrote, 'demonstrated the justice and the necessity of establishing social, civil, and political equality'[27]—the American Revolution, and then the French Revolution. At this point, 'an old and great nation' set about the task of regenerating itself and in so doing became 'the tribune of the universe'.

What followed was an account of how that potential for emancipation had failed to be realized, the key moment for Cabet being the introduction of the distinction between active and passive citizens. This was a theme he returned to time and time again in his long narrative, its significance being that it excluded the people from the Revolution and opened the door to the emergence of a new 'aristocracy of wealth'. In summary, Cabet praised the National Assembly of 1789–91 for its proclamation of the Déclaration des Droits de l'Homme and for its affirmation of the principles of equality and the sovereignty of the people, but condemned it for not having had the courage to press forward towards social and political equality. Corrupted by 'the ambitious, by intriguers, aristocrats, renegades, and traitors', it had established 'an aristocratic bourgeoisie and a bourgeois aristocracy' and from this flowed 'the greater part of the terrible struggles that were to follow'.

Given this betrayal, Cabet absolved the people of all blame for the massacres that were subsequently to occur, repeatedly challenging Thiers's depiction of their barbarous behaviour and eulogizing their devotion to the cause of liberty, equality, and the *patrie*. In like fashion, he poured scorn upon Thiers's praise of the Girondins, condemning them for their cowardice, their hypocrisy, their lack of morality, their vanity and self-interest. Had the Girondins remained in power, Cabet insisted, their weakness and treachery would have ensured that France would have been lost. 'In reality', he maintained, 'it was the Girondins who were responsible for the Terror and for its consequences.'[28] Danton fared little better. If he had displayed audacity, it had only been to enrich himself. He was, Cabet wrote, 'perhaps the most striking example there is of the disastrous influence of

---

[26] Cabet, *Histoire Populaire de la Révolution Française de 1789 à 1830*, 145–6.
[27] Ibid. 150.   [28] Ibid. iii. 328.

corruption, of immorality, and of the infernal temptation of the love of money'.[29] Danton's opposition to the Committee of Public Safety, he concluded, had been 'a political crime' of enormous magnitude.

Thus it was that Robespierre and the Jacobins were singled out for special praise. When contrasted with the traitors and conspirators around them, they were principled and beyond corruption. They alone had possessed the courage and heroism required to defend France and had understood 'the horrible necessity of destroying their enemies in order not to be destroyed themselves'. When they came to power, the distinction between active and passive citizens had been abolished. The measures they implemented in order to win the war had amounted to the introduction of the common ownership of property. More than this, the Jacobins identified the goal of the Revolution to be that of 'radically regenerating France and Humanity' and of securing the reign of 'eternal Justice'.[30] Assuredly, Robespierre was not a perfect human being, but had he been a tyrant? Rather, it had been his enemies and assassins who had been the tyrants. Robespierre had spurned personal power and had wanted to bring the Terror to an end as quickly as possible. Had he been cruel and merciless? No one, Cabet replied, had been more devoted to the happiness of the people and it was because he had preferred kindness to violence that he had perished. In brief, from 1789 until the moment of his downfall Robespierre had been 'the most faithful instrument of the Revolution and the truest representative of the People'. Indeed, he had been their very incarnation.[31]

Thus, with Robespierre's execution, the movement towards equality and the eradication of poverty came to an end and Robespierre himself was to be treated as nothing more than a brigand and a monster, the perpetrator of unimaginable crimes and excesses. Nothing less had been required if the meaning of the Revolution was to be disfigured and its memory shrouded in calumny. What remained of Cabet's history is outside our compass. His tale was one of France's decline into violence and immorality under the Directory, dishonour and criminality under the Consulate, and, finally, despotism and conquest under the Empire. The Revolution, Cabet concluded, had been 'vanquished'. What lies within our compass is how Cabet related this experience to his own views about the radical reform of society.[32]

Cabet had not a good word to say for the political order that emerged after Thermidor. It was, in his view, the embodiment of everything that was malign and repressive. Reduced to despair, the people, and especially those of the poorer quarters of Paris, had seen no alternative other than that of insurrection. None was remotely successful and all were subject to brutal repression but it had been this experience, Cabet acknowledged, that had given rise to Babeuf's conspiracy. Cabet had known Buonarroti personally and, as he commented in his text, he did not for one minute doubt either his sincerity or disinterestedness, but was his account of Babeuf's devotion to the people sufficient reason for 'blindly' adopting his ideas and

---

[29] Ibid. 571.   [30] Ibid. iv. 6–8.   [31] Ibid. 108.

[32] For Cabet's own account of the emergence of socialist and communist ideas in France see *État de la Question Sociale en Angleterre, en Ecosse, en Irlande et en France* (1843), 58–94.

for turning Babouvism 'into some sort of cult'?[33] Cabet's answer was in the negative. Babeuf, he argued, had not invented the doctrine of communism. This honour went to Lycurgus and the Greek philosophers, to Jesus Christ and the early Christians, and, later, to such writers as Thomas More, Morelly, and Mably. Moreover, it was Cabet's contention that, for all their opposition to the 'inopportune' and 'atheistic' proposals of the Hébertists, both Robespierre and Saint-Just had been advocates of 'real equality' and of communism and that they had intended to march towards these goals by means better suited to success. Second, Babeuf's conspiracy had been imprudent and incompetently organized. It was destined to end in catastrophe. It was a 'fatal error' to believe that an uprising, even if it were defeated, advanced the cause of the people. If the ideal of communism was in no way 'chimerical' or 'impracticable', Cabet concluded, 'we are at the same time deeply convinced that a minority cannot establish it through violence and that it is realizable only through the power of public opinion'.[34]

Cabet was in no doubt as to the principal lesson that was to be learnt and he never tired of repeating it. If the communist society of the future could not be instituted as a result of one violent and impulsive revolutionary *coup*, it would rather require the establishment of a transitionary and preparatory regime lasting for perhaps as long as fifty years.[35] During that time the right to private property would continue to exist but all legislation would have as its goal to 'diminish superfluity, to improve the condition of the poor and progressively to establish equality in everything'.[36] The transition would be effected through civic education and a reformed political structure resting upon a sovereignty of the people made real through the existence of 1,000 deliberative assemblies scattered across the Republic. It would equate, Cabet avowed, to something like 'a pure democracy', with the executive branch of government firmly subordinated to the legislature and never consigned to one person. All citizens would be eligible to vote and to stand for election. There would be no upper chamber full of aristocrats.

Cabet described this process of transition in a variety of different ways, at times outlining its general principles, less frequently doing so as part of a utopian vision. The latter received its most vivid and extended expression in Cabet's *Voyage en Icarie*, first published in 1839. Here the stylistic device employed was that of a voyage by a rich English aristocrat, Lord Carisdall, to the distant island of Icarie, his journal being presented as a portrayal of an imaginary ideal society. Cabet provided a detailed picture of virtually every aspect of the new social order, depicting its towns, its public monuments, its theatres, its housing, the clothing and diet of its inhabitants, as well as a multitude of other facets of its existence right down to the benefits of cremation. As might be readily imagined, there would be no money; nothing would be bought and sold; and production would be carried out communally. All would work equally and all would be rewarded equally, new working practices ensuring the creation of material abundance. There would, of course, be

---

[33] *Histoire Populaire*, iv. 328.   [34] Ibid. 333–4.
[35] e.g. ibid. 333; *Comment je suis communiste* (1845), 6–7; *Voyage en Icarie* (1842), 343, 357–71.
[36] *Voyage en Icarie*, 359.

virtually no crime; the streets would be clean; and everyone would live long and healthy lives. Indeed, one of the few surprises in this otherwise predictable montage was Cabet's enthusiastic endorsement of heterosexual marriage and the family.[37] Icarie also had neighbouring colonies, each conquered peacefully as well as to the delight of their 'savage' inhabitants, now brought gratefully into the arc of civilization.

Several points are worthy of remark. The first is that in such texts as *Comment je suis communiste* and *Mon credo communiste* Cabet set out identical principles without recourse to a utopian framework. Paradoxically, his very point was that, now more than ever before, the establishment of a communist society was a practical possibility made daily more feasible by advances in production and machinery. Second, when Cabet sketched the history of Icarie's successful transition to communism he framed it explicitly in terms of France's own revolution of 1789. Imagined was a bloody struggle lasting two days, followed by 'a terrible war' against a foreign coalition, leaving the revolution and the people ultimately victorious. More intriguing was Cabet's description of the emergence of the 'immortal' Icar as a 'dictator' inspired by a boundless love of the people and concern for their well-being. 'It was he, as dictator,' Cabet wrote, 'who recommended social and political equality, common ownership and the democratic Republic to his fellow citizens.'[38] The parallel with Robespierre was presumably not lost on Cabet's audience. Next, Cabet saw his imagined egalitarian society as a fulfilment of the hopes and aspirations of 1789. Here was a system of government, born of the revolutionary barricades, which remained true to its origins and which saw that all the vices of society—poverty, idleness, immorality, opulence, adultery, hatred, and war—had their source in the unequal ownership of property. The guiding maxims of the new society, therefore, were to be equality, community, and association. Where did liberty fit into this picture? It is true, Cabet wrote, that the desire for liberty was now a 'universal passion' but such a 'blind passion', he countered, was 'an error, a vice, a grave evil', born of 'violent hatred'. As the goal was to 'produce wealth and happiness' it was only right that society 'should subject all wills and all actions to its rules, its laws, and its discipline'.[39] The 'lying liberty' associated with freedom of the press would be brought to an end through the establishment of one single newspaper whose function it would be to express public opinion.[40] Finally, if Cabet located his argument firmly within an Enlightenment framework that assumed the perfectibility, innate sociability, and natural goodness of human beings, he did not hesitate to equate the advocates of communism to the 'disciples, the imitators, and continuators of Jesus Christ'.[41] In fact, he suggested that communism was 'the true Christianity'.[42]

[37] For a fuller statement of Cabet's views on this subject see *La Femme* (1844). See also Pamela Pilbeam, *French Socialists before Marx: Workers, Women, and the Social Question in France* (Teddington, 2000), 75–106.
[38] *Voyage en Icarie*, 217.   [39] Ibid. 403–4.   [40] Ibid. 197–8.
[41] Ibid. 567.   [42] Cabet, *Le Vrai Christianisme suivant Jésus-Christ* (1846).

Quite remarkably, there was little that was unusual in this opinion. Similar sentiments were found, for example, in Alphonse Esquiros's *L'Évangile du peuple défendu*[43] and in Pierre Leroux's *De l'Humanité*.[44] Indeed, framing the case for socialism or communism in the language of Christianity was something of a commonplace among left-wing opinion during the 1840s.[45] Nor was it mere window dressing designed to give moral lustre to a secular ethic or Rousseau-style civil religion. Rather, writers such as Cabet were entirely sincere when they affirmed that the doctrines, morality, and conduct of Jesus Christ provided inspiration and guidance for everyone who wished to deliver humanity from the evils afflicting it. When practised in accord with the 'true' spirit of Christ himself, Cabet argued, no one would refuse to describe themselves as a Christian.[46] The argument, as might be guessed, was that the precept of love thy neighbour was a divine expression of the call to fraternity. This was then bolstered by a portrayal of Christ as a man of the people, always living among the sick, the poor, and the persecuted. The reign of God would mean no more rich and poor, no more masters and slaves, no more oppressors and oppressed. Crucially, however, Cabet and those like him located the promise of salvation in this world rather than the next, the transition to the 'new Jerusalem' or 'holy City' being placed invariably on the immediate horizon.

Just as intriguing was the question of why a religious characterization of aspirations towards social justice and equality held out such appeal to its proponents as well as to its audience. At least four considerations came into play. Stripped of its impurities and returned to its original doctrinal core, Christianity was perceived as a motivating and inspirational force. 'If the doctrine of Christ is a Religion of Hope', Cabet wrote, 'it is also a Religion of Activity and of Courage'.[47] Christianity provided much-needed evidence to support the view that it was not by violence or insurrection that humanity was to be set free and that emancipation was better achieved through the moral transformation and resurrection, first, of the oppressed and, then, of their oppressors.[48] Likewise, it provided ammunition to refute the charge—made, for example, by Alexis de Tocqueville—that socialism and communism were immoral and materialistic doctrines. Last, but not least, it enabled those advocating radical reform to mount a sustained critique of a society deemed to be increasingly in the grip of individualism (the word was coined by Pierre Leroux), economic anarchy, and plutocracy.[49] Jesus, it was pointed out, was no friend of the merchants. He was not a king but a liberator and revolutionary, a democrat and believer in equality.

---

[43] Alphonse Esquiros, *L'Évangile du peuple défendu* (1841).

[44] Pierre Leroux, *De l'Humanité, de son principe et de son avenir, ou se trouve exposé la vraie définition de la religion* (1840).

[45] See Edward Berenson, *Populist Religion and Left-Wing Politics in France, 1830–1852* (Princeton, NJ, 1984).

[46] Cabet, *Le Vrai Christianisme*, 4.

[47] Ibid. 351.

[48] See Michèle Riot-Sarcey, *Le Réel de l'utopie: Essai sur le politique au XIXe siècle* (1998).

[49] See Cabet, *Le Salut est dans l'union: La Concurrence est la ruine* (1845), 1–2, and Pierre Leroux, *De la Ploutocratie ou du gouvernement des riches* (Boussac, 1848).

The socialism of the 1840s was redolent with these themes, its growing number of adherents frequently characterizing the new creed as the realization of Christ's message of justice and brotherhood. Expositions of the doctrines of socialism were often set out in the form of a catechism. However, the hard-nosed realities of industrialization and the pauperization of the working class were increasingly to make themselves felt and nowhere more so than in the writings of Louis Blanc. Blanc's prolific outpourings were not immune from the religious drives and inclinations of the period—he always retained a faith in Christian ethics and what he termed 'the immortal laws of the Gospel'[50]—but he devoted his attention primarily to what became known as the social question. As Tony Judt has observed,[51] at the centre of socialist discourse in the 1830s and 1840s was the issue of whether work was a duty or a right. Seen as a duty, it provided grounds for a moral critique of the bourgeoisie and of the idle rich. Seen as a right, on the other hand, it placed economic reform and the organization of labour at the forefront of the agenda. Blanc, through his tireless advocacy and not inconsiderable influence within the French labour movement, played a key role in effecting the shift from the former to the latter.

This he did most obviously in *L'Organisation du travail*.[52] The basic premise upon which its argument rested was simply stated: economic competition was a 'system of extermination'. The facts proved, Blanc asserted, that unbridled competition led to a systematic lowering of salaries, to a reduction in production, to crime, to the dissolution of the family, to child labour, and to 'a frightening moral corruption'. It also gave rise to civil war and 'necessarily' to international war.

The solution lay in the intervention of the State. This would entail not the ownership of the means of production but rather funding to allow the establishment of *ateliers sociaux*—workers' co-operatives—with the State acting as the ultimate regulator and coordinator of their activities. Blanc's assumption was that, over time, these co-operative ventures would supplant those of private enterprise, an intricate web of social workshops gradually taking shape across industry as a whole. In place of private monopoly—always something of an obsession in socialist literature—the guiding principles would be those of association and solidarity. A similar arrangement would operate for agriculture.

In this way, Blanc imagined that a new social and economic order would come into existence 'without usurpation, without injustice' and, above all, without violence. He also believed that, in contrast to the radical proposals of 1793, these practical reforms would endure. The chance to test these suppositions came in 1848 when, following the February Revolution, Blanc found himself a member of the Provisional Government and head of what became known as the Luxembourg Commission.[53] His allotted task was to find the means of implementing the right to work.[54] The result was a dismal failure. Instead of Blanc's *ateliers sociaux*, the

---

[50] *Catéchisme des Socialistes* (1849).   [51] *Marxism and the French Left*, 65–8.
[52] Blanc, *L'Organisation du travail* (1840).
[53] For Blanc's own account see *Histoire de la révolution de 1848* (1848).
[54] For the debate between Blanc and Adolphe Thiers on this issue see pp. 57–8 above.

government set up state-run *ateliers nationaux* designed primarily to provide poor relief for the Parisian unemployed. Opened in February 1848, their closure was announced on 21 June of that year (Blanc's Luxembourg Commission had been shut down the previous month): two days later barricades were raised in the poorer quarters of eastern Paris and the short, bloody, and ultimately doomed insurrection began. Class war, as the ever-prescient Alexis de Tocqueville recognized, had returned to the streets.[55] Threatened with prosecution, Blanc went into exile in England, not returning until the fall of the Second Empire in 1870.

Despite this abject defeat, Blanc was a key figure in the development of socialist thought in France. Blanc, as we have already seen, set out a vision of the republic resting upon the sovereignty of the people mediated through parliamentary representation. When applied to an analysis of the social and economic condition of France, this endorsement of the claims of universal suffrage and the ballot box was sufficiently strong as to bind him to a vision of democratic socialism. It was this commitment to both socialism and democracy that was to be a defining feature of the labour movement in the early years of the Third Republic. But as we also saw, Blanc was an unashamed advocate of political centralization, of the republic one and indivisible. The corollary was that socialism could only be implemented through the capture of the State. In part, this followed from Blanc's conviction that the reform of society was such an enormous undertaking that it would require the 'full force' of government intervention, but it also reflected his belief that the State was in the hands of socialism's enemies. 'Seize hold of power', he advised, 'if you do not want it to crush you. Use it as an instrument lest you meet it as an obstacle.'[56] This was the conclusion he reached as a historian of both the French Revolution and the July Monarchy.[57]

Blanc's view was that 1789 had begun the domination of the bourgeoisie and that 1830 had served to continue it. There were, he argued, three general principles operating in the world: those of authority, individualism, and fraternity. Completing a process begun with Luther, 1789 had destroyed the authority of the Church, and in its place a triumphant bourgeoisie had installed the principle of individualism. If the principle of fraternity had been announced by the Mountain, it had been swept away by the 'storm' and silenced with the *coup* of Thermidor. On Blanc's account, therefore, there had been two quite distinct revolutions, one bearing the imprint of Voltaire, the other that of Rousseau, but it had been the former, that of a bourgeoisie fully armed with its own distinct conception of politics, philosophy, and the economy, that had taken root and that now ruled the present.[58] This analysis was confirmed by Blanc's reading of the first decade of the July Monarchy's existence. The 1830s, he affirmed, had been nothing else than the rule of the bourgeoisie. Blinded by an ignoble preoccupation with its own well-being, the

---

[55] *Souvenirs* (1999), 182.
[56] *Organisation du travail*, 95.
[57] See *Histoire de la Révolution française,* 12 vols. (1849–62), and *Histoire de Dix Ans 1830–1840,* 6 vols. (Brussels, 1843).
[58] This argument is primarily set out in vol. i of *Histoire de la Révolution française.*

bourgeoisie had allied itself with the monarchy only out of self-interest, believing that this course of action would help keep the people in check. The July Monarchy, Blanc continued, was a regime marked by the complete abandonment of the poor and their subjection to the impersonal and invisible tyranny of the market. It was also a regime that in its egoism and cowardice was not worthy of France.

It was Blanc's view that the days of the bourgeoisie, and consequently of the principle of individualism, were numbered and that the future lay with the principle of fraternity. To argue thus, of course, meant that the Revolution needed to be cast as a source of inspiration for later socialists and this unavoidably involved him in some deft reasoning with regard to the Terror. His argument was that the violence and the fury of the Revolution had their origin as a response to counter-revolution[59] and that the Terror was not a 'system' of government self-consciously invented by the Jacobins but rather a temporary expedient born of necessity out of the 'entrails' of a desperate and exceptional situation.[60] To believe otherwise was mistakenly to dismiss the heroic efforts and achievements of those involved as little more than attempts to forge a permanent dictatorship.

Blanc insisted that this was no apology for terrorism and that its crimes and excesses were to be condemned unreservedly, as were those individuals who had been motivated by the passions of hatred and vengeance. The latter Blanc referred to as 'the Caligulas of *sans-culottisme*'. The terrible character of the means employed had served only to hide the grandeur of the goal pursued and had served not to save the Revolution but to extinguish the very life out of it. More than this, and as he made clear from the first pages of his history of the Revolution,[61] Blanc's view was that the violence and repression of the Terror had been such as to ensure that they would never be resorted to again. And so, according to Blanc, what was 'truly admirable' about the Revolution was its advocacy of the twin principles of individual and social rights. If the first had been the religion for which the Girondins had lived and died, the second had been that for which the Mountain had suffered the same fate, and if, therefore, the Revolution had never succeeded in bringing both principles into harmony, this was to be the task of socialism.

With the advent of the Second Republic in 1848, issues relating to the organization and extension of the franchise again irresistibly came to the fore.[62] As we have seen, Louis Blanc set himself against proposals for direct democracy, fearing that the outcome would be chaos and what he did not hesitate to describe as the reign of ignorance. But these were not the only ideas that Blanc felt compelled to combat at this time. For some on the left, revolution of the kind recently witnessed presented not so much an opportunity to seize hold and democratize the State as an occasion to destroy it altogether. The most forceful advocate of this view during the short life of the Second Republic was Pierre-Joseph Proudhon. We will return to Proudhon when we consider those from whom the Jacobin model of social and political transformation was never able to obtain general assent, but here it is sufficient to

---

[59] Ibid. iv. 308–9.   [60] Ibid. x. 5.   [61] Ibid. i 1–6.
[62] Piero Craveri, *Genesi di une constituzione: libertà e socialismo el dibattio constituzionale del 1848* (Naples, 1985). See also Considérant, *La Solution du gouvernement direct du peuple* (1850).

indicate that Proudhon charged Blanc with being a supporter of despotism. Blanc's indignant response to this accusation—for the most part voiced in his short-lived journal, *Le Nouveau Monde*—served, if nothing else, to highlight a fundamental and enduring fissure in socialist thought in France. Blanc's argument was that Proudhon's vision of a society without a state—anarchy—would give rise to 'tyranny in chaos', to the domination of the strongest, whereas his own under-standing of a state in a democratic regime would engender what he termed an 'État-serviteur' where, through the practice of universal suffrage and representation, the State and the people would merge into one. The words state and liberty, he argued, were mutually related.[63]

The counter-argument was that the State would always remain the instrument of a ruling class and that it would always play the role of master rather than that of servant. The introduction of (male) universal suffrage would make no appreciable difference to the situation. Indeed, this conclusion seemed to be proved by experi-ence. The calamitous result of extending the franchise to include a largely unedu-cated electorate was the election of Louis Napoleon to the presidency, an event followed by the inauguration of the Second Empire and the descent into 'césar-isme'. The impact upon the left of this disastrous experiment was profound. If for some it instilled a profound distrust of a strong executive power, for others it undermined their faith in voter competence and the electoral process as a whole. This bitterness was only enhanced as a result of further disappointment following the inception of the Third Republic. Universal suffrage again failed to deliver significant social and economic reform. To this was then added disenchantment with the parliamentary regime itself. Rather than the superior capacity of the political elite, all that was evident was plain incompetence and corruption. In this context, it is interesting to note that the word 'politician' made its entry into the French vocabulary at the end of the 1870s and that it quickly developed a negative connotation, the by-word for self-interest and self-importance.[64]

This situation elicited a variety of responses, none of which unfortunately can be explored here in the detail they deserve. Some in the forever-fractured socialist movement turned their backs on politics altogether, raising *ouvriérisme* to a matter of high principle.[65] This was true, for example, of the Parti ouvrier socialiste révolutionnaire, founded by Jean Allemane in 1891.[66] Others, especially those associated with the orthodox Jules Guesde, sought to construct a 'class party' that would be immune from the blandishments of parliamentary intrigue and ambition.[67] Of crucial importance here was the gradual assimilation and

---

[63] See esp. 'Hommes du Peuple, L'État, c'est vous! Réponse au citoyen Proudhon', *Le Nouveau Monde*, 5 (15 Nov. 1849), 195–207, and 'L'État-Anarchie du citoyen Proudhon', *Le Nouveau Monde*, 7 (15 Jan. 1850), 302–7.

[64] Tuula Varakallio, *'Rotten to the Core': Variations of French Anti-System Rhetoric* (Jyvaskyla, 2004), 34–71.

[65] See e.g. Gustave Lefrançais, *République et Révolution: De l'Attitude à prendre par le prolétariat en présence des partis politiques* (Geneva, n.d.).

[66] See Jean Allemane, *Notre Programme* (1895).

[67] See Claude Willard, *Les Guesdistes: Le Mouvement socialiste en France (1893–1905)* (1965). See also Marc Angenot, *Jules Guesde, ou la fabrication du marxisme orthodoxe* (Montreal, 1997).

misappropriation of Marxist ideas that occurred in France from the 1880s onwards. Marx's writings were increasingly made available in (often inaccurate) French translation and his ideas subjected to detailed discussion in such reviews as *Le Devenir social* and, after the turn of the century, Hubert Lagardelle's *Le Mouvement socialiste*. Electoral success, however, could not hide the fact that in the hands of Guesde and his colleagues, Marxism was reduced to an arid and formulaic doctrine resting upon a crude economic determinism and an advocacy of class struggle, the inevitability of collectivism, and the seizure, by force if necessary, of the State. Somewhat reassuringly for Guesde's loyal supporters, it was imagined that the capitalist system would soon come to an end in a crisis of overproduction. The next Revolution, unlike that of 1789, was to be not the Revolution of property owners, of financiers, and of the bourgeoisie but of the Fourth Estate. In such circumstances, there was to be no room for ideological deviation. Nevertheless, between August 1914 and the end of 1916 Guesde served in the national unity government of René Viviani as Minister without Portfolio, patriotism having got the better of his intransigence and dogmatism.[68]

Still others, most notably Jean Jaurès and Charles Andler, tried manfully to reinvigorate the principles of democratic socialism. To pass over the formidable figure of Jaurès in a few sentences is to do a grave injustice to a man whose memory still looms large in the imaginations of many French socialists. An impassioned anti-militarist, if for nothing else he is remembered because of his assassination at the hands of a young nationalist on the very eve of the First World War. His life, however, was a remarkable one, his political commitment and rhetorical skills matched by his immense erudition and scholarship. Jaurès's views on politics were best summarized in his *Études socialistes*, a collection of wide-ranging essays he first published in Charles Péguy's *Cahiers de la Quinzaine* in 1901, and then in book form a year later. Distancing himself from the Marxist orthodoxy of Guesde, Jaurès's view was that the emancipation of the proletariat would best be achieved through 'the methodical and legal organization of its own forces under a regime of democracy and universal suffrage'.[69] This he defined as a process of 'revolutionary evolution'. Gradually, through the implementation of an extensive programme of reforms, the proletariat was to take hold of the means of production and the State, the new society slowly emerging from the dissolution of the old order. Such a radical transformation was not to be the work of a minority. 'A revolutionary minority,' Jaurès wrote, 'no matter how intelligent and energetic it might be, is not able in a modern society to carry out a revolution. It requires the support and collaboration of the majority, indeed of the overwhelming majority.'[70] The Revolution of 1789, Jaurès added, had been the work of the majority.

---

[68] For a selection of Guesde's writings see *Collectivisme et Révolution* (1908), *Questions d'Hier et d'aujourd'hui* (1911), and *Essai de catéchisme socialiste* (1912). Also of interest is the famous debate held with Jean Jaurès in 1900 and available as *Les Deux Méthodes* (1925).

[69] *Études socialistes* (1902), p. li. A selection of Jaurès's work can be found in Jean-Pierre Rioux (ed.), *Jaurès: Rallumer tous les soleils* (2006).

[70] *Études socialistes*, 43.

It should come as no surprise that Jaurès was also the author and editor of a multi-volume *Histoire socialiste de la Révolution française*, written in the years following the loss of his parliamentary seat in 1898. In historiographical terms, the novelty of Jaurès's account lay in its attempt to be both a social and political history of the Revolution, to draw inspiration, as he himself said, from the approaches of Marx, Michelet, and Plutarch.[71] Unlike many of his forebears Jaurès did not identify himself with any of the actors in the great drama, expressing no preference for either Danton or Robespierre, although he was unremittingly critical of the scheming of the royal family and of the self-interested machinations of the Girondins. Above all, he saw the Revolution as the consequence of the rise to economic dominance of the bourgeoisie in the eighteenth century and for that reason was unambiguous in his conviction, announced in the very first paragraph of his first volume, that it 'marked, at bottom, the political advent of the bourgeois class'. Nevertheless at no point did Jaurès reduce his argument to one of crude economic determinism. Rather, he saw the growing complexity of the Revolution and of the class struggle internal to it, and in so doing also saw that the people had played a decisive role in shaping its outcome. 'The Revolution', Jaurès wrote, 'had a logic and an impulse that not even the blindness and the narrow egoism of the bourgeoisie could put a stop to.'[72] In short, in realizing what Jaurès regarded as 'the two essential conditions of socialism'—democracy and capitalism—the Revolution had also 'indirectly prepared the advent of the proletariat'.[73]

With his return to parliament in 1902, and having written only the first four volumes, Jaurès handed over the task of completing the *Histoire socialiste de la Révolution française* to others of his colleagues in the socialist movement. He did, however, write the conclusion to the twelfth and final volume, published in 1908. In doing so, he was able to reaffirm the fundamental point that had informed his account of the period from 1789 until the fall of Robespierre in 1794: democracy was the indispensable vehicle for the emancipation of the proletariat. Without ever idealizing the Revolution and without ever imagining that it could have given birth to a socialist society, Jaurès believed that the Revolution had contained the germ of an idea whose time had come, that at certain moments the Revolution had transcended the class interests of the bourgeoisie, and that, after the long struggles of the nineteenth century, the proletariat was now in a position to effect a 'new and more fundamental revolution', not only in terms of the ownership of the means of production but also with regard to the morality of society as a whole. In so arguing, Jaurès recognized that he was writing not only against the enemies of socialism but also at a time when socialists were in disagreement among themselves about their methods and goals and thus when the accord between socialism and democracy and the necessity of political action needed once again to be affirmed unambiguously.[74] The Revolution, he believed, proved the validity of this argument.

---

[71] *Histoire Socialiste 1789–1900* (1902), i. 3.   [72] Ibid. ii. 1049.   [73] Ibid. i. 3.

[74] For a sense of these disagreements, in addition to *Les Deux Méthodes*, see Jaurès, *L'Action du parti socialiste* (1908).

Not the least of the many lessons that Jaurès imagined might be drawn from a study of the Revolution was that socialism had no need or desire to make permanent enemies. As a doctrine it was able to embrace both the material and moral aspirations of the whole of humanity. The ambitions of socialism, in other words, went beyond that of divesting the bourgeoisie of their property and were focused upon the creation of a more equitable society and one where individuals would live harmoniously together. All were to be treated with equal moral dignity.

It was this moral dimension of socialism that was brought to the fore by Charles Andler, most notably in his essay *La Civilisation socialiste*.[75] 'To be a socialist', he there wrote, 'is to have passed through a complete inner regeneration and through a process of spiritual rebirth.'[76] Unlike Jaurès, Andler never attained political prominence within the socialist movement but he did exercise considerable influence in intellectual circles. An academic working first at the École Normale Supérieure and later at the Sorbonne, he had written his doctoral thesis on the origins of state socialism in Germany and, as a fluent German speaker, was perfectly placed to engage with the writings of Marx and his followers.[77] In 1901 he published a long historical introduction and commentary on *The Communist Manifesto*.[78] He was however unreservedly critical of orthodox Marxism, believing it to be flawed in terms of both theory and practice. Marxist metaphysics, he argued, rested upon a series of 'unprovable hypotheses' and it was incapable of generating an adequate moral theory. As early as 1897 he had diagnosed what he termed 'the decomposition of Marxism'.[79]

In its stead, Andler, like others of his left-leaning colleagues at the École Normale Supérieure, was prepared to look to the example of Fabian socialism in England[80] and, as a group, they came to recommend the attainment of socialism through consumers' co-operatives, educational programmes for the working class, the municipalization of public services, and the state ownership of the means of production. They were opposed to the control of industry by the workers themselves, on the grounds that it was both impracticable and undesirable. An institution would be required to coordinate production and this would inevitably be some form of state. To counter the fear that this would lead to the creation of a centralized and autocratic bureaucracy, an emphasis was placed upon occupational associations as vital intermediaries between individuals and the government. However, this gradualist programme clearly envisaged an enhanced role for the State.

A key ingredient in this argument was that capitalism was a chaotic, wasteful, and anarchic system and, by implication, that socialism would provide greater

---

[75] Charles Andler, *La Civilisation socialiste* (1912).

[76] Ibid. 6.

[77] *Les Origines du Socialisme d'État en Allemagne* (1897).

[78] *Le Manifeste Communiste* (1901).

[79] 'La conception matérialiste de l'Histoire', *Revue de métaphysique et de morale*, 5 (1897), 644–58. See Christophe Prochasson, 'Sur la réception du Marxisme en France: Le Cas Andler (1890–1920)', *Revue de synthèse*, 4 (1989), 85–108.

[80] See e.g. Edouard Pfeiffer, *La Société Fabienne et le mouvement socialiste anglais contemporain* (1911) and Robert Hertz, 'Le Socialisme en Angleterre: La Société Fabienne', *La Revue socialiste*, 323 (1911), 426–31.

rationality in production and consumption. It was, then, perhaps no idle coincidence that the 1890s saw a marked revival of interest in the ideas of Saint-Simon, with Georges Weill and Sébastien Charléty publishing studies of his ideas between 1894 and 1896.[81] In the hands of his disciples Saint-Simonianism developed into a decidedly eccentric religious cult but there was enough in his writings to convince some at least that Saint-Simon himself could be taken as a precursor of socialism. If one of these ideas was that society should be so organized as to secure the amelioration of the condition of the poorest and most numerous class, another was that we should seek to move beyond the government of men to the administration of things. What this attraction to Saint-Simon revealed was what Célestin Bouglé was later to describe as 'the double aspect of socialism': namely, that socialism was both a doctrine of emancipation and a doctrine of organization.[82]

Another writer who was influential in developing this theme was Émile Durkheim. He was a major influence upon the socialist group at the École Normale Supérieure and many of their ideas were developed in Durkheim's journal, *L'Année sociologique*. In 1895–6 Durkheim himself gave a course of lectures on socialism and he too located Saint-Simon as a central figure in the socialist tradition.[83] Needless to say, his approach was deeply sociological, and thus socialism was explored 'as a reality' and as 'an unknown phenomenon yet to be explored'. Durkheim's starting point, however, was that socialism was a 'cry of anguish and, sometimes, of anger uttered by the men who most keenly feel our collective malaise'[84] and, most importantly, that it was a response to the economic disorganization arising from industrialization. In contrast to communism, which Durkheim saw as a pre-industrial form of utopianism akin to Christian asceticism, the primary drive behind socialism was to overcome economic anarchy and the injustice which arose from it. 'We define as socialist', Durkheim wrote, 'every doctrine which calls for the connection of all the economic functions, or of certain among them, which are currently diffuse, to the directing and conscious centres of society.'[85] He stressed that 'connection' did not mean 'subordination' but the crucial point was that the amelioration of the condition of the workers was only the by-product and consequence of the reorganization of the economy. Socialism, in brief, went beyond 'the question of the workers' and entailed more than the introduction of a 'higher morality': it consisted 'in the organization and centralization of economic life'.[86]

On this account, socialism was not concerned to secure the dominance of the proletariat or the negation of private property but was conceived primarily as an aspiration to so restructure the economy that it would serve the greater interests of the collectivity. The State was not seen as something that was antagonistic towards

---

[81] Weill, *Un Précurseur du Socialisme: Saint-Simon et son œuvre* (1894); *L'École saint-simonienne, son histoire, son influence jusqu'à nos jours* (1896); and Charléty, *Essai sur l'Histoire du saint-simonisme* (1896).

[82] 'Préface', to Élie Halévy, *L'Ère des tyrannies* (1938), 10.

[83] See *Le Socialisme* (1992). A selection of Durkheim's writings on socialism can be found in Anthony Giddens (ed.), *Durkheim on Politics and the State* (Cambridge, 1986), 97–153.

[84] *Le Socialisme*, 37.   [85] Ibid. 49.   [86] Ibid. 75.

the individual but rather as an instrument that would allow the overcoming of economic anomie. Socialism was not a doctrine of class war.

It is therefore not without interest that Durkheim was also very critical of the ideas then being developed by the theorists of revolutionary syndicalism. This was made most evident in 1906 when Durkheim debated the issue of anti-patriotism with the editor of *Le Mouvement socialiste*, Hubert Lagardelle.[87] Durkheim raised three objections to the ideas advanced by Lagardelle. First, Durkheim believed that it was possible for legal and moral institutions to progress in parallel to and in harmony with progress in the economy and therefore that it was not necessary to destroy the present economic order. Second, he argued that revolutionary syndicalism rested upon the false premise that 'the worker is exclusively a producer'. In Durkheim's opinion, the worker also possessed an intellectual and moral life. Finally, and most seriously, he believed that the syndicalist project of destroying society would bring about a return to barbarism. Far from creating a new civilization, we would 'enter into a time of darkness'. Underpinning each of these arguments was Durkheim's conviction that there was far more uniting the bourgeois and the worker in society than the anti-patriotic Lagardelle would allow.

If Durkheim always kept his distance from the socialist movement, this was not true of his academic followers in Paris.[88] Predominantly bourgeois in background they were drawn to socialism out of a sense of moral obligation and as intellectuals armed with the discoveries of social science. Another important factor driving their political commitment was the Dreyfus Affair and the momentous events that surrounded it. When the campaign to release Captain Dreyfus began in the mid-1890s the initial reaction across the left was one of indifference, if not downright hostility. What, it was asked, had the wrongful imprisonment of a member of the bourgeoisie to do with the cause of the proletariat? Such was the response of Jules Guesde and his colleagues in the Parti ouvrier français. It was Jaurès who, almost single-handedly, changed this view. In a series of newspaper articles—later published as *Les Preuves*—he set out to convince his fellow socialists that not only was Dreyfus innocent, but that if, as Jaurès argued powerfully, the cause of socialism was that of justice and humanity, then he deserved their support, irrespective of his class. 'Without compromising our principles and without abandoning the class struggle', he wrote, 'we can hear the call of pity.'[89]

As a result, the forces of the left mobilized in great numbers and one year later, in June 1899, Pierre Waldeck-Rousseau formed a government of 'republican defence'. Among the members of that government, as Minister of Commerce and Industry, was the socialist deputy Alexandre Millerand. Again there was division on the left, the Guesdists and others condemning what they saw as a politics of compromise and deviation. It was indeed true that, in 1892, Millerand had made a famous speech at Saint-Mandé on the outskirts of Paris where he had outlined 'a minimum

---

[87] *Libres entretiens* (11 Mar. 1906), 389–436.

[88] See the special issue devoted to 'Les Durkheimiens', *Revue Française de Sociologie*, 20 (1979).

[89] Quoted in Vincent Duclert, 'L'Affaire Dreyfus et la gauche', in J.-J. Becker and G. Candar, *Histoire des gauches en France* (2004), ii. 207.

programme' of reforms to be pursued by socialists,[90] but the broader question raised by these developments was whether the socialist movement could be indifferent to the fate of the Republic. Those who answered in the negative did so in the belief that the Republic remained the most favourable institutional structure within which socialists could pursue their desired reforms. In Millerand's formulation this meant that the Republic was the political form of socialism, whilst socialism was the economic and social expression of the Republic. For others, the entry of a socialist into government meant accepting that, for all their doubts about the bourgeois republic, socialism was an offspring of the traditions of republican democracy. The harder part of the equation was that of embracing the daily reality of reformism and of cooperation with the bourgeoisie. Worst of all, and as the most astute observers saw clearly, the yawning divide between revolutionary rhetoric and reformist practice ran the risk of reducing socialism to nothing more than meaningless gestures and verbalism.

These divisions and debates were not without an important international dimension.[91] From the late 1860s onwards, the congresses of both the First and Second Internationals frequently revealed the deep schism that existed over the respective claims of political and economic action and these tensions were only to be accentuated by the rise to prominence (above all, in Germany) of Marxism during the final decades of the century. Matters came to a head when Eduard Bernstein began to challenge the very foundations of historical materialism. Beginning with a series of articles published in *Die Neue Zeit* in 1896, he plunged German Marxism into the crisis of revisionism, arguing that the historical necessity of socialism could not be derived from the evolution of capitalism. At bottom, this was a difference of opinion about the process and mechanics of revolution. If democracy was the end, Bernstein believed, so also it should be the means. The strategy of the dictatorship of the proletariat had to be abandoned. In the French case, it also denoted a deep-seated disagreement about the nature of the Revolution. The fractured heritage of 1789 was again to come into play.

III

To begin our analysis of what is often referred to as the 'second left',[92] we might turn our attention to Charles Fourier's *Théorie des Quatre Mouvements*, first published in 1808.[93] With its accounts of copulating planets, the sea tasting of lemonade, and the nine degrees of cuckoldry, this is undoubtedly one of the

---

[90] See Millerand, *Le Socialisme réformiste français* (1903), 19–35.
[91] See Emmanuel Jousse, *Réviser le marxisme? D'Edouard Bernstein à Albert Thomas, 1896–1914* (2007).
[92] See Vincent Duclert, 'La Deuxième gauche', in Becker and Candar, *Histoire des gauches*, ii. 175–89.
[93] See *Œuvres Complètes de Charles Fourier* (1846), i. This text is available in English tr. as *The Theory of the Four Movements* (Cambridge, 1996). See Jonathan Beecher, *Charles Fourier: The Visionary and his World* (Berkeley, Calif., 1986).

strangest books ever written. Beneath these numerous oddities, however, lay an audacious attempt to refashion the principles of social organization following what Fourier described unequivocally as 'the catastrophe of 1793'. The Revolution, according to Fourier, was a direct consequence of the 'systematic thoughtlessness' of the moral and political sciences. The *philosophes*, he wrote, had been like 'children playing with fireworks amidst barrels of gunpowder'.[94] They had forgotten that 'liberty is illusory if the common people lack wealth', that equality was a 'chimera' where the right to work did not exist, and that there could be no 'fraternity between sybarites steeped in refinements and our coarse, hungry peasants covered in rags'.[95] The result had been 'civilized chaos, barbarism, and savagery'.

In response, Fourier's ambition was to sketch out the details of an 'Ordre Sociétaire' that would permit the transition 'from incoherence to social combination', 'universal harmony', and 'a state of great happiness'. This he did through the formulation of a highly complex theory of 'passionate attraction and repulsion'. Hitherto, Fourier argued, the passions had been seen as sources of discord: his theory, in contrast, would 'appeal to the passions common to everybody' and its success would be guaranteed through 'the allurements of profit and sensual pleasure'.[96] There is no need to analyse Fourier's taxonomy of what he took to be our 'luxurious', 'affective', and 'distributive' passions, nor to dissect his classification of the 810 personality types which derived from it: the point was that Fourier believed that it was a mistake to repress the passions. This explains why he allotted such a central place to 'amorous freedom' and what he termed 'combined gastronomy'. If, as Fourier believed, sensual pleasure was the primary and immutable source of human activity, the trick was so to arrange society that it should be maximized. Exquisite food and a rich diet of sexual partners would secure social harmony.

Fourier was not much read until around 1829, the year in which he published *Le Nouveau Monde industriel et sociétaire*.[97] If the basic principle of Fourier's argument remained unchanged—'it will be proven', he wrote, 'that true happiness consists in the enjoyment of great riches and an infinite variety of pleasures'[98]—the emphasis upon 'amorous corporation' was much less evident. 'The vice of our so-called regenerators', Fourier wrote, 'is to condemn this or that abuse instead of condemning civilization in its entirety, for the latter is nothing but a vicious circle of abuses.'[99] The remedy to these vices, he continued, lay 'in the discovery of a mechanism of industrial attraction' which would transform work into a pleasure and guarantee a minimum income to all members of the community. Labour was no longer to be regarded as a duty but as an enjoyable and satisfying activity structured in such a way as to ensure that all necessary tasks would be accomplished without coercion.

---

[94] *Œuvres Complètes de Charles Fourier*, 284.
[95] Jonathan Beecher and Richard Bienvenu (eds.), *The Utopian Vision of Charles Fourier* (London, 1972), 160–2.
[96] *Œuvres Complètes de Charles Fourier*, 8.
[97] Ibid. vi.   [98] Ibid., p. xiv.   [99] Ibid., p. xv.

Needless to say, Fourier provided a detailed breakdown of how this would be done—work was to be of infinite variety, of short duration, and carried out in clean surroundings, for example—but the fundamental principle underlying the whole operation was arguably best discerned in the proposal that children—the 'little hordes'—should perform such unsavoury tasks as cleaning the drains and shifting manure.[100] The trick, in other words, was to align the job with the natural propensities of those involved (in this case, the 'love of dirt' dear to so many pre-adolescents). Crucially, such work was to be undertaken in the new material conditions provided by the *phalange*, an association of approximately 1,600 in-dividuals—twice the number of identified personality types—the physical and organizational arrangements of which Fourier planned down to the last detail. For the most part these aspects of Fourier's argument, intriguing as they are, can be passed over but we should perhaps note that members were to live in a condition of what was described as 'graduated inequality' and that remuneration was to be made according to a complicated formula taking into account labour performed, capital invested, and talent displayed. Placed in a rural setting, at the centre of the *phalange* would be a vast Palace of Harmony or *phalanstère*. The architectural drawings used to adorn various Fourierist publications indicate that this magnificent edifice, replete with dining rooms, libraries, workshops, ballrooms, private apartments, and street gallery, would bear a marked resemblance to the palaces of Versailles and the Louvre.

The organizational difficulties arising from such arrangements are presumably self-evident. It is, therefore, all the more important to understand that Fourier believed his proposals to be far from utopian. Indeed, he insisted that he had revealed the principles of a new 'social science' and that his discoveries bore comparison with Newton's theory of gravitational attraction. By the same token he was unfailingly critical of what he saw as the impractical schemes put forward by Robert Owen and the various Saint-Simonian sects.[101] Moreover, it was as a doctrine which located society's ills within the social system that Fourier's ideas were taken up by his growing number of followers.[102]

Fourier's big breakthrough came in 1831 when the schism within the Saint-Simonian movement led to the conversion of sizeable numbers of its members to Fourierism. The following year saw the creation of a weekly journal, *Le Phalanstère*, edited jointly by Jules Lechevalier, Victor Considérant, and Fourier himself. That year also saw the first concerted attempt to create a model community, located not far from Paris. Early optimism quickly gave way to personal acrimony and the disciples distanced themselves more and more from their troublesome master. As a consequence Fourierism was gradually purged of many of its wilder eccentricities. This was especially so after Fourier's death in 1837. *Le Phalanstère* was superseded by Considérant's *La Phalange: Journal de la Science Sociale* and by the daily *La*

---

[100] *Œuvres Complètes de Charles Fourier*, 207.

[101] See e.g. Fourier's *Pièges et charlatanisme des sectes Saint-Simon et Owen* (1831).

[102] See Jonathan Beecher, *Victor Considerant and the Rise and Fall of French Romantic Socialism* (Berkeley, Calif., 2001).

Démocratie pacifique in 1843. Although never as large as that achieved by Cabet's *Le Populaire*, their audience was substantial, and the École Sociétaire (as Fourierism was now known) secured a sizeable following across France into the 1840s.

Ultimately what emerged from this process of transition was a vague form of democratic socialism much removed from Fourier's original intentions. A place was found for the State—in the form of a Ministry of Progress—and Considérant's vision of the future was noticeably more egalitarian than that of his former master. It was, moreover, a socialism which (echoing the familiar refrain of the time) saw itself as 'the social realization of Christianity'. The commitment to a 'peaceful democracy' also entailed a willingness to engage in electoral politics.[103] Here it was Considérant, now the effective leader of the movement, who led the way. Having first stood for election in 1839, he became a member of the National Assembly in 1848 and there championed both the right to work and female suffrage. Although deeply unsettled by the popular violence of 1848–9, he was arrested in June 1849 and, like so many other radicals, went into Belgian exile. Four years later, following a visit to the United States in 1852, Considérant published *Au Texas*,[104] a detailed report and programme for the establishment of an experimental colony on American soil. Buoyed up by the enthusiastic reception his ideas received, on 15 January 1855 he set sail again for the New World, from whence he did not return until 1869. Predictably, the new settlement on the banks of the Trinity River near Dallas was rapidly to fall prey to feuds and factions, with the result that a discouraged and disenchanted Considérant spent the remainder of his American sojourn as a farmer near San Antonio.

This sorry end to a tale fuelled by such exalted expectations should not blind us to what was of intellectual significance in the Fourierist movement. Fourier and those who followed him saw that the profound ills afflicting society derived not from any defects intrinsic to human beings or from causes that had political solutions but from evils inherent to a system of industrial organization characterized by disorder, oppression, and deceit. They concluded that abstract political rights were of little import when placed beside claims to a right to work and to a basic minimum subsistence and that violent revolution and insurrection was the route least likely to engender a 'perfect social state' resting upon the 'sacred principles of justice, liberty, and humanity'. Rather than relying upon what Considérant portrayed as 'the eruption of a popular volcano', they saw themselves as 'social engineers' intent on securing 'universal union' through the progressive application of the principles of voluntary association. From this standpoint, it became possible to conceive of a new set of social arrangements where everyone would work 'freely and passionately' for the general good and where everyone would identify that good with his or her own personal

---

[103] In addition to the various Fourierist journals already cited, see Victor Considérant, *Bases de la Politique Positive* (1842); *Exposition abrégée du système phalanstérien de Fourier* (1845); *Principes du socialisme: manifeste de la démocratie au XIXe siècle* (1847); and *Le Socialisme devant le vieux monde* (1848).

[104] Considérant, *Au Texas* (1854).

well-being. It was these truths that were repeated incessantly in Fourierist tracts and periodicals, in lectures and in speeches, and in the press, but which also resolutely escaped practical application.

Considérant was prepared to accept that his conception of socialism was anti-revolutionary, if not counter-revolutionary, and he went to great lengths to demonstrate that socialism should not seek to imitate the bloody and destructive example provided by the emancipation of the bourgeoisie in 1789. The violent, subversive, and conspiratorial socialism of Babeuf, he wrote, would 'immolate' liberty and destroy all personal spontaneity, putting in its place 'the absolute despotism of the law'. The communism of Cabet, he likewise argued, drew inspiration from the 'democratic and political tradition' of the Revolution and accordingly paid little attention to the immense difficulties posed by the organization of society and of collective labour. 'To invoke fraternity', Considérant wrote, 'is to resolve nothing.' As for the 'errors' of Louis Blanc, Considérant was of the opinion that his distinguished colleague had no other idea than that of 'imposing his egalitarian socialism through the exercise of authority and by surprise'. Relying solely upon the instrument of the State, Blanc intended to bring socialism into existence by decree.[105]

Another fellow socialist for whom Considérant had few kind words was Pierre-Joseph Proudhon.[106] His 'portrait of the beast' revealed a man of paradox who delighted in self-contradiction and argument and this, with some justification, has remained the view of almost all those who have subsequently read his work. 'I distrust an author', Proudhon wrote, 'who pretends to be consistent with himself after an interval of twenty-five years.'[107] Something of an autodidact, Proudhon possessed a capacity to arouse controversy—it was in his *Qu'est-ce que la propriété?* of 1840 that he launched his famous slogan that 'property is theft'—and he continued in this vein until the end of his life in 1865. Never a supporter of feminism, it was Proudhon's opinion that the choice facing women was that of being either housewives or courtesans. Like many a radical of his day, he published a series of newspapers, of which the most successful was *Le Représentant du peuple*, launched in February 1848. He also spent three years in prison (where he both married and fathered a child) and a further four years in exile. He was a man of notoriously poor political judgement—believing, for a short time, that Louis Napoleon Bonaparte might serve the cause of revolution—and frequent ill-humour. Nevertheless, in the hydra-headed world of the socialism of the 1840s not only did Proudhon achieve sufficient prominence as to attract the attention (and briefly admiration) of Karl Marx but his ideas were also able to secure a powerful sway over

[105] *Le Socialisme devant le vieux monde*, 21–2, 31–2, 33–4, 59–61, 87–91.
[106] In English the standard text is George Woodcock, *Pierre-Joseph Proudhon: A Biography* (London, 1956). See also Alan Irving Ritter, *The Political Thought of Pierre-Joseph Proudhon* (Princeton, NJ, 1969); Edward Hyams, *Pierre-Joseph Proudhon: His Revolutionary Life, Mind and Works* (London, 1979); and K. Steven Vincent, *Pierre-Joseph Proudhon and the Rise of French Republican Socialism* (Oxford, 1984).
[107] Quoted in Woodcock, *Pierre-Joseph Proudhon*, 277.

the French labour movement. This was an influence that was to endure up to the First World War, if not beyond.

Lurking beneath all of Proudhon's writings was a fierce and unbending moralism. This was disclosed in a variety of ways: a hatred of plutocracy, a belief in the nobility of manual work, an opposition to divorce, distaste for bohemian life, and undisguised contempt for the materialistic civilization of America. Proudhon also believed that France had entered a period of decline and decay. Above all, it was revealed through his abiding preoccupation with the nature of justice and the manner in which it was expressed in the different aspects of our lives. Proudhon's views on this subject changed over time but were to come to fruition in the three weighty volumes he published in 1858 entitled *De la Justice dans la Révolution et dans l'Église*.[108]

This, as summarized by Proudhon himself, was the core of the argument. Among primitive peoples, justice took the form of a supernatural commandment supported by religion. In this form it became aristocratic and, with the arrival of Christianity, led to the 'degradation of humanity'. In short, justice was seen by the Church to be transcendental, to have its origins outside man, and to be known only through revelation. According to Proudhon, true justice was immanent to man and was innate to human consciousness, constituting his very essence. 'Justice', Proudhon wrote, 'is human, completely human, and nothing but human.'[109] This being the case, what was the substance of justice? The point of departure, Proudhon argued, was our 'sentiment of personal dignity' which, when generalized through our exchanges with others, produced an affirmation of 'the respect, spontaneously felt and reciprocally guaranteed, for human dignity, in whatever person and in whatever circumstances it finds itself compromised and at whatever risk its defence exposes us to'.[110] From this flowed the principles of right and duty. 'Right', Proudhon stated, 'is for each individual the faculty of requiring in others respect for the human dignity of his person; duty, the obligation to respect this dignity in another.'[111]

The remainder of Proudhon's text explored the various dimensions of this argument as they applied to the activity of work, education, love, marriage, and so on, but the central idea informing this discussion was that the very purpose of what he termed the Revolution was to be the realization of such a concept of justice. It was with the Revolution that a new age for humanity would be opened up where justice, previously only vaguely understood and perceived, appeared in all its 'purity and plenitude'.

The key issue was how this bore upon the social and political organization of society. No clearer statement of Proudhon's views on this matter can be found than in the final paragraphs of his *Idée générale de la Révolution au XIXe siècle*, published in 1851. 'To be governed', he there proclaimed, was 'to be watched over, inspected, spied upon, directed, legislated for, regulated, confined, indoctrinated, preached at, controlled, numbered, valued, censured, and commanded, by people who have

---

[108] Proudhon, *De la Justice dans la Révolution et dans l'Église*, 3 vols. (1858).
[109] Ibid. i. 85.   [110] Ibid. 182–3.   [111] Ibid. 183.

neither the right nor the wisdom nor the virtue to do so.'[112] Proudhon continued this list of repressive activities for the best part of a page, adding *inter alia* being shot, deported, robbed, taxed, and imprisoned, but his overall point was that this was the nature of government, this its conception of justice, and this its morality. On this view, government performed no functions that could not be better undertaken by individuals; it created not order but disorder; it neither defended liberty nor protected the weak but fostered privilege and safeguarded the rich; it impoverished and indebted the people; it perpetuated antagonism and inequality in society. Faced then with the question of what form of government was required, Proudhon's answer was unequivocal: 'No authority, no government, not even popular'.[113] The solution lay in anarchy. 'Liberty, always liberty, and nothing but liberty', Proudhon wrote, 'there is the revolutionary catechism in its entirety.'[114] The problem was that we had become so infatuated with power and so liked being governed, that we could no longer imagine what it would be to live freely.

It was this that explained why the Revolution of 1789 had only done half its work. The Revolution had succeeded in destroying the feudal order but it had not created a new form of economic organization and this was so because the revolutionaries had not been able to free themselves of the prejudice in favour of government. All that had occurred was a change in 'governmental metaphysics'. One might say, Proudhon argued, that 'the nobility, clergy, and monarchy disappeared only so as to make way for another governing faction composed of Anglomaniac constitutionalists, classical republicans, and authoritarian democrats, all infatuated with the Romans and the Spartans and, above all, with themselves'.[115] An attempt had been made to solve an abuse by an abuse and it was thus no surprise that 'the bloody struggles and failures' of 1793 had ended in the reestablishment of tyranny. 'To sum up', Proudhon wrote, 'the society which the Revolution of 89 should have created does not as yet exist. What we have had for sixty years is but a superficial, factitious order, barely concealing the most frightful chaos and demoralization.'[116]

It was Proudhon's view, therefore, that since 1789 France had been subjected to a series of attempted constitutional fixes, all of which had been doomed to failure and all of which had been built upon a series of myths or fictions.[117] Despite changes in the external form, in each case the ambition had been to centralize power and to govern the people as if they were a conquered nation. If this was true of the Napoleonic Empire—Napoleon, Proudhon acknowledged, 'was the centralizer *par excellence*'—so also it was true of the government that emerged under the Second Republic. Here Proudhon spoke from bitter personal experience. In June 1848 he had been elected to the National Assembly and

---

[112] *Idée générale de la Révolution au XIXe siècle* (1923), 344.
[113] Ibid. 199.
[114] *Les Confessions d'un Révolutionnaire, pour servir à l'Histoire de la Révolution de Fevrier* (1929), 251.
[115] *Idée générale de la Révolution*, 126–7.
[116] Ibid. 127.
[117] *Contradictions politiques: Théorie du mouvement constitutionnel au XIXe siècle* (1952).

quickly found himself condemned to what he was later to describe as 'a life of hell'. When retold in his *Confessions d'un Révolutionnaire*, the experience was taken to provide clinching evidence of the futility of attempting a 'revolution from above' and of endeavouring to reform society through the instruments of the State. This, he declared, was nothing less than revolution through dictatorship and despotism and no one was subjected to more severe criticism in this regard than Louis Blanc and his neo-Jacobin version of 'governmental socialism'.

For his part, Proudhon wanted a 'revolution from below', a revolution made not in the name of the masses but by the masses themselves, a revolution whose intention was not to strengthen the authority of government but to secure the abolition of all authority, a revolution that prioritized not the seizure of political power by either insurrection or the ballot box but the transformation of the economic organization of society through the direct action of the workers, a revolution characterized by popular spontaneity and not rigid utopian dogma. Between this 'democratic' socialism and the hierarchical and centralizing socialism of Louis Blanc, Proudhon insisted, there existed a veritable abyss and one that could never be bridged.

The alternative presented by Proudhon was that of mutualism. 'Whoever says mutuality', Proudhon wrote, 'envisions the sharing of the land, the division of property, the independence of work, the separation of industries, the specialism of functions, and individual and collective responsibility.'[118] Under such a system, the worker would no longer be a slave to the State or be 'swallowed up by a communitarian ocean' but would be a free and truly sovereign individual. Society would be conceived in terms of equilibrium and balance rather than hierarchy and compulsion. The evils of unrestricted competition would be countered by the benefits of association and of equitable exchange. If private property would be retained, it would be purged of its abuses, thus, in Proudhon's view, putting an end to the economic exploitation of man by man and providing a bulwark against the unwarranted intrusions of the State. In political terms, mutualism entailed federalism, localism, and an end to the dominance of Paris and the unitary state. The individual would govern himself and the principle of the sovereignty of the people would be 'applied to the letter'. 'In contrast to the demands made by Rousseau for the government of his republic', Proudhon wrote, 'in the mutualist confederation the citizen would give up nothing of his liberty.'[119]

The manner in which the process of 'social liquidation' would be undertaken was sketched out on numerous occasions by Proudhon. One frequently voiced proposal was for the creation of a Bank of Exchange, later called the People's Bank. The plan was to set up a bank on mutualist principles with the intention of supplying cheap credit and thereby undermining the capitalist financial system. For a few months in 1849 such a bank actually existed, attracting as many as 27,000 subscribers. In the years of government repression that were to follow there was little possibility for further initiatives of this kind; but, from the early 1860s onwards, the workers'

---

[118] *De la Capacité politique des classes ouvrières* (1924).   [119] Ibid. 219.

movement gradually came back to life. Strikes became more frequent and associations of various kinds—mutual aid societies, co-operatives, and so on—sprang into existence. Of equal significance was the publication of the Manifesto of the Sixty in February 1864.[120] Written by Henri Tolain and signed, as its name suggests, by sixty workers from the Seine region, it argued not only that equal political rights entailed equal social rights but also that 'we who have no other property but our hands' had need of 'direct representation' and therefore that 'working-class candidates' should be prepared to stand for election. It was these developments that led Proudhon to write his last and most influential book: *De la Capacité politique des classes ouvrières*.

Proudhon advanced three propositions. First, if the working class were to possess 'political capacity', it needed to acquire consciousness of itself and of its distinctiveness from the bourgeoisie. This it had accomplished with the Revolution of 1848. Second, the working class needed to affirm an 'idea' of the conditions of its own existence and of its destiny and goals. This it had done but only partially. Third, and most importantly, the working class had to arrive at conclusions about how to put this 'idea' into practice. This it had not yet done.[121] But the lesson to be drawn was clear enough: the interests of the workers would not be advanced by members of any other social class but their own.

This idea was subsequently to have an enormous impact upon the French labour movement. After Proudhon's death in 1865, his friends and disciples took up the message of working-class autonomy and did so in an increasingly receptive environment. Certainly, the failure of the Second Republic to deliver on its promises of radical reform encouraged a growing scepticism about the effectiveness of political action on the part of the working class. When combined with what amounted to their banishment from the political realm during the Second Empire, the result was a growing distance between what was more and more recognizable as an industrial proletariat and the world of bourgeois republicanism. In these circumstances, the language of emancipation through politics, the Republic and the State carried less and less conviction. As the Manifesto of the Sixty had announced: 'It has been repeated time and time again: there are no more classes and since 1789 all Frenchmen are equal before the law. Yet for us . . . it is not easy to believe such an assertion.' The universalistic rhetoric of republicanism, in other words, had scant purchase when placed alongside the sociological realities of a French society where the working class found itself marginalized and from which, as citizens, it was excluded.

To what extent the Paris Commune of 1871 was an expression of such sentiments has been an open question ever since the moment of its brief existence and bloody repression.[122] No sooner was it crushed by the forces of the French

---

[120] A tr. can be found in Eugene Schulkind, *The Paris Commune of 1871: The View from the Left* (London, 1972), 61–2. In French see *De la Capacité politique des classes ouvrières*, 409–17.

[121] Ibid. 91–2.

[122] See Jacques Rougerie, 'La Commune et la gauche', in Becker and Candar, *Histoire des gauches*, i. 95–112.

government sitting comfortably in Versailles than its inheritance was claimed by virtually all sections of radical opinion. If Karl Marx led the way, others were quick to follow, not least former Communards who rapidly succeeded in creating a myth around what many were prepared to see as the first example of an authentic workers' state. The truth of the matter is that no one—neither Marxists, nor Proudhonians nor neo-Jacobins—could rightly claim the Commune as being exclusively their own. For all its proclamation of the abolition of the standing army and the separation of Church and State, its prevailing mood was one of moderate and patriotic republicanism combined with what was undoubtedly a genuine desire to reverse what its official programme denounced as 'the despotic, ignorant, or arbitrary centralization' of the French state. It also saw itself as heralding 'the end of the old government and clerical world; of militarism, bureaucracy, exploitation, speculation, monopolies and privilege'.[123]

If anything it was the conclusions drawn in the aftermath of the Commune that were of most significance. The deaths of an estimated 20,000 Parisians during the so-called *semaine sanglante* provided convincing proof for many that class war was a reality and that there could be no possibility of a political alliance with the bourgeoisie. This was only confirmed by the subsequent execution and imprisonment of Communards and the repression of the labour movement that continued through the next decade. Second, the overwhelming military superiority of the forces at the disposal of the government indicated that the hallowed tradition of revolutionary street fighting might well be over.

It was in this context that a sterner, and altogether more uncompromising, strategy was developed by the French trade union movement in the shape of revolutionary syndicalism. If the roots of this wholesale rejection of the political process go back to the writings of Proudhon, it also received intellectual sustenance from an increasingly vibrant anarchist movement in France. Once the futility of the tactic of propaganda by the deed became self-evident, there was many a former libertarian who sought a way of adapting the anarchist principles of spontaneous and decentralized action to the conditions of an industrialized economy.[124] However, it took the political betrayals of the Third Republic to turn irregular protests into a coherent and articulate stance.

Following the legalization of trade unions in 1884, revolutionary syndicalism was arguably at its height in the first decade of the twentieth century.[125] At the centre of its doctrine lay the conception of the trade union movement as 'le parti du travail'.[126] The *syndicat* united workers according to their economic interests and these were considered more real and permanent than any other considerations that

---

[123] 'An Official Programme of the Commune', in Schulkind, *Paris Commune*, 149–51.

[124] See Jean Maitron, *Histoire du mouvement anarchiste en France (1880–1914)*, 2 vols. (1975). See also Gaetano Manfredonia, *Les Anarchistes et la Révolution française* (1996) and Daniel Guérin, *La Révolution française et nous* (1976).

[125] In addition to my *Syndicalism in France*, see Jacques Julliard, *Autonomie ouvrière: Études sur le syndicalisme d'Action directe* (1988). For a selection of texts see Miguel Chueca (ed.), *Déposséder les possédants: La Grève générale aux 'temps héroïques' du syndicalisme révolutionnaire* (2008).

[126] Émile Pouget, *Le Parti du travail* (1905).

an individual might entertain. 'The *syndicat*', Émile Pouget, one of the leaders of the movement, wrote, 'groups together those who work against those who live by human exploitation: it brings together interests and not opinions.'[127] By implication the *syndicats* could only be open to members of the proletariat, thus excluding middle-class politicians and intellectuals whose immediate interests were taken to be in conflict with those of the workers.

In terms of both membership and organizational structure, the class-based nature of the *syndicat* was deemed to be in marked contrast to the political party. What characterized the political party (including those of the left) was that they grouped people together in terms of opinions rather than interests and therefore at best political parties possessed a fragile unity that could be easily broken when interests collided and personal ambition intervened. Parties, Pouget wrote, 'are an incoherent mishmash of men whose interests were in opposition'.[128] Stated by the practitioners of revolutionary syndicalism the point was a simple one: the *syndicat*, and not the political party, was the natural expression of the real needs and aspirations of the working class and for as long as it grouped together only members of that class it would not be deflected from pursuing the end of the exploitation created by capitalism. 'In opposition to the present society which knows only the *citizen*', Pouget wrote, 'stands from now on the *producer*.'[129]

To scorn politics was not only to be committed to the elucidation and employment of new tactics—in this case, those of direct action—but also to display contempt for the dominant revolutionary tradition drawing inspiration from the events of 1789 and the Jacobin experience. To establish the merits of the general strike, in other words, the French Revolution itself had to undergo a process of demystification. However, there was no *one* syndicalist critique of the Revolution drawing upon a series of set themes. Nor was it the case that only one practical or strategic conclusion was drawn from a rejection of the 1789 model. Rather, and as befitted a movement characterized by intellectual diversity, there was something akin to a continuous debate about the significance of the Revolution, frequently operating as a backdrop to broader tactical or ideological considerations.

Born in 1867, Fernand Pelloutier came to syndicalism via provincial radical republicanism and then orthodox Marxism. His break with Guesdism came in 1892 when, with Aristide Briand, he jointly defended the use of the general strike and thereafter he consistently advocated the organization of society as an association of free producers. Moreover, as secretary of the Fédération des Bourses du Travail from 1895 until his death in 1901, he was instrumental in creating the institutional basis of an autonomous working-class movement that, in the first decade of the twentieth century, appeared to threaten the very existence of the Third Republic.[130]

---

[127] Émile Pouget, *Le Parti du travail* (1905), 2.
[128] Ibid. 3.
[129] Émile Pouget, *L'Action directe* (1910), 1.
[130] See Jacques Julliard, *Fernard Pelloutier et les origines du syndicalisme directe* (1971). Pelloutier's most substantial written work was *La Vie ouvrière en France* (1900) and his posthumously publ. *Histoire des Bourses du Travail* (1902).

For Pelloutier, the goal of the proletariat was that 'of overturning a social organism which cannot adapt itself to the new morality and that no amount of modification could sufficiently improve and of substituting an essentially egalitarian economic regime'.[131] The central question faced by Pelloutier, therefore, was how such a transformation could be brought about. Even in his earliest writings, Pelloutier sought to distance the working class from the parliamentary process, arguing that suffrage was a complete irrelevance, but from this he moved towards a broader critique of the socialist and republican traditions. In his newspaper articles written for *La Démocratie de l'Ouest*, for example, he frequently returned to the theme that the Republic, for all its democratic façade, had failed to satisfy the hopes of the working class and this led Pelloutier to ask, in an article entitled 'L'Oeuvre de 1789', whether people were more free under the Republic than they had been under the *ancien régime*? 'Free to die of hunger, certainly. . . . Free to resist oppression? Just let the workers try to make use of their liberty' was his reply.[132] One was led to ask, Pelloutier concluded, if only the bourgeoisie had benefited from 1789.

Pelloutier specifically extended his criticisms to include the tactic, still prevalent as part of Guesdist rhetoric, of the insurrectionary seizure of state power. Pelloutier's objections to this strategy were based upon two considerations. First, the beneficiaries of past revolutions had never included the proletariat. 'The people', he wrote, 'have attempted on many occasions since the French Revolution to complete the work of 1793 and with each of these attempts we have seen politicians, profiting from the blood that has been spilt, climb over the corpses towards an assault on power.' Second, the advance of military technology, the improvement in communications, the rebuilding and modernization of cities, had turned the seizure of power by a determined revolutionary minority into an impossibility: all the advantages, most notably fire power, now lay with the State.[133]

Having belittled the achievements of the Revolution and rejected the tactics bequeathed by it to the French left, Pelloutier next commenced the formulation of what he hoped would be an alternative and also more effective means of proletarian emancipation: the general strike.[134] Conceived initially as a peaceful event which would require only a 'coalition du repos' of two weeks' duration, Pelloutier subsequently conceded that a general strike could not be confined to a passive refusal to work on the part of the proletariat. The main attraction of the general strike, however, always remained that it avoided the pitfalls of a revolutionary insurrection on the Jacobin model. While the army could be deployed against 30,000 insurgents, it was ineffective against a rebellion that was both 'everywhere and nowhere'. The army could not protect every factory and every railway line.

---

[131] Pelloutier, 'De la Révolution par la grève générale', unpubl. manuscript, 1892, in Julliard, *Fernard Pelloutier*, 280.

[132] Pelloutier, 'L'Oeuvre de 1789', *La Démocratie de l'Ouest* (24 Sept. 1892).

[133] See esp. 'De la Révolution par la grève générale', 285–95; 'La Motion de Tours', *La Démocratie de l'Ouest* (9 Sept. 1892), in Julliard, *Fernard Pelloutier*, 306–7; 'Réplique au "Temps"', ibid. 307–8; 'La semaine politique', *L'Avenir social* (19 Nov. 1893); 'Qu'est-ce que la grève générale?' (1895), in Julliard, *Fernard Pelloutier*, 326.

[134] See esp. 'Qu'est-ce que la grève générale?', 319–33.

Debate about the precise nature and detail of the tactics to be employed by the syndicalist movement continued into the first decade of the twentieth century, but the focus remained the worker as producer and not as a citizen. Combined with a recognition of the primacy of class interests this pushed the leadership of the Confédération Générale du Travail (CGT) towards the advocacy of new strategies involving sabotage,[135] strike action, consumer boycotts, go-slows, and walk-outs and away from a republican regime drawing inspiration from the principles of 1789, a process formalized in 1906 with the endorsement of the Charte d'Amiens.[136] Anti-republican sentiment permeated syndicalist propaganda. Marianne, the female symbol of republican virtue, was described by Pouget as *une salope*. 'In place of the Marianne of their dreams', he wrote, 'the people have seen a horrible seductress saving her embraces for upper-class swine.'[137] Victor Griffuelhes, another of the movement's principal figures, argued that the workers wanted the substance of emancipation and not its hollow form, the bourgeois Republic.[138] Alphonse Merrheim, recounting details of a lengthy strike in Hennebont, described how the authorities had placed the Breton town under virtual military occupation. The workers, he argued, had understood that 'the priest, the owner of the château, the director of the factory, the Republic, in their *mutual complicity*, were in equal measure the *Masters* that must be removed'.[139] A full-page cartoon printed on the front cover of the CGT's official organ, *La Voix du Peuple*, showing Georges Clemenceau, Prime Minister of the day, balancing two scales of blood and which read 'Last year I massacred the peasants of Narbonne with cavalry from Paris! This year I'm massacring the workers of Paris with cavalry from the Midi. That's Equality', perfectly encapsulated the deep antipathy felt by revolutionary syndicalists towards what they saw as the empty principles of the Republic and of 1789.[140] Pouget, pressing home the case against the use of the army to intimidate striking workers, vilified the description of conscription, the 'blood tax', as an achievement of the Revolution. 'The bourgeois revolutionaries', he wrote, 'gave the name of *right* to that which under the *ancien régime* was always called *slavery*.'[141]

After the army came a rejection of the very idea of the nation and of what was contemptuously characterized as 'le préjugé patriotard'. For the vast majority of syndicalist leaders—as an Enquête sur l'Idée de Patrie et la Classe ouvrière organized by Hubert Lagardelle's Le Mouvement socialiste revealed—talk of the superior virtues of the French nation and of the duty of all Frenchmen to defend the cultural patrimony of France was gibberish. 'I am a stranger', Griffuelhes wrote,

---

[135] See Pouget, *Le Sabotage* (1910).

[136] On the Charte d'Amiens see 'Le Syndicalisme révolutionnaire: La Charte d'Amiens a cent ans', special issue, *Mil Neuf Cent*, 24 (2006); Michel Pigenet and Pierre Robin (eds.), *Victor, Emile, Georges, Fernand et les autres ... Regards sur le syndicalisme révolutionnaire* (Bouloc, 2007).

[137] Pouget, 'Marianne la salope', in Roger Langlais (ed.), *Le Père Peinard* (1976), 194–6.

[138] Griffuelhes, 'Le Fond et la forme', *La Voix du Peuple* (29 Mar. 1903).

[139] Merrheim, 'Un grand conflit social: La Grève d'Hennebont', *Le Mouvement socialiste*, 20 (1906), 378–9.

[140] Special issue, 'L'Appel de la classe', *La Voix du Peuple* (Sept. 1908).

[141] Pouget, 'La Conscription', special issue, *La Voix du Peuple* (Jan. 1904).

'to everything that constitutes the moral dimension of our nation. I possess nothing: I must sell my labour in order to satisfy even my smallest needs. Therefore nothing which for some people forms a homeland exists for me. I cannot be a patriot.'[142]

Syndicalists, in brief, did not merely question the substance of the democratic liberties as they had come to be expressed in the Third Republic; they went further, rejecting the rhetoric, imagery, and symbolism of the Revolution itself. But was their break with the Revolution complete? The evidence would seem to suggest that it was not. An intriguing example is provided by Émile Pouget. Not only was Pouget the editor of *La Voix du Peuple* from 1900 to 1908 but his career, first as anarchist and then as syndicalist activist, stretched back to 1882. In 1889 he established a paper entitled *Le Père Peinard*, subtitled *Réflecs d'un gniaff* and written in Parisian *argot*. It was specifically modelled on Jacques Hébert's inflammatory and obscene *Le Père Duchesne*, mouthpiece of the *sans-culottes* during the Revolution. The standard fare of *Le Père Peinard* was anticlericalism, anti-parliamentarianism, and anti-militarism, and to this was added support for feminism and educational reform. However, the year of its launch provided Pouget with an ideal opportunity to berate the Revolution for its failures at the very moment of its centenary celebrations.

What the people of 1789 had wanted, Pouget wrote, was to live better than they had done under the *ancien régime*. They wanted to sit on their backsides; to fill their bellies; and 'no more be under the thumb of nobles, priests and the bourgeois'.[143] Alas, they had been 'conned' by the politicians, 'the filthy good-for-nothings' who, from Mirabeau to Robespierre, were excellent at making speeches but 'lacked courage': the Revolution had been side-tracked by 'vermin'. But it was clear how 'le populo' intended to get what they wanted. 'The burning of toll-gates', Pouget wrote, 'blazing torches thrown at sweatshops, a convent sacked and pillaged, the houses of the wealthy put under threat, all this indicates better than the storming of the Bastille what the Revolution should have been.'

Pouget's line on the Revolution did not alter significantly over the next decade. His *L'Almanach du Père Peinard*, published in 1894 and from 1896 to 1899, utilized the revolutionary calendar, its first number boldly dated as 'An 102'. An article entitled 'Ce que je vous souhaite? La Liberté!', which appeared in the 1898 issue, proclaimed in Pouget's typically vivid style: 'Whereas the framers of laws churned out a Déclaration des droits that was bloody nonsensical, [*Le Père Duchesne*] didn't mince words and gave birth to a tip-top Déclaration that boils down to this—"Don't shit on me!"' The sentiment still applied, Pouget maintained, and nothing needed to be added to it.[144] Likewise, when faced with divisions between rural and industrial workers in the first decade of the twentieth century, Pouget

[142] Griffuelhes, 'Enquête sur l'idée de patrie et la classe ouvrière', *Le Mouvement socialiste*, 16 (1905), 443.
[143] Pouget, 'La Prise de la Bastille', in Langlais, *Le Père Peinard*, 83–7.
[144] *L'Almanach du Père Peinard pour 1898*, 2.

appealed to the example of 1789–93 to show that if the Revolution had only been the work of city-dwellers it would have been no more than a riot or insurrection.[145]

These ambiguities of response towards the Revolution of 1789 were best seen in *Comment nous ferons la Révolution*, written by Pouget in collaboration with electricians' leader Émile Pataud and published in 1909.[146] Pouget and Pataud's text offered a fictional account of what its authors presumed a revolution based upon syndicalist principles would look like. Griffuelhes, a close associate of Pouget for many years, dismissed it as a piece of 'literary and imaginative fantasy' but Pouget, in reply to similar criticisms voiced by Jean Jaurès, suggested that even the most far-fetched aspects of the tale should be taken seriously.[147] Emphasized was the manner in which a revolutionary situation could be generated out of one incident—in this case, the 'massacre' of a group of workers by soldiers reduced to 'automata'—and how from this a general strike, at first spontaneous, later more organized, could arise. Demonstrations, electricity black-outs, and acts of sabotage follow as the strike spreads from Paris to the provinces and the countryside. Discipline breaks down in the army; troops side with the strikers, leading the way for a final assault upon parliament and the dissolution of both the State and the capitalist system.

Yet the constant point of reference was the revolutionary experience of 1789–93 and so much so that the two authors felt able to remark that 'revolutionary tactics have a constant identity which recurs in different times modified only by diversity of place'.[148] They also spoke of the people 'imitating the revolutionaries of the eighteenth century'.[149] Thus, at the decisive moment when hunger threatens to drive the strikers back to work, they storm the shops, taking the provisions they require. The workers arm themselves and, like their forebears, keep hold of their weapons. Rural agitation produces another *Jacquerie* and 'a re-edition of the Great Fear of 1789'. But the most striking dimension of this parallelism is to be found in the discussion of the international repercussions of the revolution. Events in France, the account continued, would engender enthusiasm from the peoples of Europe, but their governments, supported by capitalist émigrés and the forces of internal reaction, would try to kill the revolution at birth. 'The bourgeoisie of the twentieth century', Pouget and Pataud commented, 'ape the aristocracy of the eighteenth century and parody the army of Condé.'[150] France is invaded, but the revolution would be defended not by the formation of a regular army—this would imply a return to the *ancien régime*—but by the development and employment of highly sophisticated weapons which would not only crush the enemy but also effectively put an end to war.[151] Victory, however, recalled the Revolution's finest

[145] Pouget, 'Les Paysans et la Révolution', *L'Almanach de la Révolution pour 1906*, 22–6.

[146] Pouget and Émile Pataud, *Comment nous ferons la Révolution* (1909).

[147] Griffuelhes, 'A propos d'un livre', *La Vie ouvrière*, 1 (1909), 274–5; Pouget, 'L'Élève Pouget au prof. Jaurès', *La Guerre sociale* (1 Dec. 1909). The 2nd edn. of Pataud and Pouget's book (1911), pp. v–xi, had a preface by Peter Kropotkin in which he argued that, like Proudhon, the authors had provided 'a general idea of the Revolution'.

[148] Pouget and Pataud, *Comment nous ferons la Révolution*, 136.

[149] Ibid. 194.   [150] Ibid. 245.   [151] Ibid. 247–8.

hour: 'Better than on the evening of Valmy did the prophetic words of Goethe suit the occasion: "Here begins a new epoch of history".'[152]

In August 1914, after years of anti-militarist campaigning, the CGT launched neither a general strike nor an insurrection in the face of the outbreak of war. Léon Jouhaux, its general secretary, made it clear that France was fighting not a war of conquest but a war of defence against German imperialism and despotism: it was 'a war of revolution and not of reaction, truly in the tradition of 1792'.[153] Pouget, despite having been the most consistent of the syndicalists in his denunciation of the republican regime, shared these sentiments. His regular mouthpiece, *La Guerre sociale*, edited by the most vociferous of anti-patriots, Gustave Hervé, immediately announced that its title would be changed to *La Victoire* and declared that it would not seek to sabotage the defence of 'the country of Revolution'. For his part, Pouget wrote a column entitled 'La Rue', intended to catch the mood of the people in the streets. 'There is', he wrote, 'heroism in the air. The populace is saturated with it.' The people saw that theirs was a war of civilization against barbarism. '1914', Pouget announced, 'continues 1792 . . . our year is going to be a harbinger of liberty'.[154]

This is not the place to analyse in detail either the reasons for the defeat of the CGT's anti-militarist strategy or its capitulation before the wave of nationalist sentiment unleashed in the summer of 1914, but the inability of the leaders of the CGT to free themselves entirely from a residual revolutionary patriotism would seem to have been a contributory factor in both cases. If the Revolution had been betrayed by the bourgeoisie and the Third Republic was only a fallen woman who had deceived the people, there remained the experience of the *grandes journées*, of popular upheaval and protest against oppression, and, above all, of the people of France defeating the forces of counter-revolution and carrying the flag of liberty across the continent of Europe. Here was a door that allowed entry into the *union sacrée*.

One supporter of syndicalism for whom the 'poetry' of the 'epic of the wars against the coalition and that of the *journées populaires*'[155] never held any attraction was Georges Sorel. He let be known that he had not come to socialism via Jacobinism, that he did not share the 'veneration' for the men who made the French Revolution, indeed that he loathed those he called 'the terrorists of 1793'. Evidence of this profound distaste for the Revolution can be traced back to the days prior to 1892 when Sorel was employed as a civil servant in the southern town of Perpignan. In those writings, most notably *Le Procès de Socrate* of 1889 but also the numerous articles of historical analysis devoted to the study of the Revolution in the

---

[152] Ibid. 261.
[153] See Jouhaux, 'Paroles de solidarité', *La Bataille syndicaliste* (23 Aug. 1914); 'Le Prolétariat et la guerre: Des raisons de notre attitude', *La Bataille syndicaliste* (26 Sept. 1914); 'Le Prolétariat et la guerre: L'Alliance des peuples', *La Bataille syndicaliste* (27 Sept. 1914); 'A l'Assaut de l'Impérialisme allemand', *La Bataille syndicaliste* (10 Oct. 1914).
[154] Pouget's column ran from 7 Aug. to 6 Sept. 1914. See esp. the articles of 8, 18, and 21 Aug.
[155] Sorel, *Réflexions sur la violence* (1908), 116–17.

Pyrénées-Orientales region,[156] can be discerned a hatred of the Jacobin tradition, its bourgeois adherents, and their passion for dictatorial state power. Sorel himself, writing in *Réflexions sur la violence*, traced this antipathy towards the Revolution back to what he saw as the disastrous consequences of the last great upsurge of Jacobinism, the Paris Commune; the earliest of Sorel's writings that survives, a letter written in February 1872, spoke of 'the crimes of the Commune' and of 'la jésuitière rouge'.[157] Sorel's general point was that, stripped of its unwarranted prestige, all that remained of the Revolution were 'police operations, prescriptions, and the sittings of servile law courts'.[158]

The mature Sorel concentrated his criticisms of the Revolution upon three related aspects of its ideology and practice. First, if Sorel recognized that Rousseau was not responsible for the Terror and for the actions of Robespierre, he did believe that certain key Rousseauian notions had been passed on via the Revolution into contemporary democratic and republican theory. Specifically, Sorel believed that the concept of the general will had been used to justify the idea of 'government by all the citizens' despite the fact that the whole thing was nothing but a 'fiction'. 'Never', Sorel wrote, 'has anyone tried to justify the singular paradox according to which the vote of a *chaotic majority* leads to the appearance of what Rousseau calls a general will that cannot err.'[159] Further, a vote was not an indication of a deliberate and rational choice: it was 'rather an *abdication* by people who recognize their own incompetence and incapacity to act'.[160] The reality was that, during the Revolution, every *salon*, then every Jacobin leader, had come to believe that they possessed the secret of the general will, while in contemporary France that conceit was now entertained by a class of intellectuals and politicians who had turned themselves into the people's masters.[161]

The second line of criticism detailed what Sorel took to be a set of attitudes that contemporary socialism had absorbed either directly or indirectly from the Revolution.[162] Foremost among these was the idea of 'Parisian dictatorship', with the Revolution cast as 'a school of docility'. 'Even today', Sorel wrote, 'many socialists believe that if power were to fall into their hands it would be easy to impose their programme, their new morals, and their new ideas upon France.' Related to this, and exemplified in the use by the socialists of the expression 'féodalité capitaliste',

---

[156] See 'Les Représentants du peuple à l'Armée des Pyrénées-Orientales', *Revue de la Révolution*, 13 (1888), 68–9, 153–72, and 14 (1889), 40–65; 'Les Girondins de Roussillon', *Société agricole, scientifique et littéraire des Pyrénées-Orientales*, 30 (1889), 142–224; 'François Ducroix; Contribution à la psychologie des Maratistes', *Société agricole*, 33 (1892), 387–437. For a discussion of these articles see the thesis by J.-C. Despax, *Georges Sorel: Historien de la Révolution française* (Université de Montpellier III, 1984).

[157] Pierre Andreu, 'Une lettre de Sorel en 1872', *Cahiers Georges Sorel*, 2 (1984), 93–107.

[158] Sorel, *Réflexions sur la violence*, 117.

[159] Sorel, 'L'Avenir socialiste des syndicats' (1898), in *Matériaux d'une théorie du prolétariat* (1921), 118.

[160] Sorel, 'Les Dissensions de la social-démocratie en Allemagne', *Revue politique et parlementaire*, 25 (1900), 49.

[161] Sorel, *Les Illusions du progrès* (1906), 106.

[162] Sorel, 'Le Socialisme et la Révolution française', *Le Pays de France*, 1 (1899), 220–8, and 'Lichtenberger:—Le Socialisme et la Révolution française', *Le Mouvement socialiste*, 1 (1899), 122–4.

was the belief that capitalism could be decreed out of existence. 'The creators of this formula', Sorel commented, 'wished simply to let it be known that one could liquidate the present order by methods as hasty as those employed by the revolutionary assemblies to suppress feudal rights.' More telling still was Sorel's contention that the Revolution had been fundamentally inegalitarian in inspiration and aspiration. It had sought to bring into existence not what Sorel termed 'a juridical idea of equality' but a purely material conception of a fuller life, and to this had been added the notion that hidden within the old society were new men of 'talent', capable of directing the new order. Thus, Sorel concluded, it was clear that those socialist politicians 'imbued with the spirit of the Revolution' wished to preserve 'the spirit of hierarchy'.

Taken together, these remarks amounted to saying that, from the perspective of a socialism modelled upon the French Revolution, all social reform could be reduced to a change of government personnel. There was to be no radical break between the political structure of the old and the new societies. It was this theme of continuity between the *ancien régime*, the Revolution, and contemporary socialism that underpinned Sorel's third major criticism of the ideology and practice of 1789–93.

'One of the fundamental ideas of the *ancien régime*', Sorel wrote in a key chapter of *Réflexions sur la violence*, 'had been the employment of penal procedures to ruin all the powers which acted as obstacles to the monarchy.'[163] The aim had not been to maintain justice but to enhance the strength of the State and in this way it had become possible to define 'negligence, ill-will, and carelessness' as 'revolts against authority, attempted crimes, and treason'. The Revolution, Sorel argued, continued this tradition, giving immense importance to imaginary crimes, guillotining those who could not satisfy the expectations aroused by public opinion, and producing the classic piece of 'Robespierrean legislation', the law of 22 Prairial, a law whose definitions of political crime were so vague as to ensure that 'no enemy of the Revolution' could escape. Here, raised to pre-eminence, was 'the doctrine of the State'. Yet, according to Sorel, these reprehensible methods had been rendered even more formidable through the addition of moral justification provided by natural law theory. Straightforward *raison d'état* now took on the appearance of an attempt to restore humankind to the principles of primitive goodness, truth, and justice through the elimination of those 'bad citizens' whose evil influence prevented the regeneration of humanity.

From Sorel's account it is not clear how this obsession with political justice migrated through the nineteenth century to find a home in the heart of parliamentary socialism. It would be strange, Sorel remarked, if all the old ideas were quite dead. He cited the experience of the Dreyfus Affair and of the actions of the Dreyfusards in power as a contemporary example of these procedures, and added that experience showed that hitherto all revolutionaries, as soon as they had come to power, had used the language of *raison d'état*. Ultimately, one is led to conclude that for Sorel the clinching piece of evidence was provided by Jaurès's equivocation

---

[163] Sorel, *Réflexions sur la violence*, 111–39.

in his *Histoire socialiste de la Révolution française* when faced with the need to account for the actions of the Jacobins. Whatever the justice of that charge, there was no doubt about the conclusion that Sorel was to draw. 'If by chance', he wrote, 'our parliamentary socialists get to power they will prove themselves to be worthy successors of the Inquisition, of the *ancien régime,* and of Robespierre.'

The point of all this was to establish that syndicalism should not be confused in any way with parliamentary socialism. Syndicalism sought to demolish the State, not to raise a 'cult' in its honour. It conceived the transmission of power not in terms of the replacement of one intellectual elite by another but as a process of displacement, spreading power out into the workers' own organizations and enhancing the capacity of the workers to direct their own affairs. In contrast to a system of universal suffrage replete with its fictitious Rousseauian baggage, the *syndicats* would provide genuine and effective representation. Most importantly of all, the violence employed by the workers in the course of the general strike, despite being the most vivid and complete expression of class struggle, would bear no relationship to the ferocious and bloodthirsty acts of jealousy and revenge associated with the massacre of political prisoners in September 1792. With the general strike, Sorel wrote, the revolution appeared as 'a revolt, pure and simple' and as such it served the 'interests of civilization'. 'We have the right to hope', he concluded, 'that a socialist revolution carried out by pure syndicalists would not be tainted by the abominations which polluted the bourgeois revolutions.'[164]

It was precisely because, in the years after 1909, the syndicalist movement appeared to endorse some kind of *rapprochement* with the forces of parliamentary socialism that Sorel withdrew his support from it, breaking with former friends and aiding royalist Jean Variot in the publication of a new periodical entitled *L'Indépendance.* The latter act in particular, coinciding as it did with attempts by Charles Maurras and the Action Française movement to gain support among the working class, was seen by some as an indication of Sorel's support for the restoration of the monarchy. In truth, Sorel's writings in the years immediately prior to the outbreak of the First World War consisted almost entirely of a series of merciless attacks upon virtually every aspect of France's republican regime: its decaying democracy, corrupt administration, superficial art, lax morals, and shallow religion. No compromise was possible with such a decadent system of government and values. Thus, unlike Pouget and other leading syndicalists, Sorel was from the outset an unremitting opponent of the *union sacrée.* 'All socialist thought', he wrote to Italian journalist Mario Missiroli in August 1914, 'has become Jacobin'.[165] The recent dismal events showed that 'the old Jacobin tradition remained alive, a tradition formed of frenzied envy, pride and puerile imaginings'. He poured scorn on calls for the workers to relive the days of 1793, to organize a *levée en masse.* In time, he concluded, 'this war will be regarded as execrable above all because of the reawakening of the Jacobin spirit it promoted'.

---

[164] Sorel, *Réflexions sur la violence,* 139.

[165] Sorel, 'Lettres à Mario Missiroli', in *Da Proudhon a Lenin e L'Europa sotto la tormenta* (Rome, 1974), 500–14.

Remarkably, it was within this perspective that Sorel first placed news of the February Revolution in Russia led by Kerensky.[166] The *cadets* he saw as Girondins, eager to continue the war. Grand-Duke Nicholas figured as the Duc d'Orléans, Philippe-Egalité, while the 'poor Tsar' seemed condemned to imitate Louis XVI. If this revolution were to succeed, Sorel commented, the chances were that Europe would be both Cossack and republican. 'For a second time', he wrote, 'Jacobinism would govern Europe but this time the Russians would play a leading role, due to them on account of their inability to understand anything but anarchy and authority.'

There remained one final episode in Sorel's battle to sever the connections between socialism and Jacobinism. Writing in early 1917, Sorel was of the opinion that Italy alone of the European nations was in a position to defend itself from the advance of Jacobinism, but subsequently he came to believe that socialism, and possibly Europe as a whole, could avoid the dire fate threatening to overwhelm it. If Sorel continued to believe that the most likely outcome of the First World War would be the triumph of plutocracy, he now became transfixed by the 'extraordinary events' of the October Revolution and the seizure of power by the Bolsheviks. For Sorel, Lenin was the very antithesis of a Russian Jacobin, while the revolution itself had been carried out according to syndicalist principles. These views were expressed in articles, letters to numerous friends, and in new sections added to three of his most important books: *Réflexions sur la violence*, *Les Illusions du progrès*, and *Matériaux d'une théorie du prolétariat*; but the most significant manifestation came in the form of an essay which, when published in 1928 after Sorel's death, bore the title 'Ultima meditazione'.

In this text, originally intended as a preface to articles Sorel had published in Italy between 1910 and 1920, the focus fell upon attempts during the nineteenth century to free socialism from 'the prestige of the French Revolution', and 'to efface the Robespierrean tradition'. The first such attempt, according to Sorel, had been utopian socialism. 'The utopians', he wrote, 'wished to spare the people a dictatorship of Jacobin charlatans analogous to the one with which they were themselves acquainted.' But the decisive break came with the failure of the Revolution of 1848. After this, Sorel argued, Jacobinism appeared as an 'archaeological fantasy' absolutely incapable of understanding the activity of the proletariat. This picture, Sorel admitted, was complicated by the fact that Marxism had never managed entirely to free itself from this pernicious inheritance but the true interpreter of what Sorel termed 'the new juridical spirit' was Pierre-Joseph Proudhon. It had been Proudhon who had understood the importance of the workers' own organizations in fostering the growth within the proletariat of an ethics of socialism. And, for Sorel, it was the very absence of such an ethic, an absence embodied and exemplified in the arbitrary actions of the Jacobin tradition, which opened up the possibility of a return to barbarism. It was Sorel's view that the organizations that now best embodied this 'neo-Proudhonian concern' with the

---

[166] Ibid. 613–14.

development of an ethics of the producers were the soviets brought into existence by the Russian Revolution.

IV

That Sorel misunderstood the significance of the Russian Revolution and the meaning of Bolshevism cannot be denied. In this he was by no means alone. Indeed, the evidence suggests that even the anarchists in France shared similar feelings of support for the Russian Revolution. As the events of 1917 unfolded and as more information about the nature of the revolution became available, Sébastien Faure and his associates behind the principal anarchist wartime publication, *Ce qu'il faut dire*, were among the first to defend the Bolsheviks. Whatever might be the creed of Bolshevism, it was argued, the revolutionary masses were pushing the Bolsheviks beyond their original programme and towards the implementation of far-reaching reforms along anarchist lines. A similar stance was taken by *Le Libertaire* when it recommenced publication in January 1919. But now the anarchists began to grapple with the issue of the role of dictatorship in the revolution. An article of 8 June 1919 specifically entitled 'La Dictature du Prolétariat' set out the revisionist argument. Before the war, its author argued, anarchists would have been against such an authoritarian notion as the dictatorship of the proletariat but, given what now had to be recognized as the likelihood of military opposition to the revolution, the reliance upon dictatorship was a necessity.

How far this argument could go was illustrated by Victor Serge. Born in Brussels in 1890 Victor Napoléon Kibaltchitch was the son of Russian émigrés. From 1905 onwards he began to collaborate with a variety of anarchist and insurrectionary papers in France. These included Gustave Hervé's *La Guerre sociale*, Jean Grave's *Les Temps modernes* as well as *Le Libertaire*. After his move to Paris he acted as editor of *L'Anarchie*. Arrested in 1912 he remained in prison until 1917 when, under threat of extradition, he moved to Spain. It was there that he adopted the name of Victor Serge. Having returned illegally to France, he was arrested and, in January 1919, was put on board ship at the French port of Dunkirk for Petrograd. In May of that year he joined the communist party. Serge's argument—stated most vigorously in *Les Anarchistes et l'expérience de la Révolution russe*[167]—was that the realities of the revolution in Russia necessitated 'the complete and methodical revision' of anarchist thinking. Above all, Serge argued, the Russian Revolution should serve to remind the anarchists of something that had been largely forgotten since France's own revolution: revolutions were bloody affairs. 'Who says revolution', Serge wrote, 'says violence, and all violence is dictatorial.' Upon pain of death, he continued, 'the most advanced minority of the proletariat' had 'immediately to take up the task of dictatorship'. No half-measures were possible. Red terror had to be used to match White terror as a war of revolutionary defence would be

---

[167] Victor Serge, *Les Anarchistes et l'expérience de la Révolution russe* (1921).

unavoidable. It was, he remarked, thanks to the Jacobin clubs that France had emerged victorious from its battles with Europe's monarchical coalition and the same lesson applied to the Bolsheviks in Russia. Moreover, 'the general lack of culture in the Russian people' entailed 'an inevitable Jacobinism'. Little of this, Serge believed, need pose any problems for anarchists because the goal of the Bolsheviks was 'the complete implementation of the communist programme', was 'libertarian communism' and 'anarchy'.

Nevertheless there emerged a consensus among the anarchists that the 'libertarian revolution' was being betrayed. Disquiet initially took the form of arguing that the revolution appeared temporarily to be locked into what one writer in *Le Libertaire* called its 'authoritarian stage', but, with each month, praise for the courage of the Bolsheviks became increasingly qualified and hedged in by doubts about their true intentions. The official break—as Faure was later to recount in one of his most heartfelt articles[168]—came in January 1921. In that month *Le Libertaire* launched a series of articles entitled 'En Russie Sovietique', written by the Spanish anarchist Wilkens and recounting his experiences during his six-month stay in Russia. The conclusions were damning. The Revolution and Bolshevism were not one and the same thing. The communist party was quickly moving towards the creation of 'a class which has interests opposed to those of the revolutionary masses'. Dictatorship was 'an instrument of oppression' in the hands of this new class. The Bolsheviks made greater use of terror than had the Tsarist regime. If a break with capitalism was being made, the proletariat were being placed under 'a new yoke'. The true revolutionaries, and specifically the anarchists, were being 'persecuted, imprisoned, and shot without trial'. The soviets were being turned into 'the instruments of bureaucracy'. The Red Army was but the tool of what increasingly looked like a militarist regime. The idea of workers' control of the factories had already been forgotten.

All of this, it should be noted, was written and published before the brutal repression of the uprising by sailors and soldiers at Kronstadt in March 1921. These tragic events were simply added to the picture as 'the best and the worst illustration' of *Le Libertaire*'s thesis that the revolution in Russia had been killed at birth. 'The massacre of the proletariat at Kronstadt', proclaimed one anonymous article, 'is a more ignominious crime than that committed by the French bourgeoisie in 1871, because this crime was committed in the name of a socialist Republic.' What is more, for the anarchists of *Le Libertaire*, the revolution of 1917 had come to resemble France's own revolution of 1789. In both cases, 'the inspired enthusiasm of the people had been redirected by the bourgeois politicians of the day to their own advantage and to that of their class'.[169]

In point of fact, the reality behind the Soviet myth was known almost from the outset and was certainly not unknown to the most important intellectuals of the left. As Christian Jelen has shown,[170] the newspaper of the then French socialist

---

[168] 'Il y a un an', *Le Libertaire* (13 Jan. 1922).
[169] Editorial, *Le Libertaire* (2 Dec. 1922).
[170] Christian Jelen, *L'Aveuglement: Les Socialistes et la naissance du mythe soviétique* (1984).

party, *L'Humanité*, was fortunate to have had a correspondent, Boris Kritchevski, in Petrograd at the moment of the October Revolution and his account of what actually occurred and of what the Bolsheviks believed subsequently proved to have been remarkably accurate. There was never any intention, Kritchevski argued, of installing a republic of the soviets; a military plot had brought the Bolsheviks to power; and there they intended to stay by any means. However, his reports quickly met with censorship from his colleagues and then the socialist daily decided to dispense with his services altogether. Similarly, between November 1918 and March 1919 the Ligue des Droits de l'Homme (an organization founded in 1898 to defend Captain Dreyfus) undertook a public inquiry into the situation in Russia. The unambiguous conclusion was that the Bolshevik regime paid scant attention to the rights of man, was undemocratic, and was a travesty of socialism. A party dictatorship, it concluded, was being established. But here, as was so often to be the case, there was an unwillingness to acknowledge that the faults were inherent to the Bolshevik model and accordingly due homage was paid to the great ideals that had inspired the revolution. Later, with the rise to power of Hitler, the Ligue des Droits de l'Homme hid behind the casuistic argument that, whereas under fascism the rights of man were denied out of conviction, under Bolshevism they were denied only out of necessity.[171]

Nonetheless, in the years that followed the USSR was not without its critics, many of them drawn from the left.[172] In 1935, former communist Boris Souvarine published his monumental and deeply critical study of Stalin[173]—arguably one of the most important books of the twentieth century—and a year later André Gide published his *Retour de l'URSS*,[174] an account that mixed admiration with a sense of the all-pervasive conformism being imposed upon Soviet society. Not even in Hitler's Germany, Gide wrote, was thought less free and more terrorized. Nor were the melons available for purchase in the shops of good quality! From within France's own dissident Marxist tradition, the Soviet Union was subsequently characterized as a 'degenerate workers' state' and then, much later, by Cornelius Castoriadis and his group Socialisme ou barbarie, as a form of 'total bureaucratic capitalism'.[175] State socialism and party capitalism were also contenders as descriptions of the reality of the Soviet Union and to this, although somewhat belatedly, was added totalitarian.[176]

The fact of the matter was that among wide sections of opinion—stretching from the far left until well into the middle of the political spectrum—the Russian Revolution enjoyed an almost immediate respect and adulation. Romain Rolland, Anatole France, and Henri Barbusse were just three of the well-known literary figures prepared to voice their support for the Bolsheviks and for what they took to

---

[171] Christian Jelen, *Hitler ou Staline: Le Prix de la paix* (1984).

[172] See Sophie Cœuré, 'Communisme et anticommunisme', in Becker and Candar, *Histoire des gauches*, ii. 487–506.

[173] *Staline, Aperçu historique du bolchévisme* (1935).

[174] André Gide, *Retour de l'URSS* (1936).

[175] See Robert Desjardins, *The Soviet Union through French Eyes* (London, 1988).

[176] See Jeannine Verdès-Leroux, *Le Reveil des somnambules, 1956–1985* (1987).

be their goals of peace and liberty. Several factors were at play here. The first, and probably the most powerful, was opposition to the carnage of the First World War, a sentiment which in many cases led to an identification with pacifism.[177] In this context, the Bolsheviks appeared to represent the hope of a new international order and it was undoubtedly the case that many of those who were among the first to rally to the PCF did so with this in mind and with scant concern for the canons of Marxism. The second consideration had even less to do with the realities of the situation in Russia. The policy of support for the national war effort had entailed collaboration with those formerly regarded as class enemies. Support for the Russian Revolution—albeit that it was someone else's revolution and on the other side of Europe—allowed for a sense of reidentification with the original principles of socialism and with the working class in general. Thus, for example, a yet-to-be-disillusioned Boris Souvarine could pen an *Éloge des Bolsheviks* in 1919 and there write: 'Let us further the superhuman effort of the heroic pioneers of the social revolution, let us glorify the courageous and intelligent innovators who have sacrificed themselves for socialism and the emancipation of the people, in the hope that we may show ourselves to be worthy of them. Let us not limit ourselves to saluting the creators of the new world but let their example inspire us.'[178]

The third motive for support of the Bolsheviks had a decidedly French angle. Lenin and his comrades were not just demonstrating that a revolution was possible but were also doing so in a manner that recalled the revolutionary experience of the French people. The problem here was that among the French left there was no agreed interpretation of the French Revolution or of the revolutionary tradition it had spawned and thus the Bolsheviks could be seen as doing a variety of different things, praiseworthy or otherwise. However, it was as early as 1920 that the socialist historian Albert Mathiez sought to portray what he saw as the resemblance between Bolshevism and Jacobinism, between Lenin and Robespierre. His *Le Bolchévisme et le Jacobinisme*[179] affirmed unequivocally that 'Jacobinism and Bolshevism are dictatorships of the same kind; both are born out of civil and foreign war; both are class dictatorships, using the same means: terror, requisitioning and price controls; and both ultimately pursue the same goal, the transformation of society, and not just the transformation of Russian and French society but of society in general.'[180] On this account the list of similarities was truly extensive. Both sought to carry the revolution abroad; both were led by men drawn from the former ruling classes; both relied upon the population of the cities and especially the capital; both had succeeded in winning over the peasantry; and both placed the rights of society over those of the individual. More than this, the 'two dictatorships' were 'eminently realistic' and both, in the 'interest of public safety', were prepared to compromise their principles. Both Lenin and Robespierre, Mathiez wrote, wished to see the

---

[177] See Nicole Racine, 'Pacifisme, socialisme et communisme naissant', *Communisme*, 18–19 (1988), 34–49. On the phenomenon of inter-war pacifism see Norman Ingram, *The Politics of Dissent: Pacifism in France 1919–1939* (Oxford, 1991).

[178] Boris Souvarine, *Éloge des Bolsheviks* (1919), 5.

[179] Albert Mathiez, *Le Bolchévisme et le Jacobinisme* (1920).

[180] Ibid. 3–4.

suppression of the death penalty but both were prepared to use it as 'a means of government'. Both were in favour of freedom of the press but both had suppressed the newspapers of the opposition. In brief, both saw that 'the end justifies the means' and for both that end was 'the happiness of the masses'. 'History', Mathiez concluded, 'never repeats itself exactly; but the resemblances revealed by our analysis of the great crises of 1793 and 1917 are neither superficial nor fortuitous. The Russian revolutionaries are intentionally and knowingly imitating the French revolutionaries. They are animated by the same spirit. They move among the same problems in an analogous atmosphere.'[181]

Blessed with such a favourable intellectual environment, a rapidly 'bolshevized' French Communist Party (PCF) had little difficulty in convincing its adherents that the USSR was the home of socialism, that Moscow (in the words of the PCF's general-secretary) was a 'holy city', and that a terrestrial Eden and 'superior civilization' was in the process of creation.[182] As time went on, there appeared to be no shortage of evidence to support these claims. Between 1917 and the Second World War no less than 125 (for the most part uncritical) accounts of visits to the Soviet Union were published in France alone. The list is even longer if the numerous novels inspired by the Soviet experience are included. Unfortunately, there is little indication that many of their writers went beyond Moscow (in some cases, beyond the Kremlin and the Hotel Lux!) or that they spoke Russian and hence were able to free themselves from the influence of the Bolshevik propaganda machine.[183] Nothing was left to chance by the Soviet authorities. Laid on for André Gide, for example, was a swimming pool full of handsome young soldiers from the Red Army and even homosexual encounters were prearranged in order that Gide could be blackmailed if necessary.[184] When Jean-Paul Sartre visited the Soviet Union in 1962 he was given the curvaceous Lena Zonina as his guide.[185] A whole series of front organizations (the most prominent of which was Les Amis de l'URSS) designed to enhance the image of the Soviet Union as the land of peace and progress complemented the PCF in its self-appointed role as the sole, authoritative source of information on the subject. When, after the Second World War, the achievements of the Red Army at Stalingrad and the sacrifices of the Russian people were translated into ideological ascendancy in such diverse fields as art, literature, philosophy, and even science, there seemed little that could shake the hold of the Soviet myth over French public and intellectual opinion.[186] As Robert Desjardins remarked in *The Soviet Union through French Eyes*: 'Any person daring to level criticism against the Soviet Union was automatically accused of playing

---

[181] Albert Mathiez, *Le Bolchévisme et le Jacobinisme* (1920), 22.

[182] Quoted in Dominique Desanti, *Les Staliniens* (1975), 34.

[183] See Fred Kupferman, *Au pays des Soviets: Le Voyage français en Union soviétique 1917–1939* (1979) and Sophie Cœuré, *La Grande lueur à l'Est: Les Français et l'union soviétique 1917–1939* (1999).

[184] Herbert Lottman, *The Left Bank* (Boston, Mass., 1982), 113–15.

[185] Carole Seymour-Jones, *A Dangerous Liaison: Simone de Beauvoir and Jean-Paul Sartre* (London, 2008), 411–29.

[186] See Jeannine Verdès-Leroux, *Au Service du parti: Le Parti Communiste, les intellectuels et la culture (1944–1956)* (1983).

into the hands of the class enemy and labelled as a member of the imperialist and fascist camp.'[187] Even the existence of the *gulag*—firmly attested after 1945 by the accounts provided by escaped German and Polish prisoners—could be denied with apparent sincerity (and not only by the PCF itself but by others such as Jean-Paul Sartre).

Once transformed into a replica of its Soviet counterpart, the PCF became the French section of the international communist movement.[188] Defining itself as *the* party of the French working class, it was rebuilt according to the twenty-one conditions that determined membership of the Comintern[189] and was committed to a rigid conception of Marxism-Leninism. Closely controlled from Moscow, it was run on democratic-centralist lines and came to establish a panoply of factory cells, trade unions, newspapers, clubs, and associations. Frequently seen as a society within a society,[190] the PCF succeeded in establishing its own distinctive style, a language (the famous *langue de bois*), a culture, and an identity all of its own.[191] It was into this worldview that the party activist would be drawn, accepting its rules, its discipline, and its objects of veneration, and so much so that no life seemed possible outside its confines.[192]

To what extent this ideological and organizational framework led inevitably to a willing embrace of the dictates of Stalinism is open to discussion (and touches upon questions that relate to the entire history of Marxism in the twentieth century), but there can be no doubt that the PCF fell victim to the personality cult: Stalin was at once the father figure, spiritual leader, sage, and undisputed expert in all fields of knowledge, the very exemplar of all that was finest in communist man. 'Comrade Stalin', acting party secretary Jacques Duclos told the PCF's 1953 national conference in a speech of deep emotion mourning their terrible loss, was 'the greatest man of his age'.[193] If the party's own leader, Maurice Thorez, received similar adulation and devotion, behind the reverence for Stalin lay a continued worship of the Soviet Union as the home of socialism. Surrounded by its enemies (and hence meriting unqualified loyalty), the USSR was the very model of a proletarian nation, a laboratory in which a new world of prosperity and emancipation for all was being forged, a civilization superior in every respect to that of capitalism, be it in the fields of art, literature, housing, science, or healthcare. No praise seemed too excessive for its heroic leaders and people.

An uncritical stance towards the Soviet Union constituted only one part of French communism's ideological identity. Another key ingredient was an unabashed nationalism. From the time of the Popular Front of the 1930s, if not

---

[187] Desjardins, *Soviet Union through French Eyes*, 13.
[188] See Nicole Racine and Louis Bodin, *Le Parti Communiste Français pendant l'entre-deux-guerres* (1972). For an account of the PCF's later history see D. S. Bell and Byron Criddle, *The French Communist Party in the Fifth Republic* (Oxford, 1994).
[189] These conditions covered party organization, doctrine, and strategy.
[190] See Annie Kriegel, *Les Communistes français* (1968).
[191] See Georges Lavau, *A quoi sert le Parti Communiste?* (1981).
[192] See e.g. Edith Thomas, *Le Témoin compromis: Mémoires* (1995).
[193] Bernard Legendre, *Le Stalinisme français: Qui a dit quoi? (1944–1956)* (1980), 66–8.

before, the PCF did not hesitate to articulate passages of astonishing lyricism in praise of France, her natural beauty, her moderate climate, her civilized culture, her generous people, her industrial ingenuity, and even the richness of her food and wine.

To this, as was illustrated by such texts as Thorez's *La Mission de la France dans le monde*,[194] was added the universalist message of France as the country of progress, liberty, and peace. Such a description necessarily entailed a particular vision of the course of French history and this inevitably involved fixing upon an interpretation of the French Revolution. Viewed from the prevailing orthodoxy within the PCF, the Revolution of 1789 was a bourgeois revolution marking the passage from feudalism to capitalism and the victory of a new industrial class over the aristocracy of the *ancien régime*. In ideological terms it denoted the triumph of the *Encyclopédistes* and of the philosophy of materialism. Yet, following the reading provided by Jean Jaurès, the Revolution was also seen to contain the potential to effect a transformation from political democracy to social democracy, to a society of justice and fraternity and one dominated by the masses. To that extent the communists were able to portray themselves as the descendants of the revolution-aries of the eighteenth century and as defenders of the 'great principles' of the Revolution, and it was this stance that allowed Thorez to place the PCF at the forefront of those celebrating its 150th anniversary in 1939.[195] More than this, 1789 also represented the moment when France affirmed herself for the first time as a nation. From here it was but a short step to an identification of the interests of the working class with those of the nation as a whole and then to a designation of any challenge to the independence of France as a direct threat to the French proletariat.[196] Patriotic rhetoric of this kind was a prefiguration of communist participation in the Resistance during the Second World War. In short, at the heart of communist ideology were to be found the twin symbols of the red flag and the tricolour.

Where did writers, philosophers, and intellectuals more generally fit into this picture?[197] As the heir to the long-established tradition of *ouvriérisme*, the PCF gloried in the celebration of proletarian values and identity. From this perspective, the party leadership was to remain under the control of its working-class activists and bourgeois intellectuals were not to be trusted to represent the workers' inter-ests. Nevertheless, the PCF saw the utility of intellectuals in its struggle to displace bourgeois cultural hegemony and to defeat its capitalist enemies. The various mechanisms used by the PCF to control a group of people it viewed with undisguised suspicion were long ago laid bare by David Caute,[198] but not everyone

---

[194] Thorez's *La Mission de la France dans le monde* (1937).

[195] See Thorez, 'Vive la grande Révolution française', *Œuvres choisies en trois volumes,* ii. *1939–1950* (1966), 125–53.

[196] See Marc Lazar, 'Damné de la terre et homme de marbre: L'Ouvrier dans l'Imaginaire du PCF du milieu des années trente à la fin des années cinquante', *Annales ESC,* 45 (1990), 1071–96.

[197] See Sudhir Hazareesingh, *Intellectuals and the French Communist Party: Disillusion and Decline* (Oxford, 1991).

[198] David Caute, *Communism and the French Intellectuals* (London, 1964).

was expected to adopt the *esprit du parti* later demanded by Central Committee member Laurent Casanova in *Le Parti Communiste, les intellectuels et la nation*.[199] Indeed, the PCF often preferred its intellectual sympathizers to remain outside the party and to play the role of *compagnon de route* or fellow-traveller. Nevertheless, the result was the imposition of a deadening uniformity, with whole swathes of French intellectual and artistic life—not least the historiography of the Revolution of 1789—reduced to stultifying orthodoxy. If the disciplines of history and philosophy were particularly affected, science too was not untouched by the absurdities of a crude dialectical materialism.[200] Worse still was the slavish subservience and bad faith witnessed with every dramatic change in party line. With one or two notable exceptions, independent and original socialist thought effectively died during these years, those remaining outside the orbit of the communist party being subject to sustained vilification.

The power and influence of the PCF over intellectual opinion in France was at its height during the Fourth Republic (1946–58). These years were also ones of considerable electoral support, with the party regularly securing between 25 and 30 per cent of the popular vote. Now, with the advent of the Cold War, to an uncritical admiration of the USSR was affixed an equally fervent anti-Americanism. In the communist imagination, the United States stood for consumerism (Coca-Cola), philistinism (the English language), economic imperialism (the Marshall Plan), and barbarism (germ warfare in the Korean War).[201] 'The awakening of the sleepwalkers', according to Jeannine Verdès-Leroux,[202] began in the mid-1950s and with the Soviet invasion of Hungary in 1956 and Khrushchev's denunciation of Stalin before the XXth Congress of the CPSU it became increasingly difficult to sustain a positive image of the USSR and, indeed, of the French Communist Party itself. For their part, many among the leftist intelligentsia drifted off into one or other variety of *gauchisme*, their faith in the Soviet Union conveniently replaced by a new-found enthusiasm for the oppressive regimes of Mao's Communist China or Fidel Castro's Cuba.[203]

For the leadership of the PCF (as well as for many of its adherents) the Soviet myth endured for almost as long as the Soviet Union itself, its leader Georges Marchais famously describing the achievements of the USSR as being 'generally positive' as late as the PCF's 23rd National Congress in 1979. How that myth was sustained and how it remained a powerful motivating force is itself a fascinating topic and says much about the human need for the certainty of ultimate victory, not to mention the capacity for self-deception. How, against all the

---

[199] Laurent Casanova, *Le Parti Communiste, les intellectuels et la nation* (1949).

[200] See Michael Kelly, *Modern French Marxism* (Oxford, 1982) and Bud Burkhard, *French Marxism between the Wars: Henri Lefebvre and the 'Philosophies'* (New York, 2000).

[201] See Richard Kuisel, *Seducing the French: The Dilemma of Americanization* (Berkeley, Calif., 1993), 15–69.

[202] Verdès-Leroux, *Le Reveil des somnambules*.

[203] See Jeannine Verdès-Leroux, *La Lune et le Caudillo: Le Rêve des intellectuels et le régime cubain (1959–1971)* (1989) and François Hourmont, *Au pays de l'Avenir radieux: Voyages des intellectuels français en URSS, à Cuba et en Chine* (2000). See also Richard Wolin, *The Wind from the East: French Intellectuals, the Cultural Revolution and the Legacy of the 1960s* (Princeton, NJ, 2010).

evidence, the passion for communism managed to retain its hold over so many French intellectuals for so long is an even more intriguing question. To the factors already cited might be added not only the laudable struggle against fascism but also the conviction held by many after the Great Depression that capitalism had no future. François Furet, in one of the most important books published in France over the last twenty years,[204] accepted both of the above explanations but added an important psychological explanation: the intellectual's love of communism was a form of bourgeois self-hatred. The 'communist idea', he argued, was sustained by an unremitting scorn for the ugliness and mediocrity of bourgeois society and for the bourgeois as an individual. Whatever the explanation, French intellectuals of the left failed in their responsibility to tell the truth about Soviet totalitarianism.[205]

Then, with astonishing speed, everything changed.[206] The language of revolutionary politics virtually vanished in the space of less than a decade. Its last gasp was Althusserian Marxism. In brief summary, Louis Althusser, the leading philosopher within the PCF, effected a brilliant reformulation of Leninism in order to prevent the de-Stalinization of the party from degenerating into a revival of the humanist language of democratic rights and social democracy. To that end, history had to be reduced to a 'process without a subject' and Stalinism was redescribed as a theoretical error.[207] By the mid-1970s, however, the game was up and only the most blinkered and self-deluded could fail to see the PCF and its spiritual fatherland for the moribund and discredited institutions that they were. In these circumstances revolution was exorcized. First, the Bolshevik Revolution and its totalitarian outcome was subjected to detailed and systematic criticism, the so-called New Philosophers (Bernard-Henri Lévy, Alain Finkielkraut, and André Glucksmann among others) claiming great credit for seeing what outside France had long been self-evident.[208] Then, and even more fundamentally, the French Revolution itself was implicated in the totalitarian nightmare. With (former Communist) François Furet at the forefront, terror was now seen as an integral and not a contingent part of the Jacobin project and hence of modern revolutionary politics. If the French and Bolshevik Revolutions were inextricably linked, it was only for them to be

---

[204] Furet, *Le Passé d'une illusion: Essai sur l'Idée communiste au XXe siècle* (1995). Furet was a member of the PCF between 1949 and 1956.

[205] Judt, *Past Imperfect: French Intellectuals 1944–56* (Berkeley, Calif., and Oxford, 1992). Judt's text was first publ. in French and was not warmly received. On the broader theme see Judt, *The Burden of Responsibility: Blum, Camus, Aron and the French Twentieth Century* (Chicago, 1998).

[206] See Sunil Khilnani, *Arguing Revolution: The Intellectual Left in Postwar France* (New Haven, Conn., 1993).

[207] Althusser's most important books were *Pour Marx* (1965) and the jointly authored *Lire 'Le Capital'* (1965). But see also his autobiographical essay *L'Avenir dure longtemps* (1992), which begins with Althusser's account of his murder of his wife. For a biography see Yann Moulier Boutang, *Louis Althusser* (1992) and for a sympathetic study see Gregory Elliot, *Althusser: The Detour of Theory* (1987). For a less sympathetic appraisal see Judt, 'French Marxism 1945–1975', *Marxism and the French Left*, 169–238.

[208] The best-known examples are Lévy's *La Barbarie à visage humain* (1977) and Glucksmann's *La Cuisinière et le mangeur d'hommes: Essai sur les rapports entre l'État, le marxisme et les camps de concentration* (1975) and *Les Maîtres penseurs* (1977).

inextricably condemned. The irony of ironies was that it was at this very moment, as its historic vision and sense of ideological identity was on the point of collapse, that in 1891 the left (with four government ministers drawn from the PCF) came to power on a programme committed to making a final break with the capitalist system. Only further disillusionment was to follow.

10

France, Intellectuals, and Engagement

I

1896 marked not the opening of the Dreyfus Affair—the innocent Captain Dreyfus had to wait a further two years before novelist Émile Zola penned his open letter 'J'accuse'—but rather another event of immense importance: the 1400th anniversary of the baptism of Clovis, first king of the Franks and founder of the Merovingian dynasty, at Rheims in 496. It was this act that had secured France's place as the 'eldest daughter' of the Church and which, when celebrated at the end of the nineteenth century, provided Catholics with the opportunity to reassert that Christianity represented the inescapable destiny of France. As Eugène Léotard stated in one of the many speeches and lectures made to celebrate the anniversary: 'France will be Christian or it will no longer be France.'[1] From this perspective, the baptismal act had tied not merely Clovis but the entire French nation to the Church, bequeathing a spiritual principle that would permanently define the collective identity of France and her history. 'Whatever have been our weaknesses and our faults', declared the Jesuit Jules Pachau before the church of Saint-Sulpice in Paris, 'the public power, word, heart and sword of France appear in history as a power, a word, a heart and a sword faithful to the cause of the Church and of God.'[2] If France should turn away from this primordial reality the result would be chaos.

For all this heartfelt celebration, the primacy accorded to the Roman Catholic religion in this description of the meaning of France ran up against one major, if not insurmountable, problem: in 1789 France had contradicted her vocation and her mission, the Revolution and the Republic denying France's ancient faith and history. Moreover, this violation of France's Catholic destiny came replete with its own conception of France's identity, one forged by the experiences of the Revolution and of the Napoleonic Empire and one resting upon less essentialist and more voluntaristic assumptions: the destiny of France was now wedded to the new doctrines of liberty, equality, and the rights of man.

Yet, in the aftermath of the defeat of 1870, France was a demoralized nation, shame at the military 'debacle' suffered by her army compounded by the loss of the

---

[1] *Le Quatorzième centenaire du baptême de la France: conférence faite aux facultés catholiques de Lyon* (Lyons, 1896), 52.
[2] *Église et Patrie* (1897), 9.

territories of Alsace and Lorraine to the new German Empire.[3] Despite the recovery and growth of her economy—as well as the air of luxury associated with the *Belle Époque*—subsequent diplomatic humiliation at the hands of Great Britain over territorial claims to the Sudan only seemed to confirm that France was a second-rate power, somewhere on a par with lowly Italy. Dishonour and cruel deception appeared to have deprived both the vision of France as the eldest daughter of the Church and that of France as the beacon of humanity of much of their meaning and substance.

Given this, it is tempting to imagine that the political thought of the period was overwhelmingly preoccupied with the military threat posed by Prussia and by a sense of France's cultural and intellectual inferiority when compared to her powerful eastern neighbour. This was certainly the view presented by Claude Digeon in *La Crise allemande de la pensée française (1870–1914)*.[4] Nor is it a view without justification. For many defeat on the battlefield derived as much from the superiority of German science and her education system as it did from the inadequacies of the French army and the folly of Napoleon III. Patriotic duty demanded not only military reorganization but also the imitation of Germany's universities. It was in this spirit that Émile Boutmy established the École Libre des Sciences Politiques. His express intention was to provide the State with the professionally trained administrators required for a modern, technically proficient civil service.[5] At another level, the romanticized picture provided by Madame de Staël of Germany as a temple of philosophy and literature was eclipsed by that of a barbarian nation, its people subject to an impersonal and hierarchical discipline, its values those of materialism, organization, and economic might. At best, there appeared to be two Germanies, one civilized, the other cruel and immoral, with an unbridgeable abyss separating the two.

It would be a mistake, however, to conclude that political thinking in France after 1870 consisted solely of an extended comparison between the relative merits of a Protestant and monarchical Germany and a Catholic and republican France. Rather, the disorientation and dismay prompted by defeat engendered not only an analysis of the causes of France's ignominious surrender and subsequent political disintegration but also a searching reappraisal of the nature of the nation and of the character of France herself. If this quest was to continue throughout much of the remainder of the life of the Third Republic it was because it fostered a debate without possible resolution. In the first place there could be no agreement about the mechanism through which national renewal was to be achieved. Was it to be through a collective display of penitence and moral renovation, or perhaps the creation of a great overseas empire, or even—perish the thought—a swiftly executed act of revenge over an ignoble enemy?[6] These were just some of the

---

[3] Published to great acclaim in 1892, *La Débâcle* was the nineteenth and penultimate volume of Émile Zola's Rougon-Macquart series of novels.

[4] Claude Digeon, *La Crise allemande de la pensée française (1870–1914)* (1959).

[5] See Pierre Favre, *Naissances de la science politique en France, 1870–1914* (1989), 19–50.

[6] See Bertrand Joly, 'La France et la Revanche', *Revue d'histoire moderne et contemporaine*, 46 (1999), 325–47.

contending views articulated at the time. Still more problematically, for as long as the deep divide separating republican and Catholic France continued to exist, there could be no end to the search for the true or real France. Between the rural France of the peasantry and the land, of the parish priest and the château—Black France—and the urban, egalitarian, and secular France of the factory worker and the cosmopolitan intellectual—Red France—there was little common ground and little room for agreement about the nation's identity.[7]

This might be illustrated by reference to the figure of Jeanne d'Arc. In his history of France, Jules Michelet had presented a potent image of Jeanne d'Arc as the embodiment of the national sentiment of the people. Scorned by the monarchy, betrayed by the Church, in his account it had been this simple peasant girl who had been the saviour of France. It was in part to counter this portrayal of Jeanne d'Arc as a secular heroine inspired by love of country rather than by religious visions that, in 1869, the Catholic Church in France began moves to secure her beatification and canonization, a process completed in 1920. In the intervening years, and as controversy raged, *la Pucelle d'Orléans* became an object of veneration for the Catholic (and Anglophobic) right, the very incarnation of the land and of national unity, the unblemished symbol of purity and spirituality. It was against this backdrop of post-1870 patriotism and increasing Catholic fervour that the novelist Anatole France wrote his own account her life and in doing so did much to deflate many of the myths surrounding her iconic status as the miraculous protector of Christian France. Anatole France attributed Jeanne d'Arc's military victories to the weaknesses of the English army rather than to any supposed act of divine intervention.[8] At the time of Jeanne d'Arc, he argued, the notion of a homeland or *patrie* had not existed and, although the sentiment had undoubtedly come into existence under the *ancien régime*, it was only with the Revolution that the idea of national unity and of the integrity of the territory became firmly fixed in people's minds. 'Twenty-three years of wars', he wrote, 'confirmed our forefathers in their love of the *patrie* and their hatred of the foreigner.'[9]

In this context, it is interesting to note that when, in 1913, the political scientist André Siegfried published his *Tableau politique de la France de l'Ouest*[10] he did so with the intention of looking beyond the 'metaphysical' divisions associated with political ideology in order to grasp what he saw as the 'infinite variety' and 'complex personality of the nation'.[11] Despite the appearance of rapid change, his detailed examination of the electoral geography of the region revealed striking levels of continuity in voting behaviour and 'political temperament' over generations. In this

---

[7] See Douglas Johnson, 'The Two Frances: The Historical Debate', in Vincent Wright (ed.), *Conflict and Consensus in France* (London, 1979), 3–10. See also Herman Lebovics, *True France: The Wars over Cultural Identity, 1900–1945* (Ithaca, NY, 1992).

[8] *Vie de Jeanne d'Arc* (1908).

[9] Ibid., p. lxxii.

[10] André Siegfried, *Tableau politique de la France de l'Ouest sous la Troisième République* (1913). See also Philippe Veitl, 'Pour une géologie des opinions: André Siegfried et la « science » des cartes', in Olivier Ihl, Martine Kaluszynski, and Gilles Pollel (eds.), *Les Sciences du gouvernement* (2003), 39–52.

[11] *Tableau politique*, pp. v–viii.

part of 'old France', he wrote, 'the battles of the past carry on'.[12] In later work Siegfried concluded similarly that party divisions were the product of 'opposing conceptions of life'. He was also of the view that a Frenchman wore 'his heart on the left and his pocket is on the right—and in practice every Frenchman has a pocket!'[13]

Next, we need to recognize that the secession of Alsace and Lorraine to Prussia induced a deep psychological trauma among many members of France's intellectual establishment. To take but one example, for Jules Michelet, now nearing the end of his life, the tearing way of France's eastern provinces was akin to a form of physical amputation, with the Germans accused of brutally removing vital organs from a living body. Of all peoples, he believed, the French were 'le moins démembrable' and thus France's 'murdered and mutilated' condition was an affront to her 'organic unity' and to her 'invincible soul'.[14] Yet dismembered France was, and despite Michelet's hopes that France's renaissance would save Europe, her dismemberment festered like an open wound in the French body politic.

If, in *La Réforme intellectuelle et morale de la France*, Ernest Renan provided articulate witness to the crisis afflicting his homeland,[15] he was equally adamant that he could dismiss Prussian claims to France's lost provinces. This he began to do as early as September 1870 in the first of two open letters to David Friedrich Strauss. Carefully avoiding any attribution of blame for the conflict, he argued that time had legitimized France's original conquest and that Prussia would be making a major error if it ignored the wishes of the people of Alsace.[16] He developed this argument, and to great effect, in a lecture given at the Sorbonne in 1882 entitled *Qu'est-ce que la nation?*[17] Prussia's justification of its possession of Alsace rested upon the claim that in terms of race, culture, and language, it was German. Renan, like the historian Fustel de Coulanges before him, disputed each of these defences. The truth of the matter, Renan argued, was that there were no pure races—France was Celtic, Iberian, and Germanic in much the same way as Germany was Germanic, Celtic, and Slav—and to base politics on ethnographic or linguistic considerations was a dangerous illusion. Similar arguments applied to attempts to define nations in terms of religious affinity, geography, or military exigencies. It was, Renan argued, more accurate to define a nation as 'a soul, a spiritual principle'. The components parts of that soul, he continued, were two-fold: a past and a present. A nation's past was a shared past, 'the possession in common of a rich legacy of memories', a past of sacrifice and devotion. 'Of all cults', Renan wrote, 'the cult of ancestors is the most legitimate, since our ancestors have made us what

---

[12] Ibid. 514.
[13] *Tableau des parties en France* (1930), 89.
[14] Michelet, 'La France devant l'Europe', *Œuvres complètes* (1987), xx. 637–712.
[15] See pp. 373–6 above.
[16] See 'Lettre à M. Strauss' and 'Nouvelle lettre à M. Strauss', in Renan, *Œuvres complètes* (1947), i. 437–62.
[17] *Qu'est-ce que la nation?* (1882); ibid. 887–906.

we are.'[18] A nation's present was one of 'actual consent', made manifest 'in the desire to live together, the will to continue the heritage that has been received'. As Renan described it, a nation was an expression of a sense of solidarity and no one should be 'a slave to his race, his language, his religion or to the courses of rivers or the direction of mountain ranges'. The existence of a nation, therefore, was an act of affirmation, 'a daily plebiscite', 'un plebiscite de tous les jours'.[19]

Renan's diagnosis of France's ills continued to find an audience in subsequent decades. In particular, his reference to the nation as a 'spiritual principle' was sufficiently vague as to appeal to all sides in any future debate about the meaning of France. Nevertheless, not everyone was prepared to go along with this definition of the nation. For example, 1886 saw the creation of the anarchist-inspired Ligue des Antipatriotes and later this anti-patriotic message was continued by firebrand Gustave Hervé, editor of *La Guerre sociale*. Writing in *Leur patrie*, published in 1906, he affirmed that a nation was no more than a means of organizing 'the shameful exploitation' of a people by 'a privileged class'. Annexation by Germany, therefore, had made little difference to the people of Alsace: the large manufacturers remained large manufacturers and the beggars remained beggars. Our country, Hervé proclaimed, is our class. As the head of the Confédération Générale du Travail Georges Yvetot likewise remarked, for the workers of France the lost provinces were not called Alsace and Lorraine but Life and Liberty.[20] Although disputed by the powerful figure of Jean Jaurès[21]—whose internationalism was combined with a deep sense of France's mission as the land of democracy and for whom the proletariat quite definitely did possess a homeland—such a reluctance to attach any significance to the fact of being French or any meaning to France's imagined vocation as a nation remained a powerful strand of opinion up to and beyond the *union sacrée* of 1914–18.

Of an altogether different hue was the charge that the very spiritual principle that defined France was being eaten away from the inside. France was suffering from internal decomposition and a loss of physical and moral vitality. One long-standing and soon to be familiar version of this argument attributed France's military defeat to the moral corrosion of her governing elite and her current malaise to the political corruption and disorder of the Third Republic.[22] Successive scandals at the heart of government—combining sex, nepotism, and money in equal measure—only served to heighten distaste for the present regime and popular nostalgia for the strong leaders of the past. At the end of the 1880s hopes of political renewal settled briefly upon the charismatic figure of General Georges Boulanger and his programme of republican 'revision', the elections of 1889 returning forty-eight *boulangiste* deputies to parliament. Although this colourful episode came to an ignominious end with the enigmatic general's suicide upon the grave of his mistress, in the immediate years that followed there was to be no diminution of

---

[18] *Qu'est-ce que la nation?* (1882), 903.   [19] Ibid. 904.
[20] *Ma Pensée libre* (1913).   [21] *L'Armée nouvelle* (1911), 545.
[22] See e.g. Arthur de Gobineau, *La Troisième République Française et ce qu'elle vaut* (1877).

anti-parliamentary sentiment and no shortage of enthusiastic patriots willing to threaten to topple the fraudsters and crooks of the Republic.

The same fetid climate of greed and corruption also gave rise to a reinvigorated and strident anti-Semitism.[23] As a body of ideas, anti-Semitism drew strength from many of the fears and anxieties of the period, most especially the sense of both cultural and demographic decline typical of the prevailing *fin-de-siècle* mood. So too anti-Semitism flourished in an atmosphere where fashionable 'scientific' theories about race and blood (for example, those associated with Gobineau, Gustave Le Bon, and Vacher de Lapouge) appeared to justify the distinction between 'inferior' and 'superior' peoples.[24] Such theories only served to strengthen the already-rich vein of Christian anti-Semitism and to give greater weight to the concerns of a Catholic France growing ever more fearful of her future de-Christianization. To this could be added the potent equation of Jews with the world of finance, thereby facilitating the picture of the Jew as the itinerant foreigner heading an international conspiracy in the name of all that represented 'anti-France': Protestants, Free-masons, the 'two-hundred families', England, and whatever else could be drawn into this fertile terrain. Jews were nomads, speculators, agents of physical and moral decay. Paradoxically, the very assimilation of French Jews and their consequent entry into positions of political and economic prominence only encouraged the myth that the Republic was itself controlled by Jews.[25]

By the 1880s such anti-Semitic views had become something of a commonplace to be found right across the political spectrum. The left, for example, was only too ready to exploit resentment against the fortune amassed by such Jewish families as the Rothschilds to further their campaign against capitalism.[26] Nevertheless, it was on the right that anti-Semitism came to the fore and nowhere was this more evident than in Edouard Drumont's *La France Juive*.[27] No stone was left unturned in this compendium of anti-Semitism: the Jews engaged in child sacrifice as part of their religious rituals; they were permanently diseased and suffered from 'a corruption of the blood'; they were cowards and robbers; they readily consigned their daughters to prostitution and did so with a view to dishonouring the sons of the French aristocracy; and so on and so on. None of this was remotely original but to these familiar cries of denigration and vilification Drumont added the late nineteenth-century theme of a war between races—'From the very beginning of time', Drumont wrote, 'the Aryan has been in conflict with the Semite'[28]—as well as the claim that it had been the Jews who had been responsible for the collapse of the *ancien régime*. 'The only person to have benefited from the Revolution', he

---

[23] Stephen Wilson, *Ideology and Experience: Antisemitism in France at the Time of the Dreyfus Affair* (Rutherford, NJ, 1982) and Vicki Caron, 'The Jewish Question from Dreyfus to Vichy', in Martin Alexander (ed.), *French History since Napoleon* (London, 1999), 172–202.

[24] See Pierre-André Taguieff, *La Couleur et le sang: Doctrines racistes à la française* (1998).

[25] See Pierre Birnbaum, *Un mythe politique: 'La République juive'* (1995).

[26] See also Michel Dreyfus, *L'Antisémitisme à gauche: Histoire d'un paradoxe de 1830 à nos jours* (2009).

[27] See Grégoire Kauffmann, *Edouard Drumont* (2008).

[28] *La France Juive* (1886), i. 7.

announced, 'is the Jew. Everything comes from the Jew and everything comes back to the Jew.'[29] The violent invasion of the Carthaginian and the Saracen, Drumont concluded, had given way to the 'silent, progressive, and slow' advance of the cunning Jew, the armed hordes of the past being replaced by 'single individuals, gradually forming themselves into little groups, working sporadically, quietly taking possession of all the posts and of all the functions in the land, from the lowest to the highest'.[30] Drumont's message was crystal clear: unless the French rediscovered their love of their country and of God there would be no alternative but to watch 'the painful agony' of a 'generous nation' brought to the edge of extinction by a foreign invader.

Published in 1886, Drumont's 'essay in contemporary history' enjoyed a phenomenal commercial success. Despite the fact that it ran to two volumes and a daunting 1200 pages, it sold 70,000 copies within two months and an estimated 150,000 copies by the end of its first year. In the following year there appeared an illustrated edition and then, in 1888, a popular edition. By 1889 *La France Juive* was in its sixty-fifth edition. Building on this success Drumont published a series of anti-Semitic tracts in rapid succession and then, in April 1892, launched a newspaper, *La Libre Parole*, dedicated to purveying the anti-Semitic message. As part of this strategy, in October 1895 the latter launched a competition to find the best 'practical means of eliminating Jewish power in France'. The winning entry (there were 145 in total) was published, along with the jury's 50-page report and a lengthy 'exposé historique' by Émile Rouyer. The front cover carried an illustration of 'the Aryan breaking the chains which held him captive to the Jew and the Freemason'.[31] As the success of Drumont's enterprise shows, anti-Semitism was big business. Not only did it have a ready audience in wide sections of the French population but it also found expression in novels, on the stage, in literary periodicals, and in the Catholic press (most notably, *La Croix*).

Anti-Semitism was also not entirely unknown among Jews. One such was a journalist and writer named Lazare Marcus Manassé Bernard, born in Nîmes in 1865 and who from 1888 chose to style himself simply as Bernard Lazare.[32] Bernard Lazare was a flamboyant and intriguing figure. Drawn to the literary avant-garde, he had strong anarchist sympathies and firmly believed that the artist should be an educator. He was also hostile to all religion, including that of his forefathers, believing that Judaism had declined into an arid rationalism. In 1890 he published two articles in a review entitled *Entretiens politiques et littéraires* in which he effectively blamed the Jews for bringing anti-Semitism upon themselves.[33] 'In summary', Bernard Lazare wrote, 'Jews are those for whom integrity, benevolence, self-sacrifice are only words and virtues that can be cashed in, those for

[29] *La France Juive* (1886),, p. vi.   [30] Ibid. 8.
[31] *La République plébiscitaire* (1897).
[32] See Nelly Wilson, *Bernard-Lazare: Antisemitism and the Problem of Jewish Identity in Late Nineteenth-Century France* (Cambridge, 1978) and Jean-Denis Bredin, *Bernard Lazare* (1992).
[33] 'Juifs et Israélites', *Entretiens politiques et littéraires*, 6 (1890), 174–9, and 'La Solidarité juive', *Entretiens politiques et littéraires*, 7 (1890), 222–32.

whom money is the end of life and the centre of the world.'[34] Then, in 1894, Bernard Lazare brought out a 400-page study devoted to anti-Semitism.[35] In very brief outline, the force of Bernard Lazare's argument was that the causes of anti-Semitism lay in Jewish separatism and exclusiveness and therefore that it would only disappear if the Jews were to assimilate into the society in which they lived. Throughout all of these texts Bernard Lazare was utterly dismissive of any sense of solidarity with his fellow Jews. An Israelite such as himself, he declared, had nothing in common with 'money changers from Frankfurt, Russian usurers, Polish tavern keepers, Galician pawnbrokers'.[36]

Among those who praised Bernard Lazare's work was none other than Édouard Drumont and thus it was that the young anarchist found himself a member of *La Libre Parole*'s jury to decide the winner of its prize competition on practical solutions to Jewish power. The experience was to prove a brief one as, on 18 June 1897, Bernard Lazare and Drumont were to fight a duel.[37] As luck would have it, neither man was injured! What made this incident all the more curious and incongruous, however, was that in February 1895 Bernard Lazare had had his first meeting with the brother-in-law of the now-imprisoned Captain Alfred Dreyfus and that, despite some initial hesitation about becoming involved, he had become convinced of the latter's innocence. He also quickly concluded that Dreyfus had been found guilty principally because he was a Jew. Dreyfus, he was to write in 1897, 'is a soldier but he is a Jew, and it is as a Jew that he was prosecuted. It is because he is a Jew that he was arrested, because he is a Jew that he was put on trial, because he is a Jew that he was convicted, and because he is a Jew that the voice of justice and of truth could not be heard in his favour.'[38] By virtue of his birth alone, Bernard Lazare affirmed, Dreyfus belonged to 'a class of pariahs'. Bernard Lazare had become the first of the Dreyfusards. No more would be heard from him about the virtues of assimilation.

In December 1894 Alfred Dreyfus, a General Staff officer of Alsatian-Jewish origin, had been found guilty of passing military secrets to the Germans.[39] For this heinous crime (which he had not committed) he was court-martialled and sentenced to life imprisonment and solitary confinement on Devil's Island.[40] The real culprit was a minor crook by the name of Major Ferdinand Esterhazy. At first there was little doubt among the public about Dreyfus's guilt and his condemnation unleashed a veritable torrent of anti-Semitic abuse in the press, the entire Jewish people being implicated in Dreyfus's guilt. No punishment was deemed too severe for the captain's venal treachery. Initially, therefore, Bernard Lazare and

[34] 'Juifs et Israélites', 178.
[35] Bernard Lazare, *L'Antisémitisme, son histoire et ses causes* (1894).
[36] 'Juifs et Israélites', 179.
[37] For Bernard Lazare's own account see *Contre l'Antisémitisme (Histoire d'une polémique)* (1896).
[38] *Une Erreur judiciaire: L'Affaire Dreyfus (Deuxième Mémoire avec des Expertises d'Ecritures)* (1897), 9.
[39] See Jean-Denis Bredin, *L'Affaire* (1983), Michael Drouin, *L'Affaire Dreyfus de A à Z* (1994) and two books by Vincent Duclert, *L'Affaire Dreyfus* (1994) and *Alfred Dreyfus: L'Honneur d'un patriote* (2006). Most recently see Ruth Harris, *The Man on Devil's Island* (London, 2010).
[40] See Alfred Dreyfus, *Cinq années de ma vie* (1901).

the Dreyfus family had little success in winning over support for their call for a retrial. Patiently and quietly they stated their case but then, in November 1896 and from the safety of Belgium, Bernard Lazare published *Une Erreur Judiciaire: La vérité sur l'Affaire Dreyfus*.[41] With meticulous attention to the evidence he demonstrated the falsity of the charges made against Dreyfus. Two more brochures followed, one in 1897 and another in early January 1898. The latter, *Comment on condamne un innocent*,[42] was published on the eve of the failed trial of Major Esterhazy. If he protested about the fate of Dreyfus, Bernard Lazare wrote, it was because 'the law had been disregarded and justice violated'. 'I spoke out', he continued, 'for the salvation of one man alone, but in the name of salvation for all.'[43]

Faced with the prospect of having to admit to a miscarriage of justice, the army now resorted to forgery and perjury. For its part, nationalist opinion attributed the campaign on behalf of Dreyfus to a vast conspiracy headed by a 'Jewish syndicate'. Across France and in French Algeria, popular violence was directed at Jewish shops and synagogues. The stage was now set for the second, and more famous part, of what ever since has been known simply as the 'Affair'.

The curtain was raised on 13 January 1898 when novelist Émile Zola published an open letter in Georges Clemenceau's newspaper, *L'Aurore*, under the banner headline 'J'accuse'. Addressed to Félix Faure, president of the Republic, it denounced the acquittal of Ferdinand Esterhazy two days earlier and all those in the army who had been responsible for the wrongful imprisonment of Dreyfus. His act of protest, Zola announced, was intended as 'a revolutionary means of hastening the explosion of truth and of justice'. The following day, the same newspaper published the first instalment of a document which subsequently became known as the manifesto of the intellectuals. Entitled 'Une protestation', it announced: 'We, the undersigned, protest against the violation of judicial procedure at [Dreyfus's] trial of 1894 and against the mystery surrounding the Esterhazy affair and persist in demanding revision.' Headed by Zola himself, with Anatole France in second place, the undersigned comprised a significant proportion of France's artistic and academic elite, many of whom proudly appended their institutional affiliation and qualifications to their names. Among the 3,000 or so signatories were to be found the names of novelist Marcel Proust and painter Claude Monet, as well as those of Charles Andler, Émile Durkheim, Georges Sorel, and Célestin Bouglé. Also present were a sizeable number of now-forgotten composers and musicians.[44]

The broader circumstances that gave rise to this dramatic 'explosion of truth' are themselves significant. As Christophe Charle has shown, the intervention by Zola marked the culmination of a long process which had seen the intellectual professions progressively disentangle themselves from the tutelage and patronage of, first, the Church and, then, the State. Charle's detailed investigations reveal conclusively

---

[41] Bernard Lazare, *Une Erreur Judiciaire: La vérité sur l'Affaire Dreyfus* (Brussels, 1896).
[42] Lazare, *Comment on condamne un innocent* (1898).
[43] Ibid., p. ii.
[44] Jane Fulcher, *French Cultural Politics and Music: From the Dreyfus Affair to the First World War* (Oxford, 1999).

that in the latter part of the nineteenth century France's intellectual elite became increasingly isolated—educationally, socially, economically, and even matrimonially—from her political and business elites.[45] This relative separation was greatly aided by their own expansion in numbers (especially in higher education), and by the increased power and wider audience of the press, journalism, and publishing in general.

Moreover, during the decade preceding the Affair, two new forms of expression had come into usage: the *enquête*, designed to elicit the opinion of notable figures on issues of perceived interest; and the signed petition or manifesto. Jean-François Sirinelli cites a petition signed by 'writers, painters, sculptors, architects and art lovers' protesting against the building of the Eiffel Tower in 1887 as the first example of the latter.[46] Both served to foster a sense of common identity and both encouraged the belief that it was legitimate for writers, critics, and scholars to voice their opinion on matters of public and political concern. A new name seemed appropriate to a new figure and that name was the intellectual. It was only now, in the weeks immediately following the publication of Zola's open letter, that the noun, previously indeterminate and uncertain of meaning, came into general usage. A national icon had been born.[47]

The manner in which the intellectuals intended to make use of their authority and position for political purposes was well illustrated by Émile Duclaux, director of the prestigious Institut Pasteur and the third of the names to appear on the petition of 13 January.[48] In his *Propos d'un Solitaire*, he provided a response to the request of the vice-president of the Senate, Auguste Scheurer-Kestner, for an assessment of the evidence used to convict Dreyfus and, as he made abundantly clear, he did so as a 'savant'. In reaching his conclusions, Duclaux stated, 'I believe that I have remained moderate and impartial. . . . I accept that Dreyfus was judged and condemned without reference to his Jewishness . . . However, I believe that I have shown that . . . the trial was carried out in conditions hostile to the discovery of the truth.'[49] This was not to attack the army, he insisted, but to establish that the original investigation had 'mistaken art for science'. It was, then, as a scientist that Duclaux exposed judicial error and as such he phrased his argument not in terms of the individual fate of Dreyfus but in the name of his own scientific expertise.[50]

---

[45] See Charle, *Les Élites de la République 1880–1900* (1987) and *Naissance des «intellectuels» 1880–1900* (1990).

[46] *Intellectuels et passions françaises: Manifestes et pétitions au XXe siècle* (1990), 21–3.

[47] See Venita Datta, *Birth of a National Icon: The Literary Avant-Garde and the Origins of the Intellectual in France* (Albany, NY, 1999).

[48] See Vincent Duclert, 'Émile Duclaux: Le Savant et l'intellectuel', *Mil neuf cent*, 11 (1993), 21–6; 'Le Savant, l'intellectuel et le politique: L'Exemple d'Émile Duclaux dans l'affaire Dreyfus', in Michel Woronoff (ed.), *Savant et société aux XIXe et XXe siècles* (Besançon, 1996), 133–58, and 'L'Engagement scientique et l'intellectuel démocratique: Le Sens de l'affaire Dreyfus', *Politix*, 48 (1999), 71–94.

[49] *Propos d'un Solitaire* (1898), 32.

[50] For a broader statement by Duclaux of the merits of science see 'Le Rôle de la science', *Revue des revues*, 32 (15 Mar. 1900), 615–23.

Not everyone was happy to display this level of political engagement and commitment. As Christophe Prochasson has shown in an article outlining the contours of 'non-engagement',[51] at the time of the Dreyfus Affair there were eminent scientists, most conspicuously Henri Poincaré, who were painfully aware of the contradictions between the demands of their professional vocation and the passions and language of politics. As Prochasson also shows, this sentiment only intensified as the disasters of Nazi and Soviet totalitarianism unfolded. Many were those who placed liberty of expression before political commitment and party loyalty. Nevertheless, Émile Duclaux was by no means alone in believing that the public esteem in which his academic achievements were held gave him both the right and the duty to pass judgement on matters beyond his professional domain and to cast himself as the defender of universal principles and verities. 'The practices of the intellectual', wrote Frédéric Paulhan, father of the future editor of the *Nouvelle Revue Française*, 'tend to create a general intelligence, an ability to understand and to appraise with less difficulty and greater certainty not only the things that he has especially studied but also those which lie beyond the sphere of his principal interests.'[52] In an age of growing specialization and the division of labour, it was the intellectual who could aspire to apprehend and defend 'the general conscience of the social body'.[53]

More, however, was at stake in the Dreyfus Affair than the professional autonomy and status of the intellectual. As the eminent historian Ernest Lavisse remarked in an article significantly entitled 'La Réconciliation nationale',[54] the 'grandeur and capital importance' of the Affair derived from the fact that it pitted 'two rival ways of understanding our national life' against each other. This was already clearly visible in Émile Zola's *Lettre à la France*, written in January 1898.[55] Deploying what were to become familiar themes, Zola's argument was that France herself was being insulted by the daily lies associated with the Dreyfus case. 'How', he asked of the French nation, 'can you want truth and justice when all your legendary virtues, the clarity of your intelligence, and the strength of your reason are being wrecked?' Worse still, France was 'turning to the Church' and was returning 'to the past of intolerance and of theocracy', a past that her 'most illustrious children' had fought 'with the gift of their intelligence and their blood' and had believed to be destroyed. France, he implored, wake up, rediscover yourself, become again *la grande France*, 'the nation of honour, the nation of humanity, of truth and of justice'.[56]

Similar arguments were set out at greater length by philosopher Célestin Bouglé.[57] 'If', he remarked before an audience in Toulouse in December 1899, 'we have been so concerned to see Dreyfus return from Devil's Island, it is because,

---

[51] Christophe Prochasson, 'Jalons pour une histoire du "non-engagement"', *Vingtième Siècle*, 60 (1998), 102–11.
[52] 'Le droit des intellectuels', *Revue du Palais* (1 Oct. 1898), 742.
[53] Ibid. 737.
[54] *Revue de Paris*, 5 (Oct. 1899), 648–68.
[55] Émile Zola, *Lettre à la France* (1898).
[56] Ibid. 3.
[57] See the collection of essays included in *Pour la Démocratie française* (1900).

on the same boat, we have wanted to see return with him to their native soil a whole body of ideas which to us are sacred.'[58] These ideas were 'the worship of the human person considered as an end in himself... All are free, all are equal. ... No individual can be treated as a means in the service of the State. ... The sovereignty of the law. ... A scrupulous respect for legality.'[59] Such, Bouglé declared, was the 'French tradition' and such, as exemplified in the treatment of Dreyfus, were the principles that were being flouted in the name of *raison d'état*. Bouglé did not go so far as to claim that France alone had invented these ideals, but he was confident that it was in France that they had attained their most human and popular form and in the French language that they had received their clearest expression. Accordingly, when the anti-Semites put on the mask of nationalism, when they invoked the old traditions of France and spoke of the genius of the country, it was a 'bloody irony' without any foundation.[60] The supporters of Dreyfus, therefore, fought 'not only for a Frenchman but for France, not only for a single citizen but for the Republic, not only for a man but for humanity'.[61]

For those more obviously situated on the left of the political spectrum, rallying to the Dreyfusard cause posed its own challenges and obstacles. Why should socialists be concerned by acts of illegality committed by the bourgeoisie against one of its own? Why should they side with their political opponents to defend the Republic when it was demonstrably a corrupt regime?[62] As late as December 1897, for example, Jean Jaurès could write that 'if the terrible sentence had fallen upon a poor man, without family, without money, and without the means to act, the excitement would be less great and the agitation less in evidence'. The quarrel over Dreyfus, he went on, was a struggle between 'two parts of the privileged class', with the Jews, Protestants, and Opportunists on one side and the supporters of the Church and the army on the other.[63] Once convinced of Dreyfus's innocence, however, Jaurès put these apprehensions to one side, arguing that no one had a bigger interest in seeing an end to the criminal illegalities committed by the French military High Command than the working class. But Jaurès also phrased his response in terms of the meaning of France. Through the sheer weight of the injustice heaped upon his person, Jaurès argued, Dreyfus had ceased to be an army officer and a bourgeois and had become 'nothing less than humanity itself'. Faced with this outrage, only one 'institution' had remained upright and that had been 'France herself'. 'For a moment', Jaurès accepted, 'she was surprised, but she is recovering possession of herself and, even if all her official lights are extinguished, her clear good sense can again dissipate the night.'[64] Never, he argued, had France been obliged to sacrifice

---

[58] 'Intellectuels et manuels', ibid. 94.
[59] 'La Tradition française', ibid. 18–20.
[60] 'Philosophie de l'antisémitisme', ibid. 70.
[61] 'Intellectuels et manuels', 94.
[62] See Madeleine Rebérioux, 'Zola, Jaurès et France: Trois Intellectuels devant l'Affaire', *Cahiers naturalistes*, 54 (1980), 266–81.
[63] 'Dreyfus-Esterhazy', originally published in *La Petite République* (11 Dec. 1897): see *Œuvres de Jean Jaurès*, vi. *L'Affaire Dreyfus*, ed. Eric Cahm (2001), 85–8.
[64] 'Les Preuves', ibid. 709.

'the legal guarantees that she instituted for all her children and her duties as a civilized nation' in the interests of 'the humiliating calculations of a false international prudence'. Justice was required in the name of 'the salvation of the innocent, the punishment of the guilty, the education of the people, and the honour of the *patrie*.[65]

Yet no sooner had the intellectuals intervened to call for Dreyfus's release and to defend the honour of France than their act was denounced by those Jaurès described as 'the reactionary intellectuals', by those who, in his memorable phrase, would only be completely happy 'when science has been repudiated by the scientist, when the spirit of criticism has been repudiated by the critic, and when thought has been prostituted before force'.[66]

Leading the way was Ferdinand Brunetière.[67] Already a controversial figure because of his article 'Après une visite au Vatican', Brunetière now added fuel to the fire in March 1898 with his anti-Dreyfusard article 'Après le Procès'.[68] Here he addressed three issues: the causes of anti-Semitism, the place of the army in France's democracy, and, finally, the claims of the 'intellectuals'. His response to the first was that the Jews themselves were 'not entirely innocent' and he did not disguise his sympathy for the 'thirty-eight million French people' who felt themselves displaced by 'the last arrivals, the most recent members of the family'.[69] On the second, his contention was not only that the army was compatible with the existence of democracy but that, in terms of its traditions and composition, 'the army of France, today as before, is France herself'. It was in perfect harmony with the 'genius' of the country.

It was Brunetière's answer to the third question that was the most controversial. Against the intellectuals, he denied their special authority to speak out on 'the most difficult questions concerning human morality, the life of nations, and the interest of society'. What, he mocked, could a professor of Tibetan be able to teach his fellow citizens about politics and why did knowledge of the properties of quinine confer a right to be obeyed?[70] But there was, he believed, an even greater danger lurking behind the protestations of the Dreyfusard intellectuals. 'Scientific method, the aristocracy of intelligence, respect for truth, all these fine phrases', he argued, 'only serve to conceal the pretensions of *Individualism*.'[71] And it was individualism and not parliamentarism, socialism, or collectivism, according to Brunetière, which was 'the great sickness of the present time'. In short, when 'intellectualism' and individualism reached 'this degree of self-infatuation' the result was anarchy.

---

[65] 'Les Preuves', 691.

[66] 'La Classe intellectuelle', ibid. vii. 515. This article was first publ. in *La Petite République* (7 Jan. 1899). See Vincent Duclert, 'Anti-intellectualisme et intellectuels pendant l'affaire Dreyfus', *Mil Neuf Cent*, 15 (1997), 69–83.

[67] See p. 378 above.

[68] *Revue des Deux Mondes*, 146 (1898), 428–46; repr. as *Après le Procès: Réponse à quelques «intellectuels»* (1898).

[69] Brunetière was consistent in his refusal to endorse a physiological theory of race. See esp. his review of Drumont's *La France juive* in the *Revue des Deux Mondes*, 75 (June 1886), 693–704.

[70] See also Brunetière's review of Zola's novel *Paris*, *Revue des Deux Mondes*, 146 (1898), 928.

[71] 'Après le Procès', *Revue des Deux Mondes*, 445.

The broader import of this argument becomes all the clearer if we look at other of Brunetière's pamphlets and speeches, most notably *L'Idée de patrie*[72] from 1896 and *Les Ennemis de l'âme française*[73] from 1899. Also of great interest is a speech delivered in 1899 entitled *Le Génie latin*.[74] In the first of these texts, Brunetière argued that the idea of a homeland had three composite parts: 'le Fondement Naturel', 'le Fondement Historique', and 'le Fondement Mystique'. The homeland was natural in the sense that we could neither survive nor flourish without it. It had a history and it was this history that made France into a reality and a person and that defined her character such that she had possessed a 'general intention' that had remained unchanged 'over ten centuries'. The mystical basis of the nation, according to Brunetière, was precisely that aspect which escaped analysis, which defied reason, and which drew upon instinct. At its heart was 'the religion of the dead'. Contrary to what was believed, Brunetière argued, such an idea of the *patrie* was not in decline but it was under attack from those 'individualists' who believed in 'the worship and idolatry of themselves'.

The basic premise of *Les Ennemis de l'âme française* was that there existed such a thing as the French soul and that it could be defined as a 'hereditary communion of sentiments and ideas'. The idea of a homeland, on this account, was not something transitory or unstable and therefore Brunetière bluntly dismissed Renan's notion of the nation as a 'daily plebiscite', pointing out that it would justify all manner of separatist claims. Rather, there were three traditions that informed this soul and it was these that ensured the continuity of France. The first was France's military tradition. Reacting against what he saw as the Dreyfusard attack on the army, Brunetière declared that there would be 'no nation without an army'.[75] The second was a 'literary and intellectual' tradition. Great literature had given the French soul a 'truthful expression, a durable expression, an immortal expression'. In *Le Génie latin* he made clear his view that the particular genius of the French was to be 'Latins in sentiment, Latins in morals, Latins in taste, Latins in spirit, Latins in language, and Latins in thought'. If we cease to be Latins, he wrote, 'we will cease at the same time to be French'.[76] The third tradition, and by far the most important, was religion. Specifying that he spoke as 'neither believer nor moralist but simply as a historian and an observer', Brunetière's conclusion was unequivocal: 'What I determine in both fact and history is that . . . in the same way that Protestantism is England and "orthodoxy" is Russia, so France is Catholicism. What I determine, in both fact and history, is that for twelve centuries the role of acting as a protector and propagandist of Catholicism has belonged to France.'[77] This, therefore, was Brunetière's conclusion: 'everything that we do, everything that we allow to be done, against Catholicism, we allow to be done and we do it to the detriment of our influence in the world, against the grain of our history, and at

[72] Brunetière, *L'Idée de patrie* (1896).
[73] Brunetière, *Les Ennemis de l'âme française* (1899).
[74] See Brunetière, *Discours de combat* (1920), 249–91.
[75] See also 'La Nation et l'armée', ibid. 215–48.
[76] 'Le Génie latin', ibid. 289–90.
[77] *Les Ennemis de l'âme française*, 57–8.

the expense of the qualities which are those of the "French soul"'.[78] You could not, Brunetière concluded, be 'French and anti-Catholic'.[79]

It was these traditions, Brunetière resumed, that had made France what she was and to that extent they were 'neither monarchical nor republican, but were French, uniquely French'. However, he was in no doubt that 'the best of governments' would always be the one which most respected French traditions and that 'the best of institutions' would be those which allowed these traditions to develop and to be renewed. Similarly, in a long footnote to his published text, Brunetière was careful to specify that being a Protestant or a Jew or a Muslim or even a 'Free-thinker' was not what he meant by being anti-Catholic: what he had in mind, he assured his readers, was the 'militant and active' anti-Catholicism of groups such as the Freemasons. He also made it clear in *L'Idée de patrie* that he did not believe that races formed nations. 'The French race', he wrote, 'is not the producer but rather the creation or, if I dare say so, the created being of the history of France.'[80] Nevertheless, and despite Brunetière's attempt to portray French history as one long unbroken continuum, it is clear that the Catholic religion was to be considered a fundamental dimension of the identity and meaning of France and that those who were not Catholics could scarcely be considered full members of the nation.

In Brunetière's view, the French soul was under attack and France was internally weakened. By whom? By politicians, intellectuals, and freethinkers was his answer. By all those who, 'in their desperate assault on all our traditions, confound a liberty of spirit with an independence of the heart'. All these had worked 'to denature the French soul', to turn the 'essentially sociable' French towards individualism. This was to be the central theme of the numerous articles that Brunetière published in the *Revue des Deux Mondes* as well as the essays that appeared in the series of volumes entitled *Discours de combat*. In these pieces can be discerned a consistent and loud objection to subjectivism, scepticism, rationalism, moral relativism, and what was repeatedly characterized as intellectual dilettantism. This translated itself into a hostility towards literary Romanticism, the theory of art for art's sake, the naturalism of Émile Zola's novels, the errors of the philosophy of the eighteenth century, Protestantism as a form of 'individual salvation', and what was described as a Nietzschean 'aristocracy of intelligence'. These texts endorsed not only the merits of tradition over novelty and the future triumph of idealism over materialism in science, art, and politics but also the idea of solidarity as 'a Christian and, above all, Catholic idea'.[81] Brunetière was equally of the opinion that there were reasons to believe in God and, moreover, that we needed to believe in God. Before this mystery, he avowed, all one could do was yield.[82] Given the universality of the Catholic faith, he did not believe in the need for a national church.[83]

---

[78] *Les Ennemis de l'âme française*, 58.   [79] Ibid. 67.

[80] *L'Idée de patrie*, 19.

[81] See esp. 'L'Idée de solidarité', in *Discours de combat* (1903), 49–83; *L'Action sociale du Christianisme* (Besançon, 1904); and 'La Renaissance de l'idéalisme', *Discours de combat* (1920), 3–57.

[82] 'Le Besoin de croire', *Revue des Deux Mondes*, 150 (1898), 702–20, and 'Les Raisons actuelles de croire', *Discours de combat* (1903), 1–48.

[83] 'Voulons-nous une église nationale?', *Revue des Deux Mondes*, 6 (1901), 277–94.

For all the ambiguities and contradictions in Brunetière's position—always the acute observer, Georges Sorel was to comment after Brunetière's death that 'this man who was so perceptive in his study of texts displayed considerable naivety in matters concerning practical life'[84]—he nevertheless provided a formidable and powerful combination of ideas of great appeal to the nationalist right. Deployed by Brunetière at the height of the Dreyfus Affair, this anti-individualist and Catholic vision of France challenged many of the basic presuppositions of republican politics and culture at the turn of the century. Where these meanings of France could lead was best illustrated by Brunetière's fellow member of the Ligue de la patrie française, Maurice Barrès,[85] author of *Scènes et doctrines du nationalisme* and one of the most popular writers of his day.

Here too there was an attempt to transcend and to encompass all aspects and features of French history, be they Catholic, revolutionary, or Bonapartist. 'Let us leave these tales', Barrès wrote, 'we find greater profit in merging ourselves together with all the moments of the history of France, in living with her dead, in not placing ourselves beyond any of her experiences.'[86] All these conflicting experiences, he continued, 'proceed from the same source and lead to the same goal: they are the development of the same seed and the fruits of the same tree'.[87] No conception of France could prevail over 'the France of flesh or blood'. Yet, this generosity of spirit and of vision quickly vanished when Barrès came to speak of Protestants, and especially of Jews. The 'Catholic world', Barrès wrote, 'is where my forebears grew to maturity and prepared the way for me. As a consequence I find it the least jarring to my nature. It can best accommodate my various roles and best promote the life suited to my nature.'[88] This was why he felt able to celebrate 'the destruction of the Protestant forces': 'I intend to preserve the benefits of this victory with all the power at my command, for it enables the tree of which I am one leaf to continue to exist.' Barrès pointed out that in Alsace and Lorraine it was the Protestants who were most likely to accept German rule.

The Jew, as a member of 'a race antagonistic to my own', fared even worse in the Barrèsian scheme of things. The Jews, Barrès argued, had no *patrie* in the way the French understood it. For them, it was not a matter of their native soil and of their ancestors but 'only a place where they find greatest profit'. Thus, Barrès had no difficulty comprehending the nature of Dreyfus's crime. 'In psychological terms', Barrès wrote, 'it is sufficient for me to know that he is capable of treason' and this he was able to 'deduce from his race'.[89] On this view, the actual guilt or otherwise of Dreyfus appeared almost irrelevant and of secondary importance. What mattered, as Barrès never tired of repeating, was that the question should be resolved 'in light of the interests of France'. And by these standards Dreyfus *was* guilty. Indeed,

[84] Review of V. Giraud, *Ferdinand Brunetière, Notes et Souvenirs*, in *Le Mouvement socialiste*, 22 (1908), 93–4.
[85] See Zeev Sternhell, *Maurice Barrès et le nationalisme français* (2000).
[86] *Scènes et doctrines du nationalisme* (1906), 82.   [87] Ibid. 83.
[88] Ibid. 60.   [89] Ibid. 152.

the 'worst crime' of Dreyfus and his supporters in their 'anti-French campaign' was that for the past five years they had weakened the army and the nation.[90]

This, according to Barrès, was an argument that the intellectuals, with their passion for metaphysics and abstract truth, could not understand. An intellectual, he announced, is 'an individual who convinces himself that society should be founded on the basis of logic and who fails to see that it rests on past exigencies that precede and are perhaps foreign to individual reason'.[91] Such was the case with the central figure in Barrès's famous novel *Les Déracinés*,[92] the professor of philosophy Paul Bouteiller. The charge was that he, and those in real life like him who taught what Barrès regarded as the official Kantian doctrine of the educational system, approached man as 'an abstract universal entity' and encouraged their students to become 'citizens of humanity, free spirits, initiates of pure reason'. As a result, all were 'uprooted' from their race and from their land. All became incapable of bearing witness to 'French truth and French justice'.[93] The intellectual thus functioned as 'the enemy of society', producing a decadence that derived from 'a lack of moral unity' and the absence of a 'common understanding of our goal, our resources, our centre'. They were 'the anarchists of the speaker's platform'.[94] 'As for ourselves', Barrès commented, 'we are happier to be intelligent than to be intellectual.'[95]

Nationalism, therefore, was defined by Barrès as the acceptance of a form of determinism.[96] It was a 'sense of descent', a way of seeing things deeply rooted in the soil of France, her history, and her 'national conscience'. Correctly understood, it provided a series of 'fixed points' and 'landmarks' that 'over the preceding centuries have educated our reflexes'. So Zola's defence of Dreyfus could be explained by the fact that he was not French but rather 'an uprooted Venetian'.[97] The outrage with regard to occupied Alsace and Lorraine was that little French children were being prevented from thinking and speaking like Frenchmen. Those 'too recently' accepted into the French nation had troubled the 'national conscience' precisely because they bore the blood of their non-French ancestors. Accordingly, it was among the people, among those uncontaminated by the aberrations of rationalism, that was to be found the authentic expression of the nation's true instincts in all their vigour and vitality.

These views carried with them a clear political programme. Nationalism, Barrès argued, necessitated a series of 'protectionist' measures designed to defend the French people. The nationality laws were to be tightened in order to reduce 'the interference of the foreigner into our politics'. Laws on the ownership of property were to be designed so as to prevent foreigners possessing 'the soil of France' and to limit their commercial and industrial activities. The 'financial feudality' comprised of Protestants and the 'kingdom of Israel'—described by Barrès as 'the dangerous plutocracy of exotics from which France might perish'—was to be challenged and

[90] *Scènes et doctrines du nationalisme* (1906), 209.   [91] Ibid. 45.
[92] Barrès, *Les Déracinés* (1897).   [93] *Scènes et doctrines du nationalisme*, 13.
[94] Ibid. 220.   [95] Ibid. 45.
[96] Ibid. 8–10.   [97] Ibid. 40.

defeated through a series of measures designed to secure the economic interests of French workers. The union of the race and of the earth was to be sealed by granting 'a corner of the land' to every French family. There was to be no room for either cosmopolitan socialism or economic liberalism. 'Our salvation', Barrès concluded, 'lies in ceasing to be uprooted and scattered individuals.'[98]

To the opinions voiced by both Brunetière and Barrès, the Dreyfusard camp made an immediate reply. Against Brunetière's *Après le Procès* was lined up Émile Duclaux's *Avant le Procès*,[99] Alphonse Darlu's *M. Brunetière et l'individualisme*,[100] and, thirdly, Émile Durkheim's *L'Individualisme et les intellectuels*.[101] If Duclaux again defended the liberty, impartiality, and competence of the 'scientific spirit' and therefore the duty of 'intellectuals' to make use of their expertise on matters of public concern,[102] Darlu, one of the founders of the *Revue de métaphysique et de morale*, was quick to point out that Brunetière had misconceived the nature of the individualism he so deplored and as a result had exaggerated its dangers. Of greater force and interest was the response of Durkheim. Like Darlu, Durkheim was of the opinion that Brunetière had mistaken individualism for 'the utilitarian egoism' of Herbert Spencer and of liberal political economy. This, Durkheim conceded, did amount to an 'egoistic cult of the self' but it was in decline and had, in any case, to be placed alongside 'another individualism', one derived from Kant, Rousseau, and the Déclaration des Droits de l'Homme of 1789. This form of individualism, he countered, saw all actions carried out for personal gain 'as the very source of evil' and saw the human person as sacred. It also held that 'there was no reason of State which can excuse an outrage against the person'.[103] So, Durkheim argued, turning the tables upon his opponents, 'not only is individualism not anarchy but henceforth it is the only system of beliefs which is able to ensure the moral unity of the country'.[104] This was so because, as societies grew in size and complexity, it was impossible to 'prevent men from becoming increasingly differentiated from one another' or 'to bring them back to the conformism of earlier times'. In those circumstances, the only viable alternative was to 'complete, extend, and organize' the individualism bequeathed by the eighteenth century, to pass beyond the 'negative ideal' of freeing the individual from the political fetters that bound him, such that we might learn properly to make use of our liberty. 'All moral education', Durkheim wrote, 'should be directed to this end.'[105]

What of Brunetière's case against the intellectual? What, as Durkheim put it, of his argument that 'intellectual and moral anarchy would be the inevitable consequence of liberalism?'[106] 'Respect for authority', Durkheim replied, 'was in no way

---

[98] Ibid. 425–77.

[99] Émile Duclaux, *Avant le Procès* (1898).

[100] Alphonse Darlu, *M. Brunetière et l'individualisme* (1898).

[101] *Revue bleue*, 10 (1898), 7–13.

[102] A year later Duclaux showed himself to be far less eager to express a view on anti-Semitism. 'It is not my habit', he explained, 'to make prophecies that scarcely fall within my field of competence': see Henri Dagan, *Enquête sur l'antisémitisme* (1898), 52.

[103] *Revue bleue*, 8–9.   [104] Ibid. 10.

[105] Ibid. 13.   [106] Ibid. 10.

incompatible with rationalism provided that authority itself was rationally ground-ed.'[107] However, the case of Dreyfus was 'one of those questions' which, by definition, pertained to the common judgement' of men. To know whether a court of justice might try a man without hearing his defence, Durkheim continued, there was no need of any 'special knowledge'. It was a matter of 'practical morality' upon which everyone of good sense was competent and about which no one could be indifferent. If, Durkheim concluded,

> a certain number of artists, but above all scientists, have believed that they ought to refuse assent to a judgement whose legality appeared to them to be suspect, it is not because... they attribute to themselves any special privileges or any exclusive right of control over the question. It is rather that, being men, they seek to exercise their entire right as men and to keep before them a matter which concerns reason alone. It is true that they have shown themselves more jealous of this right than the rest of society; but this is simply because, as a result of their professional activities, they have it nearer to heart. Accustomed by the practice of scientific method to reserve their judgement when they are not fully aware of the facts, it is natural for them to give in less easily to the enthusiasms of the crowd or to the prestige of authority.[108]

Thus, the 'individualist' who defended the rights of the individual was at the same time defending 'the vital interests of society' and, Durkheim continued, in no other country was this cause more 'truly national' than in France. To renounce it, he told his readers, would be 'to renounce ourselves', to 'diminish ourselves in the eyes of the world', to 'commit real moral suicide'.[109] It was, in other words, Brunetière who was speaking against the soul of France. To that extent, according to Dur-kheim, anti-Semitism in France, if not elsewhere, was 'the consequence and symptom of a state of social malaise'.[110]

Against Barrès stood Lucien Herr, librarian of the École Normale Supérieure and an Alsatian Protestant.[111] Writing in the Dreyfusard *La Revue blanche*,[112] he told Barrès that 'your idea is that the French soul, French integrity, is today being insulted and compromised to the advantage of foreigners, by the infernal machina-tions of other foreigners, and aided by the complicity of second-rate intellectuals de-nationalized by a second-rate culture'.[113] This, Herr believed, was nonsense. More tellingly, he also turned his fire against Barrès's conception of France. 'At the heart of your national patriotism', he continued, 'you would find not the old France... but a conquering, proud and brutal France, Napoleonic France, the jingoistic chauvinism of our large cities, the impassioned instinct for warlike glory, barbarous exaltation, hatred and the arrogance of force.'[114] This, he made plain, was not his France. 'The French soul', Herr wrote, 'has only been truly great and strong at those moments when it has been welcoming and generous'. Nor was it the

---

[107] *Revue bleue*, 8–9.   [108] Ibid.   [109] Ibid. 12.
[110] Dagan, *Enquête*, 59–63.
[111] See Charles Andler, *Vie de Lucien Herr 1864–1926* (1932) and Robert Smith, 'L'Atmosphère politique à l'École Normale Supérieure à la fin du XIXe siècle', *Revue d'histoire moderne et contemporaine*, 20 (1973), 248–68.
[112] 'A M. Maurice Barrès', *La Revue blanche*, 15 (1898), 241–5.
[113] Ibid. 242.   [114] Ibid. 243.

France of the 'young people' who had rallied to the Dreyfusard cause. They, like Barrès himself, did not claim to possess the whole truth but 'they have within themselves something which is absolute: the faith in a human ideal'.[115]

II

One of the common meeting places of these young people was the tiny bookshop and office of Charles Péguy, located in the heart of Paris's Latin Quarter in the rue Cujas.[116] It was here that, with passionate intensity, they followed the dramatic course of events and where, on the rock of the Dreyfus Affair, their friendships were ultimately to be broken. Quickly disillusioned, in their eyes the triumph of the Dreyfusard cause had been sullied by the actions of unscrupulous politicians intent upon reaping their own personal reward and upon punishing both the Roman Catholic Church and the army for their misdemeanours. This mood of disenchantment was captured well by Georges Sorel, a weekly visitor to Péguy's bookshop, in *La Révolution dreyfusienne*. Published in 1908, it was undoubtedly Sorel's worst book, but its clear message was that the policies of the victorious republicans—especially the anticlerical Émile Combes—had put an end 'to the passable functioning of the parliamentary regime' and had brought about the ascendancy of what he dubbed 'a philosophy of hypocritical cowardice'. Few were spared from Sorel's venomous and scornful bile. Émile Zola, he wrote, 'was the representative example of the buffoonery of the time . . . He can be compared to a clown parading before a fairground stall.'[117]

By Sorel's own admission, his volume caused something of 'a scandal'[118] but this was as nothing compared to the controversy evoked by Daniel Halévy's 'Apologie pour notre passé'.[119] The 'our past' of the title was the past of a small group of young men (which included future socialist prime minister Léon Blum and critic Julien Benda)[120] for whom the Dreyfus Affair had acted to define them as human beings. According to Halévy's account, they had had no opinions, occupations, or friendships prior to the Affair but within a short space of time all (and more, their hatreds) were decided upon. 'A single and redoubtable crisis', Halévy wrote, 'took hold of us and marked us.'[121] He and his friends, Halévy recalled, became involved in the Dreyfusard cause not just to save an innocent man but to save 'an innocent

---

[115] Ibid. 244.
[116] See Daniel Halévy, *Charles Péguy and Les Cahiers de la Quinzaine* (London, 1946). See Géraldi Leroy, *Péguy: Entre l'ordre et la révolution* (1981) and Alain Finkielkraut, *Le Mécontemporain: Péguy, lecteur du monde moderne* (1991).
[117] *La Révolution dreyfusienne* (1908), 35.
[118] 'Lettres de Georges Sorel à Edouard Berth: Deuxième Partie: 1909–1910', *Cahiers Georges Sorel*, 4 (1986), 86.
[119] Daniel Halévy, 'Apologie pour notre passé', *Cahiers de la quinzaine*, 10th cahier of the 11th series, 1910. See Pierre Guiral, 'Daniel Halévy, esquisse d'un itinéraire', *Contrepoint*, 20 (1976), 79–95.
[120] Both were to write at length about this experience: see Léon Blum, *Souvenirs sur l'Affaire* (1935) and Julien Benda, *La Jeunesse d'un clerc* (1936).
[121] Halévy, 'Apologie pour notre passé', 8.

France' whose honour was being betrayed by 'a small group of men poisoned by fear, by hate'. At issue, then, had been 'the salvation of the French spirit'.[122] Yet, from within their own number and as a result of their own efforts, a 'demagogic bloc' had emerged and had taken control of the State.

The potency of Halévy's text lies in the way it combined reflection and memory to turn a recent event into history—'our memories are already our masters', he wrote[123]—but if it remains known today it is largely because it elicited one of Charles Péguy's greatest works, *Notre Jeunesse*, published in 1910.[124] Here was a text that pushed eloquence and lyricism to the point where the recovery of history played little part. 'I am shocked', Sorel wrote to Halévy, 'to see the extent to which Péguy sacrifices reality (which does not seem to interest him at all) to the requirements of oratorical development.'[125] Pèguy himself did not see it that way. 'My past', he wrote, 'has no need of apology ... I have no need of being defended.'[126] Nor did he have the intention of writing 'the memoirs of a weakling, of a penitent'. Specifically, he did not recognize himself as the 'downtrodden dog' of Halévy's account. He had been mistaken and he had been fooled but he had not been beaten. Nor, he asserted, had he been a victim of an 'illusion of youth'. Rather the defence of Dreyfus—a man, Péguy believed, who would not have died for his own cause—had been something akin to a religion. A single crime, a single injustice, had been sufficient to break the social compact and thus theirs had been a struggle to restore 'the historic honour of our people, the entire historic honour of our entire race, the honour of our ancestors, the honour of our children'. 'Deep down', he wrote, 'we were men concerned with eternal salvation and our adversaries with temporal salvation. That is the true, the real division of the Dreyfus Affair.'[127] Halévy's mistake had been to presume that it was the politicians who represented the Dreyfusard movement and therefore he had forgotten the fervour and ardour that had inspired their own original commitment.

Where did what Halévy later described as Péguy's 'glorious memory of the event' lead him?[128] First, he placed Bernard Lazare at the centre of his account. A 'prophet' and 'one of the great names of the modern age', his reward had been solitude and to be forgotten.[129] Next, to explain the decline of the Dreyfusard movement into careerism and cynicism he forged his famous distinction between *mystique* and *politique*. As Péguy expressed it, one died for a *mystique* but one lived off a *politique*: the first was principled; the second was self-interested. *Politique* was the devouring of the *mystique* that gave the movement its original force. Moreover, in Péguy's view, all movements began as *mystiques* and ended as *politiques*.[130] Péguy, therefore, believed that he and his friends had been 'the mystics'; that they had always been 'the heart and the centre' of the Dreyfusard cause; and that, if

---

[122] Halévy, 'Apologie pour notre passé', 38–9.   [123] Ibid. 8.
[124] See Péguy, *Notre Jeunesse*, in *Œuvres en prose, 1909–1914* (1961), 501–655.
[125] 'Lettres de Georges Sorel à Daniel Halévy', *Mil Neuf Cent*, 12 (1994), 184.
[126] Péguy, *Notre Jeunesse*, 563.   [127] Ibid. 648.
[128] Halévy, *Charles Péguy*, 110.   [129] Péguy, *Notre Jeunesse*, 551–3.   [130] Ibid. 518.

their enemies had spoken the language of *raison d'état*, their concern had been that 'France should not fall into a state of mortal sin'.[131]

This was only the springboard for a broader digression about the condition of France. On Péguy's account, the Dreyfusard *mystique* had been inspired by the virtues of justice, charity, courage, perseverance, and self-sacrifice. These virtues, he wanted to argue, were not simply 'republican' virtues: they were also Christian virtues. The Dreyfusard movement, in other words, encompassed both the republican and Christian *mystiques*. Péguy's simple point here was that the Catholic Church, instead of opposing the Dreyfusard cause, should have recognized its religious character. His broader point was that both *mystiques* were part of what he constantly referred to as *l'ancienne France*. It was for this reason that Péguy refused to see 'the 1st January 1789 (Paris time)' as the great divide in French history.

In this Péguy was fortified by a provincial and rural education in which, as he recounted, his schoolmasters and priests, for all their 'metaphysical' differences, had taught the same morality and the same discipline, had taught the virtues of 'the French race'. Yet his argument was that this France was coming to an end. The Dreyfus Affair, he believed, represented the 'last operation of the republican *mystique*'. This was so because France was entering a period of 'demystification'. To that extent, 'de-republicanization' went hand in hand with 'de-Christianization'. The same 'sterility' was afflicting 'the city of men and the city of God'. For the first time we were living in a world 'opposed to all culture'.[132]

So, for Péguy, the dividing line came not in 1789 but 'around 1881'.[133] Up to that moment the Republic had been a 'restoration' (it had, in actual fact, been a republic of the notables, a republic without republicans) but after this, according to Péguy, it lapsed into 'cæsarism' and demagogy. Worse still, the Republic had fallen under 'the domination of the intellectual party'.[134] In *Notre Jeunesse*, and in many other texts,[135] Péguy's denunciation of this 'tyranny' knew almost no bounds. It was a system of oppression, of corruption, of depravity, of lying that, for over thirty years, had tried to overthrow God, the Church, France, the army, morality, and the law. The unfortunate Jaurès was singled out for particular condemnation and reproach as the 'bourgeois intellectual' who had subverted and corrupted the workers' movement. Péguy, in short, was perhaps the first to suspect that the intellectuals had betrayed their calling, and his bitterness was all the greater for the lofty conception he had had of their almost-sacred role. The intellectuals, he believed, had sold their souls for 'temporal domination', for riches, for honours, for privileged positions, for political power, for earthly glory.

Péguy's text contained another theme of great resonance. Péguy repeatedly stated that he and his friends had been inspired by 'warlike virtues'. And this he explained in terms of 'a need for heroism, which seized an entire generation, our generation,

---

[131] Ibid. 648.   [132] Ibid. 508–9.   [133] Ibid. 520.   [134] Ibid. 521.

[135] See esp. 'De la Situation faite au parti intellectuel dans le monde moderne', in *Œuvres en prose 1898–1908* (1959), 1031–78 and 'De la Situation faite au parti intellectuel dans le monde moderne devant les accidents de la gloire temporelle', ibid. 1115–1214.

a need for war . . . a need for sacrifice to the point of martyrdom'.[136] When the young Péguy had arrived from Orléans to pursue his studies at the École Normale Supérieure he had quickly converted to socialism and in his earliest writings had provided a description of the 'cité socialiste' as the 'cité harmonieuse'. Then his hero had been Jean Jaurès. In the cheerless aftermath of the Dreyfus Affair Péguy held fast to the purity of his earliest convictions but he there began the journey that was later to see his pilgrimage to the cathedral of Chartres and his own death in the first battle of the Marne in September 1914. In many respects the contours of this journey can best be discerned by comparing his two treatments of the figure of Jeanne d'Arc. The first, a dramatic trilogy published in 1897, ended with a plea for the 'establishment of the Universal Socialist Republic'; the second, a long prose poem entitled *Le Mystère de la Charité de Jeanne d'Arc* published in 1910, focused upon the possibility of eternal life and salvation.

For our purposes, however, we might also briefly consider Péguy's essay of 1905, *Notre Patrie*.[137] In its composition, it was typical of so many of Péguy's lyrical outpourings. It opened with a description of the sorry plight of French politics under the premiership of Émile Combes but then used the state visit of the king of Spain as a pretext for a series of reflections about the people of the Paris and the city's 'imperishable monuments'. In effect, what Péguy sought to portray was the *patrie* as a physical and enduring reality, as something at once both eternal and immortal.[138] But Péguy also saw that what was imperishable 'will inevitably perish'. Here, the political context was not unimportant. In March of that year, Kaiser Wilhelm II had made a provocative and unexpected landing at Tangiers. The intention was to humiliate France by demonstrating the hollowness of her pretensions in North Africa. To many—including Péguy—war with Germany again seemed inevitable. Convinced that invasion was imminent, he now wrote that 'a new period had begun in the history of my own life, in the history of this country, and assuredly in the history of the world'.[139] He was not to be mistaken. 'Happy', he was later to write in a premonition of his own death, 'are those who die for an earthly land, when a just war calls.'

Péguy's erstwhile friend and colleague, Georges Sorel, also believed that 'a great foreign war' might renew France's 'lost energies'. His preferred solution to France's ills,[140] however, was a renewed bout of proletarian class struggle directed against a timorous and humanitarian bourgeoisie. In much the same way as he became disillusioned with the 'Dreyfusard Revolution', he quickly became disenchanted with the workers, and thus from 1909 to 1914 found himself participating in a series of publishing initiatives that brought together thinkers from the extremes of both the left and the right.[141] One such initiative was the short-lived plan to

---

[136] *Notre Jeunesse*, 643.
[137] *Œuvres en prose 1898–1908*, 801–53.
[138] Ibid. 812–14.
[139] Ibid. 851.
[140] See p. 428 above.
[141] A more detailed discussion of these developments can be found in my *Syndicalism in France: A History of Ideas* (London, 1990), 99–113.

publish a journal called *La Cité française*. Another, more successful, project was the launch of the periodical *L'Indépendance*. The message hammered home in both was that France's classical and Christian traditions were being overturned by Protestants, by Catholic modernists, parliamentary socialists, feminists, Jews, and Freemasons. This is not the place to rehearse the arguments of Zeev Sternhell to the effect that it was here that the origins of fascism were to be found,[142] but there can be no doubt that Sorel's post-Dreyfus Affair loathing of politicians and of bourgeois intellectuals focused his attention upon the rootless and messianic Jew as the antithesis of everything that had brought greatness to France. This was most clearly evident in a 60-page article devoted to exploring 'Quelques prétentions juives'.[143] The Dreyfus Affair, Sorel contended, had shown that 'Jewish particularisms had not in any way disappeared' and that the Jews wanted to control everything. The article ended, therefore, in a menacing tone. Having praised Charles Maurras for his 'defence of French culture', Sorel commented that 'Action Française seeks to inculcate its ideas among the youth of our universities; if it succeeds in attracting a sizeable minority of students to its cause, the Jewish intellectuals will experience bad times. But perhaps the Jews will be wise enough to gag their intellectuals?' That Sorel should have drawn such conclusions from the Dreyfus Affair was all the more worthy of remark given that, at the outset, this was an aspect of the Affair upon which he had scarcely passed comment.[144]

The fact was that anti-Semitism now flourished among sections of left-wing opinion where previously it had not existed. A similar evolution, for example, was apparent in the writings of Sorel's closest associate, Edouard Berth. His *Dialogues socialistes*, published in 1901, had not only defended socialism as a 'superior civilization' but had also denounced anti-Semitism as 'the protest of the *petite bourgeoisie* against big capital'. After the Affair he argued that France, 'the most plutocratic of nations', was the subject of the 'Jewish Empire'. The Jews, he believed, were the enemies of the concrete realities of the French nation.[145]

These views, and others similar to them, were expressed by Berth in the pages of the *Cahiers du Cercle Proudhon*. It was here, moreover, that Berth was to develop an argument which allowed him both to endorse a Maurrasian vision of a monarchy that was traditional, hereditary, anti-parliamentary, and decentralized and to maintain that this was 'perfectly convergent' with his own earlier endorsement of revolutionary syndicalism. The curious logic behind this position was by no means self-evident but it had much to do with Berth's conviction that parliamentary democracy was irredeemably corrupt and that bourgeois society offered little possibility for the development of an ethics of moral seriousness. Democracy, Berth opined, was 'nominalist, subjectivist, individualistic, atomistic': it was a regime without a memory and one which scorned the bonds of

---

[142] See esp. *Ni droite ni gauche: L'Idéologie fasciste en France* (1983).

[143] *L'Indépendance*, 3 (1912), 217–36, 277–95, 317–36.

[144] See Christophe Prochasson, 'Georges Sorel: itinéraire d'un Dreyfusard antisémite', in Michel Dreyfus (ed.), *L'Affaire Dreyfus* (1998), 235–43.

[145] 'Satellites de la ploutocratie', *Cahiers du Cercle Proudhon*, 5–6 (1913), 177–213.

'blood, race, history, the land, and profession'.[146] This argument gains further significance when we realize that Berth was here saying nothing that could not be found in the articles written by the other contributors to the *Cahiers du Cercle Proudhon*, most of whom were drawn from the ranks of the anti-parliamentary and nationalist right. Its opening editorial—a text signed by Berth under the pseudonym of Jean Darville—argued that it was 'absolutely necessary to destroy democratic institutions' in order to preserve 'the moral, material, and intellectual capital of civilization'. Democracy, it continued, was 'the greatest error of the past century' and, when combined with the establishment of the capitalist regime, was substituting 'the law of money for the law of blood'.[147]

The *Cahiers du Cercle Proudhon*, like the Cercle Proudhon which spawned it, never had more than a tenuous existence. It limped on into early 1914, securing no more than 200 regular subscribers.[148] Neither its importance nor its influence should be exaggerated. However, in bringing together such young men as Georges Valois, Henri Lagrange, Edouard Berth, and others, and in doing so under the joint patronage of Charles Maurras, Georges Sorel, and, of course, Pierre-Joseph Proudhon, it provided evidence of the disillusionment with democratic politics felt in some quarters at the time. For these young men the heady idealism of the heroic days of Dreyfus Affair had little purchase. They saw nothing to admire in 'l'État judéo-républicain'. Everything around them appeared to be in a state of decline, degeneration, and decadence. Accordingly, they longed for an as yet unattained national reawakening and renaissance. And, by the same token, they believed fervently, in Berth's own words, that this would not take the 'nauseating' form of the 'humanitarian, pacifist, and rationalist ideal' purveyed by the 'Intellectuals' who now controlled the State.[149] They were to be by no means alone.

By general agreement something quite profound had changed in the intellectual mood of the time. For long the view has been that, from around 1905 onwards, a whole generation of writers and scholars was exclusively preoccupied by the military threat of Germany and by the thought of impending war.[150] It was this that gave rise to the notion of 'the generation of 1914', of an iconoclastic generation only too ready to be seduced by the charms of violence and irrationalism.[151] In truth, this has been to see events retrospectively. When war did break out, the French intellectual community was as surprised as anyone.[152] The threat posed by Germany, in other words, was only part of the picture.

---

[146] 'Le Procès de la démocratie', *Revue critique des idées et des livres*, 13 (1911), 9–46.

[147] *Cahiers du Cercle Proudhon*, 1 (Jan.–Feb. 1912), 1–2.

[148] See Georges Navet, 'Le Cercle Proudhon (1911–1914): Entre le syndicalisme révolutionnaire et l'Action française', *Mil Neuf Cent*, 10 (1992), 46–62.

[149] *Les Méfaits des intellectuels* (1914), 19.

[150] See Elizabeth Fordham, *The Adventure Years: French Intellectuals, 1905–1914* (Ph.D. thesis, European University Institute, 2006). More broadly see Michel Winock, 'Les Générations intellectuelles', *Vingtième Siècle*, 22 (1989), 17–38.

[151] See Robert Wohl, *The Generation of 1914* (London, 1980). See also Roland Stromberg, *Redemption by War: The Intellectuals and 1914* (Kansas, 1982).

[152] See Stéphane Audoin-Rouzeau and Annette Becker, *1914–1918 Understanding the Great War* (London, 2002), 94–112. The authors state that: 'For Europeans, the beginning of the war was rapid

The broader picture was most famously captured by Henri Massis and Alfred de Tarde. As we know, *enquêtes* were now extremely fashionable, and Massis and Tarde, writing under the pseudonym of Agathon, had already cut their teeth with an inquiry entitled 'L'Esprit de la Nouvelle Sorbonne' devoted to an examination of recent reforms in higher education.[153] At issue were a series of measures imposed by the Republic which, it was claimed, downgraded the French classical tradition and gave pride of place to a Germanized vocational training. The 'secte sorbonnique'— Massis and Tarde's version of Péguy's 'parti intellectuel'—was held to blame. Flushed with success and satisfied with the controversy they had aroused, Massis and Tarde quickly moved on to produce a survey of the opinions of those they described as 'la jeunesse cultivé' and as 'le jeune élite intellectuelle'. *Les Jeunes Gens d'aujourd'hui* was published in the early summer of 1912 and met with immediate approval,[154] being reprinted several times and receiving the prestigious Prix Montyon from the Académie Française the following year.

From start to finish, the point of comparison was with those Massis and Tarde defined as 'the generation of 1885'. This, Massis and Tarde decided, had been a lost generation, 'une génération sacrifiée'. It had been pessimistic, wracked by self-doubt and scepticism, consumed by an inability to act, afflicted by a distaste for life, a prey to dilettantism and an over-refined egoism. Its intellectual masters had been Taine and Renan. The new generation, by contrast, had turned its back on doubt, was guided by a spirit of affirmation and had a taste for action. It was no less intelligent but was less in love with intelligence. Scorning relativism, it sought a morality of heroism, virility, sacrifice, and discipline. In the activity of war it saw the possibility of 'an aesthetic ideal of energy and strength'.[155] Accordingly, it was a generation not without 'patriotic faith' and through it could be discerned 'a revival of national instinct'.[156] Nor was it a generation lacking religious aspiration or sentiment. Having witnessed the revival of metaphysics—the reference was to Bergson—it was ready to accept the legitimacy of religious belief and to participate in a 'Catholic renaissance'.[157] Finally, it was a generation imbued with 'political realism'.[158] It had foregone 'the cosmopolitan culture' of its predecessors and no longer thought of humanity and of the universal but of the nation. It judged political questions from the perspective of France and was unanimous in its assessment of the causes of national decline. These, it believed, were to be found in the parliamentary democracy of the Republic. What was required, however, was less a change of institutions than a reform of 'political morals'. Interestingly, Massis and Tarde conceded that both 'the intellectual amoralism' and the 'implacable logic' of Charles Maurras and the Action Française movement held little appeal for these political realists.

and unexpected, and its speed was the determining factor in the way the groundwork was laid for support of the war. The evidence suggests that the groundwork was established in a few hours, perhaps even less.' Ibid. 94.

[153] *La Nouvelle Sorbonne* (1911).
[154] First serialized in *L'Opinion* between 13 Apr. and 30 June, it was publ. in book form in 1913.
[155] Ibid. 31.　　[156] Ibid. 28–31.　　[157] Ibid. 65.　　[158] Ibid. 94.

The picture presented by Massis and Tarde, therefore, was of a young generation which had turned its back on the scientism and positivism of the past and which exuded a sense of moral and spiritual idealism. For all its methodological limitations—only a small number of individuals were actually cited as evidence and many of these were Massis's own contemporaries—few people appeared to doubt the accuracy of their portrayal of the new representatives of French youth. Nor did they have reason to, as this was a description for which supporting evidence could be found.

To take but one example, these years saw an extraordinary number of conversions to Catholicism among the younger intellectual generation. If these were to include Massis himself and Charles Péguy, they were also to include such important figures as Jacques Maritain, undoubtedly one of the most prominent Catholic philosophers of the twentieth century, and many others.[159] Another development was the remarkable vogue for real-life adventure, be it in the form of the early aviators[160] or the colonial soldier. The latter was exemplified by Ernest Psichari, author of two novels[161] loosely based upon his experiences with the French army in Africa. Although dreadfully written, they were read avidly by his many admirers and did much to foster the image of military life as a source of moral grandeur. That Psichari was the grandson of Ernest Renan and that he too converted to Catholicism in 1913 only served to enhance his reputation as someone who had overcome the spiritual crisis and moral anarchy of the age. Christophe Prochasson and Anne Rasmussen are therefore correct to suggest that these years saw the appearance of 'a new type of intellectual, no longer the washed-out figure of the Dreyfusard intellectual, converted into the guardian of democracy and taken naturally to be cowardly and feminine, but rather that of the fervent defender of the values of civilization constantly threatened by the corrosion of decadence and barbarism'.[162]

Consequently, the outbreak of the First World War saw an immediate self-mobilization of the intellect behind France's war effort.[163] For those writers and scholars prepared to take this course of action—many volunteering for active service—there was more to this cause than the defence of the nation and the liberation of the lost territories of Alsace and Lorraine. France again figured as a land unlike any other, as a country whose fate was of universal significance. France's defeat would be humanity's loss.

This, for example, was the case with Maurice Barrès. Rallying to the French nation, he portrayed it, in all its diversity, as united against a common enemy and in common sacrifice. All—Catholics, Protestants, socialists, traditionalists, and Jews—merged 'their religion and their philosophy with France'. 'The old rabbi',

---

[159] See Hervé Serry, *Naissance de l'intellectuel catholique* (2004).

[160] See Robert Wohl, *A Passion for Wings: Aviation and the Western Imagination, 1908–1918* (New Haven, Conn., 1994).

[161] Ernest Psichari, *Terres de soleil et de sommeil (1908)* and *L'Appel des armes* (1913).

[162] Christophe Prochasson and Anne Rasmussen, *Au nom de la patrie: Les Intellectuels et la première guerre mondiale (1910–1919)* (1996), 9.

[163] See Martha Hanna, *The Mobilization of the Intellect: French Scholars and Writers during the Great War* (Cambridge, Mass., 1996).

Barrès wrote, 'offering a dying soldier the immortal sign of Christ on the cross is an image that will never perish.'[164] It was for an 'eternal France' and 'a more beautiful France' that the war was being fought. 'The French', Barrès concluded, 'are fighting for a land filled with their graves and for a sky where Christ reigns. . . . They are dying for France, and do so to the extent that the ends of France can be identified with the ends of God and even the ends of humanity. And it is in this way that they are making war with the passion of martyrs.'[165]

The extent and unanimity of the intellectual mobilization effected in 1914 can perhaps best be judged by looking at the composition of the Comité d'études et documents sur la guerre.[166] The intended purpose of the committee was to combat German propaganda by giving lectures and publishing pamphlets directed at neutral countries. Amongst its eleven executive members were to be found Henri Bergson, Émile Durkheim, Charles Andler, the philosopher Émile Boutroux, and two of France's most eminent historians, Charles Seignobos and Ernest Lavisse. The other five members were only slightly less distinguished and were for the most part drawn from either the Sorbonne or the Collège de France. Leading the way was Bergson. *Bergson politique*, as the late Philippe Soulez showed in a book of that title,[167] was a man deeply committed not just to the Republic but also to France. A fluent English speaker, he led several diplomatic missions to America designed to secure US entry into the war. Beyond this, he used his immense prestige as the world's most famous living philosopher to trumpet France's cause and to portray her 'idealism' as 'the essence of the French spirit'. When, as he did in a collective volume devoted to praising *La Science française*,[168] he spoke of the deepest aspirations of the 'soul of France', he spoke also of 'the need to philosophize'. Moreover, his was a rhetorical inclusiveness that placed France's soldiers in the traditions of both Jeanne d'Arc and the Revolution.[169] France, he told his audience in April 1915, had always identified herself with 'the double ideal of liberty and justice'.[170]

Many other philosophers joined the fray, the pages of France's philosophical journals being littered with articles comparing the national psychologies and philosophies of France and Germany.[171] The land of Descartes and of reason was unfailingly thought superior to a country where from Hegel, if not from Kant, to Nietzsche, philosophy had corrupted the national conscience.[172] A typical example

---

[164] *Les Diverses familles spirituelles de la France* (1917), 93.

[165] *Les Traits éternels de la France* (1916), 44–5.

[166] See Eric Thiers, 'Droit et culture de guerre 1914–1918: Le Comité d'études et documents sur la guerre', *Mil Neuf Cent*, 23 (2005), 23–48.

[167] Philippe Soulez, *Bergson politique* (1989).

[168] 'La Philosophie', *La Science française*, 1 (1915), 15–37.

[169] 'Discours en séance publique d'académie des sciences morales et politiques', in Bergson, *Mélanges* (1972), 1129.

[170] 'Allocution avant une conférence sur la guerre et la littérature de demain', ibid. 1156.

[171] See Philippe Soulez, *Les Philosophes et la guerre de 14* (1988) and Yaël Dagan, '«Justifier philosophiquement notre cause»: La *Revue de métaphysique et de morale*, 1914–1918', *Mil Neuf Cent*, 23 (2005), 49–74.

[172] On the controversy surrounding Kant see Hanna, *Mobilization of the Intellect*, 106–41.

of this genre was Émile Boutroux's *L'Idée de liberté en France et en Allemagne.*[173]
A member of the Académie Française, Boutroux had no hesitation in putting
forward the argument that the two countries operated with opposed conceptions
of liberty. The Germans, he wrote, had removed any sense of individual judgement from their definition, equating liberty with 'the power, expansion, and
domination of Germany'. By contrast, the French idea of liberty drew upon the
twin traditions of Graeco-Latin civilization and Christianity and therefore emphasized free will and the capacity of each individual to be 'master of himself'. To
the charge that this made France a country of 'ungovernable individualism', his
response, like that of so many of his colleagues, was that, through the use of
reason, the French acknowledged their duties towards their fellows and towards
humanity as a whole. 'Our flag', Boutroux affirmed, 'signifies *patrie* and liberty,
duty and right, in equal measure.'[174]

For his part, Durkheim—who was to lose a beloved son in fighting
in Macedonia—concentrated on vituperation of the enemy. For the Comité
d'études et documents sur la guerre, for example, he wrote a pamphlet entitled
'*L'Allemagne au-dessus de tout': La Mentalité allemande et la guerre.*[175] Its central
thesis was that 'the conduct of Germany during the war springs from a certain
mental attitude' and that this mentality could best be discerned by examining the
writings of Heinrich Treitschke. The Germans believed that the State was above
international law and that the defining element of the State was power. They also
believed that the State was above morality and that the sole duty of the State was
to be strong. Accordingly, they embraced the doctrine that the ends justified the
means. Finally, they believed that the State was above civil society and thus that it
was the duty of the citizen to obey. For them, the ideal statesman was someone of
limitless ambition and inflexible will. 'Germany', Durkheim concluded, 'cannot
fulfil the destiny she has assigned to herself without preventing humanity from
living in freedom.'[176]

For good measure, Durkheim also co-authored another pamphlet firmly attributing blame for the war to the Germans.[177] This was a line pursued by others of
his colleagues. For example, Charles Andler—as a Germanist someone seemingly
well-placed to pass expert judgement—argued in *Le Pangermanisme*[178] that from
the accession of Wilhelm II in 1888 German diplomacy and military planning had
turned their thoughts to territorial expansion and continental domination. Andler
also published a lengthy historical study of the doctrines of the German military
high command, castigating their readiness to disregard civilized and humane

---

[173] Émile Boutroux, *L'Idée de liberté en France et en Allemagne* (1916). By Boutroux see also
'Germanisme et Humanité', *La Grande Revue*, 19 (1915), 145–65, and 'L'Allemagne et la Guerre',
Revue des Deux Mondes, 33 (1916), 241–63.
[174] *L'Idée de liberté*, 36.
[175] Émile Durkheim, '*L'Allemagne au-dessus de tout': La Mentalité allemande et la guerre* (1915).
[176] Ibid. 47.
[177] Émile Durkheim and Ernest Denis, *Qui a voulu la guerre? Les Origines de la guerre d'après les
documents diplomatiques* (1915).
[178] Charles Andler, *Le Pangermanisme: Ses plans d'expansion allemande dans le monde* (1915).

behaviour,[179] as well as another pamphlet, co-written with Ernest Lavisse, purporting to document the authenticity of German military atrocities.[180] Entitled *Pratique et doctrine allemandes de la Guerre*,[181] it detailed the murderous brutality and cruelty of the German soldiers. To great effect, the Comité d'études et documents sur la guerre also published Joseph Bédier's *Les Crimes allemands d'après des témoignages allemands*[182] and his *Comment l'Allemagne essaye de justifier ses crimes.*[183]

With no difficulty whatsoever, it would be possible to cite many more brochures, pamphlets, lectures, speeches, and articles written and given by eminent and not so eminent writers supporting the French war effort. Indeed, enthusiasm for the war even stretched as far as the aesthetes of André Gide's *La Nouvelle Revue Française.*[184] Despite the huge loss of life and despite the vivid description of the carnage provided by Henri Barbusse's Goncourt prize-winning novel *Le Feu* of 1916, there were very few defeatists or pacifists. However, at least one more text merits our attention: Alphonse Aulard's *La Paix future d'après la Révolution.*[185] Given as a lecture at the Sorbonne in March 1915, the great historian of the Revolution of 1789 solemnly affirmed that 'the present war, the war that we are fighting against Prussian militarism . . . is nothing else but the continuation of the French Revolution'. The victory at Valmy, he told his audience drawn from the Amis de l'université de Paris, had had the victory on the Marne in 1914 as 'a distant but direct consequence'. 'Our soldiers', he went on, 'are the sons of the soldiers of Year II; they are risking their lives for the same ideal, with the same energy and with the same high spirits.'

To this extent, the Nobel prize-winning novelist Romain Rolland[186] was correct in his observation that 'since the beginning of the war, [the intellectuals] have brought so much violence and passion to bear upon it, that it might almost be called their war'.[187] Exiled in Switzerland, Rolland himself remained, as the title of his famous essay indicated, *Au-dessus de la mêlée*, producing a series of articles, open letters, and appeals which not only condemned German militarism—he was especially outraged by the damage inflicted upon the cathedrals of Louvain and Rheims—but also criticized the intellectuals of both sides for spreading 'the warlike contagion' and for an abdication of responsibility before a 'blind and menacing' public opinion.[188] The highest duty of the intellectuals, he proclaimed in February 1915, was 'to safeguard the spiritual unity of civilized humanity' but this they had

---

[179] *Les Usages de la Guerre et la Doctrine de l'Etat-Major Allemand* (1915).

[180] See John Horne and Alan Kramer, *German Atrocities, 1914: A History of Denial* (New Haven, Conn., 2001), 229–90.

[181] Andler and Ernest Lavisse, *Pratique et doctrine allemandes de la Guerre* (1915).

[182] Joseph Bédier, *Les Crimes allemands d'après des témoignages allemands* (1915).

[183] Joseph Bédier, *Comment l'Allemagne essaye de justifier ses crimes* (1915).

[184] See Yaël Dagan, *La NRF entre guerre et paix, 1914–1925* (2008).

[185] Alphonse Aulard, *La Paix future d'après la Révolution* (1915).

[186] See David James Fisher, *Romain Rolland and the Politics of Intellectual Engagement* (Berkeley and Los Angeles, Calif., 1988).

[187] *Au-dessus de la mêlée* (1915). This appeared in English as *Above the Battle* (London, 1916), 152.

[188] For a discussion of the role played by German intellectuals see Wolfgang J. Mommsen, 'German Artists, Writers and Intellectuals and the Meaning of War, 1914–1918', in John Horne (ed.), *State, Society and Mobilization in Europe during the First World War* (Cambridge, 1997), 21–38.

abandoned before the idols of '*Kultur* and Civilization, of the Germanic races and of Latinity'.[189] Never before, Rolland wrote, 'have we seen humanity throwing into the bloody arena all its intellectual and moral reserves, its priests, its thinkers, its scholars, its artists, the whole future of the spirit—wasting its geniuses as food for cannon'.[190] Nevertheless, not even Rolland could resist indulging in some familiar rhetoric. Speaking of 'the true France, the France of work and of faith', he admitted that he could never distinguish the cause of France from that of humanity, adding 'I wish France to be loved, I wish her to be victorious not only by force, not only by right . . . but by that warm and generous heart which is pre-eminently hers.'[191]

All hope that the spirit of unity forged during the war would endure after the end of hostilities was quickly dashed.[192] The signs were already there in the favourable, if understandably naïve, reception given to the Russian Revolution by large sections of the French left and the subsequent creation of the French Communist Party in 1920. Solidarity with the Russian people was often matched by a sense of alienation from domestic politics and the growing sentiment that the intellectuals who had embraced the *union sacrée* should be held to account for their actions. Certainly, the terms of post-war political debate had been set by the mid-1920s, with Bolshevism, colonialism, the renewed threat of war, and, later, the rise of fascism galvanizing intellectuals into action. On all sides, 'vigilance' became the watchword.

In January 1919 Henri Barbusse published his *Manifeste des intellectuels combattants* and later that year, in May, he launched Clarté, described as 'A league of intellectual solidarity for the victory of the international cause'.[193] Barbusse's launch of Clarté in its turn provoked the publication by Romain Rolland of another manifesto, subsequently known as the 'Déclaration d'indépendance de l'esprit'. Upon this occasion, the target was those intellectuals who, during the war, 'had put their science, their art, their reason in the service of governments'. In so doing, the manifesto proclaimed, 'they had disfigured, debased, cheapened, and degraded thought'. Intellectuals, it argued, should be servants only of the 'mind' and should serve no other master, be it a state, a country, or a class. 'Our duty, our role', the signatories affirmed, 'is to preserve a fixed point, to reveal the pole star in the midst of the disorder of the passions of the night.'[194]

Although Barbusse signed this manifesto (along with Benedetto Croce, Bertrand Russell, Heinrich Mann, Albert Einstein, and many others) it was soon clear that he was out of sympathy with its ethos. In the years that followed he and his group canvassed for active support of the Russian Revolution whilst Barbusse[195] sought to redefine the role of the intellectual, emphasizing not just the need for 'lucidity'

---

[189] *Above the Battle*, 119.
[190] Ibid. 167.   [191] Ibid. 100.
[192] For an example of the way in which the extreme right quickly abandoned the spirit of the *union sacrée* see Charles Maurras, *Les Chefs socialistes pendant la guerre* (1918). Maurras specifically challenged the attempt to paint Jaurès as a patriot.
[193] See Jean Ralinger, *Henri Barbusse, écrivain combattant* (1994).
[194] The text of this manifesto can be found in Rolland, *Quinze Ans de combat (1919–1934)* (1935), 1–6.
[195] See Barbusse, *Le Couteau entre les dents* (1921).

but for intellectuals, the 'workers of the mind', to be prepared to subordinate themselves to the needs and political will of the masses. Whoever is not with us, Barbusse intoned, is against us; whoever wills the ends wills the means; the use of violence by the oppressed was 'the reality of social justice'.[196]

Barbusse sought political commitment from intellectuals—as exemplified by his own membership of the Communist Party in 1923—and in so doing he made it clear that he had little sympathy for the abstract humanitarianism and pacifism he labelled derogatively as 'Rollandism'. The disagreement came to a head in 1921–2, when Rolland refused to support the new journal of the Clarté group and Barbusse in turn declined to participate in Rolland's planned international congress of intellectuals. What followed was a heated exchange of open letters between the two men, with Rolland asserting that he looked for a form of commitment that allowed the intellectual to act as an independent moral conscience.[197] As Rolland specified in a letter to the Communist Party daily, *L'Humanité*: 'I am with the proletariat when they respect truth and humanity. I am against the proletariat every time they violate truth and humanity. There are no class privileges, either high or low, in the face of supreme values.'[198] The clash between Barbusse and Rolland was to foreshadow a debate about the commitment of the intellectual that was to flourish for decades to come.

Only a matter of weeks after the publication of Rolland's manifesto the nationalist (and, for the most part, Catholic) right published its own manifesto on 19 July 1919. 'Pour une parti de l'intelligence', written by Henri Massis,[199] proclaimed the necessity of defending the intellectual and spiritual heritage of the Christian West from the forces of 'liberal and anarchic disorder'. Against 'the Bolsheviks of literature' and against 'the party of organized ignorance', the 'guardians of civilization' proposed a principle that was straightforward and simple: 'national intelligence in the service of the national interest'. With this in mind, the following year saw the launch of the *Revue universelle* under the editorship of Massis and monarchist historian Jacques Bainville. Defining its goal as the achievement of an 'intellectual and national Renaissance' and as placing France at the head of 'a civilizing mission', its opening statement made clear that no distinction was to be made between the 'service of France and the service of humanity'.[200]

Left and right clashed again in 1925 over the Rif war in North Africa. Once more Barbusse was in the vanguard, publishing an anti-colonialist manifesto entitled 'Aux travailleurs intellectuels: Oui ou non, condamnez-vous la guerre?' which proclaimed 'the right of peoples, of all peoples, of whatever race they belong, to govern themselves'.[201] Aligned by the side of Barbusse and his Clarté group were writers from *La Révolution surréaliste* (including Louis Aragon and André Breton) and the group of young philosophers associated with Georges Politzer. The right

[196] Ibid. 36, 46, 47.
[197] See Rolland, *Quinze Ans*, 33–58.
[198] Quoted in Fisher, *Romain Rolland*, 101.
[199] The text is repr. in Sirinelli, *Intellectuels et passions françaises*, 43–7.
[200] 'Notre Programme', *Revue universelle*, 1 (1920), 1–4.
[201] Sirinelli, *Intellectuels et passions françaises*, 62–4.

responded with 'Les Intellectuels aux côtés de la patrie', a petition addressed 'to the French troops who fight in Morocco for Law, Civilization and Peace' and which specifically condemned those 'who have the audacity to disfigure the lofty and generous duty towards progress and humanity displayed by France on the soil of Africa'. The same people, it pointed out, had not thought fit to raise their voices in defence of the thousands of people who had been 'tortured and executed by the executioners of Bolshevism'.[202]

Ten years later it was the Italian invasion of Ethiopia and the threat of sanctions imposed by the League of Nations against the aggressors that provided the opportunity for a virtual rerun of the same arguments, although with some new participants. The right produced a 'Manifeste des intellectuels pour la défense de l'Occident' signed not only by sixteen members of the Académie Française but also by such luminaries as Robert Brasillach, Pierre Drieu la Rochelle, Pierre Gaxotte, Thierry Maulnier, and Charles Maurras. Condemning what it described as 'a false legal universalism which sets the superior and the inferior, the civilized person and the barbarian, on the same equal footing', it justified the right of all European nations to possess colonies in the name of the advancement and protection of Western civilization.[203] The response came first in the form of an appeal headed by the writer Jules Romains and then a 'Manifeste pour la justice et la paix', penned by philosopher Jacques Maritain and signed by, among others, Emmanuel Mounier. Both texts supported the League of Nations, but the latter in particular denied that the 'mission of the people of the West' could be accomplished by force of arms. Casting themselves as 'the true representatives of French intelligence', the signatories called for all governments to respect international law and to work for peace.[204] The following three years—1936–8—saw similar petitions in response to the Spanish civil war, those for and against Franco, those for or against the Spanish Republic, those for or against intervention, claiming to defend civilization against either communism or military dictatorship. Interestingly, and as was the case with the war in Ethiopia, among those supporting the cause of the Spanish people were young Catholic writers such as François Mauriac and Georges Bernanos.

The inter-war years, therefore, saw no evidence of de-mobilization on the part of France's intellectuals. Indeed, if anything, their involvement in public affairs only intensified as France limped from one economic or diplomatic crisis to another and as disenchantment with the political system grew among the electorate. Curiously, if for the most part the participants in these debates now all seemed happy to describe themselves as intellectuals, discussion of the proper role of the intellectual in no way diminished. This was most clearly visible in Julien Benda's text of 1927, *La Trahison des clercs*, and in Paul Nizan's later polemical riposte, *Les Chiens de garde*.[205]

When the quarrel between Daniel Halèvy and Charles Péguy broke out, one of the people who had acted as an intermediary was Julien Benda. He had been

[202] Sirinelli, *Intellectuels et passions françaises*, 64–5.   [203] Ibid. 92–4.   [204] Ibid. 96–8.
[205] See Ray Nichols, *Treason, Tradition and the Intellectual: Julien Benda and Political Discourse* (Lawrence, Kan., 1978) and David L. Schalk, *The Spectrum of Political Engagement* (Princeton, 1979).

drawn into Péguy's circle at an early age and like them had thrown his weight behind the Dreyfusard cause. The mental outlook that had informed this political commitment was later spelt out by Benda in a volume of memoirs entitled *La Jeunesse d'un clerc*. It was this same outlook that informed the argument of his more famous essay on the betrayal of the intellectuals.

The first two sections of *La Jeunesse d'un clerc* focused upon Benda's family upbringing and his school years. What emerged was a picture of someone whose Jewishness was felt through an attachment to certain abstract values rather than as a religion and where those values—civil equality, the elimination of privilege, individual liberty, and the religious neutrality of the State—were also the values of the Republic. His republican education further reinforced his sense of loyalty to these values, producing a 'mandarin' with no sense of 'the particularity of his nation, his ancestors, or his race'.[206] The result was a vision of the intellectual consciously modelled upon the medieval cleric withdrawn from the daily realities of the world and whose function it was to meditate and to reflect, 'not to act but to think'.[207] As Benda later explained, the task of the 'true intellectual' was 'to think correctly and to find the truth, without concern with what will happen to the planet as a result'.[208]

'Not everyone', Benda wrote, 'has the opportunity at the threshold of their lives to make an abrupt choice between two very different moralities and to know what they are.'[209] This was what the Dreyfus Affair had enabled him to do. 'In a flash', Benda wrote, he had understood 'the hierarchy of values' that formed 'his very essence' and 'the visceral hatred' he felt for opposing views. From this point onwards he had held firm to the belief that truth and justice were 'abstract values' separate from the interests of either time or place. He had therefore opposed the position taken by Barrès not simply because it was 'profoundly anti-French' but also on the grounds that it constituted 'the systematic destruction' of everything since Socrates that had sought to raise human beings above their 'individual or group egoisms'.[210] Similarly Benda had no time for those Dreyfusards who were motivated by human compassion for the innocent Dreyfus languishing on Devil's Island. His protest, Benda wrote, had been an act of 'pure intellectuality', an affirmation of truth in the face of error.

This was the position that underpinned the argument advanced in *La Trahison des clercs*. Restated in more polemical terms he here defined the *clercs* as 'all those whose activity in essence is not the pursuit of practical ends and who, seeking their joy in the pursuit of an art or a science or in metaphysical speculation, in short, in the possession of non-temporal advantages, say in a certain manner: "My kingdom is not of this world"'.[211] This was not intended as a purely prescriptive account of how the intellectual ought to act, as this, Benda believed, was precisely how the *clercs* had operated in the past. 'Thanks to them', Benda wrote, 'it might be said that if, for over thousand years, humanity did evil it had honoured the good.'[212]

---

[206] *La Jeunesse d'un clerc* (1936), 50.   [207] Ibid. 121.
[208] *Précision (1930–1937)* (1937), 19.   [209] *La Jeunesse d'un clerc*, 203–4.
[210] Ibid. 198.   [211] *La Trahison des clercs* (1977), 194.   [212] Ibid. 195.

Moreover, it was precisely in this manner, according to Benda, that men such as Zola and Duclaux had acted during the Dreyfus Affair. 'They had been', Benda argued, 'the officiants of abstract justice and had not been sullied by any passion for a worldly objective.'[213]

Benda's complaint, however, was that 'at the end of the nineteenth century' the *clercs* had ceased to exist as 'a class of men' separate and distinct from the multitude and that they had subordinated their mission to the service of political passions. In so doing, they had abased the values of knowledge before the values of action and the cult of success. Doing nothing to resist the passions of race, class, and nationality, Benda affirmed, the 'modern *clercs* . . . had set about proclaiming that the intellectual function is respectable only to the extent that it is connected to the pursuit of concrete advantage and that the intelligence which is disinterested in these ends is to be scorned'.[214] The list of culprits was extensive and was not exclusively French—both Rudyard Kipling and Friedrich Nietzsche were cited by Benda, for example—but among the French writers accused of proclaiming the superiority of instinct, the unconscious, and the will over intelligence were Brunetière, Barrès, Maurras, Georges Sorel, and Péguy.

How could this 'great betrayal' be explained? Benda proffered three principal explanations. The first, and most important, was that the present age was the age of politics, the 'century of the intellectual organization of political hatreds'.[215] 'Today', Benda wrote, 'political passions possess a degree of universality, of coherence, of homogeneity, of precision, of continuity, of preponderance over other passions, not previously known.'[216] The *clercs* had come to share these passions and hatreds and to embrace what Benda termed 'the realism of the masses'. The second cause identified by Benda was 'the decline in the study of classical literature' and with that a lesser appreciation of what was 'human in its universal aspect'.[217] In effect, the charge was one of a loss of intellectual discipline. The third explanation drew upon an altogether different conjecture, and one that has since informed many critiques of the intellectual's supposed autonomy: the *clercs* had descended to the market place 'in the interests of their careers'.[218] Rather than the pursuit of knowledge as an end in itself, their goals were now fame, honours, and social status. 'The Bohemian man of letters', Benda wrote, is 'a figure who has practically disappeared'.[219] In similar vein, elsewhere Benda wrote that 'one of the great treasons of the modern *clerc* is marriage'.[220]

La Trahison des clercs was a deeply flawed book. It was also a self-serving book, designed not only to justify the position taken by Benda during the Dreyfus Affair but also his support of the French war effort in 1914. Roman Rolland, for example, was criticized for his 'mystic pacifism'. It also proved to be a controversial book and one to which Benda himself had to return on numerous subsequent occasions as he sought to steer a course through the turbulent political environment of the 1930s and 1940s. To the end, he believed that he had remained true to his original

---

[213] *La Trahison des clercs* (1977), 200.   [214] Ibid. 293.   [215] Ibid. 180–1.
[216] Ibid. 182.   [217] Ibid. 312.   [218] Ibid. 303.   [219] Ibid. 306.
[220] 'Le Clerc et la famille', *Précision*, 9.

principles, writing in the preface to the 1946 edition of *La Trahison des clercs* that 'when injustice becomes master of the world and the entire universe kneels before it, the *clerc* must remain standing and confront it with the human conscience'.[221] It was, on the other hand, precisely this argument that provoked the blistering attack directed against Benda by Paul Nizan in *Les Chiens de garde*.

Born in 1905 into a petit-bourgeois provincial family,[222] Paul Nizan entered the École Normale Supérieure in Paris in 1924 to study for the *agrégation* in philosophy. One of his fellow students (and soon to be a close friend) was Jean-Paul Sartre.[223] Unlike his more famous colleague, Nizan was quickly attracted to Marxism and in 1927 he joined the French Communist Party, subsequently writing for *La Revue Marxiste* and a series of other left-wing publications.[224] In 1931 he published *Aden Arabie* and then, a year later, *Les Chiens de garde*. The former drew upon his experiences in the British colony of Aden where, in 1926, he had secured a post working for Antonin Besse.[225] Nizan's first-hand experience of colonial exploitation did much to confirm his hostility towards capitalism but the early chapters of *Aden Arabie* also provided a vivid, and unreservedly hostile, portrayal of his own education. It was an account that differed markedly from that provided by Benda in *La Jeunesse d'un clerc*. Of his fellow students at the École Normale Supérieure, he wrote that they were 'exhausted by their years at the *lycée*, were corrupted by the humanities and by the bourgeois morals and cooking of their families'.[226] They were nothing else, in Nizan's opinion, than elitist hypocrites. As for his professors, they were men who believed that 'problems will no longer exist when the terms of debate are conveniently defined' and that the Good amounted to keeping the people in a position of subservience.[227] They acted, Nizan wrote, as 'watchdogs of vocabulary'.

The starting point of *Les Chiens de garde* was that all philosophies had a bearing upon the world. 'Every philosopher,' Nizan argued, 'though he may consider that he does not, participates in the impure reality of his age.'[228] Moreover, all philosophies were either beneficial or detrimental to the interests of humankind. There was, therefore, 'a philosophy for the oppressors and a philosophy for the oppressed'.[229] Thus, to speak of the abstract and eternal notions of Truth and Justice—which, in any case, did not exist—was to divert attention from the things that really mattered to the inhabitants of the earth—'war, colonialism, the rationalization of industry, love, the varieties of death, unemployment'—and was to put up a smokescreen before the economic, social, and political realities constituting the everyday oppression of ordinary people. If, then, as Nizan believed, the proper

---

[221] *La Trahison*, 135–6.
[222] On Nizan see W. D. Redfern, *Paul Nizan: Committed Literature in a Conspirational World* (Princeton, NJ, 1972) and Annie Cohen-Solal, *Paul Nizan, communiste impossible* (1980).
[223] When Nizan married in 1927 his two witnesses at the ceremony were Sartre and Raymond Aron.
[224] See Jean-Jacques Brochier (ed.), *Paul Nizan: Intellectuel Communiste 1926–1940* (2001).
[225] Besse subsequently provided the money to establish St Antony's College, Oxford.
[226] *Aden Arabie* (1931), 16. [227] Ibid. 14, 18.
[228] *Les Chiens de garde* (1998), 34. [229] Ibid. 57.

function of philosophy was to serve the real interests of real people, to adopt a position of 'impartiality or indifference' was to take sides. From this he concluded that 'the desire to be a *clerc* and only a *clerc* is less a choice made by an eternal man than the decision of a partisan. To abstain is to make a choice and to express a preference.'[230]

This was the charge levelled against those Nizan described as 'the fraternal enemies' who made up the world of French philosophy: Benda certainly, but also Bergson and Émile Boutroux, and, above all, Léon Brunschvicg from the Sorbonne. 'The audacity of their philosophy', Nizan affirmed, 'consists in identifying human society, all possible human societies, with bourgeois society, and human reason, all possible forms of human reason, with bourgeois reason.'[231] Nor did Nizan leave his readers in any doubt as to the consequences of such hollow bourgeois rhetoric. Arguing that to have defended Dreyfus was to have supported the bourgeoisie, he claimed that 'when the victim of a violation of justice is a proletarian there is no reaction at all from philosophy'.[232] More than this, it had been these very same men who had provided the philosophical justification for France's war against Germany. 'These *clercs*', Nizan fumed, 'simply emulated the crowd and followed the orders of the generals and the politicians. These men, most of whom were not subject to mobilization, meekly went along with the forces of ignorance and exhorted those who had been mobilized to give up their lives. Every one of their students who fell in battle was a martyr to their philosophy.'[233]

Nizan's explanation of this duplicity demolished any claim to autonomy on the part of the bourgeois intellectual. 'It is especially worthy of note', Nizan observed, 'that, generally speaking, our thinkers are salaried employees of the State, that the leading opinions in this country are produced in exchange for public monies and are backed by government sanctions.'[234] The Republic, in other words, had successfully replaced the spiritual guardians of the old monarchical and ecclesiastical order with a 'secular clergy'. This new clergy, Nizan continued, now discharged exactly the same functions as its predecessor, generating 'all the forms of moral suasion, all the spiritual propaganda which the State might require'.[235] Intellectuals—and specifically France's humanist philosophers—were nothing else but the purveyors of 'the philosophy of the State'.[236]

Nizan's claim therefore was that it was in their attachment to the world of the bourgeoisie that lay the real 'trahison des clercs'.[237] For that reason an alternative model to the 'contemplative *clerc*' of 'bourgeois thought' was required and this, Nizan believed, was to be found in the Leninist idea of the professional revolutionary, of the philosopher as 'the technician of revolutionary philosophy'.[238] 'His sole mission', Nizan wrote, 'will be to denounce all the conditions which prevent men from being human, to explain and describe these conditions so clearly that all those who do not yet understand how they live will attain consciousness of their situation.'[239] And this, Nizan argued, would only be possible if the

---

[230] *Les Chiens de garde* (1998), 59.   [231] Ibid. 73.   [232] Ibid. 149.
[233] Ibid. 52.   [234] Ibid. 117.   [235] Ibid. 119.   [236] Ibid. 116.
[237] Ibid. 151.   [238] Ibid. 154.   [239] Ibid. 152.

philosopher identified himself with both the class and the party which were the bearers of revolution. 'Today's philosophers', Nizan concluded, 'are still too embarrassed to admit that they have betrayed mankind for the bourgeoisie. If we betray the bourgeoisie for the sake of mankind, let us not be ashamed to admit that we are traitors.'[240]

During the 1930s Nizan continued to betray his own class. Abandoning his teaching career, he worked as a journalist for the Communist Party press, writing for both *L'Humanité* and *Ce Soir*, and in 1934 made the obligatory visit to the Soviet Union.[241] He wrote three brilliant novels, two of which, *Antonin Bloyé* and *La Conspiration*, explored aspects of betrayal. In the first, Nizan portrayed his anti-hero's abandonment of the working class for the comforts of bourgeois life: in the second, his subject was collaboration with the police by a young member of the Communist Party. As an opponent of the policy of appeasement, in 1939 he published *Chronique de septembre*, a biting denunciation of the Munich accord signed by Hitler, Neville Chamberlain, and the French premier, Édouard Daladier. However, he failed to anticipate one further act of betrayal: the signing of the Nazi–Soviet non-aggression pact in August 1939. Already mobilized into the French army, Nizan resigned from the PCF immediately. He died near Dunkirk with the fall of France in May 1940. What Nizan left behind was the first fully formulated statement of the concept of commitment and engagement and it was this that was to be taken up by writers in post-war France with such enthusiasm. But his name was also to be shrouded in controversy. Even before his death, the PCF had placed him among the opportunists and careerists who had deserted the Party and to this was added the unfounded rumour that Nizan had been in the pay of the police. When from the pen of Louis Aragon, recently promoted to the Académie Française, the PCF persisted in this slander, a small group of writers felt compelled to defend Nizan's memory, indicating that the PCF should either provide proof of its accusation or shut up. Among the signatories of this open letter of 29 March 1947 were Raymond Aron, Simone de Beauvoir, Albert Camus, Maurice Merleau-Ponty, Jean-Paul Sartre, and . . . Julien Benda.[242]

III

In 1932 a 19-year-old Albert Camus published an article entitled 'La Philosophie du siècle' in an Algerian journal, *Sud*.[243] It was a review of Henri Bergson's recently published *Les Deux Sources de la morale et de la religion*. This, Camus began, was a book that he had been eagerly anticipating. What he had hoped for was an 'effective application' of the Bergsonian method to ethics and, thereby, the exposition of a

---

[240] Ibid. 155.
[241] See Cohen-Solal, *Paul Nizan*, 137–82 and Sophie Cœuré, 'Les Récits de l'URSS de Paul Nizan: A la recherche d'un réalisme socialiste de témoignage', *Sociétés et Représentations*, 15 (2002), 97–111.
[242] Brochier (ed.), *Paul Nizan*, 13–17, and Pascal Ory, *Nizan: Destin d'un révolté* (1980), 237–54.
[243] *Cahiers Albert Camus* (1973), 145–8.

philosophy that ought 'to have been able to play the role of religion in our century'. In this, however, he had been disappointed. Whilst Bergson's was still 'the most beautiful' of all philosophies, the 'sublime conclusion' to his work had not been provided. Given Bergson's 'advanced age', Camus surmised correctly, it was doubtful that he would ever complete this task. 'But', Camus concluded, 'perhaps another philosopher will come along, younger, more daring, who will declare himself Bergson's heir. He will turn Bergsonism into an established fact and then move towards its immediate realization. Then perhaps we will have the philosophy-religion, that gospel of the century, for lack of which the contemporary mind wanders so painfully. Is this, in truth, too much to ask?'[244]

Camus, we might assume, probably imagined that he would be that young and daring philosopher. Certainly his later writings returned again and again to the questions he had been hoping that Bergson would answer. But was Camus right in his assessment of Bergson's text? Was it a failure or was Camus himself asking too much? Bergson's starting point was a discussion of the role of habit in social life and of the way in which people came to think of social norms as having such an unquestionable force that we felt obliged to obey them. As a consequence, for the greater part of our existence we acted unthinkingly, automatically, in state of passive lethargy, simply accepting the social rules that society had imposed upon us out of a sense of self-protection. 'Obedience to duty', Bergson wrote, 'means resistance to self.'[245] Bergson developed this argument by next suggesting that, corresponding to this state of mind, there existed both a 'closed morality' and a 'closed society'. A closed morality was one firmly rooted in our daily habits and one which called for an unthinking discharge of our duties. It was an impersonal morality, one imposed upon us from the outside and which we ourselves did not create. A closed society was characterized by the dominance of these social norms and obligations. Such a society, Bergson contended, was an inward-looking society, a society which could not transcend its own norms and values and one, consequently, where there existed a gap between itself and humanity. 'The closed society', Bergson wrote, 'is one whose members stand together, indifferent to the rest of humanity, always ready for attack or self-defence, one compelled, in short, to adopt an attitude of combat'.[246] Such, Bergson added, was 'human society when it emerged from the hands of nature'. It was the human equivalent of an ant-hill or a bee-hive.

The full force of this argument only became apparent when Bergson introduced the comparison with an open morality and an open society. An open morality was a form of morality based not upon habit but upon moral awareness and personal decision, a morality that was dynamic and creative. It was outward-looking and turned its gaze not towards family, party, or nation but towards humanity as a whole. As for an open society, it would rest not upon hierarchy and authority but upon democracy. 'Of all political conceptions', Bergson wrote, democracy was 'the

---

[244] *Cahiers Albert Camus* (1973), 147.
[245] *Les Deux Sources de la morale et de la religion* (1932), 14.
[246] Ibid. 287.

furthest removed from nature, the only one which transcends, at least in intention, the conditions of the "closed society"'.[247] Such a vision, Bergson conceded, had to be considered only as an ideal or, more accurately, as a direction in which humanity might be travelling, but it was nevertheless a vision which 'proclaims liberty, demands equality, and which reconciles these two hostile sisters by reminding them that they are sisters and by placing fraternity above everything else'.[248] Bergson, in short, offered a philosophically sophisticated defence of the Republic (and, as it turned out, the League of Nations).

However, there was far more to the argument of *Les Deux Sources de la morale et de la religion* than this. In his text, Bergson repeatedly emphasized that the difference between a closed and an open morality was not one of degree but of kind, and therefore that we would not pass from one to the other by a process of the expansion of the self or by a progressive widening of the bounds of the city to include humanity. Rather, what amounted to a leap from one to the other would arise from a powerful and joyous liberation of the soul from the grip of nature and through this would emerge an intuition into the unity of humanity. For Bergson this amounted to a mystical experience. Furthermore, in his view, the most 'complete mysticism' was to be found among the Christian mystics. To be clear, Bergson's conception of what he described as a dynamic religion was far from Catholic orthodoxy but, in specifying that religion was a crystallization of what mysticism 'had poured, white hot, into the soul of man', he opened up the way for a new moral aspiration which would have God firmly fixed at its centre and which would contradict the ideas, customs, and institutions of a closed society.

One can readily imagine Camus's dissatisfaction when he saw that Bergson's conclusion to what he unhesitatingly categorized as a 'long series of brilliant works' amounted to letting God back in through the philosophical back door. 'We already knew', Camus wrote, 'that instinct could render the whole truth. We all knew the advantages of the intuitive method. We were simply waiting for its consequences.'[249] Bergson's embrace of the Catholic faith was probably not one of the consequences that Camus had anticipated and it was certainly a step that he himself was not prepared to contemplate. Such a course of action was to require a faith that was no longer possible. Nevertheless, perhaps the young student was being unduly dismissive of both Bergson's achievement and of his conclusions; for, in a very real sense, Bergson had laid down the philosophical agenda that was to preoccupy the post-war generation. By turning away from intellectualism, Bergson had shown that morality could not be deduced from first principles and in doing so he had posed anew the question of the rationality of our ethical (and therefore political) commitments.

Although they were to disagree with Bergson's own answer and its religious tone, it was this question with which Jean-Paul Sartre, Maurice Merleau-Ponty, Simone de Beauvoir, Camus, and others were to grapple at great length, and with fateful consequences. Bergson's emphasis upon the superiority of an open morality in

---

[247] Ibid. 304.   [248] Ibid.   [249] 'La Philosophie du siècle', 147.

particular was to find a powerful echo in the important distinction between a habitual and impersonal morality and one that was authentic and creative of values. 'It is quite certain', Merleau-Ponty was later to write, 'that Bergson, had we read him carefully, would have taught us things that ten or fifteen years later we believed to be discoveries made by the philosophy of existence itself.'[250] Contrary to Camus's opinion, *Les Deux Sources de la morale et de la religion* should be seen as one of the most significant and portentous philosophical works of the last century.

The fact of the matter, however, was that, although Bergson continued to have his admirers,[251] his work largely fell from philosophical favour during the 1930s. This was so for a variety of reasons, but one of the most important was his frequent characterization as the philosopher of the bourgeoisie. In 1928, for example, Robert Louzon published an article in *La Révolution prolétarienne* entitled 'Henri Bergson, philosophe de l'homme d'affaires'[252] in which this very charge was forcefully articulated and, as we know, something very similar was argued by Nizan in *Les Chiens de garde*. The accusation received its clearest and most articulate expression in Georges Politzer's *La Fin d'une parade philosophique*. A young and enthusiastic Marxist, Politzer did not pull his punches.[253] Bergson, he wrote, 'has always been the enthusiastic ally of the State and of the class for which it is the instrument'. He had openly supported the war, had been against the Russian Revolution, and had not shown the slightest interest in rebellion. 'His entire life', Politzer concluded, 'enables us to see that he has given himself over entirely to the values of the bourgeoisie.'[254]

There was, however, a more original and interesting thesis contained within Politzer's attack. Bergsonian philosophy, he argued, could be refuted in a number of different ways. Its claims to be in accord with the findings of science could be challenged. Its theory of knowledge could be subjected to criticism. But, above all, it could be asked whether Bergsonism had understood 'the concrete'. 'If the answer is yes', Politzer wrote, 'Bergsonism is a great philosophy; if the answer is no, there must be a scandalous artifice at the heart of Bergsonism.'[255] Politzer's reply was in the negative and he therefore concluded that his task was 'to show what was hidden in the elegant box of the conjuror'.[256] What was hidden, in his view, was a new form of Pharisaism, a new form of hypocrisy, designed to hide 'the daily comedy of the bourgeoisie'.

The force of this argument derived from the fact that, in Politzer's words, everyone was talking about the concrete: it was, as he put it, 'la tarte à la crème'. To fail to talk about or to take into account the concrete was, therefore, automatically to invalidate a body of ideas. In this assessment of the thinking of the day, Politzer was undoubtedly correct and this became ever more the case as the 1930s

---

[250] Quoted in Gary Gutting, *French Philosophy in the Twentieth Century* (Cambridge, 2001), 114.
[251] See e.g. Vladimir Jankélévitch, *Bergson* (1931).
[252] *La Révolution prolétarienne*, 69 (1928), 1–2.
[253] Born in Hungary, in 1929 Politzer had been one of the founders of the *Revue Marxiste*. As a member of the Resistance he was executed in May 1942.
[254] *La Fin d'une parade philosophique* (1932), 10.
[255] Ibid. 12–13.   [256] Ibid. 97.

progressed. To that extent, the debate which came to dominate this decade was not one between left and right but one between those who persisted in clinging to what was castigated as the abstract individualism of bourgeois society and those who sought a moral and political renewal through the rediscovery of what was frequently referred to as either *l'homme réel* or *l'homme concret*. It is in this context that Jean-Louis Loubet del Bayle has spoken of *les non-conformistes des années trente*,[257] meaning by this the generation of young intellectuals who, from a variety of different perspectives and in a plethora of new and often short-lived reviews, sought to escape from what they regarded as a crisis of civilization. Often critical of Communism and of the Soviet Union, they were similarly hostile towards what was seen as the cancer of productivism and materialism typical of modern American society. In both cases, man was being crushed by the tyranny of the machine. The prevailing mood, then, was anti-capitalist, anti-liberal, and also anti-parliamentary. It was also one unsympathetic to the ideology of 1789.

No publication perhaps better exemplified this mood than *Esprit*, the review founded by Emmanuel Mounier in 1932.[258] Drawn largely from Catholicism, its contributors focused their ire upon what most commonly they referred to either as 'bourgeois and individualist civilization' or as the 'established disorder'. This was the society born of 1789, one in which individuals had been distanced and abstracted from their communal bonds and where the activity of work had become a burden and source of exploitation. It was a society in decline, one dominated by avarice and the power of money and characterized by the spiritual impoverishment and 'depersonalization' of its citizens. By way of reply, *Esprit* called for a new economic order giving primacy to work over capital, to personal responsibility over bureaucracy, to service over profit, and to decentralization over centralization. But more than this, *Esprit* called for a spiritual renovation and moral revolution. A political revolution, Mounier and his colleagues believed, would serve no purpose if it only succeeded to replacing one regime by another, if it did not effect a transformation of the moral conscience of man.

Reworking a formula first devised by Jacques Maritain, primacy was to be given to the spiritual over the material. This quite definitely did not entail an endorsement of bourgeois idealism (Mounier spoke of an 'anaemic idealism') or indeed of a bogus reactionary spiritualism, but was rather to be grounded upon what Mounier referred to as 'the concrete' or 'living individual'. It was for this reason that Mounier defined the doctrine of *Esprit* as that of 'personalism'. 'A personalist civilization', Mounier explained,

> is a civilization whose structures and intelligence are directed towards enabling all those individuals who comprise it to become persons. Natural collectivities are there recognized as realities, as possessing their own purpose, as being different from the sum of individual interests and as being superior to the interests of the individual. Nevertheless they have as their ultimate goal that of placing each person in a condition where they

---

[257] Jean-Louis Loubet del Bayle, *Les Non-Conformistes des années trente* (1969).
[258] See Michel Winock, *Histoire Politique de la Revue 'Esprit' 1930–1950* (1975) and Loubet del Bayle, *Les Non-Conformistes*, 121–57.

can live as a person, where they can enjoy the maximum of initiative, of responsibility, and of spiritual life.[259]

Aligned to this would be a 'personalist democracy' which, as Mounier was at pains to point out, would be far removed from 'a liberal and parliamentary democracy' resting upon 'the postulate of popular sovereignty' and 'the myth of the will of the people'.[260]

Such views fed into a powerful sense of dissatisfaction with the democratic institutions of what Albert Thibaudet termed the 'République des professeurs'.[261] Contempt for politicians, for political parties, and for politics in general now became almost the norm as government after government failed to meet the challenges posed by France's domestic and international problems. This malaise received graphic illustration with the right-wing riots of 6 February 1934 in Paris, interpreted by many as an abortive fascist *coup*. The intellectuals of the left responded with the creation of the Comité de vigilance des intellectuelles antifascistes, whilst the electorate voted into power the left-wing Popular Front government in 1936. The extreme right, now with Jewish premier Léon Blum as one of their principal targets and scapegoats—'Rather Hitler than Blum' read the famous slogan—only intensified their campaign against what they saw as a corrupt and degenerate political regime. This ill-tempered frame of mind was captured brilliantly in Robert Brasillach's autobiographical account, *Notre avant-guerre*, published in 1941 and dated '6 February Year VII. National Revolution'.[262] For Brasillach, the Popular Front was nothing less than a 'revolution of intellectuals' leading to 'the ruin of the State' and the 'vulgarization of immorality'. Never had stupidity, pedantry, and mediocrity been more in evidence. Out of this 'extraordinary bedlam' the workers had become convinced that they had no need to work and that everything would be provided by the government. Hope for France, he therefore believed, lay in abandoning 'the promises of liberalism, the equality of man, and the will of the people' and in following the example of Nazi Germany. There, he wrote, we have seen the 'birth of fascist man', young, virile, proud of 'his race and of his nation'. Here was the basis of an intellectual collaboration that followed the fall of France in 1940[263] and which, in Brasillach's own case, led to his execution for treason in 1945.

There is a question mark over how extensive such collaboration was.[264] Jeannine Verdès-Leroux, for example, has argued that there were 'few true writers ready to declare themselves as collaborators'.[265] Those that did, she believes, were mostly second-rate and there is no evidence to suggest that writers were queuing up to be invited to the Institut allemand in Paris. Others would disagree, pointing to the

---

[259] 'Manifeste au service du personnalisme', in *Œuvres de Mounier* (1961), i. 523.
[260] Ibid. 619.
[261] Albert Thibaudet, *La République des professeurs* (1927).
[262] Robert Brasillach, *Notre avant-guerre* (1941).
[263] See Julian Jackson, *The Fall of France: The Nazi Invasion of 1940* (Oxford, 2003). See also the classic text by Marc Bloch, *L'Étrange Défaite* (1946).
[264] See Albrecht Betz and Stefan Martens (eds.), *Les Intellectuels et l'Occupation 1940–1944: Collaborer, partir, résister* (2004).
[265] *Refus et violences: Politique et littérature à l'extrême droite des années trente aux retombées de la Libération* (1996), 216.

examples of Drieu la Rochelle, Henry de Montherlant, and Lucien Rebatet as evidence of widespread collaboration. What is undoubtedly true is that the world of wartime intellectual collaboration was constituted by a curious hotchpotch of convinced fascists (of one sort or another),[266] pacifists, defeatists, anti-Semites, anti-Communists, outright opportunists, and, later, anti-Gaullists. What is also clear is that those who were prepared to cast themselves as the ideologues of the National Revolution[267] instituted by Marshal Pétain's Vichy regime[268] were drawn from both the right and the left and that they were prepared to call upon a very diverse set of sources as guides to the intellectual character and inspiration of the New Europe. In 1942, for example, the writer Alfred Fabre-Luce published an *Anthologie de la Nouvelle Europe*.[269] In addition to readings taken from Hitler, Mussolini, Gobineau, Nietzsche, Richard Wagner, and others of a similar hue, he also selected texts from Renan, Georges Sorel, Charles Péguy, Paul Nizan, specifically arguing in his preface that 'Proudhon, Michelet, Quinet, sons of 89 and active participants in 1848, had already treated national socialist themes: respect for force, a counter-religion, the cult of the family and of the homeland.'[270]

It was arguably the monarchist doctrines of Action Française and of its principal theoretician, Charles Maurras, rather than the temptations of fascism, which received the greatest interest from those eager to save something from the wreckage of humiliating defeat. For Maurras, the defeat of 1940 amounted to 'a divine surprise'. Despite his anti-Germanism, he had no hesitation in calling for unconditional support of Marshal Pétain and the Vichy regime. Writing in *La Seule France*, he sought to blame France's defeat upon disunity and to protect the armed forces from any blame, arguing that 'the government of parties is the symbol of our divisions'. 'In France', he proclaimed, 'the Republic is the reign of the Foreigner.'[271] Accordingly, the restoration of both the State and the nation would require putting an end to 'the enormous power and monstrous influence exercised in France by people of a foreign birth and culture'. Maurras therefore supported the anti-Semitic and anti-Masonic legislation associated with the National Revolution, defended measures to strengthen the family, advocated educational reform designed to give greater influence to the Church, called for an end to democratic liberties, and promoted a series of industrial measures intended to forge a community of interests between workers and owners. Yet, as the abject failure (not to mention corruption and political infighting) of Vichy's political programme revealed, Maurras's own conception of France, of the 'pays réel', no longer had any significant purchase upon the real world. The clock could not be turned back to pre-1789. Ironically, Maurras himself was a perfect illustration of the problem, for his (as we might recall) was a Catholicism without faith. He was an unbeliever.

---

[266] See Philippe Burrin, *La Dérive fasciste: Doriot, Déat, Bergery, 1933–1945* (1986).
[267] See Philippe Burrin, 'The Ideology of the National Revolution', in Edward J. Arnold (ed.), *The Development of the Radical Right in France* (Houndmills, 2000), 135–52.
[268] See Julian Jackson, *France: The Dark Years 1940–1944* (Oxford, 2001).
[269] Alfred Fabre-Luce, *Anthologie de la nouvelle Europe* (1942).
[270] Ibid., pp. ii–iii. See Daniel Lindenberg, *Les Années souterraines 1937–1947* (1990).
[271] *La Seule France* (1941), 136.

There are two further aspects of intellectual collaboration meriting our brief attention. The first concerns attitudes towards the French Revolution. It should come as no surprise that pro-Vichy and pro-Nazi sympathizers were, in the main, hostile to the Revolution of 1789. In their view, the Revolution had been illegitimate, bequeathing a political regime characterized by chronic instability and a society in the grip of moral decadence. In a special edition of the review *Je suis partout* marking the 150th anniversary of the Revolution, for example, Robert Brasillach wrote that there was no reason to believe that the leaders of the Revolution had been any less corrupt than the politicians of the Third Republic, whilst right-wing historian Pierre Gaxotte defined the Revolution as 'an exercise in expropriation and extermination'. The other contributions were similar in tone and strident in their denunciation of a Revolution led by Jews and Freemasons. Nevertheless, for the aspiring Fascist there was much to admire in the cold and calculating leadership of Robespierre and the dictatorial power exercised by the Jacobins. Viewed from this perspective, their hostility to the bourgeois, liberal state, their preoccupation with the nation and national defence, and their emphasis on their own discipline and purity (not to mention, their ruthless dispatch of their enemies) offered an eighteenth-century prefiguration of national-socialism. For the tormented souls dreaming of a new order, the Revolution of Year II, Robespierre's Revolution, was a form of totalitarianism *avant la lettre*.[272]

The second aspect worthy of comment was a virulent form of self-hatred. In large part this focused upon France, and what was taken to be her decadence, her bourgeois culture, her rationalism, her materialism, her supine surrender, her vanity and arrogance, her abominable political leaders. 'France', Drieu la Rochelle confided to his diary in 1942, 'is finished, a second or perhaps even a third-rate country.'[273] She had become, novelist Roger Peyrefitte wrote, 'a civilization of shop girls'.[274] To an extent these sentiments were fuelled by snobbery and by what amounted to an aristocratic contempt for the masses, but they also were fired by a form of self-loathing that went beyond a detestation of Jews and of pederasts. Again Drieu la Rochelle pointed the way. His writings displayed hatred for others and self-disgust in equal measure. However, particular opprobrium was heaped upon the intellectual as a physically weak, effeminate, impotent, and sick individual, the very embodiment of a lack of vitality and virility. Faced with his own imperfection as a disembodied subhuman, therefore, Drieu la Rochelle idealized the man of action and longed for a world of youth, vigour, life, honour, and heroism. With his realization that collaboration had failed, he descended into self-pitying pessimism. In 1944 he refused all offers of escape from France and committed suicide in March of the following year.[275]

---

[272] See George L. Mosse, 'Fascism and the French Revolution', *Journal of Contemporary History*, 24 (1989), 5–26, and Shlomo Sand, 'Les Représentations de la Révolution dans l'imaginaire historique du fascisme français', *Mil Neuf Cent*, 9 (1991), 29–48.

[273] *Journal 1939–1945* (1992), 318.

[274] Quoted in Jackson, *France: The Dark Years*, 211.

[275] See Pascal Balmand, 'Anti-Intellectualism in French Political Culture', in Jeremy Jennings (ed.), *Intellectuals in Twentieth-Century France* (Houndmills, 1993), 165–9. See also Pascal Ory,

One writer who was immune from such spiritual impoverishment was Simone Weil.[276] Born in 1909 of Jewish ancestry, Weil was educated at the prestigious Lycée Henri IV in Paris and at the École Nationale Supérieure, where she studied philosophy. Upon graduation, the naturally rebellious Weil took up a teaching post in the provincial town of Le Puy and (somewhat uneasily) managed to combine her professional duties with militant trade unionism as well as writing for both *La Révolution prolétarienne*, edited by Pierre Monatte, and Boris Souvarine's *La Critique sociale*.[277] Never an admirer of the French Communist Party or of orthodox Marxism, she set about the writing of *Oppression et liberté* and did so in the firm conviction that we were living in an age 'without a future'.[278]

Since 1789, Weil argued, each new generation had placed its hopes in revolution but such hopes could no longer be sustained. Weil based this claim upon a critique of the Soviet Union—Lenin and the Bolsheviks, in her view, had succeeded only in creating a new form of oppression imposed upon the proletariat by a state bureaucracy and a privileged intellectual caste—but, more fundamentally, and contrary to the views of Marx, she believed that the capitalist system had not 'developed within itself the material conditions required for a regime of liberty and equality'.[279] Rather, Weil was convinced that the division, specialization, and mechanization of labour typical of modern production methods fashioned the possibility of a permanent enslavement of the workers and not their free association. Never, Weil wrote, has the individual been so completely delivered up to a 'blind collectivity'. Never had the 'social machine' worked more efficiently at 'breaking hearts and crushing spirits'[280] Such a bleak vision provided few grounds for optimism, but Weil was adamant that the 'most fully human civilization' would place the dignity of 'manual labour' at its centre and as its highest value. The best that we could do in these circumstances, Weil wrote, was to 'strive to introduce a little play into the cogs of the machine that crushes us'.[281]

It was after the completion of *Oppression et liberté* in the autumn of 1934 that Weil resigned as a teacher and began working as a machine operative in a factory. This painful experience only confirmed her fatalism. The same was true of the Popular Front. Despite her initial enthusiasm and sense of joy, the strikes and factory occupations of the summer of 1936 served to convince her further that a radical social transformation was not possible. Nevertheless, with the outbreak of the civil war in Spain, Weil made her way to Barcelona to join the anarchists where, like many a volunteer, she proved to be more of a hindrance than a help. What followed was a period of profound reflection and her conversion to a deeply spiritual Christianity.

L'Anarchisme de droite ou du mépris considéré comme une morale (1985) and François Richard, *L'Anarchisme de droite dans la littérature contemporaine* (1988).

[276] See Mary G. Dietz, *Between the Human and the Divine: The Political Thought of Simone Weil* (Totowa, NJ, 1988).

[277] See Weil, *Œuvres complètes*, II/1. *L'Engagement syndical (1927–juillet 1934)* (1988).

[278] *Oppression et liberté* (1955), 58.

[279] Ibid. 63.   [280] Ibid. 142.   [281] Ibid. 158.

In the few years that were to remain to her—Weil died in Ashford, Kent, on 23 August 1943 at the age of 34—a preoccupation with the divine became ever more present in her thoughts and her writings but the realities of politics—most notably, the rise of Nazism and the fall of France in 1940—could not be avoided. Living in Marseilles, Weil left for New York in May 1942 and arrived in London in December of the same year. She there joined the Free French and, with her health in rapid decline, wrote a long and unfinished manuscript entitled 'L'Enracine- ment'.[282] Subtitled 'Prelude to a Declaration of Duties towards Mankind', it was explicitly intended as a contribution to the debates about what form of government and society was required in post-liberation France. To say the least, Weil's views did not chime with those of many of her exiled compatriots.

The manuscript itself was divided into three sections. The first explored our reciprocal duties; the second detailed the nature of the 'uprootedness' that afflicted France; and the third set out a series of incomplete proposals for a new 'rooted' society. The tone was set by the very first sentence. 'The notion of obligations', Weil wrote, 'takes precedence over that of rights, which is subordinate and relative to the former.'[283] This, she affirmed, was something that the 'men of 1789' had not understood. Next came the claim that our obligations should correspond to 'the needs of the soul'. The latter were listed as a set of 'antithetical pairs' and were said to include the need for order and liberty, obedience and responsibility, equality and hierarchy, honour and punishment, security and risk, private and collective prop- erty, freedom of opinion and truth. 'The need of truth', Weil wrote, 'is more sacred than any other need.'[284] Nevertheless, the most pressing need facing the French population, Weil believed, was the need for roots. 'To be rooted', Weil argued, 'is perhaps the most important and the least recognized need of the human soul.' It was also, she continued, one of the most difficult to define. Thus, she argued, 'a human being has roots by virtue of his real, active, and natural participation in the life of a community which preserves in living shape certain particular treasures of the past and certain particular expectations for the future'.[285] As the 'sudden collapse' of France in the summer of 1940 indicated, it was precisely this sense of rootedness that the French people lacked. The urban proletariat, Weil wrote, had been reduced to a 'state of apathetic stupor'. The peasantry had been 'brutally' uprooted from the land. More generally, Weil argued, 'money and the State have come to replace all other bonds of attachment'.[286] This was the crux of her argument.

The focus of much of Weil's ire was the French state. 'The State', she wrote, 'is a cold thing which cannot be loved but it kills and eliminates everything that could be; thus one is forced to love it because there is nothing else.'[287] In the French case, since Richelieu in the seventeenth century, the ambition had been 'systematically to kill all spontaneous life in the country'. France was ruled like 'a conquered territory'. If, in 1789, those who had been French by force became so by consent,

---

[282] *L'Enracinement* (1949).   [283] Ibid. 9.   [284] Ibid. 38.
[285] Ibid. 45.   [286] Ibid. 90.   [287] Ibid. 102.

the Revolution 'melted all the peoples subject to the French crown into one single mass'. It thus succeeded in establishing 'the most violent break with the country's past'.[288] Each successive regime only continued the process of destroying local and regional life. If it was the fashion before 1940 to speak of 'eternal France', Weil remarked, such was the level of uprootedness that 'no Frenchman had the slightest qualms about robbing or cheating the State in matters relating to customs duties, taxes, subsidies, or anything else'.[289]

The task facing the Free French, therefore, was nothing less than that of 'refashioning the soul of the country'. And this could be done only if the people were provided with a country to which they felt that they really belonged. A spiritual and moral void had to be filled. Accordingly, Weil recommended a series of measures designed to secure 'the abolition of the proletarian lot'. Large factories were to be abolished. Every worker would own a house and a piece of land. Through education and land reform the peasant was to be freed of his inferiority complex and was to be reacquainted with the 'pure poetry' of working the fields. More vaguely, Weil argued that four 'obstacles' had to be overcome: 'our false conception of greatness; the degradation of the sentiment of justice; our idolisation of money; and our lack of religious inspiration'.[290] As David McLellan observed, 'it is extremely difficult to characterize the kind of politics that Weil is advocating'.[291] What we can be sure of, however, is that it was not the kind of politics that emerged at the end of the war.

With the Liberation of France from German occupation came what was known euphemistically as 'l'épuration'.[292] Under the aegis of the self-appointed Comité national des écrivains, lists were drawn up of those writers deemed to have collaborated with the enemy, those experiencing this misfortune being effectively prevented from publishing their work. Similar lists were drawn up for publishers and the press more generally. Those deemed to be the worst offenders were put on trial. In this often tawdry process the desire for vengeance was never far from the surface and, in some quarters at least, deep unease about the arbitrary punishments meted out was not slow to appear.[293] The whole episode did, however, bring the question of the responsibility of the intellectual into sharp relief. Could one write without consequences? Did the responsibility of the writer extend so far as to include the possible loss of his or her life? Were writers any guiltier than the innumerable engineers, civil servants, builders, and entrepreneurs who had worked to build the coastal sea defences against Allied invasion? As writers faced imprisonment and possible execution, these were not idle speculations.

Liberation also brought with it a not insignificant reconfiguration of the intellectual landscape. Discredited and silenced, the right temporarily vacated the stage, leaving it to be filled by those who had either fought in the Resistance or who had

---

[288] Ibid. 98.   [289] Ibid. 107.   [290] Ibid. 187.

[291] *Simone Weil: Utopian Pessimist* (Houndmills, 1989), 257.

[292] See Pierre Assouline, *L'Épuration des intellectuels* (Brussels, 1985). See also Ariane Chebel d'Appollonia, *Histoire politique des intellectuels en France 1944–1954*, 2 vols. (Brussels, 1991).

[293] More than one critic has seen a parallel with the Terror of the Revolution of 1789: see Lindenberg, *Les Années souterraines*, 259–60.

successfully negotiated the complexities of cultural life in Occupied France. Post-war euphoria was ideally suited to facilitate the emergence of a new generation of writers and philosophers, a generation ready to capitalize on the widespread yearning for renovation and change. What followed is a story too well-known to need recounting in any detail. The 'existentialist offensive' was about to begin.

Jean-Paul Sartre and Simone de Beauvoir had almost prospered during the Occupation.[294] Despite its physical hardships and privations, they were gainfully employed as teachers and continued to write, broadcast on the radio, and publish under the conditions of German censorship. In 1943, for example, Beauvoir published her first novel, *L'Invitée*, whilst Sartre published his monumental philosophical tract, *L'Être et le néant*. Neither, until the very end of the German occupation, showed the least interest in joining the Resistance. Nor was this out of character. Unlike many of his fellows, as a student at the École Normale Supérieure Sartre remained resolutely apolitical and in the elections which brought the Popular Front to power in June 1936 he did not bother to vote. Nothing was allowed to get in the way of the summer holiday he was sharing with Beauvoir in Italy. 'What I remember best', Sartre was later to write of these pre-war years, 'is the unique atmosphere of intellectual power and gaiety which enshrouded us.'[295] To that end, in 1933 he went to Nazi Germany to study philosophy. How this came about was captured wonderfully by Simone de Beauvoir in the second volume of her memoirs.[296] It is an oft-quoted passage but one that merits rereading, such is its candour and insouciance. When Raymond Aron came back from his studies at the French Institute in Berlin, Beauvoir reported, 'we spent an evening together . . . in the Rue Montparnasse. We ordered the speciality of the house, apricot cocktails; Aron said, pointing to his glass: "you see, my dear fellow, if you are a phenomenologist, you can talk about this cocktail and make philosophy out of it!" Sartre turned pale with emotion at this. Here was just the thing he had been longing to achieve for years—to describe objects as he saw and touched them, and extract philosophy from the process.'

It would be to do an injustice to the richness of Sartre's writings to suggest that the only outcome of his encounter with the work of Husserl and Heidegger was *L'Être et le néant*—the same themes were evident in his novels (most obviously *La Nausée* of 1939), his short stories, and his plays—but it was undoubtedly here that were set out most clearly the central themes of his existential phenomenology. For our purposes, there is no need to dwell upon Sartre's explorations of the key concepts of consciousness, being, nothingness, the self, and bad faith, but in order better to understand his later political journey it might be of use to comment briefly on the general tenor of his argument. The first point would be that, from Sartre's understanding of consciousness, it followed that we have no essence and therefore that we were free to be what we chose to be. The second is that, according to Sartre, our freedom induces in us a deep sense of dread and anxiety and therefore that we attempt to deny our freedom by resorting to bad faith. The two best-known

[294] See Gilbert Joseph, *Une si douce occupation* (1991).
[295] *War Diaries* (London, 1984), 175.
[296] *The Prime of Life* (Harmondsworth, 1983), 135.

examples of this provided by Sartre (both redolent of his own 'situation') were that of the café waiter who through his exaggerated movements plays at being a waiter and of the young girl who refuses to notice that she is being seduced by her lover. Such forms of bad faith were an aspect of what Sartre termed being-for-others. People were acting out a role given to them by others. Crucially, there was no way out of this, for it was in the nature of our consciousness that we wished to dominate others as, in the same way, they sought to dominate us. 'Conflict', Sartre wrote, 'is the original meaning of being-for-others.'[297] Could love overcome this conflict? According to Sartre, our concrete relations with others could only take the forms of indifference, sadism, or masochism.

On the face of it, Sartre's existentialism offered no grounds for optimism, presenting us with a bleak picture of individuals locked in an unending conflict from which there was no escape. Yet the same text also hinted at the possibility of a new ethical theory. The morally good life was clearly associated with freedom and authenticity: the immoral life was defined by conformism and bad faith. But what was to be the content of this morality? Apart from a few hints at the very end of the text, Sartre did not make this clear, promising only 'a future work' devoted to 'the ethical plane'. Certainly, Sartre offered no solution to the anxiety and conflict arising from our freedom. Nor was this something that did not go unobserved. Once again Beauvoir's memoirs provide enlightenment. 'At a party in Lausanne', she recounted, 'Sartre had met a young man called Gorz, who knew all his writings like the back of his hand and talked very knowledgeably about them. In Geneva we saw him again. Taking *L'Être et le néant* as his starting point, he could not see how one choice could justifiably be given preference over another and consequently Sartre's commitment troubled him. "That's because you're Swiss", Sartre told him.' As a matter of fact, Beauvoir added without a hint of levity, he was an Austrian Jew.[298]

Sartre did his best to answer this criticism in his celebrated lecture of 1945, *L'Existentialisme est un humanisme*, where he argued, implausibly, that existentialism did not confine man 'within his own subjectivity' and that 'no doctrine is more optimistic'. 'What is at the very heart and centre of existentialism', Sartre proclaimed, 'is the absolute character of the free commitment by which every man realizes himself in realizing a type of humanity.'[299] The more serious response was Sartre's endeavour to redefine himself as a 'writer who resisted'. This he did to great effect and with remarkable audacity. By sleight of hand Sartre positioned himself within the Resistance, equating the passive resistance of those who had 'had to remain silent' with the heroic deeds of those who had risked and lost their lives, and so much so that when in the very first edition of *Les Temps modernes* he proclaimed that 'I hold Flaubert and Goncourt responsible for the repression which followed the Commune because they did not write one line to prevent it' no one imagined that the same thing might have been said with some justification of Sartre's own literary career during the Occupation. Having successfully taken this

[297] *Being and Nothingness* (London, 1972), 364.
[298] *Force of Circumstance* (Harmondsworth, 1968), 100–1.
[299] *Existentialism and Humanism* (London, 1975), 47.

step, Sartre's next move was to sketch out the philosophical and political grounds of what he saw as an engaged literature.

This Sartre did most thoroughly in *Qu'est-ce que la littérature?*, published in 1948. In both tone and content it bore a striking resemblance to the argument advanced in Nizan's *Les Chiens de garde*. Denouncing 'the aesthetic purity' of bourgeois literature and the 'lay morality' taught by such 'petit-bourgeois professors' as Durkheim and Brunschvicg, Sartre affirmed that 'the author writes in order to address himself to the freedom of readers' and from this, he argued, it followed that the question facing the writer was:'Why have you spoken of this rather than that, and—since you speak in order to about change—why do you want to change this rather than that?'[300] At the heart of literature, in other words, there lay 'a moral imperative'. This did not mean that, like Benda's *clerc*, the writer was to be 'the guardian of universal values'. Rather, Sartre affirmed, the poet, the essayist, and the novelist were to write for the proletariat because the proletariat alone was capable of transforming the possibility of freedom into an actuality. The committed writer, Sartre stated, knew that words were action.

The writer, then, was enjoined to embrace his epoch and it was precisely this that Sartre himself attempted to do for the remainder of his life, attaining a level of celebrity for his demonstrations of political commitment that few have ever matched. The intellectual, he never tired of repeating in subsequent years, was obliged to take sides, 'to commit himself to every one of the conflicts of our time', to recognize that all such conflicts—be they class, national, or racial—were struggles between particular groups for the 'statute of universality'. The 'true' intellectual's most immediate enemy was the 'false intellectual', the defender of 'bourgeois humanism' and of 'a false bourgeois universality'.[301]

More striking still was Sartre's conversion to Marxism and his effective abandonment of existentialism.[302] This was a long process, culminating in the publication of the *Critique de la raison dialectique* in 1960. Marxism, he now declared, was 'the untranscendable philosophy of our time'. The philosophical intricacies of this lengthy tome might best be summarized by suggesting that Sartre here relocated the existential struggle between one individual and another at the level of consciousness described in *L'Être et le néant* with a struggle determined, above all, by economic scarcity. 'Nothing, not even wild beasts or microbes,' Sartre now wrote, 'could be more terrifying for man than a species which is intelligent, carnivorous, and cruel, and which can understand and outwit human intelligence and whose aim is precisely the destruction of man. This, however, is obviously our own species as perceived in others by each of its members in the context of scarcity.'[303] In those circumstances—in effect, the circumstances of capitalism and of a society divided into classes—human beings lived in a condition of 'alterity', one in which our

---

[300] *What is Literature?* (London, 1970), 15.

[301] See e.g. 'A Plea for Intellectuals', in Sartre, *Between Existentialism and Humanism* (London, 1983), 228–85.

[302] See Mark Poster, *Existential Marxism in Postwar France: From Sartre to Althusser* (Princeton, NJ, 1975).

[303] *Critique of Dialectical Reason* (London, 1982), 132.

relations with others were those of separation rather than reciprocity and where society took the form of a 'series' or 'collective' characterized by a lack of community. Sartre illustrated this beautifully with the example of a queue of people in the place Saint-Germain waiting for a bus. Although they possessed a common goal, the people in the queue existed in isolation.

The greater part of the *Critique de la raison dialectique* explored the manner in which we might escape this condition of alterity and seriality. Sartre offered two possibilities. The first entailed the overcoming of scarcity through the economic reorganization of society and the abolition of capitalism. The second was more intriguing. What Sartre described was the transition from the series to the 'fused group', a situation in which there existed an absolute identity of interests between its members and where other people would become a source for, rather than an obstacle to, our freedom. Such a condition most typically emerged in circumstances of external danger or actual revolution. To illustrate the point Sartre chose as his example the storming of the Bastille on 14 July 1789 by the people of Paris. 'In this behaviour', Sartre wrote, 'everyone sees his own future in the Other and, on that basis, discovers his present action in that of the Other.'[304]

Yet written into the *Critique de la raison dialectique* was a vaguely tragic vision of our fate. After the revolution, Sartre argued, it should be our aim to preserve the group and to avoid lapsing back into the chaotic condition of seriality in which individuals are at war with one another. But Sartre recognized that the existence of the group was at best unstable and fleeting. Under constant threat from outside and from disunity within, the group would turn itself into an organization, into an 'institution', where there would exist a division of labour and where certain people would hold positions of authority. Mutuality and reciprocity would give way to the re-emergence of hierarchy and inertia. This time the principal example cited by Sartre was the descent into Terror experienced after 1789.

Did this mean that Sartre's analysis of the dialectic was ultimately redundant? If it did nothing else, it allowed Sartre to establish a critique of all those institutions which embodied seriality and thus to show that his vision of the future in a post-capitalist society was far removed from that of actual existing socialism in the Soviet bloc. The dictatorship of the proletariat, he wrote, was 'a bastard compromise between the active sovereignty of the group and passive seriality' leading to bureaucratic terror and the cult of personality. The internal contradictions of the socialist world, he continued, brought forth 'the objective exigency for de-bureaucratization, decentralization, and democratization'.[305] Likewise, it was the participatory 'group-in-fusion', rather than the elite Leninist political party, that was to be the proper mode of revolutionary praxis. From this it was but a short step to Sartre's support of the student demonstrations of May 68 and the violent tactics of Maoism.[306]

---

[304] Ibid. 354.   [305] Ibid. 661–2.

[306] For three comprehensive biographies of Sartre see Annie-Cohen Solal, *Sartre: A Life* (London, 1985); Ronald Hayman, *Writing Against: A Biography of Sartre* (London, 1986); and Bernard Henri-Lévy, *Le Siècle de Sartre* (2000).

It is impossible to speak of Sartre without mentioning Simone de Beauvoir.[307] Hers was a life as remarkable and her achievements were as significant. She, like Sartre, led the existentialist offensive and she, like him, underwent a radical conversion in the post-war years. She too expressed her ideas in a variety of literary forms: novels, plays, essays, and philosophical treatises. In some respects, however, her most substantial literary achievement was her three-volume autobiography, published between 1958 and 1963.[308] Here was an account of a life that was no less candid and high-minded than it was humourless and self-serving. Only marginally less memorable was her Goncourt prize-winning novel, *Les Mandarins*, a *roman à clef* which, despite Beauvoir's claims to the contrary, chronicled the lives of Sartre, Camus, herself. and other inhabitants of the incestuous world of the Parisian Left Bank. The title, Beauvoir later recalled, was chosen to reflect the fact that, as intellectuals, they existed as 'a race apart', the only remaining nobility in France.

In 1943 Beauvoir began writing an essay entitled *Pyrrhus et Cinéas*. It was intended to be a companion piece to Sartre's *L'Être et le néant* and sought (unsuccessfully) to define an ethics of freedom. Four years later, and encouraged by the favourable reception her first essay had received, she again took up the challenge of basing a morality upon Sartre's text in her most sustained philosophical work, *Pour une morale de l'ambiguité*. Her intention, she subsequently explained in her memoirs, was to refute the charge that existentialism was a 'nihilistic philosophy, wilfully pessimistic, frivolous, licentious, despairing, and ignoble'. Again, however, it was something of a failure. 'I was in error', she wrote in 1963, 'when I thought that I could define a morality independent of a social context.'[309] Sartre, as we know, was experiencing similar problems. Infinitely more successful, however, was Beauvoir's attempt to apply the lessons of existentialism to an examination of the condition of women.

The impact of existentialism upon the argument of *Le Deuxième Sexe* was visible in three primary ways. First, Beauvoir was able to argue that women possessed no fixed nature or essence. This was the argument that informed her famous statement that: 'One is not born but one becomes a woman. No biological, psychological, or economic fate determines the figure that the human female presents in society.'[310] Second, existentialist ethics stipulated that women, as much as men, were free and autonomous beings and therefore that they were capable of transcending their present condition and of living a life of authenticity rather than one of immanence and stagnation. Third, and most importantly, existentialism provided an explanation of the cause of the original subjection of women. This phenomenon was a

[307] On Beauvoir see Deidre Bair, *Simone de Beauvoir: A Biography* (London, 1990). On Sartre and Simone de Beauvoir, see Hazel Rowley, *Tête-à-Tête: The Tumultuous Lives and Loves of Simone de Beauvoir and Jean-Paul Sartre* (London, 2006) and Carole Seymour Jones, *A Dangerous Liaison: Simone de Beauvoir and Jean-Paul Sartre* (London, 2008).

[308] See *Mémoires d'une jeune fille rangée* (1958); *La Force de l'âge* (1960); and *La Force des choses* (1963).

[309] Beauvoir, *Force of Circumstance*, 76. See Anne Whitmarsh, *Simone de Beauvoir and the Limits of Commitment* (Cambridge, 1981) and Penelope Deutscher, *The Philosophy of Simone de Beauvoir: Ambiguity, Conversion, Resistance* (Cambridge, 2008).

[310] *The Second Sex* (Harmondsworth, 1984), 295.

'result of the imperialism of the human consciousness'. If, Beauvoir explained, 'the human consciousness had not included the original category of the Other and an original aspiration to dominate the Other, the invention of the bronze tool could not have caused the oppression of women'.[311] Women, in other words, found themselves in a world where men compelled them to adopt the status of the Other.

Less evident was the manner in which existentialism might enable women to overcome their subordinate position. A change in women's economic condition alone would not be sufficient to effect this transformation. Nevertheless, Beauvoir placed great emphasis upon the emergence of 'the independent woman'. She similarly stressed the need to engage in an activity of demystification and to avoid gender stereotyping. Crucially, however, she insisted that 'legends notwithstanding, no physiological destiny imposes an eternal hostility upon Male and Female as such'.[312] Accordingly, Beauvoir affirmed, the present condition endured by women could be surmounted and, as she continued her ascent, an 'inner metamorphosis' would occur heralding the arrival of the 'new women'. When this occurred, women and men would live in a condition of reciprocity and mutuality. Nor, she concluded movingly, would this do away with the 'miracles' of 'desire, love, possession, dream, adventure' that arose from the division of human being into two categories. 'On the contrary', she wrote, 'when we abolish the slavery of half of humanity, together with the whole system of hypocrisy that it implies, the "division" of humanity will reveal its genuine significance and the human couple will find its true form.'[313]

When *Le Deuxième Sexe* was published in 1949 it sold 20,000 copies in its first week. It also provoked a well-nigh unprecedented outpouring of criticism and abuse.[314] It is not difficult to understand why. The second part of *Le Deuxième Sexe*, exploring 'women's lived experience', was devoted to a detailed examination of such topics as menstruation, sexual initiation, lesbianism, pregnancy, marriage, and motherhood, the like of which had probably never been published before and certainly not as a work of philosophy. Conservative critics condemned it as a work of pornography. Many on the left—especially within the French Communist Party—were similarly shocked and dismissive. Nevertheless, for all its undoubted faults, *Le Deuxième Sexe* must rank as one of the most significant and important texts to be published in post-war France. Not only did it establish Simone de Beauvoir as a figure and a thinker in her own right, but it also provided the impetus for her own subsequent involvement in the feminist movement during the 1970s.

In the words of Simone de Beauvoir, both she and Sartre had the impression that Frantz Fanon 'must be one of the most remarkable personalities of our time'.[315] When they first met, however, Fanon was already dying of the leukaemia that would kill him in 1961 at the early age of 36. Fanon had been drawn early to Sartre's writings and especially to the argument advanced in his *Réflexions sur la question juive* that it was not the Jewish character that provoked anti-Semitism but

[311] Ibid. 88–9.   [312] Ibid. 725.   [313] Ibid. 741.
[314] See Ingrid Galster (ed.), *Le Deuxième Sexe de Simone de Beauvoir* (2004).
[315] Beauvoir, *Force of Circumstance*, 597, 605–11.

rather the anti-Semite who created the Jew.[316] For his part, from 1948 onwards Sartre was increasingly preoccupied with the issue of colonialism and the emerging anti-colonial struggles in Africa and Asia.[317]

On the face it, there was something deeply incongruous about a Republic possessing a colonial empire.[318] How could a regime founded upon rights, equality, and the rule of law be reconciled to a system of exclusion, discrimination, and violence? Yet the establishment of an overseas empire had been an integral, rather than a marginal, dimension of the republican project from the early years of the Third Republic onwards. In part, this policy was driven by the desire to replicate the lost empire of the *ancien régime* and to match the British Empire, but after the military defeat of 1870 empire-building was likewise fostered by the need to restore national pride and honour. The French were also not without a taste for exoticism. However, in the eyes of its proponents, the French Empire was to be marked out from its competitors by the spirit of generosity in which it was to be created and by its 'civilizing mission'. Instead of oppression, there was to be liberty; instead of exploitation there was to be emancipation. What is more, this sense of mission was born of the two Frances. As the eldest daughter of the Church, France was under an obligation to spread the Christian message: as the inheritor and embodiment of the traditions of 1789, she was under a duty to save the oppressed and to export fraternity. Armed thus, it became possible for generations of sincere republicans and of devout Catholics to denounce the iniquities and abuses of colonialism[319] and yet remain ardent defenders of a system whose self-proclaimed task was that of freeing the indigenous colonized peoples from savagery and ignorance and of providing both education and health. The instruments of colonization, therefore, were not only to be the soldier, the administrator, and the settler, but also the teacher, the priest, and the doctor. To what extent this vision of empire bore any relation to reality is not a question that needs to be answered here. It is sufficient for us to know that, as France sought to re-establish her empire in Indo-China and North Africa after the Second World War, it was a vision that became increasingly difficult to sustain.

Frantz Fanon was born in the French Caribbean island of Martinique and was a descendant of slaves. He completed his studies in psychiatry in Paris and Lyons and in 1952 took up a post in French Algeria as a doctor. The following year he married a white French woman. It was in the year of his appointment to Algeria that Fanon published *Peau Noir, Masques Blancs*.[320] Described by Fanon as a 'clinical study', its subject was the position of the black person in relation to the white colonizer. It owed much to the phenomenological arguments of Sartrean existentialism. In brief, Fanon analysed the numerous ways in which the black person was persuaded to feel

---

[316] Sartre, *Réflexions sur la question juive* (1946).
[317] See Azzedine Haddour, Steve Brewer, and Terry McWilliams (eds.), *Sartre: Colonialism and Neocolonialism* (London, 2001). This includes Sartre's introduction to Fanon's *Les Damnés de la terre*.
[318] See Raoul Girardet, *L'Idée coloniale en France de 1871 à 1961* (1972) and Nicolas Bancel, Pascal Blanchard, and Françoise Vergès, *La République coloniale: Essai sur une utopie* (2003).
[319] See e.g. André Gide's *Voyage au Congo* (1927) and *Le Retour du Chad* (1928).
[320] Frantz Fanon, *Peau Noir, Masques Blancs* (1952).

inferior to the white colonizer and how he became ashamed of his own colour, language, and culture. Fanon also looked at the 'arsenal of complexes' that intruded their way into the sexual relationships between black and white persons, in the process exposing the supposed anatomical superiority of the black male as a myth. His overall conclusion was that, in the colonized world, the choice facing the black person was that of 'turn white or disappear'. As Fanon wrote, 'the Negro will become proportionately whiter—that is, he will become closer to being a real human being—in direct ratio to his mastery of the French language'.[321] The challenge facing the black person, therefore, was to choose authenticity and freedom. This could be achieved through nothing less than the removal of the colonial environment.

It is clear that if Fanon, at this point, was not so naïve as to believe that such a 'restructuring of the world' could be brought about by appeals to reason and the dignity of man, he did imagine that it was possible to envisage 'a healthy encounter between black and white'.[322] In this sense, there were clear parallels to the positions then being developed by both Sartre on the proletariat and Beauvoir on the position of women. Like them, however, Fanon too was to undergo a radical conversion in the years which immediately followed. In his case, the decisive factor was his first-hand familiarity with the Algerian rebellion. Begun in 1954 and ending in 1961, this turned into a conflict of awful ferocity. Moreover, as a doctor, Fanon was to be witness to the victims of torture.

It was this experience that led to the publication of Fanon's *Les Damnés de la terre* in 1961[323] and also caused Fanon to appreciate fully the nature of colonialism.[324] Fanon now wrote that colonialism 'is not a thinking machine, nor a body endowed with reasoning faculties. It is violence in its natural state and it will only yield when confronted with great violence.'[325] Accordingly, Fanon addressed two major themes by way of response: the use of violence by the oppressed and the definition of those best placed to use violence. The tenor of Fanon's argument can be judged by his statement that 'when the native hears a speech about Western culture he pulls out the knife—or at least makes sure it is within easy reach'.[326] In other words, Fanon went beyond recommending that violence could be employed for strategic reasons and insisted upon its value as a means of purification. 'At the level of individuals', he wrote, 'violence is a cleansing force. It frees the native from his inferiority complex and from his despair and inaction; it makes him fearless and restores his self-respect.'[327] Violence, Fanon argued, would do more than 'songs, poems, and folklore' to restore an oppressed people's national culture.

Concerning the perpetrators of these acts, Fanon took the decisive step not only of relocating the revolutionary class from the white proletariat in Europe to the

[321] *Black Skin, White Masks* (London, 1970), 13.

[322] Ibid. 57.

[323] Frantz Fanon, *Les Damnés de la terre* (1961).

[324] See also Fanon's *L'An V de la révolution algérienne* (Paris, 1961) and *Pour la révolution africaine* (1964).

[325] *The Wretched of the Earth* (Harmondsworth, 1971), 48.

[326] Ibid. 32.   [327] Ibid. 74.

colonies but of also discounting the native bourgeoisie and the colonized intellectual. Indeed, Fanon discounted all those who had begun to benefit from the
colonial set up. According to Fanon, it was the peasantry who were revolutionary
and this was so because they had nothing to lose and everything to gain. As the
'urban spearhead' of the revolution, however, Fanon added the lumpen-proletariat,
'the hopeless dregs of humanity', the uprooted of the shanty towns. These people,
he wrote, are 'like a horde of rats; you may kick them and you may throw stones at
them, but despite your efforts they'll go on gnawing at the roots of the tree'.[328]
'Now', Fanon concluded, 'the fellah, the unemployed man, the starving native do
not lay claim to the truth; they do not say that they represent the truth, for they are
the truth.'[329]

Simone de Beauvoir reported that relations with Fanon could often be very
difficult—Fanon, she wrote, 'could not forget that Sartre was French and he
blamed him for not having expiated that crime sufficiently'[330]—but it was Sartre
who wrote a long preface for *Les Damnés de la terre*. What this text demonstrated
was the concordance of their views, for Sartre too believed that colonialism was a
system with its own internal necessities, that it could not be reformed, and that it
infected France herself with racism. It also heralded the emergence of 'tiers-
mondisme' as an ideology and of a 'new left' which throughout the 1960s focused
its attention upon the liberation struggles taking place in Africa, Asia, and Latin
America and increasingly turned away from what it saw as the obsolete and ossified
communism embodied in the PCF and the USSR. On this view, capitalist imperialism would be defeated in Algiers, Hanoi, or Havana rather than in Paris, London,
or Moscow. Third, Sartre's preface gave him a further opportunity to condemn
those who deplored the violence used by *both* sides in the Algerian conflict.
The violence of colonialism, he affirmed, could only be destroyed by violence.
To shoot a European was 'to kill two birds with one stone, to destroy an oppressor
and the man he oppresses'.[331] Consequently, Sartre had no time for what he
contemptuously dismissed as 'Chatter, chatter: liberty, equality, fraternity, love,
honour, patriotism, and what have you.'[332] The abstract universalism of 'racist
humanitarian', he concluded, failed to understand that 'the European has only been
able to become a man through creating slaves and monsters'.[333] Among those
Sartre undoubtedly had in mind was his former friend, Albert Camus, born in
Algeria of *pied noir* parents.

When Albert Camus died in a car accident on his way back to Paris in January
1960 he had effectively fallen into silence.[334] The winner of the 1957 Nobel prize
for literature had simply been overwhelmed by events in Algeria and by the
conflicting demands made upon him, in his famous phrase, by the claims of justice

---

[328] *The Wretched of the Earth* (Harmondsworth, 1971), 103.   [329] Ibid. 39.
[330] Beauvoir, *Force of Circumstance*, 610.
[331] Sartre, 'Preface' to Fanon, *The Wretched*, 19.
[332] Ibid. 22.   [333] Ibid.
[334] See Herbert R. Lottman, *Camus: A Biography* (London, 1979) and Olivier Todd, *Albert Camus:
Une vie* (1996). See Tony Judt, *The Burden of Responsibility: Blum, Camus, Aron, and the French
Twentieth Century* (Chicago, 1998), 87–135.

and the desire to defend his mother.[335] Prior to this, however, he had been bested in a quarrel with Sartre ostensibly over his essay of 1951, *L'Homme révolté*.[336] The tale of Camus's split with Sartre is well known but it merits brief discussion if only to clarify the political issues that were at stake in post-war France.

By the age of twenty-eight Camus had written three masterpieces: his play, *Caligula*; his novel, *L'Étranger*; and his philosophical essay, *Le Mythe de Sisyphe*. Not only did he have these achievements to his name, but by 1943 he had become editor-in-chief of the leading Resistance newspaper, *Combat*.[337] It was in this same year that Camus met Sartre and Simone de Beauvoir, quickly becoming a member of their intimate circle of friends. They appeared to have much in common and, not without some good cause, Camus too was seen as an existentialist. *Le Mythe de Sisyphe*, published in 1942, argued that, in a world of the absurd where we could make no appeal to universal or transcendental values, 'the one truly philosophical problem' was that of suicide. The absurd man, Camus wrote, was 'he who does nothing for the eternal'. For all that, the message of *Le Mythe de Sisyphe* was that suicide was 'acceptance pushed to its extreme' and that it was revolt against the absurd which restored 'majesty' to life. It was for this reason that Camus believed that Sisyphus, condemned by the gods to 'futile and hopeless labour', must be imagined to be happy.

Yet the differences between Camus and Sartre were not slow to emerge. Although he had been an active member of the Resistance, Camus became deeply troubled by the post-Liberation *épuration*. He (unlike Sartre) campaigned against the execution of Robert Brasillach. Likewise, whilst he situated himself on the left and was eager to see the radical reform of post-war France, Camus had no sympathy for the communists and was not prepared to overlook the crimes and oppression that were taking place behind the emerging Iron Curtain. In a series of essays entitled 'Ni victimes ni bourreaux', published in *Combat* at the end of 1946,[338] he therefore advocated the need for a new way of thinking that would be 'politically modest, freed of all messianism, and without any nostalgia for an earthly paradise'. He specifically denounced the 'political realism' endorsed by those who believed that the end justified the means.

This, however, was precisely what the young philosopher Maurice Merleau-Ponty, now a member of the Sartre circle, appeared to be doing. In a series of articles in *Les Temps modernes*, later to be published under the title of *Humanisme et terreur*,[339] Merleau-Ponty took issue with Arthur Koestler's denunciation of the Moscow show trials and argued they could be justified in terms of the ultimate victory of communism. Morality, in good Jacobin fashion, was to be subordinated to the judgement of history. Camus, according to Simone de Beauvoir's memoirs,

---

[335] See *Actuelles III: Chroniques algériennes 1939–1958* (1959).
[336] Camus, *L'Homme révolté* (1951). See Ronald Aronson, *Camus and Sartre: The Story of a Friendship and the Quarrel that Ended it* (Chicago, 2004).
[337] See Jacqueline Lévi-Valensi (ed), *Camus à Combat: Editoriaux et articles d'Albert Camus 1944–1947* (2002).
[338] Camus, *Actuelles: Chroniques 1944–1948* (1950), 139–79.
[339] Merleau-Ponty, *Humanisme et terreur* (1947).

was furious, going so far as to challenge Merleau-Ponty publicly at a party one evening. For Sartre and his friends, in Beauvoir's phrase, Merleau-Ponty's argument helped them cross the Rubicon: they could now see that moralism was 'the last bastion of bourgeois idealism'.[340] For his part, Camus refused to make a choice between the Soviet Union and America, believing it possible to find a neutral course of action. He was, for example, an enthusiastic supporter of Gary Davis, the American airman who declared himself a citizen of the world. Moreover, as the Cold War intensified, it was abundantly clear that Camus saw the USSR rather than the USA as the principal threat to peace and freedom.

Matters came to a head with the publication of Camus's *L'Homme révolté* in 1951. This was an immensely impressive, if flawed, work which sought 'to follow into the realm of murder and revolt a mode of thinking which began with suicide and the idea of the absurd'.[341] If Camus began his text with a discussion of the 'metaphysical rebellion' of the Marquis de Sade—a 'monstrous form of revenge', Camus argued, that could only be assuaged by the creation of a 'kingdom of servitude'—his first substantive point was that 1789 had marked 'the turning point of modern times' and that this was so because the revolutionaries had 'added to traditional tyrannicide the concept of calculated deicide'.[342] Having executed both the king and God, they then set about the building of a new temple dedicated to the divinity of the people and it was through this that crime, in the form of state terrorism, had received its justification. In this way, according to Camus, revolution became a form of moral nihilism.

As a result, in the twentieth century to act was to murder. There were, Camus maintained, two political ideologies that had embodied this absurdist position: Nazism and Marxism. 'Hitler', Camus wrote, 'presents an example which is perhaps unique in history of a tyrant who has left absolutely no trace of his activities. For himself, for his people, and for the world, he was nothing but the epitome of suicide and murder.'[343] He represented 'complete annihilation'. In terms of Camus's own trajectory, it might be said that Hitler was a modern-day Caligula. Yet, Camus asserted, the 'Fascist mystics' had had no pretensions to create a world empire. This, he claimed, was quite definitely not the case with Russian communism.

Camus's critique of Marxism was marvellously perceptive. Even though Camus acknowledged Marx's good intentions he saw that Marxism as a doctrine could only lead to 'the direst consequences'. This was the case because all actions were permitted as long as they furthered the emergence of the future 'golden age'. 'When good and evil are reintegrated in time and confused with events', Camus wrote, 'nothing is any longer good or bad, but only either premature or out of date.'[344] The result, as the Russian Revolution showed, would be dictatorship and rational terror. 'By dint of argument, incessant struggle, polemics, excommunications, persecutions conducted and suffered', Camus argued. 'the universal city of free

---

[340] Beauvoir, *Force of Circumstance*, 115.
[341] *L'Homme révolté*, 15.
[342] Ibid. 143.   [343] Ibid. 154.   [344] Ibid. 259.

and fraternal man is slowly diverted and gives way to the only universe in which history and expediency can, in fact, be elevated to the position of judges: the universe of the trial.'[345] The city of man was replaced by the city of ends: injustice and crime could be justified through the promise of a miracle.

Camus's difficulties started when he began to sketch out an alternative to such revolutionary violence and when he tried to establish a realm of 'limited culpability' which would enable us to avoid 'universal murder'. He did so by focusing upon the act of rebellion rather than that of revolution. 'Rebellion', he wrote, 'though apparently negative since it creates nothing, is profoundly positive in that it reveals the part of man which must always be defended.'[346] The act of true rebellion came into operation when we refused to see another human being abused and humiliated any further. But how were we to prevent this act itself becoming a form of tyranny? Rebellion after all implied murder. Camus's answer was that the rebel did not claim the freedom to commit universal murder. Rather, he accepted that he could only rebel, if he also accepted the loss of his own life. 'The rebel', Camus wrote, 'has only one way of reconciling himself with his act of murder if he allows himself to be led into performing it: to accept his own death and sacrifice.'[347] Measure and limit were indispensable. Somewhat vaguely, Camus ended with a vision of what he described as Mediterranean moderation.

What followed was a very public and very nasty quarrel between Sartre and Camus, the details of which can be thankfully passed over. It was, however, to be a quarrel of long-term significance. Camus had, in fact, written a companion piece to *L'Homme révolté*. His play, *Les Justes*, took as its subject the terrorists of late nineteenth-century Russia. The same people figured in *L'Homme révolté*. In both works they were praised for the moral scrupulousness with which they had resorted to acts of terror. They stood as a counter-example to the ruthlessness of Lenin and the Bolsheviks. In *L'Homme révolté* Camus also made favourable reference to an indigenous tradition of radical activism: the libertarian socialism of Fernand Pelloutier and Georges Sorel. It was with this tradition that his true sympathies lay.[348] Sartre had no liking for such ideas and, as he was to put it in *Les Communistes et la paix*, 'an anti-communist' was, in his view, 'a dog'. If he proved himself only too willing to protest about the execution in America of the convicted Soviet spies Julius and Ethel Rosenberg in 1953, he remained silent about the shooting of workers in communist-controlled East Berlin in the same year. Nothing was to be done, as he famously remarked, to disillusion the workers of the Renault car factory at Billancourt outside Paris. What makes this important is that Sartre was not alone in displaying an unwillingness to condemn Stalinism. Indeed, if we are to believe Tony Judt, Sartre was broadly representative of a 'collective myopia' exhibited by the greater part of the Parisian intelligentsia.[349]

Camus, in short, not only lost the argument to Sartre but he was also quite definitely in a minority. According to Judt, the period of Sartrean dominance was characterized

[345] Ibid. 296.   [346] Ibid. 32.   [347] Ibid. 348.
[348] See Lou Marin (ed.), *Albert Camus et les libertaires* (Marseilles, 2008).
[349] Judt, *Past Imperfect, French Intellectuals 1944–1956* (Berkeley and Los Angeles, Calif., 1992), 246.

by a network of intellectual practices which had, at its centre, 'the will and the desire to believe in communism'.[350] Around this article of faith, he argued, was to be found 'a sort of epistemological double vision' which made it possible to judge the Soviet Union and its satellites by criteria not applied elsewhere. To this was added hostility to the various manifestations of individualism and modernity, often seen in the form of anti-Americanism. Providing the above with their 'political and ideological anchor', to refer to Judt again, was 'an indigenous antiliberalism'.

Remarkably, these practices persisted even when the philosophical tide began to turn against existential Marxism, as it did in the 1960s with the advent of structuralism. The anti-Sartrean dimension of structuralism was given dramatic illustration by anthropologist Claude Lévi-Strauss. Responding to the publication of the *Critique de la raison dialectique*, in the concluding chapter of *La Pensée sauvage*[351] he proclaimed that 'I believe the ultimate goal of the human sciences to be not to constitute but to dissolve man.' Sartre's praxis of the subject, he contended, represented nothing more than an unscientific subjectivism. Later, in the 'Finale' to *L'Homme nu*,[352] Lévi-Strauss continued the anti-Sartrean theme, announcing that the 'elimination of the subject represents what might be called a methodological need' and that structuralism, by reintegrating man into nature, made it 'possible to disregard the subject—that unbearably spoilt child who has occupied the philosophical scene for too long'. Existentialism, Lévi-Strauss concluded, was 'a self-admiring activity which allows contemporary man, rather gullibly, to commune with himself in ecstatic contemplation of his own being'. The allotted task of structuralism, in short, was to break with the philosophical inheritance of humanism, an aim fully articulated in the last sentence of Michel Foucault's *Les Mots et les choses*, where the reader was told that man was a recent invention who would soon disappear 'like a face drawn in sand at the edge of the sea'.

This anti-humanist position, rooted in dissatisfaction with the phenomenological theory of the subject, found a variety of expressions in the writings of structuralism. Roland Barthes, championing the reader and announcing 'the pleasure of the text', spoke of 'the death of the author'. Likewise, Jacques Lacan, reworking Freud, rebelled against the 'ego-centred' character of psychoanalysis and used the basic concepts of Ferdinand de Saussure's structural linguistics to illustrate that the conscious life of the individual did not provide the means of its own intelligibility. Althusser, as we have already seen, spoke of history as 'a process without a subject'.

Who exactly the structuralists were and whether they constituted a fixed and identifiable group or school are not questions that deflect from the fact that the 1960s was a very much the structuralist decade. Their work received immense critical (and popular) acclaim, sold in huge quantities and effectively established a new philosophical orthodoxy or paradigm. In large part, however, this success can be attributed to non-philosophical causes. The vogue for structuralism coincided with France's belated entry into the consumer society and seemed to postulate its

---

[350] Judt, *Past Imperfect, French Intellectuals 1944–1956* (Berkeley and Los Angeles, Calif., 1992), 154.
[351] Claude Lévi-Strauss. *La Pensée sauvage* (1962).
[352] Claude Lévi-Strauss, *L'Homme nu* (1971).

decisive rejection. This was most obvious in Lévi-Strauss's explicit challenge to the supposed superiority and universality of the categories of Western reason. 'The scientific spirit in its most modern form', Lévi-Strauss wrote, will serve 'to legitimize the principles of savage thought and to re-establish it in its rightful place'.[353] Similarly, the structuralist challenge to the values of the bourgeois and capitalist society of the West was evident in Lacan's ethics of desire and in Foucault's ethics of liberation. It was there too in the work of Roland Barthes. In his preface to the 1970 edition of *Mythologies*, for example, he wrote as follows: 'I had just read Saussure and as a result acquired the conviction that by treating "collective representations" as signs, one might hope to go further than the pious show of unmasking them and account *in detail* for the mystification which transforms petit-bourgeois culture into a universal nature.' And this was the conclusion he reached from the fifty-four short sketches that followed: 'the whole of France is steeped in this anonymous ideology: our press, our films, our theatre, our pulp literature, our rituals, our justice, our diplomacy, our conversations, our remarks about the weather, the cooking we dream of, the garments we wear, everything in everyday life, is dependent upon the representation which the bourgeoisie *has and makes us have* of the relations between man and the world'. The world of the bourgeoisie had been constructed as if it were the world of Eternal Man.[354]

Nevertheless, when the student protests of May 1968 rocked France to its very foundations, Lévi-Strauss, Jacques Lacan, Roland Barthes, and the other structuralists responded with what J. G. Melchior described as an 'eloquent' silence.[355] One of the many famous student slogans of the day summed up the situation admirably: 'Barthes says that structures do not take to the streets. We say: neither does Barthes.' Sartre, the intellectual hero of the hour, had his revenge.[356]

Ironically, the events of May 68 also sounded the death knell of the Sartrean model of the committed intellectual.[357] Most importantly, the very philosophical foundations that had underpinned the Sartrean model of the universal intellectual were progressively dismantled. Sartre's Marxist humanism was jettisoned in a philosophical revolution that, via post-structuralism, led ultimately to Jacques Derrida and deconstruction. In its assault upon what was taken to be the 'logocentrism' at the heart of the Western metaphysical tradition, philosophy simply ceased to be engaged in the formulation of normative theories or to concern itself with questions of public life. And thus writers like Philippe Sollers, the influential

---

[353] Lévi-Strauss, *The Savage Mind* (London: 1966), 269.

[354] Barthes, *Mythologies* (St Albans, 1973), 140.

[355] *From Prague to Paris: A Critique of Structuralist and Post-Structuralist Thought* (London, 1986).

[356] These comments on structuralism are expanded upon in my 'Structuralism', in Simon Glendinning (ed.), *The Edinburgh Encyclopedia of Continental Philosophy* (Edinburgh, 1999), 505–14. See François Dosse, *Histoire du structuralisme*, 2 vols. (1992).

[357] See François Hourmont, *Le Désenchantement des clercs: Figures de l'intellectuel dans l'après-Mai 68* (Rennes, 1997). More broadly, see Pascal Ory, *L'Entre-deux Mai: Histoire culturelle de la France Mai 68–Mai 1981* (1983); Julian Bourg, *From Revolution to Ethics: May 68 and Contemporary French Thought* (Montreal and Kingston, 2007); and Serge Audier, *La Pensée anti-68: Essai sur les origines d'une restauration intellectuelle* (2008).

editor of the literary review *Tel Quel*,[358] could break with Sartre's definition of committed literature and argue that a writer's commitment was displayed not in any message to be conveyed but in the activity of writing itself. Later, Julia Kristeva—who herself was to provide a withering description of the self-obsession of French intellectuals[359]—reduced the philosophical project to an attempt to destabilize the 'master discourses' constituting the existing symbolic order.[360] Jean-François Lyotard, the high priest of postmodernism, could likewise argue that 'The responsibility of "intellectuals" is inseparable from the (shared) idea of a universal subject. It alone gave Voltaire, Zola, Péguy, Sartre (to stay within the confines of France) the authority that has been accorded to them.' As, he continued, we no longer believed that a universal subject exists, there ought therefore no longer to be any intellectuals.[361] Gone were the days when the intellectual was able to speak out in the name of truth and, in so doing, aspire to change the world for the better.

Not only this, but the ideological climate that had sustained the 'intellectuel de gauche' appeared to evaporate. How this occurred is a complicated story, but there can be no doubt that the publication of Alexander Solzhenitsyn's *The Gulag Archipelago* in French in 1974 produced a major shock to the whole edifice, cruelly exposing the past errors and political misjudgements of France's intellectuals before Marxist totalitarianism.[362] Faced with such compelling evidence of complicity with tyranny and mass murder, the claims of the intellectuals to superior knowledge and to a greater lucidity were mercilessly stripped away, leaving behind only the image of a figure prone to folly and bouts of ideological blindness.[363] The picture was of a community of intellectuals in disarray, feeling unsure of itself and of how it should act in a world in which it no longer enjoyed automatic respect. Power and influence seemed to have slipped from its grasp.

In those circumstances, the immediate years that followed saw the publication of a veritable flotilla of books and articles devoted to the examination of the intellectual's supposed demise and its causes. Picking over the carcass of a fallen national hero, all evinced a nostalgia for a lost golden age of heroic Dreyfusard intellectuals battling against the forces of darkness and all agreed in their condemnation of a corrupted, degraded, and mediocre present. When the content of a

---

[358] Philippe Forest, *Histoire de Tel Quel, 1960–1982* (1996) and Danielle Marx-Scouras, *The Cultural Politics of Tel Quel: Literature and the Left in the Wake of Engagement* (University Park, Pa., 1996).

[359] Julia Kristeva, *Les Samouraïs* (1990).

[360] See 'A New Type of Intellectual: The Dissident', in Toril Moi (ed.), *The Kristeva Reader* (Oxford, 1986), 292–300.

[361] 'Tombeau de l'intellectuel', *Le Monde* (8 Oct. 1983). See also Lyotard, *Tombeau de l'intellectuel et autres papiers* (1984).

[362] See Michael Scott Christofferson, *French Intellectuals against the Left: The Antitotalitarian Moment of the 1970s* (New York, 2004), 89–112.

[363] See e.g. Michel-Antoine Burnier, *Le Testament de Sartre* (1982) and Jeannine Verdès-Leroux, *La Lune et le caudillo: Le Rêve des intellectuels et le régime cubain* (1989).

culture had come to be so determined by the market, Régis Debray wrote, a philosopher was not judged by his ideas but by the colour of his eyes.[364]

From among the wreckage, however, there appeared several alternative models of the intellectual. Arguably the most influential of these was that fashioned by Michel Foucault. Formulated as early as 1972 and restated on many subsequent occasions—most notably in an interview given in 1977—Foucault sought to replace the 'universal' intellectual (with Voltaire and Sartre cast as the prototype) with that of the 'specific' intellectual.[365] As with Julien Benda, there was reference to 'the great treason of the intellectuals', but here it was taken to be the inculcation of the values of 'bourgeois justice' among the proletariat. So also there were derogatory comments directed against those dismissed as 'les intellectuels professionnels parisiens'. But Foucault's central argument was that the intellectual could no longer make claim to be 'a giver of lessons' or to act as a 'moral legislator'. 'The work of the intellectual', Foucault argued, 'is not to mould the political will of others.' Rather, the role of the intellectual was 'to make visible the mechanisms of repressive power which operate in a hidden manner'. This was to be done by providing 'instruments of analysis' drawn from the intellectual's own work 'within specific sectors'.

It was, then, as 'specialists' and as 'experts' engaging in 'specific' and 'local' struggles rather than as 'universal prophets' or 'the bearers of values' that intellectuals should operate. Yet in one respect at least the work of the intellectual could take on a 'general significance' and have implications which were not 'simply professional or sectoral'. Starting from the assumption that truth was not 'the child of protracted solitude' but the product of 'multiple forms of constraint', the function of the intellectual, Foucault believed, was to struggle to destroy 'the regime of truth' integral to the structure and functioning of present society. Foucault himself sought to exemplify the role of the 'specific' intellectual not only through his own writings, most notably *Naissance de la clinique* and *Surveiller et punir*,[366] but also through his own political commitments and interventions. In 1971, for example, he established the Groupe d'information sur les prisons to secure prison reform.[367] A series of similar gestures linking his academic work to contemporary social and political issues were made by Foucault in the years before his death in 1984. It was this model that was to be taken up and developed by thinkers on the left of the political spectrum in the years to come.

As influential as Foucault's reformulation of the relationship of the intellectual to politics might have been, it provided little attraction for those who had now become—or who had always been—deeply sceptical about the supposed virtues of the revolutionary project. For this increasingly numerous and vocal group there

---

[364] See *Le Pouvoir intellectuel en France* (1979). Debray returned to this theme in *i.f. suite et fin* (2000).

[365] See e.g. 'Les Intellectuels et le pouvoir', in *Dits et écrits 1954–1988* (1994), ii. 306–15; 'Entretien avec Michel Foucault', ibid. iii. 140–60; and 'L'Intellectuel et les pouvoirs', ibid. iv. 747–52. The quotations that follow are drawn from a wide range of sources from within the 4 vols. of *Dits et écrits*.

[366] *Naissance de la clinique* (1972); *Surveiller et punir* (1975).

[367] See Didier Eribon, *Michel Foucault* (1989), 314–28.

was another and wiser source of inspiration: Raymond Aron.[368] Unlike the apoliti-cal Sartre,[369] Aron had not been blind to the dangers of the rise of fascism and in the summer of 1940, immediately following the fall of France, he had left for London to join the Free French and there became one of the editors of *La France libre*. Following the Liberation, Aron devoted himself to journalism and to the pursuit of an immensely distinguished academic career, quickly making known his opposition to communism and his support for the United States and the Atlantic Alliance. As the Cold War intensified, Aron became a leading member of the CIA-financed Congress for Cultural Freedom. If he quickly saw the futility and the 'tragedy' of the cause of French Algeria, he similarly dismissed the student protests of May 68 as a self-indulgent 'psychodrama' fuelled by 'the worst form of utopian-ism and revolutionary mythology'.[370]

Always an admirer of Montesquieu and Tocqueville (as well as a lifelong reader of Marx),[371] time and time again Aron returned to the themes of the fragility of civilization and the ever-present threat of tyranny and totalitarianism. If political thought in France, in his view, tended to be either nostalgic or utopian, then, by the same token, political action was divorced from reality and from economic necessities. The French left in particular, he believed, needed to free itself from 'the siren charms of ideal emancipation' and of its faith in both revolution and the proletariat. Both, Aron argued, were a form of 'imaginary compensation' for the successive revolutionary failures that had occurred from 1789 to 1848. The intellectuals of the left, he asserted, were in search of a secular religion.

For his pains, over many years Aron was treated as something of a pariah—better to be wrong with Sartre rather than be right with Aron was the celebrated quip—and his influence scarcely stretched beyond a small group of loyal friends and former students. His intellectual itinerary was however the mark of a philosopher and a commentator who refused to turn his back on political realities and who, in Aron's own words, had sought 'to lead the life of an active witness'. It was this willingness to look the realities of politics square in the face that underpinned his conception of the intellectual as 'a committed observer'.

The origins of this notion can be traced back to Aron's experiences in Germany during the 1930s but it was given much clearer articulation with the publication of *L'Opium des intellectuels* in 1955 and then, much later, in a series of interviews

---

[368] See Daniel J. Mahoney, *The Liberal Political Science of Raymond Aron* (Lanham, Md., 1992); Nicholas Baverez, *Raymond Aron: Un moraliste au temps des idéologies* (1993); Brian C. Anderson, *Raymond Aron: The Recovery of the Political* (Lanham, Md., 1997); and 'The Peripheral Insider: Raymond Aron and the Wages of Reason', in Judt, *Burden of Responsibility*, 137–82. Above all, see Aron's own autobiographical reflections contained in *Mémoires: 50 Ans de réflexion politique* (1983). An excellent selection of Aron's work in French is to be found in *Penser la liberté, penser la démocratie* (2005) and in English in *The Dawn of Universal History* (New York, 2002).

[369] On the relationship between the two men see Sirinelli, *Sartre et Aron: Deux intellectuels dans le siècle* (1999).

[370] See Aron, *La Révolution introuvable: Réflexions sur les événements de mai* (1968).

[371] See Aron, *Le Marxisme de Marx* (2002).

published as *Le Spectateur engagé*.[372] At its heart lay the distinction, taken from Max Weber, between an ethics of commitment and an ethics of responsibility. It also drew upon Aron's belief that there were very few occasions which possessed the moral simplicity and purity of the Dreyfus Affair. Aron asked of the intellectual, therefore, not indifference or the pose of 'l'observateur glacé', but modesty, moderation, lucidity, and prudence. Above all, he invited intellectuals to *penser la politique*, to dream not of the attractions of a perfect society but to reflect upon the difficult choices and decisions faced in an impure world by those who held power. 'The great proportion of struggles', Aron declared in 1983, 'are of an ambiguous character and intellectuals who wish to be exclusively at the service of the universal ought not to participate.'[373]

For Aron, then, politics was never a choice between absolute good and absolute evil but between what was preferable over what was detestable and in those circumstances intellectuals were called upon to act responsibly and not as the prophets of an earthly paradise. As Aron neared the end of his life and as a new generation of thinkers began the painstaking task of formulating the theoretical foundations of a distinctively French version of liberalism, there was ample evidence to suggest that this was a message that had taken root and that the days of partisan engagement in the name of abstract ideals or collective salvation were at an end. One piece of evidence to support this claim would be the creation of the Aron-inspired review *Commentaire* in 1978 under the editorship of Jean-Claude Casanova. Another would be the launch of Pierre Nora's *Le Débat* in 1980 and its proclamation of a new age of 'intellectual democracy'. Yet another would be the creation in 1985 of the Institut Raymond Aron within Paris's École des Hautes Études en Sciences Sociales, an institution which included among its members not only François Furet but also a younger generation of thinkers (amongst whom could be counted Marcel Gauchet, Pierre Manent, and Pierre Rosanvallon) sympathetic to liberal and social democratic goals and aspirations. Summarizing these and other similar developments, Mark Lilla spoke of 'the legitimacy of the liberal age'.[374]

More telling still was the so-called 'silence of the intellectuals' that caught public attention in 1983.[375] As France's socialist-led government ran into severe economic problems and saw its electoral support collapse, essayist and government spokesperson Max Gallo penned an article in France's leading newspaper, *Le Monde*, making an explicit comparison with the earlier experience of the Popular Front and asking where the intellectuals were when the beleaguered government of the left needed them. The answer was that they were nowhere to be seen. Moreover, as Philippe Boggio made clear by way of response, unlike their colleagues of the

[372] *Le Spectateur engagé: Entretiens avec Jean-Louis Missika et Dominique Wolton* (1981).
[373] 'Les Intellectuels et la politique', *Commentaire*, 22 (1983), 259–63.
[374] *New French Thought: Political Philosophy* (1994), 3–34. On the broader intellectual and cultural developments occurring during this period see Olivier Mongin, *Face au scepticisme (1976–1993): Les Mutations du paysage intellectuel ou l'invention de l'intellectuel démocratique* (1994).
[375] See the columns of *Le Monde* in the weeks following 24 July 1983.

1930s, the intellectuals of the 1980s felt disinclined to help a government that was suspected of complacency towards the Soviet Union and towards communism. Aptly summarizing the situation of those Gérard Noiriel was later to describe as 'les fils maudits de la République',[376] not long afterwards Bernard Henri-Lévy penned a hypothetical dictionary entry for the year 2000 which read as follows: '*Intellectual*, noun, masculine gender, a social and cultural category born in Paris at the moment of the Dreyfus Affair, died in Paris at the end of the twentieth century; apparently was not able to survive the decline in belief in Universals.'[377]

---

[376] *Les Fils maudits de la République: L'Avenir des intellectuels en France* (2005).
[377] Lévy, *Éloge des intellectuels* (1987), 48. See also Lévy's *Les Aventures de la liberté: Une histoire subjective des intellectuels* (1991).

Conclusion
Citizenship, Multiculturalism, and Republicanism

I

When General de Gaulle wrote his war memoirs in enforced retirement during the 1950s he began with the resounding phrase that 'France cannot be France without greatness.' The post-war years did little to confirm this hope. Fearing a return to what he dismissed as 'the regime of parties', de Gaulle resigned as head of the provisional government in January 1946 and later that year the French electorate gave its approval to a new constitution that, in nearly all essentials, resembled that of the Third Republic. 'Unless one considers total inertia as the supreme virtue of a state', Raymond Aron was later to write in 1955,[1] 'one could not possibly approve of the Fourth Republic.' The old problems of ministerial instability returned and the Fourth Republic quickly became bogged down in a series of colonial wars, bringing humiliating defeat in Indo-China and then the prolonged agony of the Algerian conflict. Reduced to powerlessness and discredited by years of failure, in May 1958 the politicians of the Fourth Republic called it a day and had no alternative but to recall General de Gaulle to power on his own terms.[2]

Those terms amounted to the creation of a Fifth Republic and a constitution which, with its emphasis on presidential power and a subordinate role for parliament, was deeply troubling to many republicans. In 1964 de Gaulle's inveterate opponent, François Mitterrand, described the new regime as a 'permanent *coup d'état*'.[3] Four years later, France was brought to a standstill by the student demonstrations of May 68 and the wave of industrial strikes accompanying them. De Gaulle momentarily lost his nerve and a year later, following defeat in a needless referendum, he resigned from office.

These years were not, however, without their successes. The task of securing Franco-German reconciliation was begun and was followed by the first tentative,

---

[1] *L'Opium des intellectuels* (2002), 75.
[2] See Michel Winock, *L'Agonie de la IVe République* (2006).
[3] *Le Coup d'état permanent* (1964).

but decisive, steps towards European integration. Just as importantly, from the late 1940s onwards France began the period of sustained economic growth that, over the next thirty years, was to transform her economy. This dramatic shift from agriculture to industry and commerce produced a modern, urbanized, consumer society. Once returned to power, de Gaulle successfully extricated France from Algeria and in subsequent years carved out an independent foreign policy built around France's nuclear strike force. Moreover, the political institutions he gave France produced stable and successful government, their durability receiving decisive confirmation when the left, led by none other than François Mitterrand, came to power in 1981.

The consequences of these dramatic developments were far-reaching. What was being witnessed, it was argued, was the end of the 'French exception'.[4] France was fast becoming a country that more resembled her neighbours. Two facts were often cited as evidence of this trend. The communist party vote, although still high, began to fall steeply. Likewise, religious observance among Catholics experienced a sudden and rapid decline. From this it was argued that the polarization between extremes that had for so long characterized French politics was on the point of extinction and that there was now emerging a consensus around a set of core democratic values. Everyone, it appeared, was a republican and, if it was possible to speak of a prevailing ideology, it was that of the rights of man and what was sometimes referred to as 'the new individualism'. Stated another way, the theatre was leaving French politics and the French (much like everybody else) were now preoccupied with such banal and mundane issues as taxation and the price of goods in the shops rather than the political legacies and divisions of the past. In some people these developments induced a sense of melancholy and nostalgia for the days of confrontation and class war, but, by general agreement, they seemed to presage the arrival of a new, less conflictual politics that would work within the parameters of social democracy and liberalism.

The chance to display this new reality came, somewhat fortuitously, in the form of the bicentennial celebrations of the French Revolution. A year before, François Mitterrand had been re-elected as socialist president of the Fifth Republic and the left, under the premiership of Michel Rocard, formed the government of the day. Mitterrand in particular cared deeply about the bicentennial and many believed that he would seek to make it the apogee of his political career. Moreover, it seemed as if, for the first time, the commemoration of the Revolution could be celebrated in a spirit of quasi-consensus broadly reflecting the stability of a constitution that had just survived its first experience of political and institutional *cohabitation*. Accordingly, the Bastille Day festivities were marked by a summit of world leaders drawn from rich and poor nations alike and by an extravagant parade down the Champs-Elysées masterminded by the designer and artist Jean-Paul Goude and featuring a rendition of the *Marseillaise* by African-American opera singer, Jessye Norman. By focusing

---

[4] See François Furet, Jacques Julliard, and Pierre Rosanvallon, *La République du centre: La Fin de l'exception française* (1988).

almost entirely upon the Déclaration des Droits de l'Homme et du Citoyen of 1789 the official celebrations all but denied all knowledge of 1793 and in order to do so were obliged to turn their gaze not towards the past but towards the present and the future: hence Goude's grandiose and outlandish spectacle.[5]

For the historical profession, the central questions raised by the experience of the French Revolution could not be so straightforwardly and effortlessly evaded and there were many, on both the left and the right, who believed that the attempt to evoke a palatable and sanitized 1789 amounted to a silencing of the Revolution, be it the Revolution that had slaughtered the people of the Vendée or that had held out the messianic promise of radical social change. It was, however, François Furet and his 'galaxy' of loyal and able colleagues who were to win the argument in 1989 and who were to produce its definitive historiographical statement: the *Dictionnaire critique de la Révolution française.*[6]

The key move was Furet's assertion, first formulated in 1978, that the 'Revolution is over'.[7] This had several dimensions, not the least of which was a dismissal of the long-established claim that the causes of the Revolution of 1789 were to be found in a set of social and economic contradictions prevailing in late eighteenth-century France. It also sought to refute the central contention of French Marxist historiography that, in the last analysis, the Revolution marked the end of the society of orders and the arrival of the bourgeoisie to a position of political and economic dominance. According to Furet, the Revolution was best seen not as 'a set of causes and consequences' but as having 'invented a type of political discourse and practice by which we have been living ever since'. What gave the Revolution its unique and universal quality was that it was 'the first experiment in democracy'.

In consequence, Furet envisaged not just a new historiography of the Revolution as 'an autonomous political and ideological movement' but also the displacement of what he termed a 'revolutionary catechism' born of the conviction that France's own Revolution had presaged the Bolshevik Revolution of 1917. Specifically, this interpretation declined to account for the Jacobin Terror in terms of the circumstances created by war, preferring to see it as inherent to the revolutionary process. More generally, it was Furet's contention that 'The Revolution was more than a "leap" from one society to another; it was also the conjunction of all the ways in which a civil society, once it had suddenly been "opened up" by a power crisis, let loose all the words and languages it contained.'[8] The intellectual reference point was not to be Karl Marx or even Jules Michelet but Alexis de Tocqueville, for it was the latter who had come to see and define the Revolution as 'a radical ideological

[5] See Steven Laurence Kaplan, *Farewell, Revolution: Disputed Legacies France, 1789/1989* (Ithaca, NY, 1995).

[6] See vol. ii by Steven Laurence Kaplan, *Farewell, Revolution: The Historians' Feud France 1789–1989* (Ithaca, NY, 1995). For an assessment of the present state of play in French Revolution studies see Michel Biard (ed.), *La Révolution française: Une histoire toujours vivante* (2010).

[7] 'The Revolution is Over', in François Furet, *Interpreting the French Revolution* (Cambridge, 1981), 1–79. See also 'La Révolution et ses fantômes', in Furet, *Un itinéraire intellectuel* (1999), 541–58.

[8] Furet, *Interpreting the French Revolution*, 130.

venture'.[9] It was also Tocqueville who had perceived the glaring discrepancy between 'the intentions of the actors and the historical role they played'.

To summarize: Furet believed that France and the French had, at last, left behind what he termed the 'revolutionary political civilization' and therefore that, for the first time, it would be possible for the historian to write a history of the Revolution that not only avoided 'mental laziness and pious rehashing' but also eschewed 'identification with the actors, . . . commemoration of the founders or . . . execration of the deviants'.[10] As Furet observed, 'No historical debate about the Revolution any longer involves real political stakes.'[11] This was a new situation, born out of political stability, economic prosperity, and increasing social homogeneity.

In these circumstances the view that France's revolutionary and republican heritage was no longer relevant to present-day realities was not slow to emerge. This has subsequently come in a variety of forms. One was to suggest that the ideology of republicanism no longer enthused or motivated the French population. This was so because the Republic's principal antagonist—an intransigent Catholic Church laying claim to an earthly authority—no longer existed in any significant form.[12] From this it was but a short step to the claim that the core republican doctrine of *laïcité* was only of relevance to what Pierre Birnbaum called 'La France imaginée', a France mistakenly believed to be prey to the political and religious cleavages of an earlier age.[13] A second, and more forceful, argument came in the form of the charge that the Republic had not delivered on its promises, that it was a charade, and that many of the citizens of the Fifth Republic were citizens in name only. This, it was stated with increasing frequency from the 1980s onwards, was especially the case with regard to women. All the evidence showed that, despite the fact that women had held the same political rights as men since 1944, they continued to be massively under-represented in positions of elected office. From this derived the (not exclusively) feminist demand to ditch the republican attachment to the equality of rights in favour of the new principle of *parité*.[14]

Similar arguments were advanced with regard to the category of citizens that came to be known as *les exclus*, the excluded.[15] In part this was a debate about who exactly the excluded were. Were they the old, the unemployed, the poor, or some other as yet undefined and unidentified part of the population? More substantively, in the eyes of some at least, the dispute served to expose the hollow rhetoric of the republican discourse of fraternity in what was described as 'the new age of inequalities'.[16] There was, in particular, a growing awareness that the young unemployed, often from

---

[9] See in particular 'Tocqueville and the Problem of the French Revolution', ibid. 132–63.

[10] See in particular 'Tocqueville and the Problem of the French Revolution', 11.   [11] Ibid. 82.

[12] See Marcel Gauchet, *La Religion dans la démocratie: Parcours de la laïcité* (1998).

[13] *La France imaginée: Declin des rêves unitaires* (1998).

[14] See Françoise Gaspard, Claude Servan-Schreiber, and Anne Le Gill, *Au pouvoir citoyennes: Liberté, égalité, parité* (1992) and Joan Wallach Scott, *Parité! Sexual Equality and the Crisis of French Universalism* (Chicago, 2005).

[15] See Jacques Donzelot, *Face à l'exclusion: Le Modèle français* (1991) and Serge Paugam, *L'Exclusion: L'État des savoirs* (1996).

[16] Jean-Paul Fitousi and Pierre Rosanvallon, *Le Nouvel Âge des inégalités* (1996). See also Rosanvallon, *La Nouvelle Question sociale: Repenser l'État-providence* (1995) and, more recently, Alain Ehrenberg, *La Société du malaise* (2010).

immigrant backgrounds and living in the suburbs of the big cities, *les banlieues*, were being failed by the traditional republican strategies of social integration—most conspicuously, the republican school system with its ethos of *civisme* and *universalisme*—and that what was taking place was the effective ghettoization of large sections of France's urban population. A very low level of voter turnout in elections in these areas was just one of the pieces of evidence cited to justify this conclusion.

This was an argument that was only to intensify with the general conflagration that engulfed most of France's major towns and cities in the autumn of 2005. Whilst there was no general agreement about the causes of the widespread looting and car-burning that night after night filled French television screens and left French politicians searching desperately for responses, these dramatic events were sufficient to raise grave doubts about the effectiveness of France's costly model of welfare provision. What is more, those involved in this debate shared an acute awareness that the republican ideal of social solidarity was under serious threat.[17]

A further, and related, challenge has arguably come from what is taken to be the process of economic globalization. France's distinctive model of social provision has had its counterpart in a form of economic management that, to date, has remained remarkably impervious to the demands of economic liberalization witnessed over the last two decades or more. During this time (the recent world economic crash notwithstanding) the French economy has been consistently outperformed by its major competitors. High levels of unemployment, mounting public debt, and low levels of economic growth have been just three of the most obvious manifestations of recent economic failure. More than this, virtually all attempts at reform (be it with regard to public service pensions, moves towards a more flexible labour market, or in the universities) have been met by (usually successful) protests and demonstrations. Not without some justification, economic commentator Nicolas Baverez chose the title of *La France qui tombe* for his study of France's economic ills.[18]

A similar argument was advanced with regard to the forces of cultural globalization. Speaking of the values of the Republic, it was argued, only made sense for as long as France continued to possess a distinct national identity and voice. But was this any longer the case? In a widely read volume entitled *La Défaite de la pensée*,[19] Alain Finkielkraut argued that the malaise afflicting France had its origin in the internationalization of culture and in the fact that France was becoming ever more

---

[17] For a selection see Yann Moulier Boutang, *La Révolte des banlieues ou les habits nus de la république* (2005); Véronique Le Gaziou and Laurent Mucchielli (eds.), *Quand les banlieues brûlent : . . . Retour sur les émeutes de novembre 2005* (2006); Hugues Lagrange and Marco Oberti (eds.), *Émeutes urbaines et protestations: Une singularité française* (2006); Alain Lefebvre and Dominique Méda, *Faut-t-il brûler le modèle social français?* (2006); Alain Renault, *Modèle social: La Chimère française* (2006); Pierre Rosanvallon *et al.*, *La Nouvelle Critique sociale* (2006) and the special issue of *Cahiers Français*, 330 (2006) devoted to 'Le modèle social français'. For a critique of the French model see Timothy B. Smith, *France in Crisis: Welfare, Inequality and Globalisation since 1980* (Cambridge, 2004). See also Peter Hall *et al.*, *Changing France: The Politics that Markets Make* (London, 2008).

[18] Nicolas Baverez, *La France qui tombe* (2003). See also Baverez, *Nouveau Monde, Vieille France* (2006); Jacques Julliard, *Le Malheur français* (2005) ; and Pierre Lellouche, *Illusions gauloises* (2006).

[19] Alain Finkielkraut, *La Défaite de la pensée* (1987).

hostile to high culture and ever more consumerist and hedonist. Seen from this perspective, France was increasingly uncertain of herself. Her national specificity had been eroded; her language was under threat; her republican political culture had been enfeebled; and her role in the world had been diminished. What did it mean to speak out in the name of France and the Republic in the age of the ubiquitous baseball cap and in an age of declining national sovereignty and prestige?

The response of France's politicians to these numerous challenges has largely been to repeat the republican mantras of the past. Whilst there have been calls for constitutional reform and some have even gone so far as to advocate a move to a Sixth Republic, for the most part riots and increasing lawlessness have been met by renewed calls for solidarity and invocations of national identity rather than innovative programmes of affirmative action and employment quotas.[20] Job losses and the relocation of industries outside France have elicited the rhetoric of 'economic patriotism' and 'national champions' and not an embrace of the demands and opportunities provided by a global market.[21] Certainly, there has been no eagerness to recommend the practices of what remains a much-despised 'Anglo-Saxon' model.[22]

The same might be said of the response provided by France's intellectual community. Cast adrift from their traditional moorings and wounded by the deceptions of the present, many of France's public intellectuals found comfort in what at times amounted to a nostalgic reaffirmation of a golden age of republicanism.[23]

II

In November 2002, for example, the Parisian intellectual and academic world experienced one of its periodic fits of ill-humour when, to great controversy, the normally amiable and unassuming figure of Daniel Lindenberg suddenly found himself catapulted to notoriety, his 90-page pamphlet *Le Rappel à l'ordre* becoming front-page news in *Le Monde*.[24] The precise details of what, at one level, amounted to something of a family quarrel need not be dwelt upon: suffice it to say that Lindenberg's text was published in a collection edited by Pierre Rosanvallon and that, with only thinly disguised contempt, it dismissed many of Rosanvallon's friends and acquaintances from the Institut Raymond Aron as the 'new reactionaries'. There was, indeed, much that was contentious about Lindenberg's analysis. Placing the diatribes against mass tourism of controversial novelist Michel Houellebecq alongside the more sober reflections upon democracy of Pierre Manent and Marcel Gauchet was at best contentious. However, Lindenberg's serious point

---

[20] See e.g. the speech made by President Jacques Chirac on 14 Nov. 2005.
[21] This was the view expressed by Prime Minister Dominique de Villepin on 25 Sept. 2006.
[22] See my 'France and the "Anglo-Saxon" Model: Contemporary and Historical Perspectives', *European Review*, 14 (2006), 537–54.
[23] See e.g. the official publication *Guide républicain: L'Idée républicain aujourd'hui* (2004).
[24] Daniel Lindenberg, *Le Rappel à l'ordre* (2002); 'Les "Nouveaux Réactionnaires": Enquête sur le paysage intellectuel', *Le Monde* (22 Nov. 2002). Lindenberg returned to this theme with the more substantial *Le Procès des Lumières* (2009).

was that many of those who had until recently embraced the causes of anti-totalitarianism and anti-Marxism were now adopting the 'corrosive' language of order, authority, and tradition. The targets of their attacks, Lindenberg suggested, were May 68, the rights of man, the belief in equality, mass culture, a multiracial society, tolerant sexual mores, and . . . Islam.

What did this strange episode reveal about the situation of political thought in contemporary France? Since the waves of strikes in protest at proposed reform of the social security system that brought France again to a standstill in the late autumn of 1995, the Parisian intelligentsia has been widely perceived as being split into two camps. On the one side have been those who supported the plans for reform and who, more generally, have recommended a break with the state-centred or Jacobin structures of the past. Broadly associated with three of the most influential reviews of the day—*Commentaire*, *Le Débat*, and *Esprit*—it has been this intellectually diverse group that has not only brought about the rediscovery of France's own liberal tradition but which has also shown itself to be open to the recent arguments and debates within the tradition of Anglo-American philosophy. If the latter has entailed a somewhat belated reading of such major thinkers as Hannah Arendt, Isaiah Berlin, and Karl Popper, it has also involved a thorough engagement with the work of John Rawls, Michael Walzer, Charles Taylor, and Richard Rorty amongst others.

On the other side has been a reinvigorated radical left associated above all with the camp of the late Pierre Bourdieu. The precise nature of this radical left has been the subject of much discussion.[25] It is heterogeneous. It is built less around political parties than around a range of single-issue organizations (for example, Les Comités des sans-papiers and Les restos de Cœur) as well as a set of clubs and associations (for example, Pétitions and Copernic, the last of which was explicitly set up to oppose the reformist Fondation Saint-Simon). It has sought (some would say, successfully) to dissociate itself from the incubus of the repressive Marxist-Leninist regimes of the past. It took a leading role in articulating opposition to the invasion of Iraq. In the eyes of critics such as Pierre Rosanvallon, it represents a 'distrust' of modernity, a 'vague' anti-establishment 'radicalism', a 'moral posture' of 'resistance', and 'a culture of criticism rather than a culture of action'.[26] For its members, however, this new radicalism draws its strength from the real problems experienced by modern society and from the need to defend the 'French model' from the destructive intrusions of the emerging technocratic world economic order. To cite Pierre Bourdieu, what was involved was 'the defence of a civilization associated with the existence of public services, a republican equality of rights, the rights to education, to healthcare, to culture, to knowledge, to art, and, above all, to work'.[27]

The disagreement between these two groups came fully out into the open in April 1998 with the publication of *Le 'Décembre' des intellectuels français*, a text

---

[25] See Bernard Poulet, 'A gauche de la gauche', *Le Débat*, 103 (1999), 39–59, and Philippe Reynaud, *L'Extrême Gauche plurielle: Entre la démocratie radicale et révolution* (2006).

[26] 'L'Esprit de 1995', *Le Débat*, 111 (2000), 118–20.

[27] *Contre-feux* (1998), 30.

authored by five of Bourdieu's supporters and directed (venomously) against the
editorial team of *Esprit*. Littered with the jargon of Bourdieu's sociological method,
it claimed that the supporters of the 1995 reforms, endowed with 'mediatic,
political, and bureaucratic capital', not only stood for 'moral conservatism' but,
in doing so, had abandoned the 'autonomy' of the intellectual and had sought to
diminish 'the prestige associated with this group since the Dreyfus Affair'. For their
part, the authors of the text did not hesitate to take up the mantle of their
Dreyfusard forebears. Armed with their 'intellectual and scientific capital', the
task of the intellectuals, it was argued, was to act as 'an autonomous collective
force'. Faced with a 'conservative' revolution resting upon 'xenophobia' and the
values of 'the traditional order', their duty was to embody 'a necessarily vigilant and
critical resistance'.

It was therefore no idle coincidence that 1998 also saw the republication of
Paul Nizan's *Les Chiens de garde* and that the 'actualité' of its criticisms of France's
intellectuals was there reaffirmed in a preface written by another of Bourdieu's
allies, the journalist Serge Halimi.[28] Several months earlier the same author had
made the identical point, but with more telling effect, with the publication of his
Les Nouveaux Chiens de garde.[29] The force of the criticism was that France's
dominant intellectuals, far from voicing lucid and independent criticism, were
floating about in 'an ocean of conformist thought' and were serving the status
quo through their constant endorsement of 'the neo-totalitarianism that is called
the democracy of the market'. Reverence before power and prudence before capital,
Halimi claimed, were their watchwords. Taken together, the charge was that the
intellectuals who had supported the government's proposed (and ultimately abandoned) reforms were the purveyors of pro-market 'pensée unique' and the unwit-
ting architects of a neo-liberal dystopia.

For their part, the targets of this criticism responded with undisguised scorn,
ridiculing the claims of the Bourdieu 'clan' to exist as a marginalized and dominated
faction in French intellectual life and as the very embodiment of 'an elevated moral
and political conscience' characterized by 'courage' and 'selfless dedication'. Not
only did they dismiss this resort to a Dreyfusard rhetoric of heroic intellectual
action, but they also pilloried the self-identification of Bourdieu with the earlier
model. 'It is striking to note', Joël Roman and Olivier Mongin wrote, 'that the
political commitment of Pierre Bourdieu reproduces exactly the most obsolete form
of commitment in French history: that of the scientist who, in the name of his
science, denounces this or that reality and supports this or that initiative.'[30]

Bourdieu had, in fact, been working towards this position for some time. Unlike
many of his contemporaries, he had never passed through the French Communist
Party nor did he participate in the *gauchisme* of the May 68 generation. Indeed, in
the early 1960s he had worked as Raymond Aron's research assistant. However,
it was Bourdieu who telephoned Michel Foucault in December 1981 to solicit his

---

[28] Paul Nizan, *Les Chiens de garde* (Marseilles, 1998).
[29] Serge Halimi, *Les Nouveaux Chiens de garde* (1997).
[30] 'Le Popularisme version Bourdieu ou la tentation du mépris', *Esprit*, 244 (1998), 158–75.

support for a petition in defence of Poland's Solidarity movement. It was when Bourdieu reflected upon this experience after Foucault's death that he not only spoke of the need for intellectuals to enjoy 'the most complete autonomy *vis-à-vis* all other powers' but also recognized that, if they were not 'the spokesmen of the universal, even less of a "universal class"', they often had 'an interest in the universal'.[31] This theme was continued by Bourdieu in a lecture he gave in 1989. There he spoke of 'the need to keep the most autonomous cultural producers from the temptation of the ivory tower by creating appropriate institutions to enable them to intervene collectively under their own specific authority'. This autonomy, Bourdieu stated, was under threat from the State, from the world of finance, and from the growth of technocratic control. By way of response, Bourdieu called for the creation of an 'International of Intellectuals', 'a large collective of intellectuals combining the talents of the ensemble of intellectuals'.[32] This project was given flesh in 1993 with the creation by Bourdieu and others of a Parlement international des écrivains. Described by Bourdieu as 'a critical countervailing force', it was to be modelled upon the Encyclopedists of the eighteenth century.[33]

The theoretical grounding of this argument was sketched out most thoroughly in Bourdieu's *Méditations pascaliennes*.[34] Recognizing that France, more than any other country, had embodied the 'imperialism' of a 'false Western universalism', Bourdieu argued that the process of autonomization that had followed the Enlightenment had allowed the development within society of sectors which had 'an interest in the universal' as well as 'an interest in being disinterested'. Crucially, this position rested upon the further supposition that within the category described by Bourdieu as the *noblesse d'État* there existed a distinction between those who defended the interests of the dominant class and who had turned a 'public' into a 'private good' and the *petite noblesse d'État* who, according to Bourdieu, continued to defend 'les acquis universels' associated with the State and the general good. If the latter deployed their 'intellectual and scientific capital' in defence of 'the victims', the former—dismissed as the 'doxosophes' by Bourdieu—comprised the vast cohort of 'mediatic' intellectuals and so-called experts who, through either cynicism, self-interest, or narcissism, colluded and collaborated with 'the dominant discourse' of globalization, exploitation, and neo-liberalism.

This was a message that did not go unheard, and so much so that, as 1998 came to a close and as Jeannine Verdès-Leroux published her *Le Savant et la politique*,[35] the question being asked—in much the same way as a century earlier it was asked

---

[31] 'Les Intellectuels et les pouvoirs', in *Michel Foucault: Une histoire de la vérité* (1985).

[32] See 'Pour une Internationale des intellectuels', in Bourdieu, *Interventions 1961–2001* (Marseilles, 2002), 257–66.

[33] See 'L'Intellectuel dans la cité: Un entretien avec Pierre Bourdieu', *Le Monde* (5 Nov. 1993) and 'Un entretien avec Pierre Bourdieu', *Le Monde* (7 Dec. 1993).

[34] Bourdieu, *Méditations pascaliennes* (1997).

[35] Jeannine Verdès-Leroux, *Le Savant et la politique: Essai sur le terrorisme sociologique de Pierre Bourdieu* (1998).

whether you were for or against Émile Zola[36]—was whether you were for or against Bourdieu.[37] What followed were a series of high-profile interventions and campaigns by Bourdieu and his supporters designed to counter globalization and the 'neo-liberal invasion' under the banner of a 'new internationalism' and in support of the unemployed, immigrants, sexual minorities, and the underprivileged. Time and time again the argument was to be heard that it was not the principles of the Republic that were responsible for the social injustices of the day but their very betrayal. Similarly, it was chorused that there was nothing inevitable about the process of globalization and that it was being used as a pretext to dismantle social welfare provision and to legitimize greater inequalities. Again, this was an argument that reached a sizeable audience. *Le Monde diplomatique*, edited by Serge Halimi, has had a readership within France of over 200,000 whilst *L'Horreur économique*,[38] published by the literary critic of *Le Monde*, Viviane Forrester, not only won the Prix Médicis but also sold well over 350,000 copies. *Une étrange dictature*, which continued Forrester's polemic against 'the fiasco of ultraliberalism', had only marginally less success.[39] Many others books and articles attacking the 'chienlit mondialiste laisser-fairiste' have appeared over the past decade or more.[40]

For all the diatribes against 'la pensée unique', in short, both free market liberal capitalism and globalization have been subject to strident attack and criticism in France over recent years. Viewed from the perspective of the accused, this was a cause for some sober reflection. 'The big error of the early years of the 1990s', Marcel Gauchet observed, 'was to conclude that the failure of communism would lead to a disappearance of anti-capitalism.'[41] More recently, Ezra Suleiman, speaking in his capacity as professor at Paris's prestigious Fondation Nationale des Sciences Politiques, spoke of the existence of 'a hegemonic anti-liberalism' in France.[42] The liberal tide, evidenced in the 1980s, appeared, and still appears, to have ebbed.

III

This has by no means been the only controversy to divide intellectual opinion in France in recent years. Nor has it been the only subject to engender debate about the meaning of the Republic. The political malaise that has afflicted France since the late 1980s has been accompanied not only by persistent economic problems but also by an increased prominence given to the issue of legal and illegal immigration.

---

[36] The centenary of Zola's intervention in defence of Dreyfus was marked by extensive press coverage, debate, and speeches: e.g. Prime Minister Lionel Jospin made a speech at Zola's tomb on 13 Jan. 1998.
[37] See the special issue of *Magazine littéraire*, 369 (Oct. 1998) devoted to 'Pierre Bourdieu: L'Intellectuel dominant'.
[38] Viviane Forrester, *L'Horreur économique* (1996).
[39] Viviane Forrester, *Une Étrange dictature* (2000).
[40] In addition to Bourdieu's own *Les Structures sociales de l'économie* (2000), see Emmanuel Todd, *L'Illusion économique* (1998).
[41] 'Les Voies secrètes de la société libérale', *Le Débat*, 111 (2000), 132.
[42] *Le Figaro* (7 Sept. 2005).

The most obvious political manifestation of this has been the persistent electoral success of Jean-Marie Le Pen's Front national. Less visible (to the foreign observer at least) has been the fifteen years of vigorous debate about the possibility (or even the desirability) of the integration of immigrants into French society and two (hotly contested) changes of legislation relating to the reform of France's nationality code.[43] Stated simply, France has had to face up to the reality of being a *de facto* multicultural society and this, it is argued, poses a set of fundamental challenges to France's republican conception of citizenship.[44]

In marked contrast to many of her European neighbours, France has for long been a country of immigration. Demographic stagnation meant that France had neither sufficient workers to fill her factories nor soldiers to secure her national defence, and thus that she needed to import, rather than export, people to survive. Consequently, from the mid-nineteenth century onwards large numbers of Poles, Italians, Central Europeans, Spaniards, and Portuguese arrived and settled permanently within her borders. Moreover, when viewed from within the republican paradigm, this policy of immigration has been regarded as a success and as a major achievement of the French Republic.[45] In much the same way (to refer to the title of Eugen Weber's well-known book) as peasants have been turned into Frenchmen, so the children of this immigrant population became citizens of the Republic, speaking the same language and sharing the same cultural and patriotic values. From within this perspective, it has been the school that has acted as the principal site of integration and also, by extension, of individual emancipation.[46] It was to be here that the future citizen of the Republic, leaving behind the dogmas and traditionalisms of family, regional, and religious life, would enter the world of progress, justice, toleration, and enlightenment.

Following the separation of Church and State in 1905 a further key component of republican ideology fell into place: the doctrine of *laïcité*. When primary education was taken out of the hands of the Catholic Church, schools were transformed into civil institutions and, no less importantly, religion was redefined as a purely private practice and institution. The consequences of this were far-reaching. If the State was deemed to be neutral towards all religion, by the same token religion was removed from the public sphere. But it was to be through the school that a republican ethos was to be inculcated and a shared public identity developed. Here the story has been more complex, and possibly less Jacobin, than has sometimes been imagined. It was only in 1923—some forty years after the initial steps to establish a secular education system—that reference to teaching

---

[43] See Patrick Weil, *How to Be French: Nationality in the Making since 1789* (Durham, NC, 2008), 152–67.

[44] See Cécile Laborde, *Critical Republicanism: The Hijab Controversy and Political Philosophy* (Oxford, 2008).

[45] See Jacqueline Costa-Lascaux, *De l'immigré au citoyen* (1989); Michèle Tribalet, *Cent ans d'immigration: Étrangers d'hier, Français d'aujourd'hui* (1991); Patrick Weil, *La France et ses étrangers: L'Aventure d'une politique de l'immigration 1938–1991* (1991); Vincent Viet, *La France immigrée: Constructions d'une politique 1914–1937* (1998).

[46] See Yves Deloye, *École et citoyenneté* (1995).

Conclusion

'duties before God' was dropped from the programme of civic education. However, from the 1880s onwards, the emphasis shifted from 'moral and religious education' to that of 'moral and civic education' and with that came a stress upon the teaching of the basic principles of a republican and universal morality.

A further dimension of this philosophy of integration has been the steadfast refusal to recognize the legal distinctiveness of ethnic communities. The Republic has consistently refused to acknowledge what it has referred to as 'the rights of minorities' and the claims of communal 'particularisms'. It has been as individuals, rather than as members of a group, that immigrants are integrated and it has never been the intention of the State to facilitate the existence of groups of persons possessing collective rights. In the same way as the Republic is conceived as being one and indivisible, so the French people is conceptualized as being one, without regard to origin.

At an official level, there has been a growing recognition that an integration of this kind has become more difficult to achieve. The traditional institutions of integration, it is acknowledged, work less efficiently than in the past.[47] Above all, there has been an awareness that, if France now experiences lower levels of immigration than it did at the beginning of the twentieth century, the character of her immigrant population has changed and she now finds herself before the challenge posed by the existence of a sizeable immigrant minority which is not only subject to social and economic exclusion but which also identifies itself strongly and publicly with the Muslim religion.[48] It is no exaggeration to say that the French state has struggled to respond positively to this new reality. Something very similar might also be said of France's intellectual community.

The debate got well and truly under way in 1989 when three young girls in the small town of Creil to the north of Paris arrived at school wearing Muslim head-scarves, thus creating what quickly became known as the *affaire du foulard islamique*. The public response to these events was almost universally hostile, seeing them as an expression of Islamic fundamentalism and as a threat to the hallowed principles of the Republic's secular educational system. The same was true of the cream of France's republican intellectuals. On 27 October, the left-leaning weekly *Le Nouvel Observateur* published an open letter signed by Elisabeth Badinter, Régis Debray, Alain Finkielkraut, Elisabeth de Fontenay, and Catherine Kintzler, urging the 'profs' not to 'capitulate' in a situation it described (not without an element of exaggeration) as 'the Munich of the republican school'. This was followed a week or so later by an article from Debray entitled 'Êtes-vous démocrate ou républicain?' in the same journal. Debray's piece merits being quoted at length as it made a series of vivid and forceful comparisons between democracy and republicanism, each designed to defend France's traditional republican model. 'The universal idea', Debray told his readers,

---

[47] See Alain Renault, 'Les Composantes de l'identité française', *Cahiers français*, 342 (2008), 63–6, and Didier Lepeyronnie, 'L'Intégration menacée? Les Grands Instruments d'intégration: Panne, crise, disparition?', *Cahiers français*, 352 (2009), 70–4.
[48] See in particular the successive reports of the Haut Conseil à l'intégration.

governs the republic. The local idea governs democracy... Reason being its supreme point of reference, the State in a republic is unitary and by its nature is centralized.... Democracy, which blossoms in the pluricultural, is federal by vocation and decentralized out of scepticism.... In a republic, there are two nerve centres in each village: the town hall, where the elected representatives deliberate in common about the common good, and the school.... In a democracy, it is the Protestant chapel (*le temple*) and the drugstore or (alternatively) the Cathedral and the stock exchange.... In a republic, society should resemble the school, whose first mission is to form citizens capable of judging all things by their natural intelligence alone. In a democracy, it is the school which resembles society, its first mission being to form products adapted to the labour market.

Somewhat remarkably Debray was able to extend this contrast over six pages of text and it would be impossible here to analyse the significance of each of his chosen comparisons. However, a sense of the overall tenor of Debray's argument was disclosed in his remark that, if *homo republicanus* had 'the faults of the masculine', then *homo democraticus* had all 'the qualities of the feminine'.

The logic underpinning this argument was made abundantly clear in another Debray text of the same year, *Que vive la République*. Here Debray argued that 'the enemies of the Republic have taken control of society' and that the old alliance between throne and altar had been replaced by that between 'money and the image'. As a consequence, the State stood 'humiliated' before 'civil society', as did 'truth' before 'opinion' and 'public office' before the 'private sector'. Politics had been reduced to 'a market of opinions'. By way of response, Debray called for the reinvigoration of the republican 'faith' in the 'transcendent goals' of liberty and equality. 'Republican idealism', he proclaimed, 'demands an intransigent rationalism.' A year later Debray indicated that that the *foulard* affair had to be seen as part of the 'dissolution' of the republican idea and the victory of 'the dictatorship of particularities'.[49]

During the 1990s this restatement of traditional republicanism was developed in a variety of different ways not only by Debray himself but by many others. All too frequently it amounted to a straightforward reaffirmation of the principles of republican citizenship filtered through a vision of an idealized past of shared civic identity. More nuanced was the response provided by Guy Coq in *Laïcité et République*.[50] A Catholic and member of the editorial team of *Esprit*, Coq was eager to establish a distinction between *la laïcité légitime* and a *laïcisme* which he saw as 'a philosophy hostile to religion'. Nevertheless, Coq accepted the basic republican premise that, without a common culture and a sense of common identity, the political as well as physical integrity of France would be threatened. The principal 'political' function of the school, he argued, was that of 'strengthening the cultural preconditions of democracy'. And here, once again, the wearing of the *foulard* was identified with religious *intégrisme* and was seen as being 'incompatible' with the

[49] 'La Laïcité: Une exception française', in Hubert Bost (ed.), *Genèse et enjeux de la laïcité* (Geneva, 1990), 201–2.
[50] Guy Coq, *Laïcité et République: Le Lien nécessaire* (1995).

Republic. 'To be welcoming', Coq concluded, 'does not mean self-abnegation.'
From others, there was an attempt to restate the integrative and assimilationist
capacities of French immigration policy. Writing in *Le Destin des immigrés*,[51] for
example, Emmanuel Todd not only rejected what he referred to contemptuously as
'la poussée différentialiste', but did so by stating that integration would take place
whatever ideological obstacles were placed in its path. A similar argument was
advanced by Christian Jelen in a text entitled *Ils feront de bons Français*.[52] Jelen's
argument was that the reasons given to suggest that the new immigrants from
North Africa could not be integrated had been earlier used against Poles, Italians,
and Jews from Central Europe, all of whom were now fully integrated into French
society. More than this, both Todd and Jelen were deeply critical of British
immigration policy and what they saw as its acceptance of the existence of distinct
ethnic communities, Todd going so far as to suggest that the British passion for a
'différentialisme de classe' had now been replaced by a 'différentialisme de race'.
They also saw calls for an acknowledgement of the 'right to difference' as part of an
'illusion multiculturaliste'.

It was this latter theme that continued to grow in prominence during the 1990s.
For the defenders of traditional republicanism, multiculturalism appeared as nothing less than a 'new tribalism'. Speaking before the Commission de la nationalité,
for example, philosopher Alain Finkielkraut commented: 'I believe that the fanatics
of cultural identity, those who raise collective difference to the level of an absolute,
do not proceed differently from racists, even if, to be accurate, the determinism
within which they enclose individuals is not genetic but historical and traditional.'[53] Finkielkraut did not hesitate, therefore, to draw a comparison between
multiculturalism and the ideas of Maurice Barrès.[54] In similar vein, Todd characterized multiculturalism as a 'reincarnation' of 'the Maurassian thematic'. Literary critic and philosopher Tzvetan Todorov continued the argument, making a
connection between multiculturalism and anti-Semitism. 'One hundred years after
the Dreyfus Affair', he wrote, 'it is truly depressing to see that it is again the anti-
Dreyfusards, those who think that the identity of an individual is entirely determined by the ethnic or biological group to which he belongs, who are winning.'[55]
Jelen, writing in *Le Débat*, simply aligned multiculturalism with the nationalist
ideology of Jean-Marie Le Pen.[56] In *Les Casseurs de la République* he took a different
tack, describing multiculturalism as the 'new opium of the left', a form of 'reactionary' leftism that had replaced the 'Marxist vulgate'. Multiculturalism's advocates, Jelen argued, wished to see a 'France babélisée' and based their arguments
upon a 'denigration' of the French nation. Calls for the recognition of difference
amounted to the toleration of polygamy and of female circumcision. Islamic law, he
predicted, would come to replace France's Civil Code, with France's immigrants

[51] Emmanuel Todd, *Le Destin des immigrés* (1994).
[52] Christian Jelen, *Ils feront de bons Français* (1991).
[53] *Être français aujourd'hui et demain: Rapport de la Commission de la nationalité* (1988), i. 597.
[54] See 'La Nation disparaît au profit des tribus', *Le Monde* (13 July 1989).
[55] 'Du culte de la différence à la sacralisation de la victime', *Esprit*, 212 (1996), 96.
[56] 'La Régression multiculturaliste', *Le Débat*, 97 (1997), 143.

being offered only a situation of permanent marginalization. Worse still were the political consequences of multiculturalism. 'Individual liberty, political democracy, the rule of law, the equality of citizens, the protection of the individual, the right to education, to health, to security, the separation of political and religious power, all', Jelen wrote, 'are threatened by multiculturalism.'[57] A France 'torn apart' and obsessed by 'racial, ethnic, and religious origins' would not be a 'charming and attractive multiplicity of cultural exchanges' but a 'tribal mosaic . . . a jungle'.

By the same token, if multiculturalism engendered a new tribalism, its critics also tarred it with the brush of 'Balkanization' and 'Lebanization'. The charge was that multiculturalism produced an inevitable descent into fratricidal civil war. The latter has been a remarkably common theme and it has been one that has fed off long-standing French fears about the fragility of their own nation. It has also drawn upon a deep disquiet associated with what has been described as the 'spectre of American multiculturalism'. There have, of course, been misconceptions here and the descriptions provided of America's recent culture wars have often been something of a caricature, but much use, it has to be acknowledged, has been made of America's own critics of multiculturalism (for example, Dinesh D'Souza's *Illiberal Education*). On this view, multiculturalism has gone hand in hand with political correctness (the horrors of which are a frequent topic of conversation among French intellectuals) and, as such, it has been linked with dogmatism, intolerance, and a form of left-wing McCarthyism. It has also been aligned with reverse discrimination, America now being adjudged not to embody Tocqueville's tyranny of the majority but a tyranny of the minority that threatened Western civilization and culture, especially in the universities. The talk was of a crisis of American identity that should not be replicated in France.[58] Multiculturalism was thus un-French. It sanctioned unequal rights. It recommended affirmative action. It countenanced the existence of communities turned in upon themselves. It placed culture before politics and groups before individuals.

The various dimensions and extent of this controversy might be illustrated by citing the opinions of two of France's most eminent scholars and public commentators. The first are those of the aforementioned Tzvetan Todorov, for whom multiculturalism denoted the 'sacralization of the victim'. Public life in America, Todorov argued, was based upon a demand for less rather than for more individual autonomy. This took three forms. Individuals 'systematically' denied responsibility for their actions. Next, they saw themselves above all as members of a group. Thirdly, they exhibited a fear of mixing with others. If the last produced a 'cultural apartheid', taken together they betokened not only a form of moral cowardice but also a reduction of the activity of politics to a conflict of particular interests rather

[57] *Les Casseurs de la République* (1997), 173.
[58] See Denis Lacorne, *La Crise de l'identité américaine: Du melting pot au multiculturalisme* (1997), 17–47, and the extended discussion of this book to be found as 'L'Avenir du multiculturalisme', *Le Débat*, 97 (1997), 132–67.

than the pursuit of the common good. Dialogue and communication with others became impossible.[59]

The second example is drawn from distinguished historian Mona Ozouf and her widely praised *Les Mots des femmes: Essai sur la singularité française*. Here, Ozouf rejected the criticism directed against the French Revolution by the 'American' historians Joan Scott and Carole Pateman, according to which, in Ozouf's words, the Revolution was seen as 'the incarnation of the universal in the particularity of the white man'. As a woman, Ozouf responded, she had little difficulty embracing the singularity of the French revolutionary experience. 'If one grants to French women', she wrote, 'the strength of this first conviction that they see themselves above all as free and equal individuals—one can understand that, armed with such a belief, they can live out sexual difference without resentment, cultivate it with good humour and irony, and refuse to "essentialize" it.'[60] This, Ozouf recognized, did not accord with the views of recent theorists of female identity, for whom the female universe was 'globally under siege', but nothing similar could be observed in France. It was not as women that French feminists claimed their rights, she argued, but as individuals. The French spirit, she concluded, was 'decidedly unamenable to communitarianism'.[61]

A more innovative response to these issues came from sociologist Dominique Schnapper, a member of the French Constitutional Council.[62] Indeed, Schnapper's work has represented the most sophisticated attempt to rethink the Republic as an ideal type and, in so doing, to reformulate the republican model of citizenship from within the republican paradigm. Schnapper's central idea, as the title of one of her books indicates,[63] is that the Republic has to be conceived as a 'community of citizens'. Crucially, Schnapper distinguishes the nation from the ethnic group, seeing the former solely as a political entity. This distinction has allowed her to argue that the nation is 'more open to others than all forms of ethnicity' and that cultural homogeneity is not necessary for the nation to exist. However, she writes, 'it is a necessary condition for the existence of the nation that its citizens accept the idea that there exists a political domain which is independent of their particular interests and that they must respect the rules governing its operation'.[64] Accordingly, the nation, and consequently the Republic, is to be seen as 'an attempt through citizenship to transcend particularist adherences', be they biological, historic, economic, social, religious, or cultural, and thus to fashion the citizen into 'an abstract individual, without identification and without particularist characteristics'. For this reason alone, Schnapper has seen no reason for the nation-state to be superseded.

Yet, for all her faith in the Republic as a set of political institutions capable of facilitating the life of a community of citizens, Schnapper also recognizes that there

---

[59] Todorov, 'Du culte de la différence', 90–102. These views were restated in Todorov's *L'Homme dépaysé* (1996), 213–31.

[60] *Les Mots des femmes: Essai sur la singularité française* (1995), 383.

[61] For a discussion of Ozouf's volume (including responses from American historians Lynn Hunt and Joan Scott) see *Le Débat*, 87 (1995), devoted to 'Femmes: Une singularité française'.

[62] See Schnapper, *Une Sociologue au Conseil Constitutionnel* (2010).

[63] *La Communauté des citoyens: Sur l'idée moderne de nation* (1994).

[64] Ibid. 44.

exists a tension between 'the universalist unity of the public domain and the real ethnic and social diversities of national society'. To a 'humiliated people', she comments, 'transcendence through citizenship appears as purely formal, having only the function of consecrating the dominance of the other under the guise of universality'.[65] And so, she has argued, it is of vital importance that 'individuals have the sentiment that their collective dignity . . . is recognized and respected'. Schnapper has thus been prepared to raise a series of questions considered anathema by traditionalist republicans. Why, she has asked, if a language is used in the home, can it not have some form of official status? Equally, however, Schnapper insists that there can be no toleration of 'cultural traditions' that do not respect the rules of a modern democracy. Recognition of the equal dignity of persons would, for example, rule out forms of cultural pluralism which treated women unfairly or which endorsed polygamy. Similarly, she is adamant that 'these particularities must not form a political identity which is recognized as such within the public space'.

These remarks indicate the qualifications that Schnapper has imposed upon her reassessment of the republican ideal. If the community of citizens envisages pushing the Republic in a more pluralist direction, so too it carries with it the fear of social disintegration as the links which have previously bound individual citizens together weaken and disappear, leaving only 'patterns of behaviour inspired by the sentiment of belonging or by identification with specific ethnic or religious communities'.[66] From this follows Schnapper's reference to the situation in the Lebanon where, she argues, 'individuals no longer exist as citizens but as representatives of a recognized community'. Here is proof of the damaging consequences of the intrusion of multiculturalism into the political sphere. Hence, also, her reference to what she describes as the 'impasse of American multiculturalism'. The present weakening of the American political community, she writes, is not due to ethnic diversity in America but to 'the tendency to recognize and to inscribe this diversity in the public sphere'.[67] So too there is Schnapper's recognition that the *affaire du foulard islamique* represents a challenge to the principles of integration embodied in the French 'civic community'. Moreover, it is clear that Schnapper believes that the policy and practices of integration continue to be relatively effective.[68] Likewise, although Schnapper is one of the few to address seriously the issue of a future European citizenship, she does not believe that it will provide a new model capable of replacing her preferred nation-based community of citizens.

How might Schnapper's reformulation of the principles of republican citizenship be summarized? A major clue can be found in an article she wrote for a special issue of *Raison Présente* devoted to the question: 'Avons-nous tort d'être universalistes?'[69] The universal, Schnapper responded, 'is a principle, an horizon, a regulatory idea'. Accordingly, for Schnapper, the universal, in the form of the Republic, becomes a

---

[65] Ibid. 121–2.   [66] Ibid. 100.

[67] 'Nation et démocratie: Entretien avec Dominique Schnapper', *La Pensée politique*, 3 (1995), 161.

[68] For two recent statements of her position see 'La Logique de la nation', *Cahiers français*, 336 (2007), 25–9, and 'La Notion d'identité nationale: Quelles significations?', *Cahiers français*, 342 (2008), 3–9.

[69] 'La Nation et l'universel', *Raison Présente*, 122 (1997), 9–19.

form of *ouverture potentielle*, where the citizen breaks with the 'given', achieves distance from a 'historical destiny' whilst not denying it. We must, she wrote, 'refuse the general, the unique, the global: we must choose the particular and therefore plurality: but by inscribing it within a reference to the universal which is the very condition of its existence and the possibility of dialogue with others'. The Republic, in short, can no longer be built upon the 'utopia' of an 'abstract humanity'.

On this reading, Schnapper shares much with some, although by no means all, of the proponents of what might be called a multicultural or modernizing republicanism.[70] A useful starting point here are the views of one of the editors of *Esprit*, Joël Roman, as the title of two of his articles best summarizes this position: 'Pour un multicultur- alisme temperé'[71] and 'Un multiculturalisme à la française'.[72] Roman shares the view that multiculturalism carries the danger of 'the closing in upon themselves of ethnic and religious communities', but such a *repli communitaire*, in his opinion, cannot best be countered by relying upon a republican ideology constructed to meet the demands of a nineteenth-century France that was predominantly rural and Catholic. The former strengths of this position, he argues, are now, in changed conditions, its weaknesses and if, therefore, there can be no question of abandoning 'republican emancipatory goals', it needs to be accepted that 'the prospect of integration is no longer presented as a commitment but is rather brandished as a threat'. Moreover, according to Roman, the principal danger facing France is not that of 'community membership' but that of 'the suffocation by the State of civil society and of its diversity'. Roman's ambition, therefore, was to 'invent a middle path' grounded upon 'a plural universal- ism'. To attain that end, Roman argued, the French had first to cease giving an 'aura' of universality to all their national particularities (be it philosophy, politics, fashion, or cooking) and needed to 'recognize the diversity of society and of the groups of which it is composed'. These differences, he continued, had to be accorded legal recognition and mutual visibility. Next, in Roman's opinion, came the 'necessity' of organizing 'the dynamic of confrontation between these groups and these differences, in order to prevent them from being differences closed in upon themselves'. The final element of Roman's argument was an endorsement of 'the provision of unequal measures designed to correct inequalities of fact and to bring about dynamics of equality'. The whole idea was summarized by Roman when he spoke of the need 'to invent a plurality of ways of being French'. French society, in other words, was not on the point of disintegration but it was diverse and what threatened it most was 'the refusal to accord a place to these differences and its forced homogenization'. Restated in a later work entitled *La Démocratie des individus*, Roman's claim was that his 'moderate multiculturalism' amounted to a move away from a 'democracy of emancipation' to a 'democracy of recognition'.[73] Citizenship, he argued, had to be reconceived as a series of lateral relationships

---

[70] See Joël Roman, *La Démocratie des individus* (1998), 17, and Dominique Schnapper and Joël Roman, 'De l'idée républicaine', *Les Cahiers du radicalisme*, 1 (1998), 13–28.
[71] *Hommes et migrations*, 1197 (1996), 18–22.
[72] *Esprit*, 212 (1995), 145–60.
[73] Roman, *La Démocratie*, 193–220.

between individuals and groups rather than as a vertical relationship between the individual and the State.

What such a *républicanisme élargi* would look like is not as yet easy to discern but there is an acknowledgement that it might entail a substantial recasting of some hallowed republican principles. There is in particular an awareness that a tension exists between the republican values of liberty and equality and the multicultural values of difference and equity.[74] The argument of some of the Republic's more severe critics, however, has been that such an accommodation is hardly likely to occur. On this view, the 'abstract universalism' of French republicanism now serves less to integrate than to dehumanize the excluded. Republicanism, it is argued, has become only more intransigent and mono-cultural as its capacity to secure adherence has weakened.

One of the more bizarre examples of this followed the triumph of France's football team in the 1998 World Cup. The talk was both of a brilliant victory and of *les bleus* as a symbol of *la France plurielle* and of *une France métissée*. For many political commentators, the triumph of the national team denoted nothing less than the success of France's republican model of integration and a confirmation of its continued relevance. For Alain Peyrefitte, editor of the right-wing *Le Figaro*, it showed that, if France was 'multiracial', she was certainly not *pluriculturelle* or *pluriethnique*.[75] The left-of-centre *Nouvel Observateur* pursued a similar line, arguing that 'the team has given back meaning to the French melting-pot'.[76] Of France's star player and 'man of the year', Zinedine Zidane, it was later to comment that he was 'Algerian by origin, Kabyle by spirit, and 100% French'.[77] Nowhere was this argument in praise of the French republican model pushed further than in the pages of the left-wing newspaper, *Libération*. Casting Zidane as 'the icon of integration', immigration specialist Michèle Tribalet could not resist reworking the old Franco-German comparison, contrasting a French squad drawn from the sons of immigrants to 'the German team, with their fair complexion and blond hair, which did not contain a single young player of Turkish origin'. Best of all was Laurent Joffrin's editorial in the same issue. Ernest Renan, he told his readers, had been right: the nation was truly 'un referendum de tous les matchs'![78]

Six weeks later *Le Monde* published an article entitled 'Républicains, n'ayons plus peur!'. It was signed by the elite of France's left-intelligentsia: Régis Debray, Max Gallo, Jacques Julliard, Blandine Kriegel, Olivier Mongin, Mona Ozouf, Anicet Le Pors, and Paul Thibaud.[79] Here the republican credo was deployed in precisely the

---

[74] See e.g. Françoise Gaspard and Farhad Khosrokhavar, *Le Foulard et la République* (1995); Michel Wieviorka (ed.), *Une société fragmentée: Le Multiculturalisme à l'épreuve* (1995); Jean-Loup Amselle, *Vers un multiculturalisme français: L'Empire de la coutume* (1996); Khosrokhavar, *L'Islam des jeunes* (1997); Alain Touraine, *Pourrons-nous vivre ensemble? Égaux et différents* (1997); Wieviorka, 'Le Multiculturalisme', *Les Cahiers du Cevipof*, 20 (1998), 104–29; Wieviorka, 'Le Multiculturalisme, est-il la réponse?', *Cahiers internationaux de sociologie*, 105 (1998), 113–51.

[75] *Le Figaro* (13 July 1998).

[76] *Le Nouvel Observateur* (16 July 1998).

[77] *Le Nouvel Observateur* (24 Dec. 1998).

[78] *Libération* (10 July 1998).

[79] *Le Monde* (4 Sept. 1998).

fashion most feared by its critics: as a threat used to intimidate those indecent enough not to adhere to the canons of republican citizenship. All the old republican shibboleths were repackaged and recast in a forthright attack upon what was taken to be the prevailing *incivisme* of daily life in France. The latent anger was easily seen in such statements as the following: '"Violence at school" begins with the use of familiar speech (*tutoiement*) towards teachers, listening to Walkmans in the school yard, and the wearing of deliberately provocative clothing in the classroom.' The authors therefore demanded a re-establishment of 'discipline' and a reawakening of 'responsibility'. Among whom? France's politicians for sure; her public servants too; but principally the young who engaged in criminal activity, badly behaved pupils who did not take their studies seriously, France's international partners who did nothing to stop the influx of illegal immigrants, and, of course, the immigrants themselves who failed to 'adhere to the minimum of republican values (in plain language: learning to speak and read French); respecting the secularism (*laïcité*) of public spaces'. As critics of the article immediately responded, the Republic now appeared to stand for a renewed call to 'moral order'.

IV

One of the central questions of political debate over the last ten years or more, therefore, has been whether one can be a good French citizen and clothe oneself in the Muslim headscarf or *hijab*.[80] That the answer was in the negative appeared to be confirmed when, in March 2004, the French parliament passed a law banning the wearing of all religious signs in French schools. Since then France has created a minister for immigration and national identity and (at the time of writing) is engaged in a government-led debate about what it means to be French. Censure has turned away from wearing of the *hijab* in the school towards those very few Muslim women in France who clothe themselves in the *burqa*. Seen in this light, citizenship of the French Republic is tied to a specific culture and to a specific national past. To be a citizen is to share a common inheritance and patrimony and to feel a strong sense of social solidarity with one's fellow citizens. The concern is that France's recent immigrants have not been (or cannot be) integrated into the values and duties of French citizenship.

But this in turn begs the question of whether the republican ideal of citizenship, forged in the cauldron of the Revolution and consolidated during the nineteenth century, is still relevant or workable when faced with the realities of an increasingly differentiated and diverse society? This issue itself has evoked a variety of responses and it needs to be acknowledged that the French state has responded to these matters in a far more pragmatic manner than is often recognized. The same can be said of the exponents of republican doctrine. Few are those who believe that the

---

[80] For two recent discussions of these themes see Jeanne-Hélène Kaltenback and Michèle Tribalet, *La République et l'islam: Entre criante et aveuglement* (2002) and Patrick Weil, *La République et sa diversité: Immigration, intégration, discriminations* (2005).

republican model, with its emphasis on the free and equal participation of all of France's citizens, needs to be completely abandoned but, putting aside 'les républicains purs et durs', there is evidence to suggest that republicanism can respond to the challenge of ethnic and religious diversity in a constructive and innovative way. As the recent book by Cécile Laborde amply shows, the question would be that of just how far republicanism and the Republic should go on the road to compromise.

Nevertheless, this unhappy experience has raised some fundamental questions that cannot be easily sidestepped by the defenders of republican principles. Is French republicanism a non-liberal or even a fundamentally illiberal doctrine? Should it be seen as a perverse form of communitarianism where a unitary conception of the common good is imposed upon the plurality of national or ethnic subgroups? To what extent does the republican conception of citizenship embody a truly universalist commitment to justice and emancipation as opposed to a particularist articulation of national values? Is the commitment to freedom of thought and conscience in a neutral public space sufficient to support and embrace cultural diversity or does it amount to a form of discrimination and oppression directed against all religious believers? Is it plausible to uphold a strong version of the duties of citizenship in a *de facto* multicultural society? To its critics, the answers to these questions suggest that there is little that can be saved from the republican project and that, as a political form, the Republic has entered its twilight years.

And yet republicanism remains the dominant language of politics in today's France and it seems to have lost little of its intellectual potency. Indeed, the vacuum created by the demise of more conventional ideologies (most notably Marxism) has been filled by a renewed enthusiasm for the republican tradition. Moreover, there is little that is substantially new in these criticisms of republican thinking. The long-standing and far from uncontroversial charge has been that the aspiration towards social unity and equality born of the Revolution of 1789 produced a democracy that was unresponsive to the demands of political, religious, and cultural pluralism. Likewise the allegation has been that the republican preoccupation with the sovereignty of the people has entailed an inability properly to conceptualize the nature of representative democracy and, indeed, to understand the activity of politics itself. Failing to see (unlike their wiser Anglo-Saxon counterparts) that questions about who gets what, when, and how are intrinsic to the politics of modern pluralistic societies, the republican tradition, it has been argued, simply imagined that that these questions could be deliberated or decreed out of existence. The result, according to this negative view, has been a succession of rather spectacular political and institutional failures and well-nigh two centuries of instability and ideological conflict.

If this exploration of political ideas in France since the eighteenth century has taken a critical eye to these developments, its primary purpose has been to explain rather than to criticize or praise. Above all, it has sought to explore the astonishing complexity of political thought in this period and to show how political problems have been repeatedly addressed through the prisms provided by both the Revolution and the Republic. Rather than consensus, there has been continuous debate and controversy, with both the events following 1789 and the institutional form of the Republic being subject to unremitting re-examination and redefinition. Nor does this analysis always confirm the Jacobin caricature of legend. If France has had its believers in the one and indivisible Republic, she has also had those within the republican camp who have been acutely aware of the need for her political institutions to be in tune with the complex socio-economic and cultural realities of the day. For these people in particular, there were no easy answers or solutions to the tensions and ambiguities within republican thinking.

So too we can see that many have stood outside this multifarious republican tradition, either as critical observers or as outright critics. To this end, they have often clung to an alternative vision of French history and of the French nation. This was especially so of Catholic writers in the nineteenth century, but again there is need to recognize that this pattern of thinking was by no means exclusively a story of religious intransigence before a sinful republic (although this undoubtedly existed) nor, for that matter, of republican aggression before an unyielding and obdurate Catholic Church.

Intriguingly, many of those who stood outside the republican tradition or who felt that the Republic had failed to fulfil its emancipatory promise turned their gaze (often longingly) towards the political traditions and institutions of other countries. If one, all-too-familiar, example of this in the twentieth century was an admiration for the achievements of the Soviet bloc and other points east, another altogether more enduring fascination has been with the 'Anglo-Saxon' world. Whether it has been England or the United States of America, this preoccupation has run like a subterranean current in French political thinking for well over two hundred years. Of especial note is the fact that even the most ardent Anglophiles rarely believed that France either could or should engage in the wholesale copying of English or American institutions. At most there were lessons to be learnt.

This latter point is worth making because, of recent years, there has been a tendency to disparage the achievements of those Walter Bagehot well over a century ago described as the 'poor French'.[81] The French republican model has for long seemed on the verge of collapse and the French state, ground down by debt and budget deficits, has looked perilously close to bankruptcy. In those circumstances, France has appeared ill-equipped to meet the challenges of the day, be they those associated with the reform of the welfare state, the future development and construction of the European Union, or the adaptation of her economy to an age of global capitalism. If these difficulties were cruelly exemplified by the presence of the Front national's Jean-Marie Le Pen in the second ballot of the 2002 presidential elections, they were only further confirmed in May 2005 when the French electorate decisively rejected the proposed European constitution in a popular referendum. The very public humiliation of losing the 2012 Olympic bid to a self-consciously multicultural and market-driven London did little to discourage the view that France's republican culture was decidedly past its sell-by date. France, her critics across the Channel averred, needed a good dose of Anglo-American

---

[81] Quoted in Georgios Varouxakis, *Victorian Political Thought on France and the French* (Houndmills, 2002), 57.

market reform and free market liberalism. Indeed, this was a view that France's new president, Nicolas Sarkozy, appeared to accept. In comparison to the grandiose designs of his predecessors, his vision of France's future seemed to be one where every Frenchman and Frenchwoman could aspire to ownership of a Rolex watch.

Of course, all of this looked far more appealing before the world banking crisis exposed the frailties of the global economy and plunged Britain and America in particular into severe recession. In these difficult and uncertain circumstances, it is not easy to assess the resources available to the French republican tradition to respond to these new challenges and it would be a mistake to underestimate the difficulties involved in the reformulation of republican principles that will undoubtedly be required in the near future and beyond. There is however little reason to believe that a republican tradition that has sustained and galvanized political thinking in France for over two centuries will not respond. For all the predictions of its impending death, it still moves.

Chronology of Modern French History

1598   Edict of Nantes: issued by King Henri IV, brings an end to the Wars of Religion by granting freedom of conscience to Protestants

1610   Murder of Henri IV

1643   Accession to the throne of Louis XIV, aged five

1695   Revocation of the Edict of Nantes by Louis XIV, declaring Protestantism illegal

1713   The Treaty of Utrecht brings an effective end to the War of the Spanish Succession and forbids the union of the French and Spanish thrones

1598   Accession to the throne of Louis XV

1756   Beginning of the Seven Years' War

1763   As a result of the Treaty of Paris, France loses possession of New France (Quebec) and of any effective power in India

1768   Following the Treaty of Versailles, Corsica becomes a part of France

1774   Accession to the throne of Louis XVI

1787   Edict of Toleration grants civil rights, including the right to practice their religion, to Protestants (29 November)

1789   Estates-General formally summoned by Louis XVI (24 January)
Estates-General convenes at Versailles (5 May)
National Assembly proclaimed (17 June)
Storming of the Bastille (14 July)
Abolition of the feudal order and of feudal privileges (4 August)
Déclaration des Droits de l'Homme et du Citoyen (26 August)

1685   Civil Constitution of the Clergy (12 July)
Fête de la Fédération (14 July)

1791   Louis XVI and his family attempt to flee France and are captured at Varennes (20 June)

Full citizenship granted to all French Jews (27 September)

1792   War declared on Austria (20 April)

Overthrow of the monarchy (10 August)

French victory at the battle of Valmy (20 September)

The legislative assembly known as the Convention comes into existence (20 September)

Proclamation of the First Republic (22 September)

1793   Execution of Louis XVI (21 January)

Beginning of the anti-revolutionary revolt in the Vendée (March)

Creation of the Committee of Public Safety (6 April)

Ratification of the Constitution of the First Republic (24 June)

Assassination of Jean-Paul Marat (13 July)

Execution of Marie-Antoinette, Queen of France (16 October)

Execution of the Girondins (31 October)

1794   Abolition of slavery in the French colonies (4 February)

Execution of Danton (5 April)

Festival of the Supreme Being (8 June)

Passing of the Law of 22 Prairial (10 June)

Fall and execution of Robespierre, known as Thermidor (27–8 July)

1795   Proclamation of the Constitution of the Year III (22 August)

Directory constituted (2 December), bringing the Convention to an end

1799   Napoleon Bonaparte overthrows the Directory in the coup of 18 Brumaire (9–10 November)

The Consulate comes into existence with Napoleon as First Consul

Proclamation of the Constitution of Year VIII (24 December)

1801   Concordat signed between Napoleon Bonaparte and Pope Pius VII (15 July)

1802   Re-introduction of slavery (20 May)

1803   France sells Louisiana to the United States of America, thereby losing her last possessions in North America

1804   Napoleon declared Emperor and First Empire established (18 May)

1805   Decisive French victory over Russia and Austria at the battle of Austerlitz (2 December)

1806   Napoleon dissolves the Holy Roman Empire and creates the Confederation of the Rhine (12 July)

1812   The invasion of Russia leads to the destruction of Napoleon's *Grande Armée*

1814   Restoration of the Bourbon Monarchy with Louis XVIII as king following the abdication of Napoleon (6 April)

1815   Napoleon returns from exile on the island of Elba (1 March)
        Napoleon defeated at the Battle of Waterloo (18 June)
        The Treaty of Paris reduces France to her territorial borders of 1790 (20 November)

1824   Accession of Charles X to the throne (16 September)

1830   Establishment of the July Monarchy with Louis-Philippe as king (26–29 July)

1840   Return of the ashes of Napoleon Bonaparte to France and their re-burial in the chapel of the Invalides in Paris

1848   Proclamation of the Second Republic (26 February)
        Definitive abolition of slavery in the French colonies (27 April)
        Popular uprising known as the June Days (23–26 June)
        Election of Louis Napoleon Bonaparte as President of the Second Republic (12 December)

1850   The Falloux law restores the influence of the Catholic Church in the educational system (15 March)

1851   Coup d'état of Louis Napoleon Bonaparte, dissolving the National Assembly (2 December)

1852   Proclamation of the Second Empire (2 December)

1870   Franco-Prussian War (19 July–10 May 1871)
        Proclamation of the Third Republic (19 September)

1871   Paris Commune (18 March–28 May)

France signs the Treaty of Frankfurt, ceding the territories of Alsace and Lorraine to Germany (10 May)

1877   Dissolution of parliament by President Patrice de MacMahon in a failed attempt to secure the return of the monarchy (16 May)

1879   The Marseillaise is reinstated as France's national anthem

1882   The so-called Jules Ferry laws of this and the previous year establish free, mandatory and secular public education

1884   Trade unions are legalized

1889   Centenial celebration of the French Revolution, marked by the *Exposition Universelle* in Paris and the inauguration of the Eiffel Tower (31 March)

1891   Pope Leo XIII's encyclical Rerum Novarum calls upon Roman Catholics to 'rally' to the Republic

1894   Assassination of President Sadi Carnot (24 June)

Arrest of Captain Alfred Dreyfus for treason (15 October)

1898   Publication of Émile Zola's article 'J'accuse' (13 January)

1903   First staging of the *Tour de France*

1905   Law establishing the separation of Church and State (9 December)

1906   The innocence of Alfred Dreyfus is formally announced by the Court of Cassation (12 July)

1914   Creation of the *union sacrée* government at the beginning of the First World War (August)

1918   France regains possession of the territories of Alsace and Lorraine at the end of the Great War, in which France suffers over 1.3 million military deaths

1920   Foundation of the French Communist Party (PCF) at the Congress of Tours (25–30 December)

1934   Antiparliamentary riots by far-right leagues in Paris (6 February)

1936   Election of the Popular Front Government led by socialist Léon Blum (3 May)

1940   Fall of France brings into existence the Vichy Government led by Marshal Philippe Pétain

1944   Liberation of Paris (25 August)
Creation of the Provisional Government led by Charles de Gaulle
Suffrage extended to include women (21 April)

1946   Charles de Gaulle resigns as head of the Provisional Government (20 January)
Proclamation of the Constitution of the Fourth Republic (13 October)

1954   French army defeated at the battle of Dien Bien Phu, heralding the departure of France from Indo-China (March–May)
Beginning of the Algerian War (November)

1957   France signs the Treaty of Rome establishing the European Economic Community (March 25)

1958   Proclamation of the Constitution of the Fifth Republic (4 October)
Election of Charles de Gaulle as President (21 December)

1962   Algeria obtains independence from France (3 July)

1968   Wave of protests by students and workers (May)

1969   Resignation of Charles de Gaulle as President (28 April)

1974   Following the death of Georges Pompidou, Valéry Giscard d'Estaing is elected President (27 May)

1975   Abortion is legalized with the passing of the law proposed by Minister of Health Simone Veil (17 January)

1981   Election of socialist François Mitterrand as President and victory of the left in parliamentary elections.

1988   François Mitterrand re-elected as President (8 May)

1995   Election of Jacques Chirac as President

1998   France's national team wins football's World Cup in the Stade de France (12 July)

2004   Law passed banning the wearing of conspicuous religious symbols in French state-controlled primary and secondary schools (15 March)

2005   In a referendum the French electorate votes against ratification of the Constitution of the European Union (29 May)

2007   Election of Nicolas Sarkozy as President

Index